Psychology: A Study of a Science

STUDY II. EMPIRICAL SUBSTRUCTURE
AND RELATIONS WITH OTHER SCIENCES

Volume 6. Investigations of Man as Socius:

Their Place in Psychology and

the Social Sciences

PSYCHOLOGY: A STUDY OF A SCIENCE

STUDY II. EMPIRICAL SUBSTRUCTURE
AND RELATIONS WITH OTHER SCIENCES

Volume 4. **Biologically Oriented Fields: Their Place in Psychology and in Biological Science**

CONTRIBUTORS: *Fred Attneave, Paul R. David and Laurence H. Snyder, R. C. Davis, I. T. Diamond and K. L. Chow, C. H. Graham and Philburn Ratoosh, William H. Ittelson, Robert B. Livingston, Carl Pfaffmann, Karl H. Pribram, Floyd Ratliff, W. A. Rosenblith and Eda B. Vidale, Burton S. Rosner, Gerhardt von Bonin, Karl Zener and Mercedes Gaffron*

Volume 5. **The Process Areas, the Person, and Some Applied Fields: Their Place in Psychology and in Science**

CONTRIBUTORS: *D. E. Berlyne, Irvin L. Child, Paul M. Fitts, Norman Guttman, Ernest R. Hilgard, Douglas H. Lawrence, Robert W. Leeper, Daniel R. Miller, Leo Postman, Eliot H. Rodnick, Julian B. Rotter, Nevitt Sanford, W. N. Schoenfeld and W. W. Cumming, Franklin V. Taylor*

Volume 6. **Investigations of Man as Socius: Their Place in Psychology and the Social Sciences**

CONTRIBUTORS: *Kenneth J. Arrow, Donald T. Campbell, David French, A. Irving Hallowell, Alex Inkeles, George Katona, William W. Lambert, Robert E. Lane, F. G. Lounsbury, Charles E. Osgood, Muzafer Sherif, Herbert A. Simon, George and Louise Spindler, James Tobin and F. Trenery Dolbear, Jr.*

POSTSCRIPT TO THE STUDY
(This title in preparation)

Volume 7. **Psychology and the Human Agent** (*by Sigmund Koch*)

Psychology: A Study of a Science

STUDY II. EMPIRICAL SUBSTRUCTURE
AND RELATIONS WITH OTHER SCIENCES

Volume 6. Investigations of Man as Socius: Their Place in Psychology and the Social Sciences

Edited by Sigmund Koch

DUKE UNIVERSITY

McGRAW-HILL BOOK COMPANY, INC.

New York   San Francisco   Toronto   London

PSYCHOLOGY: A STUDY OF A SCIENCE was made possible by funds granted by the National Science Foundation to the American Psychological Association, and carried out under the sponsorship of the latter organization. Neither agency, however, is to be construed as endorsing any of the published findings or conclusions of the Study.

PREFACE

When one looks back over the history of science, the successes are likely to be stressed and the failures forgotten. Thus one tends to see science as starting with a sure sense of direction and progressing neatly to its present form: or so it is for the older and well-established branches of science, but not for psychology. Psychology has not one sure sense of direction but several quite unsure directions. Growth is erratic, and there is much casting about for the most crucial problems and the most powerful methods. These apparent differences between psychology and the older branches of science may result from the difficulty of developing a science of man; it is perhaps significant that many of the problems of psychology were not attacked by the methods of science until so late a date in history. Or the differences may be an illusion resulting from the much closer view we have of the beginning struggles to develop a science of psychology than we now have of the beginning efforts in the older sciences.

Certainly psychology has its problems, and they are not easy. Nevertheless, knowledge has grown rapidly in the short history of man's efforts to develop a science of behavior, and the time seems appropriate for a major effort to examine the progress that has been made in attempting to find a way, or ways, to the attainment of the explanatory power that we like to think of as characteristic of science. A growing body of empirical information, a serious concern over methodological issues, and a variety of efforts to bring a selected body of fact into the organizing framework of theory all emphasize the need for that line of questioning—always going on in science—which explores the shape of knowledge, the range and inner connections of the ideas through which it has been developed and organized, the changing substructures of empirical data, and their emerging relations to each other and to the findings of other sciences. The seven volumes of *Psychology: A Study of a Science* are a response to this need.

The first three volumes, which bear the collective title *Study I. Conceptual and Systematic,* are concerned with many of the systematic formulations of recent and current influence which psychologists have developed to account for the phenomena in which they are interested.

Each systematic position is analyzed by its originator, or a person connected with its development, in a way which gives attention to the problems it seeks to solve, the empirical basis on which it rests, its degree of success, and its relations to other formulations.

A second set of three volumes, collectively called *Study II. Empirical Substructure and Relations with Other Sciences,* inquires, again through the efforts of creatively active investigators, into the organization of various fields of empirical knowledge, the relations of one to another, and to work going forward in other sciences. It also examines such problems in reverse through the participation of social and biological scientists who consider the relations of their own special fields to various parts of psychology.

Volume 7—*Psychology and the Human Agent*—will present the Study Director's view of certain problems of psychological inquiry in the light of the findings of the project.

Primary credit for the initiation of these studies goes to the Association's Policy and Planning Board, which decided in 1952 that the time had come for a thorough and critical examination of the status and development of psychology. The National Science Foundation agreed upon the desirability of such an undertaking and has generously supported the effort. When funds from the National Science Foundation were found to be insufficient for all of the expenses of the studies, the American Psychological Association provided the supplementary funds necessary to complete the work.

From the beginning, the study was divided into two parts. One part dealt with the education of psychologists and the factors conducive to research productivity in psychology. That part was directed by Professor Kenneth Clark of the University of Minnesota—now Dean Clark of the University of Colorado—who has reported the findings in *America's Psychologists: A Survey of a Growing Profession,* published by the American Psychological Association in 1957.

The other part, the part with which the present series of volumes is concerned, has dealt with the substance of psychological thought and data. Professor Sigmund Koch of Duke University has been responsible for this part of the study. Working closely with him has been a panel of consultants consisting of Lyle H. Lanier, Howard H. Kendler, Conrad G. Mueller, and Karl E. Zener. These men, but chiefly Dr. Koch, have planned, organized, interpreted, and edited the work, and successfully enlisted the cooperation of the approximately eighty authors whose original papers constitute the basic material of the series.

In the background—at a safe distance from the labors that have sometimes engulfed Dr. Koch, his panel of consultants, and the primary authors—has been a steering committee on which I had the pleasure of serving as chairman, and having as colleagues Clarence H. Graham, Lyle H. Lanier, Robert B. MacLeod, Eliot H. Rodnick, M. Brewster Smith, and Robert L. Thorndike. The steering committee helped to make administrative arrangements and helped to decide on the scope of the studies, but takes no credit for their successful completion.

In the preface to *America's Psychologists* we have already acknowledged our gratitude to Kenneth Clark and his collaborators who helped to produce that volume. It is our final pleasant duty to express our thanks to Duke University for making Dr. Koch's time available; to the National Science Foundation for its necessary and generous financial support and for the counsel and support of John T. Wilson, Assistant Director for the Biological Sciences; to Lyle H. Lanier, Howard H. Kendler, Conrad G. Mueller, and Karl E. Zener for their critical and devoted help; to all the authors whose names appear on the title pages for their original contributions; and—most of all—to Sigmund Koch for directing and driving through to completion what we hope will be an oft-consulted aid to the scholars and research workers who are striving to increase the rigor and further the development of scientific psychology.

Dael Wolfle, CHAIRMAN
STEERING COMMITTEE
POLICY AND PLANNING BOARD

CONTENTS

INTRODUCTION TO STUDY II

Psychology: A Study of a Science is a report of the inquiries of many men into the status and tendency of psychological science. There were two major contexts of inquiry: *Study I* sought analytic understanding of many systematic formulations of current influence, while *Study II* sought insight into the structure, mutual interrelations, and associations with other sciences of the main empirical areas in which psychological research proceeds. The findings of *Study I. Conceptual and Systematic* have already been published as the first three volumes of *Psychology: A Study of a Science*. This sixth volume, along with the fourth and fifth, comprise *Study II. Empirical Substructure and Relations with Other Sciences*. A postscript volume by the Study Director completes the series.

Many motives can bring—and apparently have brought—readers to the series. It can be approached as a group of handbooks, textbooks, or as an encyclopedia; as a complement to the education of the student and a supplement to that of the advanced worker; as a repository of remedial reading for the repentant specialist or the overdiffuse generalist; as a guide to the recent history of the science; as a source work for the comparative analysis and assessment of theory, method, research strategies; as a detailed index to the emerging structure of the science; as data for the mapping of research within special fields and of cross-field interrelations; as an aid to inferences concerning the achievements, shortcomings, trends, prospects of our science. There is much in this Study that can nourish all such motives, as indeed many others. But first and foremost the Study is a *study* with its own milieu of aims, values, methods, questions—its own biography. Most of that biography was set forth in Volume 1, which contains the General Introduction to the Series (pages 1–18) and an Introduction to Study I (pages 19–40). The present Introduction to Study II will complete the story—happily with some dispatch because of the availability of the material just cited.

Each *study, volume, essay* is a self-contained unit which may be read with profit. But a nice appreciation of any of the units demands that it be seen in relation to the total Study. Study II, for instance, differs in problematic incidence from Study I, but it is animated by similar values and is not without overlap in subject matter, the difference be-

1

tween the "systematic" and the "empirical" being, after all, something less than absolute. Moreover, the two studies were designed so as to complement each other in certain respects—some of them obvious and some perhaps not immediately apparent. For instance, substantive areas thinly sampled in Study I were somewhat more fully represented in Study II. Again, systematic influence—necessarily one of the stronger selective criteria for contributors to Study I—resulted in a high proportion of senior contributors; the differing incidence of Study II made it possible to invite a larger proportion of younger investigators (though we make no claim to the satisfaction of "New-Frontier" standards). Points such as these are easily clarified in the present introduction. But if the reader is fully to realize any of the varied aims which may bring him to this Study, it is well that he see it in the first instance *as* a study, bearing its full burden of identity. For *that,* the reader must see this Introduction to Study II in relation to the introductions in Volume 1.

In this introduction, we consider briefly (1) the plan of the over-all Study, (2) the history and rationale of Study II, (3) the factors determining the composition of the contributor group and the coverage of this study, and (4) certain anticipations concerning the character of the findings.

RÉSUMÉ OF DESIGN OF "PSYCHOLOGY: A STUDY OF A SCIENCE"

For the immediate orientation of the reader, the next few paragraphs are given over to a résumé of the Study's plan.

Study I. Conceptual and Systematic

This study involved the intensive analysis of thirty-four "systematic formulations" of widely varying type and subject-matter reference, and all of established influence in recent psychology. A systematic formulation was defined quite generally as "any set of sentences formulated as a tool for ordering knowledge with respect to some specified domain of events, or furthering the discovery of such knowledge": in applying this definition, care was taken that no formulation be precluded by nonconformity to standardized conceptions of the nature of "theory." Since each systematic formulation is the end product of a human effort to see and state order in a given domain, each analysis was made either by the originator(s) of the formulation in question or (in a few cases) by individuals creatively associated with the *development* of formulations of which they were not the primary authors.

Each systematist was invited to approach his work with certain common *themes of analysis* in mind. These were designed to invite a convergence of insight on problems of systematization which had emerged from the practice of the past three decades, more or less. Some of the suggested problems had been conspicuous in previous "metasystematic" discussion, but required, in our opinion, exposure to a wider range of systematically schooled sensibilities. Others were problems that seemed critically posed by recent systematic work, yet ones which had received little or no explicit attention.

The dominating hope was for analyses that might illumine the relations between the creative *processes* of systematizing and their publicly expressed *products*. It was thus hoped that the atmosphere of the study might encourage as much concern with background influences, orienting presuppositions, and working methods as with conceptual content, research achievements, and prospects. It was felt that analysis of this order could itself have creative consequences; reflective scrutiny of the extent and depth envisaged means *re*thinking. The primary intent of the discussion themes (and indeed, the constant aim of editorial effort) was to realize an atmosphere that might invite such emphases. Authors were requested to make explicit reference to the themes in their writing only to an extent they deemed appropriate or congenial. The use of the themes for facilitating the collation of findings was thus a secondary, if still important, aim. As matters turned out, most authors adhered to them sufficiently to give the reader an excellent purchase for the detection of similarities and differences on key issues.

The grounds for the selection of the thirty-four formulations included in Study I are given in Volume 1 (pages 21–27). The aim was a reasonably balanced diversification of formulations (as judged by many consultants) with respect to (1) subject-matter reference, and (2) conceptual and methodological "type." Many significant formulations that we would have wished to represent in the original list were excluded by spatial and other arbitrary restrictions. Nor was it possible to include in the final domain all formulations originally chosen. Though the proportion of inclusions is remarkable, there were some individuals who could not participate. We do not, then, claim "representativeness" even in an informal and impressionistic sense. We do, however, claim sufficient diversity to extend markedly the range of formulations which in recent years have been given sustained analytic attention.

Study II. Empirical Substructure and Relations with Other Sciences

This study seeks increased understanding of the internal structure of psychological science and its place in the matrix of scientific activity. A large number of distinguished investigators in psychology proper and in related biological and social sciences were invited to write papers which examine the organization of empirical knowledge within subareas of these disciplines and chart their cross-connections. Psychologist contributors were asked to consider the relations between their own fields of special competence and the rest of psychology and, if they wished, to inquire also into relations with relevant segments of other sciences. Social and biological scientists were asked to examine the relations between their own fields and psychology.

All who were invited are individuals whose research interests have bridged conventionally discriminated fields of knowledge. Each was asked to place special emphasis on those "bridging problems" which had been central in his own research experience. As in the case of Study I, certain common themes of analysis were proposed. The "themes" for Study II comprise a detailed breakdown of the senses in which questions of "mapping" subject-matter structure and exploring field interrelations might be entertained. The analytic themes were intended to play rather different roles in the two studies. Because in Study I the analytic unit was typically a circumscribed "systematic formulation," it was reasonable to encourage adherence to the themes in some degree. In Study II, the scope of the topics made it impossible for any author to embark on more than a few of the many analytic directions that could be pursued in considering subject-matter interrelations. The analytic themes were thus offered primarily as an illustrative check list in the hope that concrete and differentiated questioning might be encouraged, and that certain perhaps promising modes of analysis of a sort not often carried out be at least considered.

Though the topography of a science is too vast and labile for comprehensive or final mapping, this very fact makes it more important to assay the contours of knowledge as best we can. Study II exploits the only resource available in such problems—individual vision. It assumes that a pool of expert, specialized minds can give insight of a sort not ordinarily available into the emerging structure of a science. Forty-two essays have been contributed by fifty authors (counting collaborators) whose interests have signally spanned subdivisions of psychology, or of social or biological science on the one hand, and psychology on the other. Just as in the case of Study I, contributors and topics are not meant to be "representative"—whatever that can mean—of their respective populations: the intention is to extend the range of areas which have been considered from a perspective like that of Study II, the range of sensibilities which have been trained on such interrelational questions, and the range of analytic approaches that have been made. The hope is that the study will not only extend knowledge of the developing structure of our science, but will highlight the importance of explicit questioning concerning the articulation of knowledge and recommend to the reader, by the rhetoric of its insights, the habit of such questioning.

Psychology and the Human Agent

This volume is a postscript to the Study, representing certain views formed by the director in its course. The book (1) records those attitudes toward *a* science and science which necessarily color the spirit of the Study, (2) constructs trends from the massive findings of the two group studies, and (3) considers, in the light of the Study's premises and apparent trends, certain problems of psychological inquiry suggested by the practice of the past several decades.

HISTORY AND RATIONALE OF STUDY II

Psychology: A Study of a Science is the result of a project sponsored by the American Psychological Association and subsidized jointly by the National Science Foundation and the sponsoring organization. The project, known as "Project A of the APA Study of the Status and Development of Psychology," was inaugurated in the fall of 1952. It, and a separately administered sister project ("Project B") had their origin in proposals of the Association's Policy and Planning Board concerning the desirability of a series of investigations into psychological knowledge and the institutional and occupational arrangements which had evolved in its pursuit. It was the Board's energetic advocacy of such a program (especially under the chairmanship of Lyle H. Lanier in 1951–1952) that eventuated in the constitution of the two projects: Project A to be concerned with the "methodological, theoretical, and empirical status of psychological science," and Project B with "occupational, educational, and institutional problems."

Kenneth Clark served as Director of Project B (and has already reported its results in his book, *America's Psychologists*[1]). The present editor served as Director of Project A. Both projects profited from the counsel of an advisory committee under the chairmanship of Dael Wolfle. Each director also had the advice of a panel of consultants. Dr. Wolfle has described the relations of these groups to the project in his *Preface*.

Certain of the stages in the process of translating the general mandate for the project into the detailed plan for *Psychology: A Study of a Science* have been described in the General Introduction to the series (Volume 1, pages 6–14). Let it suffice here to reduce an intricate story to a few words.

From the beginning it was decided to proceed gradually: to set no plan into action until it was clear that it could stir a reasonable community of imaginations, and until there was at least some evidence for its practicability. After a lengthy planning process involving an intricate

---

[1] K. E. Clark, *America's Psychologists: A Survey of a Growing Profession,* Washington, American Psychological Association, 1957.

give-and-take between the director, the committee, panel, and selected consultants, the investigation that was to become *Study I. Conceptual and Systematic* was launched in the fall of 1953. Further planning concerning Study II and, to some extent, the more slender venture of the director's book continued through October, 1954. The present study was initiated at that time.

In planning, it was felt important to arrive at relatively limited, if still challenging, objects of study: to avoid the kind of grandiosity on which group investigations can so easily founder. Moreover, objects of inquiry were sought which might most profit from the circumstances of group inquiry. If grandiosity was thus held under control, exuberance was another matter! Many such objects suggested themselves during the planning, too many. Their range is barely suggested in the discussion of "rationale" given in the Volume 1 general introduction (pages 7–14). The ideas for the present study (as those for Study I) thus represent a selection from a wide array of possibilities.

Among the many types of questions that can be asked about a science, none could well be more important than those concerning the relations among its chief fields of inquiry and its interpenetrations with other disciplines concerned with overlapping objects of study. Yet in psychology few questions have been pursued with less vigor. It has long been a platitude to lament the growing specialism and insulation of research areas in our science. But the lament has occasioned not much more than discomfort and perhaps not enough of that.

Nevertheless, the investigator who wishes to environ his work with meaning has necessarily held certain beliefs about such matters. These, however, have often been so thin as to be tantamount to a brushing aside of the type of problem they address. Thus, for instance, it has been fairly fashionable to assume that the traditional, so to say, "process fields" of psychology (as e.g., perception, learning, motivation) are essentially chapter headings, having no systematic significance. The frequent corollary is that whatever is viable in the various fields will somehow be integrated in some future theory. But whether a theory can integrate research in diverse and largely insulated fields without the theorist keeping carefully in view from an early stage the detailed relations which obtain among them is not often considered. Certainly those theorists of the recent past who assumed that all significant problems of psychology could be solved via postulates local to a single research area have not in the results of their work increased confidence in such a position.

The relatively superficial concern with interrelationship issues often reflects a judgment that such problems cannot be solved within the terms given by the state of psychology. It is held that the main areas distinguished by convention are essentially distinctions of investigative convenience and with this it is usual to presume that analysis would show each such field to be a loose congeries of research findings having little rational coherence. But since the analysis is almost never made, it is impossible to test the *coherence* of field boundaries and thus arrive at more significant organizations. *Psychology: A Study of a Science* has constantly emphasized a view which sees most things in science as an uneven compound of the rational and extrarational, but certainly the relative proportion may be made to vary.

There is no way out of it. Even were the "field" distinctions wholly ones of "convenience," it would be well to know whether and to what extent they *are* convenient. But one can doubt the story to be that simple. The rather crassly defined fields into which convention parcels psychological knowledge could be distinctions of convenience, yet not of *mere* convenience. Certainly if we trace fields like perception, learning, cognition, motivation, emotion, into the history of psychology, near or remote, it becomes clear that such fields were premised on analyses of psychological phenomena meant to have systematic and even a crude ontological significance. The late nineteenth-century psychologists who talked about cognition, conation, and affection, for instance, thought they were talking about dimensions of analysis which in some sense fitted psychological phenomena and were adequate to them. The conventionalist and nominalist sensibility of recent psychology prefers to see its subareas as collections of functional relationships among characteristic (but often not character*ized*) classes of variables. It is perhaps this nominalism which, at some level in the inquirer's personality, has supported the rather nonchalant attitude toward interrelational problems. But, whether these collections of functional relationships are seen as having "functional," systematic, or even ontological force or not, their relation must be taken seriously if we are to have a meaningful science. Plural inquiries must stand in some kind of relationship if we are to have a science. If they stand in none, we have no science.

Despite such tendencies to evade interrelational problems, they have not been bypassed. They cannot be. They are constantly thrust upon us by the exigencies of research planning, pedagogy, and administration. The upshot is that we are content with superficial levels of analysis and cognitively thin stereotypes. For example, it has not in recent memory been rare for a theorist to champion either a "purely behavioral" or a "physiological" frame of reference for his concepts and translate this preference into the grain of an ambitious theory *before* essaying detailed analysis of actual and possible relations between physiology and psychology. Indeed, there have been cases when, say, a dogmatic "empty organism" approach has become an embarrassment after the "purely behavioral" theory begins to generate psychophysiological analyses and research.

To pursue the area of this illustration a bit further: For a long time in recent history, consideration of relations between psychology and physiology was left pretty much to philosophers of science, a group not eminently qualified in either field. The philosophers proceeded from a context established by the traditional "mind-body problem." For a period —coinciding with the hegemony of positivism—of some twenty-five years, it was something of a fashion to show that this problem becomes meaningful only upon translation into questions concerning the relations between the "language systems" of psychology and physiology. But actual analysis of these relations, if not eschewed, was approached in a way that could yield little of value to the empirical scientist. In effect, the philosophers called for an analysis they did not make, while the psychologists posited stereotypes (e.g., "All explanations must come from physiology," "No explanations can come from physiology," "Psychological laws are derivable in principle from physiology but psychology must first develop at its own level") for which they did not even *invite* analysis. In the course of what discussion took place, the issue was addressed in hopelessly global form: e.g., *prescriptions* recommending some desirable future relationship between the two disciplines were not distinguished from *description* of extant relations, or either of these from *prediction,* based on apparent trends, of probable future relations. Again, much of the discussion seemed to presume that the relations of psychology to the biological sciences *in general* would be established once the matter was got straight for physiology: that specific relations with other biological disciplines need not be considered.

The century has seen considerably more attention given to relations of psychology and the social sciences than to its relations with the biological sciences. Much of this has come from within the social sciences where, for obvious historical reasons, the need to establish identity is great and where psychology is readily seen as some kind of base line against which a *persona* may be traced. And social psychology, a specifically twentieth-century product, has perforce faced the same problem in reverse. But here, too, thinking has tended to be dominated by stereotype. For instance, it is often claimed that psychology and sociology deal with behavior at different levels of abstraction, independently of efforts to specify the formal or contentual characteristics of the abstractive levels in question. Assumptions may be made to the effect that it *is* or *is not* legitimate to transfer concepts from a psychological to a sociological (or political-science, or anthropological) context, or vice versa, with little clear analysis of the grounds for the one belief or the other. Again, much enthusiasm has gone into programs toward the "interdisciplinary" integration of psychology and the social sciences, with little prior exploration of the nature and degree of integration of the relevant sciences taken separately.

But questions concerning interrelations among the *subparts of psychology* have been slighted even more than those concerning relations with its bordering sciences. Conventionally discriminated areas of psychological science are variously held to be supplementary, independent, reducible one to the other, related according to one or another set of "bridging laws" or improperly subdivided, but such positions are rarely backed up by intensive analyses of the areas in question. Not seldom, workers in a given field are victims of an irresistible tendency to see their specialty as embracing the entire science; in the embrace, the rest of the science is often squeezed to death. Students of sensory process have been known to see no room for perceptual process; of learning, no room for either; of all, none for personality; of personality, none for all: men are easily drugged by the grandeur of their solipsisms. And in each such area there are subareas and sub-subareas within which solipsisms of descending magnitude may be achieved.

Crosscutting such substantive areas, discriminations such as the "pure" versus the "applied" figure with increasing importance in recent history, especially with the growth of vast professional groupings like the clinical. Here again it can be said that though many dogmas exist with regard to interrelations—of knowledge, training, professional roles, etc.—these dogmas have not often been backed by sustained and differentiated analysis.

The preceding account of certain of the circumstances which invite a study like this may impress the reader as rather more bleak than it need be. For instance, especially over the last ten or fifteen years, a number of research clusters which relate variables usually assigned to discrete fields have become conspicuous. There was the "new look" in perception and, more generally, the cluster of concerns with relations between motivational and perceptual variables. Another cluster has involved relations between perception and personality. Perhaps most conspicuous has been a massive concentration of interest—heavily documented in the present study but certainly evident outside it—in relations between perception and learning. This increase of interstitial interest no doubt announces a changing atmosphere and is certainly encouraging. But the depth of the earlier neglect and the thinness *still* of the present interest could not well be better documented than by the *character* of the newer interstitial research. The research that has been done on the relations of motivational and perceptual variables, or perceptual and socalled "personality variables," however valuable, has by and large involved narrow and adventitiously selected sets of variables and has been correlated with few far-reaching or searching examinations of relations between the fields from which they derive. As for the present interest in learning-perception relations, this admirable development, it must be recalled, occurred only after the field of perception itself had been all but legislated out of existence (at least in this country) for a period of roughly thirty years. Learning had *preempted* perception during the hegemony of behaviorism and neobehaviorism; neo-neobehaviorism, in willing peception back to life, is at the same time drawing attention to what can happen in the history of a science as a result of piecemeal viewing.

Words like "fields," "areas," "research clusters," "disciplines," are deceptive. The terms in which we talk about the architecture of knowledge inevitably suggest knowledge to be more architectonic than it is. Study II supposes that more explicit and intensive interest in the emerging structure of psychology is desirable. But it is well that an investigation into the "structure" of knowledge commence with a profound appreciation of the limits upon any such enterprise.

The study does not, for instance, suppose that everything that has been or is being done in psychology can fall into place, or in some way be "salvaged," in the terms of some happy and even-tempered interrelational scheme. Far from it—much that happens in a science is expendable (would that we knew precisely what!) ; much that is not expendable may fall at a given time into no orderly relations with any consistent map. The study does not presume that what is currently called psychology is best regarded as a single cohesive field of knowledge; rather, it stresses the importance of asking at all times penetrating questions about the degree of integration or fractionation of the field relative to prevailing definitions. The study does not even suppose that all *significant* knowledge need now or ever fall into one systematic or rational pattern; nothing says that differing universes of discourse, or even disparate "levels" of analysis must be commensurable. The study does not suppose that there is any privileged route to the conquest of interrelational problems or any special methodological gimmickry that can either enhance or replace individual vision. Though the units of study are units of "empirical" subject matter, it sees no absolute distinction between what is called the "theoretical" and the "empirical," and it is as eager to encourage exploration of interrelations via theoretical integrations or realignments as it is to encourage attempts at charting relations among empirical variables approached in a systematically more neutral way.

The study, of course, supposes that any single study addressed to the problems at issue can make only modest progress and that the progress is to be measured more in terms of the habits of thinking it recommends to its readers than its particular findings. It does not pretend to address every field of psychology distinguished by current convention or even every important field. Though it has assembled the views of many creative and knowledgeable men, it has no intention of fusing them into some single "standard" view of the structure and associations of our science. On the contrary, it has sought to ensure against the emergence of an "official" map by arranging that most sectors of the terrain of study be inspected by a plurality of viewers. In the end, what matters to this study is that the individual reader enrich his *own* view of the science, in his own way. If the study provides materials which in any degree will enable this, its purpose will have been well accomplished.

COVERAGE, CONTRIBUTOR GROUP, AND WORKING ATMOSPHERE

In planning the study, we sought to ensure far-ranging coverage of subject matter and to encourage concrete and differentiated analysis, but to allow the specific representation of cross-field topics and analytic questions to be determined by the authors' predilections. The pattern of this study is thus very largely a pattern of its authors' sensibilities playing, each in its own mode, upon problems that interest them.

The units of subject matter available to the study for the initiation of its inquiries can, of course, be no more "rationally" bounded than the "fields" distinguished by current convention. The purpose, after all, is to explore, not prejudge, the structure of the science. Inclusion of a field implied no commitment as to its *actual* degree of coherence—whether in respect to the character of its empirical variables, its problems, its methods, its role in the systematic analysis of behavior or experience, or any other attribute. In establishing the general framework of coverage, it was felt best to select subject-matter areas of relatively broad scope (say, "learning," rather than "conditioning" or "verbal learning") or, in the case of cross-science relations, entire disciplines. These units were meant to set the framework for the inclusion of contributors; as will be seen, the role of contributors was not necessarily to consider the cross-field problems raised by the *entire* (crassly defined) area they represented, but rather to stress *specific* bridging problems in the line of their primary interests and research. In the choice of "intra-psychological" fields, it was felt wisest to concentrate on areas conventionally allocated to *fundamental* psychology but, because of the importance of stimulating more explicit interest in the relations between pure and applied psychology, to include as well at least two applied fields.

Against such a background, the "fields" ultimately arrived at for consideration in their relationships were (1) from within *psychology—*

sensory psychology, perception, physiological psychology, learning, motivation, personality, social psychology, psycholinguistics, clinical psychology, and human engineering; (2) from within *biological science*—aspects of physiology, neuroanatomy, and genetics; and (3) from within *social science*—aspects of sociology, anthropology, linguistics, economics, and political science. It need hardly be added that the study does not regard this list of fields as exhausting its domain; even for psychology *per se*, there are obviously so many incidences from which crosscutting and overlapping breakdowns can be derived that it is not possible to say what "exhaustiveness" could mean in such a connection.

The design of Study II called for individuals whose primary professional background was in some one of the "fields" indicated above to consider its relations to some one or combination of the others. In the terminology of the study, the field which the analyst represents, by virtue of professional affiliation, is the "field of primary reference"; the "field(s) of secondary reference" is the domain(s) whose relationship to his "own" field the analyst proposes to explore. The *specific* bounding, for purposes of the analysis, of *both* fields of reference is of course the option of the analyst, an option always influenced by his particular cross-field research history. Though each author was asked to place special emphasis on those "bridging problems" which had been central in his own research experience, he was encouraged also to reach out from this core and bound his field of concern as generally as he might wish.

A *plurality* of individuals of differing background, systematic predilection, or specialized cross-area interest, was invited to "represent" *each* field of primary reference. The hope was that—depending on the breadth and density of the given field—it might be represented by between two and five individuals. For most of the fields of primary reference, this hope was realized.

It should be emphasized that though a contributor was always invited to "represent" a given field of primary reference, his field(s) of secondary reference was never specified. Rather, he was asked to pursue the analysis of cross-field relations in whatever directions he might wish. Thus the pattern of specific cross-field relationships considered in the study was largely *author-determined*. Any attempt to compose the domain of study by some arbitrary combination and permutation of the fields of reference would have been close to meaningless. The chances of nontrivial knowledge about cross-field relations being won by an analyst who had not already established intimate interests in the relevant problems would be very slight. A major strength of the present study is precisely that it taps the knowledge and insight of authors in the *particular* contexts in which they are in fact most knowledgeable and insightful.

It will be noted also that the way in which the study's coverage was planned makes it possible for two (or more) authors to elect the same primary and secondary reference-field combination. Such overlap, when it occurs, is often more apparent than real, in that the meaning of "same" in such a context can be markedly qualified by the different perceptions that two analysts may have of their fields of reference. Be this as it may, provision for overlaps of this sort was considered another strength of the plan. The play of differing scientific sensibilities on the same substantive issues (be they *really* the same or only nominally so) can be highly illuminating. Moreover, patterns of convergence on given cross-field combinations and on given fields of secondary reference would to some extent be diagnostic of the distribution of interest in interstitial problems of the field at large; any clusterings of interest would mean clusterings of analysis at precisely those points which require maximum attention if a just picture of the status of the science is to be derived. In administering the study, it was standard policy to advise authors to plan their essays without regard to the possibility of overlaps with the topics of their colleagues.

A few words are now in order about the arduous process of converting these framework decisions into the *actual* coverage of the study. The initial step was to begin—with the help of the Project A panel and many consultants, each expert in some field of the study—a list of contributor candidates. A few months of intensive thought and interchange produced a list of imposing architecture. Like all such lists, it never did become fully stable: it required frequent adjustments to the exigencies of the study.

The more obvious criteria of election to the list were research distinction in the field of primary reference, significant evidence of scholarly and analytic ability, and established interest—preferably as realized in a long-range research program—in problems of a cross-field or cross-discipline nature. Among the more subtle criteria was a preference for men of especially self-determining cast.

In the background were a number of considerations of a more special sort. One was the hope that a number of men known to have original and stimulating ideas but not noted for their readiness to appear in the literature might be persuaded to participate. Others were addressed as much to the interests of the project as a whole as to those of Study II. Thus, because Study I had been populated by a high proportion of contributors in the "elder-statesman" category, it was hoped that the balance might be redressed by including a reasonable number of younger, if still mature, contributors in Study II. Another such consideration had much to do with the relative number of candidates sought to represent each area. This was the desire to represent more fully in the present study certain of the areas (e.g., physiological psychology) that had been only thinly sampled in Study I. Contrariwise, one of the fields especially widely covered in the first study (learning) was represented in the second by rather fewer contributors than might otherwise have been appropriate.

The numbers of contributors ultimately representing each of the study's fields of primary reference were conditioned by many factors, some planned and some outside our control. As already mentioned, it was envisaged at the outset that each field should be represented by between two and five contributors. Within these limits, efforts were made to represent subfields of fundamental psychology in a density roughly reflecting their extent and current importance. For each of the two applied fields (clinical psychology and human engineering), two contributors were to be sought. There were to be between two and three contributors for each of the biological and social sciences included as primary reference fields —this for a number of pragmatic reasons, such as the need to limit the study's size and the expected difficulty of enlisting nonpsychologist contributors.

Reference to the tables of contents will show that in a rough way these framework requirements were satisfied in the final distribution of contributors. The main disappointments were the failure to obtain plural representation of the three biological sciences included as fields of primary reference and of sociology. To some extent this is compensated for by the very large number of biologically oriented *psychologists* who consider relations with biological science, and the fairly large number of personality and social psychologists who entertain questions of relationship with sociology.

For areas having multiple representation, the constant effort was to achieve *diversified groups* of contributors—men who, by virtue of differences in systematic approach, research background, or scientific temperament, would be likely to see their problems in different ways. Obviously, for groups of the size involved and characteristics of the subtlety at issue, there could be no thought of some principle of diversification. If, however, inferences can be made from the essays to characteristics of their authors, it is fairly evident that this aspect of the planning was not frustrated.

So much for the *planning* of the representation. The final roster was not, of course, uninfluenced by the availability (and in a few cases the pertinacity) of authors. About as many people refused to participate as the number who ultimately did. This 50 per cent rate of refusals is, we think, fairly modest for a study of the present character, and was not out of line with expectation. In Study I, there had been a markedly lower rate. But in Study I the unit of analysis had been given systematic formulations and the men approached were in most instances their owners. Not only a vested interest in the objects of analysis but an expectation (not always borne out) that they need not go far afield in the preparation of their analysis, worked toward acceptance. In the present study, equally overcommitted people were being asked to take on a task which, though in the line of their interest, could not call on identifications of comparable power and which, moreover, was of a sort that often required extensive scholarly preparation. Despite these circumstances, relatively few of the Study II refusals came from the psychologist candidates. By far the largest number came from the "related" disciplines and, among these, most from the biologists.

These reality conditions of the present study are significant for understanding the character of the final domain but are instructive, too, as positive findings relative to the problems broached by the study. Thus, for instance, the almost standard pattern of the refusals from the biological scientists and, to a lesser extent, the social scientists, was to express enthusiasm for the aims of the study but to plead an almost total lack of knowledge concerning the area of secondary reference (psychology). If the editor is any judge of correspondence, he can report that these protestations were characteristically of the most sincere sort, even if it be supposed that their authors could sometimes have discovered supplementary grounds for refusing. When it is realized that each of these candidates was a distinguished investigator, known largely for work which had bridged over into psychology, and further, that the group as a whole (especially the biologists) represented a large proportion of those in their fields known at the time to be doing such interrelational work, a number of conclusions become fairly compelling. It becomes fairly evident that those committed to interdisciplinary work are not in general combining plural disciplines into single skulls (as the slogan of interdisciplinary training executives would have it) but tend to be crossing field boundaries rather adventitiously in the pursuit of problems originating in the home territory. One gets little impression of a concern with a broader environment of interrelationships which might condition the significance of the specific cross-field variables under study. Whether this state of affairs is regrettable is not here the issue. What *is* the issue is that we have here an important descriptive fact concerning the status of interdisciplinary thinking—one which can give pause to confidence in the imminence of sweeping interdisciplinary "integrations" and lend realism to interdisciplinary training schemes. But more appropriate to the immediate purpose, the reader approaching Study II may derive from the present finding some useful perspective. Questions of field and discipline relationships *have* been neglected, neglected even by many of those whose work is by way of erecting those relationships. These problems are *not* easy. Vision can and must be trained on them but will not readily come to focus.

The story of our working methods is the story of an *atmosphere* of work. For such tasks as are addressed by the study there are no secret weapons: there is only the hope of inviting the play of specialized, creative minds on the objects and issues which they most prize. The hope was to realize an atmosphere that invited self-determination, freshness, spontaneity, *and* intellectual craftsmanship.

As is already evident, a central awareness of the study was the desirability of a more differentiated attack on interrelationship issues than had been usual. To a large extent the design of the study guarantees this, in that the main basis for bounding topics is the authors' more or less specialized cross-field research interests. But it was hoped that a set toward differentiated questioning could be sharpened by working out a detailed breakdown of the *types* of analytic questions that can be asked about the relations between any two fields of knowledge. These "themes of analysis" were among the materials explaining the study that were sent to all authors before their work began. They were offered essentially as an illustrative check list of the *range* of questions that might be asked. It was made clear that the themes had no legislative intent, that in the analyses they could be responded to selectively or not at all.

The themes of analysis discriminate a large number of highly specified questions which fall into six categories: (1) "mapping," in terms of definitive variable-constellations and in other ways, the fields of primary and secondary reference; (2) realignments, resulting from the analyses of 1, of conventional "field" boundaries; (3) "bridging laws" (i.e., cross-area functional dependencies) and formal relationships; (4) interrelations of methods, both research and systematic; (5) knowledge overlaps, including transpositions *and* duplications of findings, as between the areas of primary and secondary reference; (6) collaborative, administrative, and educational mechanisms as these have affected or promise to affect the interrelations of the fields under analysis.

The problem addressed by such a breakdown is not, of course, the sort that has a unique solution. What can be claimed for the breakdown arrived at is that it separates issues which heretofore have often been considered in deceptively global form into constituent *particular* questions. It strives also to ask a sufficient range of questions to do some degree of justice to the many different things that can be meant by a "field" or "area" of a science. A field, after all, can be approached as a body of formulated knowledge, the totality of the inquiring action that has generated that knowledge, the methods—empirical and formal—that are definitive, or the institutional, ideological, and material arrangements that in some way may be characteristic. The field may be approached as a collection of lawful or lawlike functional relationships, as a characteristic family or constellation of *empirical* variables, as a group of *systematic* variables assigned some general common property or function in a theory, as the collectivity of all systematic variables discriminated by all theories addressed to a cluster of empirical problems believed in some sense cohesive, as a class of processes, phenomena, or empirical problems believed unified by a relatively cohesive set of empirical laws, as a class of processes having some relatively independent causal influence on organismic functioning, etc. In characterizing a field, or a relationship between fields as defined in any of these ways, one can raise questions of history, of present status, or of indicated trend for the future. One can raise *descriptive* questions, or *normative* ones concerning *desirable* future status or relationship.

The *nature* of the relations that may be asserted or explored as between any of the given units that result from the above multifarious criteria may itself be looked into from quite different incidences. One might, for instance, look into primarily *formal* relationships (as, e.g., independence, deducibility, subsumability, translatability, etc.)—a type of consideration, incidentally, which in too many earlier analyses tended to preempt other more useful lines of approach. Again, one can try to discern, or perhaps hypothesize, empirical, or for that matter, systematic, laws which bridge between variables in the one domain and the other. Or one can inquire into "methodic" relations (in several senses of the methodic) between any two areas, even when these are not *defined* against a methodic criterion. One can entertain questions about interrelations (as e.g., influence lines) between the institutional, ideological, or administrative factors which environ inquiry in the fields under analysis. And many other questions.

Not all such questions are equally significant but more than a few are quite significant. *None* are at all significant unless posed in at least fairly clear independence of the others. The themes of analysis are a selection from among such contexts of questioning as are implicit in the above illustrations. The items are formulated with some explicitness and often supplemented with rather full explanation. The result is a not unformidable document. It appears as an appendix to this volume and is offered to the reader in the same spirit it was to the authors—as a device for encouraging differentiated thinking about questions of structure and relationship, if not in these particular terms, at least in some *particular* terms.

To ensure that the themes be considered with a certain high seriousness, they were submitted to authors as a kind of ideal discussion outline which—we were quick to point out—"no . . . analyst can hope fully to satisfy." The items were in fact developed and sequenced in such a way as to set the terms of something pretty close to an "ideal" analysis, given infinite time, intelligence, and indefatigability of soul. Since the relata of analysis were sizable fields of knowledge, it was not, of course, expected that any given one of the items was susceptible to full answer, let alone any marked number of them. It was emphasized in the introduction to the outline that the task defined was "in any literal sense, impossible," and that "the condition of psychological knowledge is such that only modest increments of insight into issues of the sort here envisaged are attainable." Other escape exits were lushly distributed throughout the themes of analysis, and even more so in the letter of invitation and ensuing correspondence with contributors. Moreover, unlike the practice in Study I, where the themes of analysis played a somewhat different role, no editorial response to Study II manuscripts was ever directed toward increasing, or even encouraging, adherence to the themes. That the escape exits were effective is fairly evident from the fact that the architecture of the outline is visible in precisely none of the essays.

The themes did, we think, play pretty much the role expected of them. At the most general level, the earnestness of their intent elicited earnestness in return. Again, the atmosphere of the themes certainly has encouraged *intensive* analysis—short of which few considerations of interrelationship issues can achieve much more than the circulation of stereotype. And finally, the evidence of the essays argues the probability that a wider range of questions, and more highly specified ones, have been asked than has characterized the *genre* of interrelational analyses in the past.

Did the themes have a "grooving effect"? The evidence says "No," while the range of the themes, and the variety of ways they comprehend of looking at the structure of the science, is such that they could hardly have constricted thinking.

But the themes should not detain us. What is important is not the questions men can raise but those they do raise, especially the questions that most recommend themselves to committed men at the frontiers of their fields. Whatever force this study has is gathered from the willingness of many such men searchingly to look *across* these frontiers at approximately the same time in history in directions set by their own curiosities. The emerging shape of a science is the emerging shape of what such men do and of what they see. If there has been anything happy about the study's conduct, this has been its disposition to hem in vision as little as possible, to depend on "mechanism" to a minimum, and to employ what mechanism it does for liberating ends.

The atmospheres of the study was the fifty atmospheres of the relationships, long-continued ones, with the individual authors. If any generalizations can be made about these, the main thing of note was the gallantry and forbearance of those on the productive side of the relationships. All gave the work their best effort and for most this meant exceedingly strenuous and long-continued effort. Many—however they approached their topic—found that the demands of such structural or interrelational problems as they were addressing were rather crueller than they had anticipated. Yet they pushed on without complaint. Virtually all were issue-centered, amiable, even appreciative, when editorial suggestions were made, no matter how obsessive the latter. The universal quantifier must, we fear, be dropped when it comes to the matter of promptness in meeting deadlines. A few men were model, a fair number finished within the secret timetable that most editors perforce sew in the lining of their Inverness, but not inconsiderable numbers worked agonizingly through their sixth, eighth, and even dozenth deadlines. This may sound like the kind of secret to which all editors are privy, but the present one doubts that extrapolation from normal editorial experience can give a sense of what can happen when there are fifty authors working on tasks so challenging as those posed by this study. Whatever the elements of anguish in these thoughts, it is by way of further praise of the authors that we mention them. For the rather considerable scatter in the receipt of manuscripts made it desirable to suggest that those received earlier be brought up to date. Of the many men thus penalized for their own virtue, almost all gave their uncomplaining cooperation.

At the editorial end of these fifty relationships, the main consistency was that such problems as the study was engaging could only be advanced by a pluralism of the widest excursion, by an utterly free play of the contributors' sensibilities within the quite general frame of the study's objectives. No goal or analytic direction that an author wished to pursue was ever discouraged. Whether the author wished to approach his topic via a theoretical or pretheoretical integration of the fields at issue, or primarily by empirical survey; whether he wished to stress one type of relationship question or many; whether he chose one field of secondary reference or several, or indeed, to train attention on the structure of the field of primary reference per se—all such matters were entirely his own option. Length of manuscript (short of flagrant indecency relative to the size of the volumes) was always his option, though we did, of course, uniformly express a preference for *detailed* analysis. In editing manuscripts, the editor's conception of his role was that of putting himself at the service of the particular objectives which the contributor had set. His suggestions were addressed to such ends as clarity, sound scholarship, consistency, occasionally style, and most generally, how best to strengthen or develop the author's argument.

A few *technical* injunctions were fairly consistently, though not inflexibly, asserted. Mention of these may give the reader some useful fore-knowledge about the character of the essays. One was that essays be written at a level which, though not necessarily nontechnical, would be clear to nonspecialized readers. Along with this went a constant concern that essays be written in a self-contained way and not lean too heavily on mere citations of the literature, especially literature not likely to be known to the nonspecialist. A related concern was that authors describe in at least a little detail empirical studies on which exposition or argument hinged in any important way. Finally, since almost all of the essays perform in part the function of a review article, authors were urged to prepare generous and careful bibliographies. As a result, whatever utility the study may have for handbook purposes—and it is a not inconsiderable one—has been maximized.

SOME ANTICIPATIONS

The value of the essays is in their detail—details of analysis, creative thinking, and scholarship, which are best left unblurred by synoptic survey or the manufacture of some synthetic pattern. Volume 7, the postscript volume of *Psychology: A Study of a Science,* will consider findings from various of the essays and even trends suggested by certain groupings of them, but with no disposition toward the manufacture of a "total pattern." Here we consider a miscellany of matters which may in some measure prepare the reader for navigating among the findings.

First, a few words about the grouping of the essays into the three volumes. The intention of the tripartite bounding is clear enough. Volume 4 is meant to embrace the essays of the biologists and those psychologists whose fields of primary reference are in most intimate contact with the biological sciences. Volume 5 demarcates those essays in which the primary fields of reference belong more strictly to "psychological psychology"; this does not imply that these areas are *unrelated* to biological science (or social science for that matter), either in principle or as seen by the authors of the essays. The final volume is of course meant to comprehend essays in which social psychology is taken as the primary reference field and those in which aspects of social science play this role. Here again, there is no implication that these fields are independent of the other groupings.

If there is an element of arbitrariness in the tripartite-volume breakdown, there is a greater one in the assignment of certain of the essays to given volumes. For instance, of the four essays in which perception is the field of primary reference, three appear in Volume 4; one (Postman's) in Volume 5. It is not at all clear that Postman's treatment of perception and learning is any further from biology than, say, Ittelson's presentation of perception and transactional psychology, but it was appropriate to put Postman's essay in Volume 5 because it forms a natural cluster with the essays in which learning is field of primary reference. Again, the essays in which personality is field of primary reference (especially Miller's, Sanford's, Child's) could have clustered about as well with the essays of Volume 6 as they do with those of Volume 5, where they are situated, but there were considerations of balancing the size of volumes. Nor, it may be added, is it an unrefreshing idea to interrupt the customary wedlock between personality and social psychology and assign one of the cowering partners to a volume which will come under the gaze of fundamental psychologists.

What is mainly to be emphasized *re* the "packaging" of the essays is that the unit of planning was the total study, not the individual volume. Indeed, a necessary consequence of the interrelational objectives is that the contents of each volume range freely (if with variable bias) over the entire breadth of psychology and related sciences. The fields of *secondary reference* were, it will be recalled, taken in any directions the authors wished to pursue. Thus, for instance, the geneticists David and Snyder (Volume 4) look toward personality, abnormal psychology, and individual differences, among other directions. The physiological psychologists Diamond and Chow (Volume 4) look largely toward learning. An essay by the anthropologist A. Irving Hallowell (Volume 6) is as firmly rooted in biological science as any of the papers in Volume 4. Another anthropologist, David French (Volume 6) looks toward perception and cognition. Donald T. Campbell (Volume 6), with social psychology as field of primary reference, pursues relationships with learning, perception, and certain developments in the neurological area. Psychology *as a whole* is inescapable in each of these volumes and the purity of the reader's specialism is nowhere without risk of violation.

The fact that fields of secondary reference were spontaneously chosen by the authors affords an instructive opportunity to gauge—from the distribution of choices—the directions in which bridging interests are going in the field at large. Though we do not argue that as the study goes, so goes the science, it is hardly likely that the choices of a group of authors so large, so influential, and so varied in field of primary affiliation would not, in some appreciable degree, be diagnostic of the general situation. In this connection, one of the most impressive general findings of the study is the convergence of bridging interests toward *perception*. Every author who took learning as field of primary reference (Guttman, Lawrence, Leeper, and Schoenfeld and Cumming in Volume 5) chose to consider relations with perception. One author, Postman (also in Volume 5), who was expected to take learning as his field of primary reference decided instead to put perception in its place and transpose learning to the secondary field. And the choice of perception as the main, or one of the main, fields of secondary reference by authors representing areas as diverse as neurophysiology, physiological psychology, sensory psychology, personality, human engineering, social psychology, anthropology, and linguistics will not of course escape the reader's notice. That the last several years have seen a quickening of interest in perception is evident from the general literature. What this study suggests is that perception is by way of becoming the "basic" field of psychological interest and the foundation field of its conceptualizations—indeed, that it has by now almost certainly supplanted learning in these respects.

An interesting by-product of the concentration of author interest on perception is that the reader can look forward to what amounts to a virtual subanthology on the topic of extending learning and behavior theories to this empirical domain. This is not only Postman's, Guttman's, Lawrence's, and Schoenfeld and Cumming's major theme, but it is conspicuously addressed also by Graham and Ratoosh, Ratliff, and Attneave (Volume 4), and Campbell and Osgood (Volume 6), and, in rather different spirit, by Zener and Gaffron, and Ittelson (Volume 4), and Leeper (Volume 5). Such a subanthology should have for the reader not only the drama of timeliness, but more substantial values. After all, agreement now seems general that among the things a psychologist cannot avoid coming to terms with are the problems and phenomena of perception. Moreover, no psychologist, especially if he be an American one, can avoid coming to terms with behaviorism. And the distinctive mark of the *present phase* of behaviorism—the "neo-neobehaviorism" that began to emerge in the early fifties—is in fact the concern with perceptual, and more generally, central process. It is well, then, that the particular intersection of theoretical and problematic interests at issue be viewed with utmost care and from many angles. It is well, also, that it be viewed both in celebrant mood (there is much to celebrate at the return of the repressed) *and* critically. Precisely such viewing is afforded by the study, though, because of the fortuities of representation, the volume of celebration exceeds that of the criticism. To compensate for this imbalance, may the editor suggest that such critical consideration of the rationale of behavioristic analyses of perception as exemplified, say, in the methodological section of the Zener-Gaffron paper, be given especial attention by the reader.

Turning now to the individual papers, the happiest generalization that can be made is that few can be made. The papers are widely varied in character but each in its own way realizes such qualities as we have seen to be definitive of the study's atmosphere. Some of them give primary emphasis to theoretical ideas intended to integrate or reveal the relatedness of discrete fields; others give the main concern to tracing cross-field relations among empirical variables. Some of the analyses are process-centered, some focus on the organization of extant clusters of knowledge, others are method-centered. Some papers accent emerging substantive and formal relationships as between fields at different levels of analysis; others focus on interstitial *problems* upon which a plurality of fields may bear in complementary fashion; still others concentrate on the structure of single large areas (e.g., personality) on the assumption that extrafield relations will be most naturally revealed when structure lines are drawn with sufficient fineness. Some of the papers approach their topics historically; others in terms of current status, or indeed, *sub species aeternitatis*. Some of the essays adopt the strategy of detailed analysis of "samples" of the literature in the areas under consideration; others are developed in a somewhat less Baconian fashion. In each, a man is speaking for himself, addressing his own problems in his own accents.

Though length and scope of the essays vary, even the shorter of them do not frustrate the hope for detailed and sustained analysis. That the essays raise far more differentiated structural and interrelational questions than has been customary in discussions of this sort is obvious. That such differentiated inquiry is important to our science and should be among its continuing responsibilities is made plain, if only from the complexities, the sometimes unsuspected moot alternatives, that emerge when *specific* questioning is pursued. Readers, say, of Volume 4, will find any of the textbook slogans concerning the "nature" or "role" of physiological psychology they may bring with them evaporating into a degree of triviality worse than emptiness before completing a few dozen pages. And, taking the study as a whole, similar claims might be made with respect to the time-worn textbook slogans concerning relations between perception and motivation, personality and perception, motivation and learning, social psychology and psychology, given social sciences and psychology, applied and pure psychology, etc.

Perhaps the major dimension of variation in authors' conceptions of their tasks had to do with whether they aimed primarily toward a theoretical integration of the fields comprising the relata of analysis, or a systematically more neutral survey of empirical structure or relations. This, it should be noted, is no simple continuum—especially if it be recognized that even the grouping of *empirical* variables local to specific studies into more general classes is a theory-like process. And, of course, there is no metric for the "degree of the theoretical," or decision rule which neatly separates "theory" and "pretheory." Whatever continuum such qualifications permit to exist is populated in virtually every segment by the essays of the present study.

Closest to that extreme which marks empirical survey as the method of preference are Lambert's paper on social psychology (Volume 6) and

Davis' on physiological psychology (Volume 4). Both of these men make an intensive effort to explore the structure and associations of their fields by reconstructing from characteristic samples of the relevant literature the chief empirical variable-classes that have set the terms of research. Comparable to such an approach are those parts of Rosner's essay on psychophysics and neurophysiology (Volume 4) in which he seeks to reconstruct the chief empirical and systematic variables characteristic of both fields of reference. Other articles, which focus primarily (but certainly not exclusively) on empirical interrelations, may be exemplified by David and Snyder's discussion of psychology and genetics, Diamond and Chow's of biological psychology (Volume 4); Berlyne's essay on exploratory behavior, Taylor's and Fitts' on human engineering (Volume 5); Sherif's essay on social psychology, French's and the Spindlers' essays on the relations between psychology and anthropology, Katona's on relations with economics (Volume 6).

By far the most typical approach is one which gives approximately equal weight to theoretical analysis and empirical survey. Good examples might be as follows: Volume 4—Rosner's paper (taken as a whole), Ratliff on joint relations of physics, physiology, and psychology for vision, Graham and Ratoosh on sensory psychology and perception, Livingston on psychology and neurophysiology, von Bonin on neuroanatomy and psychology, Zener and Gaffron on perception, Ittelson on perception and transactional psychology; Volume 5—Postman on perception and learning, Hilgard on motivation and learning, Leeper on learning, perception, and personality, Sanford on personality, Child on personality in relation to anthropology and sociology; Volume 6—Osgood on psycholinguistics, Inkeles on sociology and psychology, Hallowell on personality, culture, and society in behavioral evolution, Lane on political science and psychology, Simon on economics and psychology.

Finally, we have essays which in high (but varying) degree stress theoretical modes of analysis. Among the purest cases—though none are uncontaminated with the empirical—are Attneave's consideration of perception and related areas (Volume 4); Lawrence on learning and perception, Schoenfeld and Cumming on behavior and perception, and Miller on social aspects of motivation (Volume 5); Campbell on social attitudes and acquired behavioral dispositions, and Arrow on utility in economic behavior (Volume 6).

It is to be emphasized that both theoretical and (relatively speaking) "theoretically neutral" modes of analysis have their place in considering problems of field structure and relationships. "Theoretical integration" impresses one as the *mode par excellence*—especially if the analysis can disclose meaningful relations between fields, or parts thereof, which previously seemed discrete. But if it be the most dashing mode, it is not always feasible; still less often is it the mode of choice in the present state of the science. There are stages before theoretical integration (in any strong sense of "theory") is possible, at which analysis of cross-field relations at relatively empirical levels is a necessary condition to meaningful theoretical advance.

From the typing of the essays just offered, it should be clear that there are important continuities between Study I and Study II. In Study I, the unit of analysis was the individual theory ("systematic formulation," in our preferred phrase); in Study II, it is the research area(s). The body psychological being finite, these disparate cuts will overlap. Almost every essay of Study II makes reference—usually extensive reference—to theoretical materials, and some develop theoretical ideas in a focal way. Contrariwise, few of the analyses of Study I neglect considering the bearing of the systematic formulation at issue on a plurality of empirical domains, and thus on cross-field relations. Efficient use of the series requires that the reader keep in mind this complementarity of the two studies. With respect to *either* of the major types of question posed by the different studies, both taken together will give far fuller and better-balanced coverage than will the study of primary relevance per se.

In an earlier part of this introduction, it was indicated that though the conventionalized field distinctions are in many ways adventitious and arbitrary, certain of them derive historically from analyses which in some sense were considered ontologically significant. To put this in the most vulgarly direct terms, there was a time when perception or learning or motivation or emotion was unembarrassedly considered as in the first instance a real part-process (not, of course, an independent or self-subsistent one) within the process flux mediating real actions and even real experiences of a real organism in a real world. As the present century progressed, such uncouth ontologizing was displaced by the sophisticated and hygienic imagery of variables and functions, data languages and construct languages, along with the presumption that only fools could find the confines of the linguacentric predicament chafing. During this nominalist and conventionalist deflection in the recent history of our epistemology, it became almost a matter of course to ask questions not about subject matter, but about collectivities of sentences that the "literature" had deposited concerning subject matter. Or perhaps one *did* ask first-order questions, but the object of inquiry was so filmy and assumptional—so much a fiction based on an illegitimate inference—that one did not much care *what* questions.

Against this background, it is most refreshing to note in the present study a tendency to take *process,* and more generally, the *objects* of psychological knowledge seriously. In discussing field structure or interrelations, most of our authors are not merely revising or creating filing systems for indifferent units of knowledge, but are in fact looking beyond the bits and pieces of research that have emerged in the academic workshop toward a psychological universe to which research must be adequate. That universe is once more acknowledged, and desire to render it intelligible seems burgeoning. Such changes are not evident in all essays in the same degree, but in some degree they are evident in all.

This new serious concern with process is perhaps most evident in Volume 4. By and large, the physiological psychologists represented in this study seem to have a compelling feeling that the brain (and to some extent the rest of the organism) is *there*. Our three biologists express this feeling perhaps even more uninhibitedly (some going so far as to speculate about the relation between brain and mind, brain and consciousness, mind and body), but for biologists who always *were* "naïve," this is no departure. A similar concern for process, however, can be seen in many ways among the other contributors, the more strictly "psychological" psychologists. There is, for instance, virtually not a single empty-organism position expressed in the study: Learning theorists and even personality and social psychologists all not only acknowledge the organism in some general way, but often lean rather heavily on the recent advances in the neurological and neurophysiological disciplines. Again, the already noted interest in perception on the part of S-R and learning theorists seems another acknowledgement that a universe of actual problems exists.

Important among the developments here at issue is the tendency of not a few of the authors to approach their topics not first and foremost in terms of the exploration or realignment of extant bodies of knowledge, but in what might be characterized as "process-centered" terms. Thus, for instance, Zener and Gaffron (Volume 4) ask as their main question: What specifically is perception as a process phase in the economy of the organism—an organism which experiences in a significant sense, which acts, and which does both relative to a world and to itself? This is an ancient kind of question but one which we have too long been too "sophisticated" to re-raise. In raising it anew, the authors are led to certain methodic suggestions, theoretical vistas, and empirical observations, all far from old. From a quite different perspective, Attneave (also Volume 4) addresses perception in a process-centered way, in this case performing the remarkable feat of saying many things which seem substantively apt or plausible about the real organism in terms largely of *information theory*. Other largely process-centered analyses are Ittelson's on perception and transactional psychology (Volume 4); Berlyne's on exploratory behavior, and Leeper's on learning-perception relations (Volume 5); Campbell's on acquired behavioral dispositions, Hallowell's on personality, culture, and society, Lounsbury's on linguistics and psychology, Katona's on economics and psychology (Volume 6)—to mention but a sample.

The authors of Study II—as of Study I—are not merely recording history; they are extending history. Analysis of the shape and relational texture of knowledge as conceived by the study is not "mere" analysis. To see knowledge in new ways, to test the knowledge in a field against the objects of that field, to realign knowledge, is to *create* new knowledge. Those already acquainted in any degree with *Psychology: A Study of a Science* will know that one of its fondest aims has been to advance a conception of analysis which sees it as a joint analytico-creative task. This objective is well realized by the essays of Study II.

Few of the authors were left unchanged by the practice of such analysis: for the reader this means that he can expect something fresh in virtually every essay. In the course of their analyses, many of the authors make important theoretical and methodological contributions which had not before seen the light of day. Examples are to be seen in the papers by Rosner, Rosenblith and Vidale, Zener and Gaffron, Attneave (Volume 4); Guttman, Lawrence, Schoenfeld and Cumming, Leeper, Miller (Volume 5); Campbell, Hallowell, and Lane (Volume 6). In other cases, positions previously established are significantly extended or brought to bear on new ranges of subject matter. Conspicuous examples are the papers of Pfaffmann and of Graham and Ratoosh (Volume 4); Postman, Berlyne, Child, Rodnick (Volume 5); Sherif, Osgood, Inkeles, Katona, and Arrow (Volume 6). In still other cases, we get an essentially new way of viewing the content and organization of an interstitial area: e.g., the papers of Pribram and Davis (Volume 4); of Sanford and of Rotter (Volume 5); of Lambert, French, and Simon (Volume 6). Again, certain of the papers are unique in that they address interrelational topics which have never before been considered in any direct or extensive way: cases in point are Ratliff's consideration of physics, physiology (especially single-receptor physiology), and psychology relative to vision (Volume 4); the extended discussions in Volume 5 of the relations between human engineering and general psychology by Taylor and by Fitts; the evolutionary consideration of relations among personality, culture, and society in the mode of Hallowell, or the Spindlers' consideration of the specific problems of culture change in relation to psychology (Volume 6). These sources of creative novelty are not, of course, mutually exclusive: many, indeed most, of the papers present them in combination.

In these paragraphs we have been trying to anticipate certain of the qualities of the findings, yet protect the reader's freshness of vision by not constructing trends upon the findings. In minor violation of this restraint, may we raise an issue which the reader very probably already has in mind. What of psychology's current classification of "fields" (i.e., fields as defined at the level of generality of perception, learning, and the other "primary" reference areas of this study)? Does the study suggest some new and super-rational breakdown—a comfortable and tidy geography in which everything will find its place?

The study does not. Indeed, the study would tend to suggest that the perennial and poignant thirst of psychologists for a set of new-fangled field breakdowns is doomed to perennial and poignant frustration. The editor doubts that the findings of this study are a necessary condition to the verdict, but they are certainly confirmatory.

Field names are labels, variably applied, to what is seen by men as related clusters of inquiry. The flux of history, the variability of individual vision, and the unsystematic variety of senses in which a field itself can be defined, inevitably makes these labels highly ambiguous. Different men will—and *should*—continue to see fields differently relative to their own systematic beliefs and options.

Any new classification arrived at must be an organization dictated by the terms of some systematic view or theory. Until a "theory" sufficiently compelling to command general acceptance comes along, there can be no breakdown of fields any more serviceable than the present one. A theory of the requisite scope, analytic power, and adequacy to *warrant* any extensive realignment of fields is not exactly imminent and, indeed, may be unachievable in principle.

Whatever the degree of theoretical integration psychology ultimately achieves, it is well to recognize that certain of the fields currently demarcated cut into events from different incidences—incidences dictated by different universes of discourse. Different universes of discourse are not necessarily different "levels"; they *can* be just different—unsystematically so. This lugubrious circumstance is, we think, made evident, explicitly or implicitly, in many of the essays in these volumes. Given problematic ends in view—in life as in science—*are* often incommensurable; they require incommensurable concepts, methods, and will inevitably beget incommensurable answers. Much of what is comprehended, say, in social psychology, personality, or psychopathology, will probably not fall into the grain of any single conceptual language that might unite, say, aspects of sensory psychology, perception, and learning. Psychology will progress more rapidly toward whatever "rationality" of organization or conceptual integration may be possible, if such framework limits are clearly acknowledged and understood.

There are other (and not unrelated) expectations which, when carried into investigations of the shape and texture of knowledge, can work toward a trivial, if not illusory, outcome. An obvious one is the assumption that there are necessarily vast submerged riches in our attained backlog of research which, if only extracted by some felicitous culling, could lift us to a new level of knowledge. About such a hope we need perspective. There may indeed be in the history of our science hidden leads—even findings—of great value. But the history of our science also tells us that only a narrow and adventitiously chosen range of questions has been asked. This is not to our discredit. After all, we have had the courage to address a subject matter having the most awesome amplitude of any in the history of institutionalized knowledge-seeking.

The *realistic* likelihood is that the truly important advances in our science will come from new knowledge, based on new problematic sensitivities, and new ways of addressing questions. To this, a necessary condition is ceaselessly to look at past knowledge in a way at once faithful yet unconstrained, critical yet creative—by constant attention, that is, to some such questions of structure and relationship as have been raised in the present study. It is this consideration which defines the significance of the pursuits posed by Study II. The best use that the reader can make of the study is to approach it for such an end.

Recently the editor has had occasion to indulge his penchant for neologism by discriminating a syndrome called "ameaningful thinking." Ameaningful thought or inquiry "regards knowledge as the result of 'processing' rather than discovery; it presumes that knowledge is an almost automatic result of a gimmickry, an assembly line, a 'methodology'; it assumes that inquiring behavior is so rigidly and fully regulated by *rule,* that in its conception of inquiry it sometimes allows the rules totally to displace their human users. Presuming as it does that knowledge is 'generated' by processing, its conception of knowledge is fictionalistic, conventionalistic, 'a-ontological.' So strongly does it see knowledge under such aspects that it sometimes seems to suppose that the object of inquiry is an ungainly and annoying irrelevance, that knowledge can be created by fiat."

Ameaningful thinking is a specific yet highly complex syndrome, which requires far more subtle and extended description than can be given here. But psychologists will already have noted that such a trend is pervasive in the culture at large and, if they be heroically honest, that it is not unknown in the recent history of that subculture formed by "psychology." Perhaps the most direct and telling way to convey the special hope of a study like the present one is that it might serve, however modestly, *as a counterforce to ameaning in our science.* The tendency in past decades to raise questions concerning the shape of knowledge only intermittently and halfheartedly can be seen as related to an ameaningful habit of inquiry. For, in considering questions of structure and relationship, what are we doing other than setting local inquiry into a broader environment of meanings? And what *can* we be doing as inquirers if we do not at least try to do *that?*

SOCIAL PSYCHOLOGY: PROBLEMS AND TRENDS IN INTERDISCIPLINARY RELATIONSHIPS[1]

MUZAFER SHERIF

Institute of Group Relations
University of Oklahoma

[1] Carolyn W. Sherif, Research Associate, Institute of Group Relations, collaborated in writing this chapter. B. J. White, now of the University of Utah, W. R. Hood, now of Texas A. & I. College, and Lawrence La Fave, now of the Department of Research and Statistics, Cook County Department of Public Aid, Chicago, were on the staff of the Institute of Group Relations, University of Oklahoma, at the time this study was made and assisted in surveying literature.

INTRODUCTION

The topic of social psychology in relation to cognate social disciplines is so broad that it is necessary to delimit the task undertaken here at the outset. The first task of this chapter will be to define social psychology. This definition will point to the distinctive concepts of social psychology vis-à-vis the concepts of other social disciplines. The units of analysis implied in the definition have direct bearing on effective interdisciplinary efforts. Then the present formative state of social psychology will be discussed.

Following this general discussion, a few illustrative topics which have preoccupied social psychologists, sociologists, and cultural anthropologists alike will be summarized. Both divergence and convergence will be noted.

Finally, general trends of convergence in social psychology that appear to be most promising will be presented briefly. Interdisciplinary contributions to these developing trends will be indicated.

SOCIAL PSYCHOLOGY AND INTERDISCIPLINARY EFFORTS

Interdisciplinary attacks on problem areas of mutual concern to sociologists, cultural anthropologists, and psychologists date at least to the turn of this century [90, p. 173]. During the twenties and especially the thirties, collaboration by these disciplines was encouraged by institutionalization and financial support [132, 274]. Since World War II, interdisciplinary conferences, large-scale interdisciplinary research projects supported by government, business, or foundations, and even interdisciplinary academic units have become commonplace. Today social psychologists have more and more traffic with sociologists and anthropologists, as well as with psychiatrists, social workers, and others in applied fields of endeavor.

It is not always clear to participants in interdisciplinary efforts what distinguishes the various disciplines other than preferences for distinctive terminology. Certainly the topics of interest do not serve as a clear-cut basis. Yet it is precisely when social psychologists attempt interdisciplinary collaboration that a clear conception of their discipline becomes most essential.

What distinguishes social psychology from cognate social disciplines? What are its appropriate and most productive relations with sociology and anthropology? An answer to the first question implies at least the directions that the second will take. Accordingly our first task is to arrive at an adequate characterization of social psychology.

DEVELOPMENTS IN DEFINING SOCIAL PSYCHOLOGY

In 1908 two books on social psychology appeared, the earliest formal textbooks in the field. One author, the sociologist Edward A. Ross [207], set social psychology squarely upon the study of collective behavior. The psychologist William McDougall [163] conceived with equal vigor a social psychology focused on the individual as the main determinant of social life.

In social psychology, it seems, the textbook has probably been the most frequent and influential vehicle for systematic efforts. Although formal definitions do not impart the full viewpoint and contents, substantial differences in definition usually reflect variations in both. Following social psychology's double debut, some 15 texts accumulated by 1930. The definitions differed considerably. We find social psychology defined as "the science of the motives of people living in social relations" [270]; as "the science which studies the behavior of the individual in so far as his behavior stimulates other individuals, or is itself a reaction to their behavior" [1]; as "essentially group psychology" [59]; as "the study of the individual as he develops cultural behavior equipment" [117]; as dealing "with those human characteristics that make political life inevitable" [175].

Under the circumstances it was not surprising that social psychology became chary in committing itself. Thus, Cottrell and Gallagher stated that "one of the most clearly marked trends in social psychology" during the subsequent decade (1930–1940) "has been the consistent refusal by social psychologists to define and limit their subject with any exactness" [51, p. 3].

Since 1940, over 20 textbooks on social psychology have been published in the United States, excluding readings and handbooks. Differences in formal definition persist, along with variations in content [10, 57, 136, 196]. However, since 1940, definitions in texts tend to cluster around a few points of emphasis rather than many. All include the terms "individual" or "behavior" (referring to an individual) in contrast to its neglect in some earlier definitions. Most authors [e.g., 94, 130, 184, 211, 273] include the term "interaction" either in formal definition or subsequent elaboration.

About one-third of the definitions since 1940 specifically mention groups and social institutions as principal stimulating influences in social psychology [e.g., 29, 65, 140, 153]. Approximately another third do not mention groups in formal definition, but treat groups in the text [e.g., 184, 196]. Only about a fifth of the formal definitions designate stimulating conditions broadly enough to include other individuals, groups, institutions, and other cultural and technological products [e.g., 10, 26, 222], although most authors do include many, if not all, of these as social-stimulus conditions in their texts.

A DEFINITION OF SOCIAL PSYCHOLOGY

Taking account of the converging definitions of our discipline, an adequate characterization of social psychology includes the conception that it is an integral part of psychology (otherwise the designation "social *psychology*" has very little meaning). The characterization must also indicate that its specialization is *social*.

If psychological notions were ancillary to analysis of social organization and its cultural products, the area could be designated "psychological sociology" or "psychological ethnology," as the case might be. In stating that the individual is the unit of analysis in social psychology, there is no implication that psychology is more central or more established than other disciplines. The insistence here is on clarification of the appropriate level of analysis in social psychology and hence the nature of its conceptual tools. Its concepts or "principles" need not bear the trademark of any of today's competing schools of psychology. I refer to concepts and generalizations that have been or will be established on the basis of demonstrated validity, regardless of special preferences of any school. Admittedly a rounded psychology is far from accomplished fact, especially in areas of closest concern to man's social relations—motivation, learning, conceptual functioning, and other processes traditionally termed "higher mental processes" [cf. 133].

It seems to me that the following definition satisfies the above requirements and offers a clear basis for fruitful give and take with the social sciences: *Social psychology is the scientific study of the experience and behavior of individuals in relation to social-stimulus situations.*

Consideration of the main terms of this definition will provide smoother passage to problems of social psychology—social science relationships. Social psychology is termed a "scientific study" to stress the fact that its empirical data are obtained through reproducible and verifiable procedures and that it aims at achieving a consistent and communicable set of concepts and definitions, so that any hypothesis or generalization advanced can be tested by anyone with adequate training.

As noted above, the concepts of social psychology are necessarily in terms of "experience and behavior of the individual," that is, his judging, perceiving, imaging, learning, remembering, thinking, behaving, or act-

ing. It is the individual who judges, discriminates, perceives, learns, remembers, and thinks. The unit of analysis in social psychology, as in all
psychology, is the individual, whether he is alone, participating in
interpersonal, in-group, or intergroup relations, or acting in the frenzy
of a mob situation.

The psychological activity of the individual, from simplest judgment
through more complex activities of problem solving and thinking in
social situations, is not solely an outcome of external-stimulus agents
(social or nonsocial), nor is it an outcome solely of internal impulses
(motives, attitudes, ego-involvements). Ordinarily, psychological activity
(perception, learning, memory, and so on) is a product of interrelated
factors coming both from the external field of stimulation and from
internal influences.

Therefore, it becomes meaningless to take sides as culture-group
(environment) determinists or as "instinct," "need," or individual
determinists. For this reason, the definition of social psychology stated
that experience and behavior are studied "in relation to" social-stimulus
situations, rather than "as determined by" social-stimulus situations. The
direction of influences linking individual and social setting is not one
way, but reciprocal.

Social-stimulus Situations

Now we come to the final words in the definition, namely, "social-
stimulus situations." Here I use "stimulus situations" as a generic term
for factors which at a given time are external to the individual, the
skin being the usual limit for externality. Although the ambiguity of the
word "stimulus" increases by the year, a distinction between internal and
external factors is analytically necessary in social psychology, particularly
in dealing with problems of socialization and conformity. Of course,
certain external objects may become internal through swallowing or sub-
cutaneous insult; but extraceptive, introceptive, and proprioceptive impulses can be designated as such without using the stimulus symbol.
Conceiving stimulus situations as external to the individual, it seems to
me that sound conceptions of the properties of social-stimulus situations
will go a long way toward building a social psychology commensurate
with the activities of the individual in the actualities of his social setting.
Furthermore, it will provide guideposts for delimiting the focus of social
psychology vis-à-vis cognate social disciplines and an explicit rationale
for their interdisciplinary relationship.

For that matter, the general problem of stimulus properties is one
of the basic problems for all psychology. Until fairly recently, highly
influential behavioristic schools of psychology made no systematic issue
of the properties of stimulus objects and situations confronting the in-

dividual. This neglect almost amounted to assuming that cues or stimuli had absolute values for the reacting individual, irrespective of the relations of the stimuli in the particular conditions. It was sometimes assumed that only a designated set of elements, and not others surrounding them, were stimulating agents.

A description of the above state of affairs was recently made by Melton:

Finally, I wish to mention a specific characteristic of our contemporary S-R theory that, it seems to me, must be overcome if progress is to be made. I refer to the assumption throughout much theory and experimentation, especially on the simpler forms of learning in the rat and in human conditioning, that the stimulus is a simple punctiform affair, something that can be dealt with as though it occurred without context, as though it were the stimulation of a single receptor. This comment is certainly not new. It has been made by the critics of S-R theories of behavior since the first such theory was formulated. But it is also one to which some dominant S-R theories have not adjusted adaptively. We have had Hull's principle of afferent neural interaction stated, but nothing much has been done about it either experimentally or through revision of theory. [169, p. 281].

The conception of stimulus situation that has functional significance in social psychology deals with objects and situations in their contextual relationships. Writers in the social sciences have consistently stressed the desirability of conceptualizing the social field in such terms. For example, sociologists like Durkheim [61] and W. I. Thomas [246] and social philosophers like George H. Mead [168] were groping in this direction, each in his way.

In the experimental work of gestalt psychologists and of psychologists investigating judgment, it became evident that relations among various items, even in simple judgment and perception situations, are as important as the component items themselves. The psychological significance of any item cannot be determined independently of others which constitute a functional system, variously called a "whole" or a "reference scale" as the case might be [134, 135, 259, 265, 266].

Emphasis on the relationships of parts within patterned wholes becomes indispensable in characterization of social-stimulus situations for purposes of social-psychological analysis. The individual experiences and reacts to social objects, persons, groups, cultural items (furniture, tools, words, music, and so on) in terms of meaningful relations prevailing in the characteristic patterning of these stimulus agents. It has been demonstrated that experience of meaning of social stimuli is prior to singling out particular elements or associations [37, 252]. There is a psychological basis, therefore, for approaching social-stimulus situations on a meaningful level, in terms of their patterning and properties studied by social science.

In writing social psychology books, some authors centered upon interpersonal relations as the primary concern of social psychology, to the neglect of social structures within which interpersonal relations ordinarily function. Naturally, students of culture found little of relevance to their work. Other authors elaborated on social groups and organizations to the neglect of interpersonal relations. Some authors were fixated on culture and its effects. The products offered as social psychology with primary emphasis on a single variety of social-stimulus situations resembled the well-known descriptions of the elephant examined by the blind men, as Sargent has noted [211, chap. 1]. To be sure, experience and behavior do not follow altogether different principles in different stimulus situations. However, the validity of such basic principles can be established only by testing them in the gamut of stimulus situations, from interpersonal to intergroup and cultural.

Recognizing the importance of the properties and varieties of social-stimulus situations, a social psychologist is confronted with some distinctions which were historically important in the development of social science and which still survive in the claims of some sociologists and cultural anthropologists. Traditionally, those investigators called "anthropologists" were concerned with cultures and peoples who were considered distant, primitive, bizarre, and esoteric. On the whole, sociologists traditionally dealt with contemporary societies. Because of their respective historical developments and preoccupations, an assumption arose that anthropology is primarily concerned with the study of culture and sociology with society or social systems.

When we examine representative studies of a given people, we find that they could be presented either as sociology or as anthropology if we did not know that the author calls himself a sociologist or anthropologist. One of the anthropologist's interests has been kinship systems. Is not the study of kinship exactly a study in social organization? Durkheim's analysis of religious forms [60] is claimed both by sociologists and anthropologists. The Lynds' Middletown study [160] or the Yankee City studies by Warner and his associates [e.g., 262] can be classified with equal justification as sociology or anthropology. Both sociology and anthropology are concerned with social structure or systems and with their cultural products (value systems, institutions, etc.). Cultural products such as values or norms are products of a group. The set of norms pertaining to status and role arrangements in the groups is at least partly accountable for the perpetuation of its social system or organization. Such considerations raise a question as to the usefulness of categorizing these aspects of the situation in which a person ("actor") is behaving as (1) "non-social, that is, physical objects or accumulated cultural resources, or (2) social objects, that is, individual actors and collectivities" [190, p. 5, cf. Kluckhohn's comment, pp. 26–27].

Following the above rationale, we may list the varieties of social-stimulus situations in the following general categories:

1. Other people
    a. Other individuals—represented in interpersonal relations
    b. Groups—represented in the individual's (a) intragroup (in-group) relations and (b) intergroup relations
    c. Collective interaction situations—represented by fluid and critical situations which need not be identical with in-group or intergroup relations of more stable times
2. Cultural products: products of human interaction in the past or present
    a. Material culture
    b. Nonmaterial culture

Needless to say, the varieties of social-stimulus situations listed above are not mutually exclusive. At times, the individual is confronted with representatives of all of them on a single occasion. For example, a wedding ceremony, a political convention, or a protest rally may involve most of them. I shall comment on each variety. A more extensive discussion of each variety is available [228, pp. 11–28].

Other individuals as stimuli. To be sure, interpersonal relations in which two or more individuals serve as stimuli for each other are examples *par excellence* of day-to-day social interactions. The motivational claims of individuals are in relation to one another (for bodily care, for companionship, for a sense of belongingness, for proving one's worth, for recognition, for love, and so on). Development of one's notion of himself as a human individual is unthinkable apart from his relations with other individuals. However, ordinarily, reciprocal personal expectations as friends, as companions, as parent and offspring, as husband and wife, as sweethearts, as business partners, as employer and employee, and even as equals in given capacities take place within more or less stabilized organizational patterns and sets of values (norms) of a given sociocultural setting.

Groups as stimulus situations. As a stimulus situation for an individual, a group (e.g., a clique, gang, club, or labor or management organization) has unmistakable structural properties. These structural properties are represented by a particular pattern of status and role relations which is reflected even in the intimacy of interpersonal contacts of the individual members. It is the implications of these structural properties for the reciprocal expectations and behaviors of individual members that brought the study of groups irrevocably to the foreground. A group —conceived as a delineated social unit in which individual members occupy identifiable positions and roles and share a set of values—is a concept at the sociological level of analysis. Since all groups within differentiated societies are functionally related to other groups and are parts of larger organizational structures, relations between groups are likewise ubiquitous and consequential as social-stimulus situations.

Collective interaction situations. Collective interaction (represented by rallies, crowds, mobs) cannot be properly classified as interpersonal interaction. For one thing, the number of individuals involved is greater than the usual scope of face-to-face relations. Likewise, it is difficult to subsume collective interaction under group situations. At least initially, a collective-interaction situation lacks stabilized, orderly status and role delineations embracing all participating individuals. It should be noted, however, that closely knit nuclei composed of a smaller number of individuals may be mainly responsible for initiating and influencing the course of events in such collectivities.

Collective-interaction situations usually take place under conditions of crisis, fluidity, or out-of-the-ordinary events. At times, the "cake of custom" is shattered and new values or norms arise in the form of short-cut formulations, dicta, and slogans [28, 60, 107, 144]. Out-of-the-ordinary type of behavior and emergent products of collective-interaction situations have been described dramatically by various authors [e.g., 46, 144, 207]. Such occasions give rise to accentuated expression of motives and frustrations on the one hand. On the other, they also produce emergent types of behavior which are conducive at times to the stabilization of new social values and new patterns of human relationships. For these reasons, collective-interaction situations should provide fertile soil for joint cultivation by social psychologists and social scientists.

The two varieties of stimulus situations yet to be discussed pertain to parts of culture as stimulus situations. I have deliberately chosen the wording "parts of culture" rather than the generic term "culture." Especially in modern societies, no one individual is confronted with the whole of a culture even during the course of an entire lifetime. His acquaintance with culture is confined to his experience.

The topic is a controversial one. Some students today are busily engaged in defining culture, primarily in individual and psychodynamic terms in an effort to divorce themselves from the grand theorizing and reifications of "Culture" by past anthropological systematizers. It is easy to swing too far in the opposite direction. Then culture is seen only within the confines of discrete interpersonal relations or in the unique personality characteristics of informants or a select number of "natives" responding to psychological questionnaires and projective tests. These psychological data can, of course, be valuable. But they become valuable when viewed in terms of the more fundamental problem of what constitutes sociocultural stimulus situations for the individual.

If all the social objects that the individual utilized in his day-to-day activities were *mediated* only through other persons, if his conception of them were molded *only* by the words and example of other individuals, then it might be possible to study cultural stimulus situations only in terms of interpersonal and group contacts. However, the individual is confronted from birth on with furniture, buildings, tools, melodies, means of transportation, and mass communication. Such man-made structures do exert an unmistakable influence in shaping his scales of magnitude, his sense of appropriate proportions, his notion of the tempo of events— whether or not they are mediated through other individuals.

Social psychology must be concerned with the socialization process through which the infant becomes in time an individual member of a particular sociocultural setting. Adequate analysis of this process requires a clear conceptual distinction between the sociocultural situations he faces and his particular psychological processes and products at a given time. Without this conceptual distinction, the historical error of attributing social attitudes and traits to an unfolding and fixed "human nature" is repeated over and over. Defining culture as the "man-made part of the environment" [98, p. 17] permits specification and analysis of the sociocultural setting of the newly born member of a society.

To be sure, if there were no human beings to interact, there would be no culture, no social organization, no value system, no means of communication, transportation, or production, and no technology. But once such products come into existence and accumulate through generations, they take their appropriate places as stimulus conditions, setting certain limits and forming the basis for perspectives of human beings. It is man who made machines; we can also say that machines, in turn, make man. It is man who created social organization; we can also say that it is social organization that recasts man. Man is in the beginning of things, but his products are not man himself. His products (social organization, technology, language, etc.) become subject matters in their own right, and these subject matters can be and are studied on their own level in a meaningful way without reference to single individuals. Thus economics is a discipline in its own right, and so are ethnology, linguistics, archaeology, and musicology. To think otherwise would lead us to an untenable solipsism which would assert that everything is psychology, including physics and chemistry.

Reduction of social-stimulus agents to only psychological terms—

leaving out their material setting and the value or norm system which regulates even man's most intimate relationships—would mean omitting crucial factors which enter into shaping the individual's mentality and behavior. The perspectives and the reference scales which the individual forms during his encounters with man-made parts of his surroundings and the categorizing effects of the structure of his language are among the significant components of the bounds of his mentality. The "sociology of knowledge" has called attention to these components in an impressive way [e.g., 166].

Against this background, parts of culture can be discussed as social-stimulus situations under the two remaining headings.

Parts of material culture as stimulus situations.   Products of human interaction and labor are parts of the material culture. Furniture, dwellings, facilities for cooking and sleeping, plumbing, streets, playgrounds, means of transportation (oxcart, car, train, bus, boat, plane), means of communication (books, newspapers, radio, television), and other technological products (machines) used in producing means of livelihood are parts of material culture.

Man's works reveal a great deal about his designs for living, his attainments, his standards of living, his modes of thinking, and his tastes. The foreigner who enters New York Harbor and takes a taxi to a hotel does not need to be told of the riches and industrial might of the United States. The skyline of the city, the shop windows, the density of traffic, the unceasing hustle and bustle are more eloquent than any words. Through archaeological findings we learn a great deal about the modes of living, thinking, and feeling in extinct societies.

Our notions of space and time, our standards of living, the radius of our psychological world—all are influenced by the material culture which confronts us. On the whole, this area is sadly neglected in social-psychological works. Yet items of material culture are stimulus situations, and some of the individual's significant reference scales can be effectively studied in relation to them. He uses such reference scales in appraising, for example, what is "too primitive" to bear or what is "splendid" beyond his wildest dreams. We learn from the historian Webb that the introduction of barbed-wire fencing had an appreciable effect on the development of agricultural activities, social organizations, and individual attitudes on the American Great Plains [263, pp. 270–318]. Or, to take one more example, we learn from the anthropologist Lang that the work of Chinese youngsters in industrial plants appreciably affected the pattern of role relations of the traditional Chinese family [139, p. 206].

Several decades ago, the anthropologist Sapir called attention to the effects of technological changes on human relations:

Every profound change in the flow of civilization, particularly every change in its economic bases, tends to bring about an unsettling and readjustment of culture values. Old culture forms, habitual types of reaction, tend to persist through the force of inertia. The maladjustment of these habitual reactions to their new civilizational environment brings with it a measure of spiritual disharmony, which the more sensitive individuals feel eventually as a fundamental lack of culture. Sometimes the maladjustment corrects itself with great rapidity, at other times it may persist for generations, as in the case of America, where a chronic state of cultural maladjustment has for so long a period reduced much of our higher life to sterile externality [210, pp. 317–318].

The point of emphasis here is not akin to the unbridled technological determinism advocated some time ago by the exponents of "technocracy." Material culture seldom, if ever, affects social relations singlehandedly. Its effects have to be considered in conjunction with other parts of the social setting as these are related to the motivational directions and goals of the people involved. As Quincy Wright stated: "The effect of a particular technological invention or importation upon a particular social order depends upon the way in which it is utilized, and that utilization is in large measure influenced by the values and culture of the social order" [271, p. 177].

The study of the effects of material culture, though often neglected, has decided advantages as a problem area for interdisciplinary cooperation between social scientist and psychologist. Items of material culture are suitable for quantitative specification, and they can be studied with considerable precision as stimulus conditions (independent variables) in relation to reference scales or perspectives which the individual forms internally and utilizes in his judgments and appraisals, along the lines suggested by Volkmann [258, pp. 288–294].

Items of nonmaterial culture as stimulus situations.   Material culture is not all of the man-made part of the individual's environment. Even from birth, he is confronted with lullabies and feeding and sleeping schedules which change according to medical and nonmedical vogues. In a few years, the infant learns that he is a boy or a girl, that certain toys are appropriate for boys, certain others for girls; that certain qualities (e.g., being brave or coy) and certain activities are more appropriate for a boy or a girl. A little later he internalizes certain regularities shaping his role expectations and behavior. These are only a few of the items of nonmaterial culture that a child in any group faces.

Since he is initially rather mercurial in his goal-directedness, and since his conceptual and motor capacities are not fully developed, it takes years to internalize these social items. This internalization is not merely

a "stamping" process involving rewards and coercive measures applied
by grown-ups. It includes active processes involving the individual's
particular selectivity and gradually his strivings to become like others
and do what others are doing. Such strivings emerge as the child's conceptual capacities develop, as he interacts with others, and as he acquires
a grasp of the language system. The crucial importance of language is
only hinted at here; as several authors have emphasized, language is
not merely another item of culture, but rather the scaffolding and vehicle
for the formation and perpetuation of culture [153, 168, 210].

The would-be member of a society is literally immersed in items of
nonmaterial culture. They include a language system, social organization,
religion and its organization, art forms, music forms, schedules regulating
vital activities, conceptions of man and the world around him. One
ubiquitous area of nonmaterial culture is a system of values or norms
which includes items pertinent to every important phase of his interpersonal, social, religious, educational, and work activities.

Some parts of nonmaterial culture are fairly concrete in perceptual
form and sequence (e.g., nursery rhythms, regularity of daily activities,
authority of parents in the family group). Some are more abstract (e.g.,
sentence structure of the particular language; notions of past and future,
of town, state, and nation, of the values and organization of school,
church, and profession).

The growing individual does not immediately detect all the items
in his nonmaterial culture in the tangible way that he recognizes items
of material culture, which he can literally bump into. Nevertheless, all
items of the nonmaterial culture are initially external to him. As Emile
Durkheim [61] so rightly insisted, the exteriority of social values or norms
can be unmistakably demonstrated through the consequences of observance or nonobservance of these norms by an individual member of
a group. Reactions of fellow members to deviation *beyond the range of
acceptable behavior* (within which individual variations are permissible)
are one of the best indexes of the external reality of a social value or norm
[e.g., 61, 72, 219]. Reactions to deviation tend to become standardized
in a group, depending on the nature and severity of deviation. Once a
social norm is clearly established, even the leader is not outside the demands of members to behave within the latitude of acceptable behavior
which it defines [e.g., 268, pp. 262 ff].

Insistence on recognizing the external reality of social products is
not an idle issue, nor is it overenthusiasm for supraindividual group properties. Traditionally, two sorts of psychology were recognized—one
dealing with individualistic processes in elementaristic terms which allowed for no emergent properties in experience and behavior, the other
dealing with group or collective processes in which emergences were

recognized. Here we part company with Durkheim, whose exteriority criterion of group norms was cited above.

There are not two sorts of psychology—one for individual processes and one for collective processes. The psychology of the emergence of social norms as products of interaction among individuals is embedded in the basic psychology of the individual, and this basic psychology is the same in all cultures. Whenever the individual faces a stimulus situation where clear alternatives for established modes of action are lacking, his reactions tend toward stabilization, revealing emergent properties [e.g., 221]. The weighty evidence from child psychology [170, 194] and research on clique and gang formations [e.g., 247, 268] warrants this conclusion: whenever individuals interact without established or adequate norms to deal with a problem situation with strong appeal value to them, they produce new values or norms for behavior.

The external reality of social products is stressed here to delineate the nature of concepts and facts appropriate for analysis at the sociological level and at the psychological level. Clear delineation of the nature of our data and concepts can bring order to the confusing mixture that is prevalent today in both social psychology and cognate disciplines. This does not place the sociologist (or anthropologist) and the psychologist in sealed and separated compartments. On the contrary, it makes interdisciplinary give and take a necessity.

I will illustrate the delineation of sociological and psychological analysis briefly by discussing the concepts of social norm and social attitude. *Social norm* is a sociological concept denoting expected or even ideal modes of behavior inferred from similarities of behavior by group members and from their reactions to deviation [72]. Social attitudes are formed by the individual in relation to social norms. *Social attitude* is a psychological concept inferred from the individual's characteristic modes of response to relevant situations [36, 224]. The term "internalization" or "interiorization," used widely by social psychologists in discussing social norms, is symptomatic of the stage of development in social psychology. The term implies that a social attitude is formed in relation to a social norm, or that a social item (e.g., social norm) is learned.

Recognition of the exteriority of social norms does not imply that there is a mechanical imprint of these norms on the individual. It does not obliterate the individual's active part in forming norm-regulated behavior. On the contrary, exteriority provides a baseline which facilitates more adequate study of the psychological problems. Here the baseline is the range of acceptable behavior in terms of the "expected" or "ideal," as defined by the value or norm. Limits can be established by observing the points at which deviation elicits correctives from the identified members of the group. Within the latitude of acceptance variations provide data concerning the unique individualities of members who are within the range of conformity. Individuals exhibiting behavior outside the latitude of acceptable behavior in a given respect are the nonconformists in that respect.

Once the relative positions of individuals within and without the latitude of acceptable behavior are established, we can proceed to the comparison of personality characteristics of conformist and non-conformist individuals as intensively as we wish. Conformity and non-conformity are not absolute qualities. The very terms are relative to a baseline which is defined by a value or norm. There must first be a sociological definition of the norm, independently of the behavior of any particular individual.

In the process of becoming a "good" member of the groups in his sociocultural setting, the individual forms social attitudes in relation to parts of the sociocultural setting. These social attitudes enter into the patterning of his experience and behavior as regulating factors in relevant matters. The constant presence of coercive pressures from other group members and the threat of correctives are supplanted in most instances by his own inner promptings. In fact, as he forms attitudes relative to central values of his group (defining the belongingness and status of members), these attitudes become part of a functioning system of relatedness to his environment which is termed "ego" or "self." Thus the central values of his group become the individual's own personal values. (For example, the individual says, "I am an American," or "I am a college man," or "I am white," with all that these statements imply.)

SOME PROBLEMS OF INTERDISCIPLINARY APPROACHES

Since social psychology studies experience and behavior in relation to social-stimulus situations, it necessarily becomes dependent upon cognate social disciplines for an understanding of its stimulus situations. On the other hand, when sociologists and anthropologists become interested in change and conflict, invention and diffusion, assimilation and acculturation, enculturation and role changes, they inevitably encounter some of the central problems in social psychology [e.g., 177, 210]. The interdependence of the social disciplines in seeking solutions of many central problems has been seriously discussed in numerous interdisciplinary conferences [e.g., 82, 108, 172, 205, 212, 230]. As one result, both traditionally individualistic psychological approaches and the rubber-stamp tradition of cultural determination have become somewhat passé.

Despite the current fashion of "behavioral science," dreams of interdisciplinary integration are far from realized. Too frequently, it is assumed that each contributor represents a unified discipline, and that his approach and conceptual tools are "the" approach and concepts of psychology, sociology, or anthropology, as the case might be. At times, interdisciplinary contact results in wholesale borrowing of concepts to be sprinkled through one's writing at random or tacked onto one's research report as a friendly gesture.

Progress toward a genuinely interdisciplinary approach may be materially speeded through recognizing the levels of analysis of the various disciplines [10, 227]. The social sciences (sociology, anthropology, economics, etc.) and social psychology are approaching related problems at two different levels, each employing appropriate units of analysis. Various problems of the social system are studied by historians, economists, sociologists, anthropologists, linguists, and others of the traditional social sciences. Their units of analysis are not individual man, but man's social organization, his productive and distributive relationships, his technological products and relations, his music and art forms, his language systems, his kinships systems, his values, and so on. The unit of analysis employed requires appropriate concepts for handling relevant variables.

The human individual is the smallest unit of this functioning social system, and he himself is also a functioning system. The scientist who studies his experience and behavior necessarily turns to those investigating various aspects of the individual system—the biochemist, the geneticist, and the physiologist. He also needs to know the conditions in which the individual functions. If he is a social psychologist, this means learning about social-stimulus situations faced by the individual; he must turn to the sociologist, anthropologist, linguist, historian, economist, and others studying man's social environment. But what he learns from them is not social psychology. Social-psychological analysis must be made in terms of the individual's functioning in relation to these social-stimulus situations. Thus many of the most useful concepts in social psychology are relational terms.

The direction of influences between individual and individual and between individual and groups and their products (culture) is reciprocal. The process is interaction rather than simple reaction. The social psychologist may find himself concerned with regularities and patterns of interaction which the sociologist may not have investigated. When the social psychologist investigates these regularities, he is working at the sociological level of analysis. Likewise, when the sociologist or anthropologist becomes preoccupied with the component parts of the social organization (individuals), he is working on a psychological level.

Cross-disciplinary Checking

While the notion of levels is no panacea, its consistent utilization would help to eliminate a number of obstacles to effective interdisciplinary cooperation. Such practice provides invaluable checks on the validity of findings and conclusions. If a generalization reached at one level of analysis is valid, it is not contradicted by valid generalizations reached at another level. For example, the sociologist's generalization (of several decades' standing) that collective action of a group has properties peculiar to the group level [60, 101, 247] should be supported by psychologists' findings concerning individuals when participating as members of a group. This support may be found in psychological research over several decades concerning differential experience and behavior by the individual performing tasks in a social setting [e.g., 1, 53, 125].

On the other hand, a psychologist may conclude that human social patterns in aggression or dominance relations, for example, are basically like the pecking order of domestic fowl or dominance relations in subhuman primates. Scientists familiar with properties of human social organization can document in detail the significant differences between them—differences traceable to differing capacities and underlying processes in the respective species [216, pp. 70–73]. As Schneirla [214, 215] has suggested, if the comparative psychologist were equally concerned with differences and similarities produced by evolutionary processes, he could contribute to the genuinely comparative study of life to the mutual benefit of all disciplines. But if the differences are not taken into account, his contribution is likely to be a caricature of human behavior and human social organization.

Sequence of Analysis

A sequence of study appropriate for problems of interdisciplinary concern derives from the concept of levels of analysis. An observation by the anthropologist Malinowski is pertinent. When Malinowski wrote about a rather complicated system of exchange called "Kula" among island groups in the Western Pacific, he commented that individuals participate effectively in the complex exchange relationships without ever grasping the nature of the "total outline" of the system itself. The individuals involved

. . . know their own motives, know the purpose of individual actions and rules which apply to them; but . . . not even the most intelligent native has any clear idea of the Kula as a big, organized social construction. . . . If you were to ask him what the Kula is, he would answer by giving a few details, most likely by giving his personal experience and subjective views of the Kula . . . . For the integral picture does not exist in his mind; he is in it, and cannot see the whole from the outside [165, p. 83].

If a social psychologist were to study the behavior of single individuals in these Pacific islands without knowing about the Kula as an organized system of relationships, he would be likely to draw erroneous conclusions. True, if he were genuinely concerned with a functional analysis of these behaviors, he would start observing the interactions of the individuals in pertinent activities and eventually arrive at an over-all description of the Kula system, as Malinowski did. But if he persisted in a strictly individual approach to this behavior without first relating it to the patterned relationships of the Kula system, he would have little basis for distinguishing individual variations, individual contributions, or innovations. In short, a primary task in social psychology is learning the properties and functioning of social organizations with their culture patterns. Once the social-stimulus situations are studied, the social psychologist is prepared to investigate individual functioning in relation to them.

Suppose his problem concerns suicide, that individual act of self-destruction which Durkheim [62] so eloquently incorporated into the realm of the "socially determined." If he looked for a careful ecological analysis of a city, such as a recent investigation in London [209], he would find that areas of social isolation, mobility, and "disorganization" contribute significantly to suicide statistics. He would also find that the incidence of this individual act, like most individual acts, is not determined entirely by these over-all sociocultural conditions. In the study noted, at least a quarter of the suicides could not be attributed readily to such conditions. The social psychologist would want to investigate both samples, the sample of individuals who had not been affected by these grossly defined social conditions, and the sample of individuals who seemed to have been significantly affected by them. He would need to frame his analysis within over-all sociocultural conditions to grasp the interrelationships of immediate environmental factors, unique personal characteristics, and variations in life history from birth onward. If such a sequential analysis seems inordinately demanding for the social psychologist, one can only reflect that this is the required task if he wants his social psychology to be *social*.

SOCIAL PSYCHOLOGY IS STILL IN A FORMATIVE STAGE

The integration of findings from psychological and sociocultural levels necessary for an integrated social-psychological theory is still far from attainment. This conclusion will surprise no one whose enthusiasm has not blurred his perspective. As a scientific discipline, social psychology is still in its formative stage.

In handling the current flood of research data, the social psychologist faces a plethora of contradictory and overlapping concepts. Turning to sociology and anthropology for help, he finds disciplines which themselves lack unity in approach and conceptual tools. For example, sociology may seem topically compartmentalized (into urban and rural, theory and social problems, crime and marriage, etc.). To borrow a phrase from the sociologist Becker [21], it may seem to be devoted to "self-inflicted shortsightedness." In anthropology, he finds statements of conceptual unity [177], but contradictory approaches to important problems [25] and serious doubts about the reliability of many empirical findings in the field [e.g., 131, 152].

From the turn of the century, some social psychologists have had their training in and are identified with academic departments of sociology; some have developed in departments of psychology. In terms of this classification, roughly a third of the textbooks in the field since 1908 were written by sociologists and about two-thirds by psychologists. Courses are taught today in departments of both sociology and psychology.

While little can be said here about the general character of sociology and psychology, reference to important trends which influenced social psychology is necessary. During the first decades of this century, some sociologists became seriously concerned with problems of individual functioning, notably in the area of motivation.

Alongside the domain of "bare existence" in which "structuralists" of the time moved so elegantly [e.g., 250], the rise of behaviorism in psychology brought a further trend away from those problems of individual functioning which most interested sociologists. By the 1920s, the predominant trend in psychology, despite McDougall and despite Freud, concerned reflexes, habits, and performance. Motivational problems were touched lightly or motivational concepts were translated into behavioristic terminology, e.g., "pre-potent reflexes" [1]. Sociological concern with motivational problems continued. This is reflected in a comparison between the page references to 12 motivational concepts in the indexes of 5 introductory psychology texts [40, 89, 143, 173, 193] and 5 introductory sociology texts published in the 1920s [58, 93, 159, 208, 261]. The concepts are *drive, emotion, Four Wishes, instinct, interest, libido, motive, sentiments, will to power, attitudes, self, prejudice.* "Drive" was not included in any of the sociology texts. "Four Wishes," "libido," "sentiments," and "prejudice" were omitted from all the psychology texts. The psychology texts had an average of 32 page references per book to these concepts, while the sociology texts averaged 61 page references per book.

Thus, in this period, social psychology proceeded along two different paths [22, 64, 119, 201]. On the one hand, there were the interactionists such as James Mark Baldwin, John Dewey, the sociologist C. H. Cooley, G. H. Mead, W. I. Thomas, Ellsworth Faris; on the other hand, there was a general tide of behaviorism in academic psychology as epitomized in the 1920s by F. H. Allport's text [1]. It is well to note that each discipline was influenced to some extent by the other, even though the differences between the two approaches can be termed "fundamental" and "irreconcilable" [201]. The 1927 *Sourcebook for Social Psychology*, edited by the sociologist Kimball Young [272], included six chapters on "Psychological Foundations of Social Behavior" with selections written predominantly by psychologists. And Murphy and Murphy's first *Experimental Social Psychology* in 1931 [181], summarizing research largely from the psychological laboratory, defined social psychology as the study of "interaction among individuals."

In academic psychology, a heavy emphasis on biological evolution continued side by side with behaviorism. For example, in Murchison's 1935 *Handbook of Social Psychology* [176] almost half of the pages were devoted to evolutionary problems ranging from bacteria to human life. Less than 5 per cent of the contents of the *Sourcebook* (edited eight years earlier by Kimball Young, whose affiliations had been in sociology) concerned such topics. In contrast to the Murchison *Handbook,* with its chapters on age, sex, maladjustment, and childhood, Young's volume contained sections on personality and social behavior, including selections on self, two chapters on prejudice, two chapters on social groups and their standards, and sections entitled "Leadership and Prestige" and "Collective Behavior," with chapters on public opinion and propaganda. The closest overlap between these two volumes was the topic of attitudes. In comparing the two volumes today, one cannot help noting that the topic headings in Young's 1927 volume sound more contemporary and reflect concern with actualities of social behavior not apparent in most of the 1935 Murchison *Handbook*. In fact, Robert French [75] noted in his review of the more recent Lindzey-edited *Handbook of Social Psychology* that about three-quarters of the papers in the 1935 volume were devoted to "topics of scant concern" today. Social psychologists trained in academic psychology manifested less concern than did their sociological colleagues with social actualities or applied problems until the thirties [38].

Some present converging trends in social psychology will be noted later in this chapter, but it should be noted here that their background is more complex than that of the two approaches sketched above. Besides the more traditional interactionist and behavioristic viewpoints, new trends arose in behaviorism itself, including attempts to digest Freudian conceptions [56]. In general, the influence of Freudian theories became more evident in sociology [35], in psychology, and in cultural anthropology [90]. Psychologists became aware that anthropological findings in exotic cultures had relevance for their work, some of them embracing cultural relativism without full awareness of the implications of such a position for social psychology [cf., 179]. Gestalt psychology made itself known in this country and influenced a number of social psychologists during the 1930s. There was much more to complicate this background, but this is perhaps sufficient to indicate the widened horizons and rapid pace of social psychology in the 1930s, as it hustled off in several directions.

With World War II, social psychology was "in demand" by government and military agencies. Studies on propaganda and morale, leadership selection, and "national character" were needed. Social psychologists were put to work side by side with colleagues who had considered themselves experimental psychologists or sociologists or anthropologists or political scientists. Cartwright wrote: "Practical problems of social engineering sprang up overnight which required solution before lunch" [43, p. 67].

Regardless of how one evaluates the results [e.g., 121], there can be little doubt that the research opportunities and facilities supplied during and since World War II by government and military, industrial, and private agencies have given more impetus to social psychology than could any professional efforts, no matter how dedicated. Literature on social-psychological investigations was classified by the *Psychological Abstracts* under "Social Psychology" for the first time in 1947 (after two decades as "Social Functions of the Individual" and one decade of "General Social Processes: Including Aesthetics"), but it has overflowed into almost every topical classification.

The sudden demand, broadened opportunities, and heightened interest in academic circles and outside brought social psychologists closer to the social actualities against which they must eventually test their theories. But a rash of hastily conceived investigations on topics of current interest inevitably tended to obscure any solid advance upon central problems in research and theory. In the interest of keeping the research grants coming and the research reputation of one's university or school rising, a problem suggested by one's next of academic kin was frequently investigated, with little attempt to relate the findings to earlier studies or to related topics.

Here the picture is deliberately drawn black and white to point up the glaring discrepancies and contradictions which anyone who surveys current literature is bound to find. Any pride in the achievements of social psychology over the past three decades must be tempered with awareness that considerable research is not channeled into coherent theory. Conceptual tools are still controversial. Research and theorizing flourish in certain specialized areas without recognition of their relevance to more general problems.

In progressing toward greater maturity as a scientific discipline, one necessary task is unification of conceptual tools. For example, the term *perception* is currently augmented by *social perception, sociometric perception, subception, perceptual defense, perceptual offense,* as well as W. I. Thomas's "definition of the situation," which is preferred by some in academic sociology. This is only one example of a problem area with overlapping and duplicating conceptual tools. The empirical referents of a number of historically important concepts might profitably be reexamined with the view of determining which of the present excessive number are more useful in handling relevant data, including the accumulating experimental results.

SOME PERSISTENT PROBLEMS OF INTERDISCIPLINARY INTEREST

Thus far, a definition of social psychology and its appropriate relations to cognate social disciplines have been suggested and the development of social psychology discussed. The necessity of interdisciplinary give and take became apparent in this discussion. These major points can be articulated through two illustrative problem areas which have persistently concerned all these disciplines, both in the past and at the present time. The problem areas concern small groups and individual-society relationship, including culture and personality.

Small Groups

Today the study of small groups is one of the most active research areas; it is "in vogue" in every sense. The mounting volume of publications in periodicals and books is an index of this trend. Leadership, supervision, and productivity in industrial plants, solidarity and morale, "group cohesion," problem solving, communication and decision-making processes are among the aspects being busily investigated. Considerably more space is now devoted to small-group research in collaborative volumes in social psychology [e.g., 155, 161, 244]. Recently several books appeared dealing explicitly with small groups [19, 30, 44, 92, 187, 239, 245]. Surveys have been devoted wholly or largely to small-group studies [e.g., 2, 51, 66, 125, 200, 206]. In 1954, Strodtbeck and Hare [243] compiled a bibliography of small-group studies listing 1,407 publications.

The sources contributing to the increased activities related to small groups are diverse. A glance at the products reveals diversity of research and practical interests, confusion in the multiplicity of concepts and procedures used, and yet unmistakable leads for eventual unification of problems and concepts.

One source with healthy impact on current research stems from sociological studies such as those of Thrasher [247], Anderson [7], Clifford Shaw [219, 220], Hiller [100], Zorbaugh [275], and Whyte [268]. Most of these studies were carried out in the 1920s at the University of Chicago, primarily inspired by the searching mind of Robert E. Park.

Another important influence on small-group research stems from the concern of business and industrial agencies with efficiency in supervision and production. The results of this concern are well indicated by the work that has been done by Elton Mayo and his associates since the late 1920s [167, 203], and by centers established later at Yale, Chicago, Cornell, and other universities. The movement is sometimes referred to as the "human-relations approach" in industry. As Arensberg pointed out, the development of the human-relations approach received added impetus in the 1930s from the practical concerns created by "labor unrest" [9]. A few years after World War II, a book appeared under the title *Human Relations in Modern Business: a Guide for Action Sponsored by American Business Leaders* [115]. It reflected the active interest of business circles in this research movement and its approach.

Another factor contributing to the study of group processes has certainly been the considerable interest of military organizations both in the United States and other countries in discovering quick and efficient techniques for selecting unit leaders [e.g., 8, 113, 189].

There were other important sources stimulating interest in small-group research. W. E. Newstetter and his associates utilized experimental manipulation and measurement techniques in summer camps [186], and their group studies had considerable influence in arousing interest in "group work" in the social work profession.

In academic psychology, F. H. Allport [1] followed German predecessors with an extensive series of studies which inspired other investigations. However, the works of Moreno [174] and Kurt Lewin and collaborators [147, 151] probably had more direct effect in academic psychology in arousing interest in small-group research. Moreno's sociometric technique, which appeared in the United States in the mid-thirties, provided tangible representation of friendship choices among interacting individuals. A few years later, the demonstration by Kurt Lewin and his associates [147, 151] that various group atmospheres affect behavior differentially was highly effective in gaining acceptance among psychologists for the importance of group properties and encouraging their investigation.

The impact of these investigations in psychology may be difficult to comprehend without appreciation of their audience. The notion of emergent qualities in social-interaction situations, which Durkheim and other social scientists had emphasized and indicated empirically for years, fell upon deaf ears as long as most psychologists were preoccupied with models based on "mental chemistry" or "conditioned reflex." The emergence of social norms in social interaction had to be demonstrated in the laboratory before it was incorporated into the general repertory of psychology [cf. 185]. The experimental findings on groups appeared to be "old hat" to a good many sociologists, although increasing numbers became impressed by the methodological advantages of experimental investigation.

Certain findings, however, were common in all of the foregoing movements in small-group research, and these findings provide the needed criteria for a sound definition of "group." Without some clear criteria, we are caught between rival definitions and descriptions, each claiming acceptance on the basis of particular views and research operations of its proponents. Stated broadly, it was repeatedly confirmed that stability and change of an individual's behavior in so many significant aspects of his living is inextricably related to his group ties. These ties are defined in terms of his group belongingness, his particular status and role relations within groups, and the group values or norms which he internalizes as his own.

In view of this general finding, it is not surprising that those studying supervision and productivity in factories soon found that serious headway required investigation of the organization (structure) and the set of norms that the workers considered their own [203]. Investigators of industrial relations found that incentive systems in a plant are effective for the rank and file within the acceptable bounds of rate setting established in their formally or informally organized groups. To the groups in question, rate setting is a protective measure defining the rate of work and production under given labor-management relations, financial arrangements, and technological conditions. As Whyte demonstrated in his recent book *Money and Motivation* [269], one is always confronted with the fact that incentives and machines exert their influence within the framework of groups with more or less definite organizations and values.

Several investigators of attitude change on social issues have independently reached a similar conclusion concerning the significance of the individual's place in a group with definite values [106, 150, 183]. And as studies of leadership progressed, investigators started to face the fact that apart from the structural (organizational) and normative properties of groups, the study of leadership runs into a dead end of total situational or task relativism [e.g., 41, 81].

When the study of groups starts with fragmentary factors and techniques, fragmentary data are obtained. Building a conception of groups from operations carried out on that basis is likely to end in defining aspects of more or less specific interaction episodes. The essential properties of groups, which have made their study so significant for social psychology, are necessarily obscured.

Investigations of groups actually functioning for more than a transitory interaction episode have demonstrated that a group structure (organization) which defines differentiated role and status relations of individual members and a set of norms (standards, values) are among their minimum properties [e.g., 101, 138, 219, 247, 268]. It can be said that the "groupness" of a group is proportional to the prevalence of such distinctive properties. Of course, there are other attributes of a group which should be studied exhaustively. But open-ended enumeration of dimensions and subsequent attempts at compounding them have not so far produced conceptions that are useful in handling social behavior in natural settings. There are limiting factors in every system, and they affect the main character of the system. If they are defined, then analysis of other properties and their interrelationships may proceed more effectively.

A survey of sociological studies of small groups, especially those in urban areas, provides inexhaustible leads for experimental testing. Briefly, such findings suggest the following account of group formation and its effects on individuals involved: individuals who experience motives, aspirations, deprivations, or frustrations as common tend to interact with one another with a high frequency. If the common motives are not directed toward goals whose attainment by one individual precludes attainment by the others, interaction tends to persist over a period of time. In the course of their interaction, statuses and roles are differentiated. Over a period of time, these relationships tend to stabilize in varying degrees (depending upon the individuals involved, extrinsic factors, and the relative effectiveness of group activities). The stabilization of status and role relations constitutes the group organization or structure. As group structure forms, norms are standardized, at least in matters with relevance to the common motives and aspirations which brought individuals together or which developed in the course of their interaction. In these matters, at least, the activities of the individual member are regulated internally by his membership in the structure, his particular status and role, and the group's norms.

Unless the group in question is totally isolated, it is bound to come into functional contact with other groups, small and large. Here the close examination of sociological findings on relations between groups [e.g., 24, 84, 162] reveals that the particular pattern of intergroup relations established by a group in dealing with others is reflected in that group's norms for behavior. Accordingly, the individual member perceives members of an out-group in a friendly or hostile fashion, depending upon the norms toward the out-group established in his group [227].

Sociological studies of groups are replete with more specific findings which provide leads for experimental investigation. For example, the observation that the group members judge the performance of a low-ranking member with a consistent error of underestimation [268] was the basis of experimental work dealing with judgmental variations as a function of the status of the individual performing the task [96, 229]. Similarly, observed instances of exaggeration of in-group achievements and depreciation of out-group performance suggested propositions for experimental testing concerning the effects of group membership and intergroup conflict upon judgment by members of the groups involved [97, 226].

Unfortunately, there has been intellectual discontinuity in small-group studies, as Shils pointed out so emphatically [232, pp. 26, 42]. In practice, many psychologists in recent years have ignored the intellectual heritage, rich in data suggestive of significant problems and hypotheses, with direct bearing on man's relations in actual groups. Neglect of these group data, accumulated throughout many years in diverse localities, can hardly be justified on the grounds that social psychologists are interested in individuals and not in groups as such. These facts, primarily on the sociological level, give the social psychologist necessary information concerning the individual's relative place in the scheme of relationships that really count for him.

Of course, the social psychologist cannot stop at this point. He must proceed from this "microsociological level," borrowing a phrase from Newcomb [185], to detailed analysis of the individual, his life history, the exact stimulus conditions confronting him, and his attitudes and motives operative at the time. At this psychological level of analysis, sheer improvisation from sociological data has not been notably helpful. On this score Strodtbeck and Hare's remarks concerning the neglect of experimental knowledge in social psychology are well taken [243, p. 109]. The investigator who goes to the considerable trouble of surveying available sociological data and then proceeds to more detailed analysis of individuals on the psychological level finds that the two levels of analysis are not contradictory. In fact, as we have seen, findings at one level serve as checks for the validity of findings on the other. For example, in *The Jack Roller,* Stanley's autobiography and the detailed life history and psychiatric reports contain detailed substantiation of the general trends of sociological data concerning the formation of groups and regulation of members' behavior within them [219].

The methodological advantage of studying the individual's particular role and status in his group(s) prior to detailed analysis of his behavior can be illustrated briefly through the recent controversy over generality or specificity of leadership from situation to situation. The results of various leadership studies have been rather inconclusive. Some results, notably those of "leaderless-group" studies, favor the conclusion that leadership behavior is specific to given interaction and task situations. Other results point to continuity and consistency in leadership over a period of time. It seems likely that the results will be coherent if they are evaluated in terms of the relative stabilization of status and role reciprocities among the participating individuals at the time their behavior is assessed. Is the behavior in question being studied in a group with given structure and integration, or is the behavior occurring in a new interaction situation among previously unrelated individuals?

Present evidence indicates that when there are no established reciprocities among individuals, leadership behavior is more closely related to the relative proficiency of individuals in the task at hand, thus rather specific to given situations [41, 81]. On the other hand, if the individuals are members of a closely knit group, the relative weight of single tasks and situations in determining leader-follower behaviors is considerably reduced [e.g., 170, 227, 251, 268]. In this case leadership is more likely to be general from one situation to the next. The emphasis on organizational settings of leadership by Ohio State investigators and others [192, 217, 238] is a significant advance in study of these problems.

Reference groups. Discussion of some problems of interdisciplinary approach in small-group research requires consideration of the problems which brought the concept of reference groups to the foreground. The concept is widely used today by both psychologists and sociologists [94, 99, 153, 171, 184, 222, 231, 254].

In modern societies, small groups are not self-contained closed systems. The individual member of a group has perceptual and/or conceptual access to a number of groups. The directions and goals of these various groups may be compatible or incompatible with one another. For this reason, no amount of exclusive concentration on face-to-face interaction processes within a single group furnishes a complete guide for studying behavior of an individual member.

Reference groups, that is, the groups to which an individual relates himself or aspires to relate himself as a part psychologically may or may not be the groups in which he is actually seen or is registered as a member. An individual's reference groups may include membership groups or nonmembership groups. The social bases of the individual's standards of judgment, gratification, and attainment can be assessed only through ascertaining his reference groups. For this reason, the reexamination of a variety of attitudes of American soldiers studied during World War II [241] in terms of the reference-group concept by Merton and Kitt [171] marks a conceptual advance in attitude studies.

Analysis of the individual's reference groups is a significant step in understanding the influence of groups to which he does not actually belong in shaping his tastes, attitudes, and aspirations. Particularly in a vertically mobile multigroup society, many individuals set their goals in terms of more powerful and highly placed groups to which they privately aspire [e.g., 71, 114, 256].

Once the significance of the individual's psychological relatedness to various groups is ascertained, it will be easier to explain his compliance to group pressures, either with or without inner acceptance. This persistent problem was treated extensively by Piaget, who utilized the concepts "autonomy" (i.e., regulation of one's behavior through rules cherished as one's own) and "heteronomy" (i.e., regulation of behavior through rules attributed to sources of authority) [194]. The problem was raised more recently by Festinger [67] in terms of "compliant behavior" with or without private acceptance.

Analysis of the individual's reference groups is, therefore, helpful in understanding the consistency of his behavior from day to day. It is equally valuable in analysis of inconsistent or contradictory behavior exhibited by the same individual in two different settings. For example, the individual member of a group with a nondiscrimination policy may reveal no prejudice while participating in deliberations of that group, but later may participate in a riot as an identified member of a neighborhood group, as observed during the Detroit race riots of 1943.

The concept of reference groups is a relational one. Analysis in terms of reference groups obviously requires collaboration at both sociological and psychological levels. Significantly, the term's first use by Hyman [109] was directly tied to laboratory findings on the effects of reference points in judgment; its subsequent modification was based on sociological findings of the anchoring effect of in-group standards [222], and after a period of some confusion [cf. 124], this usage is prevalent today both in sociology [153, 231, 254] and psychology [94, 99].

Individual-Society Relationship

The general problem of individual-society relationship towers over other common problems encountered by psychologists and social scientists. Persistent issues were inherited from philosophers, theologians, and political theorists of the past. The problem has been discussed under the labels "individual and the group," "culture and personality," "individual and society," and other paired polarities.

Until recently, major theories of individual-society relationship posited a picture of "original human nature" largely in the image of the prevailing temper and ideology of the times. The particular conception of "human nature" set the lines of the theory. At one extreme, human nature was depicted as an unfolding of biologically determined impulses and instincts. At the other, human nature was considered an infinitely plastic raw material molded in the image of a reified culture. Conflict was primarily between interested parties that were committed to unverified premises. No real progress was possible.

In recent years various scholars have attempted to reconcile the rival theories. For example, Homans [104, pp. 316–333] grouped the historically significant theories under the headings "The Social Contract Theory" (Hobbes, Rousseau), "The Social Mold Theory" (Durkheim), and "Culture and Personality." He offered a reconciliation of these dichotomous approaches. These traditional theories place almost exclusive responsibility on either individual or the group for prevailing social life and man's fortunes or misfortunes within it. Homan's reconciliation recognizes that each of the various one-sided theories can account for phenomena in certain periods of time, but that a complete account of individual-society relationships requires bringing all of these time periods into the picture.

The picture of human nature which is emerging considers the human being as he functions at a given time in a particular society as a biosocial product [e.g., 10, 13, 168, 178]. The individual's consistent modes of behavior in personal and group relations and his persistent strivings toward values and goals are shaped interdependently by both his biological endowment and sociocultural influences. In this view, a conception of original human nature as an entity apart from the interaction of an individual in his social setting has proven to be untenable.

Some notion of original human nature was necessary as long as man's lasting and recurrent strivings were attributed primarily to biological endowment, as they were in McDougall's list of instincts [164] or Freud's classification of "sexual instincts" and "death instinct" [76, pp. 54 ff., 67]. In such a doctrine, social organization, culture, and the entire scheme of human relations become matters of applied psychology. There is hardly place for emergence of social structure and other items of culture, or a human personality which is not reducible to the vicissitudes of instinctual impulses.

Concept of ego (self). When the individual's persistent motivational patterns manifested in characteristic modes of behavior are conceived as products of interrelated biosocial influences, preoccupation with an original human nature becomes unnecessary. If what is termed "personality structure" is revealed in anything, it is in the individual's characteristic modes of behavior. The focus of study in this area becomes, therefore, the problem of consistency in goal-directed behavior over a time span.

The regulative pattern lending characteristic consistency to the individual's goal-directed behaviors and to his performance of tasks in interaction with other individuals has been conceptualized in terms of the formation and functioning of the individual's ego or self. The concept of ego or self current in social psychology has nothing to do with the mystic halo surrounding the term historically. It has nothing to do with "homuncular entities" warring for domination of man's behavior [13]. It is not akin to the notion of an "executive agent" that intrudes in ongoing psychological activity. Rather, it refers to a psychological formation that is an outcome of man's interaction with his surroundings. The biosocial formation termed "ego" or "self" consists of a system of relatedness to one's surroundings, including social-stimulus situations with which one has contact perceptually or conceptually. In this system of relatedness, reciprocal expectations and ties with other people are crucial components.

Many psychologists and sociologists since William James's treatment of "social self" [112] have contributed to a concept of ego or self as a developmental formation relating the individual to his surroundings [224, pp. 156–199]. It is no accident that the authors who have offered theories of ego or self have been particularly interested in psychology-sociology relationships.

J. M. Baldwin described the development of self in terms of a "dialectic" process reflected in his dictum that "ego and alter are . . . born together" [16, cf. 17]. The sociologist C. H. Cooley presented an interactionist account of self as early as 1902 in his *Human Nature and the Social Order* [49]. Cooley unmistakably related development of self to the formation of "primary group" ties by the growing individual [119, p. 300].

Probably the most thoroughly interactionist of the early twentieth-century social philosophers was George Herbert Mead [168]. Mead's "act" was not an isolated behavior unit, but referred to the complete pattern of interaction. In his words:

> The social act is not explained by building it up out of stimulus plus response; it must be taken as a dynamic whole—as something going on—no part of which can be considered or understood by itself—a complex organic process implied by each individual stimulus and response involved in it [168, p. 7].

His theory of self dealt with an individual immersed in social "transactions." As an outcome of these transactions according to Strauss in his *The Social Psychology of George Herbert Mead*—

> . . . the child learns not only to assume multiple positions vis-à-vis himself but to organize these positions into a system. Childhood games, Mead suggests, are among the situations in which the child acquires the ability to

do this. This generalized system of attitudes is termed "the generalized other." Mead's most distinctive characterization of self is in terms of the "generalized other" [242, p. xiv].

In the writings of Baldwin, Cooley, Mead, and some of their contemporaries, we find insightful attempts at viewing social behavior in terms of an ongoing interaction process in which a biosocial self or ego emerges. By and large, however, their brilliant insights were not conceptualized in a way permitting ready translation into a research program. The views of Lindesmith and Strauss were strongly influenced by Mead [e.g., 153, 242], but Strauss comments: "There have been attempts to draw out of Mead's work very specific implications for empirical testing, but this has not proved very effective, at least as yet" [242, p. xiv].

The conception of ego or self that is currently developing is based squarely on converging findings from a variety of research. The main outlines of this conception are derived from child development studies, experiments on ego-involvements, and anthropological findings.

Accumulating studies of child development [e.g., 13, 79, 194, 224, 233, 260] contain ample evidence that an individual's ego or self is not innately given. Rather, their findings reveal the formation by the individual of relatedness to particular aspects of his life. This formation is not an immutable entity completely and finally structured by the age of six or the age of ten. Studies of adolescence [14, 105, 116, 137] show that noteworthy changes in the system of personal relatedness may occur during this transition period. Such changes may be intensified in sociocultural settings which are undergoing social change at an accelerated tempo [e.g., 54, 139]. Changes may also occur in later life if the individual is confronted with serious problems which arouse conflict with present expectations and values in professional or other significant aspects of living. Old age in many societies is a transition period conducive to alterations in various components of the individual's ego formation.

Study of changes in the ego formation with changing social roles at given periods of life is helpful in achieving a formulation of ego or self which is generally applicable. This study implies an understanding of both the sequence and kind of developmental stages through which individuals pass in a society. It follows that cross-cultural comparisons are invaluable checks against an ethnocentric picture of self. The social psychologist finds relevant data in anthropological field work [e.g., 197, 198, 202, 255].

In recent years, laboratory studies have demonstrated significant effects of ego-involvement in various psychological activities. The findings suggest the utility of the concept of ego in handling the consistency of characteristic modes of behavior and strivings. Are the behavior and strivings of the individual relatively consistent from situation to situation? There is evidence indicating consistency over a time span and, on the other hand, there is evidence of specificity of behavior to given situations. Certainly more experimentation and research are needed for any conclusive generalization. However, available experimental findings concerning the setting of goals [e.g., 103, 149], confidence [126], and specificity or generality of personal characteristics indicate that the person's behavior is consistent if the situation is ego-involving for him and is more variable if he is not ego-involved in the issue or situation at hand. Such experimental evidence led G. W. Allport, one of the outstanding "trait" psychologists of the thirties who favored the "generality" of personality traits [3], to conclude that a trait may be general or specific depending on the degree of ego-involvement of the person in that respect [4, pp. 472–474].

The conclusion reached here acquires added significance from relevant findings in child psychology. The growing child does not follow goals consistently until he becomes capable of setting up standards for his own behavior—an aspect of ego formation requiring conceptual development and mastery of language [79, 85]. Similar development is necessary for the appearance of consistent patterns of competitive behavior [88, 102, 145] and consistently cooperative behavior [23, 191]. During this same period, in a sociocultural setting where social distance is maintained toward certain out-groups, the child begins to exhibit prejudice in the consistent fashion prescribed in social definition [e.g., 47, 87]. The appearance of such consistent modes of behavior implies an internal patterning of motives which is here termed "ego" or "self."

There are, of course, inconsistencies in behavior in situations where the individual is ego-involved. In the brief discussion of reference groups, an example was given of personal inconsistency when the individual related himself to different reference groups with contradictory norms. Thoroughgoing study of behavioral inconsistencies needs to consider conflicting components of the individual's personal relatedness as they are situationally aroused over a period of time. However, it should also be noted that severe deprivations or frustrations usually produce striking inconsistencies of behavior in terms of the individual's "accustomed" self [e.g., 228, pp. 433–443].

The conception of ego or self derived from the above findings can be summarized. *Ego* or *self* is a developmental formation in the psychological makeup of the individual, consisting of *interrelated attitudes* which are acquired in relation to his own body, to his own abilities, to objects, persons, family, groups, social norms, and institutions and which define and regulate his relatedness to them in a number of concrete situations.

This conception takes into account cultural variations in ego formation inferred from observations in societies where individual behavior is predominantly competitive or primarily cooperative or primarily power-oriented or submissive, as the case may be. By relating ego formation to the individual's specific reference groups during his development, differences in modal behavior which are characteristic in the multiple and opposing groups of differentiated societies are amenable to psychological investigation. Changes, even transformations, in motivational patterns and behavior occurring in adolescence, in professional or marital life, in old age, and in critical situations can be analyzed without contradicting basic assumptions.

Conceiving of the individual's ego formation as a constellation of interrelated parts (attitudes) permits investigation of ego problems in specific dimensions. Unit parts (attitudes) of the ego formation are not fragmentary elements, but are interrelated. Being interrelated, the various parts may be conducive to an integrated pattern of motivation and hence behavior. Likewise, being interrelated, incompatible attitudes formed by the same individual become an important source of personal conflicts, as exemplified by the plight of many a professional woman who is torn between attitudes toward husband and home and attitudes toward her career.

Because the term "attitude" has been used in different senses historically and has at times been devoid of motivational character, additional words are necessary about the unit parts, which may be called "ego-attitudes." As used here, "attitude" denotes an internal variable, namely, a state of readiness which is learned and which involves a subject-object relationship. Characteristically, the individual in this subject-object relationship takes a positive or negative stand conducive to goal-directed behavior in relation to persons, groups, institutions, values, and other *classes* of objects. As such, attitudes do refer to acquired or sociogenic motives. As W. I. Thomas showed in the factually rich context of *The Polish Peasant in Europe and America* [246], a social attitude is always formed in relation to social stimuli, among which social values or norms constitute an important class.

In their recent book *Opinions and Personality,* Smith, Bruner, and White defined attitude in a similar way: "We define an attitude as a predisposition to experience a class of objects in certain ways, with characteristic affect; to be motivated by this class of objects in characteristic ways; and to act with respect to these objects in a characteristic fashion" [235, p. 33].

To psychologists of varying descriptions [e.g., 99, 178, 236], it is becoming evident that a psychology of human motivation requires some such concept as ego or self. Amidst current neologisms positing dynamics of all sorts, it may sound a little pedestrian to make attitudes component parts of a concept such as ego or self. However, the individual's social attitudes, as components of his ego, do have motivational character. They affect his selectivity and goal-directedness even when other more "dependable" [130] or "biogenic" motives are aroused. For a human adult, sexual activity is not only a means of releasing sexual tensions, but it involves a social relationship in which his attitudes concerning personal qualities of the sex object and socioeconomic class may be of crucial importance [70]. Likewise, eating, dressing, choice of dwelling are not only instances of tension reduction, but occasions for proving one's worth and distinction, as revealed in the choice of an eating place, the importance of the label in one's garment, the location of one's residence on this or the other side of the tracks [256]. The attitudes implied operate on a conceptual level and are not governed simply by homeostatic states of the organism.

If ego or self functions as a regulating agent from situation to situation, if relevant ego-attitudes normally regulate the functioning of other motives, shall we posit instinctive propensities at its basis? As noted earlier in this section, longitudinal studies of child development offer little justification for an instinctivist position. Without positing an instinctive basis, the motivational character of ego-attitudes can be studied through analysis of the effects of disrupting their subject-object relationships. Even in adulthood, our sense of personal stability continues to be dependent upon the perceived stability of the subject-object relationships implied in important ego-attitudes. Disruption of these relationships and out-of-the-ordinary events are conducive to feelings of uncertainty, insecurity, and anxiety. Experimental evidence has shown that even temporary disruption of physical anchorages for bodily orientation produces feelings of uncertainty, resulting in highly variable behavior [225]. These crucial points, which indicate the feasibility of analyzing the motivational bases of ego-involvement without positing innate propensities, cannot be elaborated here [228, pp. 600–606]. But a caution can be sounded against repeating the retreat of McDougall when he posited innate propensities for dominance, submission (self-abasement), etc., alongside a developmental picture of the "self-regarding sentiment" which remains to this day one of the most penetrating accounts of ego formation available [164].

"Culture and personality" approach to the problem. Among the most prominent interdisciplinary activities exploring individual-society relationships during the last two decades have been those labeled "culture and personality" and "national character" studies. The former have usually focused on smaller, less-developed societies, while investigations of similar problems in modern nations are termed studies of "national character." For purposes of the present discussion, distinction between the two movements is unnecessary.

Contemporary enthusiasm for studying culture and personality received its greatest impetus in the 1930s from the linguist-anthropologist Edward Sapir [210, pp. 357–364, 507–597]. In calling for study of "tangible problems of behavior rather than selected problems set by recognized disciplines" [210, p. 513], Sapir hoped for the development of a genuinely "social" psychology which would leave the sociocultural investigator "free to study the rationale of group forms, group functions, group changes and group interrelationships from a formal or cultural point of view" [210, p. 364]. The sociologist W. I. Thomas, whose interest in individual-society relationship was further stimulated by Sapir [132, p. xiii], contributed research orientation and conceptualizations in this area [257]. His influence was particularly apparent in the treatment of attitude-value relationships by Linton [156], who also found Mead's concept of role useful in his development of "status personality" [cf. 20, p. 150].

Gaining prominence and significantly deflecting the above influences, psychoanalytic orientation became predominant in "culture and personality" literature [90, pp. 202–209; 234, pp. 37, 56]. Comparatively few anthropologists find strictly Freudian interpretations of culture [77] palatable, and few would agree with the recommendation that psychoanalysis is necessary preparation for understanding problems of culture and personality [e.g., 204, pp. 587–588]. However, the psychoanalytic influence on their studies persists. Its most widespread effect, even on nonpsychoanalytic writers, has been severe limitation of the problems chosen for study, the kind of variables investigated, and, consequently, the range of discussion and debate.

Typical research problems have concerned influences during very early childhood, particularly the effects of adult methods and manner of child rearing [e.g., 78, 118, 154, 267]. Literally all sorts of social attitudes and their relative salience for individuals in a given society have been attributed to hypothesized effects of adult treatment in early childhood. Yet serious questions remain concerning the influence of child rearing methods in personal development and the relationships between early childhood experiences and adult functioning [154, 188, 218].

When research focus shifts to actual study of "modal personality" [e.g., 110, 156], conceived as statistical expression of characteristics common to individuals in a group, the resulting evidence of group regularities may be proper data for sociocultural analysis. The modal personality thus attained will be a sociological construct even though it carries the "personality" label. In mutual accommodation to fundamentally conflicting assumptions, sociocultural investigators and psychoanalysts have sometimes arrived at formulations strikingly similar to the venerable dichotomy between individual and society. Thus in some of the literature, the "basic personality," "modal personality," or "social character" structure appears side by side with the "authentic individual," "the real self," or "deeper layers" of personality [78, 118, 156]. The latter is presumably immune to societal influences [cf. 154, pp. 590 f.].

If studies of culture and personality or national character are to be viewed as more than exciting literary adventures, sooner or later investigators will have to respect major methodological criticisms in their actual practice. Such criticisms have pertained to adequateness of sample within a society, reproducibility of procedures, and taking "responsibility" for stated hypotheses [e.g., 63, 110,, 129, 131]. In particular, the existence of multiple groups in modern complex societies, and even in preliterate societies, requires specification of the group membership of individuals studied and of the range of group values within a society. Investigations oriented toward problems of multiple-group membership may very well lead to revision of concepts designating uniform or common characteristics for an entire society. Methodological improvements alone, however, do not guarantee more catholic selection of problems. Nor will technical refinements provide an escape from the theoretical confusion inherent in trying to reconcile "individualistic" or "reductionist" schemes of psychology with the fundamental premises of sociocultural study [90, pp. 95 f., pp. 207 f.].

If, as suggested in previous sections, a crucial problem of individual-society relationships concerns the consistency of the individual's characteristic motivational patterns, the concept of ego or self discussed there can aid in making research inroads in this area more rapid. While not identical with the totality of psychological organization usually designated as "personality," the concept deals with personal organization in terms amenable to the dimensional analysis necessary in actual research and in studying the interrelationships among evaluative dimensions. A concept of self was profitably employed by Gillin and Raimy in a research study and has been discussed in terms of culture and personality studies by Hallowell [83, 90].

It is suggested here that conceiving ego or self as a constellation of interrelated attitudes linked with identifiable reference groups will be particularly useful in studying psychological problems associated with culture change or acculturation [31, 98, 249]. Though not formulated in these terms, the Gillin and Raimy study consisted of eliciting responses to identify the individual's reference groups in order to explicate his self-conception. In a recent design for studying reactions to culture change [237), the hypotheses concerned the relative incidence of "symptoms of personality disorganization" for individuals in "transitional categories" and those still closely related to traditional groups in a society. Further specification of conflicts in reference-group ties in terms of a particular individual's relevant ego-attitudes may be useful in delineating relationships between culture change and personality disorganization.

It should be noted that the currently developing concept of ego or self includes attitudes assigned, in orthodox psychoanalytic terminology, to a "superego." The inclusion of these attitudes, which incorporate values from authority figures as part of the ego constellation, is in harmony with anthropological findings that the relative frequency and social referents of feelings of guilt and shame following violations of social values vary from culture to culture, as do other ego-involved experiences [e.g., 15, 129].

SOME CONVERGING TRENDS IN SOCIAL PSYCHOLOGY

A backward glance at this discussion of social psychology and the social sciences will bring the remainder of the chapter into better perspective. As noted, social psychology as a scientific discipline is still in a formative stage. It cannot be asserted that even its subject matter is clearly delineated, as a glance at its textbooks readily indicates. The first task of this chapter, therefore, was an attempt to attain a workable definition of social psychology in order to talk about its relationships with cognate social disciplines. The main terms of the definition were derived from developments in psychology and social science, specified in their appropriate contexts. Social psychology was defined as the scientific study of the experience and behavior of the individual in relation to social-stimulus situations.

One of the main terms in the definition, namely, "social-stimulus situations," was the basis for articulation of social psychology—social science relationships. The give and take between the individual and the social-stimulus situations confronting him is on a meaningful, patterned level. Varieties of social-stimulus situations (including human groups and their culture, material and nonmaterial), are subject matters of sociology, cultural anthropology, and other social sciences. Analysis of social-stimulus situations as patterned events in space and time requires that the social psychologist borrow from the work of the social scientists. On the other hand, the study of experience and behavior necessarily takes the individual as its unit of analysis. Here, in turn, the social scientist is dependent on the psychologist. Illustrative problem areas where such a conception of distinctive yet complementary levels of analysis has or could prove fruitful were discussed briefly.

Despite continuing confusion and controversy over important concepts and preferred research orientations, there are convergences in social psychology today which can best be referred to as over-all trends. On the whole, these trends are sufficiently general to transcend differences in preferred concepts and research topics. It should be noted, however, that they do not receive the same emphasis from all social psychologists. The emphasis of a given social psychologist may be on one or another of these trends, occasionally to the neglect of others. But it seems likely that every social psychologist has some concern and some part in all these trends and that social psychologists and social scientists have influenced one another.

Social psychologists of various persuasions seem to be concerned with the following trends:

1. A growing emphasis on studying social behavior within a framework of interacting influences, rather than concentrating exclusively on either internal factors (motives, effects of past experience, organismic states, etc.) or external factors (e.g., groups, culture) as supreme determinants

2. Positive efforts through cross-cultural and intergroup comparisons to achieve the perspective necessary to guard against ethnocentrism in drawing generalizations

3. Increased utilization of scientific methods and techniques

Studying Behavior as Product of Interrelated External and Internal Influences

Not too many years ago, controversies between exponents of an individualistic approach and exponents of a group or culture-bound approach seemed endless. But a healthy conception emerged. It is that social behavior is not accountable solely on the basis of influences coming from the individual or solely on the basis of influences from groups and their culture. Rather, behavior becomes accountable when studied within the framework of interrelated external (e.g., social) and internal factors operative at a given time. In recent textbooks on social psychology, this conception of the joint determination of behavior is expressed in one form or another, with varying emphasis and with varying degrees of success in its application to the topics covered. The trend is reflected in textbooks by Krech and Crutchfield [136], Newcomb [184], Hartley and Hartley [94], Asch [10], and Klineberg [130], to cite a few psychologists; it is reflected in the books of Faris [65], Lindesmith and Strauss [153], and Kimball Young [273], to cite a few sociologists.

In bringing this trend to the foreground, gestalt psychologists contributed substantially [e.g., 32, 135, 146]. George Herbert Mead's conceptualization of the human "act," with emphasis on "outer" and "inner" aspects, was certainly influential, especially through his teaching [168]. Bartlett's investigations of memory were conceived in terms of such joint determination and were striking evidence of the utility of this approach to some American investigators [18]. Despite differences in terminology, the basic assumption of all psychologists who have contributed to the flourishing experimental investigation of "social perception" [e.g., 34, 42, 157, 158, 195, 213, 221] and "social judgment" [e.g., 45, 96] is that experience and behavior are jointly determined by external and internal factors. Such experimentation could not make headway without the assumption that reduced structure of the stimulus field permits maximal effect of internal influences (e.g., attitudes) in psychological structuring. I trust that these examples are sufficient to indicate the scope and interdisciplinary nature of this general trend; it has been variously stated, for example, in the writings of Cottrell [50], Kluckhohn and Murray [132, p. xi], and Murphy [178].

The current need of research and theoretical development is a straightforward formulation of the frame of reference, consisting of functional relations among the interrelated external (stimulus) and internal factors that participate in shaping behavior. A diagram may be the simplest way to present the functional relationships of the frame of reference of an observed behavior. It is a representation of the main terms and the sequence of relationships. Interrelationships cannot be represented so simply. This diagram is a conceptual representation of a mode of analysis; it is not a picture of anything.

I will first note the sequence of relationships and then briefly characterize the main terms, basing my discussion on material presented in greater detail elsewhere [227, chap. 6; 228, chaps. 2, 3]. Here generalizations are stated in categorical form. By necessity, they are given without qualifications and supporting evidence. We have found the scheme most useful in developing a program to study social interaction and individual functioning in an interrelated way [223].

Note the direction of arrows in the diagram. Observed behavior, verbal or nonverbal, is not directly determined by external or internal influences. Observed behavior follows central psychological structuring, or patterning, of internal and external factors. Phenomenally, psychological structuring is revealed in perceiving, judging, remembering, imagining, and the like. In various situations, the relative weights of external and internal factors in psychological structuring differ, as will be mentioned presently.

Relations among external and internal factors constitute the frame of reference of a behavior or act, which can be adequately understood only within the frame of reference of which it is a part. Thus conceived, an item of behavior (verbal or nonverbal) is a unit of psychological analysis. This has been the working conception in research practice for a good many psychologists for some time. Such a conception makes distinctions between fragmentary and unrelated reactions and an act (considered as situationally related and goal-directed) both unnecessary and confusing [e.g., 190, chap. 1]. Such a label as "act" might have been needed by George H. Mead to refer to the nonfragmentary and

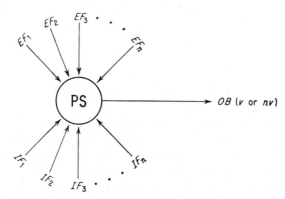

Fig. 1. Diagrammatic representation of the frame of reference of an observed behavior at a given time. *OB* (*v* or *nv*): Observed behavior (verbal or nonverbal). *EF*: External factors (objects, persons, groups, cultural products, etc., in the external stimulus situation). *IF*: Internal factors (attitudes, emotions, states of the organism, linguistic concepts, effects of past experience, etc.). *PS*: Psychological (perceptual) structuring.

interrelated nature of human behavior during the decades when psychologists were dealing with behavior in terms of atomistic S-R bonds or sensations and images as elements of mental life.

Since an observed behavior follows central psychological structuring or patterning, experience and behavior constitute a unity [178]. Differences obtained between an expressed attitude on an issue and actual behavior in a relevant situation do not require a divorce of attitude (internal factor) from overt behavior. Rather, such contradictions imply a changed constellation of factors in the structuring of experience from the time when the individual was asked to respond to a direct question and the time when he confronted a relevant problem situation. Almost always different external factors are involved and internal factors other than the attitude in question are aroused.

"External factors" refer to stimulating situations outside the individual at a given time—objects, events, groups and their cultural products, including tools and other technological items. "Internal factors" refer to bodily states (fatigue, drowsiness, thirst), emotions, effects of past experience (including, as an important class, concepts derived from the language), attitudes, interests, and other social motives formed at the time. Internal factors are not observed directly. They are necessarily inferred from behavior (verbal or nonverbal) in relation to given stimulating conditions.

Psychological structuring is determined jointly by external and internal factors contributing in varying degrees in given conditions. In 1929, Köhler stressed the "bipolar character" of psychological structuring in these words: "Apart from drowsiness and similar states of low vitality, the organization of the total field will almost always have just that bipolar character, the self being directed to something else or from it" [135, p. 323].

In the joint determination of psychological patterning, we find a sound basis for *psychological selectivity*. The facts of psychological selectivity make it difficult to conceive of perception or judgment as simply cognitive affairs. In the "open" stimulus field encountered by the individual from day to day, in contrast to the "constricted" stimulus field presented in a laboratory experiment, what stands out for the individual as figure and what is relegated to the background are determined to a significant extent by motivational factors. Laboratory experiments for many decades have shown that only a limited number of stimulus items can be attended to, perceived, judged, or remembered at a given time. Which items are singled out of an open stimulus field is determined not merely by the compelling properties of the stimulus, but to a great extent by the motivational or attitudinal relevance of the stimulus to the individual. In this area, the social psychologist's findings on effects of attitudes or ego-involvement and the social scientist's findings on the patterned properties of social-stimulus situations can supplement one another.

The primary psychological tendency is toward structuring experience, and structuring ordinarily precedes the analysis of parts. (This is the reason why, during the period when analysis of elements was considered the main objective of psychology, graduate students had to be trained rigorously as observers before they could single out elements to report.) Internal structuring or patterning is not an additive affair. Objects and events in the external field are perceived or judged in terms of the relations of their parts rather than as discrete items. Likewise, internal factors contribute as related parts, rather than as isolated sovereign "movers" of behavior. External factors and internal factors contributing to psychological structuring become interrelated. Any item (external or internal) functioning in the system of relations, which constitutes the frame of reference at a given time, is affected by other factors. Herein lies the psychological basis of the differential or "emergent" effects of social situations as compared with individual situations.

Stimulus situations which are themselves highly structured, clear cut, or unequivocal set limits for alternatives in psychological structuring. Compelling stimulus structure in a given dimension permits comparatively little variation in the way people perceive or judge that dimension. Consensus of opinion concerning highly structured dimensions of a stimulus situation is reached very rapidly [253]. The implications of this point are apparent in connection with the effects of material culture. Attempts to influence the individual toward an alternative which is contradicted by properties of stimulus situations are increasingly unsuccessful as the discriminated aspect becomes more clear cut; even individuals who are influenced are likely to see the situation as bizarre [11].

On the other hand, in stimulus situations lacking objective structure in one or several dimensions, alternatives for psychological structuring are increased. An application of this general principle for social psychology is that in social situations with ambiguous or equivocal aspects, the individual is more easily influenced by suggestions from others in perceiving or judging those aspects. This finding provides the sociologist with a psychological basis for some of his own recurring observations. The sociologist has observed that times of social instability and crises are fertile grounds for the rise and standardization of new slogans, new norms, and new forms of social organization [28, 60]. The norm-formation experiments, which utilized the autokinetic effect as a situation lacking objective structure in a given dimension, were based both on the above psychological principle and on the observations by sociologists concerning such new standardizations [221].

Experiments systematically varying external stimulus structure and covarying internal factors will clarify some problems of individual-society relationship. Promising starts have been made in this direction, as exemplified by the works of Coffin [48], Luchins [157, 158], and J. D. Thrasher [248]. To summarize just one experiment, Thrasher covaried external stimulus structure in a given dimension and the nature of interpersonal relationships (friendship and nonfriendship between subjects). His results show that when the external stimulus field is relatively more structured, external stimulus factors weigh more heavily in determining judgment of the stimulus; but as the stimulus dimension being judged becomes less structured, the influence of internal factors (attitudes toward a friend) is relatively greater.

While denying the sovereign power of any set of factors for every instance of psychological structuring, the conception of joint determination outlined here implies that various factors in the frame of reference have differing *relative weights* at a given time. Such relative weights are not absolute, of course, being affected by interrelationships among various operative factors. Nevertheless, studies of social influence and motive arousal in situations of varying objective structure, such as those mentioned above, suggest a regularity or lawfulness of the conditions in which external factors or internal factors carry greater relative weights. Doubtless systematic variation of factors affecting psychological selectivity will clarify further regularities.

In any specific research, it is necessary to recognize that certain factors function as *limiting* influences. Such limiting factors are decisive in determining salient characteristics of psychological patterning and hence behavior. They are referred to as "anchorages" or "anchoring agents." The currently developing concept of reference groups stemmed from a study of judgments of status [109] which extended psychophysical experiments on reference scales and anchorages by using different groups as the standard for judgment. A reference group is conceived as a major anchorage for the individual in his social ties [228]. With a shift in reference groups, significant changes occur in the individual's evaluation of various aspects of social life [e.g., 150, 171, 183]. Systematic investigation of the relative weights of factors under varying conditions is the most difficult but essential task of future research.

Checks against Effects of Ethnocentrism

Perception and judgment of objects, persons, and events of the social world are influenced by the individual's internal standards or attitudes formed through contact with the social norms of his reference groups. As a result, there is a tendency to see things from the viewpoint of one's own group and to evaluate them in terms of its major premises. This tendency, referred to as "ethnocentrism" since Sumner's days, is not peculiar to members of any particular culture. Scientists are not immune to errors and distortions stemming from their ethnocentrisms. Scientists whose subject matter concerns human individuals, groups, and their products are necessarily in greater jeopardy than others from this source.

Anthropological studies like those of Malinowski, Boas, and Margaret Mead were profoundly influential in making social psychologists aware of the pitfalls of universalizing research findings obtained within their own sociocultural settings. Research on measurement of abilities and traits was also important in this respect. In the decades preceding the 1930s, research findings ranking various human groupings in terms of "superiority" and "inferiority" of intelligence were presented. The comparative and longitudinal research by Klineberg [127, 128] and others demonstrated convincingly that these rankings were altered when the findings were related to sociocultural conditions.

Subsequently, prominent investigators of psychological measurement have become aware that their tests are standardized on the basis of performance by individuals in specific societies and usually within a rather narrow segment of the population. The tasks chosen are those significant in the particular cultural group [e.g., 86]. Following their extensive survey of "individual and group differences in behavior," Anastasi and Foley concluded:

> Since all types of behavior are influenced by the subject's stimulational background, it follows that psychological data obtained within any one cultural group cannot be generalized to cover all human behavior. Many statements offered under the heading of general psychology are not general at all, but are based upon human behavior as it develops within a single culture [6, p. 838].

Anastasi [5] has suggested that "culture-free" tests of abilities and traits are not feasible and that this can be demonstrated through contrasting results obtained when a trait or performance is selected in terms of its importance to a particular group. For example, a Draw-a-horse test standardized on performance by American Indian children worked to the decided disadvantage of white American children. Evidence indicates that similar differences result from evaluation of "personality" tests based on norms of different socioeconomic classes [12] or different cultural groups [129]. It has been suggested that awareness of such sociocultural variations implies revision, possibly radical revision, in many concepts used in the study of abilities and personality. A concrete example is furnished by findings on intelligence testing in Peru where mental age and consequently intelligence quotient for school children are "in an inverse relationship with their Chronological Age" [27, p. 38].

Effects of ethnocentrism on drawing conclusions from social-psychological research can be illustrated briefly in the area of group research. During the decades 1910–1930, various scholars reported experimental results which on the whole seemed to indicate a tendency toward mediocrity of performance in groups. More recently it has been shown repeatedly that interaction in groups may result in improved performance and changed attitudes of individual members in socially desirable directions. Thus it cannot be concluded that leveling of performance toward the group mean is an inevitable consequence of group interaction. The results of performance in any particular group are dependent both on the nature of the task and on the properties of the group in question [cf. 125]. Similarly, studies of the "group-decision" method for changing attitudes and behavior developed by Lewin and his associates [148] suggest limitations in drawing general conclusions concerning its superiority over other techniques. Briefly, group-decision studies in the American setting reported more frequent attitude change and persistence of change when individuals participated actively in making a decision with an informal "resource person" than when given a lecture presenting information in favor of the advocated change. However, both for Hindu and German individuals, the group-decision technique proved relatively ineffective [180, pp. 114–115; 264, pp. 66–67].

The fact that such checks have been made on these and other topics is evidence of the growing awareness among social psychologists that definite procedures are necessary to guard against ethnocentric conclusions. Since the social psychologist, like any human being, is psychologically related to certain groups—a national group, a socioeconomic class, a school of thought, or a laboratory atmosphere—checks on the effects of his ethnocentrisms are becoming standard procedure in evaluating his conclusions. The checks generally recognized as helpful in minimizing ethnocentric generalizations and actually employed for this purpose include (1) cross-cultural comparisons, (2) comparisons among groups within differentiated societies, and (3) historical comparisons within the same culture.

All such checks imply clear specification of the social-stimulus conditions under which findings are obtained. This is one reason why social-stimulus situations have been discussed rather extensively in this chapter and why their specification as external factors was stressed as an initial step, prior to investigation of their contribution in psychological structuring. As Daniel Katz has suggested, the "phenomenological bias" in much contemporary social psychology is sometimes responsible for serious neglect of important properties of social-stimulus conditions [120, 123].

Cross-cultural, intergroup, and historical comparisons as checks against ethnocentrism do not imply an unbridled cultural or historical relativism. Cultural relativism notes observed cultural variations in behavior but carries the further unwarranted assumption that principles governing behavior have to be derived separately on the basis of each culture. Such a view amounts to assuming total determination of behavior by social organization and culture [cf. 95]. On the contrary, social psychology is proceeding more and more on the assumption that basic principles of psychological functioning are the same for all individuals, and that variations in behavior in different cultures are governed by the same principles. *In fact, cross-cultural and historical comparisons are necessary in order that general laws and principles can be attained in social psychology.*

The adolescent period represents a rather well-documented example to clarify the above point. Early investigators of adolescence in the

United States, such as G. Stanley Hall, presented adolescence as a universal period of storm and stress. More recently, anthropological field work reported societies in which adolescence was a *relatively* smooth transition from childhood to adulthood. As a result, the view that adolescence was not a distinctive period of development except under highly restrictive and delaying sociocultural conditions prevailed. Careful inspection of comparative findings revealed, however, that even when relatively smooth, this transitional period was distinguished by interrelated internal changes (notably physiological) and changes in socially prescribed roles and statuses, both of which precipitate a process of re-formation of the individual's ego or self-constellation. The content, manner, and extent of change in ego-attitudes do vary from culture to culture. But recognition of basic uniformities permits active investigation of processes underlying reorganization during this period [14, pp. xiii, 22].

Increased Use of Scientific Methods and Techniques

Social psychology today is characterized by its active research orientation. Its textbooks, written by authors both from psychology and sociology departments, attempt to utilize research data whenever available, in contrast to the more speculative content of much influential literature of earlier periods. Efforts to devise more refined methods and techniques for obtaining data and for measuring and analyzing data have been a characteristic activity in the field in recent years. Particularly during the last decade, publications surveying problems and methods of research designs, of techniques employed, of actual conduct of research and treatment of data are distinctive evidence of this trend in social psychology [e.g., 111, 122, 155].

It would be unfortunate to leave the impression that in social psychology scientific method is conceived in terms of research design and measurement techniques, independent of theory and concepts. It has been noted that development of integrative theory with direct bearing on actual research data is not proceeding as rapidly as refinement of techniques [e.g., 33]. However, as Crutchfield [52] and Robert French [75] noted in their annual reviews in 1954 and 1956, respectively, the construction of theoretical models on a small scale is increasingly prevalent. Some of these efforts have attempted to propose mathematical definitions and postulates. As research and measurement techniques become more precise, the construction of mathematical models is likely to increase. At this stage of development in social psychology, J. R. P. French's statement of the frequent dilemma encountered in such attempts is pertinent. As he noted, "The very precision which gives power to the theory also tends to oversimplify it. For reasons of mathematical convenience one tends to make simple assumptions which so restrict the theory that it seems unrealistic compared to the complexity observed in social behavior" [74, p. 181].

One notable feature of the trend toward refined procedures, techniques, and modes of analysis is its marked interdisciplinary character. Social psychology has borrowed techniques freely from research developments in fellow disciplines (e.g., content analysis, participant observation, analysis of interaction process, and several other "field" methods). Social psychologists have mingled freely with sociologists, political scientists, and investigators in applied areas in developing more refined survey methods, interviewing of various kinds, a variety of questionnaires, rating scales, attitude scales, and tests. They have been sensitive to techniques developed in child psychology (e.g., observation methods), experimental psychology, and clinical psychology (e.g., "projective" techniques), and prone to adapt them for use in their own research problems.

Because many of its investigators were nurtured in psychological laboratories, experimentation in social psychology has been a prominent activity, even more so since Murphy, Murphy, and Newcomb's *Experimental Social Psychology* in 1937 [182]. The advantages and prestige of laboratory experimentation have continued to attract social psychologists, whatever their academic origins, and to attract sociologists, notably those interested in small groups. While the range of topics investigated in the laboratory has greatly expanded, a growing number of investigators display healthy caution against unqualified reliance solely on the laboratory experiment. It has been noted that some "crucial variables and relationships cannot be reproduced under laboratory conditions" [111, p. 337] and that in establishing necessary controls and manipulating conditions in the laboratory artifice may be the end product [e.g., 68]. As a result, serious discussions of the roles of the laboratory and the field in social-psychological research have been under way [e.g., 199]. The problem of discussion has centered largely around when and how each method should be used to speed continued development of valid general principles.

The value of field research for laboratory experimentation is recognized both as a source of new hypotheses and as a check on the validity of conclusions [cf. 68, p. 141]. Field work can, as in Newcomb's Bennington study [183], provide crucial evidence of hypothesized relationships between social-stimulus conditions and psychological variables or, as in the analysis of survey data by Lazarsfeld and his associates [142], it can indicate relationships obscured in the multifaceted nature of social life. Again, the participant observer can bring from his intensive and longitudinal study of social groupings a rounded "natural history," such as Whyte's *Street Corner Society* [268]. Here in the field of actual life are the variables and the relationships we must ultimately deal with. But how are we to bring them into the laboratory without mutilating their essential properties? And how are we to specify and refine our understanding of them without greater control than the field ordinarily permits?

There is, of course, no single solution, and explorations will continue. In the meantime, several steps seem to be proceeding simultaneously. On the one hand, design of laboratory experiments becomes more ingenious, and care in guarding against the possibilities of artifice is increasingly evident [e.g., 52, 69]. On the other hand, efforts to improve the standards and techniques used in the field continue; the extensive use and improvement of sociometric techniques is only one example. In addition, at least since the Western Electric studies, there has been applied research or action research introducing changed conditions in the field [73]. Such investigations, as well as detailed studies of "natural" change, like *The Invasion from Mars* [39], are indispensable in keeping theory in close touch with real life and in suggesting hypotheses for further research. Yet applied research has some built-in handicaps. The investigator seldom has sufficient control to manipulate variables to the extent possible in the laboratory. He is sometimes under considerable pressure from the sponsors to restrict his research to problems which appear practical to them and which may or may not be practical in long-range terms [cf. 121, 240].

There is another possibility—that field and laboratory may be integrated in single research designs by establishing thoroughgoing control over a lifelike situation and by manipulating conditions to produce the social conditions found in the field, at least in their most essential aspects [223]. Such an approach cannot supplant field investigations, but it can bring the laboratory and its methods of control and techniques into the field when the problems of study are amenable to investigation in manageable social units.

An example of the above approach is our series of experiments on group formation and intergroup relations started in 1948 [226, 227, 229, 228, chaps. 6, 9]. One of the main theoretical objectives of these studies was demonstration of the feasibility of experimentation on intergroup relations. Initially, extensive surveys were made of empirical findings on friendship and hostility, and cooperation and competition between groups and their individual members. These surveys led to the generalization that a prerequisite for the experimental study of intergroup relations is the formation of delineated groups. Before it can be said that there are relations between groups, there have to be identifiable group organizations or structures.

Therefore, the design of the experiments was in successive stages to be carried out over a period of time. The first stage was devoted to the experimental formation of groups among previously unacquainted individuals. To control subject selection and ensure that backgrounds of subjects be homogeneous in crucial respects and to control conditions of interaction during the experiments, the location of facilities, and the timing of events, summer camps for boys in isolated sites were established as the experimental settings.

The group-formation hypothesis predicted that when individuals interact in a series of problem situations embodying goals that require coordination of activities for their attainment, a group would form, consisting of an organization of differentiated status positions and a set of norms peculiar to the group [227]. Example of such a problem situation: Preparing ingredients available in bulk form, cooking them, and serving a meal when everyone was hungry.

Clearly, specific criteria had to be used for determining when groups were formed. In line with the discussion of small groups earlier in this chapter, the criteria included in the hypothesis for this purpose were (1) the rise of an identifiable status structure or organization, as measured by the relative frequency of effective initiative displayed by each member, and (2) the rise of an identifiable set of rules or norms, as measured by frequency and regularity of their observance and the spontaneous application of correctives by fellow members for behavior deviating beyond the latitude of acceptable behavior defined by the rules or norms.

When the criteria were satisfied by the formation of two groups, the second stage of the experiments was devoted to study of relations between groups thus formed. The hypotheses concerned the conditions of interaction between groups which would be conducive to hostility between them and to its reduction. Therefore, the two groups came into functional contact in a series of situations which involved competition and in which the attainment of goals by one group implied the deprivation or frustration of the other group. Example: A tournament of team games with prizes to the victorious group. As a result of successive win-or-lose encounters of this sort, readily identifiable unfavorable attitudes and consistently hostile actions developed between the groups. Operationally, unfavorable attitudes were measured by the frequency and stabilization of negative stereotypes of the out-group and its members, the "social distance" maintained between the groups, and manifest attempts toward hostile encounters.

In the last experiments [226], the final stage was devoted to conditions proposed as conducive to reduction of intergroup conflict. First, a series of situations was introduced involving physical *contiguity* in pleasant activities which each individual in the separate groups actively wanted. Examples: A sumptuous meal or an entertainment to which the two groups were invited to enjoy in the same hall. These occasions for contact, which required no coordination of efforts to attain the desired activity, were utilized by each group for further recrimination and fights with the other.

In the second period of conditions for the reduction of intergroup hostility, a series of goals which were compelling and highly desired by both groups was introduced in apparently natural situations. The goal was attainable only through the joint efforts of the two groups. Examples: A threatened water shortage owing to dysfunction of the supply system; preparations for a much-desired outing which required greater efforts and resources than either group could provide separately. Such goals were termed "superordinate goals."

A series of situations embodying superordinate goals over a period of time did bring about a reduction of intergroup hostility and an increase in friendly relations between the groups, as measured by the reduction of unfavorable stereotypes and an increase in favorable conceptions of the other group and its members, as well as actions toward collaborating with the other group observed in situations prepared to test such reactions.

The advantages gained by integrating field and laboratory approaches when feasible are these:

1. By painstaking efforts, the naturalness of real life situations in the eyes of individual participants can be attained. In the group experiments mentioned above, the subjects perceived the experimental situation as a summer camp and did not suspect that from the beginning the conditions and activities in which they interacted were being controlled and manipulated. They were not aware that their behavior was constantly observed and rated. Every effort was made to make measurement techniques a natural part of the situation by presenting them in the form of activities appropriate in the situation.

2. Because experimental control extends to choice of subjects in accordance with specified criteria and to location of the experiment and activities engaged in, the precision of laboratory manipulation of variables need not be sacrificed. Since intergroup relations were focal in these studies, subjects were chosen to constitute homogeneous samples in order that differences in background (e.g., socioeconomic, religious, ethnic, educational) and personal characteristics (e.g., intelligence, modes of social "adjustment") would be minimized as prior sources of antagonism or friendship among them. Experimental locations were isolated and completely under the investigators' control. The proximity of subjects to one another and their activities could be varied according to predetermined plans. Thus, rather clear-cut evidence was obtained to test hypotheses

based on sociological observations of the conditions of group formation and of specified intergroup relations [cf. 55, pp. 113–115]. By introducing over a period of time activities and goals which required interdependent efforts by a number of individuals, social groups essentially similar to those of real life were produced among individuals who were not previously acquainted. These experimental conditions were sufficient for group formation, even when individuals had not initially expressed natural liking (in the form of sociometric choices) for other members.

In order to rule out possible explanation of group formation in terms of variables other than the experimental conditions, the stage of group formation in the first experiment in 1949 [227] was preceded by a period of freedom in the choice of associates in various activities. As a result, friendship clusters of two or three individuals began to form. In dividing subjects for the stage of group formation, these friendship clusters were deliberately split by assigning best friends to different groups. Thus, at the beginning of the period of group formation, only a third of the friendship choices were for individuals in the same group, while two-thirds were directed toward individuals in the other group. Following conditions introduced as conducive to group formation, the friendship choices were reversed and restricted almost exclusively to fellow members of one's own group [227, p. 268].

When conditions of initial contact between groups were planned so that one group could achieve the goal only by preventing the other group from doing so, group conflict resulted, as predicted. In the more recent experiment, the group conflict thus engendered was experimentally reduced through the introduction of a *series* of superordinate goals which were compelling and highly desired by members of both groups, but attainable only through the joint efforts of the two groups working together [226].

3. Because subject backgrounds and experimental conditions and their alteration are controlled, it becomes possible to specify crucial stimulus variables in the formation of social attitudes and to assess the psychological effects of these attitudes as a function of developing group membership through precise laboratory techniques suitably adapted to the phenomenally natural situations of the subjects. The group experiments utilized primarily judgmental reactions in relation to performance of laboratory-type tasks which could be introduced at critical choice points in the experimental design without unnecessarily cluttering the natural flow of interaction [228, chaps. 6, 9]. Such techniques yield data in quantitative form.

In the highly complex setting of the field, in the laboratory-in-the-field, or even in some aspect of the field created in the laboratory, it is recognized that the selectivity of the investigator may influence the kind of data obtained and thus the kind of conclusions drawn. The most effective safeguard at present is the use of a combination of methods whose results can be checked one against another [cf. 122, 141, 223]. Thus in the group experiments referred to above, results obtained by participant observers were checked against independent ratings of other observers, sociometric techniques, stereotype ratings by the subjects, and several techniques adapted from the laboratory. The use of a combination of methods, continual cross-checking of laboratory and field findings, and feasible measures to integrate field and laboratory approaches may be among the steps toward ensuring the validity of generalizations based on social-psychological research.

REFERENCES

1. Allport, F. H. *Social psychology.* Boston: Houghton Mifflin, 1924.
2. Allport, F. H. Methods in the study of collective action phenomena. *J. soc. Psychol. S.P.S.S.I. Bull.,* 1942, 15, 165–185.
3. Allport, G. W. *Personality: a psychological interpretation.* New York: Holt, 1937.
4. Allport, G. W. The ego in contemporary psychology. *Psychol. Rev.,* 1943, 50, 451–478.
5. Anastasi, A. Psychological traits and group relations. In M. Sherif & M. O. Wilson (Eds.), *Group relations at the crossroads.* New York: Harper, 1953.
6. Anastasi, A., & Foley, J. P. *Differential psychology.* (Rev. ed.) New York: Macmillan, 1949.
7. Anderson, N. *The hobo: the sociology of the homeless man.* Chicago: Univer. Chicago Press, 1923.
8. Ansbacher, H. L. The history of the leaderless group discussion technique. *Psychol. Bull.,* 1951, 48, 383–391.
9. Arensberg, C. M. Behavior and organization: industrial studies. In J. H. Rohrer & M. Sherif (Eds.), *Social psychology at the crossroads.* New York: Harper, 1951.
10. Asch, S. E. *Social psychology.* Englewood Cliffs, N.J.: Prentice-Hall, 1952.
11. Asch, S. E. Studies of independence and conformity. 1. A minority of one against a unanimous majority. *Psychol. Monogr.,* 1956, 70, No. 9.
12. Auld, Frank, Jr. Influence of social class on personality test responses. *Psychol. Bull.,* 1952, 49, 318–332.
13. Ausubel, D. P. *Ego development and the personality disorders.* New York: Grune & Stratton, 1952.
14. Ausubel, D. P. *Theory and problems of adolescent development.* New York: Grune & Stratton, 1954.
15. Ausubel, D. P. Relationships between shame and guilt in the socializing process. *Psychol. Rev.,* 1955, 62, 378–390.

16. Baldwin, J. M. *Mental development in the child and the race.* New York: Macmillan, 1895.
17. Baldwin, J. M. *The individual and society.* Boston: Badger, 1911.
18. Bartlett, F. C. *Remembering: a study in experimental and social psychology.* New York: Cambridge, 1932.
19. Bass, B. M. *Leadership, psychology, and organizational behavior.* New York: Harper, 1960.
20. Becker, H. Anthropology and sociology. In J. Gillin (Ed.), *For a science of social man.* New York: Macmillan, 1954.
21. Becker, H. Field work among Scottish shepherds and German peasants: "wholes" and their handicaps. *Soc. Forces,* 1956, **35,** 10–15.
22. Bernard, L. L. Recent discussions regarding social psychology. *Amer. J. Sociol.,* 1942, **48,** 13–27.
23. Berne, E. V. C. An experimental investigation of social behavior patterns in young children. *Univer. Iowa Stud. Child Welf.,* 1930, **4,** No. 3.
24. Berry, B. *Race relations.* Boston: Houghton Mifflin, 1951.
25. Bidney, D. Towards a psychocultural definition of the concept of personality. In S. S. Sargent & M. W. Smith (Eds.), *Culture and personality.* New York: Viking Fund, 1949.
26. Bird, C. *Social psychology.* New York: Appleton-Century-Crofts, 1940.
27. Blumenfeld, W. Educational psychology in Peru. In On present-day psychology and education in the Americas. *Inter-Amer. Soc. Psychol. Monogr.* 1956, I. Pp. 34–41.
28. Blumer, H. Collective behavior. In A. M. Lee (Ed.), *New outline of the principles of sociology.* New York: Barnes & Noble, 1946.
29. Bonner, H. *Social psychology.* New York: American Book, 1953.
30. Bonner, H. *Group dynamics: principles and applications.* New York: Ronald, 1959.
31. Broom, L., Siegel, B. J., Vogt, E. Z., & Watson, J. B. Acculturation: an exploratory formulation. The Social Science Research Council summer session on acculturation, 1953. *Amer. Anthrop.,* 1954, **56,** 973–1000.
32. Brown, J. F. *Psychology and the social order.* New York: McGraw-Hill, 1936.
33. Bruner, J. S. Social psychology and group processes. *Annu. Rev. Psychol.,* 1950, **1,** 119–150.
34. Bruner, J. S., & Goodman, C. C. Value and need as organizing factors in perception. *J. abnorm. soc. Psychol.,* 1947, **42,** 33–44.
35. Burgess, E. W. The influence of Sigmund Freud upon sociology in the United States. *Amer. J. Sociol.,* 1939–40, **45,** 356–374.
36. Campbell, D. T. The indirect assessment of social attitudes. *Psychol. Bull.,* 1950, **47,** 15–38.
37. Cantril, H. General and specific attitudes. *Psychol. Monogr.,* 1932, No. 192.
38. Cantril, H. The social psychology of everyday life. *Psychol. Bull.,* 1934, **31,** 297–330.

39. Cantril, H. *The invasion from Mars.* Princeton, N.J.: Princeton Univer. Press, 1940.
40. Carr, H. A. *Psychology: a study of mental activity.* New York: Longmans, 1925.
41. Carter, L. F. Leadership and small group behavior. In M. Sherif & M. O. Wilson (Eds.), *Group relations at the crossroads.* New York: Harper, 1953.
42. Carter, L. F., & Schooler, K. Value, need and other factors in perception. *Psychol. Rev.,* 1949, **56,** 200–207.
43. Cartwright, D. American social psychology and the war. *J. consult. Psychol.,* 1945, **9,** 67–72.
44. Cartwright, D., & Zander, A. F. (Eds.) *Group dynamics: research and theory.* Evanston, Ill.: Row, Peterson, 1953.
45. Chapman, D. W., & Volkmann, J. A social determinant of the level of aspiration. *J. abnorm. soc. Psychol.,* 1939, **34,** 225–238.
46. Chapman, J., & Eckstein, M. A social-psychological study of the alleged visitation of the Virgin Mary in Puerto Rico. *Yearb. Amer. phil. Soc.,* 1954, 203–206.
47. Clark, K. B., & Clark, M. K. Racial identification and preference in Negro children. In T. M. Newcomb & E. L. Hartley (Eds.), *Readings in social psychology.* New York: Holt, 1947.
48. Coffin, T. E. Some conditions of suggestion and suggestibility: study of some attitudinal and situational factors influencing the process of suggestion. *Psychol. Monogr.,* 1941, 63, No. 241.
49. Cooley, C. H. *Human nature and the social order.* New York: Scribner, 1902.
50. Cottrell, L. S., Jr. The analysis of situational fields in social psychology. *Amer. sociol. Rev.,* 1942, **7,** 370–382.
51. Cottrell, L. S., & Gallagher, R. Developments in social psychology, 1930–1940. *Sociometry Monogr.,* 1941, No. 1.
52. Crutchfield, R. S. Social psychology and group processes. *Annu. Rev. Psychol.,* 1954, **5,** 171–202.
53. Dashiell, J. F. Experimental studies of the influence of social situations on the behavior of individual human adults. In C. Murchison (Ed.), *Handbook of social psychology.* Worcester, Mass.: Clark Univer. Press, 1935.
54. Davis, K. The sociology of parent-youth conflict. *Amer. sociol. Rev.,* 1940, **5,** 523–535.
55. Doby, J. F., Suchman, E. A., McKinney, J. C., Francis, R. G., & Dean, J. P. *An introduction to social research.* Harrisburg, Pa.: Stackpole, 1954.
56. Dollard, J., et al. *Frustration and aggression.* New Haven, Conn.: Yale Univer. Press, 1939.
57. Doob, L. W. *Social psychology.* New York: Holt, 1952.
58. Dow, G. S. *Society and its problems: introduction to the principles of sociology.* New York: Crowell, 1922.

59. Dunlap, K. *Social psychology.* Baltimore, Md.: Williams & Wilkins, 1925.
60. Durkheim, E. *The elementary forms of religious life.* London: G. Allen, 1915.
61. Durkheim, E. *The rules of sociological method.* Chicago: Univer. Chicago Press, 1938.
62. Durkheim, E. *Suicide: a study in sociology.* Glencoe, Ill.: Free Press, 1951.
63. Farber, M. L. The study of national character: 1955. *J. soc. Issues,* 1955, **11,** 52–56.
64. Faris, E. The beginnings of social psychology. *Amer. J. Sociol.,* 1945, **50,** 422–428.
65. Faris, R. E. L. *Social psychology.* New York: Ronald, 1952.
66. Faris, R. E. L. Development of the small group research movement. In M. Sherif & M. O. Wilson (Eds.), *Group relations at the crossroads.* New York: Harper, 1953.
67. Festinger, L. An analysis of compliant behavior. In M. Sherif & M. O. Wilson (Eds.), *Group relations at the crossroads.* New York: Harper, 1953.
68. Festinger, L. Laboratory experiments. In L. Festinger & D. Katz (Eds.), *Research methods in the behavioral sciences.* New York: Dryden, 1953.
69. Festinger, L. Social psychology and group processes. *Annu. Rev. Psychol.,* 1955, **6,** 187–216.
70. Ford, C. S., & Beach, F. A. *Patterns of sexual behavior.* New York: Harper, 1951.
71. Frazier, F. *Bourgeoisie noire.* Paris: Librairie Plon, 1955.
72. Freedman, R., Hawley, A. H., Landecker, W. S., & Miner, H. M. *Principles of sociology.* New York: Holt, 1952.
73. French, J. R. P., Jr. Experiments in field settings. In L. Festinger & D. Katz (Eds.), *Research methods in the behavioral sciences.* New York: Dryden, 1953.
74. French, J. R. P., Jr. A formal theory of social power. *Psychol. Rev.,* 1956, **63,** 181–194.
75. French, R. L. Social psychology and group processes. *Annu. Rev. Psychol.,* 1956, **7,** 63–94.
76. Freud, S. *The ego and the id.* London: Hogarth, 1927.
77. Freud, S. *Totem and taboo.* In *The basic writings of Sigmund Freud.* New York: Modern Library, 1938.
78. Fromm, E. Psychoanalytic characterology and its application to the understanding of culture. In S. S. Sargent & M. W. Smith (Eds.), *Culture and personality.* New York: Viking Fund, 1949.
79. Gesell, A., & Ilg, F. L. *Infant and child in the culture of today.* New York: Harper, 1943.
80. Gesell, A., & Thompson, H. *The psychology of early growth.* New York: Macmillan, 1938.
81. Gibb, C. A. Leadership. In G. Lindzey (Ed.), *Handbook of social psychology.* Vol. 2. Reading, Mass: Addison-Wesley, 1954.

82. Gillin, J. (Ed.) *For a science of social man.* New York: Macmillan, 1954.
83. Gillin, J., & Raimy, V. Acculturation and personality. *Amer. sociol. Rev.,* 1940, **5,** 371–380.
84. Goldstein, N. F. *The roots of prejudice against the Negro in the United States.* Boston: Boston Univer. Press, 1948.
85. Goodenough, F. L. *Developmental psychology.* (2nd ed.) New York: Appleton-Century-Crofts, 1945.
86. Goodenough, F. L., & Harris, D. B. Studies in the psychology of children's drawings: II. 1928–1949. *Psychol. Bull.,* 1950, **47,** 394–399.
87. Goodman, M. E. *Race awareness in young children.* Reading, Mass.: Addison-Wesley, 1952.
88. Greenberg, P. J. Competition in children: an experimental study. *Amer. J. Psychol.,* 1932, **44,** 221–248.
89. Griffith, C. R. *General introduction to psychology.* New York: Macmillan, 1923.
90. Hallowell, A. I. Psychology and anthropology. In J. Gillin (Ed.), *For a science of social man.* New York: Macmillan, 1954.
91. Hallowell, A. I. The self and its behavioral environment. *Explorations,* 1954, **1,** 108–165.
92. Hare, A. P., Borgatta, E. F., & Bales, R. E. *Small groups.* New York: Knopf, 1955.
93. Hart, H. N. *The science of social relations: an introduction to sociology.* New York: Holt, 1927.
94. Hartley, E. L., & Hartley, R. E. *Fundamentals of social psychology.* New York: Knopf, 1952.
95. Hartung, F. E. Cultural relativity and moral judgments. *Phil. Sci.,* 1954, **21,** 118–126.
96. Harvey, O. J. An experimental approach to the study of status relations in informal groups. *Amer. sociol. Rev.,* 1953, **18,** 357–367.
97. Harvey, O. J. An experimental investigation of negative and positive relations between small groups through judgmental indices. *Sociometry,* 1956, **19,** 201–209.
98. Herskovits, M. J. *Man and his works.* New York: Knopf, 1949.
99. Hilgard, E. R. *Introduction to psychology.* New York: Harcourt, Brace, 1953.
100. Hiller, E. T. *The strike.* Chicago: Univer. Chicago Press, 1928.
101. Hiller, E. T. *Social relations and structure.* New York: Harper, 1947.
102. Hirota, K. Experimental studies of competition. *Jap. J. Psychol.,* 1951, **21,** 70–81. Abstracted in *Psychol. Abstr.,* 1953, **27,** 351.
103. Holt, R. R. Effects of ego-involvement upon levels of aspiration. *Psychiatry,* 1945, **3,** 299–317.
104. Homans, G. C. *The human group.* New York: Harcourt, Brace, 1950. Chap. 12.
105. Horrocks, J. E. *The psychology of adolescence.* Boston: Houghton Mifflin, 1951.

106. Hovland, C. I., Janis, I. L., & Kelley, H. H. *Communication and persuasion.* New Haven, Conn.: Yale Univer. Press, 1953. Chap. 5.
107. Hughes, E. C. Institutions in process. In A. M. Lee (Ed.), *New outline of the principles of sociology.* New York: Barnes & Noble, 1946.
108. Hulett, J. E., Jr., & Stagner, R. *Problems in social psychology.* Urbana, Ill.: Univer. Ill., 1956.
109. Hyman, H. H. The psychology of status. *Arch. Psychol.,* 1942, No. 269.
110. Inkeles, A., & Levinson, D. J. National character: the study of modal personality and sociocultural systems. In G. Lindzey (Ed.), *Handbook of social psychology.* Vol. 2. Reading, Mass.: Addison-Wesley, 1954.
111. Jahoda, M., Deutsch, M., & Cook, S. W. *Research methods in social relations. Part One: Basic processes.* New York: Dryden, 1951.
112. James, W. *Principles of psychology.* New York: Holt, 1890.
113. Jenkins, W. O. A review of leadership studies with particular reference to military problems. *Psychol. Bull.,* 1947, **44,** 54–87.
114. Johnson, C. W. *Growing up in the black belt.* Washington: American Council on Education, 1941.
115. Johnson, R. W., et al. *Human relations in modern business: a guide for action sponsored by American business leaders.* Englewood Cliffs, N.J.: Prentice-Hall, 1949.
116. Jones, H. E. *Development in adolescence.* New York: Appleton-Century-Crofts, 1943.
117. Kantor, J. R. *An outline of social psychology.* Chicago: Follett, 1929.
118. Kardiner, A. The concept of basic personality structure as an operational tool in the social sciences. In R. Linton (Ed.), *The science of man in the world crisis.* New York: Columbia Univer. Press, 1945.
119. Karpf, F. B. *American social psychology.* New York: McGraw-Hill, 1932.
120. Katz, Daniel. Social psychology and group processes. *Annu. Rev. Psychol.,* 1951, **2,** 137–172.
121. Katz, D. Studies in social psychology in World War II. *Psychol. Bull.* 1951, **48,** 512–519.
122. Katz, D. Field studies. In L. Festinger & D. Katz (Eds.), *Research methods in the behavioral sciences.* New York: Dryden, 1953.
123. Katz, D. Special review. *Psychol. Bull.* 1955, **52,** 346–353.
124. Kelley, H. H. Two functions of reference groups. In G. E. Swanson, T. M. Newcomb, & E. L. Hartley (Eds.), *Readings in social psychology.* (Rev. ed.) New York: Holt, 1952.
125. Kelley, H. H., & Thibaut, J. W. Experimental studies of group problem solving and process. In G. Lindzey (Ed.), *Handbook of social psychology.* Vol. 2. Reading, Mass.: Addison-Wesley, 1954.
126. Klein, G. S., & Schoenfeld, N. The influence of ego-involvement on confidence. *J. abnorm. soc. Psychol.,* 1941, **36,** 249–258.
127. Klineberg, O. *Negro intelligence and selective migration.* New York: Columbia Univer. Press, 1935.
128. Klineberg, O. *Race differences.* New York: Harper, 1935.
129. Klineberg, O. Recent studies of national character. In S. S. Sargent &

M. W. Smith (Eds.), *Culture and personality.* New York: Viking Fund, 1949.

130. Klineberg, O. *Social psychology.* (Rev. ed.) New York: Holt, 1954.
131. Kluckhohn, C. Needed refinements in the biographical approach. In S. S. Sargent & M. W. Smith (Eds.), *Culture and personality.* New York: Viking Fund, 1949.
132. Kluckhohn, C., & Murray, H. A. (Eds.), *Personality in nature, society, and culture.* New York: Knopf, 1948.
133. Koch, S. Behavior as "intrinsically" regulated: work notes toward a pre-theory of phenomena called "motivational." In M. R. Jones (Ed.), *Nebraska symposium on motivation.* Lincoln, Neb.: Univer. Nebr. Press, 1956.
134. Koffka, K. *Principles of gestalt psychology.* New York: Harcourt, Brace, 1935.
135. Köhler, W. *Gestalt psychology.* New York: Liveright, 1929.
136. Krech, D., & Crutchfield, R. S. *Theory and problems of social psychology.* New York: McGraw-Hill, 1948.
137. Kuhlen, R. G. *The psychology of adolescent development.* New York: Harper, 1951.
138. Landesco, J. Organized crime in Chicago. In *The Illinois crime survey.* Illinois Assoc. for Criminal Justice. Chicago: Blakeley, 1929.
139. Lang, O. *Chinese family and society.* New Haven, Conn.: Yale Univer. Press, 1946.
140. La Pierre, R. T., & Farnsworth, P. R. *Social psychology.* (3rd ed.) New York: McGraw-Hill, 1949.
141. Lazarsfeld, P. F. The controversy over detailed interviews: an offer for negotiation. *Publ. Opin. Quart.,* 1944, **8,** 38–60.
142. Lazarsfeld, P. F., & Rosenberg, M. (Eds.) *The language of social research.* Glencoe, Ill.: Free Press, 1955.
143. Leary, D. B. *Modern psychology. Normal and abnormal. A behaviorism of personality.* New York: Lippincott, 1928.
144. Le Bon, G. *The crowd.* London: T. Fisher Unwin, 1897.
145. Leuba, C. J. An experimental study of rivalry in young children. *J. comp. Psychol.,* 1933, **16,** 367–378.
146. Lewin, K. *Dynamic theory of personality.* New York: McGraw-Hill, 1935.
147. Lewin, K. Field theory and experiment in social psychology: concepts and methods. *Amer. J. Sociol.,* 1939, **44,** 868–896.
148. Lewin, K. Group decision. In G. E. Swanson, T. M. Newcomb, & E. L. Hartley (Eds.), *Readings in social psychology.* (Rev. ed.) New York: Holt, 1952.
149. Lewin, K., Dembo, T., Festinger, L., & Sears, P. S. Level of aspiration. In J. McV. Hunt (Ed.), *Personality and the behavior disorders.* New York: Ronald, 1944.
150. Lewin, K., & Grabbe, P. Conduct, knowledge and acceptance of new values. *J. soc. Issues,* 1945, **1,** 53–64.
151. Lewin, K., Lippitt, R., & White, R. K. Patterns of aggressive behavior

in experimentally created "social climates." *J. soc. Psychol.*, 1939, **10**, 271–299.

152. Lewis, O. Discussion. In J. E. Hulett, Jr., & R. Stagner (Eds.), *Problems in social psychology*. Urbana, Ill.: Univer. Ill., 1952.

153. Lindesmith, A. R., & Strauss, A. *Social psychology*. New York: Dryden, 1949; 1956.

154. Lindesmith, A. R., & Strauss, A. Critique of culture-personality writings. *Amer. sociol. Rev.*, 1950, **15**, 587–599.

155. Lindzey, G. (Ed.) *Handbook of social psychology*. Reading, Mass.: Addison-Wesley, 1954. 2 vols.

156. Linton, R. *The cultural background of personality*. New York: Appleton-Century-Crofts, 1945.

157. Luchins, A. S. On agreement with another's judgment. *J. abnorm. soc. Psychol.*, 1944, **39**, 97–111.

158. Luchins, A. S. Social influences on perception of complex drawings. *J. soc. Psychol.*, 1945, **21**, 257–273.

159. Lumley, F. E. *Principles of sociology*. New York: McGraw-Hill, 1928.

160. Lynd, R. S., & Lynd, H. M. *Middletown in transition*. New York: Harcourt, Brace, 1937.

161. Maccoby, E. E., Newcomb, T. M., & Hartley, E. L. *Readings in social psychology*. (3rd ed.) New York: Holt, 1958.

162. MacCrone, I. D. *Race attitudes in South Africa*. New York: Oxford, 1937.

163. McDougall, W. *An introduction to social psychology*. London: Methuen, 1908.

164. McDougall, W. *Outline of psychology*. New York: Scribner, 1923.

165. Malinowski, B. *Argonauts of the Western Pacific*. London: Routledge, 1922.

166. Mannheim, K. *Ideology and Utopia: an introduction to the sociology of knowledge*. New York: Harcourt, Brace, 1936.

167. Mayo, E. *The human problems of an industrial civilization*. New York: Macmillan, 1933.

168. Mead, G. H. *Mind, self, and society*. Chicago: Univer. Chicago Press, 1934.

169. Melton, A. W. Present accomplishments and future trends in problem solving and learning theory. *Amer. Psychologist*, 1956, **11**, 278–281.

170. Merei, F. Group leadership and institutionalization. *Hum. Relat.*, 1949, **2**, 23–29.

171. Merton, R. K., & Kitt, A. S. Contributions to the theory of reference group behavior. In R. K. Merton & P. F. Lazarsfeld (Eds.), *Continuities in social research: studies in the scope and method of the American soldier*. Glencoe, Ill.: Free Press, 1950.

172. Miller, J. G. (Ed.) *Experiments in social process*. New York: McGraw-Hill, 1950.

173. Moore, J. S. *The foundations of psychology*. Princeton, N.J.: Princeton Univer. Press, 1922.

174. Moreno, J. L. Who shall survive? *Nerv. ment. Dis. Monogr. Series,* No. 58, 1934; (Rev. ed.) New York: Beacon House, 1953.

175. Murchison, C. *Social psychology: the psychology of political domination.* Worcester, Mass.: Clark Univer. Press, 1927.

176. Murchison, C. *Handbook of social psychology.* Worcester, Mass.: Clark Univer. Press, 1935.

177. Murdock, G. P. Sociology and anthropology. In J. Gillin (Ed.), *For a science of social man.* New York: Macmillan, 1954.

178. Murphy, G. *Personality: a biosocial approach to origins and structure.* New York: Harper, 1947.

179. Murphy, G. *Historical introduction to modern psychology.* (Rev. ed.) New York: Harcourt, Brace, 1949.

180. Murphy, G. *In the minds of men.* New York: Basic Books, 1953.

181. Murphy, G., & Murphy, L. B. *Experimental social psychology.* New York: Harper, 1931.

182. Murphy, G., Murphy, L. B., & Newcomb, T. M. *Experimental social psychology.* (Rev. ed.) New York: Harper, 1937.

183. Newcomb, T. M. *Personality and social change.* New York: Dryden, 1943.

184. Newcomb, T. M. *Social psychology.* New York: Dryden, 1950.

185. Newcomb, T. M. Sociology and psychology. In J. Gillin (Ed.), *For a science of social man.* New York: Macmillan, 1954.

186. Newstetter, W. I., Feldstein, M. J., & Newcomb, T. M. *Group adjustment: a study in experimental sociology.* Cleveland, Ohio: Western Reserve Univer., Sch. Appl. Soc. Sci., 1938.

187. Olmstead, M. S. *The small group.* New York: Random House, 1959.

188. Orlansky, H. Infant care and personality. *Psychol. Bull.,* 1949, **40,** 1–48.

189. O.S.S. Assessment Staff. *Assessment of men.* New York: Holt, 1948.

190. Parsons, T., & Shils, E. A. (Eds.) *Toward a general theory of action.* Cambridge, Mass.: Harvard Univer. Press, 1951. Chap. 1.

191. Parten, M. B. Social play among pre-school children. *J. abnorm. soc. Psychol.,* 1933, **28,** 136–147.

192. Pelz, D. C. Leadership within a hierarchical organization. *J. soc. Issues,* 1951, **7,** 49–55.

193. Perrin, F. A. C., & Klein, D. B. *Psychology: its methods and principles.* New York: Holt, 1926.

194. Piaget, J. *The moral judgment of the child.* London: Kegan Paul, Trench, Trubner & Co., 1932.

195. Proshansky, H., & Murphy, G. The effects of reward and punishment on perception. *J. Psychol.,* 1942, **13,** 295–305.

196. Queener, E. L. *Introduction to social psychology.* New York: Sloane, 1951.

197. Radcliffe-Brown, A. *Andaman Islanders.* New York: Cambridge, 1922.

198. Radin, P. *Primitive religion, its nature and origin.* New York: Viking, 1937.

199. Riecken, H. W. (Chairman), et al. Narrowing the gap between field

studies and laboratory experiments in social psychology: a statement by the summer seminar. *SSRC Items,* 1954, **8,** (4), 37–42.

200. Riecken, H. W. & Homans, G. C. Psychological aspects of social structure. In G. Lindzey (Ed.), *Handbook of social psychology.* Vol. 2. Reading, Mass.: Addison-Wesley, 1954.

201. Reuter, E. B. Some observations on the status of social psychology. *Amer. J. Sociol.,* 1940, **46,** 293–304.

202. Rivers, W. H. R. *History of Melanesian society.* Vol. 1. New York: Cambridge, 1924.

203. Roethlisberger, F. J., & Dickson, W. J. *Management and the worker.* Cambridge, Mass.: Harvard Univer. Press, 1939.

204. Roheim, G. Psychoanalysis and anthropology. In D. G. Haring (Ed.), *Personal character and cultural milieu.* (Rev. ed.) Syracuse, N.Y.: Syracuse Univ. Press, 1949.

205. Rohrer, J. H., & Sherif, M. (Eds.) *Social psychology at the crossroads.* New York: Harper, 1951.

206. Roseborough, M. E. Experimental studies of small groups. *Psychol. Bull.,* 1953, **50,** 275–303.

207. Ross, E. A. *Social psychology.* New York: Macmillan, 1908.

208. Ross, E. A. *Outlines of sociology.* New York: Century, 1923.

209. Saintsbury, P. *Suicide in London: an ecological study.* London: Institute of Psychiatry, 1955.

210. Sapir, E. *Selected writings of Edward Sapir.* D. G. Mandelbaum (Ed.). Berkeley, Calif.: Univer. of Calif. Press, 1949.

211. Sargent, S. S. *Social psychology.* New York: Ronald, 1950.

212. Sargent, S. S., & Smith, M. W. (Eds.) *Culture and personality.* New York: Viking Fund, 1949.

213. Schafer, R., & Murphy, G. The role of autism in a visual figure-ground relationship. *J. exp. Psychol.,* 1943, **32,** 335–343.

214. Schneirla, T. C. Problems in the biopsychology of social organization. *J. abnorm. soc. Psychol.,* 1946, **41,** 385–402.

215. Schneirla, T. C. A consideration of some conceptual trends in comparative psychology. *Psychol. Bull.,* 1952, **49,** 559–597.

216. Schneirla, T. C. The concept of levels in the study of social phenomena. In M. Sherif & C. W. Sherif, *Groups in harmony and tension.* New York: Harper, 1953, pp. 54–75.

217. Scott, E. L. *Status expectations and organizational behavior.* Columbus, Ohio: Ohio State Univer. Res. Found., 1953.

218. Sewell, W. H. Infant training and the personality of the child. *Amer. J. Sociol.,* 1952, **58,** 150–159.

219. Shaw, C. R. *The jack roller.* Chicago: Univer. Chicago Press, 1930.

220. Shaw, C. R. *The natural history of a delinquent career.* Chicago: Univer. Chicago Press, 1931.

221. Sherif, M. *The psychology of social norms.* New York: Harper, 1936.

222. Sherif, M. *An outline of social psychology.* New York: Harper, 1948.

223. Sherif, M. Integrating field work and laboratory in small group research. *Amer. sociol. Rev.,* 1954, **19,** 759–771.

224. Sherif, M., & Cantril, H. *The psychology of ego-involvements.* New York: Wiley, 1947.
225. Sherif, M., & Harvey, O. J. A study in ego functioning: elimination of stable anchorages in individual and group situations. *Sociometry,* 1952, **15,** 272–305.
226. Sherif, M., Harvey, O. J., White, B. J., Hood, W. R., & Sherif, C. W. *Intergroup conflict and cooperation: The Robbers Cave experiment.* Norman, Okla.: Univer. Okla. Book Exchange, 1961.
227. Sherif, M., & Sherif, C. W. *Groups in harmony and tension.* New York: Harper, 1953.
228. Sherif, M., & Sherif, C. W. *An outline of social psychology.* (Rev. ed.) New York: Harper, 1956.
229. Sherif, M., White, B. J., & Harvey, O. J. Status in experimentally produced groups. *Amer. J. Sociol.,* 1955, **60,** 370–379.
230. Sherif, M., & Wilson, M. O. (Eds.) *Group relations at the crossroads.* New York: Harper, 1953.
231. Shibutani, T. Reference groups as perspectives. *Amer. J. Sociol.,* 1955, **60,** 562–569.
232. Shils, E. *The present state of American sociology.* Glencoe, Ill.: Free Press, 1948.
233. Shinn, M. W. *Notes on the development of a child.* Berkeley, Calif.: Univer. Calif. Press, Vol. 1, 1899; Vol. 2, 1907.
234. Smith, M. B. Anthropology and psychology. In J. Gillin (Ed.), *For a science of social man.* New York: Macmillan, 1954.
235. Smith, M. B., Bruner, J. S., & White, R. W. *Opinions and personality.* New York: Wiley, 1956.
236. Snygg, D., & Combs, A. W. *Individual behavior: a new frame of reference for psychology.* New York: Harper, 1949.
237. Spindler, G., & Goldschmidt, W. Experimental design in the study of culture change. *S.W. J. Anthrop.,* 1952, **8,** 68–83.
238. Stogdill, R. M. Leadership, membership and organization. *Psychol. Bull.,* 1950, **47,** 1–14.
239. Stogdill, R. M. *Individual behavior and group achievement.* New York: Oxford, 1959.
240. Stouffer, S. A. Some afterthoughts of a contributor to "The American soldier." In R. K. Merton & P. F. Lazarsfeld (Eds.), *Continuities in social research.* Glencoe, Ill.: Free Press, 1950.
241. Stouffer, S. A., et al. *The American soldier combat and its aftermath.* Princeton, N.J.: Princeton Univer. Press, 1949.
242. Strauss, A. (Ed.) *The social psychology of George Herbert Mead.* Chicago: Univer. Chicago Press (Phoenix Books), 1956.
243. Strodtbeck, F. L., & Hare, A. P. Bibliography of small group research. *Sociometry,* 1954, **17,** 107–178.
244. Swanson, G. E., Newcomb, T. M., & Hartley, E. L. (Eds.) *Readings in social psychology.* (Rev. ed.) New York: Holt, 1952.
245. Thibaut, J. W., & Kelley, H. H. *The social psychology of groups.* New York: Wiley, 1959.

246. Thomas, W. I., & Znaniecki, F. *The Polish peasant in Europe and America.* Chicago: Univer. Chicago Press, 1918.
247. Thrasher, F. M. *The gang.* Chicago: Univer. Chicago Press, 1927.
248. Thrasher, J. D. Interpersonal relations and gradations of stimulus structure as factors in judgment variations: an experimental approach. *Sociometry,* 1954, **17,** 228–241.
249. Thurnwald, R. The psychology of acculturation. *Amer. Anthrop.,* 1932, **34,** 557–569.
250. Titchener, E. P. *Systematic psychology: prologomena.* New York: Macmillan, 1929.
251. Toki, K. The leader-follower structure in the school class. *Jap. J. Psychol.,* 1935, **10,** 27–56. Summarized in [94].
252. Tolman, E. C. More concerning the temporal relations of meaning imagery. *Psychol. Rev.,* 1917, **24,** 114–138.
253. Tresselt, M. E., & Volkmann, J. The production of uniform opinion by nonsocial stimulation. *J. abnorm. soc. Psychol.,* 1942, **37,** 234–243.
254. Turner, R. H. Role-taking, role standpoint and reference group behavior. *Amer. J. Sociol.,* 1956, **61,** 316–328.
255. Van Gennep, A. *Les rites de passage.* Paris: E. Noury, 1909.
256. Veblen, T. *The theory of the leisure class.* New York: Macmillan, 1899.
257. Volkart, E. (Ed.) *Social behavior and personality, contributions of W. I. Thomas to theory and social research.* New York: Social Science Research Council, 1951.
258. Volkmann, J. The anchoring of absolute scales. *Psychol. Bull.,* 1936, **33,** 742–743.
259. Volkmann, J. Scales of judgment and their implications for social psychology. In J. H. Rohrer & M. Sherif (Eds.), *Social psychology at the crossroads.* New York: Harper, 1951.
260. Wallon, H. *Les origines du caractère chez l'enfant.* Paris: Presses Universitaire de France, 1933.
261. Ward, L. F. *Outlines of sociology.* New York: Macmillan, 1928 imprint.
262. Warner, W. L., & Lunt, P. S. *The social life of a modern community.* New Haven, Conn.: Yale Univer. Press, 1941.
263. Webb, W. P. *The Great Plains.* Boston: Houghton Mifflin, 1936.
264. Weiss, R. S. A structure-function approach to organization. *J. soc. Issues,* 1956, **12,** 66–67.
265. Wertheimer, M. Laws of perceptual forms. In W. D. Ellis (Ed.), *A sourcebook of gestalt psychology.* New York: Harcourt, Brace, 1939.
266. Wever, E. G., & Zener, K. E. Method of absolute judgment in psychophysics. *Psychol. Rev.,* 1928, **35,** 466–493.
267. Whiting, J. W. M., & Child, I. L. *Child training and personality.* New Haven, Conn.: Yale Univer. Press, 1953.
268. Whyte, W. F. *Street corner society.* Chicago: Univer. Chicago Press, 1943.
269. Whyte, W. F. *Money and motivation.* New York: Harper, 1955.

270. Williams, J. M. *Principles of social psychology.* New York: Knopf, 1922.
271. Wright, Q. Modern technology and the world order. In W. F. Ogburn (Ed.), *Technology and international relations.* Chicago: Univer. Chicago Press, 1949.
272. Young, K. (Ed.) *Sourcebook for social psychology.* New York: Knopf, 1927.
273. Young, K. *Social psychology.* (3rd ed.) New York: Appleton-Century-Crofts, 1956.
274. Zetterberg, H. L. *Sociology in the United States of America.* Paris: UNESCO, 1956.
275. Zorbaugh, H. W. *The Gold Coast and the slum.* Chicago: Univer. Chicago Press, 1929.

SOCIAL ATTITUDES AND OTHER ACQUIRED BEHAVIORAL DISPOSITIONS

DONALD T. CAMPBELL
Department of Psychology
Northwestern University

I. INTRODUCTION

Social attitude provides a traditional theme in social psychology at the levels of both theory and empirical research. Gordon Allport [3] and W. I. Thomas [159] have called it social psychology's central problem. In several of the decades of quantitative social psychology's brief history, research on social attitudes has been the dominating concern [e.g., 121, pp. 889–1046]. While not so in this past decade, the topic remains nonetheless of substantial importance. Particularly is this so if one includes consideration of the neologisms which introduce the old problem in modern works.

The field of primary reference for this chapter is thus a subtopic in social psychology, to wit, the theory and measurement of social attitudes. The fields of secondary reference chosen for this study of interrelationship issues come primarily from general psychology. Perception and learning theory are the most prominent of these, entering as sources of the major competing theoretical interpretations of social attitudes. The field of individual differences and their measurement provides a third psychological reference field. Sociology enters in two ways: (1) social-attitude research has been as important a part of sociology as of psychology; and (2) sociology is invoked for a description of the environmental attributes to which the social attitudes refer and in contact with which they have been learned.

The interrelationship issues broached are these:

1. An effort to define social attitude places this concept among a large and growing group of social science concepts, all referring to acquired behavioral dispositions and all functionally definable in essentially the same terms, even though in dictionary meanings the concepts may be quite incommensurable. The center of discussion shifts at this point to the generic acquired behavioral disposition.

2. The conditions of data collection in social psychology are judged to generate a divisive influence on the conceptualizations of social psychologists, dividing them into behaviorist and quasi-phenomenological camps, according to whether they observe or interview their subjects. An

effort is made to demonstrate the empirical convergence or equivalence of the two types of dispositional concepts resulting and to provide translation between them. The concept of attitude is judged a valuable intermediary just because it has the multiple connotations of "view of the world" and "predisposition to respond."

3. In a similar way, conceptualizations distinguishing means and ends are examined, and the ubiquity of ends connotation is argued.

4. Finally, the theoretical orientation is related to the practices of attitude measurement and the issue of attitude inconsistency.

The interrelationship issues to be dealt with and the integrative resolution attempted can be introduced by quoting from an effort to define social attitudes made by the present writer over ten years ago [20, pp. 31–32]:

Research on social attitudes has been justly criticized for a lack of common definition of the concept, and for a failure to integrate definition and measurement procedures. This diversity of definition has been in odd contrast with the obvious similarity of research procedures. This paradox arises from definitional attempts which confound *explanations* of the phenomena with the process of *pointing to* the phenomena. It is the contention of the present writer that agreement on the implicit operational (or pointing) definition of attitudes is already present. As a tentative formulation the following is offered: *A social attitude is (or is evidenced by) consistency in response to social objects.* If we look at definitions utilizing concepts of set, or readiness to respond—for example, Allport [3]: "An attitude is a mental and neural state of readiness, organized through experience and exerting a directive or dynamic influence upon the individual's response to all objects and situations to which it is related"—and ask for the evidence of a "mental and neural state of readiness," the symptoms of a "directive or dynamic influence," criteria as to the "objects and situations to which it is related," these evidences will be, in final analysis, consistency or predictability among responses. *An individual's social attitude is a syndrome of response consistency with regard to social objects.* And even those whose behavioristic orientation leads to a rejection of such mentalistic definitions as Allport's and who would say with Bain [7] and Horowitz [72, p. 142], "Essentially . . . the attitude must be considered a response rather than a set to respond,"—in research practice do not equate *isolated* responses with attitudes; but on the contrary, look for the appearance of *response consistencies.* This is dramatically evidenced by Horowitz's [71] use of the appearance of consistent differentiated response to photographs of Negro and white children to mark the occurrence of race prejudice in children.

This definitional effort seemed to have the advantage of conveying the common meanings in the principal efforts at formal definition and the implicit definitions of research usage. But the definition has the weakness of being equally appropriate to a very large number of social science concepts, ranging from sentiment to expectancy to *Anschauung* to social habit. This unsatisfactory state of affairs might be resolved in several ways. One might declare this whole host of terms synonyms or one might look for the more specific definitional qualifiers which would differentiate each from the others. The strategy of this paper partakes of both. It looks to the generic concept for which this definitional effort is appropriate, a concept for which attitude, expectancy, habit, and the like, would all be subspecies. It then tentatively hypothesizes that all of these terms are synonyms until operational evidence distinguishing them be brought forth.

No name for the whole genus of terms is in common usage, but "disposition" has been used occasionally in psychology and sociology for this purpose, as by Stout in 1899 [155, pp. 76–81] and by Faris in 1931 [47, p. 7]. If we add a qualifier and make it "behavioral disposition," the usage is not out of keeping with that of philosophy. Since in the area of social psychology, we today regard attitude and most of the other dispositional constructs as learned or acquired, the total phrase "acquired behavioral dispositions" will be used to indicate the genus of interest. The section which follows will deal with this genus in terms of three subtopics. The first will look to that ubiquitous aspect of these acquired-behavioral-disposition terms which refer to their status as *residues of experience.* The second will deal with that aspect of them all which refers to the *coordination of behavior in environments,* and with the particular problem of diagnosing dispositions after they have been acquired. The third subtopic will attempt to offer an expanded perspective on *modes of acquiring and expressing* acquired behavioral dispositions.

II. ACQUIRED BEHAVIOIRAL DISPOSITIONS

Common Characteristic: Residues of Experience

It is a commonplace observation that for human and other organisms, *behavior is modified as a result of experience,* that somehow a person *retains residues of experience of such a nature as to guide, bias, or otherwise influence later behavior.* This pervasive fact has been noted and conceptualized by most social scientists. Individually and collectively, they have given the process many and diverse labels. Today there is a surfeit of such concepts, and each new theoretical effort seems to increase the number.

It seems that the multiplicity of such conceptualizations has increased in recent decades, that efforts to coordinate terminology may have decreased, and that the student in the social sciences is today faced with more confusing alternative sets of competing languages than he might have faced at the turn of the century when physiologists, psychologists, and sociologists, for example, were all willing to speak of habits with some feeling of mutual understanding. Such an increased number of terms might reflect an increase in the scope of the behavioral sciences, an expanding of boundaries, and an incorporation of new fields, so that the increase in concepts represents an increase in the number of processes described and in the number of facts accumulated. On the other hand, it might be possible that the increase in the number of concepts is due solely to the increase in the number of social scientists. In an area of science in which the discipline of experimentation is not present and in which the temptations of narcissistic pseudoinnovation are strong, an increase in the number of persons active in the field might in itself increase the number of schools and terminologies. The social scientist of today seems to feel quite justified in creating a new terminology without any effort to translate his neologisms into the terms of others or into concepts so traditional that they no longer bear the label of any one man's theoretical thinking. There may be some truth in both of these explanations. However, it seems probable that a more important reason for the multiplicity of terms at the current moment is that we are going through a phase in which the inadequacy of the older conceptualizations has become clear, with a resulting diversity of explorations for better conceptualizations.

Terms thus referring to the residues of experience are so diverse in nature and so apparently dissimilar that an illustration may help to justify the present effort to treat them under the same rubric. Let us take a simple example of a child who is allowed to explore a room that contains a number of boxes. Box C always contains candy; box S gives a shock whenever it is opened. With sufficient time in the room the child accumulates experience which serves to modify behavior in certain uniform and predictable ways. This process might be characterized by varying behavioral scientists in some of the following ways:

A descriptive behaviorist of the Skinner [144] or Brunswik [17, 18] variety might describe the change or the learning in terms of the *probability values* of certain responses to objects on the part of the child. As a result of the experience, the probability of the child's touching box C has gone up, and the probability of the child's touching box S has gone down.

Kurt Lewin [93] might have described the situation as a change in the *life space* of the child. Whereas initially the life space of the child was undifferentiated, with no such objects as A, B, C, or S existing in it, after the experience, the life space has become more structured, and the two objects and regions C and S have emerged in it with clear-cut positive and negative *valences*. These valences induce forces which will result in the child's locomotion away from region S and toward region C. Lewin would emphasize that you cannot predict the child's behavior simply by knowing that he is in a room in which there are objects *A, B, C,* and *S,* but that you must know in addition how these objects appear in the child's life space, what kinds of valences they have, and what resulting forces impel him toward or away from them. Knowing how the child structures its life space, we can then predict behavior. Inferences as to this structuring may be made by observing the behavior, using essentially the same data as that recorded by the descriptive behaviorist. Hallowell [60], using Kofka's concept of the *behavioral environment,* might make a similar description.

George Herbert Mead [106] would perhaps have summarized the experience in terms of the development of the *objects S* and *C* for the person and would have emphasized that in the image of the object was contained its rewardingness, punishingness, or general utility; that in the image of the object were the potentialities or readinesses for response to it.

In conditioning theory as elaborated by Hull [75] and Spence [149, 150], for example, one might speak of the development of two *habits* in which the stimulus *C* led to the response of touching and the stimulus *S* led to the response of withdrawing or running away, emphasizing the effects of the reinforcements of candy and shock on certain of the low-strength initial stimulus-response connections which were involved in the original exploration. Within this same tradition one might also speak of *acquired drives* instigated by the boxes or of the *secondary reinforcement* value which they had acquired.

In the Freudian tradition, one might describe the resultants of the experience in motivational terms, saying that a positive *cathexis* had been developed toward box *C* and a negative cathexis toward box *S,* or one might use the term *fixation,* although admittedly these potent terms might be reluctantly applied to such a trivial instance.

In the language of one of the most influential postwar developments in social psychology as practiced in psychology departments, there is emphasis upon the effects of experience, particularly motive-relevant experience, upon perceptual thresholds. Bruner [16] and Postman [134] might speak in this situation of the child's *sensitization* to box *C* or the lowered *perceptual threshold* for seeing box *C,* with implicitly the greater likelihood of responding to box *C* because of its greater perceptual prominence. (In the case of box *S,* the application of their theory is less clear. Some presentations lead to the expectation of a heightened *perceptual defense* for box *S,* other presentations to *perceptual vigilance.*)

In older languages of social science we might be willing to discuss the content of the child's *idea* of *C,* and *idea* of *S;* or the child's *images* of *C* and *S,* and the manner in which they have been built up by contiguity with shock and candy. Or in a more general humanistic tradition we might be willing to say that the child had acquired *knowledge* of *C* and *S;* that whereas initially they had no *meaning* for the child they now had acquired meaning, or that they now represented *values* to the child. We could similarly speak of the *orientations* and *attitudes* which the child had developed, of innovations in his *definition of the situation,* etc. We could speak about his *anticipations, expectations,* or *expectancies* with regard to the future if the courses of action of touching C or S were taken, of the altered nature of his *Weltanschauung,* of his *beliefs* or *dispositions* with regard to these objects, etc.

This simple-minded illustration certainly cannot be taken as demonstrating the equivalence of the terms. Few of the theorists cited would accept in detail this utilization of their terminology. Many of the terms were developed to emphasize nuances in much more complex situations and in quite other arenas of human behavior. Nonetheless, it is hoped that the illustration makes plausible the possibility of overlap, of some mutual relevance among these conceptualizations at least sufficient to justify more detailed exploration into the terminological forest. It is hoped also that the illustration makes it conceivable that superficially quite dissimilar terminologies may be describing essentially the same facts and processes. Coutu's [39] discussion is also to this point. To further illustrate the multiplicity of concepts available, here is a list of terms, all of which—in part, at least—call attention to the fact that experience has modified the behavioral tendencies of the organism:

acquired drive	determining tendency	memory
adaptation	disposition	mental image
adjustment	engram	motive
Anschauung	evaluation	need disposition
anticipation	expectancy	neurobiotaxis
apperceptive mass	expectation	notion
association	experience	object
attitude	fixation	opinion
behavioral environ-	frame of reference	orientation
ment	goal	past history of rein-
belief	hab	forcement
bent	habit	perceptual sensitiza-
canalization	hypothesis	tion
cathectic orientation	idea	percept
cathexis	imprinting	perseveration
cell assembly	integrative field	personality trait
cognitive map	intention	predisposition (ac-
cognitive structure	interest	quired)
concept	judgment	prejudgment
conditioned reflex	knowledge	representation
conviction	learning	response disposition
definition of the situ-	life space	response latency
ation	meaning	response probability

response threshold	stereotype	tinsit
role perception	synaptic threshold	trace
schema	change	valence
sentiment	tendency	value
set		

Common Characteristic: Coordinators of Behavior in Environments

The social scientist frequently makes bold to diagnose acquired behavioral dispositions in specific organisms without having observed the past history of the organism. This constitutes a major part of the research activity in social attitudes. Most of the specific acquired behavioral dispositions mentioned above are similar in this respect. We can in some instances diagnose the orientations, expectations, cathexes, habits, sets, etc., of organisms whose past histories and environments we have not known. These diagnostic procedures in some sense constitute an operational definition of the disposition. The present argument is that all acquired behavioral dispositions share a generic form of operational definition.

In the quotation cited above, social attitude was defined as (or as evidenced by) "consistency in response to social objects," or as "a syndrome of response consistency with regard to social objects." But in spite of the acceptance which this definition has had, it seems to have a hidden circularity, or to beg the question. How, for example, do we operationally decide what is a social object for the organism if not by response consistency? How do we determine what molecular responses are equivalent and can be treated as a unit? If we have already diagnosed for an individual his response equivalents and his social objects, have we not done most of the attitude diagnosis? Does not the definition thus *assume* rather than *denote* the crucial step?

Like many psychologists, I find my epistemology clarified by turning to the animal analogy. In particular, I have found the following parable of help. Dealing with rats, it considers habits rather than attitudes. For the most part, habits have been studied only by observing their gradual development, and then only in the specific situation in which they have been learned. The learning theorist has rarely faced the problem of specifying what the habit was about, or what habits an animal has. He has been able to limit himself to a study of the degree of habitualization of a certain series of behaviors occurring within the artificial limits imposed by the apparatus and recording procedures. But the problem of the social scientist, the anthropologist, or the clinical psychologist is different; it is to diagnose the residues of experience in persons whose prior life history he has not observed and whose prior mazes he has not seen.

To parallel this problem, let us pose to a hypothetical animal psychologist the problem of diagnosing the habits of an aged and experienced rat shipped to him from another laboratory. What would happen? The process would be a hit-or-miss, random, trial-and-error procedure. The foreign rat under varying degrees of deprivation would be placed in all the likely pieces of apparatus available in the diagnostic laboratory. Knowledge that the rat shared some common culture, i.e., that it was a university-psychology rat, would make the selections of apparatus somewhat less random. The rat would be tried in a lever-pressing Skinner box, while buzzers buzzed and lights flashed, and any combinations that resulted in increased lever pressing would be taken as symptoms of some habit. The rat might be placed on a Lashley jumping stand while various colors and designs were placed in the card slots; and if jumping occurred, an effort would be made to find to which cue cards the jumping was most consistent. Multiple T and Y maze segments would be tried. The process would be one of random search, and the presence of a common culture merely serves to limit the range of things tried or to make certain guesses more probable. And no matter how clever the research, there would still be the possibility that important and highly routinized habits of the rat went unnoticed by the diagnostician.

The diagnostician makes the initial definition of stimuli and the initial classification of response. They represent classes of objects and behaviors which the experimenter can consistently discriminate, and which he guesses the animal might also. Once he finds some evidence of the stimulus-response consistency on the part of the rat, the experimenter would typically start varying stimuli and varying his classification of muscle movements in order to approximate more closely the appropriate genus proximum for the habit; that is, he would try and find out whether certain subtleties discriminable by him were also discriminable and being discriminated by the rat. Thus, if he found that the rat jumped to a yellow circle, he would start varying the shape and the color of the stimulus card to find which degree of yellow, if any, maximized the response, which shape maximized it, or whether shape made any difference. At the same time, he would strive to learn the appropriate classification of the consistency of response. Was it a consistency of muscle contraction, or a consistency of locomotor achievement, an object consistency, etc.? Gradually, by trial and error, the diagnostician would obtain a more specific and appropriately labeled stimulus-response correlation. The final classification, however, would still be in the scientist's terms, and would be limited to discriminations that the scientist could make. Occasionally in a search for the sources of consistent behavior in the animal, the scientist may have to add to his own natural senses. This seems to be the case in studies of homing behavior in bees, in which cues from the polarization of sunlight are utilized [49]. A similar quandary might be observed were a scientist to be given a job of diagnosing the habits or stimulus-response consistencies on the part of Berkeley's [9] mechanical squirrel, which responds differently to lights impulsed by alternating and direct current. By mechanically adding to his discriminatory capacities, the scientist might find out toward what the machine is responding consistently via a trial-and-error process, with no solution guaranteed. Improving of the fit of the habit diagnosis is just as much trial-and-error process as was the initial hitting upon evidence of some stimulus-response correlation. By the same token, there is no guarantee that the habit would ever be diagnosed perfectly or even noticed at all.

Although the definition of stimulus and response are in the experimenter's language, there still is a verifiability to his diagnosis. This proof is the simple actuarial matter of a co-occurrence of stimuli and response at a great enough frequency to rise above the general "noise level." The experimenter can legitimately claim that he has located a stimulus-response consistency if certain actuarial standards are reached. What he cannot claim is that his is the optimal classification of the stimulus and response for maximum predictability. If, however, two experimenters differ in their diagnoses or in their classification of stimulus and response, the same actuarial approach can say which experimenter's classification scheme is the most efficient and, in this sense, the more nearly correct or implicitly closer to the "animal's own" definition of stimulus and response [21].

There are some other technical problems that would be involved, and these potentially have epistemological implications too. Once the experimenter had achieved a definition of stimulus and response that seemed to maximize predictability for the rat, it would be necessary to cross-validate this on a new sample of the rat's behavior in which all stimulus conditions except those deemed relevant were varied; the same procedure would be used for response opportunities. As observed in test-construction work, the degree of fit achieved from repeatedly reanalyzing a limited bit of the animal's behavior would involve considerable capitalization on chance, and cross validation would be necessary to demonstrate that an effective genus had been designated.

An equally important technical problem is that rats may acquire new habits during the testing for the old ones, or that old habits may be extinguished if learned stimuli are introduced without expected rewards. Thus, if the testing procedure is very long and the habits weak, it would soon become impossible to distinguish between newly acquired habits and the residues of the original experience. Methodologically, the cleanest approach would be to have the training school supply a large number of rats with equivalent experience, so that the habits diagnosed on one rat could be cross-validated on other rats who were uncontaminated by the residues of the experience from the inappropriate diagnostic efforts. While farfetched, this seems to suggest a legitimate precaution in anthropological studies, i.e., that a group of the best potential informants be set aside, not to be interviewed or observed until the anthropologist has learned the culture in first approximation.

Note a general limitation on this process: the diagnosis of the rat's behavior is only possible in so far as the rat and the scientist to some extent overlap in their classifications of the environment into things. Were the rat indeed to be responding to constellations of molecules or atoms sharing no boundaries with the constellations the scientist was able to discriminate, the diagnosis of the rat's habits would be impossible.

TABLE 1. TALLY OF OUTCOMES FOR ONE ORGANISM IN A SERIES OF ONE-STIMULUS–ONE-RESPONSE OBSERVATIONAL SITUATIONS

Stimuli	Responses					
	m	n	o	p	q	r
A	1	1	111		1	
B	1	1111	1	1	11	111
C	1111		1111	1	11	11
D	1		1	1111	1111	
E	1111	1	1111	11	11	11
F	11	1111	1	11	11	111

A final technical difficulty: in terms of the procedures described, one could not distinguish between a stimulus-response consistency which the animal had acquired through experience and an innate one universal to the species. The procedure we have just described would be most appropriate if one had shipped some newborn rats to the training school for their education, while retaining litter mates in the diagnostic laboratory to provide information as to the basic genetic stock and the inherited response dispositions characteristic of the strain. In practice, this restriction is probably not an important one for the social sciences.

The operational approach to the diagnosis of habit may be epitomized in the following diagrams. Table 1 implies essentially experimental conditions; the experimenter chooses to classify his stimuli so that only one of the stimuli to which he is paying attention is present at any one instance. These various stimuli are separately presented on numerous occasions, and a single response to each of them is classified in the experimenter's terms. Eventually a matrix such as Table 1 might emerge, in which each tally represents a separate experimental occasion. For some of the cells, the frequency may rise above the chance level that would be inferred from taking the stimulus and the response marginals jointly. In terms of the kinds of actuarial tests employed in chi-square, some of these concentrations would be taken as evidence of systematic stimulus-response connections. From such a table suggestions would also emerge for lumping stimulus and response categories into larger equivalence groupings (e.g., *C* and *E* and *m* and *o* in the table). Little suggestion is offered for subdividing categories, and this would have to be done on a trial-and-error basis, concentrating upon those cells (and the stimulus and response categories associated with them) which rise a little above chance expectancy but do not achieve any high degree of consistency.

TABLE 2. STIMULUS-RESPONSE TALLY SHEET

Observa-tional time units	Stimuli						Responses					
	A	*B*	*C*	*D*	*E*	*F*	*m*	*n*	*o*	*p*	*q*	*r*
1	1	1		1		1	1	1			1	
2	1	1		1		1				1	1	
3			1			1					1	1
4			1			1	1				1	1
5						1	1				1	
6			1			1					1	1
7	1					1					1	

But the Table 1 matrix is not the ideal model for actuarial investigation because it implicitly assumes a single stimulus and a single response of relevance for each situation. A more generalized actuarial model would recognize that many stimuli discriminable by the experimenter are present simultaneously, and that a number of discriminable responses may be emitted in a short time segment by the organism, without any variation in the discriminable stimulus context. Table 2 shows the basic data protocol that might be involved. Upon such a table, one could make a number of analyses involving simple relationships between stimuli and responses taken singly and simultaneously, various degrees of time displacement between stimulus and response, or higher-order relationships, as the correlation of stimulus D with response m when stimulus A is present, etc. Stimulus C and response r seem to constitute a simple disposition. Note that for any correlation to be observed, there must be occasions of both presence and absence for both stimuli and response. This rules out any conclusions about stimuli E or F and responses o and q of Table 2. Correlational evidence of the type computable from Table 2 will be taken as a prototypic operational diagnosis of a habit.

It is the present writer's allegation that most of the acquired behavioral dispositions can be diagnosed occasionally, even if not typically, by such behavioral observation, with guessing as to categories and actuarial documentation of contingency. Certainly goals, motives, and attitudes are all occasionally so observable.

The social scientist will want to point out that the diagnosis of dispositions goes on continually in his field, that primarily it is done by asking the person about his habits, even though it is conceivable that the actuarial approach here described might be used. He will also point out that we would hit upon these verifiable stimulus-response consistencies much more easily if—instead of resorting to the experimenter's trial and error of categorizations—we interviewed the person to find out how he organizes his world and then test the fit of the categorizations thus suggested. In terms of practical research approaches, these are valid points, but they do not alter the basic formal operational definition. Indeed, one person learns another's language in just the way the scientist has been described as diagnosing habits. The learner makes guesses that objects or stimulus configurations which he can discriminate are discriminated in the other's language. These guesses are tried out in terms of the kinds of classifications of response he deems relevant. Learning another language would be impossible if there were not some common overlap between the learner and those who already know the language in the discriminable contours of matter and uniformities of response. Furthermore, through either observation or interview, the scientist can diagnose dispositions of which the speaker is not aware. Usually the scientist does this by regrouping stimulus and response into syndromes of stimulus and response equivalents not so conceived by the subject.

In summary, acquired behavioral dispositions provide coordinations of behavior with reference to environmental settings. They may be epitomized as correlations between objects and acts or between stimuli and responses. They can be diagnosed through the observation of stimulus-response consistency. An essential part of diagnosis is the formation of hypotheses as to stimulus equivalents and response equivalents.

Modes of Acquiring Behavioral Dispositions

The initial illustration of the child in the room with the boxes, and the setting of the problem of operational diagnosis may have seemed to bias the presentation in favor of the animal behaviorists. This section will attempt to correct this narrowness of perspective. To do so, it will be convenient to employ another physical psychology illustration. I am reminded of the multiple-unit maze for humans which Prof. Warner Brown [15] used to have at Berkeley—a trough maze with 3-inch high pathway edges through which one shuffled. Socialized human beings acquiring behavioral dispositions in this trough maze and in the room of boxes will provide the concrete illustrations as we examine the several ways in which these behavioral dispositions can be acquired.

1. *Blind trial and error—locomotor exploration.* Shuffling blindfolded and with ears covered, the individual could learn Warner Brown's maze without benefit of distance receptors. And the child in the room with the boxes could have acquired some behavioral dispositions, even if he were blind. Animals in tunnel mazes or in puzzle boxes where vision is useless acquire habits in this fashion. If the person starts with no initial behavioral dispositions, blind trial and error is the only method of approach. This is the mode of learning built by Ashby into his homeostat [6]. And, as is argued elsewhere [24], this is the only mode of learning that is systematically investigated in learning theory—perhaps on the grounds that the simplest processes should be studied first. While this approach is clearly not modal for the socialized human being, it does seem in some sense basic, the ultimate resort.

2. *Perception.* Were one not blinded in Warner Brown's maze, one acquired the appropriate behavioral disposition so rapidly that the process eluded study. The fact that perception may be substituted for blind trial and error is so ubiquitous as to go unrecognized, but it has received attention from Tolman in his concept of perceptual expectancies as coordinate with mnemonic expectancies [165]. It can also be interpreted as a major part of the demonstration of the delayed-reaction studies. Certainly one who has vision acquires in one glance behavioral coordinations which a blind person tediously achieves by trial-and-error learning.

Since a major purpose of the argument is to establish the equivalence of these modes of acquisition in leading to the same behavioral coordination or disposition, let us specify that the subject be allowed to see the maze, explore it visually, and then run the maze blindfolded, as does the person learning the maze by blind trial and error. Could observing diagnosticians distinguish the final behavioral dispositions had they not seen the acquisition trials?

The argument here is that the socialized human being can learn mazes and acquired dispositions by vision, in addition to blind trial and error. The claim is not made that all can be so learned. The issue is avoided as to whether such visual cognition must have been preceded by and based upon achievements of blind trial and error, which might have established, for instance, the rewardingness of the candy and the electrical coil.

3. *Perceptual observation of another person's responses.* Behavioral dispositions may also be learned by observation of another organism's responses to stimuli. This is the traditional social science mode of behavioral-disposition acquisition, known as imitation of responses. It has been demonstrated by Miller and Dollard [111] and designated matched dependent behavior. Let us suppose that we permit an observer to watch a person who already has learned the maze run it repeatedly. And let us suppose that the observer can see the choice-point stimuli but not the clues for distinguishing blind alleys and main paths. By memorizing the responses and then imitating them, the observer might acquire a behavioral disposition externally identical to that which others had acquired by perception of the maze or by blind trial and error.

4. *Perceptual observation of the outcomes of another's explorations.* The previous mode referred to the observation of another only after he had already acquired an asymptotic behavioral disposition; it represented a learning of responses. The present mode refers to observing another only during his initial exploration of the environment; it refers to learning about the environment and its rewardingness rather than about responses. Thus a child who sees another child get shocked from the shock box does not imitate the explorer's response. Nonetheless, he acquires the same behavioral disposition of avoidance which the explorer acquired by learning about the nature of the box. Phylogenetically, this is an extremely important kind of learning for social animals for, even if the explorer does not survive the experience and has thus learned nothing, the observers may have acquired an adaptive disposition representing the fruits of the explorer's trial and error. This is vicarious trial and error in its most literal sense, i.e., letting a vicar do one's exploring.

In approach-learning situations, this mode of dispositional acquisition is apt to be confounded with the perceptual observation of responses, unless specific tests are introduced to separate them, as in studies [111] which demonstrate that the learned response is associated with the responses of the lead animal and not with the clues which the lead animal is employing. That both can occur has, of course, also been indicated [37]. An interesting test of the relative strength of the two would be provided by giving the lead animal a painful shock after the matched dependent behavior had been well established and observing the subsequent depression of the imitative response tendency.

While their experimental design is not adequate for their conclusions, Herbert and Harsh [66] provide a fascinating and relevant study in which the observation of another cat's trial-and-error process accelerated subsequent learning more than did the observation of error-free performances. In a sense, observation led to extinction in the observing animal of maladaptive response tendencies, which were also being extinguished in the model animal, as well as to an increase of those response tendencies being reinforced in the lead animal. Such conclusions cannot be predicted from the matched-dependent behavior model but require some sort of postulate such as the present one.

The emphasis upon dispositional acquisition through observation of outcome is in accordance with Asch's [5, p. 392; 28] emphasis upon cognitive factors in imitation situations and with his rejection of matched-dependent behavior as the fundamental process involved. However, the principle need not lack behavioristic support. Assuming a tendency for fractional or subliminal motor mimicry (motor empathy) on the part of the observer, reinforcement or extinction of such fractional responses might plausibly occur in the observer. G. H. Mead [106], Logan et al. [100, p. 150], and Osgood [129] describe such processes.

5. *Verbal instruction about responses to stimuli.* Accepting the adult or socialized child as he is and skipping for the moment the problem of language learning, it is obvious that adaptive behavioral dispositions can be acquired by verbal instruction. We can instruct a person as to what response to make at the first and second choice points, etc., so that he can run the maze blindfolded, perfectly the first time, with overt behavior which is not distinguishable from that of other modes of acquisition. While there have been many treatments of language learning in learning-theory terms, the induction of locomotor habits through language has only begun to receive treatment. Outstanding in this regard is Mowrer's paper [117], in which he epitomizes the prototypic sentence as conveying to the listener a habit, designating both a stimulus and a response to it. Certainly such sentences are one typical means by which the dispositions we call "social attitudes" are induced, even those social attitudes symptomatized by such nonverbal locomotor behavior as throwing stones or running away.

6. *Verbal instruction about the characteristics of objects.* For purposes of a balance to be made clear later, it should be emphasized that behavioral dispositions can be verbally induced by means of descriptions of the objects with no mention of responses. Instead of saying "Turn right," one can say "The left path is blocked, the right one open." In-

stead of saying, "Open the black box and avoid the green one," one can say "The black box contains candy, the green one a shocking coil." Certainly both modes of linguistic disposition-induction are employed. Which is the more typical, the most linguistically primitive, must be determined through analyses not yet made. For the purposes of this presentation, it is enough to emphasize that to some extent they are equivalent and produce results comparable to those which might be obtained through blind trial and error, perception, etc.

Composite dispositions.   Not only are the results of these different modes of dispositional acquisition comparable, they also combine in ways that so far seem to be additive, or at least monotonically cumulative, or decremental, as the case may be. Thus, one is more certain (has a stronger disposition) when both individual exploration and verbal reports of the outcomes experienced by others are in agreement than when the two sources are discrepant. The exploration of the details of such combinatorial processes represents a most important problem area in social psychology. In addition, it seems profitable to interpret many traditional topics as studies of composite dispositions.

Directly relevant is a neglected classic by Hilgard [67] in which modes 1 (trial-and-error learning) and 5 and 6 (verbal instruction about responses to stimuli and the nature of stimuli) are studied singly and in combination. Hilgard attempts to discover algebraically the relative weights of each required to predict the combined effects in an eyelid-conditioning situation. While a simple additive model does not provide a perfect fit, the results are very encouraging. Response strength is strongest where both modes induce the same disposition, weakest where the dispositions induced are in opposition. His paper should be a classic in social psychology because of its clear establishment of social sources of dispositional strength comparable to and combinable with those of a more purely individual nature.

The experimental conformity literature can be interpreted profitably as a composite-disposition situation in which the experimenter has created the ecologically atypical situation of placing the individual dispositional sources (modes 1 and 2) in opposition to or in decremental combination with the social sources (modes 3, 4, 5, and 6). Interpreting this as a composite-disposition problem leads to the obvious prediction that anything weakening modes 1 or 2 or strengthening modes 3, 4, 5, or 6 will increase the relative weighting of the latter, an outcome commonly labeled "conformity." The large research literature on situational and individual-differences factors in conformity is coherently summarizable in these terms [28]. The mode of composite, whether a "resolved composite" or a more aggregative "compromised composite," provides one of the few empirically specifiable disagreements between behaviorist and gestalt theories in social psychology, even though the data to date are equivocal [28].

While these are the main illustrations of composites across modes of acquisition, the composite-dispositional orientation is important also for dispositions acquired through a single mode. It is characteristic of social situations that the behavior of the moment is a net result of numerous dispositions, incompletely learned in settings only partially similar to the current one. The long-standing study of approach-avoidance conflict and displacement [14, 45, 92, 93, 110] is a composite-dispositional study. So are the retroactive and proactive inhibition studies in learning. The problem of primacy versus recency effects in persuasion become resolved when viewed in this light [112]. Exaggeration of social-group differences when the individual members of the groups are imperfectly known becomes an inevitable prediction from laws of learning applied in composite form [23].

Modes of Expressing Acquired Behavioral Dispositions: Diagnostic Symptoms

The major point of the preceding section was that behavioral dispositions acquired in such varied ways could all have similar expression, i.e., could all be manifest in locomotor behavior, and might well be indistinguishable when so expressed. To return to the operational diagnosis of dispositions not observed during acquisition, and with a reminder of the unguaranteed nature of that process in any instance, it can be stated that dispositions acquired through any of these means are potentially so diagnosable.

In this section a parallel point is aimed at, the intersubstitutability of modes of expression of the acquired behavioral dispositions. For the socialized human being, many behavioral dispositions can be expressed by locomotor behavior, by verbal statements of stimulus-response sequences, and by verbal descriptions of the environment and the objects in it. Once the child has, as by blind trial and error, learned about the boxes, he can express the acquired dispositions by locomoting around and manipulating the boxes or by reporting what he does when he comes to a given box or by reporting what the boxes are like. He can instruct another person about the maze he has learned through statements about responses to make or about the nature of the maze parts.

While this substantial intersubstitutability and multiple symptomatology is the major emphasis needed for purposes of integrative conceptualization in this area, this should not be understood as total. Research has indeed shown that persons may not be able to draw or describe accurately a maze through which they can locomote perfectly. Similarly, verbally acquired dispositions may be expressed more perfectly verbally than through locomotion. Some degree of common variance between similar input and output modes may be recognized without negating the point of substantial intersubstitutability.

III. INTEGRATING PERCEPTUAL AND RESPONSE DISPOSITIONAL CONCEPTS

Learning theory and perception theory lead relatively autonomous and uncompetitive existences in general psychology, where their supporting and disciplining data lie, but both have been analogized as explanatory systems into social psychology. Here they are in direct competition, being used as translations of the same phenomena, summarizing and explaining the same aspects of social behavior. Thus, in the 1930s one was asked to understand social attitudes as "conditioned reflexes," in the 1940s as "social perceptions."

In the pages which follow, these points will be argued: (1) In *social* psychology, the S-R and perceptual-cognitive-phenomenological languages are functionally synonymous—not only competing in the same arena, but in general making the same predictions; (2) the confusion of terminologies is a needless obstacle to the cumulative development of the field; and (3) the concept of attitude is an excellent integrative acquired behavioral dispositional construct just because of its multiple connotations, rather than in spite of its varied definitions.

The Possibility of Equivalence between Perceptually Oriented Terms and Response-oriented Terms

In the earlier discussion of the hypothetical experience of the child in the room full of boxes, the case was begun for the possibility that theorists employing languages as widely divergent as the perceptual and the behavioral might be summarizing the same facts in ways that are operationally or predictively indistinguishable. The challenge has also been made that acquired behavioral dispositions stated in terms with phenomenal connotations could be diagnosed through the S-R correlational model, providing a generic operational definition for all behavioral dispositions.

It should be noted, however, that the assumption of possible equivalence of these processes challenges a well-established division of labor within the field of experimental psychology. Through publications and the careers of individual scientists, we note that general experimental psychology treats perception and learning as two independent fields of inquiry that have some complementary relationship to each other but no equivalence of function or synonymity of data. The recently popular social-perception orientation in social psychology has furthered this tacit assumption, which may be thought to lead to the implicit model of the central nervous system shown in Fig. 1. On the one hand, there is a perceptual projection screen; on the other hand, there is a series of levers eliciting various motor responses. In between is a homunculus, I, the decision maker, who views the projection screen and pulls an appropriate lever. For the unification of theory in psychology, we need to replace the homunculus with integrative concepts, and we need explicit recognition that the formal processes involved in studying the partial concepts of perception and habit are the same [21, 55, 79, 147].

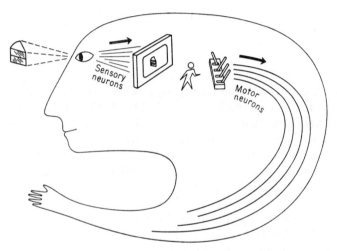

Fig. 1. A too-frequent implicit model of the central nervous system.

One may protest. On the one hand, nobody really uses the homunculus model. On the other hand, the difference between perception and habit is obvious—they are entirely different—at most, they influence one another. But the "obviousness" of this difference may be an unfortunate consequence of the conditions of conscious experience. This is not to quarrel with studying receptor and effector processes as separate processes. But in most studies and theories of perception and learning— and universally in their extensions into social psychology—it is a total integrative process lying between receptor and effector that is being studied, while interpretation tends misleadingly to refer to either the receptor or motor side exclusively and leads to an artificial dichotomization of any central integrative processes in our psychological language and theory.

Empirical Convergence in Perceptual Threshold Research

Perhaps most of the 80-odd acquired behavioral disposition terms listed earlier occur in social science settings in which there has been no accumulation of empirical regularities. However, if essentially equivalent concepts are duplicated or independently invented, and if empirical laws develop around each of these concepts, then the equivalence should show up in an identity or overlap of the empirical regularities. Were social psychology and the social sciences able to be fully experimental— were each seriously proposed theoretical system pretested by developing empirical relationships employing its terms—then empirical convergence would produce clarification of terminology and integration of theory, and the argumentative approach here employed would be superfluous. However, both the difficulties of research in the social sciences and the tremendous social pressure for theory in the absence of disciplining fact rule out any rapid achievement of integration by empirical convergence.

Within our domain of constructs, however, the development of empirical laws has occasionally occurred. The Bruner and Postman social-motivational-perceptual movement provides an excellent example for our purpose. Including the previous research upon which they built and the subsequent confirmatory and elaborative studies, hundreds of empirical researches are involved. The central focuses were on perceptual thresholds and perceived magnitudes, as influenced by need, value, etc. In midstream they provided two summaries [16, 134] of the empirical regularities, introducing the dispositional construct of "perceptual hypothesis." The striking convergence to habit theory apparent in these reports has been noted by several persons including Postman himself [e.g., 21, 44, 135, 138, 180]; it is detailed here for its value as an illustration of the integrative effect of systematic experimental exploration of theories:

Bruner and Postman	*Habit-theory equivalent*
1. The stronger a (perceptual) hypothesis, the greater its likelihood of arousal in a given situation.	1. The stronger the habit, the more probable the response, and the greater the likelihood that stimuli will occur which are close enough to the original stimulus on the generalization gradient to elicit the response.
2. The greater the strength of a hypothesis, the less appropriate information necessary to confirm it.	2. The stronger the habit, the weaker can be the stimulus which will still elicit the response.
3. The greater the strength of a hypothesis, the more inappropriate or contradictory information necessary to infirm it.	3. The stronger the habit, the more the response will appear in inappropriate situations or the more resistant it is to extinction.

Bruner and Postman	*Habit-theory equivalent*
4. The more frequently a hypothesis or expectancy has been confirmed in the past, the greater will be its strength.	4. The more frequently a response to a stimulus has been reinforced in the past, the greater its strength.
5. The more basic the confirmation of a hypothesis is to carrying out a goal-striving activity, the greater its strength.	5. The stronger the reinforcement of the response to the stimulus has been in the past, the stronger the response.
6. The hypothesis may be strengthened by virtue of its agreement with the hypotheses of other observers to whom the perceiver may turn.	6. (This requires extension of S-R theory in the manner of modes of acquisition 3, 4, 5, and 6 in Sec. II plus consideration of composite dispositions.)
7. The smaller the number of alternative hypotheses held by the person concerning his environment at a given moment, the greater their strength will be.	7. The fewer the competing habits in the situation, the greater the likelihood of a given response being elicited.
8. The larger the number of supporting hypotheses, the stronger the hypothesis.	8. The more stimuli in the situation all eliciting the same response, the greater the likelihood of that response.

It seems likely that in the early phases of this enthusiastic movement, this convergence occurred initially without awareness of the similarity on the part of these perception theorists and that it emerged more or less directly from the discipline of data. Postman in a subsequent review [135] has explicitly recognized the appearance of the traditional laws of association, and has relabeled the perceptual hypotheses as perceptual response dispositions.

While Postman's leadership both as an initiator of the perceptual sensitization movement and as an advocate of the associative learning interpretation should have been sufficient, a more recent review [76] indicates such a total neglect of this achievement that it seems well to emphasize the convergence in further detail. Let us consider a situation in which a stimulus is presented at such a tachistoscopic threshold that it is not clearly recognizable, presentations with and without the stimulus present being randomly mixed. If the stimulus represents a food object, and the response a food-appropriate response, the baseline situation for a nonhungry S might be of this nature:

	RESPONSE		
STIMULUS	Absent	Present	
Present	17	33	50
Absent	33	17	50
	50	50	

Of these data, the top row represents the typical threshold data, the proportion of "correct" responses when the stimulus was actually present. Let us suppose that, in agreement with the voluminous data on the problem, this top row changes in the direction of more "correct" responses when S is hungry, as follows:

	RESPONSE		
STIMULUS	Absent	Present	
Present	10	40	50

This shift can be a part of an increased accuracy or precision of perception (in traditional psychophysics, a steepening of the ogive, a reduction of the standard error) or it can be a part of a general increase in the frequency of the response, uncontingent on stimulus presence or absence. These two fourfold tables illustrate the alternatives:

	RESPONSE					RESPONSE		
STIMULUS	Absent	Present			STIMULUS	Absent	Present	
Present	10	40	50		Present	10	40	50
Absent	40	10	50		Absent	25	25	50
	50	50				35	65	
	Increased accuracy					Increased responsiveness		

Using the tetrachoric r as an over-all index of accuracy, the nonhungry table has a value of .50, as does the increased-responsiveness table. In the increased-accuracy illustration, the response marginals are held as before, and the tetrachoric index goes up to .81. Other indexes of accuracy which pay attention to frequency of responding when the stimulus is not actually present (as a crude per cent of error or a contingency coefficient) would give a similar picture. Which of these conditions actually obtains in the motivation and perception literature? We get a hint from noting that under the increased-responsiveness condition not only has the top-row accuracy increased, but also that the bottom-row errors have increased (from 17 to 25). This corresponds to the autistic perceptions of Murphy [120] and to the value-resonant errors discovered by Postman, Bruner, and their co-workers in many situations [e.g., 136]. Thus, instead of two principles, one for the top row (perceptual sensitization) and one for the bottom row (value-resonant errors), a single principle of increased associative strength or increased responsiveness might be substituted.

While such data strongly presaged the outcome, Zeitlin [180] undertook a direct test of the increased-accuracy versus increased-responsiveness interpretations. In a training period involving above-threshold presentations, two nonsense syllables out of six were associated with the gift of 3 pennies for one group, with a loud and painful noise for another, and given no special treatment for the control group. Subsequently, the syllables were presented in random orders tachistoscopically, with the Ss forced to guess from among the six syllables. Reinforcement, both reward and punishment, increased the frequency of naming the reinforced syllable when the reinforced syllable was presented (the usual evidence for perceptual sensitization or selectivity), increased the naming of reinforced syllables when other syllables were presented, and increased the naming of the reinforced syllables when a blank screen was presented (a finding which Goldiamond [54] has also elegantly demonstrated). On the other hand, a tetrachoric score for accuracy computed for each subject for each reinforced syllable showed no significant increase as a result of reinforcement, nor did the percentage of correct responses among the total responses of reinforced syllables (i.e., a score based upon the right-hand column of the fourfold table). The results thus strongly supported the increased-responsiveness interpretation.

To note the convergence in another form, it can be said that Hullian theory anticipates the major findings in the perceptual-threshold area, once it is recognized that increased responsiveness means lower perceptual thresholds in the ascending method of limits. This Hullian formula can be used: sE_R (response probability) $= D$ (drive level) $\times K$ (incentive motivation, magnitude of reward on previous trials) $\times sH_R$ (frequency of making the response to the stimulus in the past). This formula thus predicts perceptual sensitization in the presence of high drive, strong values (K, as in Zeitlin's study), and frequency or familiarity. This last factor has turned out to be a very strong one, both in perceptual threshold studies and in learning studies. Hullian theory likewise predicts, under varying conditions, both increased and decreased responsiveness for noxious stimuli, i.e., both perceptual vigilance and defense.

To increase the ability of phenomenological and behavioristic social psychologists to understand each other, it seems best to interpret these developments as a *convergence between two equally justified theoretical systems*. Important critiques of this literature [e.g., 51, 53] tend to use similar evidence to infer that the students of social and motivational effects upon perception made a *mistake in interpreting the effects as perceptual*, since the results were specific to certain psychological methods (e.g., were found with the ascending method of limits but not with the constant method) and could be demonstrated through response manipulation in the absence of stimulus variation [54, 87, 180]. This point of view is acceptable if perceptual processes be defined in advance as excluding associative processes and as independent of phenomenological reports. However, such a purified view of perception is obviously not what is being referred to in the perceptual-cognitive-phenomenological social psychologies. And even though many of the personality and perception experiments have not used a phenomenological methodology in that they have forced or encouraged guessing, their results have confirmed the abundant testimony of phenomenological reports as to the selective effects of drive and meaning upon conscious contents, whereas the imperturbable thresholds found by the constant method have not.

Convergence between Hull and Lewin

The Bruner and Postman social-perception instance is the only striking empirical convergence we have to offer. Nevertheless, it seems worthwhile to call attention to a partial line of convergence between Lewinian and Hullian theory, which developed at the instigation of research in learning theory with animals, rather than from empirical developments making use of Lewinian theory.

To compare the two at all, one must make explicit certain aspects of the Lewinian theory to which Lewin himself gave little emphasis. We must include an external environment in addition to the life space; we must concede that aspects of the present life space are in some sense products of past experiences in so far as they have contemporaneous representations in the individual; and we must interpret the life-space diagram as predicting overt behavior at least in some instances. With regard to the first, if Lewin's statement that behavior is a function of the life space, which, in turn, is a function of the person and the environment, $B = f(L) = f(P,E)$ [93, pp. 12, 216; 95, p. 240] is not to be taken as meaningless, then E and L are *not* to be regarded as synonymous. Lewin did not deny the relevance of the external (physical and social) environment; rather, he insisted upon representing the behavior-influencing aspects of it through the life space. Physical facts are to be represented in it, but "only to the extent and in the manner in which they affect the individual in his momentary state" [93, p. 24]. Indeed, when he wished to manipulate the life space experimentally, he usually did so by manipulating the external environment.[1]

---

[1] Taking his discussions of environment as a whole, Lewin is not clear on this subject. Where he refers to "psychological environment," he is clearly referring to the phenomenally nonself aspects of the life space rather than to an external environment or to aspects of an external environment externally definable. The present interpretation of Lewin is in essential agreement with Deutsch [43], Bronfenbrenner [13], and Leeper [89, pp. 207–210], although Leeper regards the interpretation as a needed editing of Lewin. Cartwright does not so interpret Lewin and seems to identify the E and the L of the above formula [35, p. 67], which is consistent with interpreting the formula as dividing the life space into two parts, P and E. Actually, the formula $B = f(P,E)$ antedates the life-space formulation [92, p. 73]. But whether or not the present writer is correct in interpreting

When in early stages of his theory, Hull added the distinction between $_sH_R$ and $_sE_R$, he provided for something of the detachment of response from the physical-stimulus presence emphasized by the concept of life space. Life space thus functions as the explanatory and predictive equivalent of D, K, and $_sH_R$. D and tension system are easily equated, and both theories allow for both physiological and acquired drives, quasi needs, induced tensions. The newly prominent concept K, forced upon Hull by performance changes resulting from changes in magnitude of reward, is in striking convergence with Lewin's concept of valence. Both represent the knowledge of the goodness or tension-satisfying qualities of the goal region. In this regard, the K of Hullian theory seems more economical in that in the performance formula, it is independent of contemporaneous drive, whereas Lewinian valence is a part function of the momentary state of the tension system. (The Lewinian valence must also be a function of something other than tension level, something which could perhaps be called "potential valence," which would need to be specified in a complete system.) Hull's $_sE_R$ and Lewin's force vector converge, both being products of tensions, valences, and mediational knowledge. The directional feature of the force vector is equivalent to the specification of the response involved, the length of the vector to the strength of the response tendency. To complete the equivalences, the structured pathways to the goal region are here interpreted as analogues of $_sH_R$, which for this purpose is translated as knowledge of means (with K as knowledge of ends), or as familiarity with the responses to make if you want to make them.

The identification of structure with $_sH_R$ is undoubtedly the least plausible of these identifications. Nevertheless, I believe it is one which Kurt Lewin himself would have made had he been asked about the current version of Hull's theory, in which the former H has been separated into H and K. Indeed, regarding the derivation of his own notions from older associationistic doctrines, he stated:

The attempts were all based upon the assumption of the classical laws of association as stated, e.g., by G. E. Müller. The experiments, however, seemed to prove conclusively, contrary to my expectation, that this assumption had to be abandoned or decidedly modified. It was necessary to distinguish two rather different types of habits (associations): "need habits" (like alcoholism) and "execution habits" (like pulling a lever up rather than

---

the E of this little-used formula as "external environment," there are numerous passages [e.g., 92, pp. 70–74] which make it clear that Lewin emphasized rather than ruled out the effects of an external environment. He did insist that the external environments be represented in the prediction of behavior only as perceived, interpreted, and understood by the person. But this is far from the position that it should be totally disregarded.

down). The first type represents a tension (source of energy), a need such as hunger, which demands satisfaction either directly or through substitution. The execution habit, on the other hand, is in itself no source of action. It is equivalent to a pattern of restraining forces determining a certain path. Without need or quasi-need, the execution habit does not lead to action [94, p. 13].

Note particularly the identification of "execution habit" with "path," and the recognition that, without motivational components, the habit does not result in behavior, i.e., the same evidence that forced Hull in the evolution of his theory to separate from $_sH_R$ both D and K in turn.

In spite of this convergence, one can, of course, note differences in the focuses of the theories. The convergence is in the performance formula. Most of the effort in learning theory is upon the acquisition and extinction of the component variables, upon how valences and life spaces are acquired and changed, if you will. This emphasis is almost totally lacking in Lewin, and his a-historical emphasis argues against it. Lewin was the more interested in the allocative or composite-disposition problem, in the situation that elicited a number of already developed habits in various degrees of conflict with each other. Where Hullian theory has dealt with the multiple-habit situation, as in approach-avoidance conflict [14], the convergence has even reached the level of cross-school citation.

Convergences in Research on Bias

The instances of convergence between behavioristic and perceptual concepts in this section are less compelling than those previously cited in that only one parameter from each theory, rather than several, is involved in any one study. Noting them briefly, however, may emphasize the ubiquity of possible integrations. For example, take the Levine and Murphy [90] experiment in which anti-Communists find it hard to memorize a pro-Communist passage, and vice versa. The original interpretation emphasized the function of attitude as a perceptual filter which selectively modifies contact with the world. However, an alternative statement is available; it would explain the effect in terms of proactive inhibition, or negative transfer, when antagonistic responses are to be learned to familiar stimuli. Thus the preexperimental learning of the pro-Communists might be epitomized as a paired association of "Communist-good," having positive transfer to the similar pro-Communist selection, but negative transfer to "Communist-bad" pairing of the anti-Communist passage.

This is the area in which I have longest attempted to express research findings in both languages. The first of these studies [178] examined a decrement in accurate perception resulting from premature guessing. The initial inspiration for the study came from the perceptual *Einstellung* tradition, but Wyatt and I had no difficulty in translating the findings into the learning-theory terms of negative transfer resulting from the strengthening of an incorrect response tendency. Note the superficial dissimilarity from a cognitive statement in terms of the effect of one cognitive structure in making the achievement of restructuring more difficult.

In the study of another cognitive bias, the tendency to exaggerate group differences, enhancement of contrast, was examined. The phenomenon was first studied as the tendency for white school children to exaggerate the difference between the classroom examination scores of their Negro and white classmates [Clarke and Campbell, 38]. Subsequently [23] an enhancement of contrast for similarity families of nonsense syllables was demonstrated in a learning situation in which each syllable was paired to a specific location on a spatial continuum. Here again, the conceptualization of the phenomenon came initially from analogies to visual space perception. It turned out, however, that the effect could be elegantly derived from learning-theory considerations. The tendency for stimuli sharing common elements to elicit the same response predicts a "homogenization" within similarity groups, and a resultant enhancement of contrast between groups. The practical equivalence for social psychology of "perceived as" and "responded to as to" was explicitly pointed out in the discussion.

A predisposition toward oversimplification in early stages of cognition or learning constitutes a very pervasive bias tendency which is integral to the phenomenon of stereotyping. Gruen and I [32] illustrated this bias experimentally for spatial maze learning, and attempted to state the effect in both cognitive and behavioral terms. Furthermore, in many situations and for stereotypes about social objects, the learning-theory concepts of stimulus generalization and broader generalization gradients in early learning generate predictions of a bias toward cognizing one's world in terms of as few entities as possible. A broad generalization gradient indicates that many different stimuli are being responded to as though equivalent.

In an extensive review of perceptual, cognitive, and communicative biases [27], I have attempted to interpret the specific phenomena in both perceptual-cognitive and learning terms. Of the many biases enumerated, this duality seemed impossible for only one. (This one was the contrast error, or stimulus-relativism effect, which can, of course, be incorporated into learning theory, as through Hull's V, the stimulus-intensity dynamism.) In a series of papers on attitudes toward authority figures, Burwen, Chapman and I [19, 29, 30] explicitly attempted to state the problem in both cognitive and S-R terms. Biased perceptions were equated with biased response tendencies. We expected a respondent's view of his father to influence his perception of his boss in a new situation or, in *S-R* terms, learned responses to father should transfer to boss.

These several scattered notations of equivalence would not be compelling in their own right, but they may add depth and generality to the implications of the two multiparametered convergences.

Practicing Translation: Causal Perception and Conditioning

If social psychology is to develop a cumulative and integrative theory of acquired behavioral dispositions, it would seem wise to practice translations across the semantic barrier created by the implicit homunculus model of conscious experience. When a respondent is diagnosed as having such and such a view of the world, one would then try to translate this as a tendency to make such responses to such stimuli, and vice versa. This exercise would seem desirable for both readers and authors of research reports.

Such exercises have led me to a bizarre instance of potential synonymity between causal perception and the conditioned response. Developments in gestalt psychology have led to a psychological attack on an old philosophical problem. Heider [65] in this country and Michotte [108] in Belgium have undertaken experimental investigations of causal perception. They find that when two events are appropriately coincidental in time, space, and sequence, an unavoidable and indivisible experience of causality occurs. With regard to the older philosophical issues, they find against Hume and for Kant as to the primitiveness, indivisibility, and immediacy of the experience. However, the conditions under which the experience occurs are those described by Hume for the coincidence we call causality. And the temporal requirements bear a strong superficial identity to those required for conditioning. Now, if there were to be a subjective perceptual counterpart to conditioning (particularly in one-trial learning), would it not be a perception of causality? On the other hand, if one sought to describe the external behavior of one perceiving a causal sequence in which he himself was involved, would not this look like a conditioned response?

Let us look at Watson and Raynor's [171] classic case of Albert and the white rat. Startled by a fearful noise right after the appearance of the rat, the child subsequently gave as a conditioned response to the rat the fear responses he had originally shown to the noise. Yet had some perceptually oriented social psychologist been able to interview Albert (he was but eleven months), had he been able to describe the situation as he saw it, would it not have turned out that Albert mistakenly perceived the rat as being to blame for the frightening noise, under temporal conditions appropriate for the perception of causality? We lack actual cases in which both conceptual approaches have been applied to the same specific instances, yet it is hoped that this unlikely illustration can alert us to the possibility of identities in process being obscured by the great superficial differences in conceptualizations.

Possible Empirical Distinctions between Perceptual Dispositions and Response Dispositions

I have argued for the possible equivalence between dispositional constructs employing a subjective language and constructs employing response terms. So far, I have dealt with theorists who have limited themselves to a single vocabulary. It should be pointed out, however, that a number of theorists have posited two separate processes: a learning process involving perceptual dispositions, and a learning process involving motor coordination. It is possible that the general equivalence between theories suggested here might hold in some instances, but that there might still be a bona fide distinction between "modified views of the world" and "modified readinesses to respond."

Leonard Doob in his paper "The Behavior of Attitudes" [46] posits at least two separate learning processes: afferent habit strength and efferent habit strength. Doob sees an attitude as a learned implicit response bound to a stimulus pattern by a certain degree of afferent habit strength and bound to a motor pattern by a certain degree of efferent habit strength. He also has two other constructs with learned dispositional attributes, in the familiarity of the stimulus pattern and in the learned motor-pattern coordination. It turns out, however, that his conceptual scheme offers no challenge to an argument for a single acquired behavioral disposition, inasmuch as Doob provides no operations whereby one could distinguish between the afferent habit-strength component and the efferent component. As a matter of fact, he treats these as a team which he never unyokes. An actuarial approach to synonymity through observing the frequency with which terms are used in parallel hitch would score the two concepts as highly synonymous. For example: "Response to each question is not only a function of how closely the question approximates the original learning situation but also of the afferent habit strength of the attitude, its efferent habit strength and the interaction occurring at the time the replies are given" [46, p. 146]. In this and other illustrations, he shows how both are involved in any attitude diagnostic process; furthermore, he shows that the same reinforcing state of affairs would modify both. A single integrative concept, which might as well be called habit as attitude, could be substituted for the two or five here involved without loss of any operational distinctions or illustrative subtleties suggested by Doob.

James Olds [128], going beyond Hebb's theory, has explicitly hypothesized separate learned perceptual phase sequences and motor phase
sequences. However, he has not yet operationally justified the hypo-
statization of these two processes, and it may be unlikely that he will be
able to do so. But as he presents it, the idea will be appealing to a
number of psychologists who wish thus to reconcile the disparate trends
in theorizing.

As a third illustration of explicitly separate acquired perceptual dispositions and acquired response dispositions, J. J. Gibson's distinction
between two kinds of set can be offered. Gibson makes a sharp contrast
between set as an anticipation of a certain stimulus as opposed to set as
an intention to respond in a specific way. He emphasizes that the distinction is important, neglected, and demonstrable [52, p. 784]. He cites
several studies to this end. The first of these is that of Lindner [97] to
whom he refers as having established an expectation both with and without an accompanying motor intention to react. On reexamination, however, the study does not seem to be crucial to the existence of two separate
set processes.

Lindner's data are of a retrospective-introspective sort. Unlike other
studies of set, there are no reaction times or other behavioristic comparison data, nor is there any effort to define the difference operationally.
In his "perceptive anticipation" situation, a single click antecedes the
illumination of a rolling landscape and a double click antecedes a
mountainous scene. The subjects gradually become aware of this correlation, and their anticipations are reported introspectively after the scenes
have been presented. In his actional anticipation study, the number of
clicks antecedes and serves as a cue as to which of three chutes will emit
a ball which the subject is to catch. Once the ball is caught, there is
retrospective introspection as to what went on during the period between
the click and the catching of the ball (the period of anticipation, once
the correlation had been learned). Although the experimental setups
were different, there is nothing in the report to justify Gibson's interpretation that data are available to discriminate the two types of set.
Lindner himself does not draw this interpretation. He reports

. . . as between the two experiments then we have found a smaller difference
than we expected . . . the result is an intermediate between perceiving and
acting, with perceiving the closer affiliate [for the motor anticipation study]
. . . . It may well be that a re-examination of remembering and imagining,
expecially of those forms of imagining common in artistic and inventive
production, would reveal similar intermediaries with action.

Lindner's position is highly sympathetic with the orientation here
presented in that he sees these anticipatory images as intermediaries to
action.

The second study cited by Gibson is a conditioning experiment by Hilgard and Humphreys [68] which was designed to illustrate the interaction of an instructional set with a conditioned response. Previous research had illustrated that conditioning was modified by instructions or expectancies or set as to the stimulus conditions (i.e., telling the subjects which cues would be related to which unconditioned stimuli, etc.). Hilgard and Humphreys studied the effects on conditioning of an instruction to inhibit or augment the response. Their findings showed that these instructions also would interact with the conditioned response and would either augment or suppress it. Nowhere, however, are any data provided to demonstrate that this is a different kind of set than that shown in earlier studies, where the instructions introduced expectations as to stimulation. And it is Gibson, not Hilgard and Humphreys, who makes the claim. In terms of the orientation of this review, Hilgard and Humphreys's studies are on the combination of two behavioral dispositions, one resulting from locomotor exploration (the conditioning experience), the other induced by verbal instruction about responses or, in the earlier work, by verbal instruction about stimuli. While the two types of experiments are thus clearly distinct as to the mode of set induction, no evidence is introduced to show that the sets thus differently induced have different effects, and indeed the data argue for the functional identity of the two types of set.

Gibson's distinction is clear and appealing, but the studies he cites seem to show no justification for the implied functional distinction. He seems to have overlooked the possibility that the "set to see" and the "set to respond" could be operationally identical and he persistently criticizes previous writers for having failed to note his distinction. For example, in referring to a study by Mowrer [115], Gibson says, "Mowrer assumes that the irregularity [of stimulus presentation] affects reaction time by weakening the expectancy of a stimulus, but the effect could equally well be explained as the weakening of the intention to react." The emphasis of the present discussion would be on the probable equivalence of these two statements. If there are two functionally separable set processes, they have not as yet been demonstrated, and the available evidence argues against the dual-process notion.

Labeling the Internuncials

While neither the operationalist learning theorists like Spence [149] nor the operationalist perceptionists like Postman [135] believe in the employment of literal physiological brain-mechanism constructs, there is this much anatomy of learning upon which we all probably agree. There are sensory neurons reaching the brain. There are motor neurons conducting impulses from brain to muscle. In between the sensory and motor neurons

in the brain, there are frequently internuncial neurons. Some of these internuncials are involved in the learning process. Without entering into
debate as to whether neurological speculation is premature or harmful in
psychology, and certainly without any necessary disagreement with the
positions taken by Spence and Postman on this issue, I should like to use
this oversimplified neurology as a heuristic device to indicate in Fig. 2
the specious nature of much of terminological confusion in social psychology today. Unless operationally specified and shown to be otherwise,
disagreements in terminology can be suspected of being nothing more
than annexational labeling tendencies with regard to the functions of

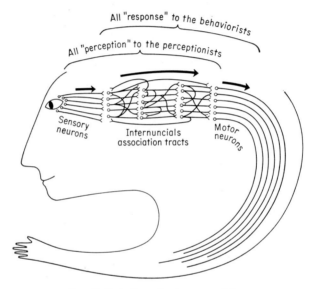

Fig. 2. Labeling the internuncials.

the internuncials. The perceptual-cognitive-phenomenologists employ
terms of afferent connotation [even when, atypically, they specifically
eschew phenomenological evidence, e.g., 135], terming internuncial
processes "expectancies," "perceptual hypotheses," "frames of reference,"
"definitions of the situation," "perceptual selectivities," "meanings engendered upon the world," etc. The stimulus-response theorist labels
central or internuncial functions with motor terms such as "fractional
anticipatory goal response," "mediation response," "pure stimulus act,"
"subliminal cue producing response," etc. (Indeed, every synaptic transmission represents a response and a response-produced stimulus.) For
social psychology, and possibly for psychology in general, we need central
concepts, concepts which are neither sensory nor motor, neither afferent
nor efferent.

This is not to deny that there may be genuine disagreements among theories or construct systems. After the terminological clouds are cleared away, there may be testable predictive differences, as Spence [147] and I [21] have indicated even while making this general point of specious disagreement. These differences are probably rare, however, in the aspects of acquired behavioral dispositional theory which are employed in social psychology. In any event, let us substitute real differences and innovations for terminological pseudoinnovations.

The Location of Conscious Experience in the Central Nervous System

The social scientist surveying the terminological fads and feuds in an undisciplined area such as social psychology is rightly tempted to interpretations of the sociology-of-knowledge type. There are many directions in which this could go. For instance, current preference for subjective conceptualizations might be regarded as a part of the more general antimechanistic reaction created by the tragedy of two scientifically fought world wars and the anticipations of a third. Asch [5], and Krech and Crutchfield [81] may stand vis-à-vis the Floyd Allport of 1924 [2] as Aldous Huxley stands vis-à-vis H. G. Wells. While these historical trends are worthy of more detailed analysis in their own right, I wish to turn the sociology-of-knowledge spotlight on a more persistent ecological condition and a corresponding correlation.

We can note that the animal psychologist uses only one of the three available processes for diagnosing behavioral dispositions, i.e., observation of overt responses in the presence of external stimuli. Even here, he finds statements about responses more dependable and intersubjectively communicable than statements about stimuli. These ecological conditions of data collection tend to be reflected in his constructs at the connotative if not the operational level. Such observational diagnostic procedures are generally impossible for the social psychologist. For many purposes, he can learn of the animal's acquired behavioral dispositions only by asking it directly. Now even this approach need not bias the social psychologist away from the stimulus-response language. The respondent animal could report, for example, "When I see stimulus A I've learned to make response B." Were all or most reports from respondents of this nature, the data pressures would probably lead to a construct language very similar to that of the animal psychologists. Probably, however, most reports from respondents are in the form of the third type of diagnostic symptom, i.e., reports on the nature of environmental objects as the respondent, through learning, has come to know them, that is, as he "sees" them. It may be that in so far as animals are aware of their own acquired-response dispositions, they are aware of them in the form of views of the world rather than tendencies to respond. The nature of conscious experience seems relevant to the existence of any such data pressure. The most objective recent tabulation of the conditions and character of conscious experience of which I know has been assembled by Penfield and his collaborators. This report will primarily depend upon Penfield and Rasmussen [132]. They electrically stimulate the cortex of epileptic patients under brain surgery, eliciting reports of conscious experience and motor movements as a part of a diagnostic process to guide their operations. While it is dangerous to generalize from such patients to normals, their data are sufficiently stimulating to tempt me to do so.

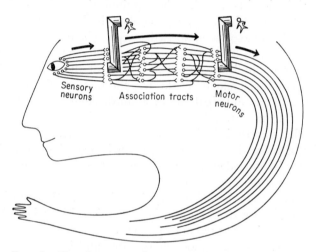

Fig. 3. Conscious experience conceived as periscopes lowered into the central nervous system.

If one takes as a temporary expedient an explicitly epiphenomenal point of view regarding conscious experience (or a more sophisticated "synthetic identity" or "double knowledge" position [48]) one can analogize to wiretaps, or to periscopes lowered into the neural stream of the previous diagram, resulting in Fig. 3, in which the homunculus has been moved out of the main stream to the position of periscope watcher. If one then considers the preponderant directionality of nervous transmission (toward the brain for sensory neurons, away from the brain for motor neurons, and predominantly from sensory to motor for internuncials), it would seem that any tapping or monitoring of this stream would be receiving impulses from the afferent direction and any periscope put into the stream would be looking upstream, even if it were placed among the motor neurons. There are thus grounds for expecting conscious contents to be primarily afferent in their orientation, no matter what aspect of central nervous flow they correspond to.

This is indeed what Penfield and Rasmussen report. In all patients, in the sensory and motor projection areas that lie along the Rolandic fissure, dependable sensory and motor excitation loci are found. The stimulation of the sensory points produces conscious experiences (tactile in somatic projection area, visual or auditory elsewhere). The stimulation of the motor points brings movement without any awareness of tendency to movement, intent to move, or the like. Motor movement gets into conscious experience only through the subsequent sensory feedbacks, such as "I felt my finger move," etc.

These universally found activation loci represent fragmentary sensations rather than perceptions on the one hand, and muscle twitches rather than coordinated acts on the other. It would be much more relevant to our question if cortical stimulation were to activate acquired behavioral dispositions or the residues of past experience and if we could examine the related conscious contents. In general, electrical stimulation of the association areas produces no effect. However, in some cases of focal epilepsies, stimulation spots can be found which do induce meaningful perceptual and memory content. Here also, the conscious contents are totally afferent or perceptual in their orientation. Most typically, perhaps, the patient relives a past occasion with hallucinatory vividness and immediacy of experience. In some cases, the electrical stimulation produces a meaningful, memory-related distortion of objects and persons present in the immediate situation. Sometimes these conscious contents are the same as those found in the patient's preseizure aura; in such cases, the motor aspects of epileptic seizure may follow, initiated perhaps by coordinated motor movements appropriate to the contents of the hallucination (which rapidly give way to uncoordinated convulsions). No cases are reported in which electrical stimulation of association areas produced coordinated meaningful motor effects without conscious concomitants.

These instances represent the only electrical elicitation of meaningful perceptions or memories or coordinated meaningful motor responses. If, in their explorations, Penfield and Rasmussen have activated any acquired behavioral dispositions, these are the ones. It is tempting to interpret these results (short of the convulsions) as typical, being accessible in the focal epileptics only because of an exceptionally low threshold of activation for the particular disposition. If typical, these conclusions may be justified. When acquired behavioral dispositions are activated, they have conscious contents of a view-of-the-world nature. The conscious view of the world and the corresponding response pattern are elicited together and are but two aspects of a single process. George Herbert

Mead—a social behaviorist preoccupied with the fact of conscious experience—long ago noted the asymmetry of conscious experience to which I am calling attention. Criticizing Wundt's psychophysical parallelism, he said: "The required parallelism is not in fact complete on the psychical side, since *only the sensory and not the motor phase of the physiological process of experience has a psychic correlate*" [106, p. 42].

Be it also noted that conscious experience, as an epiphenomenal wiretap on the afferent-to-efferent neural stream, taps in both in the primary sensory projection area (the "upstream periscope") and subsequent to the association area (the "downstream periscope") and no doubt elsewhere. This point is relevant to a debate within the cognitive-perceptual-phenomenological orientations, in which some of the pure gestaltists have objected to the notion that needs and past experience influence perception [e.g., 169]. However, when Asch [5], Köhler [80], and others are talking about meaning and the phenomenology of action, they invoke a type of conscious experience that carries the influence of value and past learnings. Generally speaking, when employed in social psychology, all of the cognitive-perceptual-phenomenological orientations focus on the content of the downstream periscope and on sensory input as filtered through the residues of past experience in the association areas.

If this sampling of conscious contents is at all representative, then indeed those clinical psychologists, social psychologists, and sociologists who study the residues of past experience or acquired behavioral dispositions through interviews will be under a persistent pressure from the raw material of their studies toward a view-of-the-world construct language. The animal researchers will similarly be pressed toward external stimulus-response conceptualizations. These conflicting pressures are permanently with us and will persist as a divisive force in the study of behavior unless deliberate efforts are made to avoid it. A major contribution can be made along this line by deliberately attempting to employ both terminologies in studies of human beings. An improved lexicon of view-of-the-world to response-tendency translations is also needed.

The Isomorphism of Experience and Action

In his most stimulating *Social Psychology*, Asch introduces the concept of the "isomorphism of experience and action":

To justify this conclusion it is necessary to assume that there is an intrinsic correspondence between experience and action, that they are *isomorphic*. The assumption of isomorphism was first formulated in psychology by Wertheimer and Köhler for the relation between physical brain events and the conscious experiences which accompany them. The present discussion refers to an extension of the isomorphic relation to include the relation between brain processes and their conscious accompaniments on the one hand and the actions of the individual on the other [5, p. 159].

He introduces the concept in the specific and limited setting of how we are able to understand the conscious experiences of others through their facial expressions. It seems legitimate and convenient, however, to extend the label to Asch's more general position: "We act and choose on the basis of what we see, feel, and believe . . . when we are mistaken about things we act in terms of our erroneous notions, not in terms of things as they are" [5, pp. 64–65]. In a similar vein, Murphy [120, p. 354] has spoken of "the unity of perception and action," and Sherif [143, p. 72] of the "unity of experience and behavior." It is judged that this dramatic concept helps resolve the difference between cognitive and *S-R* theories, making laws predicting responses (or acts) equivalent to laws predicting the isomorphic conscious contents.

This is not, of course, how the gestaltists would see it. The very point of the unity of experience and action is apt to be made in the course of a scathing rejection of *S-R* explanations, as in the second quotation from Asch, above [5, pp. 64–65]. Several comments on this can be made. First, it seems probable that the unity or isomorphism is introduced in part as an empirically verifiable relationship between verbal reports on conscious contents and overt action (rather than as a purely definitional or axiomatic tautology). If so, this would be equivalent to the statement made earlier concerning the joint diagnosability of dispositions from overt behavior and from verbal description of the environment. While isomorphism is too strong a term for this correlation, the point of such joint diagnosability is one to which attention should be called, and one which has indeed been systematically neglected by the behaviorists.

More typically, however, the emphasis on the necessity of phenomenal description for the prediction of behavior implies the rejection of a behaviorist straw man. According to the gestaltists, the behaviorists imply a rigid reflex relationship between stimulus and response for all persons, regardless of their life histories, and thus expect a given stimulus to have the same "meaning" for every person. On the contrary, say the gestaltists, it is not enough to know what the stimulus is: to predict behavior one must know in addition how the person perceives the situation, what his life space is, what his frame of reference is, what meaning the stimulus has for him, the content of his phenomenal field, etc. Asch criticizes the honesty studies of Hartshorne and May [63] as behaviorist bad examples, for "we cannot suppose that the identical situation had the same meaning for all children, or that the 'same' response in different children was psychologically identical" [5, p. 63] and also Floyd Allport's early experiments [2] on effects of group situations, in which he—

. . . assumes that there is a fixed meaning to the condition of being alone
and that it can be produced by the simple expedient of placing people in
separate rooms . . . . Reference to phenomenal facts would have revealed
that one can at times feel close to others when physically alone, that one
can be lonely or asocial when with others, and that the sheer putting of
people in the same space does not have a constant meaning [5, pp. 66–67].

In such typical emphases the gestalt social psychologist has actually
reversed the emphases of gestalt physical psychology on two important
counts: interest in individual differences, and denial of the predictability
of conscious contents from the external stimulus field. Whereas in describing the perception of the physical world, individual differences are
neglected (as are past experiences and motivational factors), the
gestaltist as social psychologist suddenly becomes interested in the idiosyncratic character of each individual. And unless free will or arbitrary
indeterminacy or status as the prime mover is implied for the phenomenal
field, these idiosyncratic personal meanings must be due to the idiosyncratic life histories of the persons. In discussing the gestalt principles
for the perception of the physical world, Asch himself emphasizes the
lawful field determination of phenomenal contents, dealing with relationships between the total external stimulus field and perception which
are coercive, to which no man is exempt. Knowing the total physical
field, and knowing the gestalt laws of perception, one can predict conscious contents for a stranger entering the laboratory for the first time;
one can tell which item will appear stationary, which moving, which
figure, which ground, which straight up, etc. [5, pp. 48–60]. How different this is from Asch's protestations about stimuli in social situations,
where his emphasis is upon the uniqueness and unpredictability of conscious contents or behavior from knowledge of the stimulus field alone.

Asch's interests in the social setting are actually more like those of
the behaviorist learning theorist than those of the classical gestaltist. If
we examine the crucial term *meaning* and put it through the tests of
Sec. II, it turns out that meaning is a synonym for acquired behavioral
disposition. The behaviorist's translations for the phenomenalist's protest
might be: "To predict behavior it is not enough to know what the
physical stimulus is. One must know in addition what habits the stimulus
evokes, what response tendencies the person has associated with this
stimulus, what the person's past history of reinforcement is with regard
to this stimulus, what other stimuli with strong associated responses are
also present in the situation, what the person's drive level is, etc." Thus
translated, this is a statement with which any behaviorist would agree.
It is, in fact, characteristic of learning theorists to emphasize the uniqueness of individuals in so far as this uniqueness is lawfully related to the
uniqueness of their past histories of reinforcement. Of course Hartshorne
and May expected to find children differing in their response to situa-

tional contexts. Of course the temptation to cheat had different meanings or past associations to different children. Of course this made sense to a learning theorist. (Of the inconsistency of Hartshorne and May's children, more in the section on measurement which follows.)

The allegation that to the behaviorist, a given physical stimulus is expected to have the same meaning for each person is nonsense, for it translates into the expectation that every person will make the same response to the stimulus: persons will only have the same response to a given stimulus when they have had equivalent past histories of reinforcement, i.e., when the stimulus has the same meaning to them. If there is any point of view in psychology that expects the same response from all individuals in the presence of the same stimulus field, it is the classical gestalt psychology, focused on the pure perceptual problems of the upstream periscope, uncontaminated by filtration through the residues of past experience.

The bold postulation of an isomorphism of experience and action makes clear a programmatic weakness in gestalt social psychology, tied in no doubt with its occasionally militant ahistoricism [81, 92]. If experience and action are now known to be completely isomorphic, the development of laws relating them seems completed. For a behavior theory that is not a tautology, it then becomes glaringly apparent that laws predicting the contents of conscious experience are needed. Classical gestalt psychology has these. So does behavioristic learning theory if we are allowed to extend it to predicting conscious contents by employing in reverse the powerful postulate of the isomorphism of experience and action. (The behaviorist's laws predicting behavior thus become laws predicting the corresponding conscious experiences.) For the classical gestalt psychologists and for the behaviorist, statements about the nature of the external physical stimuli are essential in this prediction. For the behaviorist, just because he is interested in the learned or idiosyncratic aspects of behavior, there is also the need for statements about past stimulus situations and their outcomes. Will not the gestalt social psychologist also need laws relating these same variables to present conscious contents, and hence to behavior?

The bold postulation of isomorphism between experience and action will probably do much to unify social-psychological theory and to substitute genuine predictive disagreements among theories (and there are undoubtedly such) for specious semantic squabbles. Convinced as I am that the greatest bulk of data available to the student of social attitudes will come in the form of linguistic references to conscious contents of the view-of-the-world type, the development of a specific lexicon translating views of the world into response patterns becomes an important and unfinished empirical business. Thus, in spite of his misleading attacks on behaviorism, Asch has made an important contribution to a cumulative theory of acquired behavioral dispositions, as to other problems not covered in this document, such as the rationality of making use of information provided by others in so-called "conformity" or "suggestibility" situations [5, 28] and the coordination of persons in joint undertakings.

The Need for Multiple Connotation in Acquired Behavioral Disposition Terms

Considering the support from the conditions of data collection, it seems unlikely that the terminological alternatives which face social psychology today will be eliminated by the imperialistic domination of one point of view over the other. And even were it possible, it would represent a loss. Hopes for integration would seem more likely to lie in the utilization of acquired behavioral dispositional terms that have explicitly both connotations, are both response tendencies and views of the world. The concept of habit as described by Dewey in 1922 [42] had to a very considerable extent these dual aspects, unlikely as this may seem in terms of today's usages. The concept of "object," as uniquely used by G. H. Mead [106], had these connotations, for Mead emphasized that not only did the object contain such characteristics as color and form, but also the organism's readiness to respond to it, the object's utility, its rewardingness, or punishingness, etc. Thus the image of the chair was made up not only of form and color, but contained also, and equally inherently for a socialized human being, the character of sit-in-ableness. Preeminently among acquired behavioral disposition terms available to the social psychologist, the term attitude has such dual connotations.

While the great bulk of the formal definitions of attitude emphasize the response side, the general discussion and usage has traditionally included both. Allport has defined attitude as " . . . a mental and neural state of readiness, organized through experience, exerting a directive or dynamic influence upon the individual's response to all objects and situations with which it is related" [3, p. 810]. Although this has primarily a motor orientation, in discussion Allport also tells us—

> Without guiding attitudes the individual is confused and baffled. Some kind of preparation is essential before he can make a satisfactory observation, pass suitable judgment, or make any but the most primitive reflex type of response. Attitudes determine for each individual what he will see and hear, what he will think and what he will do. To borrow a phrase from William James, they "engender meaning upon the world"; they draw lines about and segregate an otherwise chaotic environment; they are our methods for finding our way about in an ambiguous universe [3, p. 806].

Faris, writing as a sociologist in 1931, uses Dewey's definition of habit for a definition of attitude, "an acquired predisposition to ways or modes of response," and then goes on to say, as though elaborating on this thought, "The attitude is a way of conceiving an object; it is the mental counterpart of an object . . . . One cannot experience a new object without experiencing at the same time a new attitude" [47, pp. 8–10].

While neither of these authors was attempting to make the point we are considering, these quotations are enough to illustrate the dual aspect of the concept. Further illustration of the point comes from the inspection of the kinds of items that attitude-test constructors have intuitively put into their tests—probably working more closely with a common-sense understanding of the concept than with their formal definitions. In all of the social-attitude scales I have inspected, except the purely social-distance scales, there are items stating a generalized predisposition to respond in a given way, such as "I would not patronize a hotel that accommodates Negroes" [Hinkley-Thurstone test, 161, item A-14], and items describing the view held of the social object, such as "Inherently, the Negro and the white man are equal" [161, item A-8]. If anything, items of the latter kind are the most numerous—all items reproducing popular stereotypes are of this form. Furthermore, there is no evidence that such a combination has interfered with the achievement of homogeneous attitude scales [91, 96, 153]. Factorial studies by Gage [50] and by Kahn [77] on attitudes toward the Negro show both kinds of items reflecting the same general factor.

Another dividing line among acquired behavioral dispositions has to do with the presence or absence of motivational or goal attributes. Attitude in many of its definitions and usages has this additional connotation, further enhancing its value as an integrating dispositional concept in social psychology. This very multiplicity of connotation has, however, contributed substantially to the abandonment of the term [e.g., 156]. The nominalist currents dominant in the social sciences tend to demand both singular and rigid definitions for each construct, and lead toward the reification of each attribute as a separate process or entity. Were each of the connotations of attitude functionally separable, this would, of course, be justified. But where the several attributes are aspects of a common syndrome, appropriate multiple connotation becomes an asset.

IV. MEANS DISPOSITIONS AND ENDS DISPOSITIONS: THE OBJECT-CONSISTENT RESPONSE

The theme of this section is that all constructs referring to responses or to mediational dispositions also have goal or motive quality. This theme is relevant to the unification of dispositional constructs in several ways. While the empirical convergences noted in the previous section pointed toward agreement on two types of learned constructs, even this duality is challenged here. In addition, a further contribution is made to the problem of the central nervous system and conscious experience con-comitants of the behavioral regularities described by the behaviorists.

The empirical convergences of the previous section have pointed to two basic acquired dispositional constructs: an acquired-means con-struct, and an acquired-goals construct. The reappearance of these two in such different theoretical traditions lends considerable implication of validity to the notion that these two at least are required, that reduction in the number of terms should not go beyond this point. Further con-ceptual convergence upon this duality abounds—Myrdal's beliefs and valuations [125, p. 1027]; Parsons and Shils's [131] cognitive orientations versus cathectic orientations; Tolman's [165] means-ends readiness and expectancies, etc. Rosenberg [139] and Carlson [34] have made a com-parable distinction within the social-attitude area per se. To tie their system into the previous discussion, their particular concept of attitude can be identified with Lewin's force vector and Hull's sE_R. Attitude thus conceived is demonstrated by them to be a joint function of value satis-faction associated with the outcome, to be identified with Lewin's valence and Hull's K, and the perceived instrumentality, to be identified with Lewin's structure of the life space and Hull's sH_R. Furthermore, in discussions of values in both philosophy and social science, the distinc-tion between means and ends is recurrent and, no doubt, useful.

If I were to undertake at the present moment the kind of integration of concepts appropriate for an introductory text in social psychology, I should certainly retain these two components to the behavioral formula. There nonetheless remains the feeling that a basic redundancy exists among the three concepts of tension, valence, and structure in Lewin's system and D, K, and sH_R in Hull's. Making this point requires a detour into the details of the concept of response in its most readily objectified setting of overt animal behavior. First, we must distinguish between muscle-consistent and object-consistent modes of response. This not only provides a background for the major problem, but also deals with one important factor which has led to the rejection of the dis-positional constructs of Pavlov and Watson by social scientists. Since most modern learning theorists employ object-consistent responses, many of the traditional reasons for rejecting stimulus-response theories are no longer applicable.

The second point is more difficult. Since object-consistent responses are characteristic of most (although not all) learned behavioral dis-positions, it is appropriate to characterize such dispositions as acquired purposes, motives, or goals. If this second point can be made acceptably, it will provide a bridge between the two classes of dispositional constructs, the means concepts referring to acquired behavioral routines, to pro-grams or sequences of response, to schedules for behavior, and the ends concepts stated in terms of acquired drives, motives, goals, purposes, needs, need-dispositions, cathectic orientations, and the like. The unification would be achieved by alleging that all of the acquired behavioral dispositions in which social psychology is interested—be they called habits or attitudes or sets or cathexes—have both aspects. Whereas the unification efforts of the previous section may have seemed biased toward the behaviorist, the net bias of this section may seem to be toward a perceptual point of view, ending up as it does with a tentative argument that for every object-consistent response, there is something like a stored image in the central nervous system. However, for behaviorists properly agnostic as to how the central nervous system achieves the dependable regularities they observe, no incompatibility is present.

Molar Response versus Reflex: Convenient Level of Abstraction or Empirically Demonstrable Distinction

Watson and the early behaviorists thought of learned behavior as learned muscle contractions. This description of the learning process is one of the reasons why his orientation has seemed inadequate to social scientists for predicting the behavior of socialized human beings. The typical social scientist often fails to realize that Watson's description is of proven inadequacy even for the learned dispositions of rats, and that it has been almost totally abandoned in modern learning theory.

A distinction between types of responses has been made by a number of writers. Tolman [165], Hull [75], and Spence [148] have epitomized it as the difference between the study of molar and molecular behavior. Guthrie [57, 58] has expressed it clearly in his early distinction between acts and movements and in his more recent distinction between advertent and inadvertent responses. Brunswik's [17, 18] distinction is between distal and proximal responses. Skinner [144] has always been clear that he dealt with molar responses rather than muscle contractions, and his distinction between operant and respondent behavior has some similarity, although drawn for another purpose. The present writer [21, 22, 24] has employed the concepts of object-consistent versus muscle-consistent response.

It is typical of the dominant philosophy of science in our field that many who accept the molar level of analysis as characteristic of their own research regard this as a mere experimental convenience, as the utilization of one arbitrary classification system as opposed to another. The attitude has seemed to be that any level of analysis would do, the molar level merely being the most convenient from a data-collection standpoint. The molar response has been regarded as just a larger classification category representing the arbitrary pooling of a number of molecular responses. The weakness is that this orientation often allows the learning theorist to assume that his explanatory problem is the same, whether he uses a molecular response analysis or a molar one, and it allows him to regard an explanatory construct which might be adequate for a muscle consistency as equally adequate for an object consistency.

Such an orientation is clearly incompatible with the history of the problem. As has been reviewed in detail elsewhere [145, 21], Watson specifically committed himself to a learned muscle-contraction theory of maze learning. His conclusion generated a spate of experiments that clearly disproved this point of view. Clear evidence that what rats had learned about a maze was not muscle contractions led Lashley [85, 86] to abandon Watson's theory at a time when he was Watson's leading student. Experiments by Warner [170], Dennis [40], Macfarlane [104], and others were equally clear-cut. In attempting to epitomize the learned response invariance, identifying it as an invariance in muscle contractions was clearly wrong in most instances. The invariances present were rather invariances in effects, in places reached, in objects avoided or manipulated, etc. To express the matter in Brunswik's orientation [e.g., 17, 18], while the study of learned or inherited covariances between proximal stimuli and responses is a perfectly proper scientific program, it in fact has usually discovered no laws. Instead, the demonstrable effects of learning usually turn out to be correlations between distal stimulus and distal responses.

In any given instance, the muscle-consistent versus object-consistent classifications of the learned response are rival hypotheses. In the original learning situation, they are usually confounded. But, by the employment of deliberate transposition experiments, they can be separated. When this is done, as in the experiments of Wickens [174, 175], Nissen [126], and Guthrie and Horton [58], the molar, advertent, object-consistent response is most usually found. [The instances in which muscle consistency occurs are, of course, important in their own right, and I have attempted an explanation of the exceptions elsewhere, 24.] The distinction is not, therefore, a matter of convenience in data collection, but an empirical question as to where the learned invariances actually lie.

Object-consistent Response in Evolutionary and Anatomical Perspective

In the first quarter of the nineteenth century, Bell and Magendie made one of the most stimulating discoveries of the whole century. They demonstrated the clear anatomical separation of sensory and motor nerve fibers in the spinal column. This discovery, the anatomical and clinical support which soon accumulated around it including studies of paralysis in spinal cord damage, and support from the demonstration of the unidirectional conductance of the nerve impulse, created an indelible impression upon the thinking in physiology and psychology which is still dominant. Anatomically, there is no quarrel with this position or with many of its specific implications. In our own generation, these have been amply validated by experimental embryology and anatomy in many ways, including the transplantation experiments by Weiss [172], Sperry [151], and others. But in psychology, the discovery generated a reflex-arc notion of habit in which a single sensory impulse goes into the brain, is channeled by instinctive or habitual pathways to appropriate efferent nerve fibers, which then carry an activating impulse to a specific muscle. This model, although found useful in the diagrams of the previous section, is at variance with the facts of distal object-consistent response. The misleadingness of this oversimplified anatomy as a model for behavior was seen clearly by John Dewey in 1896 [41], long before the model had achieved the dominance in learning theory which it was to attain thirty years later. There were, of course, other influences which made, and continue to make, the model attractive. For many, it seemed to be the only deterministic model, and a deterministic model has been extremely important for biologists and social scientists, who have continued to find themselves in competition with vitalistic and metaphysical theories. This particular influence may be expected to disappear within our present generation, since servomechanism or cybernetic theory has provided us with a deterministic model for the object-consistent, outcome-controlled response [22, 24, 57, 114, 116].

While the present focus is on the residues of experience in the organism's own lifetime, it should also be noted that the great bulk of so-called instinctive or inherited behavior patterns in the lower organisms consists of distal, object-consistent responses. This fact has been largely neglected, in part due to an early confusion in terminology between reflexes, instinct, and drive. A *reflex* is best defined as a proximal muscle-consistent response of specific stimulus elicitation, such as the knee jerk reflex or the Babinski reflex or other reflexes found in infants, for example. These reflexes can be artificially induced by stimulating the efferent neurons alone; they are clearly proximal. However, most instinctive behaviors of the elaborated locomotor organisms of both the arthropod and vertebrate phyla represent guided distal responses. Consider, for example, the inherited web form of the spider, achieved through a noninherited number of swings back and forth in a variable environmental context [83]. Consider the nest of the mud wasp, which fits into whatever environmental opportunities are offered and, if damaged, will be repaired [102]. Indeed, the instances of distal instinctive behavior among insects and birds are so preponderant as to make especially noteworthy the occasional occurrence of proximal responses, as for example, the egg-retrieving instinct of the bird that moves his head in appropriate pattern even when the egg has slipped away. These anomalies are indeed anomalies, and a systematic survey of instinctive behavior will show that it is adaptive just in the sense that it is not disturbed by specific relocations of the organism in question or the environmental context [160]. The distality and minor purposiveness of such behavior and its independence of muscular specificity must be clearly evident to anyone who has watched an ant carry a large piece of bread over an obstacle course of twigs and leaves. Object consistency, outcome-controlled response, is characteristic of a great deal more than learned behavior.

From the evolutionary point of view, it is likely that this must be so, for it is the feature of object consistency that has survival value. There is no point in an animal learning a habit or a species evolving an instinct which can only be applied from a specific point of application, or which is predicated upon an extreme degree of environmental stability. The ecological conditions of evolution argue that complex behavior patterns would emerge only if distal responses were possible. Behavioral complexity of a proximal sort has no survival value in the world as we know it. Thus, behavioral complexity is predicated upon distance receptors, whether this behavioral complexity be instinctive or learned.

A look at the evolution of the nervous system seems relevant here. Primitive evidence of nervous tissue is to be found in the muscular walls of the coelenterates. These nerve cells start at a skin surface and activate a muscle contraction, such as might serve to withdraw an arm of a hydra, or to contract a throat, etc. These elementary nerve fibers are certainly "fixed-wired" in the sense that the response is a uniform muscle contraction effected through a single efferent neuron. In this sense, the response is certainly proximal or muscle-consistent. But another aspect of this behavior should also be noted. The response is also stimulus-guided or object-consistent, having the effect of removing the organism from the source of stimulation in the case of a withdrawal reflex, or enclosing the source of stimulation if it is a grasping or swallowing reflex. Thus, the response is like a distal response, inasmuch as it achieves a uniform shift in the organism-environment relationship.

As a second example, let us take Jacques Loeb's [99] analysis of a simple heliotropic organism and machine in which the left eye activates the right leg, and vice versa, so that stimulation from one eye causes the opposite leg to move, and thus produces consistent locomotion toward a light. Here too there was fixed wiring and hence muscle-consistent response. However, the fixed wiring was of such a nature that the response had a consistent effect relative to the source of stimulation, moving the organism toward the light. Without going into the literal legitimacy of Loeb's model, we can emphasize the fact that the primitive nervous systems are adaptive in that they lead to responses which modify the organism-environment relationship in a consistent way and are thus object-consistent, but they are also fixed-wired or muscle-consistent. It would seem essential that in evolution the adaptive characteristics be retained at every level. Somehow in the course of evolution, behavioral complexity has been achieved through the modification of the proximal muscle consistency without losing the stimulus-guided aspect of behavior.

This analysis indicates the importance of distinguishing two functions for what are normally called stimuli. Tolman [165, p. 329], Nissen [127], Guthrie [57], and Tinbergen [163], if not others, have made the distinction. One stimulus function is that of instigator, trigger, cue, or releaser. The second is that of response guide, supporting stimulus, or maintaining stimulus. In the primitive behavioral coordination, these two functions are tied together, so that the stimulus object is both the instigator and the guide for the response. This is true for simple escape and food-gathering behavior. But at some point in the evolutionary ladder another kind of combination becomes possible; in this combination, one stimulus can serve as the instigator of the response, while other stimuli serve as guide. Experimental work on escape versus avoidance training may serve to illustrate the distinction. In escape learning, the electrical shock is both the instigator of behavior and the guide in the sense that behavior is consistent to the end of removing the shock or getting away from it. In avoidance learning, some warning stimulus becomes the cue for an avoidant response guided by other stimuli coming from the floor, walls, etc. Behavior theories in the Pavlovian tradition have focused almost entirely upon the instigator aspect of the stimulus. They have neglected the very basic and primitive attribute of stimulus as a guide to the response. Pavlovian theory presents a model in which any stimulus can be connected with any response with equal ease. From the present point of view, the natural and most frequent situation is where the stimulus is both instigator and guide, even for the higher vertebrates, as when the cat chases a rat.

Central nervous system anatomy would seem to give considerable advantage to learning stimulus-response coordinations which were naturally homogeneous in that the response was guided by the instigating stimulus. The close paralleling and the cross connections between sensory somatic and motor areas in the central nervous system, where toe sensations parallel toe movements and arm sensations parallel arm movements in an orderly fashion along the Rolandic fissure, seem to indicate some easier interconnection between stimulation of a body part and a response of that body part. Such spatial closeness has no place in the Pavlovian doctrine but could, however, be demonstrated rather easily. Suppose one took a dog in a conditioning harness and in the initial training touched the right foot and rewarded him for lifting that same foot. After that habit has been learned well, what foot will be lifted when one touches the left foot? It seems likely that the initial response would be a lifting of the left foot; that the touch stimulus is normally both a cue and a spatial guide for the response. Similarly, a dog would more easily learn to lift his right foot to a right-foot touch than to lift his left foot to a right-foot touch [see 33 for a related experiment].

This is not to deny that higher animals can learn responses to stimuli which have only instigator function. Thus one could not say that the buzzer which warns the dog to lift his leg guides his response. In this association of buzzer with leg lifting, a stimulus and response are arbitrarily associated, are nonhomogeneous. However, in most instances the leg lifting will be a distal response guided by the tactual or visual stimuli which provide knowledge of where the floor is. In many ways the Pavlovian dog, as Pavlov described it, was less adaptive to its environment than a hydra.

A study of Murphy and Miller [122] illustrates the natural tendency of animals to learn stimulus-coordinated responses and the relative difficulty animals have separating cue from response guide. In the Wisconsin general test apparatus, the monkey learns to get food by moving one of two discriminable objects which cover the food wells. In this situation, learning takes place rapidly and relearning to a changed cue relationship is almost instantaneous. Murphy and Miller modified this setup by placing the discriminated objects on a shelf 6 inches above the food wells, and covering the wells with identical white wedges. Under these conditions, one group of animals was unable to learn. A second group of animals, which had acquired the discrimination under the usual procedure, dropped to chance level of performance. It is felt that those theories of Pavlovian tradition which see in the stimulus only the cue function and not the response-guiding function are unable to predict this difficulty.

It seems obvious that human beings could have learned the Murphy and Miller discriminations. But, except for a man-made environment, such problems are extremely rare. From a functional evolutionary point of view, the ecological validity or the usefulness of such a capacity is relatively low. In nature, remote-control devices are few, and cues and guides seem usually to come together. Thus the food object provides visual instigating stimuli (cues) which are also supporting stimuli or guides. For the rat, the predatory cat represents both cue and the physical locus of threat. It is only in the experimenter's laboratory or in the push-button world constructed by modern science that the cue for an act is regularly separated from the object which guides the act. It seems a fair extension of selective survival mechanisms in the evolutionary perspective to predict that the capacity with the greatest general ecological usefulness will have emerged first and have remained most basic in the functioning of organisms.

Template for an Object-consistent Response

Guthrie was one of the earliest to recognize the importance of a clean distinction between acts and movements. He chose to study and build theory about movements rather than acts, expressing in part, no doubt, an insistence upon deterministic, materialistic explanations of behavior. Consistent to this background, he was the first of the major learning theorists to recognize the value of cybernetics or servomechanism theory in providing a deterministic explanation for responses that are controlled in terms of outcome, that are consistent in terms of results in spite of substitutability of movements. Guthrie put it this way:

In other words, association may result in acts as well as movements, and this is evident in cats as well as in men. The basic nature of the learning may be just as much an association of stimulus and response in an act that includes sustaining stimuli and cybernetic correction as it was in Pavlov's salivary responses. The automatic pilot, the thermostat, the governor of the engine—all illustrate the fact that physical analogies are available in which by setting a control we govern the later behavior of a complicated machine. In animal behavior we have only to assume that the setting, which can itself be a physical response, is itself subject to associative learning [57, p. 284].

But a thermostat setting represents the selection of an ideal locus on a single continuum. In contrast, the memories or instinctive guides that make possible an object-consistent response must be quite multidimensional. For this multidimensional thermostat setting, for this "input reference set" as a servosystem engineer might label it, for this blueprint of desired outcomes, or criteria against which to check the sensory inputs representing the *status quo,* the use of the term *template* is suggested. I am not in any way suggesting how such a central nervous system record might be carried; nonetheless it seems logically required that there be stored templates or maps for each object-consistent segment of behavior. Thus in the complex habit of lighting a cigarette, there is not only the template for cigarette in mouth, the template of warmth and smell to confirm that it is lit, but also a template for the cigarette lighter in the pocket that stops the blind fumbling among objects when that particular object is hit upon. The requirement for such templates seem to be implicit in the facts of distal behavior and in the servomechanism model for how such behavior could be achieved. If we stay at a hardware terminology like template and stay close to the servomechanism model, we seem to be on safe materialistic, deterministic grounds, but the concept may also open the back door for some prescientific conceptualizations of the storage of experience or acquired behavioral dispositions. Very often these templates are going to be built up around objects, in considerable degree will have in them requirements for the shape of the objects, and will come close to being images of objects.

A further problem arises here. In the simplest form of the servomechanism model, the template operates in terms of feedback after response. Thus, if the furnace heats too much, the thermostat turns it off; if the flywheel flies too fast, the governor cuts down on the steam. Such an operation of the template is perfectly compatible with what have been elsewhere called blind object-consistent responses [24], in which continuance of the process or its modification is dependent upon sensory feedback from the outcomes of previous response. But such a model does not seem to be complicated enough for the typical guided object-consistent response. For these responses, there seems to be a perceptual search and a perceptual checking of perceptual objects against a template, with the motor responses being guided by the discrepancy between perception and template. For organisms with vision, one needs either one template against which both vision and motor feedback are compared, or separate templates that are somehow coordinated. The single-template model seems preferable. Checking a perceptual pattern against the template (which very obviously must take place even in instinctive behavior, as in the insect recognizing a mate, or the baby chick pecking at grains of wheat) brings us closer to concepts of the storage of behavioral dispositions in terms of images. Note Uexküll's [168] use of the concept of search image, Tolman's [166] cognitive map, and Holst's [69] efference copy. Mowrer [118], and Miller, Galanter, and Pribram [109] have recently been influenced by cybernetic considerations to reintroduce the term "image," using it very much as I have done here. While the term schema [e.g., 8], like image, has been used primarily to describe perceptual processes, it likewise seems a synonym for the template guiding an object-consistent response. Such usage would further remove the lacuna between the perceptual and motor aspects of our common-sense model of the brain.

While these comments are not compelling, they may increase the possibility that, in a deterministic framework, acquired behavioral dispositions may be expressed in terms of images of objects, as well as physiological pathway routings. Such a point of view does not necessarily commit us to the kind of psychoneural isomorphism which Sperry [152] has so effectively criticized. We would agree with Hebb [64] and with McCulloch [101] that the template could be spatially distributed all through the central nervous system, as the extirpation data indicates it must be. However, it is true that a three-dimensional or two-dimensional anatomical parallelism would have many conceptual advantages were it ever to be reconciled with the anatomical findings. Woolsey's [177] data on the orderly mapping of the somatosensory projection areas, the parallel orderly mapping of the somatic motor areas, the evidence of point-to-point connections between motor and sensory areas, and the existence of duplicates for each may in the long run make a spatial paralleling of objects and templates more plausible than seems possible from Sperry's [152] resumé of the experimental anatomical evidence.

Minor Purpose and Goal in an Object-consistent Response

As Moore and Lewis [114], following the classic paper of Rosenbleuth, Weiner, and Bigelow [140], have made clear, every molar, object-consistent act is purposive or goal-oriented. Purposiveness has, of course, long been regarded by Tolman [164] as an essential characteristic of molar behavior. The animal behaves as though it had the (minor) purpose of depressing the lever, no matter how; or of getting out of the box, no matter how; or of getting to the corner and turning right, whether by 10 wading steps or 50 swimming paddlings; or of getting the finger off the spot, whether by bending the finger forward or backward. These are very minor purposes, very trivial and intermediate goals, to be sure. But in so far as we have been able to define purpose and goal operationally, these fit the definition. Since the great bulk of the learned responses studied by learning theorists have this object-consistent or molar character, their acquired behavioral dispositional terms, such as $_sE_R$ and habit, can be claimed to have the attributes of purposiveness and goal-directedness.

The minor purposes shown in object-consistent response are aspects of the flexible fitting of organism to environment found in the execution of any well-learned habit [24]. Of course, these minor purposes are only nodes of consistency in behavior sequences that encompass a larger spatial and temporal span. Thus, after learning, the rat shows an object consistency of response in pressing a lever, but a more overreaching consistency of response to a food pellet, a means object which would more usually be called a goal object than would the lever. But in lieu of a pellet, some other foodstuff would be acceptable, showing a consistency of a still more encompassing sort. These nodes of consistency or partial invariance are not to be judged arbitrary classificatory fictions. While in the initial instance they represent the experimenter's classification of response, they are actuarially verifiable as providing consistency.

By pointing to this potential series of intermediate purposes, I hope to make more plausible the description of motives and acquired drives as being of the same nature as habits, but with a broader span. Furthermore, in a given instance it may be equivocal whether a drive or a habit has been learned, and this may be decided solely by which symptoms of that learning the experimenter happens to test. Consider an avoidance learning situation in which a rat is placed in a box, a buzzer is rung, and an electric shock delivered. Something is learned, so that when the buzzer is rung again, distinctive responses appear. If these responses are jumping from the box or climbing up one wall, the learned stimulus-response connection would be called a habit (involving an object-consistent response, in that the actual movements of locomotion might vary considerably from trial to trial). If, however, this same past experience and resultant learning were to be manifest in terms of the rat's subsequent trial-and-error learning to spin a wheel to open a door so that it could get out, the initial avoidance learning would no longer be called a habit but rather an acquired drive or incentive. In this instance, it could be argued that what is learned has not changed, but merely the tested manifestations of it. The conclusion of this chapter is that motive attributes as well as means attributes characterize all learned object-consistent responses which interest the social psychologist.

The Means-end Regress

If one shifts to a social level of inquiry, one notes in the analysis of values that what may be regarded as an end for one analysis may be merely mediational for another, generating a regress of means-end relationships. In such a situation, one is offered the alternative of viewing the various elements of what becomes a means-to-a-means-to-a-means sequence not as qualitatively dissimilar categories, but as loci in a hierarchy of similar mechanisms. In so far as a unification of dispositional constructs, including drive, acquired drive, incentive motivation, and habit is essayed here, it is of this sort. Of course, acceptance of this position does not rule out using the practical distinction between superordinate purpose and subordinate purpose, or between ends and means at any one level of analysis. The notion of a hierarchical arrangement of dispositions not qualitatively different, except for position in the hierarchy, is similar to that presented by Adams [1].

In terms of the cybernetic analysis of purposive behavior [e.g., 114, 140], the rat in the maze can be seen as extending his paw until the feedbacks match a retained criterion of contacting the floor, a most minute purpose achieved; as continuing to run until the exteroceptor input matches the retained criteria of corner for right (or southwest or window-ward) turn, achieving this location by novel means of locomotion if others are blocked; as continuing to the goal region by familiar response or trial-and-error innovation until the cues with secondary reinforcing quality are present; as continuing behavior sequences until the pleasure sensory receptors associated with chewing, tasting, swallowing, and stomach inflation are activated. If necessary, the rat may substitute other turns and goal regions by extinction and trial-and-error relearning. There can be seen here a hierarchy of feedback circuits of greater and greater span, in which minor circuits become substitutable units in the service of the major ones. Smedslund [146] has suggested extending Brunswik's "lens model" [17] in a way useful here. By expanding Brunswik's diagram, the foci of vicarious functioning can be seen as occurring at several degrees of distality, as in Fig. 4. The criteria against which input is compared and the conditions of satisfaction are sometimes given

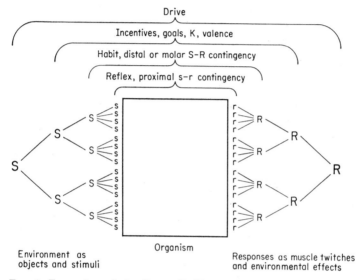

Fig. 4. Expansion of the Brunswik "lens model" to include several levels of distality. Note that in this expansion, the braces become functionally important parts of the diagram, in that a particular distal S is tied to a particular distal R at the same level of distality. In the cybernetic restatement of Brunswik's important perspective, the two-dimensional spatial separation of S and R on "opposite" sides of the "organism" becomes inappropriate.

by learning, sometimes by biological inheritance. The level which we call "drive" in studies of mammalian behavior primarily represents feedback circuits against inherited criteria. In the more instinct-ridden phyla, inherited criteria are also involved in the more proximal circuits.

Motivational, Value, and Goal Connotations in the Concept of Social Attitude

"Attitude" in the social psychology tradition has represented not only a predisposition to respond in a certain way or to view the world in a certain way; it also represents motive attributes, preferences for certain types of goals, or predilections for certain types of outcome. In the previous section, the simultaneous presence of the first two connotations has been judged insufficient grounds for splitting the concept of attitude into two constructs. Rather, attitude is to be conceived of as one process or entity with these two facets rather than as two independently manipulatable processes or entities. Can the motivational aspect be similarly handled?

As we have briefly noted, Rosenberg [139] and Carlson [34] suggest an interpretation of the concept of attitude which makes it a result of underlying components of value and perceived instrumentality. There is an analogy between their three constructs (attitude, value, and perceived instrumentality) and those of Hull (sE_R, K, and H) and those of Lewin (force vector or locomotion, valence, and path or life-space structure). Their specification of variables provides an illustration of the means-ends regress at the level of social data.

Certainly it is range of inclusiveness rather than a qualitative difference that distinguishes between attitudes such as "allowing Negroes to move into white neighborhoods," and "allowing members of the Communist party to address the public," from values such as "people sticking to their own groups," and "the open expression of disagreement between people." Certainly the former can be interpreted as values which, when combined with other instrumentalities, would produce still more specific dispositions. Certainly the latter can be interpreted as means to still more important ends. Certainly it would be unreasonable to assume a genetic priority of the more general over the more specific. Furthermore, their analyses do not justify a qualitative distinction. They have shown that both value importance and perceived instrumentality correlate with attitude, and that the composite of the first two correlates better with attitude than do either separately—but this would also be true were all three (attitude, valuation, and perceived instrumentality) cosymptoms of a single syndrome, as three alternate measures of "the same" disposition. Further, while they showed that manipulating perceived instrumentality changed attitude, it also unexpectedly changed valuation. And might not a direct effort to change the attitude have changed both? Have we as yet any evidence that value, perceived instrumentality, and attitude are independently manipulatable or that attitude is inherently the dependent variable in the triad? At very least, such considerations should warn us that the apparent empirical convergence upon two qualitatively discrete dispositional concepts, one of means and one of ends, is one of convenient dichotomization in a hierarchical system of means-to-means-to-means. In particular, the concept of social attitude in its traditional usage [e.g., 3, 142, 179] is more to be valued because it connotes both behavior-scheduling and outcome-valuing learnings, rather than rejected because it has been given such discrepant meanings.

V. MEASURED SOCIAL ATTITUDES AND OTHER ACQUIRED BEHAVIORAL DISPOSITIONS

Theory about social attitudes and measurement of social attitudes have, by and large, developed independently—even when definitional discussion and research have occurred in the same article. There are several recent discussions, however, which define social attitude in a way which is directly relevant to measurement and is consistent with the operational diagnosis of acquired behavioral dispositions as presented here. My own treatment of definition and measurement of 1950 [20] has been cited in the introduction to this chapter. In his "A Conceptual Introduction to Latent Structure Analysis" [88], Lazarsfeld effectively presents a similar orientation. Green has tied these two treatments together in his excellent contribution on attitude measurement in the *Handbook of Social Psychology* [56]. These presentations say, in effect, that an attitude is a disposition, or latent structure, which we diagnose or measure on the basis of stimulus-response contingencies. If we take attitude-test items as stimuli and respondent statements of agreement or disagreement as responses, the typical attitude test may seem to fit right into this definition. However, we are rarely interested in attitudes toward items per se, but rather in attitudes toward symbolically represented social objects, and this fact complicates the problem. The use of contingencies representing a population of respondents rather than a population of occasions for a single respondent is a further complication. In addition, one traditional attitude-test focus is upon extremeness of response, rather than upon that consistency of response which would follow most directly from the definition. These problems will be dealt with in turn.

Efforts to measure the residues of experience or acquired behavioral dispositions occur in psychology in the areas of attitude testing, opinion surveys, personality-trait measurement, projective testing, clinical diagnosis, case study reconstruction of life histories, and achievement testing. All but the last named are relevant to the discussion that follows.

Diagnostic Methods Following from the Dispositional Perspective

Before discussing actual current practice, it seems desirable to look again at our operational model for diagnosing dispositions with its related theory and to inventory the modes of attitude testing and personality diagnosis which would follow, no matter how farfetched or unfamiliar these might be.

1. *Tailing.* Following most closely from the diagnostic model of Sec. II, one would assign a detective to follow the respondent with a tally sheet of the Table 2 type, revising the stimulus and response categories in attempts to get better fit, etc. In this fashion, significant stimulus categories and response dispositions toward these stimuli would be diagnosed. This extremely costly and awkward procedure may be set up as an ideal from the point of view of a unified behavior theory. In terms of it, unconscious attitudes or attitudes of which the respondent is unaware, as well as those of which he is aware, could be diagnosed. The diagnostician would limit himself to those dispositions elicited by the life pattern of the respondent and thus might not be able to learn of the presence or absence of a specific behavioral tendency. Presumably, however, this approach would tap the dominant acquired dispositions of the person under study.

2. *Episodic recall.* While the "tailing" procedure may never actually be used, a related procedure often is employed in the psychotherapeutic interview. The respondent recounts regularly the situations he has been in during the day before or in previous years and his own reaction to these events. From these data the diagnostician attempts to construct categories of stimulus and response equivalents and stimulus-response contingencies of which the respondent himself need not be aware.

3. *Situation sampling.* In this form of field observation, the diagnostician discovers what relevant stimuli are or will be where and when. He then sets up his observational procedures so that he can make sample observations of given responses, with and without the stimuli present. The focus is not on the single individual or on a full repertory of his dispositions, but rather on the occurrence in a population of the presence or absence of a specific disposition. In the basic fourfold table, of Stimulus (Present or Absent) and Response (Present or Absent), a population of persons substitutes for the population of occasions that would be employed in the tailing procedure. The problem of having the populations equivalent except for the presence or absence of stimulus is a problem of experimental design [25] and is made much simpler if the occurrence of the stimulus is under the diagnostician's control.

4. *Contrived situations.* Where the scheduling of the behavior of the respondent is under the control of the diagnostician, series of controlled situations can be created in which the respondent's responses to specified stimuli can be observed, with the social stimuli being actual examples of the social-stimulus category toward which attitudes are being studied. It is perhaps surprising how few attitude studies have used such methods, although a few [e.g., 12, 137] dealing with attitudes toward Negroes have done so in a minor way. More general attitudes toward other persons are no doubt diagnosed in the situation tests popular in World War II [e.g., 124].

5. *Symbolic stimulus tests.* Assuming stimulus equivalence, one could adopt the diagnostic procedure of presenting substitute stimuli which would elicit response dispositions appropriate to the real social stimuli in question. Thus, photos of persons, drawings, models, verbal descriptions, names, etc., may substitute for real persons in the contrived diagnostic situations which we would now call tests. For tests in this category, we have not asked the respondent to report to us on his own response tendencies, but are still observing response tendencies in the presence or absence of stimulus classes, diagnosing response tendencies of which the respondent might himself be unaware. Many projective methods and indirect attitude tests fall into this category, most obviously those employing dolls and pictures of persons [20, 26, 29]. The Rorschach test might be regarded as consisting of images so complex and incoherent that they intersect the stimulus-equivalence gradients of many stimuli, thus being most likely to elicit responses belonging to the dispositions of greatest strength. Note that interpreting projective techniques as diagnostic of dominent dispositions leads to the expectation of parallels between test response and real life response, rather than the assumption of compensatory fantasy behavior. This is certainly the most common research finding. Where competing approach and avoidance dispositions cancel out to inaction in overt behavior because of incompatibility of final common paths, the greater freedom of the projective-test situation can, of course, allow both dispositions to be expressed.

6. *Respondent's report on own response dispositions.* Verbal behavior has been classified as response in the above section. It has been treated just as limb behavior or locomotor behavior, as another exemplification of a response disposition, as a symptom, evidence, or instance of a behavioral disposition. It is perhaps typical of the behaviorist's or operationalist's treatment of verbal report that all linguistic products are thus treated. However, in referring to human learnings of a spatial maze in Sec. II, verbal report was used to allow the respondent to report on his own overt locomotor behavioral dispositions. The use of language in this special fashion is typical of social science research techniques. The respondent becomes a collaborator in the research, a reporter, *eine Versuchsperson*, an informant. We ask, "When stimulus *A* is present, how do you respond?" If a structured test is employed, we ask, "In which of these manners do you most nearly respond when stimulus *A* is present?" This approach is typical of the direct or voluntary self-description approaches to attitude measurement in both interview and questionnaire [26]. (That verbal report can be used in this special way in diagnosing dispositions also diagnosable in other ways is, of course, an empirical hypothesis subject to test, and not an analytic presupposition.)

7. *Respondent's report on his view of the stimulus.* To reiterate a

particularly important point for the unification of attitude theory: attitudes may also be diagnosed by asking the respondent about the characteristics of the stimulus as he sees it. In the human maze illustration of Sec. II, this is represented as just as direct a form of inquiry as asking about response tendencies. Similarly, as has been noted in Sec. III, such items are frequently found in direct attitude tests. However, this approach also is characteristic of projective tests and indirect attitude measures [20, 26] in which the respondent's verbal product is taken as a symptom of response disposition rather than as a report upon response disposition.

The concept of the "isomorphism of experience and action" (Sec. III) or the equivalence of views of the world and tendencies to respond to the world, provides specific implications in the field of projective personality diagnosis. These implications are not necessarily in agreement with the quasi-Freudian similarity interpretations usually employed, but rather with Murray's [123] concept of complementary apperceptive projection. If one takes as the setting the relationship between a person's traits (interpreted as his response tendencies toward others) and the traits he attributes to others, including unknown photo persons, the typical projective notions might expect the hostile person to see others as hostile, the anxious person to see others as anxious, the rebellious person to see others as rebellious and the secretive person to see others as secretive, etc. However, if the response tendency is appropriate to (or determined by) the view of other persons, then the hostile person should see others as hostile but the anxious person should see others as threatening, the rebellious person should see others as bossy, the secretive person should see others as prying, etc. By and large, the studies of projection that have been made to date have only allowed for the appearance of similarity projection or its opposite, contrast projection, and so are silent on complementary projection. The available studies favor complementary projection where it has been placed in competition with similarity projection. Murray's original study [123] found that frightened children tended to judge photo persons as more malicious and frightening. Howard [73] found high-anxious subjects to judge photo persons as more "exacting," "strict," "cruel," and "malicious," and less "kindly," "gentle," and "lenient," as complementary projection would predict, with no significant differences on "anxious," "worried," "secure," or "serene." Hornberger [70] generated experimental anxiety through electric shock apparatus and found that this increased the tendency to describe photographed persons as "dangerous," "threatening," and "frightening," but did not increase the tendency to perceive them as "afraid," "scared," or "frightened."

To further emphasize the point of empirical convergence between different theories, it can be alleged that complementary projection is what *S-R* theory, in agreement with cognitive theory, predicts for the projection situation. The learned traits of a person are the products of experience. Stimulus generalization and habit transfer predict that one will respond to newly met or unknown photo persons as though they were the kind of persons to whom one's dominent response tendencies were originally learned. Thus a person characterized by general avoidant and withdrawal tendencies presumably learned these originally in contact with avoidworthy or punishing persons in childhood, and generalizes to novel persons by responding to them as though they were the same. The exposition seems obvious for such responses as approach and avoidance. But the attribution of character traits to others involves a very special kind of response, which we can characterize as judgment or depiction. To relate this to learning theory requires that, when considering articulate human beings, we explicitly expand our inventory of the relevant aspects of the learned response syndrome. Let us take a simple case of one trial learning. A child is burned by a hot stove. This leads to an association of the stove with the responses of withdrawal and avoidance and, in addition, and equally automatically, the responses of judging the stove to be hot, or burning, or even dangerous or bad. These verbalizable descriptions of the stove, these attitudes toward or perceptions of the stove are an intrinsic part of what has been learned or acquired by the initial contiguity of stove and pain. They may or may not be overt responses in the initial experience, but they can usually be ascertained by interview later. Or take a child to whom an adult has frequently caused pain. The original syndrome of responses learned to this adult include not only avoidance and autonomic fear reactions, but, in addition, the judgments that the adult is cruel, pain-inflicting, bad, malicious, etc. If, then, one is generalizing response tendencies from previous persons to present ones, this would include judging present persons to be similar to the previous persons that were the stimuli responsible for the dominent response tendencies. When focused on the correlation between one's dominant interpersonal tendencies and one's view of other persons, habit transfer thus also predicts a complementary relationship. The complementarity exists in the original response syndrome, as in the tendency to see approached objects as rewarding, avoided objects as punishing, etc.

The Agreement between Attitude Measurement Practice and the Diagnostic Paradigm

The parable of the rat educated at another university (Sec. II) and the approaches above have had the focuses of inventorying relevant stimulus categories, response categories, and optimal stimulus-response contingencies for *individual organisms*. In contrast, the typical attitude-measurement approach involves a diagnostician's single a priori guess as to relevant stimulus and response categorizations, and then measures the degree of stimulus-response contingency obtaining across individuals and across instances or items. There is no necessary incompatibility here. The latter can be seen as but one part of an iterative procedure in which, over a series of studies and focused upon common attitudes, successive guesses as to optimal stimulus categories and optimal response categories lead to an optimizing of the contingency. However, if we accept the validity of the original paradigm, some more specific comments upon attitude-test practice seem in order.

First, it may be noted that there are a few formal diagnostic devices available that focus on the inventorying of idiosyncratic stimulus equivalents and behavioral dispositions for single individuals. Perhaps closest to our paradigm is George Kelly's "role construct repertory test" [78]. Some uses of Q-sort procedures [154], particularly the analysis of variance within one individual's sorting, and some uses of the semantic differential [130] also seem appropriate here.

While in the revising of attitude tests the active recategorization of stimulus elements may be in evidence, there is relatively little adjustment of response categories. Approach and avoidance, with their synonyms of like and dislike, for and against, etc., dominate or exhaust the response classes found necessary. This may in part reflect our lack of ingenuity or attention to the problem, but probably speaks more generally for the nature of the animal under study.

In Sec. II, it was emphasized that at each of the iterative diagnostic steps, the classifications of stimulus and response were in the experimenter's terms, representing discriminations which the experimenter could make, classifications which the experimenter could consistently apply and recognize new instances of. This orientation favors Guttman's [59] insistence that the experimenter define an initial attitude universe, sample items from it, test the extent to which responses to these items cohere in diagnosing the same syndrome and, if this is not found, reject the universe definition as a whole, and then define a new attitude universe, sample items at random from it, and proceed as before. This is in contrast with typical item-analysis and factor-analysis procedures which may increase the homogeneity of a test, but which, if not supplemented, leave the experimenter unable to discriminate the appropriate common denominator among the items, or to generate new instances of the class. From this point of view, the item-selection purification procedure is not complete until the experimenter can identify the common denominator among the good items and provide a rule for generating more. Likewise, the factor analysis is not complete until the experimenter understands each factor in such terms that he can generate new items which will belong to it rather than to other factors.

In Sec. II it was also pointed out that no S-R contingency can be demonstrated unless the stimulus in question has both occurred and not occurred within the observational sample, and the same for the response in question. This is an obvious truism of correlational analysis, yet it is one of the most frequently neglected features of social-attitude tests. To measure attitudes specifically toward out-group A one needs to present some non-A stimulus objects and to observe whether or not the response in question occurs or does not occur. For example, in addition to attitudes toward the out-group, attitudes toward the in-group need to be asked in an ethnocentrism test to provide the non-S observations. Sullivan and Adelson [157] have pointed out how tests purporting to measure a hostility specific to minority groups cannot demonstrate this specificity if employing only minority-group stimuli, and do in fact turn out to be measuring a much more general reaction to all mankind, including self, when other stimulus items are included. In general, without both variance in S and in R, no S-R correlation, no specified behavioral disposition, can be demonstrated (this argument is detailed from a different perspective elsewhere [31]).

It is perhaps tempting to identify the kind of interitem covariance represented in reliability and Guttman's reproducibility with the S-R correlation that provides the basic evidence of disposition. However, this is not a completely legitimate identification, and a paradox of individual differences study accentuates this fact. From the basic paradigm of diagnosing a rat's dispositions, or from most of the procedures above, one could diagnose dispositions which were uniform within the population, dispositions upon which no individual differences were to be found. Thus the disposition to stand when the national anthem is played could be diagnosed by the contingency of anthem versus nonanthem situations with responses of standing versus nonstanding, even if all persons in the population showed the disposition to a perfect degree. (To demonstrate that it was an *acquired* disposition might, of course, involve cross-cultural foster-child studies.) The social psychologist who uses the typical multiple-item tests of individual differences is in a different setting, however. He cannot get internally consistent attitude measures except on topics upon which individuals in the society have significant attitudinal heterogeneity. Hoyt's [74] approach to reliability puts it well—unless the classification criterion of persons provides significant variance, the test has no reliability. Thus, what to an anthropologist or sociologist would appear to be a highly uniform well-learned attitude would prove to the student of individual differences no measurable attitude at all, whereas an attitude upon which societal indoctrination was unevenly efficient would provide reliable attitude measures and correlations with other variables, and thus attract the attentions of the student of individual differences. (Guttman scale analysis is just as subject to this weakness as are more typical psychometric approaches to individual differences.) This bias of the typical individual-differences-test approach seems a recurrent source of confusion in collaborations between sociologists or anthropologists and psychologists. The psychologist interested in a unified social science based upon a theory of acquired behavioral dispositions will be well advised not to commit himself solely to the study of social attitudes through the means of individual differences.

Two studies testing the hypothesis of a generalized attitude toward authority through examining the correlation between attitudes toward father and boss provide an illustration. In the first of these, Burwen and I [19] employed the traditional individual-differences approach, correlating the degree of favorableness toward each. To avoid confusing attitudes toward authority with a more general philanthropy-misanthropy, the several father-boss correlations were each compared with parallel correlations between attitudes toward father and attitudes toward a peer. In less than half of the 12 comparisons was the father-boss correlation the larger. From these and other data it was concluded that there was no evidence of any generalized attitude toward authority figures. This study was dependent upon genuine individual differences in attitudes for the demonstration of attitude communality, and in a homogeneous population of volunteer Air Force pilot cadets, such genuine differences might have been relatively lacking.

The second attack on the problem [30] used some of the same subjects and one of the same instruments, but set up the analysis so that the attitude generalization could have been demonstrated, even if all the respondents had identical attitudes. For this study, a single instrument was used; each respondent rated his father, his boss, and others on some 30 traits. For each respondent, several description-similarity coefficients of the Q-correlation type were computed, and for each the magnitude of the father-boss coefficient was compared with the father-subordinate correlation, etc. In this setting, some slight but highly significant evidence for a generalized attitude toward authority appeared. While the second study used more respondents, used only one instrument, and differed in other ways, the comparison of the two may serve to illustrate that covariation across occasions, across social objects, or across trait terms may frequently provide a more effective and relevant base for the demonstration of attitude communality than does covariation across respondents within a homogenous population. With this warning, the discussion will continue to concentrate upon the traditional individual-differences approaches.

Multiple Symptoms for a Disposition and Test-item Thresholds

The type of internal consistency which is the preoccupation of the attitude tester, be he Thurstone, Likert, or Guttman, is made possible by multiple-situational symptomatology for a single disposition. This model is also a part of the learning tradition. If one considers paired associates of various degrees of learning, there are at least three well-known ways of testing strength of association: (1) recall of response upon presentation of the stimulus; (2) recognition of response from a list of alternatives; and (3) savings in relearning the association. Each represents a different diagnostic situation—for each the threshold for elicitation is different. The thresholds are such that a scale of this kind could be constructed:

> Recall (highest)
> Recognition from a list of 50 alternatives
> Recognition from a list of 10 alternatives
> Some significant savings in relearning (lowest)

These would represent an ordered and consistent series of steps. An association of such strength as to be recalled would pass all lower steps. If we know that an association was so weak as to pass only two of the steps, we would be practically certain that it would be the bottom two steps, in consistency with the scale-analysis model. (In practice, taking more than one of the measures from a single respondent is cumbersome because of their mutually reactive [25] effects, but the differences in thresholds for the measures are so consistent that the point is clear.)

May and Hartshorne, in their classic paper of 1927, "First Steps toward a Scale for Measuring Attitudes" [105], envisaged such a series of situations, each with a different threshold. They dealt with the disposition to cheat. In modern Hullian terms this disposition might be considered a composite of the "intrapsychic" determinants such as familiarity with cheating procedures sH_R, degree of gratification expected from cheating K, drive level D, and competing inhibitory dispositions from the association of cheating with punishment, etc. Because of different past histories, individuals are expected to differ in the net composite. Situations offering potential opportunities to cheat differ in the difficulties they put in the way of cheating. These are primarily conceived of by May and Hartshorne as a matter of the amount of work or effort required in cheating. These situations can be regarded as having a quantitative threshold value so that the response would occur only when the response strength exceeded the situational threshold value. May and Hartshorne presented opportunities for children to cheat in scoring their own exam papers on six different occasions, with the opportunities varying in the amount of effort required. Assuming the work and other inhibitory values W to have the same rank order for all the children, and predicting a cheating response only where $D \times K \times H - W > 0$, and using hypothetical values not supplied by the original authors, Table 3 can be drawn up.

TABLE 3. THRESHOLDS FOR THE CHEATING RESPONSE

Type of change made in cheating	Hypothetical threshold value	Children and hypothetical disposition strengths						
	W	A 7	B 6	C 5	D 4	E 3	F 2	G 1
Answer in ink...............	6.5	+						
Sentence in pencil...........	5.5	+	+					
Two or three words in pencil...	4.5	+	+	+				
One word in pencil..........	3.5	+	+	+	+			
A check mark...............	2.5	+	+	+	+	+		
A digit, answers on board.....	1.5	+	+	+	+	+	+	
SCORE: Number of times cheated...........		6	5	4	3	2	1	0

It seems apparent here that the concept of scale analysis has a very direct compatibility with learning theory when the latter is applied to situations of different thresholds and to individuals of differing response strength. In the May and Hartshorne case, the empirical data confirmed the threshold hypothesis or the scale-analysis model. Ninety-six per cent of the 1,770 responses by the 295 children on the six occasions are correctly predicted by the hierarchical-threshold assumption (using Guttman's assignment of nonscale types so as to minimize error).

One early notion in attitude measurement was to order individuals in the extremity of their attitudes by means of the extremity of the attitude statements which they endorsed [162]. On the other hand, the most direct transfer of mental-test procedures to attitude measurement produces a method [e.g., 62] in which a battery of items is presented, upon each one of which a person has the opportunity of showing the attitude or not—the most extreme person is the one showing the attitude in the most instances. Accompanying this is a criterion of high interitem correlation but no attention to the relative levels of the items. In the scale-analysis model, these two scoring approaches are shown to be congruent. If the items are all symptomatizing the same disposition, then the person who shows the disposition in the situation with the highest threshold should also show it most frequently. If, in addition, within a single apparatus or item we measure not only the presence or absence of the response, but also its amplitude, à la Hull or Likert [96], then the person showing the greatest single or average response amplitude should also show the greatest response frequency. Granted individual differences in response strengths and situational or item differences in thresholds, the scale-analysis model (or the high intercorrelation among items to which its requirements reduce) is relevant to the hypothesis that a set of situation-response contingencies are aspects of the same response disposition.

The notion of a stable hierarchy of threshold probably also holds in a general way for qualitatively different response modes in a single physical setting. This hierarchy might be suggested, reading from lowest threshold to highest:

1. Autonomic-muscular readiness reaction (galvanic skin response or subliminal muscle-action currents)
2. Verbal report on perceived character of the stimulus
3. Verbal report on own response tendency
4. Overt locomotor response

Much of the literature on subception documents the lower threshold of 1 than 2. Learned inhibitions specific to 2, 3, or 4 often make for inconsistencies, but they may in general have this order, and might so be expected to scale. As Harding et al. [61] point out, in the Bettelheim and Janowitz [10] data, stereotyped views of the minority group (level 2, above) were more frequent than, and seemed to scale with, active hostility (level 3), in that those expressing hostility uniformly had the stereotype, but not vice versa.

Pseudo Inconsistency in the Attitude Literature

The allegation has been made throughout this chapter that verbal report is in some circumstances a mode of diagnosing dispositions also manifest in overt behavior. This viewpoint contrasts strikingly with the prevailing tenor of the social-attitude literature, which emphasizes the inconsistency between verbal attitude expression and overt action. Thus Logan et al. [100, p. 82], in a discussion of the use of verbal report in a context similar to the present paper, cite the classic La Piere [82] study, purportedly showing the undependability of verbal-questionnaire reports in predicting discriminatory behavior toward Chinese upon the part of restaurants and lodging places. Thus Harding et al. [61] devote a 2,400-word section, "Relationships among Intergroup Attitudes and Intergroup Behavior," to emphasizing the inconsistency shown in the literature. A whole issue of *The Journal of Social Issues* [36] has been devoted to the subject, with similar conclusions. By and large, this literature has confused correlational inconsistency with situational threshold differences, and has thus exaggerated the inconsistency present.

On an arithmetic test of four items, the child who gets only two items correct is not necessarily regarded as less consistent than the child who gets all right or all wrong. If he gets the two easiest right and the two hardest wrong, he is equally consistent. On intelligence we today think in terms of a continuum, and can conceive of consistent mediocrity. Similarly, in Table 3, the child with a score of 3, the child who cheats on some items but not on others, is not today regarded as inconsistent *if* he cheats on the three easiest items. Today, though perhaps not prior to 1927, we can regard honesty as something people have in degree, rather than as an all-or-none trait. A person of intermediate degree can be just as consistent as a person of extreme position, and his attitude can be determined from his behavior just as well. Inconsistency does, of course, occur, but from the type of analysis presented by May and Hartshorne [105] and popularized by Guttman [59], one can distinguish between consistent mediocrity and inconsistent scatter. For intelligence and honesty, we have achieved dimensionality in our thinking. For more emotion-laden topics, such as standing up for civil rights, we have not. If a university president protects a pacifist professor but fires an atheist, we call him inconsistent. If he protects a pacifist and an atheist, but fires a Communist, we accuse him of backing down under pressure. Conceptually, we have the notion of a total nondefendant of professors' rights and a total defender of professors' rights, and lack any concept of genuine mediocrity which would *in consistency* produce defense in a situation of low threshold and firing in another situation with a higher threshold value.

In terms of the scale-analysis model, let us examine the classic cases of inconsistency. In La Piere's [82] study, he and the Chinese couple were refused accommodation in .4 per cent of places stopped. The mailed questionnaire reported 92.5 per cent refusal of Chinese. The first thing we note is that the two diagnostic situations have very different thresholds. Apparently it is very hard to refuse a well-dressed Chinese couple traveling with a European in a face-to-face setting, and very easy to refuse the Chinese as a race in a mailed questionnaire. We can see easily why this would be so. But there is as yet no evidence of inconsistency. Inconsistency would be represented if those who refused face to face accepted by questionnaire, or if those who accepted by questionnaire refused face to face. There is no report that such cases occurred. The fact that 92 per cent of the cases were mediocre in their Sinophilia, having enough to get over the low hurdle but not enough to get over the high hurdle, is irrelevant to the problem of inconsistency, but rather speaks only as to the heights of the hurdles.

Minard's [113] casual comments on the Pocahontas coal miners involves two items which can be diagramed as in Fig. 5. His report clearly indicates that the settings of mine and town have markedly different situational thresholds for nondiscriminatory reactions of white miners, only 20 per cent being friendly in town, 80 per cent being friendly in the mines. He reports no instances of true inconsistency, i.e., being friendly in town and hostile in the mines. From this point of view, and considering the long-standing model of the Bogardus social distance steps [11] Harding et al. [61, p. 1032] are clearly wrong to conclude that the middle 60 per cent are persons "whose overt behavior provides no clue as to their attitudes." Their behavior clearly indicates that they

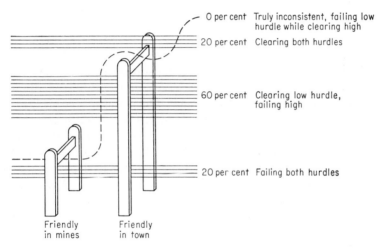

0 per cent   Truly inconsistent, failing low
             hurdle while clearing high

20 per cent Clearing both hurdles

60 per cent Clearing low hurdle,
             failing high

20 per cent Failing both hurdles

Friendly   Friendly
in mines   in town

Fɪɢ. 5. Minard's data on miners' attitudes toward Negroes.

have consistently middling attitudes. The two items, mine and town, correlate perfectly, using any index not biased by uneven item marginals (i.e., tetrachoric correlation or phi-over-maximum-phi).

Merton's [107] four "ideal types" of consistent and inconsistent liberalism are open to a similar interpretation. A verbal item, perhaps "Are you in favor of segregation?" might have a threshold of 50 per cent. One behavioral item, refusing to eat with a Negro at a businessmen's luncheon club, might be one in which it would be hard to show prejudice, perhaps only 10 per cent doing so. Another behavioral item, refusing to rent one's house to Negroes, might have a very high threshold for the liberal response, 90 per cent showing prejudice. If this were the situation, and if all persons were perfectly consistent, one would have these four types, using Merton's labels:

1. The "all weather liberal," who shows nondiscriminatory behavior in all three settings (10 per cent)

2. The "fair weather liberal," showing liberalism in words and at the luncheon, but not on the house rental (40 per cent)

3. The "fair weather illiberal," showing discrimination in words and in house rental but not at the luncheon (40 per cent)

4. "The all weather illiberal," who discriminates on all three (10 per cent)

Of this typology, Harding et al. [61, p. 1034] say, "Types 2 and 3 represent the extreme case of no dependence of behavior on attitudes." This is clearly uncalled for if no nonscale types occur (such as renting to Negroes while speaking out for segregation, etc.). If all cases are accounted for by the four types, then the three items correlate perfectly, and one can predict as well from the verbal item to either one of the behavioral items as one can from one behavioral item to the other.

Thus in the literature there has been a stubborn confusion of the fact that verbal behaviors and overt behaviors have different situational thresholds with the fact of consistency. Once this is clarified, we can look to correlational evidence of consistency. Of course, the Minard and Merton examples actually *exaggerate* this consistency. Between two measures of response strength in the animal laboratory, the correlations are far from perfect. Two social actions hypothesized to tap the same disposition will correlate far less than unity in practice, as will also one verbal statement and one overt response, or two verbal statements. The degree of correlation is, for the most part, yet to be discovered. Where the overt act of joining an ideological group has been correlated with verbal reports on own attitudes, the relationships found have been obvious and very high, as in comparisons of church members with organized atheists, conscientious objectors with ROTC members, etc. [121]. Probably the validity of attitude tests will be found higher than that of the more complex personality-trait measures when checked against overt behavior. In such studies, the unreliability and invalidity of overt-behavior measures should also be remembered and measured, and in no case should a single overt behavior be regarded as the criterion of a disposition. It would certainly be expected for the laboratory maze situation of Sec. II and for situations in which there are not special inhibitory dispositions affecting actions or words (for those situations in which the respondents are naïve or cooperating) that a positive diagnostic correlation will be obtained. Remembering that the average interitem correlation for a good verbal attitude test or intelligence test is as low as .20 or lower, we must not expect high correlations between attitude tests and *single* behavioral items.

VI. RESUMÉ

From the starting point of the concept of *social attitude,* the problem of interrelationship issues has led directly to the more general problem of *acquired behavioral dispositions.* Concepts of this type are not only already exceedingly numerous, but they predominate among the terminological innovations of new theory builders in the social sciences. Two generic features of the category are noted: first, reference to the effect of past events upon the behavior of organisms, and second, coordination of behavior in environments, i.e., stimulus-response contingency. For social science purposes, the inventory of modes of acquisition of such acquired behavioral dispositions must be expanded over that presently encompassed in learning theory to include perception, the perceptual observation of the outcomes of another's explorations, verbal instruction about responses, and verbal instruction about the nature of stimuli.

As the most recurrent and difficult conceptual problem leading to a diversity of terminology, the opposition between behavioristic and phenomenological systems is examined. It is argued that an omnipresent pressure from the raw data predisposes those working with inarticulate animals in the direction of behavioristic theories. Since conscious contents corresponding to learned dispositions are predominantly of the view-of-the-world rather than the how-I-respond nature, the data collected by those who interview articulate socialized human beings predispose them to phenomenological conceptualizations. Once it is hypothesized that acquired behavioral dispositions can have both aspects, points of articulation between such dissimilar theories can be noted, including some striking empirical convergences. While perfect agreement in all empirical predictions cannot be anticipated, in so far as examined, and especially for social psychology, the implications of the theories are surprisingly congruent. Asch's concept of the "isomorphism of experience and action" helps in the integration attempted. Theories positing both perceptual-learning and response-learning processes are judged at present to be lacking in data justifying this separation of learning processes. The concept of social attitude is judged to be a useful acquired behavioral dispositional construct for social psychology just because it connotes both a predisposition to respond and a predisposition to view the world in a given way.

A similar effort is made to integrate acquired dispositional concepts of a motivational nature with those connoting response scheduling or means knowledge. Since most learned responses are object-consistent (molar, distal, advertent), each learned response has goal or motive character. A continual regress in which means at one level of analysis become ends at another is noted as consistent with a cybernetic interpretation of complex behavior. Even though in the previous section the theories of Hull and Lewin converged upon an acquired-means concept (H or path) and an acquired-ends concept (K or valence), this distinction is interpreted as one of level rather than of kind. Likewise, the concepts of value and attitude are fundamentally similar.

Procedures for measuring social attitudes are in general found quite congruent with the dispositional concepts developed, although the theoretical perspective suggests additional diagnostic procedures and some shift of emphasis. From the dispositional perspective, the supposed absence of relationship between attitudes and behavior disappears.

At the present time, there is still a warfare of schools in social psychology. New theories are still put forth and new aspects of phenomena noted in the form of a militant rejection of other points of view. Yet there seems to be close beneath the surface an emerging convergence, and we may soon have available a composite body of theory and fact which can form the basis of a disciplined and cumulative social science. It is hoped that these fragmentary comments will have increased rather than dimmed this expectation.

REFERENCES

1. Adams, D. K. *The anatomy of personality.* New York: Doubleday, 1954.
2. Allport, F. H. *Social psychology.* New York: Houghton Mifflin, 1924.
3. Allport, G. W. Attitudes. In C. Murchison (Ed.), *A handbook of social psychology.* Worcester, Mass: Clark Univer. Press, 1935. Pp. 798–844.
4. Allport, G. W. *Personality.* New York: Holt, 1937.
5. Asch, S. E. *Social psychology.* Englewood Cliffs, N.J.: Prentice-Hall, 1952.
6. Ashby, W. R. *Design for a brain.* New York: Wiley, 1952.
7. Bain, R. An attitude on attitude research. *Amer. J. Sociol.,* 1928, **33,** 940–957.
8. Bartlett, F. C. *Remembering.* Cambridge: Cambridge Univer. Press, 1932.
9. Berkeley, E. C. Light sensitive electronic beast. *Radio electronics.* 1951, **23,** (3), 46–48.
10. Bettelheim, B., & Janowitz, M. *Dynamics of prejudice.* New York: Harper, 1950.
11. Borgardus, E. S. *Immigration and race attitudes.* Boston: Heath, 1928.
12. Bray, D. W. The prediction of behavior from two attitude scales. *J. abnorm. soc. Psychol.,* 1950, **45,** 64–84.
13. Bronfenbrenner, U. Toward an integrated theory of personality. In R. R. Blake & G. V. Ramsey (Eds.), *Perception; an approach to personality.* New York: Ronald, 1951. Pp. 206–257.

14. Brown, J. S. Principles of intrapersonal conflict. *J. Conflict Resolution,* 1957, **1,** 135–154.

15. Brown, W. Auditory and visual cues in maze learning. *Univer. Calif. Publ. Psychol.,* 1932, **5,** 115–122.

16. Bruner, J. S. Personality dynamics and the process of perceiving. In R. S. Blake & G. V. Ramsey (Eds.), *Perception, an approach to personality.* New York: Ronald, 1951. Pp. 121–149.

17. Brunswik, E. The conceptual framework of psychology. *Int. Encyc. unif. Sci.,* 1, No. 10. Chicago: Univer. Chicago Press, 1952.

18. Brunswik, E. *Perception and the representative design of psychological experiments.* Berkeley, Calif.: Univer. Calif. Press, 1956.

19. Burwen, L. S., & Campbell, D. T. The generality of attitudes toward authority and nonauthority figures. *J. abnorm. soc. Psychol.,* 1957, **54,** 24–31.

20. Campbell, D. T. The indirect assessment of social attitudes. *Psychol. Bull.,* 1950, **47,** 15–38.

21. Campbell, D. T. Operational delineation of "what is learned" via the transposition experiment. *Psychol. Rev.,* 1954, **61,** 167–174.

22. Campbell, D. T. Adaptive behavior from random response. *Behav. Sci.,* 1956, **1,** 105–110.

23. Campbell, D. T. Enhancement of contrast as composite habit. *J. abnorm. soc. Psychol.,* 1956, **53,** 350–355.

24. Campbell, D. T. Perception as substitute trial and error. *Psychol. Rev.,* 1956, **63,** 330–342.

25. Campbell, D. T. Factors relevant to the validity of experiments in social settings. *Psychol. Bull.,* 1957, **54,** 297–312.

26. Campbell, D. T. A typology of tests, projective and otherwise. *J. consult. Psychol.,* 1957, **21,** 207–210.

27. Campbell, D. T. Systematic error on the part of human links in communication systems. *Information and Control,* 1958, **1,** 334–369.

28. Campbell, D. T. Conformity in psychology's theories of acquired behavioral dispositions. In I. A. Berg & B. M. Bass (Eds.), *Conformity and deviation.* New York: Harper, 1961. Pp. 101–142.

29. Campbell, D. T., & Burwen, L. S. Trait judgments from photographs as a projective device. *J. clin. Psychol.,* 1956, **12,** 215–221.

30. Campbell, D. T., & Chapman, J. P. Testing for stimulus equivalence among authority figures by similarity in trait description. *J. consult. Psychol.,* 1957, **21,** 253–256.

31. Campbell, D. T., & Fiske, D. W. Convergent and discriminant validation by the multitrait-multimethod matrix. *Psychol. Bull.,* 1959, **56,** 81–105.

32. Campbell, D. T., & Gruen, W. Progression from simple to complex as a molar law of learning. *J. gen. Psychol.,* 1958, **59,** 237–244.

33. Campbell, D. T., Miller, N., & Diamond, A. L. Predisposition to identify instigating and guiding stimulus as revealed in transfer. *J. gen. Psychol.,* 1960, **63,** 69–74.

34. Carlson, E. R. Attitude change and attitude structure. *J. abnorm. soc. Psychol.*, 1956, **52**, 256–261.
35. Cartwright, D. Lewinian theory as a contemporary systematic framework. In S. Koch (Ed.), *Psychology: a study of a science.* Vol. 2. New York: McGraw-Hill, 1959.
36. Chein, I., Deutsch, M., Hyman, H., & Jahoda, M. (Eds.) Consistency and inconsistency in intergroup relations. *J. soc. Issues*, 1949, **5** (3), 1–63.
37. Church, R. M. Transmission of learned behavior in rats. *J. abnorm. soc. Psychol.*, 1957, **54**, 163–165.
38. Clarke, R., & Campbell, D. T. A demonstration of bias in estimates of Negro ability. *J. abnorm. soc. Psychol.*, 1955, **51**, 585–588.
39. Coutu, W. *Emergent human nature.* New York: Knopf, 1949.
40. Dennis, W. The sensory control of the maze habit in the white rat. *J. genet. Psychol.*, 1929, **36**, 59–89.
41. Dewey, J. The reflex arc concept in psychology. *Psychol. Rev.*, 1896, **3**, 358–370.
42. Dewey, J. *Human nature and conduct.* New York: Holt, 1922.
43. Deutsch, M. Field theory in social psychology. In G. Lindzey (Ed.), *Handbook of social psychology.* Reading, Mass.: Addison-Wesley, 1954. Pp. 181–222.
44. Dinsmoor, J. A. The effect of hunger on discriminated responding. *J. abnorm. soc. Psychol.*, 1952, **47**, 67–72.
45. Dollard, J., & Miller, N. E. *Personality and psychotherapy.* New York: McGraw-Hill, 1950.
46. Doob, L. W. The behavior of attitudes. *Psychol. Rev.*, 1947, **54**, 135–156.
47. Faris, E. The concept of social attitudes. In K. Young (Ed.), *Social attitudes.* New York: Holt, 1931.
48. Feigl, H. The "mental" and the "physical." In H. Feigl, M. Scriven, & G. Maxwell (Eds.), *Concepts, theories, and the mind-body problem.* Vol. 2. Minnesota Studies in the Philosophy of Science. Minneapolis, Minn.: Univer. Minn. Press, 1958.
49. Frisch, K. von. *Bees, their vision, chemical sense, and language.* Ithaca, N.Y.: Cornell Univer. Press, 1950.
50. Gage, N. L. Scaling and factorial design in opinion poll analysis. *Purdue Univer. Stud. higher Educ., further Stud. Attit.* 1948, (Ser. X), No. 61.
51. Garner, W. R., Hake, H. W., & Eriksen, C. W. Operationism and the concept of perception. *Psychol. Rev.*, 1956, **63**, 149–159.
52. Gibson, J. J. A critical review of the concept of set in contemporary experimental psychology. *Psychol. Bull.*, 1941, **38**, 781–817.
53. Goldiamond, I. Indicators of perception: I. Subliminal perception, subception, unconsious perception: an analysis in terms of psychophysical indicator methodology. *Psychol. Bull.*, 1958, **55**, 373–411.
54. Goldiamond, I. Vexierversuch: the log relationship between word-

frequency and recognition obtained in the absence of stimulus words. *J. exp. Psychol.*, 1958, 56, 457–463.

55. Graham, C. H. Behavior, perception and psychophysical methods. *Psychol. Rev.*, 1950, 57, 108–120.
56. Green, B. F. Attitude measurement. In G. Lindzey (Ed.), *Handbook of social psychology*. Reading, Mass,: Addison-Wesley, 1954. Pp. 335–369.
57. Guthrie, E. R. *The psychology of learning.* (Rev. Ed.) New York: Harper, 1952.
58. Guthrie, E. R., & Horton, G. P. *Cats in a puzzle box.* New York: Holt, Rinehart, & Winston, 1946.
59. Guttman, L. The basis for scalogram analysis. In S. A. Stouffer, L. Guttman, E. A. Suchman, P. F. Lazarsfeld, S. A. Star, & J. A. Clausen, *Measurement and prediction.* Princeton, N.J.: Princeton Univer. Press, 1950. Pp. 60–212.
60. Hallowell, A. I. *Culture and experience.* Philadelphia; Univer. Pa. Press, 1955.
61. Harding, J., Kutner, B., Proshansky, H., & Chein, I. Prejudice and ethnic relations. In G. Lindzey (Ed.), *Handbook of social psychology.* Reading, Mass.: Addison-Wesley, 1954. Pp. 1021–1061.
62. Harper, M. H. *Social beliefs and attitudes of American educators.* New York: Columbia Univer. Bureau of Publ. Teach. Coll., Contr. Educ., No. 294, 1927.
63. Hartshorne, H., & May, M. A. *Studies in the nature of character: I. Studies in deceit.* New York: Macmillan, 1928.
64. Hebb, D. O. *The organization of behavior.* New York: Wiley, 1949.
65. Heider, F. Social perception and phenomenal causality. *Psychol. Rev.*, 1944, 51, 358–374.
66. Herbert, M. J., & Harsh, C. M. Observational learning by cats. *J. comp. Psychol.*, 1944, 37, 81–95.
67. Hilgard, E. R. An algebraic analysis of conditioned discrimination in man. *Psychol. Rev.*, 1938, 45, 472–496.
68. Hilgard, E. R., & Humphreys, L. G. The effect of supporting and antagonistic voluntary instructions on conditioned discrimination. *J. exp. Psychol.*, 1938, 22, 291–304.
69. Holst, E. von. Relations between the central nervous system and the periphery. *Brit. J. anim. Behav.*, 1954, 2, 89–94.
70. Hornberger, R. H. The projective effects of fear and sexual arousal on the rating of pictures. *J. clin. Psychol.*, 1960, 16, 328–331.
71. Horowitz, E. L. The development of attitude toward the Negro. *Arch. Psychol.*, 1936, 28, No. 194.
72. Horowitz, E. L. "Race" attitudes. In O. Klineberg (Ed.), *Characteristics of the American Negro.* New York: Harper, 1944.
73. Howard, R. C. An experimental investigation of projection theory. Unpublished honors research under the direction of D. T. Campbell, Northwestern Univer., 1956.
74. Hoyt, C. Test reliability obtained by analysis of variance. *Psychometrika,* 1941, 6, 156–160.

75. Hull, C. L. *Principles of behavior*. New York: Appleton-Century-Crofts, 1943.
76. Jenkin, N. Affective processes in perception. *Psychol. Bull.*, 1957, **54**, 100–128.
77. Kahn, L. A. The organization of attitudes toward the Negro as a function of education. *Psychol. Monogr.*, 1951, 65, No. 13 (Whole No. 330), i–39.
78. Kelly, G. A. *The psychology of personal constructs*. New York: Norton, 1955.
79. Kendler, H. H. "What is learned?"—a theoretical blind alley. *Psychol. Rev.*, 1952, **59**, 269–277.
80. Köhler, W. *Gestalt psychology*. New York: Liveright, 1929.
81. Krech, D., & Crutchfield, R. S. *Theory and problems of social psychology*. New York: McGraw-Hill, 1948.
82. La Piere, R. T. Attitudes vs. actions. *Soc. Forces*, 1934, **13**, 230–237.
83. Lashley, K. S. Structural variation in the central nervous system in relation to behavior. *Psychol. Rev.*, 1947, **34**, 325–334.
84. Lashley, K. S. The problem of serial order in behavior. In L. A. Jeffress (Ed.), *Cerebral mechanisms in behavior*. New York: Wiley, 1951. Pp. 112–135.
85. Lashley, K. S., & Ball, J. Spinal conduction and kinesthetic sensitivity in the maze habit. *J. comp. Psychol.*, 1929, **9**, 71–105.
86. Lashley, K. S., & McCarthy, D. A. The survival of the maze habit after cerebral injuries. *J. comp. Psychol.* 1926, **6**, 423–432.
87. Lawrence, D. H., & Coles, G. R. Accuracy of recognition with alternatives before and after the stimulus. *J. exp. Psychol.*, 1954, **57**, 208–214.
88. Lazarsfeld, P. F. A conceptual introduction to latent structure analysis. In P. F. Lazarsfeld (Ed.), *Mathematical thinking in the social sciences*. Glencoe, Ill.: Free Press, 1954. Pp. 349–387.
89. Leeper, R. W. *Lewin's topological and vector psychology*. Eugene, Oreg.: Univer. Oreg. Press, 1943.
90. Levine, J. M., & Murphy, G. The learning and forgetting of controversial material. *J. abnorm. soc. Psychol.*, 1943, **38**, 507–517.
91. Levinson, D. J. The study of anti-Semitic ideology. In T. W. Adorno, E. Frenkel-Brunswik, D. J. Levinson, & R. N. Sanford, *The authoritarian personality*. New York: Harper, 1950. Pp. 57–101.
92. Lewin, K. *A dynamic theory of personality*. New York: McGraw-Hill, 1935.
93. Lewin, K. *Principles of topological psychology*. New York: McGraw-Hill, 1936.
94. Lewin, K. Formalization and progress in psychology. In K. Lewin et al., *Studies in topological and vector psychology*. Vol. I. Iowa City: Univer. Iowa Press, 1940.
95. Lewin, K. *Field theory in the social sciences*. New York: Harper, 1951.
96. Likert, R. A technique for the measurement of attitudes. *Arch. Psychol.*, 1932, No. 140.

97. Lindner, R. M. An experimental study of anticipation. *Amer. J. Psychol.*, 1938, 51, 253–261.

98. Lindzey, G. (Ed.) *Handbook of social psychology.* Reading, Mass.: Addison-Wesley, 1954.

99. Loeb, J. *Forced movements, tropisms, and animal conduct.* Philadelphia: Lippincott, 1918.

100. Logan, F. A., Olmstead, D. L., Rosner, B. S., Schwartz, R. D., & Stevens, C. M. *Behavior theory and social science.* New Haven, Conn.: Yale Univer. Press, 1955.

101. McCulloch, W. S. Why the mind is in the head. In L. A. Jeffress (Ed.), *Cerebral mechanisms in behavior.* New York: Wiley, 1951.

102. McDougall, K. D., & McDougall, W. Insight and foresight in various animals—monkey, racoon, rat, and wasp. *J. comp. Psychol.*, 1931, 11, 237–273.

103. McDougall, W. *The energies of men.* New York: Scribner, 1932.

104. Macfarlane, D. A. The role of kinesthesis in maze learning. *Univer. Calif. Publ. Psychol.*, 1930, 4, 277–305.

105. May, M. A., & Hartshorne, H. First steps toward a scale for measuring attitudes. *J. educ. Psychol.*, 1926, 17, 145–162.

106. Mead, G. H. *Mind, self and society.* Chicago; Univer. Chicago Press, 1934.

107. Merton, R. K. Discrimination and the American creed. In R. M. MacIver (Ed.), *Discrimination and national welfare.* New York: Institute for Religious and Social Studies, 1949. Pp. 99–126.

108. Michotte, A. E. *Études Psychologiques* Vol. 6. *La perception de la causalité.* Louvain: Institut supérieur de Philosophie, 1946. 296 pp.

109. Miller, G. A., Galanter, E., & Pribram, K. H. *Plans and the structure of behavior.* New York: Holt, Rinehart, & Winston ,1960.

110. Miller, N. E. Liberalization of basic S-R concepts: extensions to conflict behavior, motivation, and social learning. In S. Koch (Ed.), *Psychology: a study of a science.* Vol. 2. *General systematic formulations, learning, and special processes.* New York: McGraw-Hill, 1959.

111. Miller, N. E., & Dollard, J. *Social learning and imitation.* New Haven, Conn.: Yale Univer. Press, 1941.

112. Miller, N., & Campbell, D. T. Recency and primacy in persuasion as a function of the timing of speeches and measurements. *J. abnorm. soc. Psychol.*, 1959, 59, 1–9.

113. Minard, R. D. Race relationships in the Pocahontas coal field. *J. soc. Issues*, 1952, 8, (1), 29–44.

114. Moore, O. K., & Lewis, D. J. Purpose and learning theory. *Psychol. Rev.*, 1953, 60, 149–156.

115. Mowrer, O. H. Preparatory set (expectancy) some methods of measurement. *Psychol. Monogr.*, 1940, 52, No. 2.

116. Mowrer, O. H. Ego psychology, cybernetics, and learning theory. In D. K. Adams et. al., *Learning theory, personality theory, and clinical research.* New York: Wiley, 1954. Pp. 81–90.

117. Mowrer, O. H. The psychologist looks at language. *Amer. Psychologist,* 1954, **9,** 660–694.
118. Mowrer, O. H. *Learning theory and the symbolic processes.* New York: Wiley, 1960.
119. Murchison, C. *A handbook of social psychology.* Worcester, Mass.: Clark Univer. Press, 1935.
120. Murphy, G. *Personality.* New York: Harper, 1947.
121. Murphy, G., Murphy, L. B., & Newcomb, T. M. *Experimental social psychology.* (Rev. ed.) New York: Harper, 1937.
122. Murphy, J. V., & Miller, R. E. The effect of spatial contiguity of cue and reward in the object-quality learning of rhesus monkeys. *J. comp. physiol. Psychol.,* 1955, **48,** 221–224.
123. Murray, H. A. The effect of fear upon the estimates of the maliciousness of other personalities. *J. soc. Psychol.,* 1933, **4,** 310–329.
124. Murray, H. A., et. al. *The assessment of men.* New York: Holt, Rinehart, & Winston, 1948.
125. Myrdal, G. *An American dilemma.* New York: Harper, 1944.
126. Nissen, H. W. Description of the learned response in discrimination behavior. *Psychol. Rev.,* 1950, **57,** 121–131.
127. Nissen, H. W. The nature of drive as innate determinant of behavioral organization. In M. R. Jones (Ed.), *Nebraska symposium on motivation, 1954.* Lincoln, Neb.: Univer. Neb. Press, 1954. Pp. 281–320.
128. Olds, J. A neural model for sign gestalt theory. *Psychol. Rev.,* 1954, **61,** 59–72.
129. Osgood, C. E. Behavior theory and the social sciences. *Behav. Sci.,* 1956, 1, 167–185.
130. Osgood, C. E., Suci, G. J., & Tannenbaum, P. *The measurement of meaning.* Urbana, Ill.: Univer. Ill. Press, 1957.
131. Parsons, T., & Shils, E. A. *Toward a general theory of action.* Cambridge, Mass.: Harvard Univer. Press, 1951.
132. Penfield, W., & Rasmussen, T. *The cerebral cortex of man.* New York: Macmillan, 1950.
133. Platt, J. R. Amplification aspects of biological response and mental activity. *Amer. Scientist,* 1956, **44,** 180–197.
134. Postman, L. Towards a general theory of cognition. In J. A. Rohrer & M. Sherif (Eds.), *Social psychology at the crossroads.* New York: Harper, 1951. Pp. 242–272.
135. Postman, L. The experimental analysis of motivational factors in perception. In J. S. Brown et al., *Current theory and research in motivation.* Lincoln, Neb.: Univer. Neb. Press, 1953.
136. Postman, L., Bruner, J. S., & McGinnies, E. Personal values as selective factors in perception. *J. abnorm. soc. Psychol.,* 1948, **43,** 142–154.
137. Rankin, R. E., & Campbell, D. T. Galvanic skin response to Negro and white experimenters. *J. abnorm. soc. Psychol.,* 1955, **51,** 30–33.
138. Reece, M. M. The effect of shock on recognition thresholds. *J. abnorm. soc. Psychol.,* 1954, **49,** 165–172.

139. Rosenberg, M. J. Cognitive structure and attitudinal affect. *J. abnorm. soc. Psychol.*, 1956, **53**, 367–372.
140. Rosenbleuth, A., Weiner, N., & Bigelow, J. Behavior, purpose, and teleology. *Phil. Sci.,* 1943, **11**, 18 24.
141. Sherif, M. *The psychology of social norms.* New York: Harper, 1936.
142. Sherif, M., & Cantril, H. The psychology of attitudes. Parts I and II. *Psychol. Rev.,* 1945, **52**, 295–319; 1946, **53**, 1–24.
143. Sherif, M., & Sherif, C. W. *An outline of social psychology.* (Rev. ed.) New York: Harper, 1956.
144. Skinner, B. F. *The behavior of organisms.* New York: Appleton-Century-Crofts, 1938.
145. Smedslund, J. The problem of "what is learned." *Psychol. Rev.,* 1953, **60**, 157–158.
146. Smedslund, J. *Multiple-probability learning.* Oslo: Akademisk Forlag, 1955.
147. Spence, K. W. Cognitive vs. stimulus-response theories of learning. *Psychol. Rev.,* 1950, **57**, 159–172.
148. Spence, K. W. Theoretical interpretations of learning. In C. P. Stone (Ed.), *Comparative psychololgy.* (3rd ed.) Englewood Cliffs, N.J.: Prentice-Hall, 1951.
149. Spence, K. W. *Behavior theory and conditioning.* New Haven, Conn.: Yale Univer. Press, 1956.
150. Spence, K. W. *Behavior theory and learning.* Englewood Cliffs, N.J.: Prentice-Hall, 1960.
151. Sperry, R. W. Mechanisms of neural maturation. In S. S. Stevens (Ed.), *Handbook of experimental psychology.* New York: Wiley, 1951. Pp. 236–280.
152. Sperry, R. W. Neurology and the mind-brain problem. *Amer. Scientist*, 1952, **40**, 293–312.
153. Star, S. Interracial tension in two areas of Chicago: an exploratory approach to the measurement of interracial tensions. Unpublished doctoral dissertation, Univer. Chicago, 1951.
154. Stephenson, W. Some observations on Q technique. *Psychol. Bull.,* 1952, **49**, 483–498.
155. Stout, G. F. *A manual of psychology.* New York: Hinds & Noble, 1899.
156. Straus, A. The concept of attitude in social psychology. *J. Psychol.,* 1945, **19**, 329–339.
157. Sullivan, P. L., & Adelson, J. Ethnocentrism and misanthropy. *J. abnorm. soc. Psychol.,* 1954, **49**, 246–250.
158. Summer, W. G. *Folkways.* Boston: Ginn, 1906.
159. Thomas, W. I., & Znaniecki, F. *The Polish peasant in Europe and America.* Vol. 1. Chicago: Univer. Chicago Press, 1918.
160. Thorpe, W. H. *Learning and instinct in animals.* London: Methuen, 1956.
161. Thurstone, L. L. (Ed.) *The measurement of social attitudes.* Chicago: Univer. Chicago Press, 1931.

162. Thurstone, L. L., & Chave, E. J. *The measurement of attitude.* Chicago: Univer. Chicago Press, 1929.
163. Tinbergen, W. *The study of instinct.* Oxford: Clarendon Press, 1951.
164. Tolman, E. C. Behaviorism and purpose. *J. Phil.,* 1925, **22,** 36–41.
165. Tolman, E. C. *Purposive behavior in animals and men.* New York: Century, 1932.
166. Tolman, E. C. Cognitive maps in rats and men. *Psychol. Rev.,* 1948, **55,** 189–208.
167. Tolman, E. C. Principles of performance. *Psychol. Rev.,* 1955, **62,** 315–326.
168. Uexküll, J. von. *Streifzuge durch die Umwelten von Tieren und Menschen.* Berlin: Springer, 1934. Translated in C. H. Schiller (Ed.), *Instinctive behavior.* New York: Int. Univer. Press, 1957.
169. Wallach, H. Some considerations concerning the relation between personality and cognition. *J. Pers.,* 1949, **28,** 6–13.
170. Warner, L. H. An experimental search for the conditioned response. *J. genet. Psychol.,* 1932, **41,** 91–115.
171. Watson, J. B., & Raynor, R. R. Conditioned emotional reactions. *J. exp. Psychol.,* 1920, **3,** 1–14.
172. Weiss, P. *Conference on genetic neurology.* Univer. Chicago Press, 1950.
173. Whorf, B. L. *Language, thought, and reality.* Cambridge, Mass.: Technology Press, 1956.
174. Wickens, D. D. The transference of conditioned excitation and conditioned inhibition from one muscle group to the antagonistic muscle group. *J. exp. Psychol.,* 1938, **22,** 101–123.
175. Wickens, D. D. Stimulus identity as related to response specificity and response generalization. *J. exp. Psychol.,* 1948, **38,** 389–394.
176. Wiener, N. *Cybernetics.* New York: Wiley, 1948.
177. Woolsey, C. N. Patterns of localization in sensory and motor areas of the cerebral cortex. In S. Cobb et al., *The biology of mental health and disease.* New York: Hoeber-Harper, 1952. Pp. 193–206.
178. Wyatt, D. F., & Campbell, D. T. On the liability of stereotype or hypothesis. *J. abnorm. soc. Psychol.,* 1951, **46,** 496–500.
179. Young, K. *Social attitudes.* New York: Holt, 1931.
180. Zeitlin, L. R. A response oriented analysis of the concepts of autism and perceptual sensitization. Unpublished doctoral dissertation, Northwestern Univer., 1954.

SOCIAL PSYCHOLOGY IN RELATION TO GENERAL PSYCHOLOGY AND OTHER BEHAVIORAL SCIENCES[1]

WILLIAM W. LAMBERT
Departments of Psychology and of Sociology and Anthropology
Cornell University

THE PROBLEM

This paper presents the results of a content analysis of a large portion of the field of social psychology and an analysis of the relation

[1] This analysis was begun while the author enjoyed the facilities of the Center for Advanced Study in the Behavioral Sciences at Palo Alto, Calif. An early draft was completed while at the University of Oslo, Norway, on a Fulbright grant. Certain suggestions from the editor of this project and his advisors have been formative. The manuscript was improved by critical reading by Prof. Wallace E. Lambert and Elisabeth C. Lambert. Other valuable criticism was received from my colleagues James J. Gibson, Leo Meltzer, Olin Smith, and Lauriston Sharp.

of this field to general experimental psychology and other areas of behavior science.

Our task is to assume the existence of a field of study called "social
psychology," to provide an approximation to an "extensional definition"
of this field in time perspective, and then to comment upon the ways in
which it is similar to or different from other major fields of study.

This task is fascinating because social psychology has such a tangled
array of relationships with other subsections of behavioral science that
one can easily begin by questioning the assumption of the existence of a
separable field of study. For example, let us list a few of these relationships of the field to other areas. Because it is concerned with attitudes,
workers in the field share methodology, theory, and problems with the
"values" students of sociology, with political pollsters, economists, and
market researchers. A mutual interest in the sources of attitudes and in
attitude change creates common ties between social psychologists and
experimental psychologists, historians, and communication theorists.
Social psychology is closely related to the study of personality and therefore to aspects of clinical psychology and psychiatry. Since one of the
oldest problems in social psychology is the socialization of children, there
is an overlap with the field of child development, with psychiatry, and
with the work of students of the relation of culture and personality.
Workers are interested in how people relate to one another, and therefore
share problems with structural sociologists and anthropologists. The emphasis on decision making in small-group research and what is called
"interaction" between people, roles, or groups renders the field very
similar to "microeconomics" and to what Newcomb has called "microsociology" [22]. Social psychology shares the problem of the meaning
of stimuli with all the behavior sciences, particularly psycholinguistics.
Finally, there is a whole series of problems relating to general experimental psychology that makes use of the adjective "social"—"social perception," "social learning," "social motives," "social expression of
emotion," and "perception of the social."

Such listings can lead the compulsive systematizer to either hope or
despair, and they recurrently do both. Certainly no systematization of
such a field will endure very long in the current tempo of data gathering
and theoretical development. Viewed in the large, therefore, social psychology is a matter of tentative programs, conceptual schemes, and,
above all, problems. It will either serve as a clearinghouse for fact and
theory for some of the problems it shares with other fields or it will slowly
disintegrate and go the ways of these several component fields which have
important applied functions in society.

For present purposes we assume that the term *social psychology* will
continue in use and we shall try to explicate some of the import of the
term, slippery as this task may be.

The most influential unit of publication in social psychology is still the small research paper, although monographs and book-length reports of research are increasing in number. Most textbooks have tended to be heuristic in value, involving loose conceptual schemes and "story lines" in an attempt to hold together an array of data rather than representing very serious attempts at formal integration of the field.

Our approach to the delineation of social psychology and its position relative to other psychological and social sciences has been to accept both this view of the programmatic nature of the field and also the fact that the research paper is the present basic unit of progress. The task we have set is to provide our approximation to an "extensional definition" of social psychology by means of an analysis of the range of interests reflected in the research papers published in two volumes of the *Journal of Abnormal and Social Psychology* separated by seven years.

This journal is one of the oldest and most respected in the field and has therefore been important in reflecting new developments. It does not represent, however, a fully adequate coverage of the field as a whole. To do this we would need to include such excellent journals as *Sociometry, Human Relations,* and the *Journal of Social Psychology.* In fact, we could not justifiably stop here, but would have to peruse all the journals of the various social sciences where things social psychological are sometimes published. Such considerations would have required some a priori criteria of inclusion which would have prejudged some of the issues we preferred to leave open. Our arbitrary decision has, however, some virtues: the journal has a high rejection rate, assuring some quality to what is published; it has been important in reflecting new developments in the field; it covers a very broad array of the problems of social psychology. Finally, by comparing the papers published in 1960 with those published in 1952, we may be able to cast some light on change in this important publishing source.

For our tentative purposes, then, social psychology will be explicitly referred to as the contents of the 61 formal papers (no "notes" or "critiques") for Vol. 47, 1952, and the same number of formal papers for 1960 (including all of Vol. 60, and the first 8 papers from No. 1, Vol. 61).

Such an analysis calls for a conceptual scheme to provide categories for grouping the broad array of detailed material. A heuristic scheme was decided upon a priori, based on an extension and partial alteration of the dyadic schemes of Miller and Dollard [17], Cottrell [6], Sears [26], and the present writer [13].

The scheme provides (1) a general point of reference for viewing the distribution of social-psychological interests reflected in the research papers, (2) a format for evaluating the writer's a priori hunch as to a useful method for displaying social-psychological interests, (3) a point of reference for viewing the fields of secondary interest—in this case the output of the *Journal of Experimental Psychology* for one year (1952, as represented by alternate issues), and (4) it serves as a foil, so to speak, for viewing social psychology's relations to sociology, anthropology, and other social science fields.

The task set here is thus to reflect interest more than to provide criteria for evaluation for specific papers. Criticism has not been totally forgotten in this endeavor, but it has been second in importance to the attempt to grasp the distribution of interests in the fields involved. Our method of sampling has perhaps at least one disadvantage—it places emphasis on the collective, across-the-board interests of the fields involved and loses the continuities of research, particularly those where a single group of authors continues refining and broadening work on a single set of variables. Our analysis probably captures the breadth of interest, but not the continuity and deeper interests which may represent the greater successes. Social psychology is presented on its less polished side. We lose much of the long-range strategies of people like Bales [3], Sears [27], Barker and Wright [4], Cottrell [9], Dollard and Miller [7], Mowrer [18], Asch [2], Lewin [14], Whyte [33], Homans [10], Festinger [8], Whiting and Child [31], Sherif [28], Newcomb [21], McClelland [16], Hovland [11], and Osgood [23], etc. Fortunately, however, it is these longe-range studies which are published in monograph or book form and as a result are more available and well known. The present writer is aware of such developments, and they will be discussed, but in a secondary manner or as they or their derivatives appear in the studies covered.

We will first outline the scheme within which we have attempted to view social psychology and the secondary fields. We will then outline the distribution of interests this analysis has shown for social psychology —the range of independent and dependent variables, the patterns of relationships studied, and the kinds of explanatory concepts utilized.

This portrait of the distribution of interests will be followed by a comparison of this field with general experimental psychology. We will then evaluate some aspects of the methodological status of social psychology, show the kinds of operations and settings studied, and return to the conceptual scheme we have adopted and evaluate the degree to which it provides a means of capturing the interests of the social psychologists studied. It is impossible for the writer to avoid suggesting directions and problems for study and these suggestions will be left where they fit most naturally.

THE DYADIC SCHEME

The scheme shown in Fig. 1 represents the general framework for our analysis of each of the relationships reported in the studies in our sample.

Our task was seemingly simple—to place each relationship reported in the literature into its place in this scheme, viewing each numbered entity as representing a broad class of empirical (or inferred) events. It becomes necessary, therefore, to explain Fig. 1, to show how our content categories emerge from it, and to give examples of the kinds of events we placed in these categories.

The scheme represents all the classes of events needed to describe the interaction of two somewhat abstract people, Alpha and Beta. Beta is

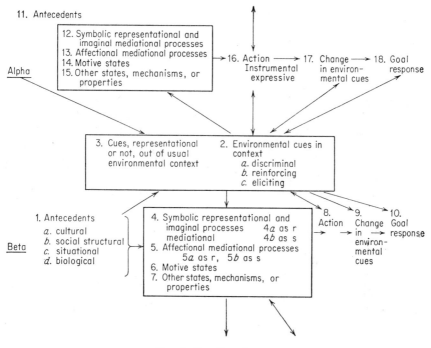

Fig. 1. Dyadic scheme.

usually the person referred to as "the subject" in social-psychological studies. Alpha is another person who is "having something to do" with Beta.

Most studies in general experimental psychology are carried out in terms of a monadic rather than a dyadic scheme, so we may start our explanation by focusing on Beta. Consider, then, the Beta section of the diagram along with the long center box which has to do with classes of stimuli or cues. It can then be seen that this is an expanded form of Miller and Dollard's "cue-drive-response-reward" formula [17], expanded to include certain antecedent events, as well as a number of intervening or inferred events—those inside the more square box.

Let us now take the concrete case where Beta is a college sophomore in a laboratory situation which is rather new to him and where he has become conditioned to respond with a finger flexion to a bell as the conditioned stimulus. The experimenter is interested in the effect of the temporal interval between the occurrence of the bell and the unconditioned stimulus, shock, on the amplitude and latency of the finger flexion. Let us use this example to outline the meaning we intend for the entities in Fig. 1.

There is much involved in such a situation, much more than ever appears in a research report. There are antecedent factors (see item 1, Fig. 1) which may be explicitly or implicitly involved. Culturally shared values (1a) may have partially decided the student to volunteer to be a subject in the experiment. His social structural history (1b) may have prepared him to bear the shock administered by a high-status person in silence. Past situational learning (1c), in conjunction with his biologically given learning mechanism, may have led him to have differentiated the sounds of bells from other noises or the feel of shock from other feels long before he entered the experiment. The stimuli (bells) become eliciting stimuli (2c), and shocks were negative reinforcers (2b) all along, and both have the properties of discriminal cues (2a). These "stimuli" are not in their usual environmental context (though this is usually a somewhat vague distinction), and the temporal relation between the two cues (the operational independent variable) is probably new to the direct experience of the subject.

The distinctions we have made under the antecedent conditions are necessary to permit us to record the main relationship studied when "culture," social structure, situational causes, or biological factors are varied in some manner. They are not meant to be the most elegant distinctions that could be made. In our present example, these factors are not relevant to categorizing the results of the study—we have merely shown how they *might* be relevant.

From the point of view of an observer, usually the experimenter, the stimuli impinge on the subject and he acts by lifting his finger (8). This is an act which is instrumental to avoidance of impending shock, again from the point of view of an informed observer, in the sense that this is a rule of the experimental "game"—the one (nonshock) is correlated to some degree with the other (finger flexion). This action in another case might be of an expressive or emotional kind, such as a sigh or a change in rate of heartbeat, and such expressive actions are undoubtedly present but are ignored by the experimenter in this case. The action leads to a change in the environmental cues (9), perhaps in this case it is simply the fact that the finger is up instead of resting on a key. In other cases, the change in environmental cues may be physically, socially, or theoretically very vital, as when an aggressive act causes hurt to someone else, or leads to a counterattack. Finally, some goal response usually occurs (10). The subject may relax, slouch back in the chair and feel proud that he has learned how to avoid the shock (this last being a complex inference which involves some of the factors in the box of intervening or mediating factors).

So much for the observable action. The psychologically mysterious matters are those events which fall under one of the rubrics in the somewhat square box. Here are the cognitions, affections, and conations, but with "modern" names with which psychologists fill their schemes of the behaving organism. In the present scheme we have found it necessary to leave the classes of intervening variables very broad and have not attempted to utilize any particular model which would be validated or invalidated by the various research reports which we wish to analyze. Such a task is both more and less ambitious than the present one. We wish merely to find classes of events which will usefully describe what is going on in all of social psychology, whereas most models attempt (ideally) to subsume some of the important relationships in a manner in which they could be shown to be wrong according to useful studies which are suggested by the model itself. The present scheme is not so specifically stated and is only vulnerable in the minor sense that we might find studies in experimental or social psychology which could not be fitted into our scheme.

To return to categories 4 to 7 in Fig. 1, category 4 refers to events of a symbolic representational or imaginal sort which are inferred by the observer to be operative in the subject and which serve to mediate between the stimuli as described (in physical or other communicative terms) by the observer, and the verbal or other actions that come from the subject. To some experimenters these are percepts or perceptual processes; to others, they are implicit habit systems or even more physiologically tinged matters like "cell assemblies." There are two subcategories under category 4. Category 4a is briefly noted as "as r," whereas category 4b is called "as s." The distinction here is simple, but it has been difficult to deal with systematically in our content analysis. In short, a percept is "as s" if it is viewed by the observer inferring it as an internal cue or stimulus which is at least partially determinative of the subject's forthcoming action. The same percept may be considered "as r," that is, a response, if the experimenter—as in many psychophysical or social-perception studies—is interested in it as itself at least partially determined by some particular external or environmental stimulus. In psychophysics, percepts are usually inferred in their role as responses; in studies of perceptual learning, they are often inferred in both roles; whereas in many cognitive studies of judgment or decision (actions), they are inferred in their property of being stimuli to such particular judgments or decisions.

This same distinction between s and r is made with regard to category 5, where the experimenter infers affective events as occurring, either as responses to some external (or other internal) stimulus, or as stimuli which mediate or partially determine some action event. When we study fear as dependent upon some stimulus or past conditions of learning, then it will fall under 5a; when such a state is viewed as a learned drive which instigates a particular action or a particular learning (change of action), then it is classified as 5b.

Under category 6 we have placed all motivational states. Here the reliability of our classifying may be somewhat lower, since this class is one of the very mysterious categories in all of behavior science. As we have noted in the paragraph above, affective states are often of interest to psychologists because of their motivational properties. Unfortunately, it is by no means clear just what such properties are supposed to be. To reinforcement theorists and some others, motives are energies or stimuli residing in the subject which lead to new learning (as a result of reduction of such energies) or merely serve to increase the probability, amplitude, or some other property of actions. To others, motives can conflict with one another, whereas for still others only the action tendencies aroused by different motives can conflict, etc. We have merely leaned on the stated intent of the reporting experimenter in deciding how to classify our studies, keeping criteria such as those just mentioned in mind. Where the experimenter has, for example, inferred fear as a response or a factor which interferes with action, it has usually been placed with "affect"; where it is evoked in its roles as stimulus or motivator in some other sense, it has usually been categorized with "motive state."

Category 7 in Fig. 1 is called "other states, mechanisms, or properties," and here we have the residual category which most descriptive schemes seem to need. In later sections we will further divide this category for different analytic purposes because it contains a great many of the kinds of events that all kinds of psychologists like to infer. To return to our sophomore in the conditioning situation, there are some who will want to talk about reinforcement, generalization, discrimination, sensory preconditioning, or operative gestalt principles as mechanisms or properties of the subject which are set off in the experimental situation. Such general behavior mechanisms are inventions of the greatest importance and most general implication to some psychologists. To others, however, there are the complex mechanisms of Freud—rationalization, projection, suppression, superego-ego conflict, etc. Although we were often tempted to engage in the useful sport of translating the one kind of thing into congeries of the other, this would have evaded our present task of describing the habits of psychologists not only as to what observables they wish to relate to what other observables, but also as to their habits of explanation. "Other states" includes all these mechanisms then, and we will have to analyze further in later sections. It also includes complex inferences like attitudes (a favorite pastime for social psychologists), except where only cognitive, affective, *or* conative functions of such entities are inferred one at a time. In short, rather than proliferate our categories beyond all counting, we have left the bins large enough to provide hope for some reliability and we will make them smaller again for specific analytic purposes.

The import of the scheme in Fig. 1 should now be somewhat clear for the lower or monadic portion of the diagram. Let us now look at the diagram as a whole, including the other party, Alpha, who is present in so many social-psychological studies. He is the second (or third or fourth) college sophomore who is called into a communication experiment with Beta. Or he is a mother feeding baby Beta, or a friend or enemy of Beta, or a doctor to the patient Beta. Or he may be the female experimenter as distinguished from the male experimenter, who is listening to the subject while he tries to see (and say) "dirty" words which are being presented in a tachistoscope.

The reader will note that categories 11 to 18 have the very same names for Alpha as did 1 to 10 for Beta, and that categories 2 and 3, which have to do with stimuli, have similar and equal import schematically for Alpha. We have merely expanded the usual psychological scheme to include the analytic elements necessary to deal with a second party. We should immediately state that there is nothing mystic in the restriction to *one* other party, and we have included a vertical arrow at the top of the page so that a third party, or another box relating to stimuli, may be imagined as being up there. Readers who are prone to like dynamic imagery may also easily imagine the boxes for Alpha and for Beta going on as far as necessary to right and to left. Such extension would be necessary to represent action or interaction at a more concrete level. For describing relationships in which social psychologists are interested, however, we are operating at a level of abstraction where "*change* in action," or even "*change* in who Alpha is" are sometimes the variables of the studies we are analyzing, so for this level of analysis the simpler scheme of Fig. 1 may be sufficient for our purposes.

The arrows in the figure need explaining. They are placed there as examples rather than in an attempt to give an exhaustive coverage of the possible relationships implied by the diagram. We have drawn all influence arrows from Alpha toward Beta as going through the long box referring to stimuli, but it is often more simple to refer to a relationship with this stricture left out, and we will sometimes do that. For example, if we are attempting to describe a study in which a speaker (Alpha) is talking to an audience with intent to change that audience's answers on a questionnaire, it is more correct to categorize it as a $16 \rightarrow 2(a,b,c) \rightarrow 8$ relationship that is under study but simpler to refer to it as a 16 (Alpha's instrumental acts of talking to an audience) leads to a change in that audience's instrumental actions (8) in answering a questionnaire, due to the ubiquity with which the stimulus box is present in all interactions. If, of course, the major independent variable is the *mode* of presentation of the speech to the audience (recorded as compared to face to face, for example), then the relationship would best be rendered as a $2 \rightarrow 8$ relationship, the 2 referring to a change in the mode of presenting the same content to Beta. As a critic, the categorizer may feel that the experimenter has overlooked variation in the goal response for the speaker or in conflicting sets in the hearer, but this is somewhat irrelevant to the major analysis in this paper. The interest or intention of the reporting experimenter is our focus, not his adequacy in terms of known methods of control and inference. In some later sections we will evaluate certain aspects of method, but just as the experimenter ignores most of what goes on in order to measure some of what goes on, so the analyst must ignore what he thinks is really going on in order to reflect honestly and succinctly what the experimenter is intending and what *he* thinks is going on.

The reader has noted that the diagram, even in its dyadic form, implies a behavioristic, nonintrospective psychology "of the other one—or two" where the experimenter's or observer's point of view is always the starting—and ending—point. Perhaps this is unfortunate in some respects, but necessary for the sanity of the person who is attempting to code so many different studies. Someone who is firmly dedicated to a phenomenological analysis of interaction might feel quite unhappy, and the present analyst might have felt rather confused if he had met a thoroughgoing analysis of that kind in the papers under study. (He did not, by the way.) Consider an analysis of a perfect social communication from a phenomenological approach. Alpha would say something to Beta which would mean A to Alpha and A' to Beta. Further, Alpha would have a notion B of what it meant to Beta, and Beta would have a notion B' of what he thought it meant to Alpha. The reader will note, possibly, the beginning of an attempt to writhe back and forth from this point of view of Alpha to that of Beta, and so on, as this kind of analysis proceeds. He is trying to be two people at once, so to speak. The present writer has two remarks about this state of affairs. Such writhing back and forth is probably often vital to obtaining a clear hypothesis regarding the factors in social interaction, just as trying to take the role of the other is a wise and sometimes even humane way to approach one's relations with others. However, and this is the second statement, once an operational design for testing the relationship has been achieved, then it can be related to a single-point-of-view diagram like Fig. 1, and we would find it possible to describe the relationship studied, at least in principle. Alpha would be inferred to have (at least) two cognitive mediators in operation, as would Beta, and the properties of these four states would be delineable in terms of some more specific dimensional scheme common to them all. In short, the multiperspectived language of subjective analysis has been utilized for obtaining a hunch or a hypothesis—a vital kind of use for a language or approach—but we do not see this as inconsistent with rendering the interaction in terms of the more stable point of view of the independent observer, once it has been set up for formal objective testing.

In explaining Fig. 1 and before putting it to our specific use, we must give some examples of how certain kinds of recurring studies in social psychology would be categorized. Consider an experiment on empathy where, for example, the past history of the subjects (category 1 in some form) is the independent variable, and each of two subjects is evaluated as responding more or less similarly to the way the other says he felt in a posttest questionnaire. The relationship under study can be regarded as involving operationally $\left.\begin{array}{c} 1 \\ 2 \end{array}\right\} \rightarrow \left.\begin{array}{c} 2a^1 \rightarrow 8 \\ 2a^2 \rightarrow 16 \end{array}\right\}$ similarity; that is, some varied antecedent factor (1), in conjunction with cues received from the "other" (2), affects the similarity of answers on two questionnaires, one in which Beta responds about himself, the other in which Alpha responds as best he can about Beta. And vice versa. To reflect the experimenter's inference, we merely add the numbers of such entities, such as the feelings or cognitions which are supposed to be similar. Then the total relationship studied may be written, in this case, as

$$\left.\begin{array}{c} 1 \\ 2 \end{array}\right\} \rightarrow \begin{array}{c} 2a^1 \xrightarrow{\hspace{1cm}} 8 \\ \text{similarity} \\ 2a^2 \xrightarrow{\hspace{1cm}} 16 \end{array}\left.\begin{array}{c} \\ \end{array}\right\} \begin{array}{c} 5 \text{ similarity} \\ \text{inferred} \end{array}$$
10

Independent variable	Dependent variable	Intervening variable

Studies of empathy are complicated matters and "require," in our sense, that numbers referring to a second party be available for a description in this way. As it stands, the inference of similar feelings in Alpha and Beta as underlying the similarity of the answers of the two subjects on the questionnaire is only one theory and only one variation in the many conditions of such studies. It may be the cognitions of Alpha that are similar to or include a symbolic content referring to the feelings of

Beta. Or the whole matter of the operational similarity on the questionnaire may be referred to a cognition or habit system termed "assumed similarity," which is similar for the two subjects and does not rest on the present cues received from the "other." Our scheme in Fig. 1 does not presume to decide such issues, but is able to reflect most of the distinctions involved, at least to the extent needed for our content analysis.

Let us consider three other social psychological problems and their relation to Fig. 1 in a somewhat less detailed fashion. Studies of thinking (complicated cognitive mediating processes or s-r sequences) of people *alone* as compared to *together* are sometimes attempted. Here the dependent variable is often the frequency with which suggested solutions (instrumental acts) occur under the two conditions which are problem stimuli *with* other people, and problem stimuli *without* other people. The inferences may have to do with matters similar to those used in empathy studies, where similarity between the mediators in the two or more subjects may be invoked, or a more statistical theory involving the increased or decreased probability of a "correct" mediator of thought in either of the subjects may be entertained.

Studies of attitude change are again in great fashion in social psychology, and often involve an attempt to measure the social influence of Alpha on Beta's action (or Beta's inferred mediators). Here the independent variables may be variations in how Alpha presents cues to Beta, what cues he presents to Beta, etc. Almost all of the entities of Fig. 1 could be exemplified in various studies of attitude change.

Social psychologists sometimes study the conditions for the development of norms of judgment or of evaluation. In terms of Fig. 1, most of these studies have used a change (over time or trials) of the behavior of two or more subjects toward greater similarity as the dependent variable. Such movement toward similarity has also been used to infer the development of the mediator, the norm, which is pictured as being some similarity on some dimensions of cognition, affect, or attitude in the two or more subjects. When norms are used as dependent variables in experiments, our diagram is adequate. But when a full-grown social norm is represented as acting as an independent variable, there is occasionally some trouble with Fig. 1.

This trouble arises because such a norm is sometimes conceptualized as involving not only shared mediators, but also tendencies to punish lack of conformity to the norm which "society" shares. Society is a rather large and complex entity and can be used with an intention which may stretch our dyad all out of recognizable shape. We can represent the notion of sanctioning response tendencies as action tendencies (mediators) in both Alpha and Beta, so that Alpha would punish Beta if Beta's actions were not in the correct class, and Beta would punish Alpha if

Alpha did not behave as called for, but this is a special case. The sanctioning power may really reside not in Alpha and Beta, but in some specialized person or agency such as a policeman or dictator, or in this third person's capacity to control the actions of a fourth person to punish Alpha and Beta, etc. So the dyad may stretch out of Fig. 1 and proliferate horizontally and vertically in order to describe society or social structure in the manner intended by some sociologists and anthropologists. Too much of this and we will need to go in search of a more complicated scheme.

There are only three things that can be done with such complicated problems: we can break them down into their dyadic elements (some psychologists seem to tend to do this); we can turn to another way of abstracting the action so that Alpha and Beta are collapsed into "one" since they are similar, and the sanctioning agent or agents can be rendered as the "other" in Fig. 1; we can utilize the extra arrows at the top and bottom of Fig. 1 and face up to the descriptive complexities of the problem. One of the aims of our content analysis is to discover how often we must resort to such devices, and thereby evaluate the adequacy of Fig. 1 for the task we have set ourselves.

One final word of explanation and perhaps apology for Fig. 1. A neobehaviorist or methodological-behaviorist bias pervades the scheme, as it does much of modern psychology. In short, we will have no argument over the existence of ideas, percepts, meanings, etc., but we see them as inferred from Alpha's or Beta's actions or movements in the presence of stimulus patterns, not as givens. This may trouble some readers, but we hope not to the exclusion of a consideration of what values may accrue from our analysis. When we categorize a percept into the bin called "symbolic representational mediational process," we are merely categorizing, not in some magical sense reducing what is largely an unknown into some a priori set of properties. We wish to use the scheme as constructively as possible rather than engage in what the present writer can only see as pretentious reduction. A percept is possibly more than—but at least as much as—a symbolic representational mediating process.

THE DEPENDENT VARIABLES

The Categories and the 1952 Distribution

All of the papers in the regular issues of the *Journal of Abnormal and Social Psychology* for 1952 and a corresponding number of papers from the 1960 issues were analyzed according to the scheme of Fig. 1. We will first discuss the 1952 sample.

In the process of analysis it was necessary to set up a few rules which

Table 1. Distribution of Relationships Studied

Dependent variables	Independent variables										
	1. Tissue or other bodily changes in Beta	2. Situation of B's action	3. Signs presented to B	4. B's cognitive processes	5. B's motives	6. B's other states	7. Validity of B's other states	8. B's expressive acts	9. B's instrumental acts	10. B's attitude toward self	11. B's action toward others
1. B's cognitive processes.....	/1.7		1.1/ .8	1.1/			/2.5		/.8	/.8	/.8
2. B's motives..............	1.1/						/ .8				
3. B's other states..........	/ .8	1.1/		1.1/			/ .8				
4. Validity of B's other states							5.3/1.7				
5. B's expressive acts........	1.1/2.5	/.8	1.1/3.4	2.1/.8	2.1/	9.6/5.9			/.8		1.1/
6. B's instrumental acts......	2.1/1.7	/.8	3.2/ .8			/2.5	3.2/3.4	1.1/	1.1/	/.8	
7. B's attitude toward self....		/.8					/1.7			/.8	
8. B's action toward others...							/ .8				/.8
9. B's action relative to other.			/ .8		/ .8	1.1/	5.3/			1.1/	
10. B's attitudes or judgments toward others...........	/ .8		/2.5	3.2/.8	2.1/	2.1/2.5				1.1/	
11. B's anticipation or achievement of environmental effects..................											
12. B's anticipation or achievement of goal response.....				1.1/			2.2/.8				
13. Attitudes or judgments of others (including those toward B).................						1.1/ .8				1.1/.8	
14. B's position relative to others..................				1.1/	1.1/ .8					1.1/	
Total 1952...............	4	1	6	8	6	22	5	1	3	4	1
Total 1960...............	9	3	10	3	4	24	2	2	0	4	2
1952, per cent...........	4.3	1.1	6.4	8.0	6.4	23.4	5.3	1.1	3.2	4.3	1.1
1960, per cent...........	7.6	2.5	8.4	2.5	3.4	20.2	1.7	1.7	0	3.4	1.7

NOTE: The numbers in the cells give the per cent of total that the relationship between the independent variable class (listed across the top of the table) and the corresponding dependent variable class (listed down the side of the table) was studied in a sample of 61 social science papers in 1952 (to the left of the diagonal) and in 1960 (to the right of the diagonal). The various variable classes are related to Fig. 1 (see Table 2). Independent variable classes 4 to 17 are the same as dependent variable classes 1 to 14. Independent variable classes 21 to 23 were added as a result of the 1960 analysis. Totals and percentages for all classes of variables for both years are presented at bottom and right-hand side of the table.

should be mentioned. Complex relationships, as in the example of empathy, were broken down into two components, one representing the first independent variable (in that case, certain unspecified antecedent conditions) and the other representing the second independent variable (in that case, the cues received from the other subject in the experiment). We also decided to leave certain relationships (where the writer reported more than one relationship of the same formal kind, according to the scheme of Fig. 1) out of consideration. If, for example, three different relationships between cue factors and judgments were studied in the same paper, only one was included in the final tabulation. This was done to avoid overrepresentation of one class of relationship because of one or two of the research papers. If either the independent or dependent variable was different, then both relationships were retained. Occasionally

BY SOCIAL PSYCHOLOGISTS IN 1952 AND 1960

Independent variables

12. B's acts relative to acts of others	13. B's attitudes toward others	14. B's anticipation or achievement of events	15. B's anticipation or achievement of goals	16. Attitudes of others toward B	17. B's relative position (including attitudes)	18. Alpha's instrumental or expressive acts toward Beta	19. Number of Alphas (or of Betas)	20. Properties of Alpha or Alphas (including familiarity or relations)	21. Cultural or historical factors	22. Alpha's relative position to Beta (including attitudes)	23. Genetic factors	Total, 1952	Total, 1960	Per cent, 1952	Per cent, 1960
	/.8	1.1/	1.1/		1.1/	1.1/ .8						6	11	6.4	9.2
					1.1/							2	1	2.1	.8
						1.1/1.7		/.8				3	5	3.2	4.2
	/.8											5	3	5.3	2.5
	/.8	1.1/.8		/.8	2.1/1.7	1.1/5.9		/1.7	/.8		/.8	22	33	23.4	27.7
	/.8	/.8	/.8		1.1/	2.1/ .8	3.2/	1.1/		/.8		17	17	18.1	14.3
				/.8		1.1/ .8			/.8			1	6	1.1	5.0
						1.1/				/1.7		1	5	1.1	4.2
/.8												7	3	7.4	2.5
/1.7	3.2/		/.8	/1.7	/1.7	/2.5	3.2/2.5	/1.7	2.1/	/.8	/2.5	16	27	17.0	22.7
						1.1/						1		1.1	
/.8			1.1/					/.8				4	3	4.3	2.5
												2	2	2.1	1.7
		/.8	1.1/			/ .8	2.1/		1.1/			7	3	7.4	2.5
0	3	2	3	0	5	13	3	4	0	0	0	94			
4	4	4	3	4	6	16	2	4	2	6	1		119		
0	3.2	2.1	3.2	0	5.3	17.0	3.2	4.3	0	0	0			100	
3.4	3.4	3.4	2.5	3.4	5.0	13.4	1.7	3.4	1.7	5.0	.8				100

we excluded relationships of a minor or subsidiary type, usually when they were brought in *post factum.* Finally, we excluded one paper from consideration *in toto,* since it reported no new data but was essentially a critical review article. With these exceptions, every relationship was analyzed according to the scheme of Fig. 1.

The final tabulation is presented in Table 1. If the reader will look down the left-hand column of the table, he will find the names of all the classes of dependent variables that were needed to reflect the relationships studied. A summary column on the far right provides a statement of the frequency (and percentage of the total number) with which each of these dependent variables appeared in the 1952 literature. The total number of dependent variables is 94, an average of about 1½ relationships which met our criteria per paper analyzed.

Let us turn to the left-hand column of the table, where the categories of dependent variables are listed. It should be noted that the categories do not simply correspond to the numbered entities of Fig. 1, but sometimes represent such combinations of these entities as were found necessary to reflect the relationships analyzed. They represent categories of dependent variables which the writer constructed from the materials available in Fig. 1 for the present purpose. A more systematic or logical listing of all the possible dependent variables of social or individual psychology which is implied by Fig. 1 awaits separate analysis and would probably be worth doing only if the model were made more substantive and vulnerable. The present listing of dependent variables does provide us with some description of the kinds of behavioral events over which

TABLE 2. ENTITIES OF THE DYAD* WHICH COORDINATE WITH THE CATEGORIES OF VARIABLES USED IN TABLE 1

Table 1 categories (names of independent variables)	Figure 1 entities (numbers in Fig. 1)
1. Tissue change or unconditioned stimulus—Beta	1c
2. Situation of Beta's action	2a
3. Sign material presented to Beta	2,3
4. Beta's cognitive mediating processes	4
5. Beta's motives	6
6. Beta's other states	7
7. Validity of Beta's states	7a
8. Beta's expressive acts	8a
9. Beta's instrumental acts	8b
10. Beta's attitudes toward self	8 (4,5) → Beta
11. Beta's action toward others	8 → Alpha
12. Beta's action relative to those of others	8 relative to 16 (Alpha)
13. Beta's attitudes toward others	8 (4,5) → Alpha
14. Beta's anticipation of environmental events	9
15. Beta's anticipation of goal responses	10
16. Attitude of other toward Beta	16 (12,13) → Beta
17. Beta's position relative to other	Beta-Alpha relationship
18. Alpha's acts toward Beta	16 → Beta
19. Number of Alphas	—
20. Properties of Alpha	12, 13, 14, 15

* See Fig. 1.

social psychologists feel they have some actual or statistical control. We can also remark upon some of the possibilities for dependent variables which are not utilized in the literature under consideration. In later sections we will be able to point out the additional categories which we must include to describe the independent variables of the studies analyzed. When we have put the two together in the matrix form of Table 1, the pattern of relationships studied in this sample of social psychology emerges. The unfilled boxes of the matrix then suggest either unfinished business for social psychology or divisions of labor which will point up the things social psychologists tend to study as compared to those chosen by other kinds of students of the behavioral sciences.

Our first task is to make clear, with examples, the categories we found necessary to describe the dependent variables of social psychology as defined by our sample of papers. To make our task easier, we have presented Table 2, which coordinates most of the named categories of Table 1 with the numbered entities in Fig. 1. We will not discuss this coordination in detail but will focus on the meanings of the categories in the left column of Table 1.

The first category of dependent variables, "B's (i.e., Beta's) cognitive processes," has a self-explanatory meaning for some psychologists. From the methodological-behavioral point of view implied in our diagram, however, such matters usually have the status of inferences and would not be operational directly measured variables. Here the analyst was caught in a dilemma. Should he drop the aim of describing the interests of the writers of research papers or should he appear to let subjectivism enter the basic operations of the field? He chose the second course because of convention and because maintaining the methodological distinction seemed overanalytic.

A gentle word of defense should, however, be permitted. Whatever a percept, judgment, thought, notion, or bit of knowledge, etc., is, subjectively speaking, it is usually very harmlessly inferred by equating it with the meaning of a verbal instrumental act of the subject (Beta). It is, in this sense, *almost* a subcategory of instrumental response, and could almost as easily have been placed in category 6, "Beta's instrumental act." But this would have swelled this category greatly and thereby lost a distinction which is considered by some students of perception to be one of kind. We did not attempt to maintain a methodological behaviorist rejection of the meaning of spoken responses in cases where such responses were recorded in psychophysical settings, in the presence of tachistoscopes, etc., where the responses were of a fairly simple sort and where the everyday meaning of such emitted words would probably be very reliably categorized by independent observers. This category, therefore, contains references to studies where the dependent variable or variables were the perceptions, thoughts, etc., of Beta, like "black-and-blue," standing for "I *perceive* the words 'black and blue' in that tachistoscope over there," or "smaller," or "larger," etc. Where the cognitive processes or hypotheses, or learned s-r bonds were involved in explanation of the occurrence of such responses, then these uses were classed as intervening variables, and will be discussed in a separate section.

Looking from the left side of Table 1 to the numbers on the far right, we see that six relationships studied in 1952 used "Beta's cognitive processes" as their dependent variables in our sense. So there are some cognitive processes, indexed by a particular kind of verbal instrumental response, which social psychologists feel that they can predict or control operationally. This was true of about 6 per cent of the relationships analyzed.

The second category has to do with attempts to change "Beta's motives," which is a category which also involves some inference. In two cases we found studies where the theoretical intent of the writer was extremely clear and the operations involved were so particularly developed for the problem that we placed them in this category. The first case involved measuring a seemingly functionally autonomous motive from the failure of an ear-scratching response to extinguish following a single application of collodion (independent variable). The second case was placed in this category because it dealt with a theoretical Lewinian tension state inferred from differences in behavior following experimental blocking of the subject. The experimental failure of a habit to extinguish appears to provide rather clear grounds for the inference of an operating O-source which deserves the name "motive"; the second case involves equating the "tension state" to a goal-deprivation operation. Such experimental operations are so conventional that these dependent variables were retained in this category to reflect the aim and intent of the writers, despite the inferences involved.

The third category concerns attempts to change or predict measured states of subjects other than simple cognitions or motives. All three of these cases involved traits measured by tests on which a good deal of validation work has been done. "Masculinity-femininity," "energy and initiative," and "secure-insecure" are the problematic names given to these dependent variables. They are included in this category because validational work had been done and could be referred to. It seems easier to accept the notion that these are measures of other states of the subjects than it does to state just *what* other states they may be measures of, and, since the category scheme in Table 1 makes no attempt to classify such other states more specifically, the particular names are irrelevant to our present purposes.

The fourth category has to do with studies where, in effect, there is an attempt merely to relate a measure of a state of Beta with another measure of that state—in short, validation studies were placed here because they should go somewhere and yet do not attempt to state relationships between two supposedly *different* entities. They do, however, all have to do with other states, such as traits, prejudices, etc. Five of these studies were found.

The fifth category, the largest, concerns the prediction or control of expressive acts of Beta by the writers of the papers concerned. The names of these acts have movements of the subject as their reference but they are not recorded because they serve the goals of Beta or because they have some predictable effect on the environment, as is the case with instrumental actions. There is an amazingly wide array of these acts. They range from aspects of the contents of dreams to stuttering, the relation of motor movements of Beta to norms for different ages, aesthetic contents of drawings, the total amount of motor activity in an audience of apathetic schizophrenics, the frequency and amount of nail biting, the length of time covered in the content of a TAT story, a measure of conditioned galvanic skin response, the relative frequency of emotional words used by Beta, etc.

The second most frequent category of dependent variables is the sixth, which has to do with aspects of instrumental actions of Beta. Here again the range of subclasses and dimensions of these actions is quite broad, including such matters as the percentage of materials recalled by Beta, the rate of pressing a bar under certain different conditions, trials required to learn nonsense syllables to a certain criterion, the speed of relearning of a visual-discrimination problem, the frequency of Beta's publications and inventions, the time taken by Beta in making a choice, the number of relevant hypotheses put forward by Beta in response to the problem of being faced with a tachistoscope, etc. Since 17 out of the 94 relations reported for 1952 in Fig. 1 involved this class of events, it is fair to say that social psychologists have considerable investment in the problems of instrumental behavior and feel that some of their independent measures are powerful in this area.

The first six categories outlined above are dependent variable categories which social psychologists share with all groups of psychologists and most other students of behavior science. The remaining categories are not so widely shared and serve to begin to differentiate the study of social psychologists from that of some other psychologists. Category 7, for example, contains only one representative—a study where Beta's attitude toward himself is the dependent variable. Attitudes are usually inferred from a class of instrumental acts and are, in a sense, special cases of category 6, but are kept separate here because the operations involved are easily classified (whether acceptable or not), and because such a separation serves our aim in making the interests of social psychologists more clear.

Category 8, "Beta's action toward others," refers to cases where there is an attempt to predict or control some aspect of Beta's social behavior, i.e., some aspect or property of that subclass of Beta's instrumental acts which have another person or persons as their environmental events or goal responses. It is exceedingly interesting to the writer that only one study deals with this potentially huge area. One might be tempted to assume that, operationally speaking, the social actor is still lost in perception and affect. This may merely reflect the difficulty and cost of measuring actual behavior in a dyadic situation. Certainly more of such work would be found in *Sociometry* and other journals.

Category 9 is related to category 8, but differs from category 8 in that the property of Beta's behavior which is predicted or controlled is merely the comparability of some aspect of Beta's behavior with that of another person or persons. We have included seven studies here. They deal with such dependent variables as whether or not Beta makes the same responses as 40 per cent of a sample of "normals" to a TAT, whether or not Beta holds an office in a social group, whether Beta is rated by others as being known more by others in a group, whether or not Beta responds the way "normals" do on the Bender-gestalt, etc. The important thing here is not content of action but the degree of comparability of action with that of some others. There seemed to be no solution but to place this kind of treatment of acts in a category by itself.

Sixteen studies fell into category 10 (as far as dependent variables are concerned). This is the classic category for social psychology, involving Beta's attitudes toward or judgments of Alpha (or Alphas). This category is similar to category 7 except that here the object of the attitude or judgment (operationally, the instrumental acts of answering questions in response to the presence of, or a sign stimulus referring to, a person or group of persons) is other than the self.

Category 11 is weakly represented by one case in our 1952 sample. It deals with an attempt to predict and change Beta's accuracy of predicting the social consequences of his own action. This is again a subclass of the general group of instrumental actions of Beta. It does not include a study of his anticipations in actual social conditions, but refers to his instrumental acts in answer to a particular questionnaire on which some validity work has been done (although the really important validity —the ecological validity—has not been dealt with in this particular case).

Category 12 (Beta's anticipation of goal responses) is represented by four relationships in which Beta's ranking of cultural objects or people in terms of the reward value he sees them as having was changed or predicted. These studies (two are involved) are placed in this category because the category is implied by the scheme in Fig. 1, and because the operations utilized represent such a small array of the possibilities on such an important aspect of behavior.

Category 13 refers to attempts to predict or change the attitude of Alpha or Alphas, including those toward Beta (as a function, for example, of Beta's attitude toward self or other states of Beta). It is closely related to category 14, which contains seven cases of relationships where prediction or change is attempted in the position or status of

Beta relative to others, indexed either by sociometric questions or by actual leadership or other status held by Beta.

These categories, taken from Fig. 1, permit us to place the studies in our sample. It remains to summarize briefly the results of this part of our analysis.

Like most psychologists, social psychologists apparently feel that their theories and studies can lead to prediction and control of various properties of the subject's instrumental and expressive acts. This is probably a common interest in all branches of psychology. Social psychology is different because of the many independent variables which are seen as controlling these two dependent categories, as we will see below.

Social psychology is notable for the number of dependent variables in which it is concerned and which are not part of a purely monadic scheme. The variables include the status of one person relative to another; the attitudes of others toward the actor; the attitude of the actor toward other people (as distinguished from cultural or symbolic or physical objects); the relative position of people with regard to adequacy or other dimensions of action, attitudes, and concepts with regard to the self; and overt behavior toward others. The existence of all these categories is the reason for a dyadic conception of the field, even when it is viewed in a cross section of a year's output. About 39 per cent of the dependent variables studied might be included in the list above.

We have noted that social psychologists see the usual behavioral categories (expressive and instrumental action) as dependent upon an especially wide array of independent variables. The same holds true for perceptual and other phenomena. This tendency challenges any restrictive definition of psychology, for new categories of variables and new views of relationships are being constantly tried out by social psychologists and others studying in this area.

It is particularly fascinating that social psychologists, even in this small sample, are challenging formulations put forward by theorists in other social sciences. It is fair to say that sociologists generally tend to view social structures (either formal or informal) as independent variables or as explanatory variables, but rarely as dependent variables.

The main focus of analysis of many sociologists is on the structures which describe the networks of relationships between people and on the functions of such structures. Although these structures may be viewed as abstractions from the thinking, perceiving, wanting, or acting of individuals, dyads, triads, etc., they are then viewed as powerful (perhaps because they are so shared that abstraction across people is possible). Therefore, they are useful as independent variables in relation to other structures or as explanatory causal factors in considering the behavior of other individuals.

Social psychologists, however, view such structures both ways—in our 1952 sample, category 14, the "Beta-Alpha relationship," is used seven times as a dependent variable and only five times as an independent one! Apparently social psychologists have as their end phenomenon for prediction or control what other people (psychologists, sociologists, or structural anthropologists) might treat as an assumption or starting point. None of the studies in our sample deals with the social structure of a total society as predictable or controllable. However, social psychology is developing a number of such approaches. Many of these are involved with the cross-cultural approach of Murdock [19]; the kind of analysis recently begun by Whiting [32], who treats puberty ceremonies as a dependent variable; and McClelland [16], who sees economic development as a dependent variable.

We can summarize the dependent variables of social psychology in 1952, as sampled here, by stating that 19 per cent of them involve the prediction or change in properties of Beta, and 42 per cent of them represent predictions or changes in Beta's overt behaviors. This largest category may partially reflect the importance placed by social psychologists on the strictures (or wisdom) of behaviorism, neo- or original. Interest in both classes of variables is shared generally with other psychologists, but there is a difference in the relationships studied. The remaining 39 per cent of the studies concern the broader range of dependent variables that involve relationship or attitudinal or interactional factors, an increasingly important area for social psychologists.

Dependent Variables: 1960 Distribution

Table 1[2] includes comparable data for the 1960 sample of papers. The main outlines of interests in prediction and control are the same, suggesting that our categories have reflected some of the more recurrent interests of the field. There are also some interesting changes in the very busy period between 1952 and 1960.

Attitudes of Beta toward others takes over second place from "B's

[2] It is interesting to consider the possibilities of matrices such as that of Table 1. They could ideally serve as summary adjuncts to the *Psychological Abstracts* or to the *Annual Review*. If agreement could be reached on a sufficiently common set of categories (no mean task in itself, of course), then the work done in the fields of psychology in any given period of time could be summarized by such a table. If a code for the classes of theory could be generally agreed upon, the table could be rendered in color or varied type. The table could then contain in the cells the direct numbered reference to the year's important bibliography. It might facilitate the speed with which a person with one specialty might pick out the papers from another specialty which would probably be of maximum interest to him. It might facilitate the study of trends, fads, and major progress or lacunae of a given area, or possibly of the field of psychology as a whole. New discoveries of a categorial kind would possibly be seen more quickly and utilized more adequately and widely.

instrumental act" in the frequency of dependent variables studied. This reflects the resurgence of interest in the experimental analysis of the conditions of attitude change, due in large part to the stimulating work of Hovland and Festinger.

Two other changes are worth noting. First, there is some increase in the study of Beta's attitudes toward others. Second, there is a decrease in the use of structural factors as dependent variables, as can be seen in the drop in category 14, and in the drop in prevalence of category 9 studies. As will be noted later, this is related to an increase in the use of such structural matters as independent variables. These categories (and particularly category 14) are probably among the more unstable categories because they reflect the seesaw of sociological versus personality issues in this interlocked field.

The over-all similarity of interests in the two samples remains the major theme, however. Exactly 42 per cent of the papers are still devoted to prediction or change in Beta's overt behaviors (expressive and instrumental), 17 per cent represent interests in Beta's properties or states, and 41 per cent represent the broader and more dyadic interests of social psychologists.

THE INDEPENDENT VARIABLES

The Distributions

The independent variables used in our sample of social-psychological studies are listed across the top of Table 1 and their frequency distribution for 1952 and for 1960 is represented in the totals along the bottom of the table. In any study of a science the classes of independent variables are interesting because they represent the assumptions regarding the causal factors of the field or, conversely, the major manipulable sources of the variance in the dependent variables. Whereas we found it necessary to construct 14 classes of dependent variables, it was found necessary to increase this number to 23 to subsume the independent variables. In fact, 20 categories were sufficient for the 1952 sample, but 3 more had to be added for the 1960 literature. All of the dependent-variable classes are included among the independent variables (4 to 17). Three classes have been added at the beginning of the list of dependent variables, and six have been added at the end. Let us begin by making these additional classes clear.

Category 1, "Tissue or other bodily changes in Beta," refers to the use of direct material applications to some part of Beta, to the use of unconditioned stimuli as independent variables, or to brain or other damage to Beta.

Category 2, "Situation of B's action," refers to studies where the setting or situation in which Beta acts is systematically varied. Although this category is represented by only one study in 1952 and three in 1960, it is potentially a very large category for social psychology, and one in which our colleagues in sociology and anthropology are quite strongly interested. In 1952, the consistency of a subject's behavior is studied as a function of whether he is behaving in a group problem-solving situation, an interview situation, or a paper-and-pencil-test situation. Potentially, however, this category may include such empirical or theoretical distinctions as personal versus formal situations, culturally patterned versus idiosyncratic situations, frequent versus infrequent situations, situations including only Beta's peers versus those including Beta's subordinates or superiors, etc. We shall return to this category because it highlights the problems of the many languages of behavioral science and shows how far we are from a generally acceptable language for describing social stimuli.

Category 3, "Signs presented to B," refers to studies in which the independent variable involves the systematic presentation of different forms of art, music, or aspects of words. This is a more easily recognizable classification of cultural stimuli but tends to include problems of less general interest to behavioral scientists, such as "Does music calm manic depressives?" or "Do 'emotional' words require more time to be perceived than 'nonemotional' words?"

As we have mentioned before, categories 4 to 17 at the top of Table 1 are the same as those listed for the dependent variables. It might be helpful to read the phrase "a difference or change in X" for each of these categories; for the dependent variables, the phrase "predicting or changing X" should be prefixed to the name of each category.

Category 18 deals with effects of others on Beta, but is called "Alpha's instrumental or expressive acts toward Beta." It refers to studies where the independent variable involves the influence of Alpha on some aspect of Beta's states or actions. This category appears quite often in social-psychological literature and represents a major investment of the field. It is here that we find the studies on the effects of parents on the personalities of children, of "important" people on the attitudes or beliefs of "less important" people (or vice versa), and studies of the effects of personal persuasion on attitude and action. This category could be subdivided into further distinctions—influence by use of formal power versus informal power, the relation of Alpha's influence to Beta's usual attitude, physical influence versus nonphysical influence, influence by threat versus influence through more direct action, influence through rewards versus influence through punishment, etc. However, the size of the present samples does not make such distinctions useful.

Category 19, "Number of Alphas," refers to studies where the independent variable involves systematic variation of the number of others, for example, where the study concerns the effect of the number of people in a group on the speed of group problem solving. Although related to category 18, this category is kept separate because it involves the more pure parameter of number of others and because it represents a lasting, though probably relatively minor, problem of social psychology.

Category 20, "Properties of Alpha," refers to studies where the independent variable involves the systematic variation of some particular property or properties of Alpha other than directly "influencing" or "manipulative" ones. Here the sex of the experimenter is systematically varied, or a speaker is presented to the audience as having—or not having—an axe to grind. Although related to category 18, this category involves systematic variation of aspects of Alphas which do not refer to what those Alphas actually and directly do which would involve influencing or manipulating Beta.

Three new categories were required to describe the 1960 sample. Category 21, "Cultural or historical factors," includes factors which the author would choose to view as involved with the larger conditions of the culture or social structure. Category 22, "Alpha's relative position to Beta (including attitudes)," refers to studies in which the causal factor might be the fact that Alpha is superordinate to Beta or another comparable factor. Category 23, the final one, is related to category 1, but deals with explicit manipulation of hereditary factors, as in a human or animal study in which intermating has been controlled for generations.

Two facts emerge regarding the categories that are common in the lists of dependent and independent variables. First, in 1952, 12 of the 14 dependent-variable categories are also represented with other than zero frequencies as independent-variable classes; this was true of 13 out of 14 in 1960. The second fact, directly related to the first, is that 61 of the independent variables recorded in the 1952 sample fall into the same classes as were used for the dependent variables (60 in 1960). One can reasonably conclude that what is an independent variable in one study crops up as a dependent variable in other studies, and that this is not totally due to the broadness of the categories as we have defined them. It clearly indicates that there is at present no general agreement in the field as to what should properly be considered its dependent and independent variables. Further inference is hazardous. It may also mean that the field is moving toward a need for some kind of overarching model in which the distinction between independent and dependent variables is not very important, perhaps some kind of "equilibrium" model. More probably, however, it means that workers in social psychology are involved with notions of several basic processes which over-lap, rendering the dependent variables of one process (i.e., learning or being motivated) as the independent variables of another (i.e., percep-tion or judgment) and probably vice versa.

Two categories of independent variables appear most often in our sample. The first is category 4, "Validity of Beta's other states." Twenty-two out of the ninty-four independent variables fell into this category in 1952, including traits of adjustment, sex differences in Betas, mental illness categories in which Betas are placed, differences in the stability of Beta's self-image, the degree of integration of two or more aspects of Beta's personality, Beta's aptitudes, variations in other traits of Beta, and variations in his age. This category represents the personality pole of social psychology, where the assumption that great causal power resides in individual differences becomes clear. Interestingly, 12 of these 22 cases of variation in other states of Beta are related (in 1952) to as-pects of the expressive and instrumental behavior of Betas (usually in-dependently measured). This is another case of the insistence of stu-dents of personality that the importance of individual differences be recognized alongside more classical general experimental treatments of overt behavior. The sample's lack of representativeness is shown, how-ever, by the fact that Beta's cognitive processes never occur as dependent upon variation in Beta's other states, or on Beta's motives. The "new look" in perception is not represented in these 1952 studies, and is pretty well past by 1960, although three 1960 studies view B's cognitive processes as dependent upon his other states (2.5 per cent).

The second most frequent is category 18, "Alpha's instrumental or expressive acts toward Beta," or the effect of others on Beta. Thirteen of the studies have this variable as causal to a wide array of dependent variance in 1952, and sixteen have it in 1960. Alphas are reported to have influenced Beta's cognitive processes, his other states, his expressive and instrumental acts, his attitudes toward himself, his actions toward others, his attitudes toward others, his anticipations of environmental effects of his actions, and his position relative to others. This is certainly a variable which is held to have broad and important effects. It is re-lated to the most wide array of dependent categories of all the inde-pendent variables in 1952, even though it ranks second in frequency of occurrence, but this does not quite hold up in 1960.

This category is of both substantive and methodological interest to social psychologists. Substantively, it reflects the interest in procedures and effects in "socializing" the child, the adolescent, or the adult. It represents, along with some of the other categories, the interest in propagandizing activities and other forms of persuasion and education. At a higher level of abstraction, category 18 represents an interest in

the social conditions of learning, or at least in the social conditions causing changes in Beta.

This substantive interest merges into a methodological one as well—
a sensitization to experimenter-subject relationships and their effects on
the measured behavior of the subjects. It is informative to note that
social-psychological literature tends to include more explicit and careful
description of conditions of the study than do most experimental journals. There is more worry shown about the ways in which the sex,
status, commonality of language community, and other properties of
the experimenter can act to influence the results of an experiment. In
fact, these sometimes become the reason for experiments. The simple
picture of the normal human adult behaving according to implacable
laws in the old psychophysics tradition has been refined, brought closer
to everyday conditions, and rendered more complex by this interest of
social psychologists.

The third most frequent category of independent variables in 1952 is
"Beta's cognitive processes," followed closely by "Beta's motives" and
"signs presented to Beta." Among the outstandingly rare variable classes
are the "situation of Beta's action" (we will comment on this later),
"Beta's action relative to others," and "Beta's anticipation or achievement of events." Although such categories as "Beta's expressive acts,"
"Beta's actions toward others," "Beta's attitudes toward others," and
"attitudes of others toward Beta" appear infrequently, much of the
interest in such dimensions may be covered by category 18, "the influence of others on Beta."

One additional point of some general importance emerges from a
consideration of the independent variables of Table 1, and it also applies
to the dependent variables. It is that most of these variables are of a
single index kind, for the most part, using only one element of the
schematic dyad. Here is one of the interesting gaps between concept and
operations in this field—many concepts call for multioperational indexes,
but most indexes are extremely simple one-measurement affairs. The
notion, for example, of "an interact" often refers to a behavior by Beta
which was anticipated by Alpha. This implies a problem of simultaneous measurement of states or behaviors in two people. "Interaction"
often refers to a complicated sequence of interacts. Yet measurements of
interaction [such as those of Bales, 3] usually evade the multimeasure-
ment problem, merely presenting a frequency distribution of *actions* of
Beta toward Alpha, etc. Such evasions of the operational implications of
terms are not rare; one of the areas for future development probably requires a more direct confrontation of the complexities of simultaneously
indexing two persons, three persons, etc.

We can summarize the frequency distribution of independent variables in social psychology for 1952 as represented here. They are more varied than the dependent variables. A large proportion of them fall into the same categories as do the independent variables. The most frequent categories are those representing the personality pole of the field and the interpersonal influence pole, respectively. Twelve per cent of them have to do with physical- or symbolic-stimulus dimensions, 52 per cent involve changes in various state, dispositional-property, or behavior aspects of Beta (interests which social psychologists share with all psychologists but with a different emphasis). Finally, 36 per cent deal with broader ranges of the dyad, which, we suggest, gives social psychology its distinct place in psychological science.

Looking along the two bottom rows of Table 1 where the proportions of studies using the various independent-variable classes are listed, the main effect is one of surprising similarity, as was found above with the distributions of the dependent variables. In fact, any measurement of the correlation of the actual proportions would be well above chance level, even though three new categories (21, 22, and 23) were added for 1960. Two of the new categories were represented by very few studies, but 22, a "structural" category involving "Alpha's relative position to Beta (including attitudes)," contained 5 per cent of the relationships reported. Whereas one low-frequency category (9, "Beta's instrumental acts") drops out altogether, two categories with zero frequencies in 1952 come into the picture in 1960 (category 12, "Beta's acts relative to acts of others" and category 16, "Attitudes of others toward Beta").

No other change in the entire group involved more than 3.6 per cent of the papers, and probably none is worth discussing; the distribution of independent variables for the two years is practically the same.

THE INDEPENDENT-DEPENDENT RELATIONSHIPS STUDIED IN SOCIAL PSYCHOLOGY

The 1952 Distribution

Whereas the independent variables found in our sample are summarized across the bottom of Table 1, and the dependent variables are summarized in the right-hand columns, the independent-dependent *relationships* are summarized in the boxes or cells in the body of the table. Let us look first at these summary proportions for 1952 and then go on to compare the distributions for the two years under study.

The most frequently studied relationship in our sample for 1952 is that between Beta's "other states" (independent) and Beta's "expressive acts" (dependent). Yet fewer than 10 per cent of the relationships fall into this most frequent category, and the concentration quickly falls to less than 6 per cent in the next two categories that stand out—our category for validation studies and the relationship between Beta's other states (independent) and his action relative to others (dependent). The main characteristic of the distribution of relationships, therefore, is scatter or dispersion. The little concentration that occurs is probably unreliable as a basis for characterizing the field, although the most frequent category for 1952 almost retains its status in 1960 (it is tied with one other category).

Table 1 gives the impression that there are many relationships to be studied in social psychology. This is undoubtedly true. It is also true that a social psychologist interested in the relationship between attempts to influence Beta, and changes in Beta's attitudes toward others (categories 18, independent, and 10, dependent) would search the whole 1952 volume for three references. Exactly the same number of references would repay the same search in 1960! Yet this is a specialization in social psychology on which careers have been spent and will be spent in the future. In short, the dispersion of relationships shown in Table 1 tells us why specialists tend to criticize the seeming irrelevance of most social-psychological literature—most of it *is* irrelevant to any given specialty—and why growing demands for replication are so rarely met. There are probably too many new aspects of the dyad yet to be explored to do much repeating.

Analysis of Table 1 provides more interesting material when we compare the distribution of independent variables with that of the dependent variables. The most frequently studied independent-variable class—Beta's other states—is only ninth in frequency as a dependent variable, and even lower in rank in 1960. This reflects the fact that sex and age are "other states" which naturally fall only into the independent class; it also reflects the costliness and difficulty of "anchoring" traits and complex mechanisms by studying them as dependent upon earlier learning or genetic conditions. At present, these traits are measured by independent but contemporaneous operations, an a-historical emphasis that is adequate as far as it goes, but one which also tends to leave important questions unanswered.

It is also intriguing that the most frequently studied dependent variable—Beta's expressive acts—is used only once in the present sample as an independent variable and twice in 1960. This again points up experimental difficulties more than it does a lack of theoretical interest. Facial expressions are often used as independent-variable stimuli for judgments (although not in the present sample), but it is very difficult to utilize Beta's emotional behavior, varying it systematically so as to ascertain its effect on others or on Beta's own instrumental action, for example. This category (Beta's expressive action) includes, for example, certain aspects of Beta's responses to TAT cards. Doubtless, the devotees of such measures consider that what is inferrable from them determines a great deal of Beta's other behavior. But it is costly to place Betas in the different measurement situations necessary to provide the basis for inferring the effects dependent upon variation in measures of emotional behavior.

The great fluidity in the actual relationships studied in social psychology will be appreciated if we look at the cells in Table 1 that are not replicated in the two years for which we have data. Leaving out of consideration the cells generated by the three new classes of independent variables, we have 280 (14×20) cells on which we can directly compare 1952 and 1960. Only 55 of these 280 cells were occupied by at least one relationship in 1952; of these, only 23—less than half—were "replicated" by at least one relationship in 1960. Forty-four additional cells that had no inhabitants in 1952 were filled by at least one case in 1960. The number should be raised to 50 if the cells added due to the three new independent-variable classes are considered. The "mobility" is considerable, betokening the almost breathless development of this field in the last decade. It would be interesting to have comparable data for the intervening years so that some stochastic model could be applied to estimate the speed with which the cells we have used are being filled, and to provide more stable evidence for identifying the "sticky" or slow-developing areas of the field.

It is also interesting to note that the rate of shifting of interest in relationships studied is greater in the larger "social" sector of Table 1 than in the "traditional psychology sector" [i.e., the 70 cells in the upper left corner of Table 1, subsuming categories 1 to 10 (independent), and categories 1 to 7 (dependent)]. Nine of the seventeen cells of the "traditional sector" which were represented by at least one study in 1952 are also filled in 1960—53 per cent. In the remainder of the table only 14 of the 1952 total of 38 were also filled in 1960—merely 37 per cent. It is in the dyadic realm that the field of social psychology is being explored most actively and with least replication at midcentury.

The Upper and Lower Boundaries of the Field of Social Psychology

Three points of some general interest emerge from a consideration of the relationships of social psychology as displayed in Fig. 1. The first is the surprising fact that the relationships can be fitted into such a simple independent-dependent scheme at all. Of course, we occasionally worked with cases where two different classes of independent variables were viewed as impinging on one dependent class, or vice versa, as when interactions were seriously studied. We merely broke this up into two or more relationships of the independent-dependent sort. But the basic image of what a publishable research paper contains remains a single-stage independent-dependent image.

It is possible that this should not be the case. Perhaps the publications in this field should have made the content analyst's task greater by presenting him with an array of chains of operations of greater complexity so that he would have had to have tables not only of "independent-dependent relationships," but also tables of "independent-dependent-dependent" relationships or of "independent-dependent-dependent-dependent" relationships, or possibly tables of studies where chains of the complexity of "$independent_1$-$dependent_1$-$independent_2$-$dependent_2$" have been recorded, if not actually systematically varied. If we take the model of Fig. 1 seriously, such complications are not difficult to imagine.

The last kind of chain mentioned would depend on a particular theory defining the two classes of independent variables as distinguished from the dependent ones, so we will not discuss that here. But the other kind of complexity is perfectly reasonable, even in our restricted discourse. For example, if a social psychologist is interested in the impact of a new child on a family, there are processes that undoubtedly occur, such as (1) arrival of a new child (sex variation of same as independent variable), (2) affects relation of older child to mother, which (3) alters relation of older child to father, etc. Such a study might have been present in the literature, but it was not. It probably would be argued that such a study was sociological rather than social-psychological. This kind of statement is very interesting in studying a science. Why would such a study be considered "sociological" and therefore not directly part of psychological science? Is it because it goes beyond a simple dyad and involves four people instead of two? This, though arbitrary, may be the root of the problem. Or is it because it deals with a problem requiring a more complicated design than usual—where more than two classes of variables are involved? It cannot be this because the possibility of multivariable designs is as well known to psychologists as to sociologists. Then, the problem remains —why are so few long chains of operations used in these studies?

Certainly our example did not need to extend the dyad. There undoubtedly occur cases—even, possibly, processes that could be replicated and named—which involve long chains of operations and yet stay within the dyad. For example, Alpha may hit Beta intentionally or unintentionally (independent variable), whereupon Beta may strike back or not (first dependent variable), depending on how he judges (second dependent variable) his chances of winning the fight. Perhaps some of the future of social psychology lies in the interaction of such sets of variables, but the operational imagination must be extended to devise a situation where the states of all three variables can be measured. Such intervening states are too often handled purely by use of theory in all of the behavioral sciences.

The second (and possibly related) point of general import that emerges from Table 1 can be raised in the context of our example. This has to do with why, to put it concisely, Alpha strikes Beta in the first place. Social psychologists tend not to be interested, at least as far as the journal studied is concerned. Note that category 18 in the in-dependent-variable list (Alpha's instrumental acts directed toward Beta does not occur in the dependent-variable list, and that the somewhat similar category 8 (dependent), where the dependent variable involves Beta acting instrumentally toward Alpha, occurs only once. This means, in terms of our example of Alpha hitting Beta, that social psychologists are interested in the effects on Beta of the hitting by Alpha, but they are not interested in viewing Alpha's hitting as dependent upon still other conditions.

For some reason, this issue appears to demark matters psychological or social psychological from those sociological and anthropological and from the "power realm" as often studied by political scientists. Psy-chologists, in short, do not tend to study all of the problems implied in the dyadic scheme. Alpha may be a dictator, a parent, or a doctor in interaction with a Beta, who may be a citizen, a child, or a patient. Psychological interests begin with the hit committed by Alpha and end with the effect of this on Beta, by and large. But why the mother spanks Beta for defecating but not for urinating or why the dictator jails one citizen rather than another is left to other specialists in the division of labor. The determinants of Alpha's actions toward Beta are left to "culture" or "social class" or "precipitates of history" or, in the case of mothers, to whether she has been educated in child psychology or has read Spock. (This latter is occasionally studied, but more often merely postulated, by social psychologists.)

In this analysis of a division of labor, we are forced back to the notions of social or cultural structures or historical events which we have already discovered are more often used (in their simpler forms) as dependent variables than as independent ones by the social psychologists studied in our 1952 sample. But the limitation of the phrase "in their simpler forms" is a very important limitation indeed, because once a psychologist begins seriously to consider the implications of these immense and largely unexplicated notions of "social structure," "culture," or "history," then Pandora's box is open, and any attempt to restrain problems into a simple dyadic image becomes a difficult endeavor indeed. Social psychologists wish to deal with aspects of such structures and as sometimes dependent upon psychological causes, but there is as yet only a thin start toward serious integration with students of change of economic, social, and cultural structures. The situation at the time of our sample can be highlighted by pondering how reasonable it is that a psychologist and an anthropologist [31] get together to write on the effects of different child training practices. But to study how these practices came to be what they are, it is better to have two anthropologists do the job together [20].

To paraphrase a famous slogan, social psychologists study the principles of how *what* propaganda, given out by *which* propagandists, will have *what* effects on *which* consumers (Betas). But the prediction of who will give out the propaganda and what its content will be rests in the hands of the social analyst or some expert who must juggle many new and strange independent variables in his considerations.

Boundaries between fields probably always involve some inconsistencies and compromises, but social psychology may reflect these in rather extreme form. There is no doubt that two kinds of things are reflected in Table 1. On the one hand, there is the kind of social psychology which stems historically from McDougall, Freud, and others, where the task is seen as one of developing methods for uncovering the nature of Beta—his drives, instincts, mechanisms, and "other states." The line is tenuous and wandering between this emphasis and the approach of "microsociology" [Newcomb, 22], where the entities become specific and complicated bundles of "expectancies," anticipated sanctions and rewards, "institutions" of beliefs and values, "definitions of total situations" or even more complicated (and often very specific) "standing waves of behavior," role behaviors, etc. Both approaches are here in Table 1, but they are far from being integrated into a single field of science.

One final general point should be made regarding the interests reflected in Table 1. Here 132 out of the total (for both years) of 213 relationships concern either an independent or dependent variable (or both) that involves a dyadic rather than a monadic or single-individual scheme. At least 60 per cent of the sample, therefore, is "social" in this sense (61 per cent for 1952, 63 for 1960). A number of the other studies in the upper left corner of Table 1 (independent-variable columns 1 to 10, and dependent-variable rows 1 to 7) would be found to have a distinctly social flavor also if they were further analyzed. This is sharply different from the informal results we obtained in reading a sample of more purely "experimental" psychological papers, where all the studies would have fallen into the upper left corner of Table 1. Relative to experimental psychology, then, social psychology is the study of the dyad. It deals with matters relevant to two subjects at a time rather than the single subject matters of the more limited field.

But, on second thought, is this one- versus two-subject characterization adequate? It seems illuminating to consider the matter in a slightly different manner. Although experimentalists use a single-person model in their own thinking, and social psychologists a dyad, an additional person is necessary in each case. In all monadic experiments there is an experimenter who has a sex, a language, and a personality and who presents stimuli, rewards and punishes, says "right" or "wrong," etc. So also in social psychology when experiments involve two subjects.

This view leads us to suggest that whereas traditional psychology proper is at least a dyadic activity which uses a monadic model, social psychology tends to be at least a triadic activity which uses a dyadic image.

This leads to an important distinction between experimental social psychology and nonexperimental or observational social psychology. When two subjects are involved in an experiment, the experimenter systematically varies the rewards, sanctions, information sent or received, etc. When two subjects are being studied through observational or sampling designs, there may be none of this systematic variation by the experimenter; he may leave this to society or culture. Society becomes, in a sense, the third person, replacing the active experimenter, who becomes an observer or recorder. Society may be called the "norm" which operates between the two subjects, the "role structure and sanctions involved in the interaction," or the "common," "shared," or "legitimately expected" factors controlling the behavior of one or both subjects. Thus, the observational (or at least nonexperimental) approach to social psychology requires an analysis of these complex and operationally difficult matters. Perhaps the relevance or usefulness of an experimental social psychology will be evaluated in terms of the goodness of fit between the experimenter's manipulations to society's manipulations. Perhaps the real complexity of observational social psychology lies in the fact that there are four kinds of people, rather than three, playing the game: the two subjects (mother-child in relation to one another) being played upon by changing cultural fashion or social norms, plus the noise-ridden observer himself.

Although the boundaries are wavering and slippery, we can summarize our main findings in this way. Social psychology appears to be an explicitly dyadic activity which is implicitly at least triadic. It is bounded on one side by psychology proper, which is explicitly monadic (but implicitly dyadic). On the other side, it is bounded by the "broader" approaches of social science which are implied by the explicit dyadic scheme, but which are conceptualized in ways that require much more complicated models than any simple dyad. Finally, it appears that social psychology cannot escape many of the implications and findings of both of these bordering areas. Social psychology may also affect both of these bordering (and really overlapping) areas. In the long run, it may affect traditional psychology by engulfing it in an explicit rendering of the implicit dyadic general case. It may affect broader social science by assisting in the operationalizing of complex concepts, by discovering psychological sources of variance in the independent (or dependent) variables of these other sciences, or by dramatizing certain phenomena of common interest by placing prototypes of these phenomena under actual experimental control.

A COMPARISON OF THE EXPLANATORY CONCEPTS USED BY SOCIAL PSYCHOLOGISTS AND BY EXPERIMENTAL PSYCHOLOGISTS

Table 1 includes only the distribution of variables which social psychologists *attempted to measure directly* during 1952 and 1960. This leaves out an important dimension of the interests of the writers of these papers, the dimension of explanatory variables and mechanisms which, though not often directly measured, are very often invoked (along with some attendant evidence for the inference) to explain the "measured" relationships of Table 1. This third dimension might have been included in Table 1, but only at the cost of making it even more complicated by the use of symbols or color codes. Therefore we have left the matter for separate treatment. In this section we will outline the changing habits of explanation of social psychologists and compare them to the similar habits of writers in experimental psychology. In the next section we will attempt to evaluate the attendant evidence which provides the ground for these inferences of causal power or efficacy as a source of variance given to the subjects under study.

Most of the explanatory concepts in both areas of psychology are functionally similar in being intervening variables or hypothetical constructs. The organism (or person) under study is usually seen as operating to mediate or "help" to determine the relationships reported.

We have not attempted to decide the theoretical status of these inferred—or sometimes fairly directly measured—O sources, since this would be a task requiring much more information than the usual paper provides. We would have to inquire as to the writers' broader intentions to discover whether they saw the particular O source as relevant to a broader array of relationships than those discussed in their publications of 1952. We would also have to quiz them as to their assumptions of the power of the explanatory concept in linking other realms of data. Otherwise we would be making judgments in a partial vacuum. The usual research reports leave too many questions of this semipersonal nature unanswered.

Our categories of classification are therefore again drawn from Fig.

1. The numbers down the left column of Table 3 represent the corresponding numbers in Fig. 1. The categories correspond to those defined when Fig. 1 was explained earlier. We have found it possible and valuable to make use of the distinction between using an O source as an implicit response and as an implicit stimulus. We have also found it necessary to add another category in each case to find a place for cases where O sources are "used" in both ways. For example, a perceptual structuring mechanism may be invoked as something aroused by a stimulus change. Therefore, in itself it functions as a response and would be so categorized in Table 3. It may also be invoked as something which functions to arouse an affect, in which case we have categorized it as an implicit stimulus. It may be used in both these senses at once, in which case it was a very busy mechanism indeed and was placed in the relevant category, "Both 1 and 2," in Table 3. Sometimes considerable judgment is needed to make these distinctions, since they are not always formally made. Our main rule in such cases was to categorize the use of the explanatory concept only as it appeared in the study under analysis, even though we knew in some cases that the author would probably use the term in a more or less "busy" sense in other papers. This is another case of our attempt to avoid making judgments about theoretical matters which went beyond the data at hand.

The first two right-hand columns of Table 3 provide the distribution of the frequency and proportion of explanatory concepts used by social psychologists in each of the categories in 1952. The next two present the corresponding distribution from the experimental literature. The final two columns provide comparable social-psychological usage in 1960. We have already described our samples of papers for social psychology. The experimental distribution comes from an analysis of all the papers in every other issue in the 1952 volume of the *Journal of Experimental Psychology*—a total of 57 papers. Time limits preclude an analysis of the distribution of the *relationships* studied in experimental psychology, but the explanatory concepts invoked for the relationships studied were rather easily obtained because of the highly formalized and consistent presentations found in the experimental journal.

It can be seen from Table 3 that in the 1952 social-psychological papers, O sources were used 103 times, an average of 1.66 times per paper, and an average of 1.10 per relationship. It is interesting to note that 87 explanatory usages emerge from the 57 experimental papers studied, an average of 1.53 per paper. This is a surprisingly similar ratio per paper. Even though this may be affected by length of paper, amount of data per paper, level of inference attempted, complexity of inference, etc., the over-all picture does not appear to provide any clear evidence that social psychologists are less parsimonious in their use of explanatory

TABLE 3. CLASSIFICATION OF *O*-SOURCE EXPLANATIONS USED BY SOCIAL AND
EXPERIMENTAL PSYCHOLOGISTS (1952) AS COMPARED TO SOCIAL
PSYCHOLOGISTS (1960)

Category*	Classification	1952, Social		1952, Experimental		1960, Social	
		No.	Per cent	No.	Per cent	No.	Per cent
	Unknown...................	1	1.0	0	0	1	1.0
4a	Symbolic mediational processes as implicit responses.............	3	2.9	3	3.4	2	2.0
4b	Symbolic mediation processes as implicit stimulus..............	3	2.9	1	1.2	4	3.9
4c	Both 1, 2	11	10.7	5	5.8	13	12.7
5a	Affectional mediation processes as implicit response	2	1.9	0	0	1	1.0
5b	Affectional mediation processes as implicit stimulus..............	2	1.9	0	0	1	1.0
5c	Both 3, 4....................	11	10.7	3	3.4	10	9.8
6a	Motive states as implicit response	4	3.9	0	0	1	1.0
6b	Motive states as implicit stimulus.	3	2.9	1	1.2	5	4.9
6c	Both 5, 6....................	5	4.9	0	0	9	8.8
7	Other states and combinations:						
	Traits.....................	17	16.5	0	0	7	6.9
	Attitudes and values (1,2,3,4, perhaps also 5 and 6)........	7	6.8	0	0	3	2.9
	Mechanisms and processes (Freudian)................	11	10.7	0	0	13	12.7
	Mental illnesses.............	6	5.8	0	0	3	2.9
	Skills (including empathic)....	1	1.0	0	0	2	2.0
	Hypnotized state............	2	1.9	0	0	1	1.0
	Instincts...................	0	0	0	0	1	1.0
	Intelligence or other abilities...	3	2.9	1	1.2	2	2.0
	General behavior and physiological processes (or model operators).................	5	4.9	70	80.0	18	17.6
	Selective memory mechanism..	2	1.9	0	0	0	0
	Personality structure (Levinian, etc.).....................	1	1.0	0	0	1	1.0
	Group or interpersonal processes (learning, thinking, culture, etc.).....................	3	2.9	2	2.3	3	2.9
	Menstruation................	0	0	0	0	1	1.0
	Total.....................	103	100	87	100	102	100

* Category numbers drawn from Fig. 1.

concepts than experimentalists. In fact, for the 1960 social psychology distribution (far right of Table 3) the invocations per paper remain at a ratio of 1.67, but the ratio per relationship has dropped to .86, possibly a sign of increasing conceptual rigor in the field over the eight-year period.

This extreme dispersion of theoretical interest that can be seen to characterize the social-psychological literature is in marked contrast with the distribution for the experimental journal. In the latter, 80 per cent of all the inferences fall into our category "General behavior and physiological processes (or model operators)." Only a scattering of perception papers—10.4 per cent in categories 4a, 4b, and 4c—and a few studies of affectional processes such as fear or anxiety provide any overlap with the social literature. It is almost humorous to note that, with all this difference in distribution, there is an almost equal use of group-thinking or cultural processes as explanatory mechanisms in the two samples for 1952.

At least two implications of general import may be made from these distributions of theoretical interests. First, even though social psychologists share empirical interests with sociologists and anthropologists, they do not share theoretical interests. In only 2.9 per cent of the cases for both years are nonindividual entities used as explanatory devices. The "group mind" has been generally ruled out in this sample of studies. There can be little wonder that sociologists and other social scientists feel that microsociology will be little served by such theory as social psychologists use, and that they must develop their own, a sociological social psychology which shares sociology's habits of explanation. We have argued above that there is real overlap in interests between social psychologists and sociologists, but it is apparent that a *rapprochement* is to be found mainly at the operational measurement level, and not at the theoretical. Our sample of social psychology literature probably dramatizes this difference in a somewhat unreliable manner. In any case, the moral is clear; social psychologists remain psychologists in their theory, by and large, and relate to others mainly through sharing dependent and independent variables with them.

This may be due to the fact that theories, like child training practices (and this is more than an analogy) change more slowly than other aspects of the culture of a science. It may also mean that, in the intellectual conflicts between broader social sciences and this presumably interstitial area of social psychology, we are experiencing the stress that occurs just before peace is restored. Surely, as empirical interests continue to overlap more and more, theoretical ones cannot lag forever. Certainly, since 1952 and before, attempts at theoretical integration have been made. If we take our present evidence seriously, however, we had best evade integration for a while and accept the more realistic aim of intertranslation through the use of shared independent and dependent variables and press for increased commonality of method and fact in interdisciplinary courses rather than for theoretical integration. Perhaps it is as hard to give up a theory as to give up a bond of identification with a favored parent. If so, we must learn to ignore our parents a bit when trying to make or keep new friends.

The second implication of Table 3 concerns the relationship of social psychologists[2] habits of explanation to those of the 1952 experimentalists. The total overlap of interest is only, at maximum, 25 per cent with the classification used here. As we will see below, this is somewhat an overstatement, but it is still a rather large and important fact. Social psychologists' habits of explanation are, though diverse in themselves, almost as different from those of experimental psychologists as they are from those of sociologists. Therefore, social psychology cannot be viewed as more specialized than the other or as an applied field in relation to experimental psychology, except to some extent in method (which we will discuss below). It ranges more widely in its independent, dependent, and intervening variables, and, despite overlap with experimental psychology, it does not see the relationships studied as special cases of the general processes studied by experimentalists. The moral here is the same as in the case of the relationship to sociology—the overlap of interest is greatest in the realms of what is measured. The extreme divergence in theoretical habits may also stem from the historical fact of different sources of personal identification.

There is a great deal of similarity in the distributions for the two years of social-psychological literature. It appears, then, that our conceptual scheme has reflected considerable stability in the "intervening" variables as well as the independent and dependent variables, despite the rather wild fluctuation in the actual relationships under study. There is some interesting change over the eight years, however. Note that the proportion of usages of motive states as *both* stimulus and response (6c) almost doubles in the 1960 sample. This reflects the interest in a little matter called "need achievement" and a stimulating notion known as "cognitive dissonance," which was merely a little cloud on the horizon when the present writer began this analysis a few years ago.

It is interesting to note two other major changes and a couple of minor ones over the eight-year span. The use of traits as explanatory entities dropped from 16.5 to a mere 6.9 per cent in this period, despite the fact that they retained pretty much their interest as independent and dependent variables (see Table 1). The other large shift in Table 3 is in general behavior and physiological processes, which grew in usage from 4.9 to 17.6 per cent over the near-decade. Perhaps (and this is the present writer's strong impression) scientific analysis in this field (and other areas of psychology) has advanced in developing what was intervening into something well enough measured to be independent or dependent. Perhaps there has been some improvement in social-psychological measurement, permitting analysis to peel away at man somewhat as one works at an onion. The writer wishes to report exactly such an eerie sensation on surveying the 1960 literature. We could explain the other shifts in Table 3 as well. Freudian mechanisms and cognitive processes have increased in use in 1960, attitudes have dropped (only as intervening matters), and mental illnesses, though still studied, are not studied as intervening matters. In short, the abstraction ladder is being ascended as measurement improves. We can only hope that "generality" is also increasing.

Having commented on the differences in interest between social psychologists and other students of man, let us comment on the similarities as well. Many social scientists do not look to social psychology as a handmaiden for their disciplines, nor do they expect social psychologists to share their theoretical interests or to compete with them. They often expect, however, that some particular problem will be solved by social psychologists—a problem such as how values are developed or internalized in the individual, or what classes of personality dimensions might conceivably affect rate of suicide, entrepreneur development, or rate of birth in a society. Seen from this reasonable perspective, social psychologists appear to be going about their business in a reasonable fashion. We have already noted their heavy interest in personality. They are unquestionably also deeply interested in the problem of motivation— though not necessarily in the way that any particular sociologist might desire. A general interest in the affectional and motivational side of the human being pervades the social-psychological literature. The trait names used, the affective component in attitudes and values, the motivational overtone in all Freudian mechanisms, and the affectional component in most diagnoses of mental illness—all can be viewed as dealing with motivation in the broad sense usually intended by sociologists and anthropologists. Viewed in this way, 73 per cent of all the explanatory attempts by social psychologists in 1952 are motivational. A similar collapsing of categories (including that of some of the general behavior processes) shows only 28 per cent of such invocations by experimentalists, pointing up a division of labor in psychology itself. With such an emphasis on motivation and personality, social psychology provides a service for other social scientists; in doing so, it retains the heavy motivational stamp placed upon it by such important theorists as Freud, Allport, Tolman, Miller, Dollard, Festinger, McClelland, and, above all, by McDougall. With regard to the last, however, it should be pointed out that Mc-

Dougall's category "Instincts" is, as such, completely empty for 1952 in Table 3, but has crept shyly back by 1960.

The most surprising fact in Table 3 is that 80 per cent of all the O-source inferences made by experimentalists fell into the category "General behavior and psychological processes." This class deserves a more refined breakdown, and this is presented in Table 4. The two most frequent subcategories in the table serve to highlight the criteria used in defining the total category. Nearly one-third of the total of the table are included in "Inhibition (including fatigue)" and "Generalization mechanism or gradients," two of the relatively refined and central mechanisms or processes of general behavior theory, particularly in the theoretical language of Hull.

TABLE 4. CLASSIFICATION OF INTERVENING GENERAL BEHAVIOR PROCESSES INVOKED BY EXPERIMENTALISTS

General behavior processes invoked	Number of invocations
"Learning" (usually "bonds" implied)	5
"Latent learning"	1
Inhibition (including fatigue)	12
Drive—primary	2
Drive—secondary (including "learned cathexes")	4
Habit strength (including S-R association or bond)	5
Expectancy, anticipation	2
Generalization mechanism or gradients	10
Discrimination mechanism	2
Response-produced phenomena	5
Change in muscle strength	1
Extinction mechanism	1
Goodness of form	1
Reinforcement mechanism—primary	2
Reinforcement mechanism—secondary (including knowledge of results)	3
Subjective standards (including scales, adaptation level, etc.)	5
Memory (perceptual or other)	1
Peripheral mechanisms	2
Threshold phenomena	2
Spontaneous recovery	1
Differential pacing	1
Goal gradient	1
Attention	1
Total	70

The remainder of the list reads like a thorough list of Hull's theoretical constructs, with a scattering of gestalt, Guthrian, and Tolmanlike terms. It gives, in fact, a fairly reasonable picture of what on other grounds seemed to be going on in experimental psychology in 1952. This makes all the more clear the difference in habits of inference between the writers in the two journals.

One might think that *rapprochement* between these two areas of psychological science might be gained by viewing these general behavior processes as genuinely and more objectively *general* than the mechanisms and traits invoked by social psychologists. Such might be the argument of some serious students of the experimental or physiological branches of psychology, suggesting hopefully that the very generality of such mechanisms as expectancies, habit strengths, discrimination mechanisms, response-produced phenomena, or goodness of form, or even cell assemblies will assure their eventual triumph in the free competition of theoretical subject-variance constructs. This may be true, and there is some evidence in the 1960 data that there may be such a trend, but the interpretation here depends in part upon the degree of generality that is stated or assumed by the writers of the social-psychological papers under review. In Table 5 we have categorized the social psychology papers in terms of the

TABLE 5. GENERALITY LEVEL AIMED AT BY 1952 SOCIAL PSYCHOLOGY PAPERS, IN PER CENT

Strictly limited to sample	5
At least social-group-wide	8
At least culture-wide, sex-wide, or illness-wide	13
General theory, probably valid across cultures	71
Unclassified	3

generality level stated or assumed. Seventy-one per cent of the papers fall into the class where the organism source of variance and also the relationship reported is at least assumed to be part of "General theory, probably valid across cultures."

This means to us that there is extreme resistance to viewing the varied theoretical interests of social psychologists as any more limited or applied or theoretically unimportant than those of any other branch of pure, generalizing science. We suggest that this resistance should be faced and accepted as a matter of fact. If one argues that threshold phenomena, generalization gradients and reinforcement mechanisms are in various senses operating in all behavior everywhere, the answer will be "Yes, but everyone has a superego, everyone has some aggressive tendencies, and sociogenic motives or social norms and values are also ubiquitous." If it is then said that a superego and a social norm and aggressive motives are extremely complex and unanalyzed entities over which it is extremely difficult to obtain experimental control or conceptual clarity, then the reply is likely to be "Yes, but there are other means of control and other designs for studies. Furthermore, discrimination mechanisms look just as complicated and conceptually murky from another point of view."

Interestingly, in such an argument experimental and social psychologists share an important assumption with which other behavioral scientists often disagree. It is that generality of theory can be discovered by a general hypotheticodeductive method, based on a limited induction. The present writer believes that psychologists, among behavior scientists, stand somewhat apart in this tendency toward generality in descriptive and theoretical language. Right or wrong, sociologists are happy to be able to describe or explain one class or society at a time. To many economists, a clear theory of Norwegian economy as a partly unique historical product is general enough. Anthropologists amass immense arrays of descriptive fact for just the Navaho Indians, hoping to see the general parameters of cultural systems emerge from this and many other case studies. Psychologists, however, study the behavior of organisms, the personality of man (and woman), or, flatly, small-group processes. The dogged and hopeful pursuit of insights that arise from induction sometimes runs head on into an equally dogged pursuit, the aim of which is the systematic probing of the implications of general theory. The meeting may be stormy, particularly if the "inductive" groups are really harboring notions of implicit but *eventually* general theory around which the search is organized.

THE EMPIRICAL STATUS OF ORGANISM INFERENCES IN SOCIAL PSYCHOLOGY

In the section above we have outlined the kinds of causal factors social psychologists see as operating in the subjects they study, and have compared the distribution of these causal organism factors with those used by some experimental psychologists. Such an analysis leaves out, as we have noted above, the logical status of such factors, that is, whether they have been introduced *post hoc,* whether they are conceived as having implications for other realms of data, whether or not they are conceived as having an independent status in some other realm than that of behavior, such as in a physiological scheme, a phenomenological or introspective scheme, or in some particular scheme of mathematical operators. We do not feel that the lack of analysis along these dimensions can be remedied, for reasons stated above. We simply do not know enough about the intentions of the writers of the papers in our sample.

We can, however, provide an analogous kind of analysis in the empirical realm. Here the focus is on empirical elegance or lack of it rather than on logical elegance. The notion of empirical elegance is a matter of considerable complexity, and it is also a frankly evaluative notion in large part. We must, therefore, make clear the dimensions of evaluation which underlie the categories which will be employed.

Briefly, we feel that the more there is empirical control over the source of variance in the organism, the less there is chance of error in designating the source as in the subject at all, and the less the error in *naming* the source, at least for the data immediately reported. Further, the more independent bases that can be presented as foundations for the inference, the less the chance of error. That is, the same thing is better seen from several vantage points than from one. Finally, the more that the name given to the inferred state or process has been validated, the less the chance of error. In this case we use the term *validated* to refer to checks on the further implications that arise because of the particular terms used to name the source, whether these are formal implications or implications arising from consideration of everyday usage of the name given to the source.

For example, let us consider the inference to intelligence as a causal organism source of variance. Most inferences would be less inelegant if the reporter had shown that the intelligence of subjects could be varied, or at least—though this is less impressive—if he could predict such variation from antecedent factors (either genetic or experiential) or from variation of statable stimulus factors (including motivational or other states). Further, an inference to intelligence as causal is more reliable if more than one source of the inference is used. One intelligence test is probably as good as two or three, since they are often validated in terms of one another, but independent validation in terms of protocols derived from direct observation of everyday problem solving would provide a further valuable basis for inference. This dimension of number of inference bases interacts with the first dimension of displayed control of variation. That is, variation in intelligence indexed in two independent ways provides a sounder inference than the same variation measured in only one way (unless, of course, the intent of the researcher is to generalize within only one measurement method). Finally, if "intelligence" is intended as referring to the everyday use of the term, then validation of the implications of the term in different situations would clearly make the inference more elegant empirically.

To many social scientists, one of the main dimensions of the empirical status of a study is the adequacy of the sampling. We do not consider this in our present analysis because we view sampling as a secondary criterion of vital practical import rather than serious analytic import. In addition, social psychologists do little more than report what sampling, if any, was done, and often have to guess what the population really was. Most studies report measurement methods and relationships which *should* apply to clearly statable populations, but the actual application is rarely achieved. These statements apply, of course, only to the basis of organism inferences—not to the empirical status of the relational propositions reported in the studies. There sampling often becomes crucial theoretically as well as practically.

The dimensions along which we chose to judge the empirical status of the major organism inferences in each of the papers are built into the 11 categories of Table 6. These categories grew out of an originally more a priori analytic set. They form a rough qualitative scale, the first representing less elegance, the eleventh representing high elegance: a rare kind of study in any branch of psychology. In category 11 there is a combination of high control over the variance source with more or less continuous independent indexing from at least one reference point other

TABLE 6. STATUS OF INFERENCE OF THE MAJOR SOURCE OF VARIANCE IN THE INDIVIDUALS STUDIED BY SOCIAL PSYCHOLOGISTS IN 1952 AND 1960

Inference of sources of variance	Number of papers	
	1952	1960
1. Merely named, or assumed, or some face validity in items is claimed	3	0
2. Named and cross-tabulated with items of similar form, measured same time (some theory)	9	1
3. Named, clinical judgment involved in the independent index	4	1
4. Named and independently indexed (not clinically)	3	7
5. Validation study—no other independent variables	8	1
6. Named, index (independently or not) "validated"	13	16
7. Named, subject "changed" using statistical controls (not independently indexed)	2	8
8. Named, subject "changed," using self as control (not independently indexed)	13	10
9. Named, subject changed with regard to intervening variable, independently indexed	2	15
10. Named, consequently validated, antecedently "anchored," with help of theory	2	1
11. Named, manipulated through antecedents, independently indexed (or could be assumed on basis of previously discovered empirical laws)	2	0
Unclear or unknown	0	1
Total	61	61

than the dependent measures themselves. Let us clarify these and all the other categories by further discussion and by giving actual examples from the 1952 sample.

The first and least empirically elegant category contains papers where the subject is seen as partially causal in some sense and where this causal factor is "merely named, or assumed, or some face validity in questionnaire items is claimed." The studies in this class can be exemplified by an intriguing relationship which is shown between the social-class position of Beta and the time covered from start to final action in Beta's thematic-apperception-test stories. Middle-class children's stories cover more time than do those of lower-class children. This relationship is viewed as due to differences in the children at the time of measurement. This source of difference is viewed as an aspect of superego, resulting from differential child training practices (not measured). The dimension of superego is not independently measured, but this is merely assumed as operative. Its empirical status in this single study is, however, not elegant.

The second category included studies where the source of variance in the subject is given a name on the basis of an item in a questionnaire or test and where a weak form of check on the naming of the item is made by cross-tabulating it with other similar items, the responses to which were recorded at the same time. In these studies the validation is open to criticism concerning response sets and other sources of bias, and the accuracy of the name given to the source in the subject has a large latitude for error. We can exemplify this group of papers by one in which an interesting empirical relationship is reported, showing a difference between the contents of the reported daydreams of men and the contents of the daydreams of women. The source of this difference in content is viewed as a difference by sex in "demand strengths," which the daydreams are seen as reflecting. Unfortunately, some of the operations involved in this study were left out in favor of the theoretical analysis of Freud's theory of dreams, but it is implied that an independent demonstration of these differential demand strengths was or could be made, showing, for example, that the women had higher demand strengths for personal attractiveness, whereas the men had higher demand strengths for vocational achievements. We presume that this was done by means of a questionnaire—an operation very similar to that used in obtaining the data from the daydreams.

The third category is very similar to the fourth, and, in fact, is merely a special group of studies where an attempt is made to provide an independent index of the subject source of variance by the use of clinical or other "expert" judges of one kind or another. In one study, for example, the different levels of anxiety of subjects were studied in their relation to the speed of conditioning and extinction of the galvanic skin response. Independent measures of the anxiety level were attempted with tests and also by the use of complicated clinical ratings. We separate out these attempts at independent indexing because they rest in part upon the often reliable but problematic use of expert judgments where the cues used by the experts are often difficult to explicate. They are a less clear, and therefore possibly less elegant, basis for inferring the organism source of variance.

The fourth category includes cases where the source of variance in the subjects is named and where a clear attempt at an independent index based on something other than clinical judgment is reported. A clear example of this is a study where the prejudice of restaurant owners was studied by first asking them by letter whether they would serve a Negro customer, then by a telephone call, and finally by facing the proprietor with an actual Negro customer. However else this study may be interpreted, it at least shows a strong attempt to get independent measures of the prejudice or discriminatory tendencies of the proprietors. The fact that each step showed less discrimination on the part of the proprietors is our reason for considering this matter of the number of bases for inference as important. The differences in the prejudice found provide a basis for limiting in a useful way the generality of any given measurement base and also give an inductive basis for trying to theorize about the complex matter of situation as an independent variable.

Our fifth category is placed near the middle of the scale because it is a special category of study altogether. It includes studies which have validation of subject-source measures as their main purpose, and, in fact, these studies rarely include any attempt to display any empirical relationship other than that between the two measures of the "same" thing. They are first steps in the direction of studying the conditions for the occurrence of the named sources. For example, in one study a major aspect involved an attempt to validate a test which is supposed to measure the typical direction in which a child tends to display aggression, e.g., toward others as compared to toward himself. The assumption is made that problem children (who are in a guidance clinic) are more frustrated than nonproblem children and are therefore more prone to aggress outwardly. It is shown that, according to the test, there is in fact a higher frequency of what is called "extropunitive" aggression in the case of problem children. Scores on the test and the "problem versus nonproblem" status of children help in making the inference of the direction tendencies more intelligible. This kind of validation—conceptual validation—leans heavily on theory or on other facts (such as the greater frustrations that might be shown in the case of problem children) in order to make the interpretation reasonable. This class also includes other validation attempts that are more direct.

The sixth category includes studies where measures of sources of organism variance are used where some *previous* validation work is referred to—studies for which those in category 5 are, so to speak, preludes. These studies usually involve more complex designs than those in category 5, attempting to show some substantive relationship with the measure which has been validated. Since some category 5 studies also attempt to show substantive relationships, while at the same time provide validation for the measure, it was a matter of judging the degree to which the substantive relationship was being used for validating the organism-source inference that kept the study in category 5 instead of category 6. Examples of category 6 studies include a number where some trait or attitude is measured, using a more or less standardized test which has been to some degree validated on populations similar to those studied in the present research report.

In all of the studies in categories 1 to 6 there is no attempt made to change the inferred state of the subjects, but merely to measure such states in one or more ways. Beginning with category 7, we find increasing emphasis on statistical or other *changes* in these states which function to provide further checks on the inference itself.

In category 7 fall a few studies in which the source of variance in Beta was named and where it was changed through the use of statistical controls. In these studies, however, there was no attempt at independent indexing of the named organism source. In one case, for example, the empirical relationship is that between the time it takes Beta to make a choice under various audience conditions, such as an audience present and seen, present and not seen, not present. The inference is to the action of "restraining forces" working in Beta to differing degrees depending upon the audience conditions. The same Beta is not studied under all of the varying conditions, but the statistical design was arranged to make up for this lack as much as possible. There is an attempt, then, to so change the audience conditions that, according to the fairly explicit theory used, the restraining forces in the subjects would vary so as to achieve predictable changes in the time required to make decisions.

Category 8 encompasses the more empirically elegant studies where the attempt to change the named states of the subjects is done "actually" with the same Betas rather than through the use of statistical controls, but, unfortunately, with no attempt at any independent measure of the state of the subject. An example may clarify this state of affairs regarding the organism source of variance. In one careful experiment an inference is made to an "opinion" state of the subjects as mediating answers on a questionnaire. A second measure of the state is taken on the same subjects after they have been given experimental treatments, such as being made suspicious of a speaker who attempts to change the opinion state. Predictions are made, and upheld, of the degree of change in the opinion state as a function of these other (independent) factors. Despite the fact that this control over the inferred opinion state is more elegant than other forms, it is less elegant than some because no attempt is made to independently index either the opinion state or the suspicion state. Several items on a questionnaire were used in evaluating the opinion state, but since they were all answered at one time, these several measures can hardly be viewed as being very independent from one another. The measurement of the controlled change in the opinion state is by no means ideal, of course, since it is only intermittently measured rather than continuously.

In category 9 fall two studies in which the source of variance in the subject is not only named and the subject changed in this regard, but in which there is also an attempt at independent indexing of the changing state. This relatively elegant empirical state of affairs occurs, for example, in a study in which a Beta's initial hostility toward an Alpha is indexed; it is then increased through having Alpha insult Beta, then is further controlled by way of either permitting or not permitting Beta to retaliate to the insult. Two measures of the aggression state of Beta were used, a more or less continuous measure derived from the aggressive content of freely written communications from Beta to Alpha, and a subsequent measure by asking Beta whether he would like to continue writing such communications. The Betas who were permitted to retaliate to the insult were happy to quit, whereas those who were not given an opportunity to retaliate desired to continue sending messages. This more or less independent index of Beta's anger state helps clarify the basic inference from the continuous measures.

Category 10 includes two studies which, though not involving control of the inferred source of variance in the Betas, achieve considerable empirical elegance by the use of validated tests to infer the state on the consequent side, and also anchor the inference by a use of theory and certain objective facts on the antecedent side. Despite the lack of direct control on the state, the total picture that emerges of the conditions for the development of the state and its exemplification in many ways is quite elegant. In one study the trait of leadership is invoked to explain the behavior of some college women. On the consequent side it is inferred from a wide array of tests in addition to the fact of holding elected office in a college group. Those women who were high on this trait, as compared to those who were low, were then studied to discover the family position of the girls which would lead to a high condition of this state. The preponderance of younger siblings being present in the family of the high-leadership girls and the presence of more brothers are interpreted as providing the conditions for development of the trait. It is the convergence of a number of bases of inference of different kinds, plus the coherence of the findings theoretically, that gives this study empirical elegance.

In category 11, we return to the control criterion, but add the criterion of manipulation of the state of the subject through antecedents, i.e., from the state's theoretical inception. The distinction here is difficult, but these studies provide a more clear basis for the inference because they do not start with a pretest measure of an already developed state

(as in categories 8 and 9) but use a pretest measure where, in a theoretically important sense, the state does not exist. It is not particularly
surprising that the two studies that fall into this class are a classical and
an operant conditioning study, respectively. The classical conditioning
study was done using human subjects and will serve as our example.
In this case the inference is to a state of strength of conditioning in subjects who had previously never had this state. The pretest shows no
depression of heart rate to a tone. This depression of heart rate to tone
is then achieved by pairing the to-be-conditioned tone to the sufficient
stimulus of shock. Once the "new state" has become theoretically relatively stable through repeated pairings of tone and shock, then the independent factors are used to study their relative effect on speed of
extinction of the state itself.

The empirically impressive things here are the presence of a fairly
continuous independent physiological measure of the inferred state, plus
the fact that the state is not present until the experimenter begins work.
In this particular case, no independent index of the state is provided,
but the empirical and theoretical background of the problem is such
that a number of such indexes could be referred to in the literature.

It is interesting to note that the empirical status of even the best
inference is far from absolute—there is no empirical basis which will
force a reader to accept the name given to the inferred source. This re-
turns us to the problems of the broader criteria by which any inference of
this kind must finally be judged, such as fruitfulness and theoretical
elegance, which are topics we have not dealt with here.

It should be emphasized that the kind of evaluation that is made
in Table 6 is an extremely limited one. There is no implication that the
papers included in the "better" categories near the bottom of the table
are the more fruitful or useful to the field of social psychology at the present
time or in 1952. A study that provides only face validity for an inference
on a single index with no control at all may, for other reasons not
judged here, prove by far to be the most important paper. We have
explicated here some classes which reflect a technical empirical type of
elegance, giving a distribution of the studies being analyzed with regard
to these limited aspects of the status of control over an important class
of variables. We have already shown that social psychologists have other
interests besides making elegant measures of "intervening" states—they
are exploring a wide range of other classes of relationships as well. To a
man who is trying to measure the effects of the naturally occurring "role
sanctions" on overt behavior in small groups, for example, criticism in
the terms presented in Table 8 might seem somewhat irrelevant and
carping, because he has many more aims and worries than merely trying
to be elegant in his organism inferences.

A number of general points emerge from considering the distribution of the studies as shown in Table 6. One way, for example, of defining an experimental psychology is to consider the interest displayed in controlling the inferred states of the subjects under study. Such an interest is clearly reflected in 19 of the 61 papers studied here—roughly one-third. As of 1952, then, social psychology cannot by this definition be termed a nonexperimental branch of psychology, and by 1960 the proportion has risen to 56 per cent.

The issue of attempts at validating inferences to the subjects as a source of variance is an intriguing one. It is interesting to note that of the 30 per cent of all the 1952 papers that strive for control through change of the subject source, only one in category 11 and two in category 9 *also* show attempts to obtain independent indexing—barely 16 per cent. Of all the other papers, however, where control through change is not attempted, 30 out of the 42, or about 70 per cent, show definite attempts at independent indexing (all of categories 3, 4, 5, 6, and 10). This leaves out of consideration, possibly unfairly, the papers which were placed in categories 1 and 2. Certainly the papers in category 2 show some attempts in this direction, and if we had attempted to evaluate the adequacy of the theory by way of which conceptual validation was attempted, the proportion would rise.

There appear, then, to be two relatively independent criteria for achieving a check on subject inferences—experimental control on the one hand, independent indexes on the other. Although obviously involved with both of these, the 1952 distribution in Table 6 tends toward the latter. This probably reflects the emphasis we have already shown on traits and other states as intervening variables. Many social psychologists are interested in the states and personality mechanisms that are suggested by the rich language of everyday discourse. And out of everyday thinking grows a criterion that if one individual is described, for example, as more aggressive than another, the designation must be upheld by some additional means of proof or it will be considered merely "calling names."

Among the most important things that this essay has to point out is that the 1960 distribution is different in this respect. There has been a significant shift toward studies which involve control through change; there has also been some re-righting of the emphasis by adding independent indexes along with, or in addition to, the use of control through experimentally induced change. This can be seen particularly in growth of category 9 from 2 papers in 1952 to 15 (nearly one-fourth of the total) in 1960. This may betoken the emergence of a science where the wisdom of the "testers" is integrated with that of the experimenters.

It is intriguing to consider why those who control the subject states through change often feel that they can ignore independence of indexing. Perhaps it is because the psychophysical experiment and the operant and respondent conditioning experiments happen to be more easily replicable and therefore more cumulative, in that one study, done with a single index, can gain seeming independence of indexes by referring to past studies which obviously apply to the present study as well. If this is the assumption, it needs testing. Such an assumption, even if true, also raises the problem of representative design, since easy replicability and seeming cumulativeness may be purchased at the price of some irrelevance as far as "representativeness" is concerned. Only with designs where the subject source of variance is studied both with control through variation and with independent indexing, *plus* adequate sampling of actual life conditions, can all these worries be dealt with. Perhaps some of the future of social psychology lies in developing more of such designs.

Many studies in both years make an effort to provide evidence for an organism inference by attempting to change the thing inferred in a short-run experiment. This is all to the good, but it reflects the general a-historical *methodological* bias of the field as a whole. It is cheaper and neater to do studies on the entities that *can* be changed in a short-run experiment. Perhaps the growth of category 9 has an added meaning in that it shows that people in this field have begun to find a new design in which (as in many "need-achievement" studies) the entity inferred can be changed to a small degree in short studies, but in which its habitual level can be independently measured, and that measure itself can be related by *other* kinds of studies to the long-run (and generally unmanipulable) conditions of human or animal development. In this way elegant research can be done not only on things where such designs are easy, but also on the more intransigeant and possibly powerful well-springs of action as well.

THE OPERATIONAL SKILLS OF SOCIAL PSYCHOLOGISTS

In describing the field of social psychology we have so far focused upon the variables which people in this area have tried to measure, manipulate, or control, the conceptual tools they utilize, and the manner in which they try to assure themselves that their inferences are reasonable. This has left out most of the information on the actual activities through which these attempts are made, and we now turn to this aspect. It is valuable for teaching new social psychologists as well as for increasing our understanding of the problems of the field to see the skills represented in the studies of our sample.

A classification of the skills or operations involved in the 122 studies under analysis is presented in Table 7. This table can be viewed as outlining what the ideal social psychologist needs to be able to do, or at least understand, in order to read and evaluate the literature in his field for a year.

TABLE 7. CLASSIFICATION OF THE OPERATIONS USED BY SOCIAL PSYCHOLOGISTS
IN SAMPLES OF PAPERS FOR 1952 AND 1960, IN PER CENT

A. Dealing with physical or cultural stimuli:
   1. Manipulating physical stimulus dimensions or patterns 17
   2. Manipulating verbal, pictorial, musical, etc., stimuli 44
   3. Preparing and/or administering questionnaires 56
   4. Administering "standardized" tests 44
B. Dealing with social stimuli:
   5. "Setting the stage" for social interaction to occur 25
   6. Arranging social situations so as to present tasks to S's 30
C. Dealing with subjects:
   7. Manipulating S's "set" through verbal or other means 27
   8. Manipulating success, rewards, punishments for S's 18
D. Dealing with responses or actions:
   9. Collecting verbatim records of interaction 11
  10. Taking latency, frequency or relearning measures 31
  11. Content analysis of symbolic response materials 23
  12. Obtaining judgments from experts 15
  13. Obtaining judgments from S's peers or other "laymen" 12
  14. Taking threshold and accuracy measures 19
E. Dealing with data:
  15. Analyzing responses to tests and questionnaires 73
F. Dealing with officials:
  16. Obtaining information from public or semipublic sources 7

We have used 16 empirically derived categories in Table 7. For each category we present the percentage of the papers which report that this operational skill was required. To facilitate reading, we have placed the categories in certain general groupings.

Our first general group refers to operations "dealing with physical or cultural stimuli." The most frequently needed skills in this group concern preparing and administering questionnaires. Then come the skills involved in administering standardized tests and the manipulation of various meaningful stimuli. Over one-third of all the papers call for these skills. The lore of the questionnaire is apparently vital to the social psychologist, as is knowledge of psychological tests. The skills of the sensory or perception psychologists in developing and presenting physical stimuli are also called for in 17 per cent of the papers, however. The skills of the complete social psychologist run a wide range with regard to stimuli.

The second general group of skills has to do with the arranging of actual social situations. A fourth of the papers call for "setting the stage for social interaction to occur"—getting people of different opinions together, or getting two people angry with one another. In addition, 30 per cent of the papers call for "arranging social situations" so as to present tasks to subjects in order to study how they solve the tasks. This may involve merely getting a group together and giving its members a task, or it may involve the more subtle skills of providing subjects with a successful group experience and an unsuccessful one, so that the task of judging preference can be studied.

Interestingly, there is a preponderance of questionnaires which often present social situations to subjects symbolically, as compared with actual social situations. A questionnaire which asks a subject what he would do or has done in a given social situation is certainly prepared with less cost and effort than would be required to present the actual social situation itself. Whether symbolically presented situations are adequate as replacements for actual situations is one of the oldest and most difficult methodological problems in social psychology. Its solution may depend upon the development of greater skill and assurance in the construction and systematic manipulation of actual situations, or in the development of better participant-observation techniques for recording what a subject does in natural settings. The solution of this conflict between the questionnaire approach and the experimental-small-groups approach may also depend upon developing explicit theory to help in the translation between the one kind of stimulus and the other (a problem on which progress can be documented by 1960).

Under category C, "Dealing with subjects," we record that 27 per cent of the studies involve the manipulation of a subject's "set" or anticipations, and that 18 per cent call for actual manipulations of some form of rewards and punishments for the subjects under study. These percentages seem to reflect the difficulties of these operations and the extremely touchy personal and ethical problems involved in administering to volunteer subjects the kinds of rewards and punishments that actual life is constantly administering. There appears to be a discrepancy between theory and research in these relatively low proportions.

It may be that the sanctions which teachers (and most researchers in this field are teachers) are permitted to manipulate, largely the cognitive feedback of "right" or "wrong," are too weak and unrepresentative of the buffetings of real life to be really adequate for the task. This has always been a problem in behavior science as well as in medical science, and depends in part for its solution on the trust and status given the researcher by the larger society. Physicians can now systematically give or withhold possibly beneficial drugs or palliatives for research purposes. It may be a long time before social psychology will be granted equal freedoms. Until that time arrives researchers can only fall back upon animal studies or become more clever in being present with measurement devices when more powerful sanctions are being legitimately used. Fraternities still turn some hopefuls down, employers fire workers for various reasons, students are asked to leave college, and people are continually dying and friends are grieving for them. Fortunately, the more positive and happy aspects of these things also occur, and if social psychologists can learn to be there in an acceptable way, more representative measurements will be taken.

Category D includes six different subcategories that have to do with obtaining or measuring responses or actions. It is a bit surprising to note that 31 per cent of the papers call for the use of the skills of the laboratory learning psychologist in reporting latency, frequency, and relearning measures. Skills of the perception laboratory are called for in the 19 per cent of the papers that report threshold and accuracy measurements. The methods of social science that overlap with methods of work in the broader humanities, i.e., the content analysis of symbolic materials, are called for in 23 per cent of the papers. The subtle problems of obtaining expert or nonexpert judgments, usually involving complex scaling procedures, are strongly represented.

Most surprising of all in this list is the tiny 11 per cent of papers which involve the collection of verbatim records of social interaction. In terms of what we have said above about the tendency to avoid experimental manipulation of sanctions, it is not a positive finding about the status of this field that the other two routes available for this kind of information, systematic observation and animal study, appear to be somewhat avoided in this otherwise extremely diverse field.

Category E reports that 73 per cent of the papers call for the statistical or quasi-clinical skills involved in analyzing responses to tests and questionnaires. Finally, in Category F we note that 7 per cent of the papers call for the more characteristically anthropological skills of knowing whom to see and how to deal with public or semipublic sources in order to obtain information.

In summary, certain general statements about this aspect of the behavior of social psychologists can be made. First, there is no doubt that social psychology, like psychology in general, is a field where people collect their own primary data. Compared to fields like economics, which rests so heavily on basic facts collected by various public agencies, social psychologists must have at their disposal the skills and operations of a basic-data-generating science.

Second, the range of skills which an ideal social psychologist needs to have at his disposal is very wide indeed, covering most of the methods and skills of psychology. We have pointed out that the conceptualizing habits of social psychologists are broad. We have also pointed out that the range of variables studied and of relationships attempted is not only distinctive from other related areas, but so broad as to include in one way or another many of the variables and relationships of those fields. Young social psychologists are, in a sense, the general psychologists of the present generation. Their training must be more broad and inclusive than that of the usual specialists of psychology, sociology, or anthropology—survey expert, expert interviewer, expert in liaison with informants, learning experimenter, test psychologist, perception or sensory psychologist, or personality psychologist. Aspects of the skills of all these specialists are represented in Table 7.

We do not mean that social psychology does not have areas of specialization—it does. People specialize in socialization, opinion change, small groups, social learning, social perception, social motivation, culture and personality, communication, etc., as well as in design of studies and in aspects of the sometimes complicated statistics called for in this field. But as a general field, or as a field where adequate training must be provided, social psychology is characterized by heterogeneity of variables, methods, and techniques. The specializations in technique overlap and shift, and careers are rarely concentrated on one problem and tied to one operational class. There seems to be too much to be explored, and the more facile one is methodologically and conceptually, the better he may be prepared to follow up a lead in the various ways necessary to provide the converging and various avenues of proof necessary in behavior science.

THE SETTINGS STUDIED BY SOCIAL PSYCHOLOGISTS

There is much talk among social psychologists about trying to obtain behavior measures in real life situations where the subjects can behave spontaneously and naturally. For some social scientists, this becomes an extremely strong value—to the extent that study design and controls are sometimes sacrificed for involvement and spontaneity of the subjects. The usual laboratory or testing sessions of psychology are criticized as unnatural and unrepresentative of real life, and generalizations from such settings are seen as extremely precarious, if not outright dangerous.

There is no doubt that vagueness enters into evaluations of this kind. This becomes particularly evident when a critic of the laboratory or test situation argues that the survey questionnaire conducted on the doorstep of the subject is an adequate solution to the problem of naturalness. There is little doubt that the users of the survey do a better job of sampling populations of people than do most psychologists and, in this limited sense, produce more representative data. But this does not mean that answering a questionnaire in one's parlor is a sufficient answer to the issue of naturalness.

Regardless of the vagueness of the value of natural behavior settings, it is a value which many behavior scientists uphold in one way or another. In a sense, some sociologists and anthropologists who use the "participant-observation" method or spend years taking notes on what the people in a village say and do have watched carefully much more behavior than many psychologists ever get around to watching. It is also true that some psychologists enjoy trying to explain everyday behavior with the use of principles derived from the rather limited inductive base of a few laboratory experiments. Other psychologists are critical of such explanatory attempts because the basic experiments do not have an adequately "representative" design.

In an interstitial field like social psychology the controversy concerning these different views of the necessary tasks or divisions of labor tends to become extreme. One of the major problems which defines this field may be mediation between those who attempt to collect and categorize the behavior of concrete people in specific everyday situations and those who attempt to study general processes under limited experimental conditions. This attempt to get the best out of both approaches can take the form of rendering the problem as empirical as possible and making studies in a wide range of settings. If "settings" is important, then differences in findings should help to decide how important this factor is.

TABLE 8. SETTINGS IN WHICH SOCIAL PSYCHOLOGY STUDIES TOOK PLACE, IN PER CENT

Settings	1952	1960
1. Naturalistic observation—"totality set"	2	0
2. Naturalistic observation—"limited set"	2	5
3. Naturalistic test or experiment	2	13
4. Test or experiment in S's usual environment (or very realistic situation)	5	23
5. Test or experiment in laboratory or clinic	45	34
6. Test or experiment in classroom	8	15
7. Questionnaire at home or usual environment	12	2
8. Questionnaire in laboratory or classroom	3	6
9. Poorly specified as to setting:		
Questionnaire	2	2
Test or experiment	18	0
Total	100	100

In Table 8 we present a set of categories focused upon the different kinds of settings social psychologists studied in 1952 and in 1960; we also present the percentage of studies which took place in these different settings. There is little in this table for 1952 to make one feel that social psychologists were making a heavy attack on obtaining a wide range of settings or that they were emphasizing naturalness in the settings they studied, but there is some improvement by 1960.

The first three categories reflect attempts at naturalistic science in social psychology. This is obviously not a major strength of the papers reported in this journal, since only 6 per cent of the papers in 1952 have this as a focus, and 18 per cent in 1960. Category 4, however, shows distinct progress; the percentage of papers where an experiment is made in the S's usual environment or where the experimental situation was very realistic jumps from 5 to 23 per cent.

Most work is still done in the laboratory or classroom, however, where the usual problems and questions of role relationships hold. Forty-nine per cent of the papers in 1960 (and fifty-three per cent in 1952) fall in categories 5 and 6. A few questionnaires are given at home or in the usual environment of the S's (fewer in 1960 than in 1952) and some questionnaires are given in the classroom or laboratory. It is pleasant to note that the specification of the setting of study (category 9) has improved markedly between 1952 and 1960. Either that or the content analyst has lowered his criteria. But the specification of settings in these studies is probably better than in most psychological journals.

One stereotype should be dented by the data in Table 8. It should be noted that the favorite mode of study by social psychologists is not the college student in the classroom. Rather, the college student is usually removed to the laboratory or clinic for study.

We have included in Table 8 only categories referring to the actual places where subjects acted. There are other meanings of "settings" upon which we can, therefore, only comment. The questionnaires used in many of these studies do attempt to take the subject into a wide array of symbolically represented settings. Behavior items on questionnaires include such questions as "How often do you attend church services?" "How often have you cheated in golf?" Although interesting, such use of "symbolic situations" is still methodologically unclear, and it does little to solve the problem of assuring naturalness and spontaneity in the measurement of different classes of overt action in different (physical-social) settings.

There is another important meaning of "setting." It denotes the place in the social system in which action takes place. The categories of Table 8 are hardly adequate to reflect how well social psychologists have covered the settings in any particular or even any theoretically generic social system, although they do distinguish between home, school, and laboratory as three such settings which might occur in some empirical classifications of social settings.

This is not the place to go into this problem of social setting at great length. We can, however, briefly point up a problem that exists here .in the relation of psychology in general, but particularly of social psychology, to sociology or even structural anthropology. The problem is that, to some sociologists, the very use of a term like *social behavior* (or particularly *role behavior*) presupposes an adequate analysis of a social system into a scheme in which the particular social behavior or role behavior can be placed. Such schemes usually (or at least ideally) involve categorizing the statuses or positions in the system, and also the important situations or settings. Unless some attempt is made at least to adumbrate the setting of action studied in this sense, the study sometimes arouses little interest in a sociological reader.

Unfortunately, although social psychologists sometimes give lip service to this ideal and do usually try to give some description of the social setting used, they do not systematically give these social-structural considerations the primary consideration which some social scientists would argue is required. Sociologists often feel, therefore, that the inference to the organism as causal in a particular setting is sometimes quite beside the point, since that behavior which the individual is seen as "causing" is more clearly seen as related to the broader structural matters which are more profitably viewed as panindividual and often, indeed, panpsychological in origin and in theoretic import.

There are reasons for both the social psychologist's occasional lip service to this ideal and his more frequent failure to live up to it. First, of course, is his tendency to prefer psychological theory, perhaps due to early scholarly training—at least in the present sample of researchers. More important, however, is the dearth of adequate structural-functional analyses to work from. Such analyses are rarely achieved. Further, when they are achieved, they often tend to be extremely specific—the social structure of Middletown or a Navajo village. Such specificity seems too limiting to the kind of people whose papers we have analyzed, who, as we have pointed out above, may feel that their explanations are very general indeed. What is needed, they tend to say, is a more bold, general, and still useful analysis of social structures—and therefore of social settings and situations.

Fortunately, in recent years there have been some sociological attempts along these lines; in turn, these have had some impact upon some social-psychological work. But as of 1952, and even now, this problem continues to hold back mutual understanding and to decrease the value that could come from more direct exchange of data and ideas.

Until some solution is achieved, social psychologists will have to choose between the languages of the two most closely allied disciplines in describing the settings they study and what they measure. In 1952, we found only one study [24] containing a direct empirical attack on the problem of settings for behavior per se, although the problem recurs again and again in the search for independent validating situations, etc. Since 1952, the work of Barker and Wright [4] has helped to stimulate empirical interest in this problem, and the work in progress by Whiting, et al. [30] is an attempt in part to obtain a general estimate of the importance of cultural and structural factors in determining spontaneous everyday behavior. With the theoretical and the empirical routes both being trod, we may eventually see the emergence of some resolution, even though it might turn out to be a new language for social psychologists which avoids both the language of general classes, or patterns of informational cues (psychology), and that of the total social systems. We can hope that if this occurs the resolution will include the positive virtues of both languages.

THE ADEQUACY OF THE DYADIC SCHEME

Before we summarize this essay, one hypothesis remains to be tested. This is our a priori assumption that the dyadic scheme outlined in Fig. 1 would be adequate, though by no means uniquely so, to capture in a descriptive sense the interests of social psychologists as seen in our sample of papers. We have already mentioned that none, or at least no more than one of the experimental psychology papers which we discussed required more than an individual scheme in order to be described. We must now see to what extent this was true generally for the social psychology papers and to what extent the dyadic scheme is inadequate to the task.

In Table 9 we have classified all of the social psychology papers according to a simple set of categories which bear on this issue. In the first category we have placed the papers which call for no more than an individual scheme for their description. In the other categories we have placed the papers which call for at least the dyad or something still more complex. Category 1 contains roughly one-third of the papers for both of the years under study. Two-thirds of the papers, therefore, in some sense call for at least the dyad for a description of the author's intent.

Let us clarify the difference between categories 2 and 3. Category 2 includes a number of papers where the author does not report the study as a "two-body study," but where, in this writer's opinion, the findings could be better placed in a dyadic scheme than in an individual one. For example, in one study—otherwise quite individual-oriented—the independent variable was the actual physical guidance of the subject (a rat) by the experimenter (a human) in solving a problem. Such a close relationship would seem to subsume some unstated but possibly important dyadic aspects. In another study, hypnotism was used as a setting condition in an otherwise individual study. Here again, the state of being hypnotized involves a number of stated (and unstated) relationships between the hypnotist and his subject, so that both should be included in the findings. In 1952, 23 per cent of the papers called for a dyad in this sense. Category 3 includes the papers which are dyadic in the judgment of both the author and the content analyst. It is interesting to note that in the period from 1952 to 1960 the percentage of papers in category 2 fell greatly, and the percentage in category 3 rose moderately. This means either that researchers have become more explicitly focused upon two-body problems (which is probably the case) or that the present writer was more sensitive to the language of the dyads when he read the papers for 1960.

TABLE 9. ADEQUACY OF "INDIVIDUAL" AND DYADIC SCHEMES FOR CATEGORIZING SOCIAL-PSYCHOLOGICAL STUDIES

Adequacy of schemes	Studies			
	1952		*1960*	
	Number	Percentage	Number	Percentage
1. Individual scheme adequate.........	20	33	19	31
2. Dyadic scheme helpful descriptively.	14	23	7	11
3. Dyadic scheme necessary conceptually..........................	19	31	26	43
4. Dyadic scheme not adequate:				
a. Referent involved more than dyad	1		3	
b. More than two people involved experimentally or in measurement..	4	13	5	15
c. Cultural or historical factors involved......................	3		1	

Category 4 is divided into three subcategories, all of which in one way or another appear to be too complicated to fit easily into a dyadic description. The first subcategory includes a paper in which the atmosphere of the family of the subject is referred to as a source of one of the measures. These atmosphere variables which are used to characterize groups tend to involve some vagueness as to their specific referent. Sometimes the intent is to characterize *all* members of the group; we say, for example, "This family has a democratic atmosphere." In this case, the problem can be solved by extending the dyad to a number of people, or, more simply, by defining Alpha in the dyad as "the modal member of this family" and providing him with a more or less specific trait which leads him to engage in democratic behavior.

Sometimes, however, the referent of the atmosphere of the group involves the *relationships* between the members of the group, where the dispositional tendency is not shared in this sense because it may not be the same from person to person. For example, the democratic atmosphere may be intended to refer to the fact that the father decides who may use the family car on the basis of a majority vote. He may be the only decider on such issues, however, the others being merely voters. Sometimes this problem can be solved by assuming that the role of the father has been internalized by each of the other members of the family, and that the father has in turn internalized the roles of each of the others. This interactional role pattern can then be abstracted as the shared and mutual expectancies that characterize all members of the group. Such a solution retains the atmosphere within a dyadic scheme since we can specify, relative to a given Beta, the Alpha, which in this case is the "democratic other" behaving according to the rules of the family. Such a solution is not always useful, however, since it leaves out the individual motives of the several Alphas, the different degrees to which they have learned the rules of the game, etc.

The second problematic group in category 4 includes four papers for 1952 (five for 1960) where more than two people are involved in an experimental study, or where more than two people's properties are involved in a measurement. In some of these a dyadic description could be retained by breaking the complicated matters down into a number of dyadic relationships. In cases, however, where the properties of several people are involved as a basis for a single measure, then either we are dealing with a "modal group property" which can be made a property of our conceptual Alpha, or we are dealing with a higher realm of variables which would be more purely sociological. In the latter case it would be proper for Beta either to disappear (along with Alpha) or to become at least a higher-order creature at the same intended level of abstraction as Alpha. In some cases where a pattern of different aspects of two or more people are used to operationalize a concept, we may be faced with a new invention, so to speak, which belongs somewhere between social psychology and sociology in a realm of concepts which we have discussed briefly elsewhere in this paper.

The final problematic category in Table 9 includes four papers which referred, in an important sense, to "cultural or historical factors." As we have pointed out earlier, these factors are often of an order of complexity which quite defeats a dyadic description. In their unique, nonrepeating sense, of course, historical and even cultural complexes do not fit the scheme of a science which is attempting to reduce its phenomena to a limited number of classes and to generalize about recurring relationships among them. But memories or reminders of historical events do sometimes determine action. In this case they can be sometimes rendered as special cases of classes of states of Alphas and Betas. Furthermore, cultural factors can often be viewed as cognitive, affective, or motivational mediators in the sense that we have used these notions in Fig. 1. In this sense, when we say that a Beta's actions are determined by such a cultural factor as a "kinship structure," then we mean that Beta, like Alpha, has learned a set of cognitive mediators—the full meaning of the kinship code—which have specifiable effects in mediating between the presence of certain people and the deference shown them, or at least the words used to refer to them. This suggestion, of course, solves no problems for the analyst of kinship systems, economic classes, or cultural values. All it does is provide a way of rendering their notions within a dyadic framework which might sometimes make their insights useful for social-psychological research. We have in no sense, however, dealt with all the rich and various meanings which the notions of "cultural" or "historical" factors can and do have to other social scientists. Some of these meanings may always evade integration with the kind of notion of social psychology which is involved in the dyad. Why should they not?

SUMMARY

In this essay we have discussed a number of aspects of the relations of contemporary social psychology to other disciplines in psychology and in other behavioral sciences. We have pursued these matters in the context of an extensional empirical definition of the field of social psychology itself which was provided by a content analysis of a year's crop of research papers published in one of the reasonably representative journals of the field, the *Journal of Abnormal and Social Psychology* for 1952, and an equal number from the same journal published in 1960. Although the papers studied represent a sample which is somewhat biased in its representation of the field, the major value of the analysis rests on the kinds of studies discovered and the changes over time more than on the particular frequency distributions uncovered. Although we assume that the frequency distributions may well fluctuate from year to year and from journal to journal, we have occasionally made general statements that depend upon the distribution found for the papers under study because these statements seemed to be true on the basis of other reading and other considerations.

The empirical data focus upon the independent, dependent, and "intervening" or organism variables which are reported in the sample of papers, and on the relationships between independent and dependent variables studied in the two years. These were all analyzed in terms of a dyadic scheme (Fig. 1) which contains the entities necessary to describe a two-person action situation from the point of view of an independent observer. This scheme helped to provide categories for the dependent variables, the independent variables and the relations between the two as represented in the sample of papers analyzed. The frequencies of occurrence of these are presented in the matrix of Table 1.

The most frequently studied classes of dependent variables have to do with the prediction of control of the instrumental or expressive actions of subjects. This is an interest which social psychologists share with all psychologists, but they appear to be different from other psychologists in the broad range of independent variables which they hypothesize that expressive and instrumental actions are dependent upon. The particular interests of social psychologists emerge most clearly in the number of studies where the dependent variables call for a dyad for their description. Thirty-nine per cent of the 1952 studies and forty-one per cent for 1960 have dependent variables such as the status of one person relative to another, the attitudes of others toward the subject, the attitude of the subject toward other people, or the overt behavior of the subject toward others, etc. Another fifth of the studies, however, deal with the more traditional psychological problems where an attempt is reported to change or predict other states of the subject, such as his traits or the workings of his Freudian mechanisms.

Social psychologists are interested in a broader array of dependent variables than those covered in traditional individualistic views of psychology. They also appear to view the traditional classes of variables as dependent upon a broader array of independent variables. Although these interests overlap with both those of traditional psychology and sociology-anthropology, there is a different emphasis. Aspects of structural factors in the relations of people tend to be studied equally or even more often as dependent variables than as independent ones. This emphasis is quite different from that in structural sociology, except possibly in studies of structural change, although there the emphasis on structure as dependent upon psychological independent variables would be more rare than in this sample. On these bases one might again generalize and suggest that part of the role of social psychologists is to create trouble for the neat compartments or limited models of other psychologists, as well as those in the broader social sciences.

The distributions of dependent variables are quite similar for 1952 and 1960, but there are some changes over the eight-year period. Attitudes are more frequently studied as dependent variables in 1960, structural factors less frequently. The major impression, however, is one of similarity in the two years in these categories.

When we look at the independent variables of social psychology we find even broader interest. The number of dependent-variable categories had to be increased by nearly one-half over the number used for the

1952 sample, and three more categories were added to handle the 1960 papers. However, nearly two-thirds of the independent variables fall into the same classes as were used for the dependent variables, which reflects the fact that what is one man's dependent variable is another man's independent variable in this field. We chose to interpret this as due to the fact that the root images in the field involve a number of nonindependent but separately conceptualized processes, such as learning, perceiving, being motivated, sending and receiving information, acting, being conditioned, reducing dissonance, etc. (although some may feel that some form of equilibrium model is called for). Since our dyadic scheme is purposefully more inclusive than any of these subprocesses, the overlapping of such subprocesses becomes manifest in an analysis of this kind.

The two most frequently studied classes of independent variables are interpreted as representing the most salient general interests of social psychologists—the effects of personality differences on action (particularly social action) and the effects of the actions of someone on somebody else. The first interest is also that of the personality researcher and of those interested in the traditional field of individual differences. The latter is most properly that of a social psychology. It is, however, in the juxtaposition of these two interests that the social psychologists are different—they see personality dependent upon social behavior, and vice versa. Since this interest is more inclusive than that of traditional monadic schemes for the study of individual differences, it may come to include this specialization. Such interest in the juxtaposition of personality and social behavior also renders logical the interest of social psychologists in parent-child relationships, culture and personality, and social structure and personality.

There is very little change in the frequency distribution of independent variables studied in 1960 when compared to 1952. In fact, in only one case was there a change of more than 3.6 per cent in the frequencies in the categories, this being a new category which had to be added in 1960 to include an increase in the number of studies where structural relationships between two people were used as an independent variable. It appears, however, that in both dependent and independent variables there is a great deal of consistency in the interests displayed over the eight-year period.

When the distribution of independent-dependent *relationships* is laid out, as it is in Table 1, the main impression is one of great diversity. It would probably require a larger sample of papers to discover the general trends because, in terms of the dyadic scheme, the number of possible relationships is probably very large indeed. Such a finding of diversity renders sensible the feeling of irrelevance which often occurs to a specialist who scans social psychological literature. It probably also explains why most general theory in social psychology is usually either extremely and even ineffectually general, or else too specific to explain more than a portion of the interests in the field.

Certain general directions do emerge, however, from consideration of the broad scatter of relationships found in the sample of studies. The first is that about 60 per cent of the relationships involve a juxtaposition of the monadic factors and the more social or dyadic factors, or of two dyadic factors, as schematized in Fig. 1. This is probably a conservative estimate of this emphasis, but it gives some meaning to the unity that does exist in the term *social psychology*.

Such a fact also lends seeming veracity to a tentative characterization of social psychology as a field which lies between psychology and the broader social sciences and tends to study explicitly two people at a time and to theorize with the dyad as a base image. It contrasts with traditional psychology, which explicitly studies one individual at a time and tends to theorize in terms of a monadic image. Both sciences, however, usually involve an additional person, the experimenter, who sets up conditions, provides rewards and punishments, etc. Traditional psychology is implicitly, therefore, dyadic, and social psychology is implicitly triadic. Since social psychologists are busily explicating the dyadic "case," so to speak, then social psychology may be emerging as merely a general psychology. Such a characterization would overlook, however, the interests of social psychologists in the still broader realms of social science. Such interests become clear when we note that sometimes the social-psychological observer gives up his active experimental role, and lets society arrange the conditions of a study or leaves to "social nature" the task of applying rewards, punishments, or other forms of stimuli. Such natural arrangements of conditions come to be called "social situations" and the rewards and punishments become "positive and negative sanctions," and the legitimately expected stimuli are the "role behaviors" or "values in action" of others in the society. Thus social psychology appears to meet individual psychology on one side; on the other side it appears to merge into sociology and the other broader social sciences.

Social psychology does not, of course, subsume these other areas. This was clarified in the empirical distributions of relationships studied in Table 1. The point here is that social psychologists attempt to predict the *effects* of the acts of another person on a subject, but they do not in turn attempt to broaden the action field so as to consider why this other person does what he does, at least not to the same degree. For example, there is great interest in social psychology in what happens to children when they are punished by their mothers, but it is left to students of society or culture to say why certain mothers punish their children more than another group. Such division of labor is in no sense final, however, and the issue of the relation of social psychology to sociology and anthropology (and thence to economics and political science) is viewed in the present essay as one either of rendering aspects of culture and social structure in the dyad, or of how the dyad can be extended to include these broader and more complicated matters. This problem is discussed in several places in the essay.

The main impression regarding the relationships studied in social psychology is that they fluctuate greatly from 1952 to 1960. In the monadic studies, 53 per cent of the relationship cells represented in 1952 were also represented in 1960, but in studies that are more clearly social or dyadic, there was only 37 per cent overlap in cells over the eight-year period. A good many of the empty cells of Table 1 have either been filled or certainly soon will be filled at this rate. By our extensional definition, social psychology is still in search of its limits, so to speak.

We have also tried to avoid some philosophical and logical issues in our description of the patterns of organism inference found in our sample of studies. Rather than discussing the logical status of such inferences we have been content to categorize them, again in terms of Fig. 1, and to evaluate their *empirical* elegance. All the social-psychological papers make such inferences. In fact, there is an average of 1.66 of them per paper analyzed in 1952 and 1.67 in 1960, which is comparable to an average of 1.53 per paper in a sample of papers from the *Journal of Experimental Psychology* for the same year. It is interesting that in the social-psychological literature, the number of relationships reported per paper rose from 1952 to 1960 and the number of inferences per relationship fell from 1.10 to .86 over the same period. The use of traits as organism inferences dropped from 16.5 to 6.9 per cent of the papers, the use of general behavior mechanisms rose from 4.9 to 17.6 per cent. Freudian mechanisms and cognitive processes increased, and attitudes and mental illnesses, though still studied in both years, were not involved explanatorily as often in 1960 as in 1952. These changes may reflect improvement in measurement procedures so that "deeper" aspects of people are being inferred, with a consequent rise in the level of abstraction.

There is a marked difference between the contents of the inferences used by the social psychologists compared to the experimentalists in 1952. The social psychologists tend to try to infer a wide variety of causal factors to the individuals being studied, with an emphasis on traits and personality mechanisms. In the experimental papers, a heavy emphasis of 80 per cent of all inferences is of extremely general behavior processes like inhibition, generalization, discrimination, expectancy, gestalt processes, and the like. After showing that the apparent intention of the social psychologists is as general as that of the experimental psychologists, the generalization is made that social psychologists' habits of inference are as different from those of experimental individual psychologists as they are from the probable explanatory habits of sociologists and anthropologists. As of 1952 the conceptualizing habits of people in these fields are far from showing much effect of the attempts to intertranslate or to integrate these various kinds of theory, although a greater use of "general-process" notions shows up in social psychology by 1960. Some suggestions are made regarding this problem, mainly that the community of interest in dependent and independent variables be made the basis of interdisciplinary discourse and training.

In our analysis of the empirical elegance of the organism inferences of social psychologists, two kinds of strategy were uncovered for 1952 which had become more merged by 1960. The first strategy is one where there is no attempt made actually to vary or control the state in the subject which is inferred (such variation or control being left to past experience or other "natural" matters), but where there is considerable attempt to provide independent ways of checking on the inference made. The second strategy involves a lack of interest in an independent check on the inference, but great emphasis on varying or controlling the state inferred, usually through experimental means. Although both strategies sometimes occur in the same study (particularly in 1960) certain recommendations are made on this problem, viewed in conjunction with the problem of representativeness of design as an additional strategy. However, a high proportion of the papers analyzed make a serious attempt at one or another of these strategies; at least 30 per cent could be characterized as "experimental" in 1952, and the proportion has grown to 56 per cent by 1960. Such facts close the circle of the following interpretation: social psychology is no less general in aim than any branch of psychology, it is certainly not nonexperimental, nor can it be viewed as derivative in its psychological theory.

Social psychology does, however, emerge as a field which borrows extremely widely for its operations. An analysis of the skills displayed in the sample of papers shows an extremely wide range, extending from psychophysics through the use of learning and other experimental operations to a careful use of informants, in the manner of cultural anthropologists. The main focus, of course, is on the skills of the questionnaire and the standardized test, and there is a heavy emphasis on statistical skills. Methodologically, then, it is a wide-ranging and complicated field, calling for the best of students and a training in techniques broader than those which existing disciplinary boundaries can often provide adequately. It is probably this sharing of techniques, as well as the sharing of interest in a broad array of independent and dependent variables, that has placed social psychologists in the forefront of the inter-disciplinary tendencies in the behavioral science of the last decade.

An analysis of the settings of the studies of social psychologists shows a lack of consistent attempt to follow up a professed interest in natural situations which permit the study of spontaneous behavior by subjects. Only one study [24] was focused on an attempt at a systematic variation of the setting or situation of subjects as an independent variable. It was suggested that this general problem is one of the most important in all of social science, underlying many of the misunderstandings between social psychologists and, for example, sociologists. More empirical work on the issue is advocated, as well as further serious attempts at conceptual *rapprochement,* once the empirical dimensions of the difficulties are made clear.

Finally, we have attempted to make an over-all evaluation of the status of our assumption that a dyadic scheme was not only necessary, but also sufficient to provide a description of the interests of social psychologists. The necessity emerges quite clearly, but the adequacy becomes somewhat questionable in cases where social-psychological interests merge into the broader areas of social science, which may call for a basic image which is much more complicated than the dyad. Our conceptual scheme can capture much of the meaning of the term *social psychology,* but, as in all science, this may only hold for a short time and for a limited space.

REFERENCES

1. Allport, G. W. The historical background of modern social psychology. In G. Lindzey (Ed.), *Handbook of social psychology.* Reading, Mass.: Addison-Wesley, 1954.
2. Asch, S. E. *Social psychology.* Englewood Cliffs, N.J.: Prentice-Hall, 1952.
3. Bales, R. F. *Interaction process analysis: a method for the study of small groups.* Reading, Mass.: Addison-Wesley, 1950.
4. Barker, R. G., & Wright, H. F. *Midwest and its children.* Evanston, Ill.: Row, Peterson, 1954.
5. Berelson, R., Lazarsfeld, P., & McPhee, W. *Voting: a study of opinion formation in a presidential campaign.* Chicago: Univer. Chicago Press, 1954.
6. Cottrell, L. S., Jr. The analysis of situational fields in social psychology. *Amer. Soc. Rev.,* 1942, **7,** No. 3.
7. Dollard, J., & Miller, N. E. *Personality and psychotherapy.* New York: McGraw-Hill, 1950.
8. Festinger, L. *A theory of cognitive dissonance.* Evanston, Ill.: Row, Peterson, 1957.

9. Foote, N., & Cottrell, L. *Identity and personal competence.* Chicago: Univer. Chicago Press, 1955.
10. Homans, G. C. *The human group.* New York: Harcourt, Brace, 1950.
11. Hovland, C. I., Janis, I., & Kelley, H. H. *Communication and persuasion.* New Haven, Conn.: Yale Univer. Press, 1953.
12. Lambert, W. W. Stimulus-response contiguity and reinforcement theory in social psychology. In G. Lindzey (Ed.), *Handbook of social psychology.* Reading, Mass.: Addison-Wesley, 1954.
13. Lambert, W. W. Foundation of human relations. In *Patterns for modern living.* Chicago: The Delphian Society, 1955. Pp. 894–945.
14. Lewin, K. *Field theory in social science.* New York: Harper, 1951.
15. McClelland, D. C. Some social consequences of achievement motivation. In M. R. Jones (Ed.), *Nebraska Symposium on Motivation: 1955.* Lincoln, Neb.: Univer. Neb. Press, 1955. Pp. 41–65.
16. McClelland, D. C., Atkinson, J. S., Clark, R. A., & Lowell, E. L. *The achievement motive.* New York: Appleton-Century-Crofts, 1953.
17. Miller, N. E., & Dollard, J. *Social learning and imitation.* New Haven, Conn.: Yale Univer. Press, 1941.
18. Mowrer, O. H. *Learning theory and personality dynamics.* New York: Ronald, 1950.
19. Murdock, G. P. *Social structure.* New York: Macmillan, 1949.
20. Murdock, G. P., & Whiting, J. W. M. Cultural determination of parental attitudes. In M. J. E. Senn (Ed.), *Problems of infancy and childhood. Transactions of the Fourth Conference, March 6–7, 1950.* New York: Josiah Macy, Jr. Foundation, 1951.
21. Newcomb, T. M. *Social psychology.* New York: Dryden, 1950.
22. Newcomb, T. M. Sociology and psychology. In J. Gillin (Ed.), *For a science of social man.* New York: Macmillan, 1954.
23. Osgood, C. *The measurement of meaning.* Urbana, Ill.: Univer. Illinois Press, 1957.
24. Salcoda, J. M. Factor analysis of OSS situational tests. *J. abnorm. soc. Psychol.,* 1952, **47,** 843–852.
25. Sears, R. R. *Survey of objective studies of psychoanalytic concepts.* New York: Social Science Research Council, 1943.
26. Sears, R. R. Social behavior and personality development. In T. Parsons & E. A. Shils (Eds.), *Toward a general theory of action.* Cambridge, Mass.: Harvard Univer. Press, 1951. Pp. 465–478.
27. Sears, R. R., Maccoby, E., & Levin, R. *Patterns of child rearing.* Evanston, Ill.: Row, Peterson, 1957.
28. Sherif, M., & Sherif, C. W. *Groups in harmony and tension.* New York: Harper, 1953.
29. Skinner, B. F. Are theories of learning necessary? *Psychol. Rev.,* 1950, **57,** 193–216.
30. Whiting, J. W. M., Child, I., Lambert, W. W., et al. *Field guide for the five-culture study.* Cambridge, Mass.: Harvard Univer., Lab. Hum. Developm., 1954. (Lithographed).

31. Whiting, J. W. M., & Child, I. *Child training and personality.* New Haven, Conn.: Yale Univer. Press, 1955.

32. Whiting, J. W. M., Kluckhohn, R., & Anthony, A. The function of male initiation ceremonies at puberty. In E. Maccoby, et al. (Eds.), *Readings in social psychology.* New York: Holt, Rinehart & Winston, 1958.

33. Whyte, W. F. Small groups and large organizations. In J. H. Rohrer & M. Sherif (Eds.), *Social psychology at the crossroads.* New York: Harper, 1951.

PSYCHOLINGUISTICS

CHARLES E. OSGOOD

*Institute of Communications Research
University of Illinois*

INTRODUCTION

The most characteristic behavior of the human species is language. It is this type of behavior more than any other that distinguishes the human from other animals. Language is the chief means of communication between members of this species, and its remarkable precision and abstractness as compared with the modes of communication employed by other species has made possible the elaborate systems of interpersonal organization we call "human culture." Given language's central role in human affairs, it is not surprising that many specialists in many fields have dealt with it. The psychologist who studies language behavior thus finds himself working in a complex web of relations with other disciplines. He stretches one hand out toward the linguist; another is extended toward the philosopher. Were he so equipped, he would extend a third hand to the communications engineer and yet another to the anthropologist. With his feet he tries to find purchase in neurology, and his head swims in a giddy exchange with journalists, political scientists, rhetoricians, content analysts, experts in stylistics, aestheticians, psychiatrists, and social theorists—to call only part of the roll of social scientists and humanists for whom language is a crucial pivot.

But what is language? The psychologist may be inclined to define it as behavior which is elicited by verbal stimuli and/or eventuates in verbal responses. This narrow definition is inadequate on several grounds. For one thing, it begs the question of what "verbal" means—certainly "verbal" does not include *all* noises produced by the human vocal apparatus, and yet it obviously must include much that is not vocal, e.g., orthography, gesture, and the Morse code. Most attempts to explicate "verbal" circle back to the notion of a *language* code. What *is* language? Charles Morris [166] has suggested five necessary criteria: We have a language when (1) a plurality of arbitrary signs (2) having a common or shared significance to a group of individuals (3) regardless of the situation in which they are used (4) can be produced by these individuals as well as received and (5) together constitute a system following certain rules of combination. Whenever the stimuli received or the responses produced satisfy these criteria, the psychologist can say he is studying "verbal" behavior.

But there is another difficulty with the narrow definition, at least as a means of delimiting the field of endeavor. As soon as the psychologist begins studying some bit of verbal behavior, he finds that it follows just about the same principles that apply to nonverbal behavior. There seems to be nothing peculiar or novel about the perception of verbal stimuli (as distinct from perceptual organization in general), about the development of talking skills (as distinct from motor skills in general), about the development of meanings of verbal signs (as distinct from perceptual signs), or even about the formation of grammatical redundancies (as distinct from what might be called a "syntax" of ordinary behavior). In other words, he soon discovers that there is no "special" theory of language behavior. Rather, the phenomena of language are perfectly and completely coextensive with the phenomena of behavior in general, and any adequate theory of one is at once an adequate theory of the other.

This means that beyond his many connections with other fields, the psychologist studying language also has very close ties with most of the specialities within his own field. For anything like a complete analysis of his own problem, he must make use of learning theory, of developmental psychology, of perception and cognition theory, of motivational dynamics, of sensorimotor-skill organization, and so on. And by the same token, the study of language behavior both sets new problems for psychological theory in general and provides some new solutions, or hints of solution, for those working in personality, social psychology, child psychology, and the like.

WHAT IS PSYCHOLINGUISTICS?

To orient ourselves in this rather complicated network of relationships, we may start with the very general model of the communication process provided by Shannon and Weaver [222]. There is communication whenever one system, a *source,* influences another system, a *destination,* by selecting among the possible signals that can be carried in the *channel* connecting them. As shown in Fig. 1 (top), a *transmitter* is required to transform the messages produced by the source into a form that can be handled in the channel, a process called *encoding;* and a *receiver* is required to transform this information back into the form that can be handled by the destination, a process called *decoding.* The familiar telephone communication system, in which variable sound pressures and frequencies are transformed into electrical signals and back again, would be a simple example. "Noise," in the most general sense, refers to variability at the destination which is not predictable from variability introduced at the source.

This model is insufficient for the study of human communication via natural languages. For one thing, the individual human functions more or less simultaneously as source and destination, as transmitter and receiver—indeed, he is regularly a decoder of messages he himself encodes through various feedback mechanisms. If we rearrange the components of Shannon's model as shown in the second diagram in Fig. 1, what might be called a "communication unit" is described, equipped to both receive and send messages. Messages from some external source (*input*) are recoded into sensory nervous impulses and integrated (*receiver*) and then decoded (*destination*); alternative messages selected by this communicating unit (*source*) are encoded as integrated motor nervous impulses and recoded (*transmitter*) into movements of vocal or other muscles which constitute messages produced (*output*). We will discuss a psychological analog of this system in a moment.

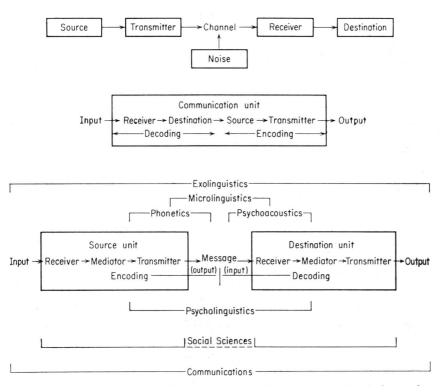

FIG. 1. A generalized model of the human communication process in relation to the science of language.

Another insufficiency of the Shannon model for our purpose is that it does not reflect the *social* nature of human language. In the third diagram in Fig. 1, two individual communicating units, a *source unit* and a *destination unit,* are shown as connected by a *message* into what may be called "an essential communication act." Messages, in the most general sense, are reactions of one individual communicating unit which produce stimuli for another communicating unit, and they may be either *immediate* (as in ordinary face-to-face communication where the vocal and facial muscle reactions of one produce auditory and visual cues for another) or *mediate* (as in written language or painting where the re-actions of one produce a more or less permanent product which may later stimulate another). It may be noted that if we start with events in the encoding system of the source unit and end with decoding events in the destination unit, via the mediation of events in the message system (channel), we have duplicated the Shannon model again.

This last model can be used to localize, at least roughly, the various disciplines which deal with human communications, including psycho-linguistics. *Descriptive linguistics* deals with the structure of messages as events independent of the characteristics of either producers or re-ceivers. Once language signals have been encoded—are "on the air," so to speak—they can be described as objective physical events in their own right. The social sciences—psychology in particular—are concerned with the characteristics of human organisms which influence the selection and interpretation of messages—their habits, motives, meanings, atti-tudes, values, roles, affiliations, and so on. The rather new discipline of psycholinguistics is concerned, in the broadest sense, with relations be-tween the structure of messages and the characteristics of the human in-dividuals who produce and receive them, i.e., *psycholinguistics is the science of encoding and decoding processes in individual communica-tors.* As such, it includes the more specialized sciences of *phonetics,* which focuses on the terminal phases of encoding, and *psychoacoustics,* which focuses on the initial phases of decoding. The much broader study of *human communications,* which really cross-cuts all of the social sci-ences, includes psycholinguistics and much more; it generalizes, for example, from the psycholinguistic processes among individual communi-cators to the effects of messages in the mass media upon mass audiences, it includes much of the traditional fields of rhetoric and aesthetics, and, ideally, it explicates those interactions upon which education, sociology, political science, and economics—even history and literature—are based.

This interpretation certainly puts communication research in a very central position in the whole picture of social and humanistic studies. The intent is not to preempt the problems and methods of traditional disciplines, but rather to suggest that what can be discovered about the process of human communication in psycholinguistics and generalized in mass communication research should be useful in understanding prob-lems of human behavior as defined by the more traditional fields. Linguistics has its roots in the humanities—in fact, it might be called the "pure science of languages"—and its methods have been, in the main, logical and analytic. Yet its main goal of economical description of the structure of natural languages as physical events has brought it into closer and closer relationship with social sciences, particularly anthro-pology (ethnolinguistics), and more recently psychology (psycholinguistics). Psychology has its roots in the biological sciences and has moved steadily into contact with the social sciences. Its methods are, in the main, experimental. Yet, truth to tell, psychology as the study of human behavior has had relatively little beyond points of view to offer the other social sciences. More than anything else, this has been because social behavior and organization (be it education or politics) is based upon communication, and until recently psychologists have done little with language behavior. It can be rather confidently predicted that to the extent that psycholinguistics is able to clarify the nature, development, and function of language, as well as produce adequate measuring devices here, psychology will have increased value to the social sciences in general.

THE "PSYCH" IN PSYCHOLINGUISTICS

It may be trite, but it is equally true, to say that language behavior is *learned* behavior. In fact, few would deny that the behavior involved in communication—from the formation and utilization of perceptual integrations and motor skills to the development and use of representational (symbolic, meaningful) processes—is by all odds the most finely differentiated learned activity of the human species. It is therefore not surprising that, although all aspects of psychology can be shown to have a bearing on language behavior, *learning theory and learning phenomena* contribute most heavily to the "psych" in psycholinguistics. However, just as theories of learning differ, so do their contributions to an understanding of language behavior. We can easily distinguish three levels of complexity in learning theory models that have been applied to language: a single-stage S-R model, a two-stage mediation S-R model, and a three-stage (or level) model that assumes both S-S and R-R associations as well as S-R associations. Each succeeding conception is at once less parsimonious but more comprehensive than its precedent; each succeeding model incorporates the assumptions of its precedents, but adds more assumptions. The motivation for this progressive complication is the felt insufficiency (but not incorrectness) of the simpler conceptions.

The Single-stage Model

Undoubtedly the most detailed and self-conscious attempts to handle verbal behavior in the single-stage S-R model is that made by Skinner (although he would not call it an S-R model), first in his William James lectures at Harvard University [228] and more recently in his book *Verbal Behavior* [229]. Rejecting meanings and all other nonobservables, Skinner sets the task of a scientific analysis of language behavior— to describe the antecedent conditions which determine the probability of emission of verbal responses. In other words, according to Skinner, the scientific job is done when we are able to state why a speaker emits a particular bit of verbal behavior at a particular time. Since he believes that verbal behavior is operant rather than respondent behavior (i.e., language responses are emitted rather than elicited), we must look for the conditions under which various stimuli can come to control or influence the probability of emission of particular verbal responses. The main condition is *reinforcement,* and one of the distinguishing characteristics of verbal behavior is that the reinforcement is usually social.

Skinner's search for the conditions which control verbal responses leads to a classification of types of verbal behavior which he considers exhaustive. The *mand* is a bit of verbal behavior that comes under the control of a particular drive state. When the hungry child cries, "Candy!" or the frightened child cries, "Come, Daddy!" and candy is given or daddy comes, these motive states are being associated with the emission of these verbal responses. Verbal behavior that is controlled by previously heard speech, and duplicates it in form, is called *echoic behavior.* Here we presume a long history of differential reinforcement by other people, particularly in the early learning of language. Verbal responses controlled by orthographic signs are called *textual behaviors.* Original reinforcements occur in the educational system, while learning how to read. A very important type is *intraverbal behavior,* where the stimulus is also verbal but the form of the response is different from that of the stimulus. The familiar word-association experiment samples such intraverbal behavior, and much of everyday language is of this sort ("How are you?" "Fine, thank you.") as is much of our educational lore e.g., "Brutus killed Caesar during the Ides of March"). *Audience variables* are another source of stimulus controls. Through subtle reinforcements we learn to modify the words selected and our style of speaking or writing as a function of the person or persons addressed. An article for a popular magazine will differ considerably from a paper for a scientific journal, even though produced by the same author. Finally, the *tact* is a bit of verbal behavior under the control of stimuli from physical objects. Again, due to diffuse reinforcements from others, the presence of a dog object increases the emission probability of saying "dog." These are what we ordinarily refer to as *labeling responses.*

The actual selection of a bit of verbal behavior at a particular moment, in competition with all other possible bits, is a case of *multiple determination.* If a child emits the response "Candy!" for example, this alternative was momentarily the most probable, but this may have been determined in part by a drive for sweets (mand), in part by having heard Mother say the word earlier (echoic), in part by the presence of Grandpa, who usually has a pocketful of jelly beans (audience variables), and in part by the sight of candy objects on the table (tact). Particularly important are antecedent contextual determinants in the speech of others or the self. On the basis of a long past history of (reinforced?) redundancies, the number of both lexical and grammatical alternatives at any given point in sequential verbal behavior is sharply reduced by what has been said or written just before.

Skinner himself has not contributed much to the empirical testing of his views about verbal behavior. In fact, Skinner's book based on his William James lectures is largely devoid of anything other than anecdotal evidence. However, in recent years a number of his followers have been demonstrating the remarkable effectiveness of reinforcement in strengthening verbal operants. Greenspoon [82] was able to increase the emission probability of plural nouns merely by murmuring "Mm-hmm" when plurals occurred in subjects instructed to give nouns. Taffel [245] was able to increase the frequency of selecting the pronouns "I" and "we" when subjects made up sentences from cards giving a verb and six pronouns by using "good" as a reinforcer. Verplank [257] was able to increase the frequency with which subjects stated opinions such as "I believe that . . . " or "I think that . . . " in ordinary conversations at ordinary times merely by agreeing with the assertion or giving it back to the subject in paraphrase. Barik and Lambert [7] were able to condition one type of complex grammatical construction (where the "that" in incomplete sentences of the form *This is the table that* . . . is reinforced when used as the subject in completions) but not in the case of another type (where the *that* is not used as the subject). Salzinger and Pisoni [214] have demonstrated verbal operant conditioning in schizophrenic subjects in interview situations; Kanfer has also studied this phenomenon under interview situations [115]. Reviews of research on verbal operant conditioning have been provided by Adams [3], Krasner [119], and Salzinger [213]. The implications of such findings for all social techniques which involve interpersonal communication, such as psychotherapy or opinion polling [cf. Hildum and Brown, 88], is obvious.

Many other types of experimental analysis reflect the Skinnerian viewpoint toward language behavior, though they do not relate directly to reinforcement. Skinner's own studies on the verbal summator as a means of studying the comparative strengths of latent verbal responses [224], in which speechlike sounds are presented at near-threshold levels until some response is made, and his papers on alliteration in Shakespeare's sonnets [226] and on sound-patterning in poetry [227], in which intraverbal determinants are explored, would be cases in point. Howes's analyses of word-recognition thresholds as functions of frequency of usage [95, 92] and his treatment of word association as a function of combinations of probabilities in various stimulus contexts [94, 93] reflect the Skinnerian point of view. So, in the main, do the researches of Bousfield [22] and Jenkins and Russell [107] on clustering and other phenomena of intraverbal associations. This is only a sample—not an exhaustive list—of experimental studies on language behavior in the tradition set by Skinner.

As is always the case, the burgeoning literature on verbal operant conditioning has been shadowed by critical studies which imply limitations and reinterpretations of the phenomenon in terms of its automaticity (learning without awareness?); its single-stage character (are not hypotheses involved?); its dependence on simple verbal reinforcement (are prestige relations between subject and experimenter involved?); its assumptions about response classes (how can classes like "active" meaning words be handled in a single-stage model?), and so forth. A series of studies by Dulany [63, 64] illustrates this critical attack: When subjects being reinforced by "mm-hmm" for plural nouns are divided into those who display awareness of the reinforcement operation versus those who do not, only the former display significant conditioning effects as compared with control subjects. In the same experiment, subjects who "hypothesized" (incorrectly, it so happens) that they were being encouraged to associate to their own previous words showed the best conditioning. Levin [134] reports an experiment showing that evidence for conditioning without awareness depends on the sensitivity of the test of awareness. As to prestige and related effects, Binder et al. [16] have reported that conditioning to emit hostile verbs is more successful when a small young lady is the experimenter than when this function is performed by a 200-pound former Marine captain!

More theoretically oriented critical reviews of Skinner's position have come from another psychologist working on language behavior [Osgood, 184], a philosopher [Morris, 167], and a linguist [Chomsky, 47]. The linguist chastises not only Skinner, but learning theorists dealing with language behavior indiscriminately for the circularity of definitions of "stimulus," "response," and "reinforcement," particularly as applied to language behavior, for the unsupported extension of principles gleaned from the animal laboratory to the complex domain of human symbolic processes, for insufficiency in handling problems of meaning, for complete naïveté with respect to grammatical mechanisms, and so forth—in an extraordinarily sophisticated fashion, especially considering that Chomsky is not formally trained in psychology.

The philosopher objects to the emphasis upon the behavior of the speaker at the expense of the listener, who seems to have significance only as a deliverer or withholder of reinforcements. Morris also remarks on the failure to deal adequately with the traditional problems of a theory of signs.

The psychologist Osgood concluded that Skinner's conception was not false, but clearly insufficient. He was also concerned about the behavior of the decoder of messages. What happens when a person reads a book silently? When he listens to a lecture? In order to bring such phenomena into his system, Skinner is forced to talk about "subaudible behavior"—in decoding a listener must make "echoic" responses to those of the speaker and a reader must make "textual" responses to the printed words. But since such subaudible behavior is seldom observed and, when it is observed, is not found to resemble overt verbal behavior [cf. Thorson, 251], the whole analysis tends to lose its objective character. Furthermore, in a very significant experiment by Lambert and Jakobovits [127], it was shown that whereas semantic satiation (see next section) occurred reliably under conditions of forced repetition of meaningful words, *it did not occur for forced repetitions of nonsense items having exactly the same vocalic response form as the meaningful words.* In other words, emission of verbal responses, overtly or covertly, does not seem to be necessary for comprehension or understanding.

Actually, there is nothing in Skinner's view (by explicit intent) that permits one to say anything about the meaning or significance of signs, and, whether one likes these words or not, symbolic processes are a central problem in language behavior. Another insufficiency of the S-R model is its failure to account for *semantic* (or mediated) *generalization.* In an unpublished study by Davis [56] in our own laboratories at Illinois, for example, subjects were reinforced by getting points on a counter if they "pecked" a button when an evaluatively favorable word was being shown, but not if they "pecked" when any other type of word was being shown. Not only was operant conditioning displayed, but it clearly generalized to words of similar meaning (but not similar form as stimuli). It is clear that generalization in such cases is based upon the similarity of some common but implicit process set in motion by the verbal stimuli, but such processes are outside the Skinnerian model. In the closing pages of *Verbal Behavior,* Skinner concedes that there must be such representational processes, otherwise there would be "certain embarrassing gaps in our account," but he prefers to let anyone else who wishes to do so "extend the analysis to his own covert behavior" [229, p. 434].

The Two-stage Mediational Model

A conception of behavior that separates decoding and encoding habits readily encompasses semantic generalization and also serves as the basis for a psychological theory of meaning. Within contemporary behavior theory, the mediational conception has its origins in Hull's "pure stimulus act" [96], an act whose function is to produce distinctive self-stimulation rather than to be instrumental in itself. At that time Hull noted that such a mechanism could serve as the basis for symbolic processes, but he did not explore this possibility himself. As a matter of fact, the only type of mediation process Hull and his students studied extensively was the anticipatory goal reaction (r_G). Recently behavior theorists have made fuller use of this mechanism. Osgood [180] has based a general theory of behavior on the mediation model; Berlyne has analyzed knowledge and human curiosity in stimulus-response terms, using the same model [14, 15]; Maltzman [152] has interpreted thinking and problem solving along the same lines; Staats [236] has applied the model to concept formation; and Dollard and Miller [61] have made extensive use of the mediation notion in their behavioristic analyses of personality and psychotherapy. Applying the two-stage model even more directly to the phenomena of language, we have the work of Cofer and his associates on semantic generalization and related phenomena [53, 50, 52], the work of Osgood and his associates on the nature of meaning [179, 193], and the more recent writings of Mowrer [171, 172] on the psychological nature of the sentence.

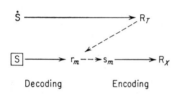

Decoding   Encoding

FIG. 2. The representational mediation process; a two-stage model of language behavior.

The essential nature of the mediation process can be described briefly in terms of the symbolic diagram in Fig. 2. Whenever some originally neutral stimulus (sign-to-be, Ⓢ) is repeatedly associated with another stimulus (significate, S) which regularly and reliably elicits a predictable pattern of total behavior (R_T), the neutral stimulus will become associated with some portion (r_m) of this total behavior as a representational mediation process. This is a conditioning postulate with a difference—namely, that the mediating reaction to the sign is not the same as that made to the significate, but rather consists of those most readily conditionable, least effortful, and least interfering components of the original overt reaction. Such a process is *representational* because the reaction made to the sign is part of the very same behavior made to the thing signified; it is *mediational* because the distinctive self-stimulation (s_m) can become associated selectively with various instrumental acts (R_x) which are appropriate to the thing signified. It is obviously adaptive biologically for such symbolic reactions to become as truncated or reduced in amplitude as possible while still generating a distinctive cue, and in the language behavior of humans we see this reduction process carried to its maximum extent.

It can be seen that what has been done, in effect, is to break the total behavioral sequence between S and R into two parts. We may refer to associations between signs and mediators ($\boxed{s} \rightarrow r_m$) as *decoding habits* and to those between mediators and overt instrumental reactions ($s_m \rightarrow R_x$) as *encoding habits*. It is assumed that all of the conceptual machinery of single-stage S-R theory (e.g., habit formation, generalization, inhibition, etc.) apply to each of the stages of the mediation model. While such a conception increases the explanatory power of learning theory tremendously, it also represents a retreat from the (ideal) objectivity of Skinner's system. This is because representational mediators are by their very nature difficult to observe, even with sensitive apparatus and even if we knew where to look. This is why such mediators are best treated as hypothetical constructs, having response properties in decoding and stimulus properties in encoding which we try to anchor to observables as securely as we can; and this is why it is so important to develop objective indexes of such processes, which are independent of the instrumental behaviors predicted from them. We will return to this problem at a later point.

How does this two-stage conception increase the explanatory power of learning theory? In the first place, as noted above, it provides directly for a psychological theory of meaning. Signs, both perceptual and linguistic, have their essential semantic or representational character because they elicit in their users part of the same behavior produced by the things signified. Given the mediational character of the process, signs can come to elicit overt instrumental acts which "take account of" the things signified. Symbolic, meaningful processes are central to all social behavior, and a learning theory which accounts for meaning is immediately more useful in the social sciences [cf. Osgood, 181].

But does the interpretation of meaningful symbolic behaviors require postulation of implicit mediational processes of this kind? In a paper titled "An Analysis of Meaning," Noble [176] defined the meaning of a sign as the average number of *associations* given to it in a minute's time (m); however, in his subsequent papers he has referred to this index as the "meaningfulness" of a sign—and appropriately enough, Jenkins and Russell [108] report a correlation of $+.71$ between Noble's m and Osgood's index of meaningfulness (polarization of semantic differential judgments, see below). The idea that meaning is nothing more than association has been taken up by Bousfield, Cohen, and Whitmarsh [27], who, in the Skinnerian tradition, state that a verbal sign produces its subvocal response, which then mediates a composite of associative verbal responses, these latter constituting the "meaning" of the original sign. A similar notion has most recently been proposed by Flavell [72, 73]. He suggests that the meaning of a sign has at least two components, a representational process reflecting the attributes of the referent itself (Osgood's r_m), and one reflecting the attributes of nonreferents frequently associated with the sign. Using judged cooccurrence in experience (C) as an index of the latter, he proceeds to demonstrate that a combination of semantic differential similarity with C predicts judged semantic similarity better than either index alone. In a paper titled "Meaning and m: Correlated but Separate," Staats and Staats [239] analyze this issue most insightfully, concluding that although the same operation (contiguities in verbal experience) tends to strengthen both representational and associative processes, accounting for both the correlation between m and semantic-differential polarization and the fact that a word tends to have the same meaning as its associates, it is also necessary that signs acquire meaning through association with nonverbal referents at some point. Deese [57] also arrives at the conclusion that what he terms "associative meaning" is separable from meaning in the more traditional senses.

The phenomenon of semantic generalization was cited as one of the major stumbling blocks for any single-stage model—how does a two-stage model handle it? Whenever physically dissimilar stimuli are associated with similar significates, they must become a hierarchy of signs having similar representational processes and thus similar meanings. This obviously applies to a class of meaningful words like *happy, gleeful, joyous,* etc. When a new overt reaction is conditioned to one of them, it is also being conditioned to the self-stimulation (s_m) of the mediation process characteristic of this sign. To the extent that the other signs elicit similar mediation processes, they will also tend to produce this new reaction in the test situation. Such semantic generalization has been demonstrated from object to sign, from sign to object, and from sign to sign; the rather extensive literature here is summarized in Osgood [180] and in Razran [207]. Apart from meaning in the usual sense, the same two-stage model has been shown to be appropriate for the analysis of cognitive phenomena more generally—in problem-solving [Cofer, 51; Judson and Cofer, 112; Judson, Cofer and Gelfand, 113], in thinking [Maltzman, 152], and certain aspects of perception [Berlyne, 13; Osgood, 182].

The main difficulty with the two-stage model, of course, lies in the postulation of processes that are difficult to observe directly. This means that we must index representational mediators in some indirect fashion (e.g., the semantic differential—cf. *Quantification of Language Data*) and test the theory through the inferred functions of such mediators in situations where a single-stage model is insufficient. The semantic generalization paradigm is one such test: Ryan [212], Dicken [59], and Baxter [8] have all demonstrated that meaningful similarity, as indexed by the semantic differential, is predictive of magnitude of mediated transfer; but these studies have also shown that other bases for mediated transfer must also be involved, such as associative tendencies and denotative similarity (for which no quantitative index exists).

Another test of the two-stage model involves the notion of selective experimental extinction of the representational reaction (r_m) itself, i.e., *semantic satiation*. If the $\boxed{s} \rightarrow r_m$ connection shares the functional properties of single-stage S-R habits, then massed repetition of it should produce temporary weakening of the connection. Using the semantic differential as an index, such weakening should be reflected in reduced polarization (intensity of extremeness) of judgments of the sign. Lambert and Jakobovits have pursued this hypothesis in a series of ingenious experiments [99, 100, 127]:

The first study demonstrated that semantic satiation did occur significantly for experimental subjects (e.g., repeat *child*, measure meaning of *child*) as compared with silence-control subjects (no repeat *child*, measure meaning of *child*), with different-word-control subjects (repeat *war*, measure meaning of *child*), or retest-control subjects (measure *child*, remeasure *child*). It was also shown that forced repetition of a nonsense item having the same vocalic form as a meaningful word did *not* produce satiation (e.g., repeat *nuka*, measure *canoe* versus repeat *canoe*, measure *canoe*).

The second study compared cross-linguistic satiation effects (e.g., repeat *house*, measure *maison*) for compound bilinguals (assumed to have the same mediation processes for translation-equivalent signs) versus coordinate bilinguals (assumed to have somewhat different mediators for translation-equivalent signs). As predicted, compound bilinguals displayed greater satiation effects than coordinates.

In the third study it was shown that forced repetition of a number prior to an addition task involving that number will significantly increase the time required by the subject to do that addition task.

Further evidence for semantic satiation, using judgments as to the occurrence of "meaninglessness" rather than semantic differential measurements, has been reported by Wertheimer [262, 263]. The first study suggested that short words and words having concrete rather than abstract referents have more resistance to satiation effects; the second suggested that words high in phonetic symbolism as compared with words low in this property (e.g., *rush* versus *write*) were more resistant.

A Three-stage (or Level) Model

There are certain important phenomena of language behavior—indeed, of behavior generally—that indicate the insufficiency of even the two-stage model. The first of these is *perceptual organization*. Few

S-R theorists have attempted—as far as I know, none have succeeded—to deal effectively with the nonmeaningful aspects of perception, such as perceptual grouping and closure. This, I think, is because a kind of sensory integration, or S-S learning, is involved here. Similarly, on the output side of behavior, we have the problem of *motor skills*. S-R theorists have usually tried to explain such skills as shoe tying, typing, and playing an instrument in terms of proprioceptive feedback—each muscle movement in a sequence producing proprioceptive self-stimulation which becomes the cue for the following movement. But the speed and complexity of such skills, particularly those of vocal speech, defy such a peripheral interpretation.

We can borrow and rephrase a notion developed by Hebb [85] in his analysis of cell assemblies, and call it an *integration principle. The greater the frequency with which stimulus events* (S-S) *or response events* (R-R) *have been paired in the input or output experience of the organism, the greater will be the tendency for their central neural correlates to activate each other.* In essence this principle states that redundancies in either the sensory input or motor output of an organism come to be mirrored in its central nervous system, presumably at some level more central than the projection systems (since the latter display both isomorphism and unmodifiability). If the input or output pairing frequency is high, the occurrence of one central event may become a sufficient condition for the central occurrence of the others with which it has been associated, and we have what could be called an *evocative integration*. On the sensory side, the completing or closure of familiar perceptions on the basis of sketchy sensory information would be an example; on the motor side, the tightly welded skill components that enter into all organized activities, like the syllables of spoken language, would be examples. If the frequency of input or output pairing is less, the occurrence of one central event may merely "tune up," or increase the probability of, the occurrence of the others with which it has been associated, and we have what might be called a *predictive integration*. Such predictive integrations provide an experience-based stability in both decoding and encoding activities of the organism. Hearing part of a familiar phrase is predictive of the remainder (cf. Skinner's intraverbal behavior); lighting a cigarette is predictive of the movement of blowing out the match—in fact we sometimes misperceive or misbehave in terms of our expectancies and dispositions. In other words, there is a syntax of perceiving and behaving, just as there is for linguistic decoding and encoding, and I am suggesting that these redundancies are based upon the formation of S-S and R-R integrations.

There is very little evidence bearing directly and critically on sensory (S-S) and motor (R-R) integration, and what I have been able to uncover is summarized in my *Nebraska Symposium on Motivation* paper [183]. All of the evidence relating visual and auditory thresholds for words to frequency of exposure to these words is relevant [Howes and Solomon, 95; Solomon and Postman, 234; Rosenzweig and Postman, 208, 209]. There is suggestive evidence that the learning of integrations is relatively independent of motivation and reinforcement. For example, Postman [202] reports an experiment by Barbara Cohn in which the frequency of both reading and pronouncing nonsense items and reinforcement consequences (reward or punishment) were varied—"the effects of frequency of exercise were considerably greater" upon recognition thresholds. That the effect of frequency of exposure upon threshold is not simply a matter of reducing the number of alternatives from which to choose is demonstrated in an ingenious experiment by Postman and Rosenzweig [204] in which frequencies of exposure to nonsense materials in both visual and auditory modalities were varied and threshold tests carried out in either the same or the other modality. Although thresholds were lowered under all conditions as compared with a control group not having pretraining (i.e., reduction of alternatives does play some role), they were lowered most when the threshold test was in the same modality as the training (i.e., there is a modality-specific effect). There is also the question of whether it is frequency of exposure to stimulus patterns [Osgood, 183] or frequency of previously emitting the response [Howes, 92]. The former view leads to the expectation that changes in threshold should be independent of pronunciation of the items; surprisingly, no unambiguous evidence seems to be available on this matter. It also implies that previous *visual* training (with pronunciation) on words should not affect visual thresholds for their homonyms (which are pronounced the same but look different); Neisser has produced just such evidence [174].

This three-stage (or level) model of behavior is certainly much more complicated than the S-R conception that Skinner uses, but one should not expect a sufficient conception (if indeed this is) of language behavior, man's most distinctive activity, to be altogether simple. Furthermore, as is suggested by Fig. 3, this more complicated model happens to match, component for component, the Shannon model for information transmission, as rearranged to constitute an individual communicating unit. Thus signs as physical-stimulus events (*Message input*) must first be *recoded* into nervous impulses at the receptor level and projected to the higher centers. This necessarily sketchy information is completed as the most probable perceptual integration in terms of past input redundancies (*Receiver*). This completed pattern of sensory impulses elicits that representational mediating reaction with which it is most strongly associated, which constitutes the decoding of the significance of the sign

(*Destination*). Turning to the output side, the mediation process as a pattern of self-stimulation (*Source*), in combination with stimulation from the integrative level, selects among alternative motor integrations, which constitutes intentional encoding. Finally, this pattern of activity in the motor nervous centers (*Transmitter*) is projected to the effector systems and recoded into the physical events which constitute behavior. Also indicated in Fig. 3 is the fact that the representational system (significances, intentions) may be short-circuited entirely, as in over-learned sensorimotor skills like reading out loud or tying one's shoes.

It should be stressed that the symbols in this model represent constructs in a behavioral theory. Identification and elaboration of their neurophysiological correlates is another matter and illustrates one of the many places where psycholinguistics impinges on other disciplines. We

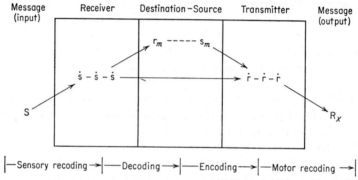

Fig. 3. A three-stage, integration-mediation model of language behavior.

will consider this and other relationships at a later point. Not shown in this diagram—which is complicated enough already—is the fact that at each level we have *hierarchies of alternatives* from which selection must be made. Thus any subset of input signals will be associated with a number of alternative integrations, each perceptual integration will be associated with a hierarchy of alternative mediators or significances, and so on. Selection from among such hierarchies (or decision in the behavior system) depends upon the momentary pattern of antecedent events at each point, in much the same manner that Skinner has analyzed the emission probabilities of verbal responses in S-R terms.

THE "LINGUISTICS" IN PSYCHOLINGUISTICS[1]

Linguistics is a descriptive science. It describes the code of any language, the set of distinctions that differentiate alternative messages,

[1] A more detailed discussion of linguistic methods is given elsewhere in this volume in a chapter by Floyd Lounsbury.

as exhaustively, economically, and elegantly as possible. Its essential method is logical analysis of functional identities and contrasts in the sound continuum. The linguist starts with the infinitely and continuously variable sounds that are actually produced (*phone sequences*) and ends with the minimum number of necessary and sufficient classes of sounds that make a difference in this particular language (*phonemes*), the rules of their combination into meaningful units (*morphemes*), and the rules of combination of these meaningful units into utterances (*syntax*). Although in theory the linguist requires nothing from the language user other than a sample of his natural speech, in actual field practices he uses judgments of sameness or difference in meaning from his informant —but, this is all. As a structural linguist he is never concerned with what things mean in a referential sense.

To get something of the flavor of linguistic analysis, let us suppose that the first space expedition from Mars lands in your own back yard and the expedition's linguist selects you as an informant. He is trained in phonetics, i.e., trained to transcribe the strange sounds he hears into some arbitrary notational system that catches even the subtle nuances— because he has no way of knowing ahead of time just what variable features in the sound continuum will prove to be significant. He has also had the "bias" trained out of his ears—the tendency to perceive signals that make a difference in one's own language but to be oblivious to those which do not. This very basic methodological matter sets some interesting psycholinguistic problems, as we shall see momentarily.

Perhaps our Martian linguist begins by pointing at various objects and having you label them *nail, tree, bush, leaf, house, mouse, pail,* and so on. He is particularly on the lookout for *minimal pairs,* phone sequences that are identical except for a single crucial distinction (which the informant agrees makes a difference in meaning). Even from the small sample of your labeling language, it would be immediately apparent to the linguist that certain distinctions between /n/ and /p/ and between /h/ and /m/ are phonemic because they provide the minimal contrast between *nail/pail* and *house/mouse,* respectively. What may be very similar sounds physically, and perhaps nonphonemic in his own language, prove to be distinctive in English—for example, the slight difference between /p/ (not voiced) and /b/ (voiced) which he notes in such contrasts as *tap/tab, slop/slob,* and *rope/robe* and which you assure him makes a difference in meaning. Occasionally he has you repeat things and notes that you may make certain changes that are apparently nonsignificant in the code—for example, on repeating the word *tag* you elongate the vowel to *ta:g* for emphasis. Such variations are said to be in *free variation*. Had our Martian linguist landed in Italy, he would have found that vowel length can be phonemic, e.g., *fatto* and *ʃaːtto* could mean different things. He also notes that /p/ at the beginning of a minimal free form in your utterances is aspirated, as in *pin,* whereas /p/ at the end is not, as in *stop.* Is this difference phonemic? Since nowhere in his rapidly growing *corpus* (sample of speech) does he find an initial /p/ that is not aspirated or a final /p/ that is, he concludes that these two forms are *allophones* of the same /p/ phoneme. In other words, these are alterations in the same signal in the code that are completely predictable from the immediate phonetic environment. Actually each phoneme in a language is a class of allophones, since the exact noise made is conditioned by the antecedent and subsequent motor states in these rapidly executed skills—and this highlights another psycholinguistic problem.

The result of such an analysis is the reduction of a near-infinity of different sounds in a language to a limited number (perhaps thirty or so in English) of phonemes which are the classes of signals that constitute the code. An even greater reduction has been achieved by analyzing these phonemes into sets of *distinctive features* [cf. Jakobson, Fant, and Halle, 103]. For example, /p/ differs from /b/, /t/ from /d/, /k/ from /g/, and /s/ from /z/—all on the basis of the same distinctive feature, nonvoicing of the former member of each pair and voicing of the latter. Other distinctive features, such as those associated with tongue position, nasalization, and the like, produce other sets of contrasts between phonemes, and we end up with each phoneme defined as a particular bundle of these distinctive features. In languages studied so far, the number of distinctive features—the minimal, irreducible signals in the code—runs to only about six to ten. This is a powerful reduction indeed.

Essentially the same method of analysis is applied to the larger units of language behavior. The grammar of a language is usually studied at two levels. *Morphology* deals with the structure of words, whereas *syntax* deals with the combination of words into phrases and sentences. A *morph* is a form composed of one or more phones which, unlike the smaller units of which it is composed, has a meaning. In strict analogy to the phoneme, the *morpheme* is a class of forms which have the same meaning. Thus the pluralizing morpheme /s/ is actually a class of somewhat different morphs which are conditionally dependent upon the antecedent context but which have the same meaning—thus the /-s/ of *cats,* the /-z/ of *boys,* and the /-iz/ of *roses.* The rules for identifying different morphemes are like those for identifying different phonemes. Morphs which have complementary distributions (like the plurals above) and hence never appear in identical contexts are collected as allomorphs of the same morpheme. Morphs which form contrasts in otherwise identical environments must be members of different morpheme classes—for example, the contrasts of all possible substitutions in the frame, —/t/ (*walk*ed, *talk*ed, *flip*ped, *sip*ped, etc.), would identify a large number of lexical morphemes and the contrasts in the frame, *man*/—/ (*-ly, -ish, -like*) would identify a smaller number of grammatical morphemes.

Syntax deals with the combination of morphemes into constructions. The boundaries of these larger syntactical units are usually identified by juncture and intonation clues, e.g., the falling intonation and relatively long silence at the end of certain types of sentences. An important notion here is that of *immediate constituents* and substitution within otherwise constant frames. Starting with a complete utterance, as identified by the above criteria, e.g., a sentence like *The wily politician keeps his eye on the public opinion polls,* the linguist finds that boundary at which the largest number of substitutions can be made according to the formal rules of English. This first set of major immediate constituents is usually the subject/predicate constituents. Retaining *the wily politician,* we can substitute almost ad infinitum for the remainder of the sentence—*eats his dinner, flew away, must have swallowed the moon,* and so on, regardless of referential sense. Similarly, retaining *keeps his eye on the public opinion polls,* we can substitute any noun phrase congruent with *his*—*he, the Mad Hatter, a roly-poly scientist,* etc.

Having established this major structural division of the English utterance, the linguist may proceed to analyze the subject segment into its immediate constituents. Since many more alternatives can be given on both sides of a boundary between *the wily* and *politician* (e.g., *the happy, the smooth, a happy, the, a,* etc.; *statesman, rabbit, bread, stone, man, child,* etc.) than on both sides of a boundary between *the* and *wily politician* (e.g., only a few alternatives can be used in place of *the,* for example, *a, one, many a, the very,* and the like), this forms a division of the subject into the head of the noun phrase and its modifiers. Continuing such analysis to morphemes as the immediate constituents of free forms and phonemes as the immediate constituents of morphemes, one arrives at a hierarchical structure of units within units.

Considerable excitement in recent years has resulted from a monograph by Noam Chomsky titled *Syntactic Structures* [46]. According to Chomsky, the grammar of a language is a theory about how its users produce and understand new sentences. It is a model that will generate all possible sentences that ordinary speakers of English, say, would accept, but it will not generate sentences unacceptable to English speakers. (Here we might enter a methodological caveat: Maclay and Sleator, [149] in an empirical study of what kinds of sentences the ordinary English-speaking person will or will not accept, find that he is indeed a very slender reed on which to rest a theory—3 out of 21 college students even accepted *Label break to calm about and* as being grammatical!)

Chomsky discards the finite-state Markov process model (according to which sentences are generated word by word in terms of the transitional dependencies associating words in past experience) on the ground that it is necessarily finite and will generate non-English sentences. He discards the phrase-structure model (according to which all sentences can be generated by expansion from a small set of "kernel" sentences by applying certain rules) as being either inefficient and inelegant (if sufficient) or insufficient (if efficient and elegant). His own transformational model adds to a basic "kernel" sentence (noun phrase/verb phrase) and its expansions a set of transformation rules which specify certain rearrangements of sentence elements under certain conditions (e.g., question transformations, passive transformations, etc.). It seems to this writer that all three levels of theory are necessary for an adequate description of the generation of sentences, and no one is sufficient. Transformations, as Chomsky shows, must operate on the units arrived at by phrase-structure analysis, and within these phrase units it appears [cf. Maclay and Osgood, 148] that transitional probabilities operate on the selection of elements.

This very brief presentation of linguistic method makes no pretense at adequacy. The classic treatise on linguistic methods was Bloomfield's *Language* [19]. A more recent elaboration of Bloomfield's techniques may be found in Harris's *Methods in Structural Linguistics* [83], and a concise summary is available in Bloch and Trager's *Outline of Linguistic Analysis* [18]. Fries's *The Structure of English* [75] applies linguistic methods to an analysis of English grammar and syntax. Nor does this presentation give any idea of the range of linguistic studies [cf. Carroll, 40]—the recording and analysis of innumerable unwritten and rapidly disappearing exotic languages, the typology of language families, the comparative analysis and historical study of major language families (e.g., Indo-European, Semitic-Hamitic, Finno-Ugrian), the analysis of relations between language and culture, bilingualism, and methods of efficient language teaching, to name only some.

QUANTIFICATION OF LANGUAGE DATA

The discrete quantal nature of linguistic units means that language behavior lends itself admirably to statistical frequency analysis. However, linguists, developing out of a philosophical-humanistic tradition, have relied on essentially nonquantitative logical methods, for the most part. Thus they have been content to state what initial clusters, including /k/, can occur in English (/kl/, /kr/, /kj/, /kw/, /sk/, /skl/, /skr/, and /skj/, as in *clay, cry, cure, quit, skill, sclerosis, scream,* and *skew,* respectively), but they have not inquired into the relative frequency of such clusters. When this is done, and frequency of clustering is described as a function of the number of distinctive features separating phonemes [cf. Saporta, 215], a very interesting relation is found for both English and Spanish, such that clustering is a normal function of feature separation. Neither very similar consonants (which would be difficult for the decoder to discriminate) nor very dissimilar consonants (which would be difficult for the encoder to produce in rapid execution) tend to appear in clusters. This nonstatistical bias often leads the linguist into what most social scientists would consider rather ludicrous situations. For example, if we list all of the pluralizing morphs that *can* occur in English, including all loan words from other languages (like the *alumni* of Latin), we end up with a monstrous number. A frequency analysis, on the other hand, yields only three major forms, the familiar /-s/, /-z/, and /-iz/. These are what the linguist calls the "productive" forms in English—those forms which the English speaker produces in linguistically unfamiliar situations (e.g., in pluralizing nonsense syllables such as *nox/iz/*, *zut/s/*, and *wuv/z/*,—we would seldom refer to a group of *nox* as *nox/i/*). This matter of productivity of grammatical stems is obviously a psycholinguistic problem—in fact, an instance of the lawful relation between amount of generalization and habit strength.

Frequency Analysis

Although some frequency studies have been made or suggested by structural linguists [cf. Carroll, 40, pp. 61–63 for a summary] and the number of such studies is now increasing rapidly as linguists are coming into more fruitful contact with social scientists, most statistical studies of language behavior have originated elsewhere. The rather magnificent regularities described by Zipf [268], for which Mandelbrot [153] has provided mathematical rationale, are a case in point. When he plots the frequency of usage of newspaper words against their rank order of frequency, both on log scales, he obtains nearly linear functions—and essentially the same relation is found for nearly all large samples of language behavior, regardless of the units studied. Skinner [225], for example, found the same relation to hold for responses in word-association tests, and I expect that the same law would hold for relative frequencies of alternative syntactical constructions. Just what *is* this type of hierarchical structure? It is one in which a small number of alternatives have a very high frequency of occurrence and a large number of alternatives have a very low frequency of occurrence. One suspects that this is the kind of habit-family hierarchy that develops naturally when the principles of learning operate freely in an open field of alternatives. Even rats display the same lawfulness; when they are turned loose in a multialternative checkerboard maze in which all choices are rewarded, they show the same hierarchical system of choices [cf. Dashiel, 55]. However, Miller, Newman, and Friedman [161] find that when a sample of written English is divided syntactically into function versus content words, the frequency/rank-frequency and frequency/rank-length functions are markedly different—not what would be expected from two random samples of the same population. Content words are longer than function words and their probabilities are relatively independent of their length.

Psychologists generally will be most familiar with the practically oriented studies of Thorndike [249] and his student Lorge [141] in counting the frequencies of words in samples of English texts. Not only has this work been of great value to educators, but it has provided the base for more strictly psychological studies on language behavior—the work of Howes and his collaborators on word recognition cited earlier is one example. It is now common practice to take into account the frequency of usage of words in any experiment using them, whether it be an association study or one on perceptual defense. Units other than words have been counted, for example, phonemes and syllables in English [Dewey, 58] and parts of speech in English [French, Carter, and Koenig, 74]. Differences in such counts as vocabulary size and diversity [Carroll, 39; Chotlos, 48], punctuation [Thorndike, 250], and verb-adjective ratios [Busemann, 37; Boder, 20] have been used to get at individual differences in *style* [see Miller, 154, for a summary of such work]. Yule [267] has contributed heavily to the statistical treatment of frequency counts and their application to style, and a recent book on such matters has been written by Herdan [87]. Actually, many linguists have criticized counts of this type [e.g., Olmsted and Moore, 178], but it is the inadequate definition of the units to be counted, not the statistical analysis itself, which deserves the criticism. Linguistic methods can do much to improve statistical approaches to language. Rubenstein and Aborn [210] provide a valuable summary of frequency studies in psycholinguistics in recent years.

Information Theory Analysis

Strictly speaking, information theory, particularly as it has been used in psychology, is not a theory in the sense of explanation and prediction. It is, rather, an extension of probability theory mathematics which provides some very useful descriptive measures of the distribution of probabilities of occurrence among alternatives. It offers a distinctive unifying concept, that of *entropy* (or, more intuitively useful for psychologists, *uncertainty*) and a highly generalizable unit of measurement, the *bit*, which equals the amount of information gained by reducing the uncertainty in a situation by half. The two fundamental measures, from which many derivatives can be made, are the *absolute uncertainty* of a set of alternatives

$$H = -\Sigma p(i) \log_2 p(i)$$

where i refers to an alternative, and the *conditional uncertainty* of a set of alternatives, given knowledge of what antecedent events have occurred

$$H_I(J) = -\Sigma p(i,j) \log_2 p_i(j),$$

where i refers to antecedent events and j to subsequent or dependent events. The H of any system is maximal when all alternatives are equally probable; it is zero when only one alternative can occur (and hence is perfectly predictable). Since the conditional uncertainty $H_I(J)$ represents the amount of unpredictability remaining in the dependent system when antecedent events are known, subtracting this value from the absolute uncertainty of the dependent system H_J immediately yields the amount of information transmitted between them (or the amount of *redundancy* in the case of sequential events). The basic notions of information theory have been treated elsewhere by Miller [155], by Quastler et al. [206], and, in particular reference to language, by Miller [154] and Wilson [192]. It has been extended to human communication problems more broadly by Osgood and Wilson [194], by Schramm [218], and by Cherry [45]. (See also the chapter by Frick in Vol. 2 of this series.)

The application of information theory measurements makes minimal assumptions about the data—essentially, that the alternatives involved in any system can be distinguished as being different and that their re-occurrences can be identified and counted. This fits the linguistic method nicely, since at each level of analysis of a language the linguist merely notes what different alternatives are possible without inquiring into how similar or different they are. Thus for any location or frame in continuous speech he can identify the substitution class, e.g., substitution in the frame, *He went* (1) *the* (2), yields mainly a set of alternative prepositions for 1 and a set of alternative nouns for 2, and someone interested in such matters can determine the relative frequencies. Computation of H for both distribution 1 and distribution 2 will indicate the absolute amount of uncertainty for each class, which in this case would undoubtedly be much greater for the noun class. Computation of $H_I J$, the conditional uncertainty, enables us to determine the degree to which the selection of nouns (J) is dependent upon or correlated with selection of prepositions (I) in such phrases; it would reflect the fact that there are certain things (nouns) we are more likely to go *in*, others that we are more likely to go *over*, and so forth.

Such a measure of *redundancy* in messages can be extended to any order of approximation to actual English messages by increasing the number of units which constitute the antecedent context. Analyses of this type have been made of sequences of vowels and consonants in written languages [Newman, 175], sequences of letters in English [Shannon, 221], and phoneme sequences in English [Osgood and Wilson, 194]. Aborn and Rubenstein [1] have studied the effect of position in sentence contexts of 6-, 11-, and 25-word length upon the frequency distributions of various word classes [nouns, verbs, adjectives, adverbs, and function words, as determined by Fries's system of classification, 75]; the distributions were remarkably similar. Aborn, Rubenstein, and Sterling [2] had subjects guess the missing word in sentences when sentence length, position in sentence, and word class of missing word were systematically varied; the major findings were that (1) predictability is inversely related to number of alternatives in a word class, and (2) a bilaterally distributed context produces greater predictability than either antecedent or subsequent contexts.

Another general type of situation in which information theory measures are used is one in which the organism is treated as a channel whose characteristics are estimated from the dependency relations between input (stimuli) to it and output (responses) from it (see Fig. 1b), again using conditional entropy H_IJ as the essential measure. Garner and Hake [76] described the basic methodology here, in relation to psychophysical judgments. Bendig [9] has applied the same model to a communication situation in which uncertainty is reduced in a modified game of Twenty Questions. Miller and Selfridge [163] have shown that ease of learning sequential words increases with their approximation to English prose. Rubenstein and Aborn [210, pp. 292–294] summarize some dozen recent experiments on recognition, learning, and skill performance which together support the generalization that increasing redundancy of input information is facilitative.

The intelligibility test is another verbal situation where the communicator is treated as a channel. Miller, Heise, and Lichten [160] showed that as the amount of information in the input (e.g., number of alternatives available) increased, the number of words decoded correctly as a constant signal-to-noise ratio went down. This leads to the question of channel capacity [cf. Miller, 156]. As the number of alternatives or amount of uncertainty in the input information increases, the selection of appropriate alternatives by the operator (individual communicating unit) at first keeps pace, then falls off, and finally becomes asymptotic, i.e., has reached its capacity. This limit is presumably set by that system within the communicator which is capable of the least fine discriminations or smallest number of discriminations per unit time. Miller has adduced a great deal of experimental data—most of it nonlinguistic, however—to show that channel capacities in many different modalities and tasks seem to run close to two or three bits of information, i.e., about seven alternatives. But, as Miller points out, capacity can be increased by organizing information into larger "chunks" in terms of internal redundancies. The sensory and motor integrations discussed earlier in learning theory terms would be one example of the organization of information into chunks in terms of internal redundancies. James G. Miller [164] has suggested that the effects of information input overload are functionally the same, whether observed at the level of the individual cell, the organ (e.g., the visual brain), the individual, or the group, and he has inquired into the mechanisms of adjustment to overload (e.g., omission, error, cueing, filtering, cutting categories).

A third type of situation in which information theory measures can be applied is that in which information in a source is transmitted to a destination via some channel (see Fig. 1c). Ordinary conversation between two individuals would be one obvious example, but another drawn from the field of communication via facial expressions [cf. Osgood, 206, pp. 374–386] will more clearly illustrate some of the limitations in information theory measurement. Forty emotional intentions, as indexed by printed words like *acute sorrow* on slips of paper given to actors, are encoded on the facial-visual channel and decoded as alternative emotional significances, as indexed by selection by judges among the same forty printed terms. Now, since we have the same alternatives in both sources and judges, it is possible to order intentions and significances in corresponding ways for both the input and output dimensions (rows and columns) of our information-transmission matrix. All cases where judges select the same emotional significance as that intended by the actors would fall in the diagonal of such a matrix—but such reordering of alternatives would in no way affect H or H_iJ. In other words, information theory measures do not distinguish between simple reduction of uncertainty (dependency) and the *correspondence* of output to input (fidelity), where correspondence can be determined by some external criterion. If all judges select *sullen anger* when the actor intended *intrigued interest,* there is just as much information transmitted as when all judges select the correct state.

Another limitation of information theory measures is that they do not take into account the *similarity* of alternatives. In the case of facial expressions, it was possible to perform a dimensional analysis which, in effect, ordered the judgments of expressions successively in terms of three similarity dimensions having a multiple r of .70 with the intentions. Thus in some cases it is possible to order input and output alternatives simultaneously in terms of similarity and in terms of correspondence, but information-transmission measures take account of neither—saying *contempt* when *disgust* was intended is just as much of a miss as saying *glee*. It is possible that this similarity problem can be handled partially in terms of *recoding* (i.e., by combining categories in proportion to their indiscriminability), but we still have the problem of applying a discrete method to essentially continuous data.

There is, finally, an important point of juncture between information measurement, linguistics, and learning theory that should be stressed. Linguistic method, as we have seen, identifies sets of discrete alternative units at each level of analysis. Learning theory models involve the central notion of associative hierarchies. At each level of behavioral organization, we must assume that particular antecedents are associated with sets of alternative subsequent events (divergent competitive hierarchies) and that particular subsequents are associated differentially with sets of antecedent events (convergent facilitative hierarchies). A major point of articulation is that between these associative hierarchies of learning theory and the substitution classes of linguistics, and information theory provides a highly generalizable method of describing the structure or degree of organization of these associative systems which result in linguistic responses. The convergent effects of antecedent context upon modifying the probabilities of alternative responses, raising the probabilities of some and lowering others, corresponds to the reduction of conditional uncertainty or entropy in information measurement.

Quantification of Meaning

So far we have considered only those objective phenomena of language which appear as overt units in the code. A single-stage S-R conception of language behavior, like Skinner's, would restrict itself to the measurement of such phenomena. However, as I have already argued, *meaning* is an important variable in behavior, particularly language behavior. A two-stage conception of language behavior postulates *representational mediation processes* as having reaction properties in decoding and stimulus properties in encoding. These processes are equated with meaning in the behavioral sense. However, if such a conception is to be anything more than a cute theoretical device, we need to have some way of measuring the nature and intensity of such mediating reactions objectively.

One possible way of indexing meanings quantitatively is reported in considerable detail in *The Measurement of Meaning* [Osgood, Suci, and Tannenbaum, 193], and only a very brief summary will be given here. This approach begins with the assumption that the apparently infinite diversity of meanings can be reduced to variations along some limited number of dimensions, these dimensions corresponding in theory to the ways in which representational mediating reactions can vary. A considerable number of factor analyses of judgments of varied concepts against large numbers of semantic scales (defined by polar adjectives) have consistently given evidence for certain major factors. The following in particular have appeared with regularity:

Evaluation—*good-bad, fair-unfair, beautiful-ugly, sweet-sour,* etc.
Potency—*strong-weak, hard-soft, heavy-light, masculine-feminine,* etc.
Activity—*active-passive, quick-slow, excitable-calm, sharp-dull,* etc.

It should be stressed that these regularly reproducible factors seem to represent the most generalizable and gross representational processes of the human animal, akin to Wundt's tridimensional theory of feeling, not the precise denotative discriminations of which this animal is capable. The aspect of the meaning of signs indexed by this technique is thus more their affect, connotation, or "feeling tone" than their denotative or referential properties—a point which has been emphasized in a critical review by the linguist Uriel Weinreich [259]. Thus the signs *nurse* and *sincere* turn out to have almost identical "meanings" by this method. Osgood [185] has discussed this distinction between denotative and connotative meaning in his reply to Weinreich's review. Although no one as yet has come up with a satisfactory quantitative index of denotative meaning which is independent of both "connotative meaning" and "associative meaning," there have been some penetrating discussions of the problems of reference [cf., Morris, 166; Brown, 31]. Along somewhat similar lines, Solley and Messick [233] have shown that when certain contingences among traits are built into the "meanings" of tribes of stick men as concepts in a probability-learning situation (e.g., 15 instances of *tall* plus *happy,* 6 of *short* plus *sad,* 3 of *short* plus *happy,* 0 of *tall* plus *sad*), the semantic differential picks up the marginal information very accurately (e.g., this tribe is *very happy* and *quite tall*) but does not reflect the internal statistical structure of the concept (e.g., that *tall* ones tend to be *happy,* and vice versa).

Measuring instruments—called "semantic differentials"—are derived from the factorial information by selecting a small number of seven-step scales representative of each factor (i.e., loading high on its factor and low on all others). Going out from the mid-position in both directions toward the polar terms (e.g., *hard* and *soft*), the three degrees of intensity are defined by the linguistic quantifiers *slightly, quite,* and *extremely.* Cliff [49] has demonstrated that these quantifiers do provide approximately equal intensity intervals when combined with a large variety of evaluative adjectives. These instruments have shown high reliability [cf. Osgood, Suci, and Tannenbaum, 193; Norman, 177], particularly for group data. The meaning of a particular concept to a particular subject at a particular time is characterized in this method of measurement by a point in an n-dimensional space defined by the factors, this point having both direction (projection onto the several factors) and polarization (distance from the origin). Similarities and differences in meaning (of two or more concepts for the same subject or group, of two or more subjects or groups for the same concept, for the same concept and subject or group at different times) can be obtained by applying the generalized distance formula of solid geometry to the sets of factor scores, i.e., this procedure measures the distance between any two points, but on the assumption of approximate orthogonality of the factors. Jenkins and his collaborators [110] have provided a useful atlas of semantic profiles for 360 words, along with a table of distances between concepts [111]. Another paper by Jenkins [106] gives factor and polarization scores for these concepts.

Meanings indexed in this fashion can be studied either as independent or dependent variables, and applications of the semantic differential technique have been made to the study of attitude change, to changes in meaning during psychotherapy, to the generality of semantic factors across language and culture, and to a variety of communication problems in aesthetics, advertising, and mass media effects [cf. Osgood, Suci and Tannenbaum, 193]. When, for example, amount of mediated generalization between items is predicted from the measured distances between their profiles [e.g., Ryan, 212; Dicken, 59; Baxter, 8; Lipton and Blanton, 140], or when difficulty in problem solving is predicted from the deviation of meanings of cues from their expected meanings [Solley, 232], or when the judged "fittingness" of visual forms to abstract verbal concepts is predicted from their semantic profiles [McMurray, 150], meaning is being treated as an independent variable. When, on the other hand, the national stereotypes held by subjects of several nationalities are measured [Prothro and Keehn, 205], or the shifts in concept meanings for the three personalities for the same woman are being gauged [Osgood and Luria, 189], or color symbolism is determined by profile correspondences of color terms and terms for various conditions and states [Hofstäter, 89, 90], meaning is being treated as a dependent variable. This is only a small sample of the range of applications that have been made of the semantic differential technique—which testifies to the significance of the meaning variable rather than to the finality of the technique.

A SAMPLE OF PSYCHOLINGUISTIC PROBLEMS

A more extensive presentation of research problems in psycholinguistics than can be presented here will be found in the monograph edited by Osgood and Sebeok [192] which was the joint product of a number of psychologists and linguists working together throughout one summer.

Psycholinguistics Units

As compared with psychologists, linguists have been remarkably successful in achieving agreement on a descriptive level. The basic units arrived at by their logically rigorous methods, phonemes and morphemes, can be determined and listed for any language with nearly perfect agreement between investigators. It is to be noted that the units established by linguistic analysis are discrete rather than continuous at all levels. An allophone of /t/ may be almost identical physically with an allophone of /d/ in certain environments, e.g., in the forms *traitor/trader,* but the decoder will hear one or the other, not any compromise. At the morphemic level, an /-s/ suffix on verbs in the present tense singular is identical with an /-s/ suffix on plural nouns, yet the former never has any pluralizing effect.

But the psycholinguist must ask a number of questions. Are these linguistic units relevant psychologically? Do they really correspond to units of selection in the process of decoding and encoding speech? Is it possible that the linguist's units correspond to decoding segments but not to encoding segments? Why is it, in any case, that the units isolated by linguists after many years of effort as being comparable and identifiable across language communities do not correspond to those "spontaneously" identified by native speakers of these languages?

The fundamental unit which the lay speaker recognizes is the word— it is also the unit that nonlinguistically trained students of language are most likely to count. The significance of the word unit to the native speaker is clearly shown by the way he puts spaces between them (i.e., unitizes them) in his written orthography; but speakers of unwritten languages also seem to have no trouble isolating and repeating single words when serving as informants. As to finer units, the linguistically naïve speaker is not likely to identify either morphemes or phonemes with any surety, but he probably does identify syllables, perhaps because they are associated with releases of air through the vocal muscles [cf. Twaddell, 255]. At any rate, when a speaker is asked to slow down, he typically inserts more time at syllabic boundaries. As to larger units than the word, something like what we call a sentence seems to be identifiable in all languages. Again, the punctuation of printed languages indicates the lay speaker's awareness of such units, and the probability of interruption by other speakers certainly goes up at such boundaries.

Linguists have generally been unsuccessful in rigorously defining these units, and many of them would question their relevance for formal structural analysis. Criteria which identify a syllable in one language do not seem to work very well with other languages. Although sentence boundaries have been defined with some success in terms of intonation patterns and types of "final juncture," one doubts if even these criteria work too well with ordinary spontaneous speech. Until very recently, the word has proved the least amenable unit of all to linguistic analysis; in fact, some linguists considered it a pseudoproblem (which, of course, explains neither how the orthography got unitized that way nor why this unit is so salient). Miller [157] has pointed up the fact that, unlike spaces in orthography, pauses at word boundaries are not such that a simple decoding machine could reliably pick them out (e.g., compare *an aim* with *a name* as spoken). Greenberg [81, chap. 2] has suggested a linguistic means of determining word boundaries which depends, in essence, upon insertion possibilities. It is characteristic of word boundaries, but not boundaries of finer units such as morphemes, that insertions are *not* specifiable and fixed in number. In the utterance *The farmer killed the ugly duckling,* for example, insertion between *The* and *farmer,* as between *farmer* and *killed,* is practically infinite (e.g., *the happy farmer, the doctor and the farmer,* and so on; *farmer quickly killed, farmer who smokes killed,* etc.). On the other hand, possibilities of insertion within word units are sharply limited by the morphological rules of the language.

The psycholinguist is particularly interested in behavioral correlates of language units. There is no question but what familiar words function as units in perception. The sequence *thelittlegirlrodeonahorse* is certainly more easily decoded than the relatively unfamiliar sequence *thepetitebipedelopedonamare,* to borrow an illustration from the *Psycholinguistics* monograph. In a more experimental vein, the demonstration that reversed letters are more difficult to perceive in familiar words than in nonsense words [Postman, Bruner, and Walk, 203] testifies to the wholistic nature of the word unit. The technique of *reversed speech* has been suggested [Saporta, 192] as one means of getting at functional units of decoding. When a subject is asked to say *boys* backwards, he usually will produce *soyb* and feel that it sounds right—yet two different allophones of /b/ have been used, the diphthong glide /oy/ has not been reversed, and the morphemic alternates, /z/ and /s/ as plurals, have been interchanged. Such evidence suggests that, at some level, phonemes rather than phones, morphemes rather than morphs, and certain sequences or clusters function as units. The fact that the rate of delayed auditory feedback at which interference with normal speech is maximal proves to be just about the average syllable interval [Fairbanks, 69] also may bear some implications for the nature of psycholinguistic units. Evidence has been found for similar interference effects on visuomotor skills under conditions of delayed visual feedback, ingeniously contrived by means of video-taping a subject's performance and substituting this information for that obtained by watching his behavior directly [Smith, McCrary, and Smith, 230].

It is also clear that *constancy* and *transposition* effects operate in language decoding. Phonemes have the same "significance" in the code, despite continuous modifications in their physical character as functions of context (allophones); the meaning of a word is constant despite changes in the pitch of the voice producing it; and the rising intonation that signals a question in English retains this significance despite variations in the carrying tone of the speaker.

Search for the functional units of encoding brings us fully into sequential psycholinguistics, which proves to be a meeting ground for learning theorists, linguists, and information theorists. In the midst of ordinary conversation, the speaker is operating rapidly and more or less smoothly on outward-moving columns of air by contracting and relaxing a set of muscles which modulate the rates and amplitudes at which this air vibrates. The learning theorist conceives of this operation as a series of responses separated one from the next by choice or decision points. At each of these points there is a hierarchy of response alternatives of varying habit strength, selection varying with momentary stimulus patterning from the antecedent context. Information theorists can, in theory at least, analyze the transitional uncertainties at such choice points, and when such measures are plotted in sequence, we have what has been called an "entropy profile." Miller and Frick [158] have described the basic procedure here, an application of the theory of stochastic processes to response sequences. But as Carroll [40] has pointed out, the situation is not quite this simple. This is because we are dealing with a hierarchical system of units within units in which the transitional probabilities of lower-order units depend upon their organization within larger units.

But how are we to get empirical estimates of these transitional probabilities? If we analyze large samples of English speech, it is feasible to compute transitional probabilities for smaller units like the phoneme, where the numbers of alternatives are relatively small, even up to the third or fourth order of approximation (amount of antecedent context). But how many mountains of English prose would we have to sample to do the equivalent job for the *word* as a unit? Miller and Selfridge [163] have shown that one can substitute the guesses of a group of subjects for such sampling, and a new cloze-procedure method [Taylor, 247] in which blanks are substituted for every nth word in the message from some source and a group of subjects tries to replace them, follows the same logic.

Psychologically, at any hierarchical level, we would expect the transitions *within* units to be characterized by stronger habits (due to frequency and redundancy factors) than transitions *between* units. Since reaction latency is a sensitive index of habit strength, we would expect the junctures (pausal phenomena) in tape-recorded spontaneous speech to give us some insight into the psycholinguistic units operating for the encoder. The junctures between words should, *on the average,* be somewhat longer than between syllables within words, the junctures between phrases should be longer than within phrases, and so on. Will the organization of encoding behavior yielded by such empirical measures correspond to those arrived at by linguistic analysis into the immediate constituents of utterances?

What evidence we have so far [Goldman-Eisler, 77; Maclay and Osgood, 148] strongly suggests that this is not the case. For example, linguistic analysis would lead one to expect that junctures at the beginning of prepositional and infinitive phrases should be longer than within such phrases, e.g., the speaker should be more likely to say *He went/ /into the house* than *He went into the/ /house,* and to say *I want/ /to indicate* rather than *I want to/ /indicate.* Intensive analysis by Maclay and Osgood of tape-recorded samples of spontaneous speech from a considerable number of speakers shows this not to be the case—rather, the longer breaks (filled and unfilled pauses, hesitation phenomena) tend to occur just before *lexical* items within such phrases, not before the function words that introduce them. Goldman-Eisler finds the predictability of words following pauses lower than that of words preceding pauses. This was predicted by Lounsbury [192, pp. 93–101]. The existing evidence on this problem, then, suggests that pausal length is a function of the uncertainty, or number of alternatives from which selection must be made, at each point. It also suggests a functional separation between at least two levels of encoding, lexical choice, and formal (grammatical, phonemic) choice.

Psychologists have never done a satisfactory job of defining the functional units of stimulus and response at the descriptive level. Perhaps we can take a hint from the linguist, who is, after all, dealing with a particular segment of the psychological domain, language, which is simultaneously the responses of one individual and stimuli for another. Is it possible that in behavior in general there are fine molecular units like the phoneme (or syllable, in encoding)—perhaps oft-repeated evocative integrations on both sensory and motor sides which enter in variable combinations into all perceptual and motor activities? At the level of meaningful units (cf. the linguist's morphemes), is it possible that we could class as functionally "the same" all stimulus patterns which, though physically distinct, elicit a common representational mediation process, e.g., have the same significance to the organism? Seeing a smiling face, hearing "Good to see you again!" and feeling a hearty clap on the back might be examples of such a class. Similarly, could we psychologists categorize as the same "behavioreme" all total response patterns elicited as alternatives by the same mediator—reaching and grasping a nearby object, walking toward a further one, and asking for it under other conditions (e.g., the response equivalence stressed by Tolman and others)? Some linguists, and others with linguistic training, have been trying to do just this for gestural communication [Birdwhistell, 17] and for social behavior generally [Pike, 200]. Although there is considerable psychological naïveté in these studies, we certainly have not as yet solved our own descriptive problem, and these approaches via the linguistic model offer some promise. The big stumbling block, of course, lies in the matter of discreteness—structural linguists have a way of making discrete by fiat that which may well be continuous, since their method requires this absoluteness.

Language Learning

This is a problem with many ramifications, but one on which psychologists, linguists, and educators find some common ground. Here we can only suggest some of the major directions of study—learning the basic signals in the code, learning the rules of combination and permutation of larger units, learning to decode and encode meanings, learning a new code (second-language learning), bilingualism, and language change. The early literature on language learning in children, which for the most part might be called "alinguistic," is reviewed *in extenso* by McCarthy [145]. More characteristically psycholinguistic approaches to language learning may be found in Berko and Brown [12].

Learning the code. The linguist is able to identify the basic signals in any language code, its phonemes, as a set of abstractions. Experimental phoneticians (on the encoding side) and specialists in psychoacoustics (on the decoding side) are trying to unravel the details of the process whereby these signals are produced and received. Although it is feasible to analyze the code as a series of discrete, segmental units (leaving aside consideration of those phonemes which are obviously suprasegmental, like intonation and stress), in the actual stream of speech there is a continuity impressed by the necessity of moving rapidly toward and from various points of articulation. Analysis may be focused on either the muscle activity of the speaker or the auditory signal produced (sound spectrograph, etc.). Although events at both loci should be highly correlated (and are), there is no perfect correspondence (e.g., there are sets of different motor positions which do not produce discriminably different sounds).

Very little seems to be known about how the young child learns to produce the fine units of his language correctly, but there is much literature on developmental stages and conditions [cf. Irwin, 98; Mc-

Carthy, 145; McCarthy, 146; Templin, 248]. We assume that differential reinforcement is operating—particularly the secondary reinforcement derived when the infant produces sounds like those produced by reward-giving adults in its environment [cf. Mowrer, 170]—to select those motor-skill patterns characteristic of the child's language community and cause them to be sufficiently practiced to develop tightly interwoven motor integrations.

However, the vocalic skills developed through babbling practice do not in themselves constitute a phonemic code, even though these skills are essential to the learning of the code. The child only begins encoding when he begins producing contrasts in his vocalizations which make differences in meaning. This point is stressed by Jakobson [Jakobson, 101; Jakobson and Halle, 104], who has even suggested that there is a period of relative silence separating babbling and code learning. He also believes that there is a lawful progression in the development of phonemic contrasts that is independent of culture and language. First there is the consonant-vowel contrast (as in syllable *pa*), then there is developed a nasal-oral opposition within the consonant group (as between *pa* and *ma*), and so forth, until the differentiations characteristic of the parental language are realized. One might expect distinction to be developed also in terms of the frequencies with which certain contrasts are made in the language, particularly in minimal pairs (e.g., *man/pan*). The Jakobson and Halle material does not give empirical evidence for these generalizations, and one can see where collecting such data would be difficult. How does one decide when babbling variations cease and meaningful distinctions begin? Leopold [132] has written a linguistically and psychologically sophisticated four-volume record of the development of language in his own bilingual child, but the material does not lend itself to a test of the hypothesis. In any case, the Jakobsonian proposition would seem to be an open invitation to the experimental psycholinguist interested in child development.

The motor integrations which characterize the adult speaker's phonetic repertoire are described in standard texts on experimental phonetics [e.g., Pike, 199] and treated in connection with more general theories of speech production [Stetson, 243]. The important role of auditory feedback in monitoring speech encoding has been stressed by Fairbanks [68]. Anything like a full understanding of how such motor skills are organized and sequenced will probably wait upon more knowledge of the neurology of the motor system. It is also probable that the learning of motor skills is intricately related to the learning of auditory discriminations, and possibly vice versa—which may account for the "silent period" that Jakobson suggests between babbling and encoding.

The search for minimal units in speech decoding has led linguists to the discovery of distinctive features. Although Jakobson, Fant, and Halle [103] depend on acoustic criteria in the main, they also describe what are assumed to be the motor correlates of these features, e.g., what is described acoustically as the *grave* versus *acute* feature (relative dominance of either the lower or higher noncentral regions of the sound spectrum) is correlated more or less with the largeness of the oral cavity. These minimal auditory cues are the critical "discriminanda" for selecting among alternatives in decoding.

The Haskins Laboratory people [Cooper, Delattre, Liberman et al., 54, 137, 138; see Liberman, 136, for summary] have developed a very ingenious method for determining the critical acoustic cues, a method in which highly simplified spectographic displays are painted on special materials, varied in certain ways, and converted to speech sounds which are judged by listeners. They have found, for example, that the frequency location of the burst following consonant constriction enables the listener to distinguish among the voiceless stops, /p/, /t/, and /k/, that the formant transitions (frequency shifts) in going from consonant to the following phone provide critical cues for distinguishing within the classes of stops and nasal consonants, and so on. Another important recent study in this area is one by Miller and Nicely [162]. The probability of confusing pairs of English consonants when heard against increasing noise levels was measured. It was shown that auditory cues serve to distinguish classes of phonemes and not one phoneme from all others (i.e., operate in terms of distinctive features). Thus, if the burst which contrasts /t/ from /k/ or /p/ is masked, subjects confuse these three phonemes but still distinguish them as a set from other consonants on the basis of the remaining cues. Such research taken together is carrying us toward an understanding of how the combinations of a small number of acoustical cues from several independent dimensions permit a relatively large number of phonemic discriminations.

Although the research outlined above tells us a great deal about the critical acoustical cues in speech decoding, it casts very little light upon the problem of how the young listener learns to react in terms of these cues. That the unit of decoding is at least as large as the word is suggested by a recent study by Brown and Hildum [32]. It was shown that initial consonant clusters occurring in actual English words (even though rare) were perceived with fewer errors than clusters in nonsense English words. In turn, these were perceived with many fewer errors than clusters that cannot occur in the initial position in English words, even though they do occur in other positions. It appears likely that discriminations of critical phonemic cues are developed "incidentally" in the course of learning to behave differentially to meaningful speech units.

It is also characteristic of any language code, as we have seen, that certain acoustical differences make a difference in the code (are phonemic) whereas others do not (are allophonic). Will the listener of a particular language come, through differential reinforcement, to make finer acoustical discriminations across phonemic boundaries than within them? Liberman, Harris, Hoffman, and Griffith [139] produced stimuli varying by small steps along the /b/-/d/-/g/ continuum and were able to show that English subjects do indeed discriminate better between stimuli lying on two sides of a phonemic boundary than between stimuli that both fall within the same phonemic category. Since other languages cut this continuum at different places, it seems likely that this is a learned rather than an innately determined discrimination. An experiment by Brown and Horowitz [reported in Berko and Brown, 12] investigated whether or not acoustic differences that make a phonemic difference in one language, but not in another, will influence categorizing behaviors indifferently in speakers of these two languages. Vowel length is phonemic in Navajo but not in English. The experimenter presented four sets of differently colored chips, two in each set, one at a time, saying *ma, ma:, mo,* or *mo:* for each of the four sets. While Harvard students generally divided the chips into two categories corresponding to the *ma, ma:/mo, mo:* distinction, Navajo subjects divided them into four sets appropriately. That this was not due to inability of the English-speaking subjects to hear the vowel-length difference is shown by the fact that they sorted "correctly" when the experimenter rejected their original classification. Many of them remarked that they had noticed some variation in the vowels originally, but had assumed it was accidental, and, as Brown observes, "there could be no better statement of the cognitive status of non-phonemic variations" as far as the referential functions of a code are concerned.

Learning the rules of combination and permutation. Here we are pretty much in the dark. Linguists [cf. Chomsky, 46] are able to describe the grammar of any language as a set of rules which will generate all of the sentences acceptable to a native speaker and none unacceptable. This has nothing to do per se with the meaningfulness of utterances, e.g., an English-speaking subject will recognize *This is a round square* as an acceptable construction but will reject *This are a round circle.* Psychologists can speculate about the formation of predictive integrations among words and larger units over longer time intervals, as I have done [192, pp. 131–135], and even talk specifically about *ordering mechanisms* (article plus adjective is most predictive of some noun form, article plus noun is most predictive of some verb form, etc.), *set mechanisms* (the repetitive affixing of past-tense tags in a continued discourse, etc.), and *congruence mechanisms* (the dependence of the /-s/ on the verb in the present tense when a singular subject has preceded, the dependence of *or* upon a previous *either*, etc.). And they can devise very clever experiments to demonstrate the grammatical meaning of certain forms. An example is Brown's [30] demonstration that the selection by children of pictures showing action, object, or substance could be readily influenced by the grammatical construction in which a nonsense label appeared, e.g., "Show me a picture of *nissing*," "Show me *a niss*," or "Show me *some niss*." But the actual process by which such grammatical redundancies and sets are learned remains obscure.

One important process here is what linguists refer to as "extension by analogy." Having practiced with such constructions as *The doggie eats his dinner,* and *The kitty chases its ball,* the speaker can easily (and "intuitively") formulate the novel construction *The professor adumbrates his thesis*—if the lexical morphemes are included in his vocabulary. Superficially, this appears to be a kind of generalization, but, if so, it is a variety of mediated generalization in which the intervening reaction (grammatical class) is difficult to identify. Again, we seem to require at least two "levels" of behavioral organization. At a grammatical level, sequences of antecedent events are predictive of *some* verb form in a particular tense, let us say, but it requires selection among alternatives at some other level (semantic) before any specific verbal item, such as *hoped,* can occur. At each point in the encoding of sequential utterances, then, the speaker is combining selections from both grammatical and semantic hierarchies.

In the language of children, extension by analogy often leads to error —"Look at my dirty foots, Daddy!"—but such errors are equally evidence that certain grammatical rules (if not their exceptions!) have been learned. The literature in many languages abounds with anecdotal evidence of such erroneous extensions by child speakers. Kahane, Kahane, and Saporta [114] have brought together such reports from several languages and systematized them. One of the difficulties with anecdotal evidence, as Berko and Brown note [12], is that much of it depends upon what the child really intended in relation to what he actually said (e.g., *Bear eat mama up,* where the child presumably meant *Bear will eat mama up*), and this distinction is difficult to make on the basis of secondhand evidence.

To surmount the difficulties in naturalistic observations of everyday child speech and yet encourage extension by analogy as a means of testing the development of grammatical rules (which, of course, are not readily verbalizable even by most adults), Berko [11] utilized nonsense words as labels for pictures, with the child subject to supply the English grammatical forms. In studying plurals, for example, the child would be shown the picture of a small nonsense animal and told "This is a *wug.*" Two such animals would then be shown, and the experimenter would say, "Now there are two of them. There are two —." At this point most children would supply the form *wugs* with the appropriate allomorph, /-z/. Beyond plurals, possessives, verbal tense and adjectival inflexions, and several derivational forms (e.g., the adjectival /-y/ in *meaty* and the agentive /-er/ in *teacher*) were studied in this fashion. In general the results show that children overregularize as compared with adult norms. They do best, therefore, on forms that are most regular and frequent in the adult language. Unlike Russian children (according to Berko and Brown), they do not use suffixes in deriving words— whereas adults said a very little *wug* might be called a *wuglet,* the children said it would be a *baby wug.* Perhaps surprisingly, there were no significant sex differences in favor of girls.

There is also evidence that syntactical structure facilitates verbal learning apart from the ordinarily concomitant factors of meaningfulness, familiarity, and transitional dependency. Epstein [66; 67] compared the ease of learning strings of nonsense words and associated grammatical markers (1) arranged to be preceived as grammatically structured (e.g., *A haky deebs reciled the dison tofently um flutest pav*) with (2) the same materials in syntactically unstructured order (e.g., *deebs haky the um flutest reciled pav a tofently dison*), and these in turn with meaningful words (3) arranged in syntactically English order but meaningless as sentences (e.g., *Wavy books worked singing clouds to empty slow lamps*) as against (4) the same materials in syntactically unstructured order (e.g., *worked clouds slow empty to wavy singing books lamps*). When these items were presented as wholes in ordinarily left-to-right reading orientation, with subjects instructed to read the sentence and then try to reproduce it, both trials to criterion and errors to criterion displayed significantly greater ease of learning the structural materials, whether nonsense or meaningful. When, however, the same materials were presented as serial items in a memory drum, no significant differences as a function of syntactical structuring were obtained, which is a puzzling thing. Interestingly enough, the serial position curves were typically bow-shaped for the memory-drum form of presentation, but decidedly not bow-shaped for the normal-sentence-reading form of presentation. This suggests that in the memory-drum situation the subjects were reacting simply in terms of a series of unrelated items. (It is also quite possible that the 2-second interitem rate, being much slower than that normal for reading, largely obliterated sequential syntactical habits.)

Semantic decoding and encoding. Although there is a sizable descriptive literature on the development of vocabulary in children [cf. McCarthy, 145], including appearance of the first word, relative frequencies of different parts of speech and of different sentence types and complexities (all difficult things to define), there is very little on the *process* whereby the meanings of verbal signs are acquired. One important exception is the Werner and Kaplan studies [261] on the accretion of meaning to artificial words by embedding them in successive meaningful contexts. Children nine to thirteen were used as subjects, giving their hypotheses after each sentence in a series, e.g., (1) *We all admire people who have much* SACKOY. (2) *You need* SACKOY *when you start to do a hard job.* . . . (6) *You need* SACKOY *to fight with a boy bigger than you.* A very detailed and productive analysis of the children's protocols was made in terms of the types of solutions and changes with age. Another exception is Roger Brown's most readable book *Words and Things* [31], which is largely concerned with problems of reference. Both words and things are analyzed as sets of categories, and the problem is to determine how these two types of categories are formed and related. Much of the material that is merely sketched in this survey is given flesh and spirit in Brown's book.

One theoretical conception of how signs acquire meaning (via the development of representational mediating processes) has already been discussed in an earlier section. Working out of this theory, but with an experimental design much like Werner and Kaplan's, Dodge [60] associated the nonsense names of fictitious tribes with adjectives having measured (semantic-differential) meanings, all in stories presumably written for the *National Geographic Magazine*. The development of assign meanings proved to be predictable from the semantic direction and intensity (frequency) of the meaningful signs with which they were associated. More conventional, if less exotic, laboratory studies of the development of assign meanings within the same theoretical frame of reference have been reported in a series of papers by Staats and his associates. Staats and Staats [238] have demonstrated that the evaluative meaning of a word (e.g., *large*) on the semantic differential can be shifted in the negative direction by conditioning a GSR to it using either shock or loud noise as the significate. By associating a CS once each with a variety of different words having only a particular meaning component in common, e.g., plus or minus evaluation, plus or minus potency, etc., the meanings of nonsense syllables, national and proper names, and other meaningful words have been modified in appropriate directions, as recorded in semantic-differential measurements [241; 237; 240]. And in yet another conditioning study of this type [242], the same relation between intensity of meaning (polarization) and number of paired presentations found by Dodge was demonstrated. Such results serve both to substantiate the inferred response-like nature of the representational mediation process and to validate the semantic differential as a measuring device.

Labels and meanings, once learned, can influence subsequent behavior, both obviously and rather subtly. On the somewhat obvious level, Campbell and Freeman [38] have shown that linking pairs of pictures with a common phrase that isolates some shared property facilitates subsequent rematching of the pairs from a scrambled set, as compared with either presenting paired pictures with separate labels or no labels at all. Somewhat less obvious, they also report that subjects in the no-label training situation rematched the pictures better than those in the separate-label situation. A more subtle influence of word meanings upon subsequent learning is displayed in an experiment by Solarz [231]. Using a display rack which could be moved either toward or away from the subjects, they were required to learn to move words of either positive or negative evaluative meaning either toward themselves or away in all possible combinations (e.g., for a given group, *nice*—away, *sour*—away, *happy*—toward, *bad*—toward) in a continuously randomized mixed list. Both latency of initiating movement and time to complete movement once initiated were recorded during the learning trials. The former were quicker for compatible (*happy*—toward, *sour*—away) than for incompatible (*nice*—away, *bad*— toward) meaning-movement relations, but the latter yielded no differences. This result again suggests a separation of mediational and instrumental responses, the former being affected by the meaning-movement compatibility or incompatibility.

If we may define [cf. Osgood, 185] denotative meanings of signs as the arbitrary and conventional correlations between nonlinguistic and linguistic events and connotative meanings of sign as their representational mediation processes (as indexed by the major factors of the semantic differential), then a recent experiment by Yavuz and Bousfield [266] seems to indicate functional independence of these two meanings of "meaning." Three sets of two-syllable Turkish words (e.g., *aslan, zahmet, demet, tezat,* etc.), six in each set, were paired respectively with evaluatively positive words (e.g., *faith, joy, sunlight*), evaluatively neutral (e.g., *heavy, slow, stout*), or evaluatively negative (e.g., *hate, trouble, steal*). Words were taken from the Jenkins et al. *Semantic Atlas,* and subjects were given to understand that the English words were the translations of the Turkish terms. Paired-associate learning of the 18 pairs in randomized orders continued through three errorless trials. One week later a test for recall of the "translations" was made. Regardless of success the subjects then had to rate the Turkish terms on the "good-bad" scale. As might be expected, the mean ratings of the nonrecall items were less polarized than those for the recalled items. Nevertheless, they were in the same (appropriate) directions. The correlation between evaluative direction of the translation and the mean rating across the 18 Turkish words was .96 for recalled items and .75 for nonrecalled items—

both values significant at beyond the .001 level. It would thus appear that the connotative "feeling tone" of a sign can persist when its denotative label has been forgotten.

The development of semantic encoding, or the "expression of ideas," was described in Allport's influential *Social Psychology* [4] as a simple conditioning process. Vocalic-skill sequences (previously practiced through "circular reflex" mechanisms) are produced imitatively while in the presence of the objects to which the labels apply and are thereby conditioned to the cues from these objects. Skinner [228] treats the same phenomenon as an instance of operant learning (his "tact" category), in which the emission probability of particular bits of verbal behavior come under the control of visual and other object cues due to generalized differential reinforcement. Both of these interpretations can handle only *sheer labeling* in the actual presence of object or situational cues.

In order to account for the abstract use of "thing" language when the "thing" is not present, Osgood [cf. 182] has argued that in the development of decoding the acquisition of perceptual significances is prior to that of linguistic significances, i.e., representational processes first become associated with the nonlinguistic visual, auditory, and other cues from objects. In everyday language, young children tend to learn the significances of what they see and hear about them (the food significance of the bottle, the security significance of mother's voice, the danger significance of a scowl, and so forth) long before they begin to learn the meanings of words. Now, given the prior establishment of representational mediators in association with the nonlinguistic cues from objects, it follows that in the reinforced association of object cues with imitative vocalizations of their labels, which both Allport and Skinner talk about, the *mediated* symbolic cues (s_m) must also be developing association with the vocal responses. Since the representational mediation process (r_m-s_m) *is* the meaning of the perceptual sign, we thus have the association of meanings with appropriate vocalizations, i.e., semantic encoding. Anything which sets the mediation process in action, with or without the physical presence of the object, is now capable of producing the label, and we have the possibility of abstract use of language. Q.E.D. and all that—but here we have much theory and little fact. Other than the simple listings of the what and when of vocabulary, I know of no experiments elucidating the process of semantic encoding [however, for an instructive analysis of the problem, see "The Original Word Game" in Brown's *Words and Things,* 31.]

Second-language learning and bilingualism. Contemporary civilization being what it is, many individuals either grow up speaking two or more languages or learn second languages after they have mastered their native tongue. This requires developing and maintaining two different codes, with all the possibilities for interference or facilitation at all levels of language organization, from phonemic skills to semantics. Linguists have taken an active interest in these problems, but stressing structural matters rather than semantic, as might be expected. Books and papers by Haugen [84], Leopold [133], and Weinreich [258] provide excellent treatments of bilingualism from a linguistic point of view. As Lambert [124] indicates, psychologists find bilingualism particularly interesting because language learning can be observed and studied much more easily than in the young child learning his first language. Transfer and interference problems appear in a very practical real life situation, and relations between linguistic and nonlinguistic behaviors like thinking and problem solving can be investigated in rather novel settings.

One of the really preliminary, yet thorny, problems in this field is the development of a satisfactory index of *degree* of bilingualism. Is a person balanced between language A and language B, dominant in language A or dominant in B, and how much? Lambert [122, 123] has investigated a variety of methods for determining degree of bilingualism, including relative reaction times for following directions, word-association tests with language to be used unspecified, and a test of pronunciation accuracy. Although such a battery discriminated undergraduate from graduate American speakers of French in the expected direction, there were still marked differences between American graduate students and native French bilinguals. Lambert, Havelka, and Gardner [126] have evaluated a number of other potential indicators. Among those correlating significantly with the criterion were speed of tachistoscopic word recognition, facility in word completion, facility in detecting words in text without spaces, ease of oral reading, and pronunciation of homographs between the two languages. The problem, of course, is to determine that type of performance which best correlates with total score on many tests of dominance and then develop a reliable and easily administered sample of it. (One can't very well run around the field with a Gerbrandt's tachistoscope!)

Another problem concerned the *type* of bilingualism. Working with the two-stage mediation model, Ervin and Osgood [192, pp. 135–146] suggested on largely theoretical grounds that two basic "types" of bilingualism should occur. *Compound bilinguals* have learned their two languages in the same context (e.g., in a fully bilingual home or under ordinary foreign-language classroom conditions) and hence develop two alternative codes associated with the same mediators. *Coordinate bilinguals* have learned their two languages in different contexts (e.g., language A at home and B at work, or A as a child and B as an adult in a different country) and hence develop somewhat distinct representational mediators for the alternative codes. Research by Lambert,

Havelka, and Crosby [125] has directly tested these notions, using the similarity of semantic-differential profiles for translation-equivalent words as the dependent variable. As predicted, subjects categorized as "compound" in terms of their language-learning history produced significantly closer profiles than those categorized as "coordinate." The fact that subjects classified as "compound" also display greater cross-linguistic semantic-satiation effects [cf. Jakobovits and Lambert, 99] than those classified as "coordinates" is also consistent with the kind of theoretical distinction being made.

The question of second-language learning is much too broad and well worked to be treated adequately in a chapter of this scope. John B. Carroll has produced many papers on second-language learning and teaching. He has recently [41] prepared a very comprehensive summary which covers methods of instruction, including new developments with teaching machines, the psychology of bilingualism, characteristics of the student as they related to foreign-language learning, and the measurement of achievement in foreign-language learning. In an earlier study, Carroll [39] attempted a predict language-learning performance by an extensive battery of tests. The tests were drawn from two instruments and administered prior to a short course in Mandarin Chinese in which subjects were enrolled. Factor analysis suggested some six factors related to subsequent language learning—linguistic interest, associative memory, and inductive ability proved to be the best predictors.

Language change. Here the linguist, his hands full of surprisingly regular facts, runs fully into the question "Why?" and hence into the arms of his social science colleagues. The experimental psychologist, using principles discovered in research on motor skills and transfer studies, is able to make some predictions about the probable loci of "stress-points" in serially produced messages. These predictions derive, in the main, from learning theory analysis of the dynamics of convergent versus divergent hierarchies and the related analysis of transfer and interference in terms of similarities among stimuli and responses [cf. *Psycholinguistics*, 192, pp. 146–163]. Similarly, theory and fact about sequential motor skills should be useful to the linguist in untangling his phenomenal threads. Greenberg [81, chap. 8] has explicitly applied such notions to a study of the relative importance of grammatical suffixing as compared to prefixing.

The social psychologist is also able to make reasonable predictions about the process of language change. When individuals are communicating under stress—particularly young members of the speech community who are learning the code—they will tend to make substitution errors at points where, in the language as a whole, probabilities favor something other than the correct unit. If such speaker "lapses" remain uncorrected by hearers—because they do not make a difference in the code or because they occur in positions of low information value— they are in effect reinforced as parts of the total communication act, become strengthened, generalize more widely, and thus gradually substitute for the "correct" forms.

Information theory also has an interesting contribution to make here. We can define the *efficiency* of any language code as the degree to which it makes full use of its information alternatives, i.e., approaches maximal entropy at all levels of units. Thus a language utilizing 32 phonemes would *need* to have only five binary distinctive features. But such a language would impose an impossible load on its users—every detail would have to be perfectly articulated by its encoders, and its decoders could not relax a moment without losing information. Natural languages take this into account by overdetermining their signals (redundancy). English, for example, uses some nine distinctive features to carry some 28 or so phonemes—an efficiency of only about 53 per cent. As to language change, we should expect a relatively lax or inefficient language code to change in the direction of losing certain overdetermining distinctive features or increasing its phonemic inventory, whereas we should expect a relatively tight, efficient language to change in the direction of either adding features or decreasing the phonemic inventory, or both. Wilson and Saporta [192, pp. 156–158] have been able to show that a number of languages for which such data are available average about 50 per cent efficiency, and values for four stages of the same language (Spanish) displayed an intriguing cyclic oscillation about this average— 49, 57, 47, and 51 per cent. Are we beginning to get the picture of a grand ebb and flow in language efficiency about its optimum balance point?

Other Psycholinguistic Problems within Psychology

We have discussed two of the traditional areas in psychology with which the newer discipline of psycholinguistics makes contact, *nature of behavioral units* (which is more notable for its lack of study traditionally!) and *learning*. Certain other overlaps with traditional psychological problems may be sketched in more briefly.

Concept formation and utilization. There are actually very few studies on concept *formation*—which, as we have seen, is essentially the problem of learning meanings. The studies of Werner and Kaplan have already been cited as exceptions to this rule. Another exception would be the many studies of the development of children's conceptions of their world by Piaget and his associates [cf. 196, 197, 198] which, despite the complexity and abstractness of the cognitive processes investigated, are still in the general area of concept formation. However, as Berko and Brown point out, "Piaget is inclined to see through words as though they were not there and to imagine that he directly studies the child mind" [12, p. 33]. Therefore, his material is not as relevant to psycholinguistics as it should be. A translation of Piaget's works that would etch their psycholinguistic significance would be most valuable; Berko makes only a beginning at this formidable task.

Yet another exception is a recent experiment by Lenneberg [130]. Four Zuni words for colors were learned by American college students; first the experimenter used these words as labels for color samples and the subject then tried to apply them correctly. For a control group, the usage of these Zuni words along the spectrum corresponded exactly to English *brown, green, blue,* and *pink,* but for various experimental groups either the slope of the usage distribution was distorted (sharpened or broadened) or the locus of the distribution was shifted along the spectrum. Although any distortion in usage from that characteristic of English increased the difficulty of the task initially, usage distributions having a steep slope (i.e., narrow spectral regions through which categories are ambiguous) were more easily learned than those with gradual slopes. Shifting spectral location by itself caused little difficulty, unless combined with slope changes.

Although not analyzed in terms of learning theory by Lenneberg, the phonemena he describes should be amenable to interpretation in terms of mediated generalization and discrimination (i.e., the acquired distinctiveness of cues). Staats [236] has made a detailed extension of two-stage mediation theory into this area of concept formation, as well as into the field of verbal operant conditioning discussed earlier. In the course of this analysis he relies heavily on the notion of *habit-family hierarchies,* both verbal and nonverbal, which are set up on the basis of the sharing of representational mediator components by antecedent signs and subsequent responses. As Staats points out, the sharing of identical stimulus elements by signs is not a necessary condition for their inclusion in the same concept, although such sharing is one of the things which facilitates the development of primary perceptual concepts. He also emphasizes the fact that the intraverbal connections established in ordinary language experience (listening to conversations, reading, etc.) can serve to modify the meanings of concepts. Although entirely different terminologies are used, Brown's [31] analysis of concept formation in terms of linguistic and nonlinguistic categories and Staats's analysis in terms of verbal and nonverbal habit-family hierarchies probably have a high degree of functional overlap.

Studies on concept *utilization*—in which the subject must first select from his supply of already available concepts those which apply and then use them as the basis for sorting, saying certain nonsense syllables, or the like—have seldom employed verbal materials (probably because words ordinarily define conceptual categories). However, if we view language behavior as something broader than the purely verbal, then much of the research on concept attainment and utilization becomes relevant. The recent book by Bruner, Goodnow, and Austin, *A Study of Thinking* [35], provides a review of this literature, a number of new experiments, and a fresh way of thinking about the problem.

Word association. The word-association technique is a tool for studying a particular type of transitional dependency in language. Because this technique has a long tradition in psychology, we have more information about this type of association hierarchy than any other. We have the early norms of Kent and Rosanoff [117] for adults and those of Woodrow and Lowell [265] for children associating to the same stimulus words. We have norms for Minnesota college students collected in 1930 by Schellenberg [217] and comparable norms for Minnesota students collected in 1953 by Russell and Jenkins [211], again for the same stimulus words. These norms display typical low-entropy hierarchical structure, i.e., a few responses having very high frequencies of occurrence and many responses having very low frequencies of occurrence. Thumb and Marbe [252] and others have demonstrated that frequency in the group is closely related to speed of association in the individual. Bousfield and Barclay [23] and Bousfield, Cohen, and Silva [26] have shown that frequency in the group is closely related to the rank order of appearance of responses in sequences produced by the individual. All of these demonstrations make such cultural data immediately more useful for checking hypotheses about associative processes in individual language users. Comparison of norms collected recently with those collected twenty or more years ago [Jenkins, 105; Jenkins and Russell, 109; Dörken, 62] reveals a startling increase in stereotypy which may well be related to the increasing role of the mass media over this period.

The existence of such normative data and the simplicity of the word-association technique have stimulated a revival of intense interest in this area. Jenkins and Russell and their associates at Minnesota have been studying the effects of associative strength upon clustering during recall, upon tachistoscopic word recognition, upon mediated generalization, and related problems [cf. 105].[2] They have also been able to demonstrate some very interesting personality correlates of "communality" (degree to which an individual subject selects responses characteristic of the group). Another team of investigators in this area, Bousfield and his associates, have employed a modified word-association technique in which subjects, given instructions to associate from some seman-

[2] Much of this work is still only available in technical reports under their contract with the Office of Naval Research (N8-onr-66216).

tic "pool" or category (e.g., four-legged animals), produce words successively and at surprisingly lawful rates [Bousfield and Barry, 24; Bousfield, 21; Bousfield and Sedgewick, 28]. Speed of successive associating decreases according to a negatively accelerated function as weaker and more remote associates must be dredged from the depths of the pool. Ripples of quickened reactions often appear where clusters of related items occur [Bousfield, 22; Bousfield and Cohen, 25]—that is, items which fall in the same general category (e.g., African jungle animals).

A somewhat related study of clustering in word-association data has recently been presented by Deese [57]. By preparing a matrix in which stimulus words form the columns and response words the rows, he has been able to analyze the networks of shared associative meaning, and factor analytic techniques have been used to study the structure of such associative networks—all in all, this is a most interesting new approach to the problem of associative structure. Osgood and Anderson [188] have subjected to test some assumptions usually taken for granted in association studies—that frequency of input pairing in experience is predictive of the mediating associative structure and that this associative structure in turn mediates organization of events in encoding. The results of an experiment—girls' names were paired with several others at varying frequencies in visual input, associative structure measured by giving each name as stimulus, and output measured by spontaneous sequential encoding—clearly substantiated these assumptions, but relations between input and output pairings were relatively low and suggested the operation of preexperimental sets.

Much of the experimental evidence on word association is only remotely relevant to psycholinguistics, so we must be choosy about our sampling. The problem of linguistic context, hinted at above, has been investigated by Howes and Osgood [94]. They used three-word antecedent contexts to show that the influence of a given context word increases with its Thorndike-Lorge frequency and decreases with its temporal separation from the cue stimulus, while the influence of the context as a whole increases with its communality of first-order associative effects. Gonzalez and Cofer [79] have manipulated linguistic context by use of modifiers (adjective-noun, verb-adverb, etc.) and have measured effects in terms of clustering in free recall [cf. Bousfield et al., 24, 21, 28]. Appropriateness of modifiers facilitated clustering and recall, and the reverse was true for inappropriateness. Another aspect of context concerns the effect of the grammatical form of the stimulus word upon the grammatical class of the associative response [cf. Saporta, 216]. The general observation is that the response most often is of the same class as the stimulus (e.g., *hard-soft*), but there are many exceptions (e.g., *dark-night*) and many items are ambiguous (e.g., *man-work*). This raises certain problems. If word associations are based simply on contingencies in the sequential linguistic input experienced, why do we not find associations like *man-who* and *butterfly-is?* Saporta terms such transitional associates "syntagmatic" (e.g., *strong-man*) and the more common type "paradigmatic" (e.g., *table-chair*), these latter being substitutible in the same paradigms or frames linguistically. Howes [93] has suggested that the function words which typically cement (and hence follow) lexical words fail to occur because of the subject's implicit instructions to react with "meaningful" words. He proceeded to demonstrate that when function words were included among the stimuli there was a 200-fold increase in their appearance as responses.

Another interesting phenomenon of the word-association experiment is the overwhelming overabundance of opposites as responses, particularly in the behavior of adults as compared with children. Osgood [180] has argued that the opposite response is essentially syntagmatic, dependent on transitional experience of high frequency, and nonsemantic in character. He uses as evidence the fact that there are many alternative similar responses to the same stimulus, as compared with usually one or two very high-frequency opposite responses. Most recently Carroll, Kjeldergaard, and Carton [43] instructed subjects to give opposites wherever they could and found that a very large component of what is referred to as the "communality" of response is based upon opposite-evoking stimuli. The article by Howes [93] already referred to has been concerned with the statistical properties of the word-association experiment generally. Following Skinner's general thesis but elaborating on it, he attempts to interpret word-association phenomena in terms of the base probabilities of word emission (as reflected in frequency-of-usage lists) and the modification of these probabilities through context (which is treated as a probability-summation problem).

Motivation. Language behavior is one of the many dependent variables influenced by energizing processes. The influence of drive level— upon facilitating associative connections at moderate levels, increasing stereotypy in behavioral hierarchies at higher levels, and producing behavioral disorganization at extreme levels [c.f. Malmo, 151; Hebb, 86; Spence, Farber, and McFann, 235]—can be seen as clearly in the psycholinguistic processes of decoding and encoding as elsewhere. Also, the specific cue effects of motivational states have been shown to be influential as antecedent contextual factors in selecting within hierarchies at all levels of organization. Many of the experiments designed to study the influence of motivation upon perceptual vigilance and defense, word associations, stuttering and other motor phenomena, and the production of intentional speech are obviously at the same time studies in psycholinguistics. Since I have summarized the literature bearing on this relation up to 1957 elsewhere [Osgood, 183], I shall not try to repeat it here. However, there are a number of relevant studies that have come to my attention since that date which should be mentioned briefly.

The word-association situation we have just been reviewing represents hierarchical organization *par excellence*. It would be expected that increasing drive level should increase the stereotypy (i.e., communality) of associations. Surprisingly, there have been no tests of this rather obvious prediction until very recently. Kanfer [116] selected high- and low-anxiety subjects in terms of the Taylor Manifest Anxiety Test (HA being above the 80th percentile and LA being below the 20th percentile); no differences in word-association communality scores were found for the two groups. Burke [36] compared the association data obtained from subjects under control conditions (using the Jenkins et al. procedures and instructions) with those obtained from subjects (1) performing under time pressure plus ego threat (informed that this was an intelligence test), and (2) performing while applying strong pressure to a rubber ball with the nonwriting hand. In both experimental groups, the communality scores increased significantly, but more so in the time-pressure and ego-anxiety group. How are we to explain the apparent discrepancy in results here? One likely possibility is that stereotypy in behavioral hierarchies is produced by *contemporary* generalized drive level, and it seems quite unlikely that this holds for high MA subjects with any consistency. Siipola, Walker, and Kolb [223] also studied word association under time pressure, and they find a significant increase in the paradigmatic (frame substitution) type of response.

This by no means completes the list of areas within psychology that have a bearing on psycholinguistics. As I said earlier in this chapter, the study of language behavior is practically coextensive with that of psychology in general—the only restriction which applies is that the stimuli or responses, or both, be linguistic. But even within this limitation there are many topics whose bearing is so remote that I have not included them, e.g., serial learning and transfer studies utilizing verbal materials, threshold studies using verbal materials where the main concern has been personality dynamics, and so forth.

THE BROADER CONTEXT OF PSYCHOLINGUISTICS

If, as I have suggested, psycholinguistics is one of the chief articulation points between the biological and social sciences, then we should expect to find the beginning of extensions of this relatively new discipline into various social science areas. Certainly, studies of the reading, listening, and looking habits of the public with respect to materials in newspapers, radio, and television, studies of the effects of such programs upon voting, buying, attending, and working behavior, studies on the opinions, beliefs, and attitudes of people, and even methodological studies on the scaling of such things are all heavily dependent upon language and hence psycholinguistically relevant. But to explore these relations in any detail would require both much more space and many more authors than are available here. Therefore I shall restrict myself to a few general comments on certain points of juncture with psycholinguistics—in neurophysiology, in the more social sciences, and in the humanities.

Psycholinguistics and Neurophysiology

The relation of psycholinguistics to neurophysiology is precisely the same as that of psychology in general to neurophysiology. On the one hand, it is clear that any adequate conception of decoding and encoding processes in human-language users must ultimately be consistent with the way the human nervous system functions—such congruence is one of the criteria in psycholinguistic theorizing. On the other hand, it seems equally clear that the psycholinguist will, for a long time, be far beyond the capacities of the neurologist in the demands he makes upon his knowledge—so the problem for the psycholinguist really is to not be inconsistent with what *is* known in the supporting field.

To the best of my knowledge there has been very little interdisciplinary activity to date between psycholinguists and neurophysiologists. One notable exception is the recent book *Plans and the Structure of Behavior* [159], written by G. A. Miller and E. Galanter, two psychologists, one of whom is certainly recognized for his contributions to psycholinguistics, and K. Pribram, a neurologist. This book is remarkable for its fresh point of view—its main theme of "subjective behaviorism" is to bring the notions of "plans" and "images" (ideas?) back into the fold via the avenues of neurology and cybernetics. It also includes a chapter on "Plans for Speaking" that relates Chomsky's theorizing about grammer to the authors' basic conceptions. This book is particularly valuable for psycholinguistics, I think, because of its suggestions about the process of sequential encoding, a problem hardly touched to date.

Another notable exception is the work that has been developing on the phenomena of *aphasia*. Being by (oversimplified) definition "disturbance of language behavior," aphasia provides a natural intersection for the interests of neurologists, clinical psychologists, speech therapists, linguists, and psycholinguists. Many people whom we associate with the study of aphasia in the past, e.g., Hughlings Jackson, Henry Head, and Sigmund Freud, have contributed both to neurology and psychology, and the same can be said for Kurt Goldstein, who has expressed his conviction that intensive, integrated work by specialists in the above fields would be necessary for understanding aphasic phenomena [78, p. 31].

The very influential linguist Roman Jakobson has indicated the important bearing of aphasic disturbances upon theories of language and language development and has contributed two major implications of linguistics for aphasia: first, that the dissolution of phonemic distinctions in aphasia will be the mirror image of the order in which the child acquires these distinctions [101]; second, that there will be two fundamental "types" of aphasia corresponding to the basic linguistic processes of metaphor and metonymy [104], the former referring to the capacity to make paradigmatic substitutions (*similarity*) and the latter to the capacity to make sequential transitions (*contiguity*). Another investigator whose work demonstrates the close interaction between neurology, psychology, and linguistics is A. R. Luria. He has recently contributed a paper relating the brain localizations of injuries to various language performances and their linguistic implications [144], and his important book *Traumatic Aphasia* [143] is soon to be translated into English. Penfield and Roberts [195] have reported the results obtained by electrical stimulation of the bared cortex of conscious subjects during surgery; some of these patients were aphasic and some not, and some were bilingual.

The rapidly increasing interest of psycholinguists in aphasia as an area of research has been shown by a recent summer seminar and conference on aphasia that involved some thirty specialists. It was sponsored by the Social Science Research Council's Committee on Linguistics and Psychology, with support from the National Institute of Mental Health.[3] Reported in these discussions were a number of on-going researches of a psycholinguistic nature. Following the lead provided by Jakobson concerning the distinction between similarity and contiguity functions, Goodglass and Mayer [80] have been able to distinguish agrammatic aphasia from other types of disturbance. Goodglass and others also have been working on gestural communication in aphasia. Howes and Geschwind reported on a series of studies being undertaken to determine the statistical properties of aphasic speech (e.g., word-frequency functions, word-association norms, threshold phenomena). On the important question of the dimensionality of aphasic disturbances, Schuell and Jenkins [219] have contributed a paper showing that much of the variance in standard tests can be accounted for by a single Guttman-type scale—implying that aphasic disturbances may be unidimensional. In addition, we have factor analytic studies by Wepman, Bock, Jones, and Van Pelt [cf. 260 and later unpublished papers] which indicate not only a dominant factor, but other independent dimensions as well. There is also an analysis of some forty cases in the classic literature by Osgood and Miron [190] which yields evidence for a symbolic versus skill-level factor, a decoding

[3] A report of this seminar and conference is presently being prepared by this writer for publication in book form.

versus encoding factor and perhaps an orthographic versus vocalic channel factor! There are several things that may account for these divergent results—types of patients studied (e.g., cerebrovascular versus traumatic injury), types of tests employed, and treatment of data. (Osgood and Miron used a procedure which, in effect, minimized differences between patients and tests in general level of disturbance and difficulty.) This is obviously only a part of this exciting area, but another chapter would be required to adequately cover what is happening in the study of aphasia.

Psycholinguistics and the Social Sciences

It is a truism to say that the social behavior of human individuals is in large part learned. If the analysis of learning made earlier in this paper is at all valid, then the most characteristic mode of learning in humans involves at least a two-stage process—learning the significance of signs and learning the instrumental acts which express intentions. Psycholinguistic analysis of meanings, stereotypes, attitudes, symbols, and the like and the development of adequate measuring techniques in these areas should therefore have value for the social sciences generally. Just as a *personality trait* can be defined as that (mediation process) which renders equivalent classes of situations and classes of behaviors [cf. Allport, 5], so a *culture trait* could be defined as that shared mediation process which renders equivalent (across people) the significances of signs, including language signs, and the classes of behaviors to be expected. *Roles,* from the viewpoint of others, are just such a set of signs or cues having a common significance. From the viewpoint of the role player, the role implies, and its learning imposes, consistent ways of perceiving situations and acting in them. A rigorous analysis of cultural phenomena through language has been begun in the study of kinship roles and their semantics [cf. Lounsbury, 142, for an illustration of this approach].

Psycholinguistic relativity versus universality. Emphasis on the uniqueness of languages and cultures seems to alternate in long-period cycles with emphasis on language universals and cultural generality. During the past two decades we have been moving through a period of heavy emphasis on uniqueness. This has been sparked scientifically by the writings of the linguist Benjamin Lee Whorf [264]. Whorf's thesis, supported mainly by comparisons between American Indian languages and Standard Average European (SAE) was that the language one uses, through the lexical and grammatical categories it sets up, somehow influences how one perceives the world around him, how one thinks, and even one's natural philosophy. This sweeping generalization would seem to impose severe limitations on the possibility of cross-cultural understanding, and it has stimulated a great deal of theoretical and, more recently, experimental activity.

On the theoretical side, Whorf's proposition of psycholinguistic relativity has been the focus of a number of conferences involving linguists, anthropologists, psychologists, and philosophers. The results of one such conference held in the summer of 1952 are summarized by Levi-Strauss, Jakobson, and Voegelin [135]; the results of another are presented in *Language and Culture,* edited by Hoijer [91]. And, of course, the theoretical implications of Whorf's thesis have been considered in a number of separate papers [cf. Feuer, 70; Lenneberg, 129]. The human infant enters this world at some point on its surface and finds itself among adults who have certain stable ways of behaving and who use a language whose lexical and grammatical code differs from other languages. More or less simultaneously he learns how to behave like others, including cognitive behavior (meanings, ways of perceiving, conceptual categories), *and* how to talk like others. Given this complete interweaving during development, it is no wonder that social scientists have difficulty disentangling all the threads—and I certainly will not try to do so here. Elsewhere I have suggested [187] that psycholinguistic relativity will hold when the arbitrary denotative or referential aspects of language are involved, and psycholinguistic generality will hold when the nonarbitrary connotative or expressive aspects of language are involved.

Experimental verification of the Whorfian hypothesis requires independent assessment of both linguistic and cognitive differences, and then demonstration of dependency of the latter upon the former. A very significant experiment has been done by Brown and Lenneberg [33]. First, it was shown that, for English-speaking subjects, color stimuli drawn from various portions of the spectrum varied in their codability (i.e., in the speed and consistency with which they were labeled). Second, it was demonstrated that ease of executing a cognitive task involving these stimuli (here, recognition) covaried with their codability. Lenneberg and Roberts [131] have demonstrated the same dependency relation for Zuni subjects—and, since the ways in which the Zuni and English languages "carve up" the spectrum differ, these two experiments taken together constitute a demonstration of psycholinguistic relativity. Van de Geer [256] has successfully replicated the Brown and Lenneberg experiment in the Netherlands. He has also extended this methodology to the domain of facial expressions, again finding that ease of recognition covaries with codability in the language. Carroll and Casagrande [42] report two experiments growing out of the Southwest Project in Comparative Psycholinguistics [cf. 44], both dealing with denotative aspects of language and both displaying psycholinguistic relativity. In the first, using Hopi versus English-speaking subjects, the effects of translation-equivalent verbs having different semantic ranges upon the categorizing of pictures was demonstrated. In the second, using Navajo-dominant versus English-dominant Navajo children as subjects, it was shown that the Navajo-speaking Navajo children tended to sort objects more in terms of shape than color—and Navajo verbs require a suffix referring to the shape of the object being discussed. Along similar lines, Flavell [71] has found that labeling tachistoscopically presented pictures with verbs (*leaping*) as compared with nouns (*a leap*) significantly influences the degree of activity attributed to them. A note of caution is injected into these generally positive results by Maclay [147]. Working with Navajo-speaking versus English-speaking subjects sorting objects in terms of shape versus alternative categories, he found no significant differences in either mode or latency of sorting behavior.

The pendulum now seems to be swinging back toward interest in language universals and psycholinguistic generality rather than relativity. This is evidenced by renewed concern with language typologies on the part of linguists [cf. Greenberg's *Essays in Linguistics,* 81]. It was also evident in the recent Conference on Language Universals (sponsored by the Social Science Research Council's Committee on Linguistics and Psychology) at which papers given by nearly a dozen linguists provided impressive evidence for universals of both absolute and statistical nature in phonology, grammar, syntax, and semantics.[4] For the development of psycholinguistics, the significance of the search for regularities among the admittedly fascinating idiosyncrasies of languages is made clear in the statement calling for this conference:

Language universals are by their very nature summary statements about characteristics or tendencies shared by all human speakers. As such they constitute the most general laws of a science of linguistics (as contrasted with a method and a set of descriptive results). Further, since language is at once both an aspect of individual behavior and an aspect of human culture, its universals provide both the major point of contact with underlying psychological principles (psycholinguistics) and the major source of implications for human culture in general (ethnolinguistics).

It is perhaps interesting, while consistent with a statement I made at the beginning of this section, that experimental evidence suggestive of psycholinguistic universality has appeared primarily for the affective or expressive (rather than referential) aspects of language. The two primary lines of research have been (1) the cross-linguistic generality of factors of "connotative" meaning, growing out of the work of Osgood and his associates, and (2) the cross-linguistic generality of tendencies toward phonetic symbolism [cf. Brown, 31]. A somewhat related direction of study has been into the similarities and differences among cultural value

---

[4] The papers prepared for this conference are to appear in book form under the editorship of Joseph Greenberg.

systems, as shown in the studies of Kluckhohn [118], Morris [168], and Morris and Jones [169].

The first study on the generality of affective meaning factors was contributed by Kumata and Schramm [121]. It compared the similarity of factor structures obtained when Japanese and Korean bilinguals (both against English) responded twice to a typical semantic differential, first in one language and then in the other, with the similarity of factors for monolingual English speakers merely taking the same form twice. Not only were the factorial correspondences extraordinarily high for all groups, but the bilinguals yielded as high correspondences as the monolinguals—clearly indicating that the language code per se does not influence semantic-factor structure. Kumata [120], for Japanese versus Americans, and Triandis and Osgood [253], for Greeks versus Americans, have compared semantic-factor structures for monolingual (and monocultural) subjects. Although the factorial correspondences are not as high as for bilinguals (where we are, after all, dealing with the same individuals), they are nevertheless significant for the first two or three dominant factors. In connection with the Southwest Project in Comparative Psycholinguistics, Suci [244] was able to demonstrate significant correspondences for at least the first two factors (evaluation and potency) for Hopi, Navajo, and Zuni nonliterates as compared with Anglos. Under auspices of the same project, Osgood [186] studied the generality of visual-verbal synesthetic tendencies among Navajo, Mexican-Spanish, Japanese, and American subjects. Not only did all groups display strong synesthetic tendencies (to associate certain visual alternatives with certain word meanings, e.g., "white" rather than "black" with *happy*), but agreements in direction of synesthetic tendency across language-culture groups were astonishingly high (e.g., 99 per cent agreement between Anglos and Japanese).

It is axiomatic among linguists that the phonemes of any language are meaningless in themselves—they merely provide the bases for differences in meaning. The "meaning" meant here is referential, not expressive, but most linguists have denied that *phonetic symbolism,* even in the expressive sense, is in any way universal. It is true that the assignments of sounds to meanings are *essentially* arbitrary; therefore any rule of phonetic symbolism (e.g., that high vowels signify *little* things and low vowels *large* things) will have many exceptions (e.g., *small* versus *big*). Yet, on the other hand, it is also true that the exceptions produced by arbitrariness may obscure the existence of general laws—particularly if the linguist insists upon absolute universality (no exceptions) as a criterion of lawfulness. In any case, experiments on the matter yield generally positive results in the statistical sense.

A number of different experimental designs have been used in testing this notion [cf. Brown and Nuttall, 34]. In two classic experiments by Sapir and Newman [cf. Brown, 31, for description], English speakers were told that nonsense syllables like *mal* and *mil* referred to tables of different sizes and that they were to decide which were large and which small. Both experiments demonstrated that the impression of magnitude increased with the size of oral cavity, lowering of vocalic resonance, and back-tongue position in producing the vowel sounds. Another procedure has been to have English-speaking subjects match words from different languages for meanings (e.g., *heavy-light* with the Chinese *ch'ing-ch'ung*—Which Chinese word goes with the English *heavy?*) Or both pairs may be from non-English languages, but with English subjects doing the judging [Brackbill and Little, 29]. Since the languages related in these ways have generally been from entirely different families, the presumption of phonetic symbolism as the basis for significantly better than chance results (even though small in absolute magnitude) seems reasonable. However, Brackbill and Little [29], Brown and Nuttall [34], and, most recently, Miron [165] have all pointed to a number of subtle factors which might contribute to such results—English-speaking experimenters have in some cases selected the other-language alternatives, frequency of usage is known to influence word length and it could correlate across languages, and so forth. Returning to the essential idea of the Sapir-Newman procedure, Miron [165] devised a set of CVC syllables which were nonsense in both English and Japanese and which permitted systematic variation of both consonants and vowels and their contexts. These nonsense materials were presented in random orders on audio tape to both American and Japanese subjects who judged the affective meanings of the syllables on a form of semantic differential (translation equivalent). The results indicated significant relations between certain articulatory-acoustic features and connoted meanings, e.g., frontness of consonant articulation and connoted "pleasantness," lowness of vowel resonance and connoted "potency," and such relations generally held across the two language/culture groups.

Universal tendencies to imitate the sounds of nature may also contribute to interlanguage similarities (e.g., the English *rumble, buzz, cock-a-doodle-doo*). In fact, any universal tendency in human culture *can* serve as the basis for a language universal. A particularly interesting example is the long-suspected tendency for baby terms referring to the female parent to involve nasal consonants, those referring to the male parent to involve oral stop consonants, and both to often involve reduplication. Murdock [173] has finally put this proposition to the test, using materials available in the Human Relations Area files and being careful to sample languages in terms of families and subfamilies. In a sample of 531 mother terms and 541 father terms thus derived, the hypothesis was strikingly verified—55 per cent of mother terms as compared with only 15 per cent of father terms involved nasals $/m/$, $/n/$, or $/ng/$, and the reverse trend held for oral stops $/p/$, $/b/$, $/t/$, or $/d/$. Why? Jakobson [102] has shown that the simple alternation between stop consonant and vowel fits his views on the first differentiations of child language development, and when one adds the biologically obvious notion that during feeding, with mouth at the breast or holding fluid, the nasal is the only possible phonation, the distinction becomes clear. Of course, psychologically one must add the notion that infants "name" their parents around the world—which becomes sensible when one observes the tendency for parents to attribute meaningful intentions to their young ones (i.e., if *nana* is heard from the child repeatedly when being fed near the mother, it is understandable that this should become the "name" for mother in baby language).

Content analysis. One of the most useful roles the psycholinguist can play in relation to the social sciences generally is that of toolmaker. This has already become apparent in the development of techniques of content analysis. The traditional method of simply counting the frequencies of occurrence of content categories, developed by Lasswell and his associates [128]—a method often identified as content analysis—has been critically evaluated by Berelson [10]. Berelson emphasized the limitations of this method and concluded, in effect, that content analysis had reached a dead end. More recently a book titled *Trends in Content Analysis,* edited by Ithiel Pool [201], has appeared which treats content analysis as a psycholinguistic problem, offers a variety of new techniques and their rationales, and creates an impression that the dead end was really just a sharp curve.

As we have defined the discipline, content analysis is clearly a psycholinguistic problem. The content analyst is interested in using events in messages as a means of either drawing inferences about their sources or making predictions about effects on their receivers. To do this, he must first discover reliable dependency relations between message events and psychological events. These dependency relations may be utilized intuitively by the sensitive qualitative analyst [cf. George in 201] or may be made explicit and tested by a variety of experimental procedures [cf. Osgood and Mahl in 201]. The dependency relation between "attention value" for source or receiver and sheer frequency of occurrence (i.e., Lasswell's method) is only one of many possible indexes. Other methods of content analysis are described and illustrated in this new book. "Evaluative Assertion Analysis" [cf. Osgood, Saporta, and Nunnally, 191] determines the evaluations of various attitude objects in messages through fairly rigorous and explicit linguistic restructuring.[5] "Speech Disturbance Analysis" employs a variety of quantifiable indicators in spontaneous speech, e.g., hesitations, corrections, and repetitions, to get at the instrumental uses of language in psychotherapeutic situations and the like [cf. Mahl in 201]. "Contingency Analysis" is designed to permit inferences about the association structure of the source from analysis of the pattern of greater-than- and less-than-chance contingencies among events in his messages [cf. Osgood in 201; Baldwin, 6]. "Cloze Procedure" deals with estimating the "readability" of a source or the "comprehension" of a receiver from the ease with which deletions in the message can be replaced by the receiver—probably a very general index of the correspondence of source and receiver language structures [cf. Wilson Taylor, 246, 247]. This brief summary by no means exhausts the possible states or characteristics of language users that might be gauged by events in the messages they exchange. The only limitation lies in the ability of psycholinguists (broadly speaking) to establish valid and reliable dependency relations.

Psycholinguistics and the Humanities

Here the potentialities seem great but the actualizations small. Again it is likely that the initial contacts will be in the form of new techniques. In this connection it is interesting that *Trends in Content Analysis* includes chapters by Saporta and Sebeok and by Armstrong in which these methods are applied to structured language materials and to folklore. A chapter by Garraty is also included. Here the prospects of such application to biography and history are discussed. Wilson Taylor [247] has applied his "Cloze Procedure" not only to the "readability" of printed prose but also to what might be called the "communicability" of visual arts.

In another recent conference on stylistics, sponsored by the Committee on Linguistics and Psychology, a major attempt to bridge the gap between the humanities and the social sciences was made. Participants included literary critics, specialists in poetics, folklorists, linguists, psychologists, and anthropologists. The book growing out of this conference, *Style in Language* [220], edited by Sebeok, illustrates both some potential points of fruitful contact and the width of the gap in orientation that exists, e.g., implicit versus explicit analysis, qualitative versus quantitative approaches, concern with uniqueness versus generality, etc. Indicative of psycholinguistic possibilities in the study of stylistics were

---

[5] Since the original writing of this chapter, several unpublished papers by David Hays of the Rand Corporation have come to my attention. This method has been elaborated and adapted for content analysis on electronic computers—which illustrates one of the values of explicit quantifiable methods.

Roger Brown's paper on an analysis of pronouns in various languages and their relation to symbols of power and solidarity, John Carroll's papers on factor analyses of both subjective judgments and objective indicators of style, Charles Osgood's paper on the prediction of stylistic differences in suicide versus ordinary notes from psycholinguistic theory, James Jenkins' paper on communality in word associations as an indicator of more general patterns of verbal behavior, and George Miller's paper, which was a psychologist's summary impressions of the Conference on Style.

It would seem to be a small step from experiments on style and the readability of literature to experiments on aesthetics more generally. Viewing aesthetic products (paintings, musical compositions, poems, and the like) as messages being exchanged between their creators (sources) and appreciators (receivers)—a mode of viewing that is by no means accepted by a majority of humanists!—one may study both the semantic aspects of this form of communication and its informational aspects. In the former case, for example, one may be interested in how various characteristics of the "message" (color, form, melodic line, harmony, meter, etc.) express the meaningful intentions or moods of the creator, on the one hand, and produce meaningful significances (denotative, connotative, emotional) in appreciators, on the other. One suspects that there is a rich lode to be mined in the related phenomena of metaphor and synesthesia. The semantic differential has been employed in a number of studies of this sort [Tucker, 254, on the factorial structure of judgments of paintings; Tannenbaum, in 193, on the connotations of visual colors and forms; Osgood, 186, on the cross-cultural generality of visual-verbal synesthetic tendencies]. As to informational aspects, one can at least speculate on the notion that there is some optimum degree of uncertainty or unpredictability (e.g., "variations on a theme") in all aesthetic products that produces maximum aesthetic enjoyment. It may be that this is the same degree of uncertainty at which there is maximum facilitation in learning. This brings us to a final area in which psycholinguistics is already having impact on the humanities—the application of psycholinguistic principles and methods to teaching languages [cf. Carroll, 40, 41; Dunkel, 65; Huse, 97]. This may seem a rather mundane matter in the immediate context of stylistics and aesthetics, but it is a point of articulation where psycholinguistics can be of considerable practical value.

SUMMARY

This chapter has been a very sketchy, and certainly insufficient, outline of what seems to be going on in psycholinguistics, a relatively new

area of science that borders on psychology. I have tried to place psycholinguistics in its proper setting within the total study of human communication and indicate its major sources of methods and viewpoints—
from learning theory, from linguistics, and from information theory.
Since it does concern itself with the processes of decoding and encoding
by human organisms, it is in a sense coextensive with psychology as a
whole, and it therefore has many implications and points of contact with
psychological science. On the other hand, because its focus is on language
behavior and because language behavior is the major point of articulation between the sciences dealing with individuals and those dealing with
society, psycholinguistics should have a very significant impact upon
the social sciences and the humanities. This impact is still largely un-
realized.

REFERENCES

1. Aborn, M., & Rubenstein, H. Word-class distribution in sentences of
   fixed length. *Language,* 1957, **32,** 666–674.
2. Aborn, M., Rubenstein, H., & Sterling, T. D. Sources of contextual
   restraint upon words in sentences. *J. exp. Psychol.,* 1959, **57,** 171–180.
3. Adams, J. Laboratory studies of behavior without awareness. *Psychol.
   Bull.,* 1957, **54,** 383–405.
4. Allport, F. H. *Social psychology.* Boston: Houghton Mifflin, 1924.
5. Allport, G. W. *Personality: a psychological interpretation.* New York:
   Holt, 1937.
6. Baldwin, A. L. Personal structure analysis: a statistical method for investigating the single personality. *J. abnorm. soc. Psychol.,* 1942, **37,**
   163–183.
7. Barik, H. C., & Lambert, W. E. Conditioning of complex verbal sequences. *Canad. J. Psychol.,* 1960, **14,** 87–95.
8. Baxter, J. C. Mediated generalization as a function of semantic differential performance. Unpublished doctoral dissertation, Univer.
   Texas, 1959.
9. Bendig, A. Twenty questions: an information analysis. *J. exp. Psychol.,*
   1953, **46,** 345–348.
10. Berelson, B. *Content analysis in communication research.* Glencoe, Ill.:
    Free Press, 1952.
11. Berko, J. The child's learning of English morphology. *Word,* 1958,
    14, 150–177.
12. Berko, J., & Brown, R. Psycholinguistic research methods. In P. H.
    Mussen (Ed.), *The handbook of research methods in child psychology,*
    in press.
13. Berlyne, D. E. Attention, perception and behavior theory. *Psychol.
    Rev.,* 1951, **58,** 137–146.
14. Berlyne, D. E. A theory of human curiosity. *Brit. J. Psychol.,* 1954,
    65, 180–191.

15. Berlyne, D. E. Knowledge and stimulus-response psychology. *Psychol. Rev.*, 1954, **61**, 245–254.
16. Binder, A., McConnell, D., & Sjoholm, N. Verbal conditioning as a function of experimenter characteristics. *J. abnorm. soc. Psychol.*, 1957, **55**, 309–314.
17. Birdwhistell, R. L. *Introduction to kinetics: an annotation system for analysis of body motion and gesture.* Washington: Dept. of State, Foreign Serv. Inst., 1952.
18. Bloch, B., & Trager, G. L. *Outline of linguistic analysis.* Baltimore, Md.: Linguistic Society of America, 1942.
19. Bloomfield, L. *Language.* New York: Holt, 1933.
20. Boder, D. P. The adjective-verb quotient; a contribution to the psychology of language. *Psychol. Rev.*, 1940, **3**, 309–343.
21. Bousfield, W. A. An empirical study of the production of affectively toned items. *J. gen. Psychol.*, 1944, **30**, 205–215.
22. Bousfield, W. A. The occurrence of clustering in the recall of randomly arranged associates. *J. gen. Psychol.*, 1953, **49**, 229–240.
23. Bousfield, W. A., & Barclay, W. D. The relationship between order and frequency of occurrence of restricted associated responses. *J. exp. Psychol.*, 1950, **40**, 643–647.
24. Bousfield, W. A., & Barry, H. Quantitative correlates of euphoria. *J. exp. Psychol.*, 1937, **21**, 218–222.
25. Bousfield, W. A., & Cohen, B. H. The effects of reinforcement on the occurrence of clustering in the recall of randomly arranged associates. *J. Psychol.*, 1953, **36**, 67–81.
26. Bousfield, W. A., Cohen, B. H., & Silva, J. G. The extension of Marbe's law to the recall of stimulus-words. *Amer. J. Psychol.*, 1956, **69**, 429–433.
27. Bousfield, W. A., Cohen, B. A., & Whitmarsh, G. A. Verbal generalization: a theoretical rationale and an experimental technique. Tech. Report, ONR Contract No. N-onr-631, 1958.
28. Bousfield, W. A., & Sedgewick, C. H. W. An analysis of sequences of restricted associative responses. *J. gen. Psychol.*, 1944, **30**, 149–165.
29. Brackbill, Y., & Little, K. B. Factors determining the guessing of meanings of foreign words. *J. abnorm. soc. Psychol.*, 1957, **54**, 312–318.
30. Brown, R. W. Linguistic determinism and the part of speech. *J. abnorm. soc. Psychol.*, 1957, **55**, 1–5.
31. Brown, R. W. *Words and things.* Glencoe, Ill.: Free Press, 1958.
32. Brown, R. W., & Hildum, D. C. Expectancy and the perception of syllables. *Language*, 1956, **32**, 411–419.
33. Brown, R. W., & Lenneberg, E. H. A study in language and cognition. *J. abnorm. soc. Psychol.*, 1954, **49**, 454–462.
34. Brown, R. W., & Nuttall, R. Method in phonetic symbolism experiments. *J. abnorm. soc. Psychol.*, 1959, **59**, 441–445.
35. Bruner, J. S., Goodnow, J. J., & Austin, G. A. *A study of thinking.* New York: Wiley, 1956.

36. Burke, C. D. Drive and word association performance. Unpublished master's thesis, Univer. Ill., 1960.
37. Busemann, A. Über typische und phasiche Unterschiede der Kategoricalen Sprach form. *Z. pädag. Psychol.,* 1926, **27,** 415–419.
38. Campbell, V., & Freeman, J. T. Some functions of experimentally-induced language in perceptual learning. *Percept. mot. Skills,* 1955, **5,** 71–79.
39. Carroll, J. B. Diversity of vocabulary and the harmonic series law of word-frequency distribution. *Psychol. Rev.,* 1938, **2,** 379–386.
40. Carroll, J. B. *The study of language.* Cambridge, Mass.: Harvard Univer. Press, 1953.
41. Carroll, J. B. Research on teaching foreign languages. In *Handbook of research on teaching,* in press.
42. Carroll, J. B., & Casagrande, J. B. The function of language classifications in behavior. In Maccoby, Newcomb & Hartley (Eds.), *Readings in social psychology.* (3rd ed.) New York: Holt, 1958. Pp. 18–31.
43. Carroll, J. B., Kjeldergaard, P. M., & Carton, A. S. Number of opposites vs. number of primaries as a response measure in free association tests. Unpublished paper, privately distributed, 1961.
44. Casagrande, J. B. The Southwest Project in comparative psycholinguistics: a progress report. *Soc. Sci. Res. Coun. Items,* 1956, **10,** 41–45.
45. Cherry, C. *On human communication: a review, a survey, and a criticism.* New York: Wiley, 1957.
46. Chomsky, N. *Syntactic structures.* 's-Gravenhage, Holland: Mouton and Co., 1957.
47. Chomsky, N. Review of *Verbal behavior,* by B. F. Skinner. *Language,* 1959, **35,** 26–58.
48. Chotlos, J. W. Studies in language behavior. IV. A statistical and comparative analysis of individual written language samples. *Psychol. Monogr.,* 1944, **56,** 77–111.
49. Cliff, N. The relation of adverb-adjective combinations to their components. Tech. Report, ONR Contract No. N-onr-1858, Yale Univer., 1957.
50. Cofer, C. N. Verbal behavior in relation to reasoning and values. In H. Guetzkow (Ed.), *Groups, leadership and men.* Pittsburgh, Pa.: Carnegie Press, 1951.
51. Cofer, C. N. The role of language in human problem solving. Paper presented at a Conference on Human Problem Solving, N.Y. Univer., 1954.
52. Cofer, C. N., & Dunn, J. T. Personality ratings as influenced by verbal stimuli. *J. Pers.,* 1952, **21,** 223–227.
53. Cofer, C. N., & Foley, J. P., Jr. Mediated generalization and the interpretation of verbal behavior. *Psychol. Rev.,* 1942, **49,** 513–540.
54. Cooper, F. S., Liberman, A. M., & Borst, J. M. The interconversation of audible and visual patterns as a basis for research in the perception of speech. *Proc. nat. Acad. Sci.,* 1951, **37,** 318–325.
55. Dashiel, J. F. Direction orientation in maze running by the white rat. *Comp. Psychol. Monogr.,* 1930, **7,** No. 32.

56. Davis, J. Unpublished research, Univer. of Ill., Dept. of Psychol., 1957.
57. Deese, J. On the structure of associative meaning. *Psychol. Rev.*, 1962, **69**, 161–175.
58. Dewey, G. *Relative frequency of English speech sounds.* Cambridge, Mass.: Harvard Univer. Press, 1923.
59. Dicken, C. F. Connotative meaning as a determinant of stimulus generalization. Unpublished doctoral dissertation, Univer. Minn., 1958.
60. Dodge, J. S. Predicting the meanings of assigns from the measured meanings of signs with which they are associated. Unpublished doctoral dissertation, Univer. Ill., 1955.
61. Dollard, J., & Miller, N. E. *Personality and psychotherapy.* New York: McGraw-Hill, 1950.
62. Dörken, H. Frequency of common association. *Psychol. Rep.*, 1956, **2**, 407–408.
63. Dulany, D. E. Reinforcement of verbal behavior. Summary report on research supported by NSF G-4461, 1960.
64. Dulany, D. E. Hypotheses and habits in verbal "operant conditioning." *Psychol. Rev.*, 1961, in press.
65. Dunkel, H. B. *Second language learning.* New York: Ginn, 1948.
66. Epstein, W. The influence of syntactical structure on learning. *Amer. J. Psychol.*, 1962, **74**, 80–85.
67. Epstein, W. A further study of the influence of syntactical structure on learning. *Amer. J. Psychol.*, 1962, **75**, 121–126.
68. Fairbanks, G. Systemic research in experimental phonetics: 1. A theory of the speech mechanism as a servosystem. *J. Speech Dis.*, 1954, **19**, 133–139.
69. Fairbanks, G. Selective vocal effects of delayed auditory feedback. *J. Speech Dis.*, 1955, **20**, 333–346.
70. Feuer, L. S. Sociological aspects of the relation between language and philosophy. *Phil. Sci.*, 1953, **20**, 85–100.
71. Flavell, J. H. A test of the Whorfian theory. *Psychol. Rep.*, 1958, **4**, 455–462.
72. Flavell, J. H. Meaning and meaning similarity: I. A theoretical reassessment. *J. gen. Psychol.*, 1961, **64**, 307–319.
73. Flavell, J. H. Meaning and meaning similarity: II. The semantic differential and co-occurrence as predictors of judged similarity in meaning. *J. gen. Psychol.*, 1961, **64**, 321–335.
74. French, N. R., Carter, C. W., & Koenig, W. The words and sounds of telephone conversations. *Bell Syst. Tech. J.*, 1930, **9**, 290–324.
75. Fries, C. C. *The structure of English: an introduction to the construction of English sentences.* New York: Harcourt, Brace, 1952.
76. Garner, W. H., & Hake, H. W. The amount of information in absolute judgments. *Psychol. Rev.*, 1951, **58**, 446–459.
77. Goldman-Eisler, F. Speech analysis and mental processes. *Lang. & Speech*, 1958, **1**, 59–75.
78. Goldstein, K. *Language and language disturbance.* New York: Grune & Stratton, 1948.

79. Gonzales, R. C., & Cofer, C. N. Exploratory studies of verbal context by means of clustering in free recall. *J. gen. Psychol.,* 1959, **95,** 293–320.

80. Goodglass, H., & Mayer, J. Agrammatism in aphasia. *J. Speech Dis.,* 1958, **23,** 99–111.

81. Greenberg, J. H. *Essays in linguistics.* Chicago: Univer. Chicago Press, 1957.

82. Greenspoon, J. The effect of verbal and non-verbal stimuli on the frequency of members of two verbal response classes. Unpublished doctoral dissertation, Indiana Univer., 1951.

83. Harris, Z. *Methods in structural linguistics.* Chicago: Univer. Chicago Press, 1951.

84. Haugen, E. *The Norwegian language in America: a study in bilingual behavior.* Philadelphia: Univer. Pa. Press, 1953.

85. Hebb, D. O. *The organization of behavior: a neurophysiological theory.* New York: Wiley, 1949.

86. Hebb, D. O. Drives and the C.N.S. (Conceptual nervous system). *Psychol. Rev.,* 1955, **62,** 243–254.

87. Herdan, G. *Language as choice and chance.* Groningen, Holland: P. Noordhoff Ltd., 1956.

88. Hildum, D. C., & Brown, R. Verbal reinforcement and interviewer bias. *J. abnorm. soc. Psychol.,* 1956, **53,** 108–111.

89. Hofstäter, P. R. Farbsymbolik und Ambivalenz. *Psychologishe Beit.,* 1956, **2,** 526–540.

90. Hofstäter, P. R. Männlich und weiblich. *Wiener Archiv für Psychol., Psychiat., und Neurol.,* 1956, **6,** 3–16.

91. Hoijer, H. (Ed.) Language and culture. *Amer. Anthrop.,* 1954, **56,** No. 6.

92. Howes, D. H. On the interpretation of word frequency as a variable affecting speed of recognition. *J. exp. Psychol.,* 1954, **48,** 106–112.

93. Howes, D. H. On the relation between the probability of a word as an associate and in general linguistic usage. *J. abnorm. soc. Psychol.,* 1957, **54,** 75–85.

94. Howes, D. H., & Osgood, C. E. On the combination of associative probabilities in linguistic contexts. *Amer. J. Psychol.,* 1954, **67,** 241–258.

95. Howes, D. H., & Solomon, R. L. Visual duration threshold as a function of word-probability. *J. exp. Psychol.,* 1951, **41,** 401–410.

96. Hull, C. L. Knowledge and purpose as habit mechanisms. *Psychol. Rev.,* 1930, **37,** 511–525.

97. Huse, H. R. *The psychology of foreign language study.* Chapel Hill, N.C.: Univer. N.C. Press, 1931.

98. Irwin, O. C. Infant speech. *Scient. Amer.,* 1949, **18,** 22–24.

99. Jakobovits, L. A., & Lambert, W. E. Semantic satiation among bilinguals. *J. exp. Psychol.,* 1961, **62,** 576–582.

100. Jakobovits, L. A., & Lambert, W. E. Semantic satiation in an addition task. *Canad. J. Psychol.,* 1962, **16,** 112–119.

101. Jakobson, R. *Kindersprache, aphasie und allgemeine lautgesetze.* Uppsala: Almquist and Wiksell, 1941.

102. Jakobson, R. Why 'mama' and 'papa'? In *Perspectives in Psychological Theory.* 1960. Pp. 124–134.

103. Jakobson, R., Fant, G. M., & Halle, M. *Preliminaries to speeech analysis: the distinctive features and their correlates.* Tech. Report No. 13, MIT, Acoustics Lab., 1952.

104. Jakobson, R. C., & Halle, M. *Fundamentals of language.* The Hague, Netherlands: Mouton, 1956.

105. Jenkins, J. J. Word association revisited. Paper read at Amer. Psychol. Ass., New York, September, 1954.

106. Jenkins, J. J. Degree of polarization and scores on the principal factors for concepts in the semantic atlas study. Unpublished manuscript, Center for Advanced Study in the Behavioral Sciences, May, 1959.

107. Jenkins, J. J., & Russell, W. A. Associative clustering during recall. *J. abnorm. soc. Psychol.,* 1952, **47,** 818–821.

108. Jenkins, J. J., & Russell, W. A. Basic studies on individual and group behavior. Tech. Report, ONR Contract No. N8-onr-66216, 1956.

109. Jenkins, J. J., & Russell, W. A. Systematic changes in word association norms: 1910–1952. *J. abnorm. soc. Psychol.,* 1960, **60,** 293–304.

110. Jenkins, J. J., Russell, W. A., & Suci, G. J. An atlas of semantic profiles for 360 words. Tech. Report, ONR Contract No. N8-onr-66216, Univer. Minn., March, 1957.

111. Jenkins, J. J., Russell, W. A., & Suci, G. J. A table of distances for the semantic atlas. *Amer. J. Psychol.,* 1959, **72,** 623–625.

112. Judson, A. J., & Cofer, C. N. Reasoning as an associative process: I. "Direction" in a simple verbal problem *Psychol. Rep.,* 1956, **2,** 469–476.

113. Judson, A. J., Cofer, C. N., & Gelfand, S. Reasoning as an associative process: II. "Direction" in problem solving as a function of prior reinforcement of relevant responses. *Psychol. Rep.,* 1956, **2,** 501–508.

114. Kahane, H., Kahane, R., & Saporta, S. Development of verbal categories in child language. *Int. J. Amer. Ling.,* 1958, **24,** (4), 1–65.

115. Kanfer, F. H. Verbal rate, content and adjustment ratings in experimentally structured interviews. *J. abnorm. soc. Psychol.,* 1959, **58,** 305–311.

116. Kanfer, F. H. Word-association and the drive hypothesis of anxiety. *J. clin. Psychol.,* 1960, **16,** 200–204.

117. Kent, G. H., & Rosanoff, A. J. A study of association in insanity. *Amer. J. Insanity,* 1910, **67,** 37–96; 317–390.

118. Kluckhohn, C. Toward a comparison of value-emphases in different cultures. In *The state of the social sciences.* Chicago: Univer. Chicago Press, 1956.

119. Krasner, L. Studies of the conditioning of verbal behavior. *Psychol. Bull.,* 1958, **55,** 148–171.

120. Kumata, H. A factor analytic investigation of the generality of semantic

structure across two selected cultures. Unpublished doctoral dissertation, Univer. Ill., 1957.

121. Kumata, H., & Schramm, W. A pilot study of cross-cultural meaning *Publ. Opin. Quart.*, 1956, **20**, 229–238.

122. Lambert, W. E. Measurement of the linguistic dominance of bilinguals. *J. abnorm. soc. Psychol.*, 1955, **50**, 197–200.

123. Lambert, W. E. Developmental aspects of second-language acquisition. *J. soc. Psychol.*, 1956, **43**, 83–104.

124. Lambert, W. E. Studies of the verbal behavior of bilinguals. Paper read at Midwest Psychol. Ass., St. Louis, May, 1956.

125. Lambert, W. E., Havelka, J., & Crosby, C. The influence of language-acquisition context on bilingualism. *J. abnorm. soc. Psychol.*, 1958, **56**, 239–244.

126. Lambert, W. E., Havelka, J., & Gardner, R. C. Linguistic manifestations of bilingualism. *Amer. J. Psychol.*, 1959, **72**, 77–82.

127. Lambert, W. E., & Jakobovits, L. A. Verbal satiation and changes in the intensity of meaning. *J. exp. Psychol.*, 1960, **60**, 376–383.

128. Lasswell, H., et al. *Language of politics.* New York: Stewart, 1949.

129. Lenneberg, E. H. Cognition in ethnolinguistics. *Language,* 1953, **29**, 463–471.

130. Lenneberg, E. H. A probabilistic approach to language learning. *Behav. Sci.*, 1957, **2**, 1–12.

131. Lenneberg, E. H., & Roberts, J. M. The language of experience: a study in methodology. Supplement to *Int. J. Amer. Ling.*, 1956, **22**, No. 13.

132. Leopold, W. F. *Speech development of a bilingual child.* Evanston, Ill.: Northwestern Univer. Press, 1947. 4 vols.

133. Leopold, W. F. The study of child language and infant bilingualism. *Word,* 1948, **4**, 1–17.

134. Levin, S. M. The effects of awareness on verbal conditioning. *J. exp. Psychol.*, 1961, **61**, 67–75.

135. Levi-Strauss, C., Jakobson, R., Voegelin, C. F., Sebeok, T. A., et al. Results of a conference of anthropologists and linguists. Supplement to *Int. J. Amer. Ling.*, 1953, **19**, No. 2.

136. Liberman, A. M. Some results of research on speech reception. *J. acoust. Soc. Amer.*, 1957, **29**, 117–123.

137. Liberman, A. M., Delattre, P. C. & Cooper, F. S. The role of selected stimulus variables in the perception of the unvoiced stop consonants. *Amer. J. Psychol.*, 1952, **65**, 497–516.

138. Liberman, A. M., Delattre, P. C., Cooper, F. S., & Gerstman, L. J. The role of consonant-vowel transitions in the perception of the stop and nasal consonants. *Psychol. Monogr.*, 1954, **68**, No. 379.

139. Liberman, A. M., Harris, K. S., Hoffman, H. S., & Griffith, B. C. The discrimination of speech sounds within and across phoneme boundaries. Unpublished report, Haskins Lab., New York, 1956.

140. Lipton, L., & Blanton, R. L. An experimental examination of the mediation hypotheses. Unpublished research, Univer. Ky., 1957.

141. Lorge, I. *The semantic count of the 570 commonest English words.* New York: Teachers Coll., Columbia Univer., Bureau of Publications, 1949.

142. Lounsbury, F. G. A semantic analysis of the Pawnee kinship usage. *Language,* 1956, **32,** 158–194.

143. Luria, A. R. *Traumatic aphasia.* Moscow: Acad. Med. Sci., 1947.

144. Luria, A. R. Brain disorders and language analysis. *Lang. & Speech,* 1958, **1,** 14–34.

145. McCarthy, D. Language development in children. In L. Carmichael (Ed.), *Manual of child psychology.* New York: Wiley, 1946.

146. McCarthy, D. Organismic interpretations of infant vocalizations. *Child Develpm.,* 1952, **23,** 273–280.

147. Maclay, H. An experimental study of language and non-linguistic behavior. *S. J. Anthrop.,* 1958, **14,** 220–229.

148. Maclay, H., & Osgood, C. E. Hesitation phenomenon in spontaneous English speech. *Word,* 1959, **15,** 19–44.

149. Maclay, H., & Sleator, M. D. Responses to language: Judgments of grammaticalness. *Int. J. Amer. Ling.,* 1960, **26,** 275–282.

150. McMurray, G. A. A study of "fittingness" of signs to words by means of the semantic differential. *J. exp. Psychol.,* 1958, **56,** 310–312.

151. Malmo, R. B. Activation: a neurophysiological dimension. *Psychol. Rev.,* 1959, **66,** 367–386.

152. Maltzman, I. Thinking: from a behavioristic point of view. *Psychol. Rev.,* 1955, **62,** 275–286.

153. Mandelbrot, B. Structure formelle des textes et communication. *Word,* 1954, **10,** 1–27.

154. Miller, G. A. *Language and communication.* New York: McGraw-Hill, 1951.

155. Miller, G. A. What is information measurement? *Amer. Psychologist,* 1953, **8,** 3–11.

156. Miller, G. A. The magical number seven, plus or minus two: Some limits on our capacity for processing information. *Psychol. Rev.,* 1956, **63,** 81–97.

157. Miller, G. A. Speech and communication. *J. acoust. Soc. Amer.,* 1958, **30,** 397–398.

158. Miller, G. A., & Frick, F. C. Statistical behavioristics and sequences of responses. *Psychol. Rev.,* 1949, **56,** 311–324.

159. Miller, G. A., Galanter, E., & Pribram, K. H. *Plans and the structure of behavior.* New York: Holt-Dryden, 1960.

160. Miller, G. A., Heise, G. A., & Lichten, W. The intelligibility of speech as a function of the context of the test materials. *J. exp. Psychol.,* 1951, **41,** 329–335.

161. Miller, G. A., Newman, E. B., & Friedman, E. A. Length-frequency statistics for written English. *Inform. & Control,* 1958, **1,** 370–389.

162. Miller, G. A., & Nicely, P. E. An analysis of perceptual confusions among some English consonants. *J. acoust. Soc. Amer.,* 1955, **27,** 338–352.

163. Miller, G. A., & Selfridge, J. A. Verbal context and the recall of meaningful material. *Amer. J. Psychol.*, 1950, **63**, 176–185.
164. Miller, J. G. Information input overload and psychopathology. *Amer. J. Psychiat.*, 1960, **116**, 695–704.
165. Miron, M. S. A cross-linguistic investigation of phonetic symbolism. *J. abnorm. soc. Psychol.*, 1961, **62**, 623–630.
166. Morris, C. *Signs, language and behavior.* Englewood Cliffs, N.J.: Prentice-Hall, 1946.
167. Morris, C. *Varieties of human value.* Chicago: Univer. Chicago Press, 1956.
168. Morris, C. Words without meaning. Review of B. F. Skinner, *Verbal behavior. Contemp. Psychol.*, 1958, **3**, 212–214.
169. Morris, C., & Jones, L. V. Value scales and dimensions. *J. abnorm. soc. Psychol.*, 1955, **51**, 523–535.
170. Mowrer, O. H. Speech development in the young child. *J. Speech Dis.*, 1952, **17**, 263–268.
171. Mowrer, O. H. The psychologist looks at language. *Amer. Psychologist*, 1954, **9**, 660–694.
172. Mowrer, O. H. The psychology of the sentence. Unpublished manuscript, Univer. Ill.: 1957. (Mimeographed)
173. Murdock, G. P. Cross-language parallels in parental kin terms. *Anthrop. Ling.*, 1959, **1**, 1–5.
174. Neisser, U. An experimental distinction between perceptual process and verbal response. *J. exp. Psychol.*, 1954, **47**, 399–402.
175. Newman, E. B. The pattern of vowels and consonants in various languages. *Amer. J. Psychol.*, 1951, **64**, 369–379.
176. Noble, C. E. An analysis of meaning. *Psychol. Rev.*, 1952, **59**, 421–430.
177. Norman, W. T. Stability characteristics of the semantic differential. Tech. Report, ONR Contract No. N8-onr-66216, Univer. Minn., 1958.
178. Olmsted, D. L., & Moore, O. K. Language, psychology and linguistics. *Psychol. Rev.*, 1952, **59**, 414–420.
179. Osgood, C. E. The nature and measurement of meaning. *Psychol. Bull.*, 1952, **49**, 197–237.
180. Osgood, C. E. *Method and theory in experimental psychology.* New York: Oxford, 1953.
181. Osgood, C. E. Behavior theory and the social sciences. *Behav. Sci.*, 1956, **1**, 167–185.
182. Osgood, C. E. A behavioristic analysis of perception and meaning as cognitive phenomena. *Symposium on cognition, University of Colorado, 1955.* Cambridge, Mass.: Harvard Univer. Press, 1957.
183. Osgood, C. E. Motivational dynamics of language behavior. In M. R. Jones (Ed.), *Nebraska Symposium on Motivation.* Lincoln, Neb.: Univer. Neb. Press, 1957.
184. Osgood, S. E. A question of sufficiency. Review of B. F. Skinner, *Verbal behavior. Contemp. Psychol.*, 1958, **3**, 209–212.
185. Osgood, C. E. Semantic space revisited: a reply to Uriel Weinreich's review of *The measurement of meaning. Word*, 1959, **15**, 192–200.

186. Osgood, C. E. The cross-cultural generality of visual-verbal synesthetic tendencies. *Behav. Sci.,* 1960, **5,** 146–169.

187. Osgood, C. E. Psycholinguistic relativity vs. universality. Paper read at Int. Congr. Psychol., Bonn, August, 1960.

188. Osgood, C. E., & Anderson, L. Certain relations among experienced contingencies, associative structure, and contingencies in encoded messages. *Amer. J. Psychol.,* 1957, **70,** 411–420.

189. Osgood, C. E., & Luria, Z. A blind analysis of a case of multiple personality using the semantic differential. *J. abnorm. soc. Psychol.,* 1954, **49,** 579–591.

190. Osgood, C. E., & Miron, M. S. Dimensionality in aphasia. Unpublished research, Univer. Ill., 1959.

191. Osgood, C. E., Saporta, S., & Nunnally, J. C. Evaluative assertion analysis. *Litera,* 1956, **3,** 47–102.

192. Osgood, C. E., & Sebeok, T. A. (Eds.) Psycholinguistics: a survey of theory and research problems. Part 2. Supplement to *J. abnorm. soc. Psychol.,* 1954, **49,** (4), 203.

193. Osgood, C. E., Suci, G. J., & Tannenbaum, P. H. *The measurement of meaning.* Urbana, Ill.: Univer. Ill. Press, 1957.

194. Osgood, C. E., & Wilson, K. V. Some terms and associated measures for talking about human communications. Unpublished research paper, Univer. Ill., 1961. (Mimeographed)

195. Penfield, W., & Roberts, L. *Speech and brain mechanisms.* Princeton, N.J.: Princeton Univer. Press, 1959.

196. Piaget, J. *The child's conception of the world.* New York: Harcourt, Brace, 1929.

197. Piaget, J. *The child's conception of physical causality.* New York: Harcourt, Brace, 1930.

198. Piaget, J. *The child's conception of number.* London: Routledge, 1952.

199. Pike, K. L. *Phonetics.* Ann Arbor, Mich.: Univer. Mich. Press, 1943.

200. Pike, K. L. *Language in relation to a unified theory of the structure of human behavior.* Glendale, Calif.: Summer Institute of Linguistics, 1954.

201. Pool, I. D. (Ed.) *Trends in content analysis.* Urbana, Ill.: Univer. Ill. Press, 1959.

202. Postman, L. The experimental analysis of motivational factors in perception. In M. R. Jones (Ed.), *Current theory and research in motivation.* Lincoln, Neb.: Univer. Neb. Press, 1953.

203. Postman, L., Bruner, J. S., & Walk, R. D. The perception of error. *Brit. J. Psychol.,* 1951, **42,** 1–10.

204. Postman, L., & Rosenzweig, M. R. Practice and transfer in the visual and auditory recognition of verbal stimuli. *Amer. J. Psychol.,* 1956, **69,** 209–226.

205. Prothro, E. T., & Keehn, J. D. Stereotypes and semantic space. *J. soc. Psychol.,* 1957, **45,** 197–209.

206. Quastler, H. (Ed.) *Information theory in psychology.* Glencoe, Ill.: Free Press, 1955.

207. Razran, G. Experimental semantics. *Trans. N.Y. Acad. Sci.*, 1952, **14** 171–177.
208. Rosenzweig, M. R., & Postman, L. Intelligibility as a function of frequency of usage. *J. exp. Psychol.*, 1957, **54**, 412–422.
209. Rosenzweig, M. R., & Postman, L. Frequency of usage and the perception of words. *Science*, 1958, **127**, 263–266.
210. Rubenstein, H., & Aborn, M. Psycholinguistics. *Annu. Rev. Psychol.*, 1960, 291–322.
211. Russell, W. A., & Jenkins, J. J. The complete Minnesota norms for responses to 100 words from the Kent-Rosanoff word association test. Tech. Report No. 11, ONR Contract No. N8-onr-66216.
212. Ryan, J. J. Comparison of verbal response transfer mediated by meaningfully similar and associated stimuli. *J. exp. Psychol.*, 1960, **60**, 408–415.
213. Salzinger, K. Experimental manipulation of verbal behavior. *J. gen. Psychol.*, 1959, **61**, 65–94.
214. Salzinger, K., & Pisoni, S. Reinforcement of affect responses of schizophrenics during the clinical interview. *J. abnorm. soc. Psychol.*, 1958, **57**, 84–90.
215. Saporta, S. Frequency of consonant clusters. *Language*, 1955, **31**, 25–30.
216. Saporta, S. Linguistic structure as a factor and as a measure in word association. Paper read at a work conference on word association, Univer. Minn., 1955.
217. Schellenberg, P. E. A group free association test for college students. Unpublished doctoral dissertation, Univer. Minn., 1930.
218. Schramm, W. Information theory and mass communication. *Journ. Quart.*, 1955, **32**, 131–146.
219. Schuell, H., & Jenkins, J. J. The nature of language deficit in asphasia. *Psychol. Rev.*, 1959, **66**, 45–67.
220. Sebeok, T. A. (Ed.) *Style in language.* New York: Wiley, 1960.
221. Shannon, C. E. Prediction and entropy of printed English. *Bell Syst. Tech. J.*, 1951, **30**, 50–64.
222. Shannon, C. E., & Weaver, W. *The mathematical theory of communication.* Urbana, Ill.: Univer. Ill. Press, 1949.
223. Siipola, E., Walker, N. M., & Kolb, D. Task attitudes in word association, projective and non-projective. *J. Pers.*, 1955, **23**, 441–459.
224. Skinner, B. F. The verbal summator and a method for the study of latent speech. *J. Psychol.*, 1936, **2**, 71–107.
225. Skinner, B. F. The distribution of associated words. *Psychol. Rev.*, 1937, **1**, 71–76.
226. Skinner, B. F. The alliteration in Shakespeare's sonnets: a study in literary behavior. *Psychol. Rev.*, 1939, **3**, 186–192.
227. Skinner, B. F. A quantitative estimate of certain types of sound-patterning in poetry. *Amer. J. Psychol.*, 1941, **54**, 64–79.
228. Skinner, B. F. Verbal behavior. *William James lectures,* Harvard Univer., 1948. (Mimeographed)

229. Skinner, B. F. *Verbal behavior*. New York: Appleton-Century-Crofts, 1957.
230. Smith, W. M., McCrary, J. W., & Smith, K. U. Delayed visual feedback and behavior. *Science*, 1960, **132**, 1013–1014.
231. Solarz, A. K. Latency of instrumental responses as a function of compatability with the meaning of eliciting verbal signs. *J. exp. Psychol.*, 1960, **59**, 239–245.
232. Solley, C. M. Problem solving difficulty as a function of deviation of "meaning" of physical cues from expected "meaning." *J. gen. Psychol.*, 1957, **57**, 165–171.
233. Solley, C. M., & Messick, S. J. Probability learning, the statistical structure of concept, and the measurement of meaning. *Amer. J. Psychol.*, 1957, **70**, 161–173.
234. Solomon, R. L., & Postman, L. Frequency of usage as a determinant of recognition thresholds for words. *J. exp. Psychol.*, 1952, **43**, 195–201.
235. Spence, K. W., Farber, I. E., & McFann, H. H. The relation of anxiety (drive) level to performance in competitional and non-competitional paired-associates learning. *J. exp. Psychol.*, 1956, **52**, 296–305.
236. Staats, A. W. Verbal habit-families, concepts, and the operant conditioning of word classes. *Psychol. Rev.*, 1961, **68**, 190–204.
237. Staats, A. W., & Staats, C. K. Attitudes established by classical conditioning. *J. abnorm. soc. Psychol.*, 1958, **57**, 37–40.
238. Staats, A. W., & Staats, C. K. First-order conditioning of word meaning. Tech. Report, No. 6, N-onr-2305 (oo), Ariz. State Coll. at Tempe, 1958.
239. Staats, A. W., & Staats, C. K. Meaning and *m*: correlated but separate. *Psychol. Rev.*, 1959, **66**, 136–144.
240. Staats, A. W., Staats, C. K., & Biggs, D. A. Meaning of verbal stimuli changed by conditioning. *Amer. J. Psychol.*, 1958, **71**, 429–431.
241. Staats, C. K., & Staats, A. W. Meaning established by classical conditioning. *J. exp. Psychol.*, 1957, **54**, 74–80.
242. Staats, C. K., & Staats, A. W. Effect of number of trials on the language conditioning of meaning. *Amer. Psychologist*, 1958, **13**, 415. (Abstract)
243. Stetson, R. H. *Motor phonetics: a study of speech movements in action.* Amsterdam: North-Holland Publishing Co., 1951.
244. Suci, G. J. A comparison of semantic structures in American Southwest culture groups. *J. abnorm. soc. Psychol.*, 1960, **60**, 25–30.
245. Taffel, C. Anxiety and the conditioning of verbal behavior. *J. abnorm. soc. Psychol.*, 1955, **51**, 496–501.
246. Taylor, W. L. 'Cloze Procedure': a new tool for measuring readibility. *Journ. Quart.*, 1953, **30**, 415–433.
247. Taylor, W. L. Recent developments in the use of 'Cloze Procedure.' *Journ. Quart.*, 1956, **33**, No. 1.
248. Templin, M. C. Certain language skills in children; their development and interrelationships. *Inst. Child Welf. Monogr.*, 1957, No. 26.
249. Thorndike, E. L. *A teacher's word book of the twenty thousand words found most frequently and widely in general reading for children and*

young people. New York: Teachers Coll., Columbia Univer., Bureau of Publications, 1932.

250. Thorndike, E. L. The psychology of pronunciation. *Amer. J. Psychol.*, 1948, **61**, 222–228.

251. Thorson, A. M. The relation of tongue movements to internal speech. *J. exp. Psychol.*, 1925, **8**, 1–32.

252. Thumb, A., & Marbe, K. *Experimentelle Untersuchungen über die psychologischen Grundlagen der sprachlichen Analogiebildung.* Leipzig: W. Engelmann, 1901.

253. Triandis, H. C., & Osgood, C. E. A comparative factor analysis of semantic structures in monolingual Greek and American college students. *J. abnorm. soc. Psychol.*, 1958, **57**, 187–196.

254. Tucker, W. T. Experiments in aesthetic communications. Unpublished doctoral dissertation, Univer. Ill., 1955.

255. Twaddell, W. F. Stetson's model and the 'supra-segmental phonemes.' *Language*, 1953, **29**, 415–453.

256. Van de Geer, J. P. Studies in codability: I. Identification and recognition of colors; II. Identification and recognition of facial expressions. Unpublished report, Psychologisch Institut van de Ruksuniversiteit te Leiden, 1960.

257. Verplanck, W. S. The control of the content of conversation: Reinforcement of statements of opinion. *J. abnorm. soc. Psychol.*, 1955, **51**, 668–676.

258. Weinreich, U. *Languages in contact.* New York: Linguistic Circle, 1953.

259. Weinreich, U. Travels through semantic space. *Word*, 1958, **14**, 346–366.

260. Wepman, J. M., Bock, R. D., Jones, L. V., & Van Pelt, D. Psycholinguistic study of aphasia. *J. Speech Dis.*, 1956, **21**, 468–477.

261. Werner, H., & Kaplan, E. The acquisition of word meanings: a developmental study. *Monogr. Soc. Res. Child Develpm.*, 1950, **15**, No. 1.

262. Wertheimer, M. The relation between the sound of a word and its meaning. *Amer. J. Psychol.*, 1958, **71**, 412–415.

263. Wertheimer, M., & Gillis, W. M. Satiation and the rate of lapse of verbal meaning. *J. gen. Psychol.*, 1958, **59**, 79–85.

264. Whorf, B. L. Language, thought and reality. In J. B. Carroll (Ed.), Selected writings of Benjamin Lee Whorf. New York: Wiley, 1956.

265. Woodrow, H., & Lowell, I. Children's association frequency tables. *Psychol. Monogr.*, 1916, **22**, No. 5.

266. Yavuz, H. S., & Bousfield, W. A. Recall of connotative meaning. *Psychol. Rep.*, 1959, **5**, 319–320.

267. Yule, G. U. *The statistical study of literary vocabulary.* New York: Cambridge, 1944.

268. Zipf, G. K. *Human behavior and the principle of least effort.* Reading, Mass.: Addison-Wesley, 1949.

SOCIOLOGY AND PSYCHOLOGY[1]

ALEX INKELES

Department of Social Relations
Harvard University

[1] I previously outlined the position taken in this paper in an article on "Personality and Social Structure" which appeared in *Sociology Today,* edited by Robert K. Merton, Leonard Broom, and Leonard S. Cottrell, Jr., and published by Basic Books of New York in 1959. Parts of this earlier effort have been incorporated in the more extended statement of my position presented here. I am particularly indebted to Daniel J. Levinson and Sigmund Koch for numerous and fruitful criticisms, observations, and suggestions.

INTRODUCTION

It would not be at all difficult to assemble a set of fifty or one hundred recent articles in social psychology, half chosen from the psychological and half from the sociological journals, which would be so much alike that no one judging without knowledge of source or author could with any precision discriminate those written by professional sociologists from those written by psychologists. Several considerations follow from this simple fact. Clearly the two disciplines cannot be defined in terms of what psychologists and sociologists respectively "do," since they so often do the same thing. Recourse to the different history and development of the disciplines, while of intrinsic interest, must be treated as irrelevant to the appropriate formulation of their present nature. In any event, this approach is merely a variant on the theme of what psychologists and sociologists do. Reference to the wide range of problems dealt with by either psychology or sociology alone is not satisfactory either, since it fails to meet the problem of overlap with which we began.

Should we then have three disciplines, psychology, sociology, and social psychology? Perhaps, but before we add to the proliferating behavioral sciences we should have exhausted every other remedy. Furthermore, many of the problems not shared today may be tomorrow, depending on the accidents of academic and scientific history. Others which do not overlap or are peripheral to either discipline are such because of accidents of national academic history, and not on logical grounds. In England, for example, anthropology has a strong sociological flavor and is there much more concerned with the study of social structure than it is in the United States. Indeed, as Kroeber points out, on the Continent "there is of course nothing corresponding to American anthropology: prehistory, ethnology and (physical) anthropology have different roots and affiliations, remain and mostly want to remain distinct" [39, p. 308].

These considerations argue strongly in favor of some other way of defining the two disciplines. By far the simplest method is to define each in terms of one central, exclusive, and independent problem or focus of interest. For purposes of this discussion, I will treat psychology as the study of the individual as a *personality* system and sociology as the study of aggregates of people, large or small, constituting a *social* system.[2] In selecting these definitions I am, of course, excluding from consideration

[2] Anthropology is conceived by some as also concerned with many features of the social system. Others define it as the study of a cultural system, in many ways conceptually quite distinct from the social system. Even this definition, however, means much overlap with typical sociological concerns, as in the study of values. Although I incline to the second definition, I have made no special attempt to keep sociological concerns distinct from anthropological.

a wide range of important theory and research customarily defined as part of psychology, such as psychoacoustics and comparable work on vision. There are various alternatives for conceptualizing the field of psychology, several of which are mainly oriented toward biology and physiology. It is not my intention here to argue the relative merits of these approaches. My assigned task in this symposium is to consider the relations of sociology and psychology from the sociologist's perspective. From that point of view, it is mainly the psychology of the human personality which is of relevance and interest.

In so far as psychology and sociology are defined mainly in terms of discrete analytic foci, many will find themselves assigned to a field quite other than the one in which they were trained and with which they identify professionally. Many psychologists concern themselves mainly with the efficiency of groups, which is a social system problem, while some trained as sociologists inquire into the personality traits which predispose one to suicide or crime, which is a personal system problem. In other words, I am classifying people according to what they do, but this principle has now been turned on its head. The discipline is not defined by what those accepting its label do. Instead, a discipline is defined in terms of a given problem or object of study and the relevant efforts to uncover the laws governing the particular phenomenon. The scholar or scientist is assigned to one or another discipline according to the problem on which he is in fact working. That many who think of themselves as sociologists will find themselves psychologists by this definition, and vice versa, is of no importance. The purpose of this discussion is to achieve conceptual clarification, not to decide on membership criteria for professional societies.

The many analogs in the study of personality and society which follow from their sharing a conception of each as a system should not obscure the basic differences in the system referent. All such systems involve component elements or properties and patterns of relation or interaction between these elements. Both social and personal systems may have patterns of development and distinctive histories. It may be important to consider the relations between the system studied and other systems of the same or a different type, and so on. These properties they share as systems do not make either the personal or the social system any less discrete. To achieve the purposes of either discipline, it may be necessary to consider certain aspects of the other, but the ultimate objects of study remain separate and distinct. Certain methods may also be held in common, and indeed certain situations might be studied by both disciplines, but in each case the data is integrated with different additional materials addressed to the solution of different problems. Psychology and sociology as here defined are similar not because person and society are "ultimately" the same object of study; the similarity lies only in the fact that both person and society are conceived of as systems of action.

The failure to recognize this distinction leads to the most serious confusion. Efforts to reduce one system to the other are sometimes justified as following from a principle of science which requires reducing more complex propositions to simpler and more "general" ones. Naïve generalization from this principle leads to absurdities. The engineering principles on which the construction of a house ultimately rests cannot be efficiently reduced to the atomic structure of the materials which compose it. This is not to say that the atomic structure is irrelevant. Indeed, knowledge of such properties of materials can have a marked effect on the kinds of structures attempted and built. Such knowledge would, however, be merely a datum available to those designing buildings rather than a principle governing their construction. Just so, knowledge of the cognitive mapping of which individuals are capable becomes a datum for the sociologist interested in the structure of opinion or the ideology dominant in a social system. Nevertheless, the pattern of cognitive mapping which characterizes individuals is not a principle of social structure. It may be a principle of personality structure, but it is only a relevant datum for the student of social structure.

It seems appropriate at this point to state the main argument of this paper in broad outline. The study of social systems can often be made much more incisive if one element in the analysis is a psychological theory, that is, a theory of the person as a system. This is true in at least three major respects. In the first instance, specification of the *consequences* of different institutional arrangements, that is, of the structural aspects of a social system, often depends on correct estimation of the given arrangements' meaning for, or effect on, the human personality. Since all institutional arrangements are ultimately mediated through individual human action, the consequences of *any* institutional arrangement will, at least *in part*, depend upon its effects on the human personality. To estimate the influence of one aspect of social structure on another one must, therefore, consider the role of the personality system as the main intervening variable. An adequate *general theory* of the personality as a system will, consequently, always be an important, and at times crucial, element in any analysis of a social system.

In the second instance, adequate assessment of the functioning of any social system, or of the maintenance and change of particular patterns within it, may in important degree depend on knowledge of the particular *personality traits*, needs, structures, and adjustments of the participants in the system. In this case it is not the general theory of personality which is critical, but rather the detailed knowledge about the distribution of particular qualities in the population. In the degree and quality of the fit between the modal personality patterns prevalent in the population and the role demands characteristic of the social system lies one of the keys to the system's functioning and one of the central points for the articulation of psychological and sociological theory.

As a third point, it seems evident that some of the more specialized psychological fields—most obviously the study of learning, but also of cognition and perception—have great potential relevance for our understanding of major social processes.

It will be noted that in each of the above points I consider only the significance of psychology for an understanding of sociological problems. To draw the conclusion that I believe sociology can be reduced to psychology would be incorrect. It would be equally wrong to assume that I do not believe sociological theory and research to be of great relevance for the solution of problems in which the personality system is the main focus of concern. In the division of labor in this symposium, however, it was decided to have each set of relations between psychology and another discipline discussed simultaneously, but separately, by a psychologist and a representative of the other discipline. By agreement with my psychological colleague, it is being left to him to discuss the implications of sociology for psychological analysis. This paper therefore concerns itself exclusively with the ways in which psychology can be used as an aid in the solution of problems which are sociological in focus. It argues that sociological research has suffered from the failure to use psychological theory and established knowledge about personality as an element in sociological analysis. In reading the lecture which I here deliver to my colleagues, the psychologist cannot hope merely to stand by and enjoy it all. An equally important part of my argument is that psychology has been woefully inadequate in providing sociologists with general knowledge about human personality, with special knowledge about more important psychological processes such as cognition, with adequate conceptualization of the particular traits of personality and techniques for measuring them adaptable to large-scale social research.

DURKHEIM'S *LE SUICIDE:* AN ILLUSTRATION

The relative exclusion of psychological factors from sociological analysis has a long history. To illustrate the consequences of that exclusion, and to suggest the advantages of correcting this position, few works can serve us more profitably than that classic of sociological research, Emile Durkheim's *Suicide* [16]. This choice enables us to see the problems in historical perspective. Yet the case is not solely of historical interest. Although this ground has been gone over many times, it seems that there are many who still do not know where the pitfalls lie. Another effort to map it is, therefore, not totally amiss. Durkheim's work is still regarded as a model of sociological research, and most sociologists would probably be proud could they produce it today. As we shall later see, it is indeed a living model beyond which more recent work has not often greatly advanced.

Durkheim noted that the mortality rate "is substantially the same for all peoples of approximately the same degree of civilization," whereas this was not true for suicide. Although the rate for any particular country varied only slightly from year to year, the rate for some countries in the same broad civilization of Western Europe was two, three, or even four times greater than in others. The rate of suicide, therefore, could be considered an attribute of a society, a characteristic index which "is peculiar to each social group" [16, p. 50]. Durkheim hoped to explain these differences in the rate of suicide, and he sought the explanation in certain other qualities or attributes of society. His goal was to discover some *general* variable cause in social structures which would in turn determine variation in the rates of suicide.

Durkheim distinguished three types of suicide, according to the conditions under which they appear, and adduced a causal or explanatory principle for each. In each case, however, the cause specified is a characteristic of the *social structure* yielding the given rate. By far the most important, fully documented, and elaborated type Durkheim called "egoistic" suicide. With an array of statistics impressive for his time, he demonstrated that suicide rates varied inversely with the "degree of integration" in the society in which the suicides were found. In "religious society," suicide rates were higher in Protestant countries and Protestant districts of particular countries than in Catholic areas. In "domestic society," the unmarried, widowed, and divorced had higher rates than did the married; childless women produced more suicides than those with children; and areas with large families yielded fewer suicides than those with smaller families. Relative to the state of integration of "political society," he showed that suicide occurred less frequently in time of war than in time of peace. Since the religious society, the family, and the nation-state are different in so many respects, the cause of suicide must lie in some quality which can be possessed in different degree by all of them. That quality Durkheim isolated and defined as "the degree of integration of the social groups of which the individual forms a part" [16, p. 209].

We are quite in agreement with Durkheim in his assertion that his study is sociological, because it seeks to explain a characteristic or "predisposition" of society. We would also agree with him that whether or not "this or that separate individual" will kill himself "concerns the psychologist, not the sociologist" [16, p. 51]. We share, as well, the conclusion that *if* "extra-social" causes such as "organic-psychic dispositions and the nature of the physical environment" could be demonstrated to bear "a regular and indisputable relation to suicide," *then* the problem would have been shown to be other than sociological. It is more difficult to assume, however, as Durkheim seemed at various points to do, that he needed no psychology of the individual to explain the leap from a "state of integration" in the society to the series of individual acts which, in sum, yield the suicide rate. Indeed, he ruled out the psychology of the individual entirely when he asserted:

We shall try to determine the productive causes of suicide *directly,* without concerning ourselves with the forms they can assume in particular individuals. Disregarding the individual as such, his motives and his ideas, we shall seek *directly* the states of the various social environments (religious confessions, family, political society, occupational groups, etc.), in terms of which the variations of suicide occur.

[And later]

Wholly different are the results we obtained when we forgot the individual and sought the causes of the suicidal aptitude of each society in the nature of the societies themselves . . . . The social suicide-rate can be explained only sociologically . . . . The victim's acts which at first seem to express only his personal temperament are really the supplement and prolongation of a social condition which they express externally [16, pp. 151, 299].

There remained, however, a logically compelling need for some mechanism to convert the state of social integration into individual acts of suicide. Despite the tone of his quoted remarks, Durkheim finally found it necessary to refer to human psychology in order to answer the question: How can suicide have such an origin? Man's psychological constitution, he said, "needs an object transcending it." Without such an object, man is "in such a state of confusion [that] the least cause of discouragement may easily give birth to desperate resolutions. If life is not worth the trouble of being lived, everything becomes a pretext to rid ourselves of it" [16, p. 213]. Society itself is the most ubiquitous of these necessary transcending objects. Where society is not integrated, there is, in effect, no such transcending object. Then the individual, having "too keen a feeling for himself and his own value . . . wishes to be his own only goal, and as such an objective cannot satisfy him, drags out languidly and indifferently an existence which henceforth seems meaningless to him" [16, p. 356].

In judging Durkheim's analysis, we should not lose sight of the fact that *Suicide* was written well before 1900, before Freud and Cooley. His psychological language was perforce that of his time. Quite apart from the issue of quaintness of expression, however, Durkheim gave little indication that he had a consistent or coherent general theory of personality, and some substantial difficulties followed therefrom. The quotations in the above paragraph suggest what might be labeled the "languishing-man" theory of suicide, one which treats suicide as the product of a kind of boredom or apathy as reflected in key words and phrases such as "discouragement," "not worth the trouble," "drags out," "languid and indifferent." This explanation does not do justice to the nature of suicide as an act by an individual. It requires an extremely definite decision, and usually a very substantial amount of effort, to commit suicide. It is a supreme act of violence, albeit against the self. This hardly seems to be the likely course for someone who exists languidly and indifferently.

At some level, Durkheim must have been aware of this, since elsewhere in his study he posited yet another, but substantially different, theory about the dynamics of human personality. At several points he speaks of the salutary-effect of an integrated society as following from its greater propensity to "control or restrain the individual." When society is strongly integrated, it "holds individuals under its control, considers them at its service and thus forbids them to dispose willfully of themselves. Accordingly it opposes their evading their duties to it through death" [16, p. 209]. I think it not unfair to state that this language implies that man has a drive to evade duties and perhaps a drive "to dispose willfully of himself" which, if not restrained by society, will lead to suicide. Thus, alongside the languishing-man theory of suicide we have a second theory, more congruent with the active nature of the act, which we may call the "desperate-prisoner" theory. This latter approach, which more orthodox Freudian theory would find congenial, was unfortunately at no point brought by Durkheim to the status of an explicit theory of personality. Yet unless we infer that Durkheim meant to posit an innate drive to self-destruction, we are left with an explanation of suicide which places the motive force outside the person. As Durkheim said, *society* "considers them at its service," and the *society* "forbids them to dispose willfully of themselves."

Durkheim was so bent on establishing the direct effect of social conditions on suicide that he greatly underplayed the mediating role of the individual who responds to the conditions and commits the act which adds to the rate. We cannot be satisfied with either the languishing-man or the desperate-prisoner theory. Whatever the correlation he demonstrated, his argument lacks the conviction which a more adequate conceptualization of personal psychology might have given him. To make this more than a mere assertion, an affirmation of faith, it is necessary to show how such a theory would better fit the data available to Durkheim or that it provides a superior explanation of some new data of the same general order. Anything less challenges the relevance of our assertion that an adequate theory of personality functioning is important for the kind of analysis Durkheim undertook.

Let us begin by doing that which Durkheim did not do, namely, looking closely and analytically at the *act* of suicide. Suicide is a conscious motivated act. It is an act against the self and reflects a desire to eliminate the self. The physical pain suffered by an extremely sick person can easily lead to such action, and we generally have little difficulty in "understanding" the suicide of a person in that situation. Most people who commit suicide, however, are not seriously physically ill at the time. *Psychic* pain could, however, be of an equivalent intensity and chronicity to account for the escape reaction. Durkheim did not deny that psychic pain may generally be a cause of suicide. He asserted, however, that since such pain is everywhere prevalent it can hardly account for the society's suicide rate. Durkheim did not ask the crucial question as to whether psychic pain sufficient to induce suicide might not be more likely to develop in one social role, setting, or condition than another. If in fact roles or situations did thus vary in their propensity to generate psychic pain, then suicide could still be viewed as having not an "individual," but rather a social cause. But the suicide would be in response neither to some disembodied state of the society, nor even to the "individual weaknesses" sought out by what Durkheim called the "strong current" of a society's tendency to suicide. Rather, the *individual* suicide would be a response to the *particular* characteristics of a *specific* role. It is not, then, a state of the system, but the specific pressures brought to bear on the incumbents of a particular role which will produce sufficient motivation for a certain number to commit suicide. The more a particular role was characterized as likely to yield its actors an abundance of psychic pain, the greater the number of suicides we would expect it to generate.

It remains then to specify more precisely what is the psychic situation of the suicide. Two elements are obviously relevant: the nature of the psychic pain experienced by the individual, and the modes for handling that pain which are objectively and subjectively available to him. By "subjectively available modes" we mean, in particular, whether a person typically reacts to the experience of being demeaned or frustrated by becoming depressed or by aggressing physically against some object; and, when aggressing, whether he tends to inhibit outward aggression and favor inward aggression, or vice versa. For the moment, however, we will rule out of consideration the modes of handling feelings which are "subjectively" available on the grounds that this is an attribute of a particular person and therefore a matter of "individual" psychology. Although we will return to this issue, let us now operate only with a general theory of personality which seeks to deal with the psychological component in suicide as it might present itself in *any* personality, quite apart from his individual or distinctive mode for handling psychic pain.

Returning to our model of the person with an acutely painful incurable illness, we note that there is no way to eliminate the source of pain, save to eliminate the self. By contrast, most psychic pain does permit escape from the situation. Young people can leave home, the married can be divorced.[3] By analogy to the case of physical illness, therefore, suicide might be described as an act of aggression against the self in response to extreme psychic pain which permits no "objective" mode of surcease except elimination of the self. In other words, the psychic pain should be seen by the actor to arise mainly from within the self, to be caused by the self, and most logically requiring for surcease the elimination of the self. Of the many types of psychic pain an individual can experience, feelings of inadequacy, of worthlessness or depravity, and of guilt would seem more likely than others to induce a drive toward self-destruction. Suicide, then, would be expected most often in social situations conducive to a feeling of inadequacy or guilt under conditions where no ready release from the feeling is objectively available as the person involved defines the situation.

Now we must ask to what degree does such a theory of personality functioning carry us further than Durkheim was able to go? To begin, does it equally well cover all the facts he explained? Durkheim held that the difference in immunity to suicide between Catholics and Protestants did not come about because the respective religions varied in the firmness with which they prohibited suicide. The crucial difference, he asserted, lay in the "intensity of collective life," which was higher for Catholics than for Protestants. In the Catholic community there existed "a number of beliefs and practices common to all, traditional and thus obligatory." In addition, Durkheim assigned importance to the lesser freedom of inquiry in Catholicism, or, in the case of the Jewish religion, to its "minutely governing all the details of life and leaving little free room to individual judgment" [16, p. 160]. There is nothing in personality theory, however, which compellingly leads one to assume that freedom of inquiry should lead to a desire to destroy oneself. There is no room here to attempt to support the argument in detail, but it should not be difficult to show that the religions in question differ profoundly both in the extent to which they make the individual's sin a matter of highly personal responsibility and in the means they provide him to secure assuagement or forgiveness for sin. In the Catholic Church, there

---

[3] Where it is permitted by custom or law. Where it is not permitted, the condition of "no escape" from psychic pain is introduced, and this should affect suicide and homicide rates. This issue is further dealt with below.

is relatively more emphasis on collective or impersonal sin, and release from guilt is infinitely easier, fuller, and more certain than in the Protestant sects. It would seem to follow that the psychic conditions for suicide we have specified would be more often experienced by Protestants than Catholics.

In the "family society" data, we meet an opportunity to show more explicitly the advantage of the use of general personality theory. In the realm of family society, there is one striking support for Durkheim's formula in the inverse association between size of household in a region and its suicide rate. It is otherwise not too clear, however, that family life confers an immunity to suicide, and Durkheim finds himself in substantial difficulty to account for the observed suicide rates in terms of societal integration. In particular, it develops that married women *without children* have a rate of suicide well in excess of that for unmarried women, although the latter presumably are less "integrated" in family society.[4] If we take the position that women generally are expected to have children, that they accept the responsibility, and that they assume it to be their fault if there are none, then it would follow that married women without children should have a higher suicide rate. The cause would, of course, be the psychic pain arising from their sense of inadequacy, reinforced by lack of support from those significant kin who share the expectation and unrelieved by any objective means of escape, since the fault is assumed to lie in oneself. Married men who were childless would not necessarily have the same reaction.[5] On the contrary, in Western society it is support of a wife rather than the ability to father children which is defined as the prime expectation for men. Childlessness is not to the same degree defined as the man's fault or responsibility. In general, therefore, a childless marriage should have a much more modest impact on the suicide rate of men than of women and should not raise their rate above that for the unmarried. Durkheim's data shows this to be the case.

Further, Durkheim himself discovered that in areas where divorce is not permitted, the suicide rate for married women is substantially *higher* than in regions where divorce is possible. The proscription of divorce may be taken as an instance of that close regulation of the individual which Durkheim holds so important as a restraint on suicide. Following his theory, therefore, we should have expected quite the opposite state of affairs. On the other hand, if such a proscription is seen as reflecting an

---

[4] Durkheim did not directly recognize a factor which might have been useful to his case, namely, that unmarried women are often members of a family, although it is the family of orientation, not procreation.

[5] Under certain circumstances, women would also be expected to respond differently. Where, for example, adoption is a recognized and culturally approved institution, the strain on a woman without children would be lessened.

objective situation and as defining the impossibility of escape should the marriage be a painful failure, then we would expect the suicide rate to be higher where divorce was not permitted.

The argument could be pressed further to reveal other instances of the difficulties which followed from Durkheim's lack of an adequate theory of personality and failure to use such a theory explicitly as the intervening variable between the social conditions he found in the societal structure and the numerous individual acts which yield the suicide rate. For example, it can be shown that it was not necessary to develop two rather different theories to account for egoistic and anomic suicide. Rather than continue along this line, however, it is perhaps more appropriate to indicate how the use of a theory of personality enables us to go beyond the problem as it presented itself to Durkheim and how it permits a wider range of generalization. For this we turn to the work of Henry and Short in *Suicide and Homicide* [31], for which we had to wait more than sixty years after Durkheim. Henry and Short utilize an explicit psychodynamic theory of suicide *and* homicide as acts of aggression. Such aggression, they hold, is produced by the frustration experienced by individuals in various social roles. They assume that the same "suicidal current," to use Durkheim's term, will affect individuals differently, depending on the roles they occupy. It will be seen that this theory is congruent with that sketched above.

Durkheim expected that even in times of prosperity suicide rates would rise, because periods of rapid change loosened social bonds. Henry and Short closely examined data on the business cycle as related to suicide, and found that Durkheim's expectation was not confirmed. Apparently suicide rises during depression, but falls in times of prosperity. Thus, Durkheim's explanation, which stresses the weakening of general social control in times of economic dislocation, must be reformulated. Henry and Short suggest instead that fuller recognition be given to the *different* "degrees of frustration which business cycles impose on differing status categories" [31, p. 24]. Again, it will be seen that this is very close to the argument suggested above.

More important, however, in relating suicide to homicide, Henry and Short were able to show how the same basic aggressive impulse which, turned inward, yields suicide, yields homicide when turned outward. This, incidentally, was an insight which Durkheim also attained but did not use. He said, "Anomy . . . begets a state of exasperation and irritated weariness which may turn against the person himself or another according to circumstances; in the first case, we have suicide, in the second, homicide" [16, p. 357]. Developing a variable they describe as the degree of "external restraint" to which the individual is subjected, Henry and Short suggest that . . .

. . . when behavior is required to conform rigidly to the demands and expectations of other persons, the probability of suicide as a response to frustration is low and the probability of homicide as a response to frustration is high. When behavior is freed from the requirement for conformity to the demands and expectations of others, the probability of suicide is high and the probability of homicide is low [31, pp. 101–102].

To support this conclusion, they present substantial evidence.

Psychological theory treats suicide and homicide as being alike in that both are seen as acts of aggression, although they differ in the object chosen. The distinctive feature of Henry and Short's analysis is that they linked Durkheim's theory about the role of social restraint to a psychological theory about aggression. By this means, they not only corrected Durkheim's analysis of suicide as it relates to economic change; they were enabled to go well beyond Durkheim in explaining the systematic relation of suicide and homicide. Here we can clearly see the crucial importance of a general theory of personality organization and functioning as an intervening variable in predicting the behavioral consequences of any aspect or quality of institutional structure. It is a testimonial both to Durkheim's extraordinary good sense and to the compelling need for such a theory that Durkheim did in fact finally come to introduce the psychology of the person into his analysis. But he did so only under pressure of need, in an *ad hoc* fashion, and more implicitly than explicitly. His great work suffered for it.

Just as he placed no systematic reliance on a general theory of personality functioning to explain the suicide rate, so Durkheim challenged the idea that it could be explained on the basis that one or another group might include more personalities predisposed to suicide. It should be noted that this was not because Durkheim was totally unaware of the conception of distinctive personalities as distinguishing one social group from another. On the contrary, he explicitly raised this issue in order to dismiss it as a major factor in determining suicide rates. Thus, he says:

. . . according to this hypothesis [that marriage makes a selection from the population at large], it would be not the family which was a protection against suicide, crime or sickness; the privileged position of married persons would be theirs *simply because only those are admitted to family life who already provide considerable guarantees of physical and moral health*" [16, p. 181; italics mine].

At another point he questions the role played by "the nature of the individuals composing the society," and concludes:

. . . a given number of suicides is not found annually in a social group just because it contains a given number of neuropathic persons . . . . It will be objected that if enough neurasthenics did not exist, social causes would not produce all their effects. But no society exists in which the various forms of nervous degeneration do not provide suicide with more than the necessary number of candidates" [16, pp. 323–324].

Durkheim is obviously in difficulty here. If the strength of the suicidogenic "current" acts on potential candidates, then we have a threshold problem. Since even weak currents take *some* people, it must be because those individuals were susceptible to even weak currents, i.e., they have a lower threshold. It follows, then, that a suicidogenic current of the *same* strength applied to populations including *different* proportions of persons with a given suicide threshold will yield *different* rates of suicide. The same rate, therefore, might result from either raising the strength of the current or reducing the average weakness in the population.

Consideration of this possibility, despite Durkheim's rejection of it, permits us to explain some of the facts about suicide with which he had most difficulty. Thus, we may assume that marriage does indeed tend to select the better adjusted, but in Western society it does so differentially by sex. This is congruent with the fact that men exercise greater initiative and have more freedom of choice in selecting a marriage partner. On the whole, therefore, married men and women should be better adjusted or less suicidogenic than the unmarried, but the contrast for men should be greater than for women. This is what Durkheim's data indicate.

Durkheim, of course, anticipated this argument about what he called "matrimonial selection," but rejected it. He did so partly on the ground that marriage, even if selective, cannot be so selective as to account for the data. He placed particular emphasis on the fact that married women without children have even higher rates than unmarried women and the fact that divorced individuals have much higher rates than the married. If marriage selects the stable person, he suggests, the childless wife and the divorced were already previously selected and should be less prone to suicide. Of course, selection can be imperfect and divorce the sign of it. But quite apart from that, Durkheim at this point seems to overlook the very cause he elsewhere stressed most heavily, namely, the strength of the "current" or the situational impetus to suicide. Marriage may indeed have selected those women less prone to suicide, but the impetus toward suicide among those who subsequently disappoint expectation by not producing children will be very great. Women without children are both more likely to feel themselves worthless and more likely to be encouraged to feel so. We can, therefore, perfectly consistently argue that marriage selects among all women those least prone to suicide, while still holding that after marriage some women, in this case the childless, will experience distinctive situational pressures which induce suicide.

The strength of the current must also be considered in explaining the rate for the divorced and widowed. Indeed, it is only by considering both personality and the situational pressures acting together that one can account for the difference in rates between these groups. Both the widowed and divorced have suicide rates higher than the married, but those for the divorced are substantially higher than for the widowed. Now Durkheim acknowledges that, on his measure of family solidarity, "widowhood is indeed as complete a disturbance of existence as divorce" [16, p. 262]. If this were so, and we introduced no further considerations, then we would expect the widowed and the divorced to have equal rates. On the other hand, if we assume that the divorced are selected from among the married on grounds of personal instability, whereas the widowed are selected for that status at random, then we must conclude that the personality of the divorced played an important factor in producing their higher rate, despite the fact that by Durkheim's measure they were subject to equal strength of the suicidogenic current. From this point of view, furthermore, it is dubious that the current *is* in fact the same. Although this would fall outside the realm of the "current" as Durkheim defined it, we must note that the divorced have more realistic basis for feeling guilty than do the widowed.

Here again the more recent study of the relation of suicide and homicide is instructive. Since suicide and homicide vary inversely, yet both are acts of aggression, groups with high suicide and low homicide rates should be those in which turning aggression inward is the basic method for handling it. Although we do not have definitive evidence, Henry and Short [31] show that there is substantial reason to believe this is the case. A strict superego formation appears to be associated with the direction of aggression against the self, whereas weak or defective superego development leads to directing aggression outward. Going beyond Henry and Short, we would hold that the development of a strict superego in Western European countries is generally more common among families of high education and status. We know that the great majority of people born into homes of professionals and the better educated will themselves enter the professions or be similarly well placed occupationally. It follows that such strata of the population would contain a disproportionately large number of individuals with strongly internalized and strict superegos who inclined to direct aggression inward. They would therefore be more likely to choose suicide as the preferred or "subjective" mode of handling aggression.

Education and occupational status *are* positively correlated with suicide, as Henry and Short show. Durkheim also noted this fact. But to explain it, he was obliged to depart from his strict formulation about the integration of society as a cause of suicide. Indeed the explanation of suicide as following from low levels of integration in society is none too convincing when applied to the professions and the well educated, who are obviously tightly integrated into society. Durkheim therefore shifted his ground. Not education itself, but something characteristic of communities in which education was extensive was assigned responsibility. This revised argument holds that the society which pursues knowledge in the process shakes accepted belief, destroys tradition, weakens faith, and thus puts man at the mercy of unsettling currents. Even this excessive stretching of the original theory will not hold. Regardless of the state of education in the society at large, the educated as a subgroup will have a higher suicide rate. Durkheim's formulation cannot account for this fact. If, however, the well educated and the professionally employed more often come from families which develop a propensity to self-punishment, then they can be expected to have a higher rate of suicide relative to other classes in the same society, quite independently of the state of the society at large.

It is to Durkheim's great credit that he made several statements which did show greater acceptance of the importance of the personality composition of a society or subgroup in determining its suicide rate. Thus, in distinguishing egoistic and anomic suicide, he asserts that "a definite moral constitution [whereby he often expressed what we call personality] corresponds to each type of suicide and is interconnected with it" [16, p. 364]. Again, when speaking of the role played by "the melancholy of civilization" in producing suicide, he declared: "For it to exist and maintain itself . . . there must be groups of individuals who more especially represent this aspect of the collective mood . . . . The part of the population which plays this role is necessarily that where ideas of suicide easily take root" [16, p. 366]. Unfortunately, Durkheim did not develop these ideas into an explicit theory of personality which could be systematically related to social forces in explaining suicide. Whatever its brilliance, Durkheim's analysis suffered from his failure to give a more systematic role to knowledge about the personalities common in the groups he studied. The fact that, in the end, he found himself making room for this factor is testimonial both to his unusual capacity and to the compelling necessity for a systematic treatment of the constituent personalities participating in any social system.

THE ROLE OF GENERAL PERSONALITY THEORY

In the early part of the twentieth century, Freud provided us with the basic foundation for a reasonably adequate general theory of personality formation and functioning. Thanks to the group of neo-Freudians, notably Horney and Fromm, and to less easily classified men of talent, such as H. S. Sullivan and Erik Erikson, that theory has been extended and developed in a manner which greatly increases its importance and relevance for sociological analysis. All of these were, of course, from psychiatry and psychoanalysis, but academic psychology has not been entirely unrepresented among those contributing in important ways. In particular Gordon Allport [4], Henry Murray [52], and Kurt Lewin [42, 43] have made significant contributions.

Many, perhaps most, of our theories of personality deal not with personality as a whole, but rather with some selected aspect or process. Freudian theory kept the whole personality more in view. In time Freud elaborated many of the elements necessary to an understanding of the total personality as a functioning system. Thus he specified the critical components of personality (e.g., id, ego, superego), the main modes of relationship between the parts, and the chief motive power in the system at large. He uncovered the main processes which characterize personality functioning, indicated the conditions under which it develops, and discriminated those influences which make for one or another end state or adjustment. Finally, he specified the conditions for the maintenance and dissolution of the personality system. In this sense his theory is relatively more complete than most, probably more so than any other.

Freud produced this general theory not out of a combination of existing elements, but largely by new creative insights. His theory therefore has a scope, a unity, and a coherence which is unmatched in psychology. Outstanding among those insights was his treatment of the role of unconscious motivation in behavior. One must also give great weight to his elaboration of the psychodynamic mechanisms, his calling attention to the crucial role of the early years, his insights into the role of the superego and values, his explorations into the meanings of symbols and symbolic behavior, and his elucidation of the importance and special character of various body zones.

Subsequent work has, of course, exposed major gaps in the system and has considerably altered the relative emphasis on one or another element. Freud's psychology, for example, was mainly concerned with the basic drives and their restraint. The theory of the ego, of the self-conception, was little developed. Despite substantial further work [Allport, 3], ego theory is still in its infancy. Freud gave prime emphasis to the early years of life and their formative influence and tended to neglect the importance of the experiences of the adolescent and adult in the networks of nonfamilial interpersonal relations. Although Sullivan, Horney, Fromm, and Lewin have all done much to remedy this condition, we still have great need for a fuller theoretical accounting of the functioning of the adult personality. Freud also left us substantially less than an adequate picture of the range and relative importance of human needs and motives. Henry Murray's work [52], and Erikson's [17] extremely perceptive discussion of typical ego problems, such as those involving trust, autonomy, and identity, have done much to give us a fuller picture of the range of human needs and their interrelations.

Considering that Freud's general theory of personality has had wide currency for at least a generation, it is striking that so little evidence can be found of its direct influence on modern sociological theory and research. In anthropology, by way of contrast, one of the main new currents, perhaps the most outstanding in modern times has been the influence of Freudian theory in shaping the study of culture and personality [Kluckhohn, 38]. Most sociologists probably accept Freud's as the foremost general theory of the human personality of our time, but this acceptance is limited to its application to the individual's psychic development and adjustment, that is, to his inner life. They do not accept it as the prime explanation of the social behavior of the individual— which they attribute more to his culture, his class, his historical time, or his immediate situation, including the network of interpersonal relations in which he is enmeshed.

Freud concentrated particularly on the more nearly ultimate causes of behavior lying in the nature of the human biological organism and less immediate causes, such as experiences in the early life history of the individual. The sociologist has generally been concerned with the more proximate causes of behavior. Ultimate human motivation and distant causes have had less interest for him. Indeed, sociologists often feel that Freud dealt less with the *causes* than with the underlying *preconditions* of social behavior. The unconscious and irrational in behavior have seemed to them of less compelling interest than the more conscious, purposeful, and rationally goal-directed behavior. This undoubtedly has been important in the sociologists' apparent attachment to Charles Cooley [11] and G. H. Mead [48], whose prime concern was with the social self arising from a matrix of interpersonal relations, and for H. S. Sullivan [68], who stressed the interpersonal element in individual action and in psychodynamic adjustment.

A second and undoubtedly important reason for the modest direct influence of Freud harks back to the old controversy between psychologism and sociologism with which Durkheim was so involved. To many sociologists, Freud and many Freudians seem to present merely a new variety of psychological reductionism which seeks to explain the most important human institutions as mere consequences of qualities or problems arising in individual psychology. Freud's general theory about the rise and maintenance of civilizations [20] and his more specific historical analyses, such as *Moses and Monotheism* [22], as well as Kardiner's [36, 37] theories about religious and other "projective" institutional systems—all would be cases in point. Levinson [41] has made the same point with regard to psychoanalytic treatment of political institutions as epiphenomena.

But our objective here is not so much to explain the impact of Freud among sociologists as to discuss the relevance and use in sociology of a general theory of personality. It is necessary to state at the outset that just as there are large segments of traditional psychological work for which social forces are largely irrelevent, so for quite a large part of what is generally accepted as standard sociology a general theory of personality is probably not of crucial importance. This is true, for example, of the special applications of demographic or ecological analysis such as those of the great Chicago school of sociology. Their main concern was with the "social mapping" of the urban community, locating the distinctive patterning of its activities and defining the laws of growth and change of the city viewed as an agglomeration of specialized urban areas. Much the same thing can be said for many of the other social-mapping activities of the sociologist. For example, the student of stratification who takes his task to be delineation of the major strata in the stratification system and the distinctive rewards allocated to each stratum is not necessarily in need of a general personality theory to discover the objective facts about each stratum. Other subfields could be added to the list.

Nevertheless, there are several problems of substantial sociological interest which would seem to require—or would certainly yield more readily through—the use of an explicit and adequate theory of personality. Outstanding are those concerned with certain general rates. These are the end products of thousands or even millions of uncoordinated individual decisions or actions which yet produce those relatively distinct stable rates such as the suicide rate which attracted Durkheim's attention. Other similar rates would be that for homicide (and other crimes), that for mental illness, and, within limits, the marriage, divorce, and birth rates. Suicide, homicide, and mental illness are much the least ambiguous examples of the probable importance of personality in social processes since they are less likely to be patterned by some specific institutionalized requirement or arrangement. By contrast, for something like divorce, a law which makes it illegal will be well-nigh decisive. Making allowances for such factors, however, we can see all of these rates as presenting problems for sociological analysis. These problems promise to yield more easily to the sociologist who can effectively use a general theory of personality to deal with the individual who intervenes between the social condition and the resultant rate.

The problem is subject to several reformulations involving the same basic elements used in different arrangements, according to the focus of study. The elements are a rate of social action R, a state of society or a set of social conditions impinging on the individuals in the system S, and a general need or action propensity of the human personality P. Sociologists generally begin with the rate, which is called to their attention because it is a social problem. Their task is generally defined as that of discovering the appropriate causal state in society, which produced the given rate. They then formulate the relationship as a sociological S-R proposition.[6] As we have seen, Durkheim began with variations in the rate of suicide R, and sought to explain them through variations in the degree of integration of society S. In the reexamination of this problem, we introduced a new element P, in our assertion that suicide is most effectively conceived as *an act of aggression against the self,* and in the further assumptions that such aggression is most likely to follow where the individual experiences an extreme sense of guilt, worthlessness, evil, or similar extreme negative self-evaluation. The sequence then becomes S-P-R. This is similar but yet not identical with Henry and Short's discussion of aggression as arising from frustration and expressed either against the self or some other, depending on the conditions of external restraint. The sequence in that case would be the more complex $S\text{-}P\diagdown\begin{subarray}{l} D_1\text{-}R_s \\ D_2\text{-}R_h \end{subarray}$. The new element D represents the degree of restraint to which the individual is subjected, with those under high restraint D_1 producing suicide R_s and those under weak restraint D_2 producing homicide R_h.

General Personality Theory and Juvenile Delinquency

To show that the human personality intervening between social condition and action rate was neglected not only during that more distant past represented by Durkheim, but also in more modern times, we may note the attempts to explain juvenile deliquency. Reacting very correctly against the old notion that criminals were a particular degenerate type, several of the sociologists of the Chicago school sought

---

[6] The use of a set of symbols and a formula identical with that of stimulus-response theory is not altogether unintended. In my opinion, the psychological stimulus-response theory has its analog in sociological state-rate theory. Both suffer seriously from the failure to utilize a specific explicit theory of human personality and its action propensities as an intervening variable between their respective S-Rs.

to demonstrate the close connection between the nature of the community and its deliquency rate. In its general form, the argument was extraordinarily similar to that which Durkheim had used more than forty years before in his explanation of suicide rates. Thus, in his classic *Delinquency Areas,* Clifford Shaw [63] asserted: "If the community is disorganized and weak in its control, it will be easy for the institutions to disintegrate and behavior will not be controlled by conventional standards" [63, p. 6]. Hence the potential for delinquency. To this potential Shaw added an additional element, the equivalent of which is not to be found in Durkheim, namely, the concept of the "delinquent area" as a subculture which transmits its ways to those who reside within it. The community in which disorganization is rife becomes the home of "delinquent gangs with persistent delinquent patterns and traditional codes and standards which are very important in determining the behavior of the members" [63, p. 7]. Summing up these forces, Shaw said:

[The] behavior of a delinquent may be in part a reflection of a family conflict which drives him into a gang in which delinquency is a traditional group pattern. The delinquent gang may reflect a disorganized community life or a community whose life is organized around delinquent patterns. The local community in its turn reflects the processes of cultural conflict and social disorganization incident to the expansion of the city and the movement and segregation of its population [63, pp. 9–10].

In support of their emphasis, Shaw and his colleagues presented a series of statistics which showed conclusively that high rates of delinquency were found mainly in areas near the center of the city. These areas were being invaded by industry and business. They contained large proportions of Negro and immigrant families living in communities characterized by physical deterioration and declining population in which neighborhood culture and local organization had largely disintegrated.

In this state of social disorganization community resistance is low. Delinquent and criminal patterns arise and are transmitted socially just as any other cultural and social pattern is transmitted. In time these delinquent patterns may become dominant and shape the attitudes and behavior of persons living in the area. Thus, the section becomes an area of delinquency [63, pp. 205–206].

In the reference to "community resistance," one senses the familiar qualities of those "currents" of suicide to which Durkheim gave such great weight. Basically the central difficulty in Durkheim's analysis affects Shaw's—his theory fails to specify the mechanisms whereby a quality of the community gets converted into the actions of individuals which, in turn, produce the delinquency rate. This is perhaps not completely fair. Shaw's formula does specify a mechanism, but hardly an adequate one. For by suggesting that community resistance, when weakened, permits more delinquency, it implies that, were it not for the force of the community, we would all be delinquents. A great deal of evidence suggests, to the contrary, that most people act properly even when there is no risk of apprehension and punishment, having *internalized* prohibitions against the violation of group norms.

Indeed, if the weakening of community resistance fosters delinquency, *most* people in the high-delinquency areas should be violators, whereas even in the worst areas only a small minority in fact transgress. A fact introduced by Shaw himself provides further evidence that there is a taint which comes to reside in the individual and, to some extent, is independent of the community's resistance. For he points out that many who contribute to delinquency in areas with generally low rates had become delinquent previously, while living in areas of high delinquency. In other words, they had acquired a personal quality, a propensity to delinquency, which they carried within them and which to some degree operated even when they lived in areas of stronger community resistance. The assumption that delinquency depends in good part on an action propensity in the individual is, of course, essential if we are to deal with the fact that some people become delinquent in the districts in which community resistance is presumably quite strong. Indeed, such districts contribute a substantial proportion of all delinquencies, and this has been a problem of growing importance since Shaw's initial study was completed. In any event, only a minority of those living even in the districts of weak control become delinquents. Clearly the weakness of community social control is therefore not a sufficient and apparently not even a necessary cause of delinquency.

A more explicit general theory of personality can be—indeed, has already shown itself to be—of substantial use. The criminal (and the delinquent before him) is violating a social norm and he knows he may be severely punished. We may rule out a strong desire to be punished as a general human motivation without denying that it could be a factor in special cases [Levinson, 40]. We have little difficulty in understanding the violation of norms when the delinquent's objective is so extraordinarily attractive and so absolutely inaccessible by other means as to warrant any risk. This is a factor we can hardly rule out entirely, especially since the delinquent often has desires which go far beyond what his social environment makes likely of attainment by the regular channels open to people of his station and skill. We might say the same thing, however, of many individuals who nevertheless do not become delinquent. Furthermore, the goals pursued by the delinquent often do not seem so extraordinarily attractive. At least in the early stages, he is after petty cash or ordinary goods stolen from shops and warehouses, automobiles stolen for joyriding, and so on. Indeed, very often the act of delinquency involves not even this gain, but is merely destructive.

Such action, violating the norms of the larger community, could be the product of encouragement by parents and others. This is what the theory of delinquency as a learned subculture in fact asserts. Frequently, indeed generally, the parents do not directly support or approve the delinquent behavior. They often actively disapprove and harshly punish, or otherwise ignore and neglect the child. The argument then rests almost entirely on the child's late learning from peers and older delinquents. That the delinquent does so learn is not to be challenged. But we must ask what the learning rests on. Does the child learn from peers and older delinquents to be *predisposed* to delinquency, or does he carry the predisposition with him and merely learn the techniques and earn the support he wants for the course he already prefers?

A close examination of the delinquent act will suggest to us some of the personality factors likely to be associated with delinquency. The delinquent engages in conscious, willful, and repeated violation of a basic social norm in the face of known risk of severe punishment. Our general theory of personality would lead us to assume such acts to be difficult or impossible for those who had successfully introjected the norms of their society—more specifically those who had an adequately active, vigorous superego.[7] In addition, the repetition of delinquent acts may be regarded as expressing hostile rejection of all constituted "parental" authority and can be closely linked to a weak superego.

We are led then to ask what special conditions might foster the development of individuals with such inadequate superego development and associated hostility to authority. Inadequate superego development can be expected in the absence of the parent, or where only intermittent, irregular, and inconsistent parental demands are met. In our culture, the effects are likely to be marked if it is the father who fits into this pattern, especially when this is linked with insufficiency of female nurturance. Inadequate superego development is also likely where the parental treatment is very harsh, especially physically, and unmixed with affec-

---

[7] This expression may be somewhat ambiguous, but space is not available to present the issue in detail. I assume with Erikson [17] that everyone, even Hitler, has a "conscience." The question is, what kind of conscience? By an adequate superego, I obviously mean here something approximating the values with regard to respect of person, property, parent, and community which are most fully evident in old, stable rural communities or the white-collar and middle classes in the city, or the traditional "self-respecting" urban working class of England and Western Europe.

tion and love. When neglect is linked with such harshness, there is likely also to be great hostility to constituted authority. Again, where the parent is extremely weak or seemingly lacking in capacity, power, prestige, or general adequacy, the consequence is likely to be weak superego development following from barriers against the internalization and valuation of the parents as role model [cf. Sears, Maccoby, and Levin, 62, pp. 362–395]. It is evident that in the marginal slum districts of great cities a high proportion of the children will experience conditions of socialization of the variety conducive to weak superego development. Children raised in this environment would more often develop the propensity toward delinquency and later learn the delinquent culture of the marginal areas.

Our general theory of personality leads us to assume that delinquency reflects inadequate superego development as well as hostility to authority and general physical aggressiveness and destructiveness. When we consider the conditions under which such weak superego development and hostile aggressiveness would be most frequently developed, we must look for homes in which certain abnormal patterns of parental behavior are manifested. Such homes are most often encountered in deteriorated slum communities. Thus, our theory leads us to the same communities to which Shaw was led by his theory. But Shaw's theory did not provide the basis for pressing the analysis further. If, however, we work with a theory of personality, we are able to go further and identify the specific homes in the community which may be expected to yield the majority of the delinquents. Since the theory holds that the superego is shaped largely by the parents and developed early in life, the delinquent should develop *specifically* in those homes where parents are unavailable, weak, or discredited role models when present, and generally fail to provide love and steady nurturance. The introjected parental image then is either weak and inadequate or harsh and self-centered—in either case, not producing a strong conscience, which restrains impulse. In addition, aggression is generated against the parents who frustrate the dependency and nurturance needs and desires of their offspring.

The theory would further suggest the importance of the delinquent gang, which does indeed seem to be highly associated with delinquency. The theory of weakened social control as the cause for delinquency offers little compelling reason why gangs should form and individuals should drift toward them. It describes the phenomenon, but offers little explanation for its manifestation. On common-sense grounds, one might expect the boys living in areas where community life has broken down to be lone-wolf types rather than to run in packs. Freudian theory suggests that the person must have some equivalent of the superego, and where it is not "internalized" and parentally derived, an "externalized" superego will be sought in a peer group. In any lasting association of this kind where the majority of the peer-group members individually lack strong superegos, the *norms* of the group will become delinquent and indeed will support and reinforce the delinquent propensities in the individual members.

It cannot be said that Shaw was totally unaware of such considerations. Indeed, in his case studies he described situations which partially fit this model. In *The Natural History of a Delinquent Career* [64], for example, the central figure came from a home which economically "afforded practically no facilities for the satisfaction of Sidney's fundamental wishes and the stimulation of wholesome play interests" [64, pp. 229–230]. In addition, the father's repeated desertions and the mother's employment outside the home meant that "the family never constituted an integrated unit capable of exercising consistent control of Sidney's behavior." Shaw did not see these environmental conditions as producing a particular quality in Sidney. He saw them mainly as indicating absence of restraint, concluding, "*In the absence of effective moral restraints in the family and in the community,* the development of [Sidney's] group relationships and his choice of companions outside of the home were almost entirely undirected" [64, p. 230; italics mine]. In this analysis, the psychological consequences of the environment for personality development remain unexplored, unsystematized, and indeed only vaguely sensed in the statement "It is possible that certain underlying factors, not disclosed in this case history, were operating to determine [Sidney's] early tendency toward delinquency" [64, p. 231].

Many researches on delinquency pointed toward the conclusion that personality played a decisive role as intervening variable between the deteriorated conditions of the slum community and the high rate of delinquency it generated [e.g., Healy and Bronner, 30]. It was twenty years before a definitive case could be made in support of this position. The imposing study of the Gluecks [25], reported in 1950, addressed itself rather directly to the problem posed by the ecological approach, and indeed charged that "to overemphasize the neighborhood matrix as a coherent whole and underemphasize or virtually ignore the biological make-up and developmental history of the different human beings who themselves contribute to the modification of that matrix is to overlook many of the factors that account for variations in the effect of the culture on the human beings . . ." [25, p. 6]. Holding the effect of community structure constant by choosing all their subjects from high-rate areas, the Gluecks sought to isolate the specific factors in the individual's environment and experience which account for delinquency. Two sets of 500 boys each, one delinquent, the other not, were closely matched on residence in a delinquent neighborhood, age, intelligence, and ethnic origin. Both sets were studied in great detail, with special reference to home environment, physique, mental qualities, and personality, the latter through use of the Rorschach and a psychiatric interview.

The Gluecks' study establishes definitely, perhaps as its outstanding finding, that delinquents come with great regularity from the kind of home environment described above as likely to lead to weak superego development and to rejection and hostility toward adult authority figures. Although there were a great many differences which were statistically significant, at the .01 level, it is particularly striking how great was the gap between the two groups on certain items relevant to the theory sketched above. For example, 90 per cent of the delinquents, as against 54 per cent of the nondelinquents, came from homes in which standards of conduct were poor because of parental drunkenness or immorality. A mere 5 per cent of the delinquents came from homes rated "good" on this score, against 38 per cent for the nondelinquents. Firm but kindly discipline, as against lax, overstrict, or erratic discipline, was characteristic of a mere 4 per cent of the mothers and 6 per cent of the fathers of delinquents, whereas for the nondelinquents the percentages were, respectively, 66 and 56. Indifference or hostility to the father was shown by 68 per cent of the delinquents and only 19 per cent felt him to have good concern for their welfare. Of the nondelinquents, 35 per cent felt hostility, 65 felt he had concern for their welfare. Only 7 per cent of the delinquents as against 65 per cent of the nondelinquents were "adequately" supervised by their mothers; 64 per cent were allowed to shift for themselves almost entirely. In evaluating these findings, the Gluecks remark:

> Character is the result of training . . . . Mechanisms of sublimation and of constructive or harmless energy-canalization, as well as "knowledge of right and wrong," are part of the apparatus of character expression . . . . Thus, the demands made upon the growing child at every level at which he is called upon to adapt his natural inclinations to the taboos, laws, and other prohibitions are neither simple nor well defined. They require a great deal of adaptive power, self-control, and self-management, the ability to choose among alternative values and to postpone immediate satisfactions for future ones—all this in a cultural milieu in which fixed points are increasingly difficult to discern and to hold to. This means that during the earliest years, when the difficult task of internalization of ideals and symbols of authority is in process, desirable attitudes and behavior standards are not clearly enough defined, or are inconsistent, leaving a confused residue in the delicate structure of personality and character [25, pp. 278–279].

In the light of the obvious inferiority of the families of the delinquents as sources of sound personality development and character formation, it is not surprising that these boys were never adequately socialized, and that they developed persistent antisocial tendencies . . . . The development of a mentally hygienic and properly oriented superego (conscience) must have been greatly hampered by the kind of parental ideals, attitudes, temperaments, and behavior found to play such a major role on the family stage of the delinquents [25, p. 281].

It must be admitted that, however convincing this argument is, the Gluecks' study does not provide the crucial link demonstrating that such poor conditions in the home environment do produce youngsters with a particular formation of the superego. The data so far presented by the Gluecks show the relation between home environment and delinquency on the one hand, and on the other between personality and delinquency, but not between home environment and personality. In addition, it is perhaps unfortunate that the instrument chosen for the personality test was the Rorschach. It is, on the one hand, imprecise as a measure of particular personality traits,[8] and on the other hand, it is extremely sensitive to the kind of psychic deprivation that all children in depressed areas experience in substantial degree. In any event, no specific rating with regard to strength or quality of superego was made. Certain of the findings were, however, strongly suggestive of the pattern we have described. In particular, 80 per cent of the nondelinquents, as against only 27 per cent of the delinquents, were rated as "submissive" to authority, meaning "abandonment of self-assertion in the attempt to gain security by submitting to others, especially to those who are believed stronger (originally often one or both of the parents) and also to the more anonymous power of institutions, public opinion, conventional usage, and so on" [25, p. 219, reprinted by permission of The Commonwealth Fund and Harvard University Press]. This measure must be recognized as very close to our description of strong superego development. The data strongly suggest that the boys raised in the homes with inadequate or harsh fathers and nonnurturant mothers failed to internalize the kind of conscience which would enable them to restrain their impulses to violate society's norms.

Of course, when we talk about the specific personality traits of those known to be delinquent, we go beyond the discussion of general personality theory to consider the distinctive traits of a population subgroup. The topic is more appropriate to a later section, where we will discuss the role of distinctive population characteristics on role performance and social system functioning. I rest my case here, for the moment, in the hope that I have shown that a general theory of personality can be extremely useful in suggesting the specific intervening variables which link the facts of social and community disorganization in urban zones of transition to the high rates of delinquency which characterize such zones.

[8] Of 1,000 cases, 256 were classified as "neutral," that is, no conclusion was ventured as to their probable delinquency. Of these 135 were delinquent.

General Personality Theory and Social Movements

Beyond its role in explaining the levels of suicide, homicide, and other forms of social action which can be expressed as population rates, a general theory of personality is of great importance in the analysis of major social movements which have so long been a central focus of sociological study.

Max Weber, perhaps the greatest sociological student of large-scale social movements, was not lacking in psychological acuity. Indeed, in many ways his analysis of the influence of Protestanism on capitalism [70] is a specification of the personality types which incline toward capitalism and were historically necessary for its initial development. Nevertheless, his basic problem—to discover what elements in the *economic ethic* of Protestantism account for its encouragement of capitalism—does not particularly require the intervention of a general theory of human personality. The personality type is given, at least implicitly, in the religious ethic, and the problem is largely one of showing the translation of the ethic into action in the economic realm.

When we move forward to more recent study of the social consequences of that capitalism whose *origins* Weber studied, the work of Eric Fromm provides an outstanding example of the application of a general theory of personality to explain social movements which arise as a consequence of particular forms of social organization. In *Escape from Freedom* [23], Fromm asks no less a question than what is the effect of capitalism as a socioeconomic system on *man* conceived according to a general theory of the human personality.

The framework of Fromm's analysis is the very general problem of "the role which psychological factors play as active forces in the social process" [23, p. 7]. He explores the problem mainly with reference to the effect of two general needs, that for relatedness to others and that for freedom or autonomy. He asserts that those needs are rooted "not in bodily processes but in the very essence of the human mode and practice of life." Of the first, "the need to avoid aloneness," he says: "This lack of relatedness to values, symbols, patterns, we may call moral aloneness and state that moral aloneness is as intolerable as the physical aloneness, or rather that physical aloneness becomes unbearable only if it implies also moral aloneness" [23, p. 19]. It is the state "which man most dreads." The quality of freedom is less precisely defined. He distinguishes two kinds of freedom. "Freedom from" suggests escape from restraints, especially those imposed by nature, by rigid traditional social organization, even by inner psychic forces, all of which act to prevent "individuation" and the "growth of self-strength." "Freedom to" apparently exists under social and cultural conditions which permit man to preserve his individuality, yet enable him "to unite himself with the world in the spontaneity of love and productive work" [23, p. 23].

Having postulated the two general needs for relatedness and for freedom, Fromm asserts that our history over some hundreds of years has been "one of conflict and strife" because "each step in the direction of growing individuation threatened people with new insecurities" [23, p. 36]. People gained freedom from the restraints of nature and rigid social organization. They were more able to understand and even to express certain of their basic impulses. But the new economic, social, and political conditions which made this freedom possible also increased the sense of insecurity and aloneness. "People have lost those ties which gave them security, [and] this lag makes freedom an unbearable burden." In response to this strain, "powerful tendencies arise to escape from this kind of freedom into submission or some kind of relationship to man and the world which promises relief from uncertainty, even if it deprives the individual of his freedom" [23, pp. 36–37].

Within this framework, Fromm traces the history of modern man, beginning with the Middle Ages and carrying through the Reformation to modern democracies and their counterpart in modern totalitarianism of the fascist variety. The Middle Ages he asserts to have been a period when relatedness was strong but freedom, especially freedom from external restraint, was extremely limited. Fromm sees the Reformation as having begun a 400-year process of breaking down the hold of the medieval world. But in doing so, it increased man's isolation and produced a "feeling of individual insignificance and powerlessness." Fromm argues that, in the process of its development, capitalist democracy freed man *from* his traditional responsibilities without providing the social foundation for freedom *to* develop his true individuality. In time, this produced "a panicky flight from freedom into new ties or at least into complete indifference" [23, pp. 37–38].

Fromm's work is extremely ambitious, attempting to fit a theory to the broad sweep of centuries of man's history. He has the historian's general advantage of being sure in advance his theory will fit the facts he selects, since he knows the outcome so well from the start. Nevertheless, Fromm definitely adds something to social history and to our understanding of modern man, and this extremely condensed account does an injustice to his work. My purpose in introducing it here, however, is not to argue in support of its thesis. The importance of Fromm's work for us, in this review, lies in his explicit use of a general theory about the human personality as an independent element in the analysis of a continuing process of social change. Specifically, his formula specifies that man must have both a high degree of relatedness to others and freedom from restraints which prevent individuation. When social contexts increase individuation but undercut relatedness, he predicts, there will be a drive to regain such relatedness by a surrender of freedom to group purposes. Presumably any period could be assessed in its potential for change according to this formula.

It is greatly to Fromm's credit that he does not try to derive the character of the economic and political structures from general human needs. He does insist, quite properly, that "psychological forces . . . have a dynamism of their own." He asserts, correctly we believe, that while "the expression of human needs . . . can be molded [they] cannot be uprooted." Nevertheless, he recognized that "economic forces must be understood not as psychological motivations but as objective conditions . . . dependent on objective factors, such as the natural productive forces, technique, [and] geographical factors" [23, p. 298]. In this respect, his work is sounder than that of Freud and that of Kardiner. The latter, while he specifically exempts economic relations, does treat the main outlines of myth, religion, and other "projective systems" as merely derived from the specific child rearing disciplines of culture.

Certain links may be here established between Fromm's work and that of Erik Erikson [17]. Erikson speaks of the entry of America, Germany, and Russia into the industrial era as creating a "need, in the youth of all these countries, for a new, a fraternal conscience" [17, p. 243]. Continuing in this vein he says:

Industrial revolution, world-wide communication, standardization, centralization, and mechanization threaten the identities which man has inherited from primitive, agrarian, feudal, and patrician cultures. What inner equilibrium these cultures had to offer is now endangered on a gigantic scale. As the fear of loss of identity dominates much of our irrational motivation, it calls upon the whole arsenal of fear which is left in each individual from the mere fact of his childhood. In this emergency masses of people become ready to seek salvation in some reactionary pseudo identity [17, p. 368].

Erikson does not develop this position systematically. The same deficiency afflicts Cantril's *The Psychology of Social Movements* [10], but it nevertheless deserves brief comment. Cantril seeks to show the relevance for social analysis of a variety of psychological concepts such as attitudes, frames of reference, and the functional autonomy of motives. He too considers certain ego needs to be of prime importance in the functioning of any personality, particularly the need for status, or self-integrity, of which he says "an individual is constantly trying to maintain or enhance his own feeling of self-regard" [10, p. 46]. In addition, he posits a need for meaning, a frame which permits man to see events as organized or structured and subject to explanation. He then seeks to explain lynching mobs, the Father Divine cult, the Oxford Group movement, the Townsend Recovery Plan, and the Nazi party as social movements which arose or were successful in part because they offered to meet these and other needs under conditions in which they were substantially unfulfilled or threatened.

For those persuaded mainly by the kind of proof which comes with successful prediction under controlled laboratory conditions, analyses such as those of Fromm, Erikson, and Cantril are not likely to be too convincing. So long as our author works with any reasonable list of human needs, he should have no great difficulty in showing that, in any situation he may select, one or more of these needs is not being met adequately. To demonstrate any *necessary* connection between the deprivation of the need and the emergence of a social movement, he would be required to show that in all other situations in which the movement did *not* arise the need had been fulfilled. Failing that improbable demonstration, it would be necessary at least to predict the emergence of specific movements in places and under conditions in which the relevant deprivation was known to be developing. This is also a most difficult task, partly because we lack adequate measures of psychosocial deprivation and those we have are expensive and difficult to use on so large a scale as a whole society. In addition, prediction is difficult because we cannot easily find a sufficient number of cases involving the same deprivation to test its general role in stimulating social movements. All this is quite apart from the problems which stem from the role of independent political, economic, or psychological forces which may suppress the development of a social movement despite marked psychological deprivations. Further difficulties inhere in the fact that deprivation of the same need may lead, in different times and cultures, to quite diverse responses which are not always easily recognized as "social movements."

Despite these massive difficulties, increased understanding of the response propensities of peoples subjected to unusual, extreme, persistent, or critical deprivation will continue to be needed and sought. The great social movements of the past will continue to demand explanation, and new movements will continuously arise to challenge the imagination. With a few notable exceptions, such as *When Prophecy Fails* [18], psychologists have done very little to meet this challenge, even though substantial and indeed rich data are available. For example, the Cargo cult or its analog[9] has been reported in a sufficiently large number of cases in widely dispersed culture areas [74] to suggest that there is some general mechanism in human nature which produces this specific type of manifestation.

[9] "Cargo cult" is the generic term applied to a type of native millenarian movement widely observed in Melanesia. A recurrent theme is the belief that cargo boats loaded with goods will arrive on the island shores to provide in abundance the goods and the associated freedom and power which the white men enjoy.

Closer study of such problems would not only promise increased under-standing of the dynamics of social movements, but would contribute equally to our understanding of the dynamics of the human personality.

Since the "psychologizing" of social organization is in bad repute with many social scientists, and perhaps deservedly so, it is important to stress certain crucial differences between the approach developed here and some which have been important in the past. Psychological theories of society and social movements have mainly been of two types. The first type derives social behavior and institutions directly from the psycho-logical properties of the individual, including, in the case of Freud, the individual's psychological prehistory. A typical, if extreme, example is the assertion that man has an aggressive instinct, therefore we have war be-tween nations [cf. T. H. Pear, 53]. The second type, which Sorokin [65] labeled the "psychologistic school" of sociology, simply reduces or trans-lates all social phenomena into psychological terms and, in its more mod-ern version, asserts that the only "real" social phenomena or variables are the personalities, the individual psychology, of those who make up any group.

Fromm, Erikson, and Cantril do not fit either of these patterns. They recognize social institutions, particularly systems of economic and political organization, to be relatively independent variables, each with its own history and laws of development, and not mere projections of personality or psychic need systems. These authors further recognize that many of the processes in political or economic systems, such as the accumulation of capital, cannot be reduced to or rendered exclusively in psychological terms. The distinctive feature of the mode of analysis they present lies in its insistence that all forms of social organization have personal meaning or psychological implications for the participants and that different so-cial systems yield different psychic effects. In their analysis, they usually posit certain general human needs or drives on the basis of personality theory and suggest in broad outline some of the psychological conse-quences of fulfilling, thwarting, displacing, or otherwise handling the needs. A particular social setting is then examined to assess its fulfillment or other response to those needs. Where the needs are not satisfied, or are met in a peculiar way, personality theory is drawn on again to suggest the typical modes of response to the distinctive pattern of frustration experi-enced in the given setting. The subsequent effects on the social system are then assessed, with special attention to the prospects for personal satis-faction or further frustration. That outcome, in turn, may set in motion a new social movement. In this model, the action propensities in the indi-vidual are not derived from society, but from a general theory of the human personality. In turn, culture and social structure are treated his-torically, and not derived from or reduced to personality factors. The link between the two systems lies in the effect of the sociocultural situation on personality and the influence of the personality's reaction back on the social system, especially as that reaction may take the form of social movements likely to change the original sociocultural system.

MODAL PERSONALITY PATTERNS

The second major point of articulation between sociology and psychology lies in the effects on any social system which follow from the distinctive or modal personality characteristics of the system's population or status incumbents. A number of problems lying at the center of sociological interest are greatly illuminated through consideration of the degree and kind of congruence between the role requirements typical of a given institution or social system and the personality patterns characteristic of those playing the roles the system provides. Since these terms and the relations they suggest are perhaps less familiar or obvious than those with which we have so far dealt, a brief elaboration is indicated.

The concept of the role is one of the central elements in sociological thinking [26, 60]. Unfortunately, it has a multiplicity of meanings and uses—which would not be a serious difficulty except for the fact that the particular meaning intended is often left unspecified by those who use the term. Its most common use is to designate the set of rights and obligations which are granted to and placed upon the incumbent of a socially recognized status. The most obvious example is found where there is a specific chart of organization, as in the military or governmental bureaucracy, where each status is precisely specified and the required and permitted acts which constitute the role are also stated with some precision.

Confusion as to the meaning of "role" has arisen from several sources. In their analysis of societies, sociologists have often found clusters of behavior which seem to go together and to be of substantial importance, even though the society's members may not be aware of the pattern nor assign it to a recognized status. These roles are constructs of the sociologist rather than clearly formulated sets of expectations held by the society's members. Another source of confusion has involved the relation between the role as a society expects the status incumbent to play it and the actual behavior characteristic of status incumbents. These often seem to be only slightly related, and many sociologists prefer to treat the actual behavior rather than the expected behavior of status incumbents as the role. Still another use of the role concept treats it mainly in terms of the consequences or *effects* of the status incumbent's behavior on others. Thus, the "role" of the father may be described as one of providing a model of authority which is introjected by the child and which forms the unconscious basis or standard for all his subsequent relations with authority. In a further extension of this approach, the concept role loses all specific reference to a particular status in a network of statuses and becomes a general quality of the person. For example, one may say of X that in most groups his role is that of a peacemaker who tries to integrate opposing currents in the group.

In the following discussion, "role" will refer mainly to the set of generally expected or normative rights and obligations allowed to and demanded of a person generally felt to be the incumbent of a recognized status by others who participate in the same social system. When the term is used in another sense, that fact will be specifically indicated.

Every society makes some broad status distinctions in accord with the biological facts of sex and age. Further, each of the major institutional complexes in any society generates a list of status designations and their accompanying roles. The kinship system, for example, always yields an array of such terms ranging from the obvious mother-father-uncle-aunt-grandparent set to less universal terms such as those for cross cousins and clan or lineage mates. The institutions concerned with religion, fraternal relations, economic activity, and political action—all generate such clusters of statuses.

Each status, then, is part of a cluster of statuses, and each role a set of actions importantly geared in with the sets of action making up other roles. Together, these sets constitute small interdependent systems of action. The term *institution* designates the subsystem which is the basic building block of sociological analysis. Institutions, like statuses, are generally but not always explicitly recognized and named by the societies in which they are found. The army or the war party, the clan, the household or family, the church or sect or cult, the nation, region, or village are generally named and known to all. They are the discernible membership units of the society, the "things" to which a person can and generally will belong in the course of his life and of which he will be a "member."

Institutions are generally organized around the problems that all societies face, such as recruitment or socialization of the young, control of the use of force, the regulation of sex, maintenance of sustenance, and defense against external attack [see Aberle, 1]. Societies will vary markedly both in the degree to which their institutions have either broad and general or highly specialized functions and in the particular combination of system problems concentrated in any given institution. Although sociologists are often naïve in the assumptions they make about the "simplicity" of primitive societies, it seems that modern large-scale societies are distinguished by the elaboration of a very large number of discrete institutions, each organized around a highly specific system need. In modern society, for example, the family is no longer a producing unit, provides little formal education, and has only rudimentary religious functions, having "lost" these responsibilities to the factory or shop, the school, the church, and so on.

The articulation of the individual's personality with the role demands of the social statuses he fills is of relevance to understanding three central problems of sociological analysis: the adequacy of role performance, the integration of the diverse institutions which make up a society, and the problem of change in social systems.

Personality and Role Performance

From the point of view of the individual, it is mainly his status *rights* that are important, since the gratifications which result from these are essential to the continued integration or maintenance of the person. From the "point of view" of the institution or social system, if we may so speak, the performance of the individual's assigned role *obligations* is the critical requirement laid on him, since others are dependent on that performance as one link in the network of such obligations. Sociologists have traditionally explained the fact that individuals do regularly perform their roles as being a logical consequence of the sanctions imposed on those who fail to meet the expectations laid on them and the rewards granted to those who do meet them. Role performance is thus typically understood by sociologists as largely dependent on factors "outside" the person. All that is posited "inside" is merely the simple desire to avoid punishment and to gain rewards.

Important as such drives may be, they are hardly sufficient to explain the complex phenomenon of differential role performance. Role performance obviously also depends on possession of the knowledge or skills a role requires and on the motivation to perform the role. In addition there may be "qualities" in the person which hinder or facilitate his role performance because they make it *intrinsically* rewarding or repugnant to him, quite apart from the formal system of sanctions. An obvious but extremely useful example which Roe [57] calls to our attention involves a neurotic symptom such as claustrophobia. Obviously a person with this characteristic cannot be employed as an elevator operator, coal miner, or underground telephone-cable repairman. Similarly, being somewhat phobic about dirt could in important degree facilitate role performance in a cleaning woman, and being somewhat compulsive might increase the pleasure a file clerk takes in his job.

Sociologists wish to explain the pattern of recruitment to statuses and subsequent performance in relevant roles as this affects the functioning of an institution or society. The measures of system functioning sociologists use are generally "efficiency" measures of some sort—production in a factory, stability or happiness in a marriage, success in bringing up children in a family. Additional measures of side effects beyond those connected with the *central* purpose of an institution are often included in the evaluation of institutional functioning. For example, even if production is high in a factory, a high rate of labor turnover or a large number of wildcat strikes will be taken as evidence of institutional malfunctioning. To explain such institutional malfunctioning, the industrial sociologist will typically seek for certain institutional defects. He may look for an inadequate flow of communications up from the bottom which prevents grievances from coming to the attention of management or he may suspect a tendency of management to shift workers without adequate consultation of their wishes and desires. Such situational factors may indeed be not merely important, but crucial, determinants of status incumbents' behavior and, consequently, institutional functioning. The objective stimulus to social action is not being challenged here.

In addition to such structural factors, however, institutional functioning may in important degree be influenced by the "qualities" of the persons who occupy the statuses in the institutional system. Furthermore, the quality of role performance is itself likely to be influenced by a prior process of differential recruitment to statuses on the basis of the personality of the candidates. We hold that the incumbents of statuses will often be found to reflect not random recruitment, but a highly selective process of assortment or assignment. To the degree that this is true, then, in order to predict the functioning of an institution of a small-scale or large-scale social system we need to know more than the system of statuses, the formal roles, the sanctions, and similar structural elements which characterize the system. We should also have knowledge of the personalities of those occupying the major statuses.

Although this proposition has great surface plausibility, it is extremely difficult to muster definitive evidence in support of it. Clearly the issues could best be investigated systematically in small groups in which it would be possible to vary both the social structure and the personality composition of the group. Although there are small-group studies which systematically vary elements of structure, such as the outstanding study of autocratic and democratic group atmospheres undertaken by Lewin and his associates [44, 46] and several which control the personality composition of the groups, there are very few in which simultaneous control of these variables is undertaken.

We may briefly cite two studies which give us the opportunity to observe the effect of varying personality patterns in a structurally constant environment. Haythorn and his associates [29] set up four-man discussion groups whose task was to compose and record a dialogue to fit a silent film they were shown on human relations in industry. The subjects had been rated on authoritarianism (F scale), and each group was composed of men who were either all high in authoritarianism *or* all low scorers. Although the structure of the two groups was alike in that no leader had been appointed and no rules for reaching an agreement specified, the behavioral patterns manifested in the groups varied significantly. In groups composed of those low on the authoritarianism scale, more positive effect was shown, there was greater concern for the feeling of others, and fewer efforts were made to direct others. In each of the two types of group there developed what the researchers describe as a distinctive "group culture." Although it derived from the modal personality patterns of the members, this culture was similar to what would have been expected had the norms of the group been formally structured as democratic or authoritarian.

A comparable but more complex pattern is represented in the work of Schutz [61]. He also composed groups by selecting members on the basis of a personality test, but the groups were arranged to be "compatible" or "incompatible." Compatible groups were made up of men who were all the same personality type, whereas in the incompatible groups two personality types were mixed. Group members were classified as either "personal" or "impersonal" in their orientation toward interpersonal relations. The "personal" were more concerned with smoothness of interpersonal relations; the "impersonal" were less considerate of the individual and good relations and more involved in getting the job done. On a variety of tasks involving problem solving by the groups, the compatible sets, those in which the members were either all "personal" or all "impersonal," had a significantly higher productivity or effectiveness score. Follow-up measures of satisfaction with the individual's experience in the group revealed more satisfaction with the group and with one's participation in it among members of the compatible groups.

In neither of these studies was the formal social structure of the group significantly varied, although in the Haythorn studies the shift from emergent to appointed leaders did introduce a structural change. Until the social structure of such groups is also brought under experimental control, sociologists will wonder how "important" these personality factors are compared to variable aspects of structure such as the pattern of leadership, the rules determining the rights of members, the methods for assigning individuals to tasks and for handling grievances, the forms for internal communication, the size of the groups, and many similar variables. Until both personality and structural variables are simultaneously controlled and the *relative* impact of each on group effectiveness is tested, sociologists will probably remain somewhat skeptical of the meaning of the statistically significant but not often absolutely large differences which emerge when groups are assembled to represent different combinations of personality types.

In addition, sociologists would stress that all of these groups were carefully and "artificially" composed of highly selected personality types. The sociologist evaluating the functioning of institutions might well feel that, in "real" groups and situations, the accidents of life history and factors other than personality which are responsible for recruitment will "randomize" personality distribution in the major social statuses sufficiently so that taking systematic account of the influence of personality composition is unnecessary.

Even if the personality composition of any group is randomly determined, random assortment would not in fact guarantee the *same* personality composition in the membership of all institutions of a given type. On the contrary, the very fact of randomness implies that the outcome would approximate a normal distribution. Consequently, some of the groups would by chance have a personality composition profoundly different from others, with possibly marked effects on the functioning of the institutions involved. Furthermore, there is no convincing evidence that randomness *does* consistently describe the assignment of personality types to major social statuses. On the contrary, there is a great deal of evidence to indicate that particular statuses often attract, or recruit preponderantly for, one or another personality characteristic and that fact has a substantial effect on individual adjustment to roles and the general quality of institutional functioning.

For example, the editorial as against the sports staff of a large college daily has been shown by Swanson [69] to be markedly stronger in tendencies toward oral passivity, anal expulsiveness, and phallic-aspiring qualities. In a study of stereopathy (a quality similar to authoritarianism as measured by the F scale), Stern, Stein, and Bloom [67] found it is markedly more prevalent among students in a military academy and a typical southern college, whereas "non-stereopaths" were rare in such groups. By contrast the "non-stereopaths," characterized by "highly personalized and individualized social relationships . . . and non-conforming flexibility in behavior" [67, 192], were markedly more common in a northern college, a liberal seminary, and among an assemblage of group dynamicists. Those high in stereopathy were very seldom found in these groups. To choose from quite a different realm, H. V. Dicks [13] showed that among German prisoners of war, those who were hard-core Nazis, as against those who gave only weak support to or even opposed Hitler, were personality types much more given to projection, marked homosexual trends, extreme antisocial sadism, and a much greater propensity to taboo the expression of tenderness. They did not, however, differ markedly in the presence or absence of anxiety, depression, or schizoid features. Among Soviet Russian refugees, Inkeles, Hanfmann, and Beier [33] found that those who had held the more favored positions of professional or administrator were markedly different from the rank and file of workers and peasants in having much greater development of strong ego defenses and in being characterized by less need for affiliation and less spontaneity and emotional expressiveness.

Such examples could be multiplied. They all indicate that occupational, political, and institutional groups may contain significantly large numbers, sometimes distinctive majorities, of a particular personality type. It may be that these types are mainly developed on the job through adult socialization, but this seems unlikely because so many of the reported differences involve depth components in the personality which are generally laid down in early life.

Whether based on recruitment or development on the job, such modal personality differences are relevant to the sociologist only if they can be shown to affect individual role performance, and consequently influence institutional functioning. Studies in which personality data and data on role performance are simultaneously reported are rare, but those available indicate marked effects of personality on role performance. In a study of the performance of nurses' aides, as judged by their supervisors in a mental hospital, Gilbert and Levinson [24] rated them as treating their patients in either a more "custodial" or a more "humanistic" fashion. The custodial designation meant that more threats were made to the patient and that the aide placed prime emphasis on keeping the ward quiet. The more "humanistic" aides were more friendly and respectful to the patients and took on more the role of a "social" therapist for their ward. For the female aides in three Boston hospitals the rank-order correlation between custodialism in the treatment of patients and score on authoritarianism in personality as measured by the F scale was .75.[10]

Several outstanding studies relate personality to school performance. Rosen [59] drew a sample of students stratified by social class from public high schools in New Haven and secured measures of achievement motivation and school performance. Those who scored high on need achievement were most likely to make good grades, 69 per cent having B or better as against 35 per cent among those with low need achievement. A test of value orientations, incidentally, failed to discriminate significantly the low- and high-grade performers. Need achievement was also very highly associated with social class, but a separate control run on class showed that it had virtually no independent effect on grade performance when achievement motivation was controlled.

Stern, Stein, and Bloom secured a series of performance measures for the students high and low on stereopathy. Intelligence accounted for

[10] The correlation in the case of the male aides, however, although in the expected direction, was only .31, just short of significance at the .05 level.

only a modest part of the variance in the stereopathy score, but any possible effect of differences in intelligence between the two groups of stereopathic and nonstereopathic students (61 in each) was controlled by matching on this dimension. On entrance and placement examinations there were marked differences in the performance of the two groups in tests on the humanities, social sciences, and English. By contrast, there was only random variation in their performance in biological sciences, physical sciences, and mathematics. The emphasis at the college concerned (presumably the University of Chicago) was on "capacity for detachment, for delaying resolution or closure, and for tolerating ambiguous relativities rather than demanding structural absolutes" [67, p. 206]. This placed a premium on qualities which were characteristic among nonstereopaths and relatively lacking in those high in stereopathy. Such qualities were, however, obviously less important in the natural sciences and mathematics examinations, for which fields the requirements and tests are also more standardized.

Striking differences also emerged in the later school performance of the two groups. At the end of the first year, 20 per cent of the stereopathic students had withdrawn from the college, whereas none of the nonstereopaths did so—a difference significant at the .001 level. Intelligence made virtually no difference in this performance. The complaints of the withdrawing stereopathic students strongly suggested their action resulted from the lack of congruence between their personalities and their consequent ambitions and hopes, on the one hand, and on the other the special requirements of the particular college they had entered. They complained most about the seeming lack of discipline, the refusal of instructors to give the "right" answers, and the separation between course content and their immediate and practical vocational interests. This outcome was largely as had been predicted from an examination of the distinctive qualities of education at the particular college and the distinctive personality attributes of the stereopathic students.

Personality and System Integration

Dealing with only one status, our problem is limited to the fit between a personality trait or set of traits and the restricted range of behavior which is distinctive for a particular role. When we consider a full-scale social system, however, the problem of the *integration* of *diverse* roles becomes prominent. Any social system which requires that individuals act in more than one role must somehow adjust to the fact that people are limited in their ability to combine in one integrated personality more than a certain number and *range* of psychic qualities or attributes. Societies can to some extent reduce the strains of integrating diverse-role requirements if they keep to a minimum the number of distinctive statuses. This is often the case with nonliterate societies; it is for this reason that we may speak of them as "simple" or relatively undifferentiated. Nevertheless, in any society each individual will have at least sex, age, and kinship roles and may have in addition others of great importance, such as specialized occupational, religious, and political roles. The task of playing so many diverse roles can be made more manageable for the individual by structural arrangements which establish sets or congeries of statuses which require similar or compatible qualities. This pattern is almost always adopted in the differentiation of the roles of men and women. It may also be used within a sex group to further differentiate subgroups. Thus war, hunting, and political roles may largely be the province of one set of men, whereas art, religion, and learning may be equally restricted to another set of individuals. Such arrangements simplify but do not eliminate the basic problem. They also raise *new* problems. The integration of a society which particularly relies on such specialized role clusters will obviously require mechanisms rather different from those required where such segmentation is less prominent.

To understand the integration of full-scale social systems with and through the personalities occupying the major statuses requires study on a scale and with resources which so far have not been mustered anywhere. For many nations one can easily assemble all sorts of impressionistic lists of personality traits alleged to characterize the population. But there is not one national population, large or small, for which we have extensive and systematic information, based on adequate sampling, which would enable us to describe accurately the modal personality traits found within it. This situation is, happily, now being remedied. In 1953, Janowitz and Marvick [34] presented data on the distribution of authoritarianism, based on a modified F scale, by age, sex, education, and occupation in the United States. This was very likely the first time anyone published the results of a national sample used to assess the nation-wide distribution of an important psychological characteristic. More recently, in connection with a national survey of adjustment, the Survey Research Center staff at Michigan [27] used a modified TAT to measure the achievement, affiliation, and power motivations in the population of the United States. The initial report on the findings of this investigation prepared by Gurin, Veroff, Atkinson and Feld [27a] firmly establishes the feasibility of using survey methods to assess personality mode in large populations.

We do have substantial data on a variety of small nonliterate societies, and some small but intensive studies of various segments of several modern large-scale societies. Although this material permits only the most tentative and exploratory hypotheses, it can be extremely important in suggesting a model of the studies we have yet to undertake. Since the problem of system integration is not a familiar one to many psychologists, the following illustrations of the relevance of modal personality patterns for such integration are discussed at some length.

Of the many studies of personality in "primitive" societies, very few have achieved the clarity and precision attained by Spindler [66] in maintaining a precise distinction between personality and the sociocultural system. His chief concern was to discern and explain personality differences in several groups of Menomini who were differentiated in degree of acculturation. Nevertheless, his study also provides a rather striking example of apparent congruence between the typical role requirements of a sociocultural system and the modal personality pattern of the society's members.

The "classical" form of Menomini culture—before the extreme acculturation during the modern period of white contact—is approximated contemporaneously in only one group. These are currently the least acculturated Menomini, and they live in the relatively isolated community of Zoar. In that community, we still see elements of the traditional Menomini life patterns. There is very little centralization of authority. The leaders are noticeably lacking in coercive power and have little interest in attaining it. The most important task of a leader is to express group consensus and to make sure that no individual's feelings are hurt. Interpersonal equality is strongly stressed, and all the folk heroes are extremely democratic. Although being a good hunter is highly valued, such attainment does not involve marked strivings or overweening achievement drives. Whatever one's success, it is extremely inappropriate to boast. Indeed, emotional expressiveness in general is dampened; in particular, the expression of aggression is under severe control. Little value is placed on, and no requirements are made for, compulsive qualities involving orderliness, regularity, or mastery over nature. Little stress or strain is imposed by the individual's statuses. The world is defined as more friendly than hostile, and provision is made for sharing food and sustaining a kind of oral optimism in other ways.

In the light of this very brief description of some of the older, more traditional Menomini culture patterns which persist in modern times, it is most revealing to examine the personality patterns revealed by the Rorschach test among 17 of the least acculturated Menomini who were largely sticking to the old ways. The test results for this group were highly homogeneous. At the lowest, 58 per cent, and on most critical dimensions 70 per cent or more, shared the same characteristics in Rorschach response (based on dichotomous cuts for the larger sample as a whole). In his summary of the Rorschach results for this group, Spindler describes the personality type:

. . . highly intratensive, sensitive to the environment but able to maintain equilibrium despite its variations, lacking generally in overt emotional responsiveness and exhibiting a high degree of rational control over it when it does appear, motivated more by biologically oriented "survival" drives than by self-projective imaginatively creative ones, intellectually uncomplicated but adequate in terms of its setting, lacking in rigidity or constriction, without evidence of the usual forms of anxiety, tension, or internal conflict [66, pp. 133–134].

Juxtaposition of this personality profile with the institutional features and role requirements of the sociocultural system suggests a number of points at which the modal personality pattern articulates significantly with important aspects of the older culture pattern. The low level of emotional responsiveness, the control over emotion, and the sensitivity to interpersonal relations obviously fit well with the cultural stress on inhibiting aggression, not striving for power, and not giving offense. At the same time, an appropriate adjustment to the environment and to the requirement of skill at hunting is provided by the strength of biologically oriented survival drives. The Menomini cosmology posits the existence of supranatural powers yielding fateful and irrevocable but generally positive outcomes. Their ideology of passive acceptance of benevolent but inscrutable nature can be seen as articulating with the personality quality of lack of tension, striving, and anxiety.

These and similar points strongly suggest that when the culture was in full form before white contact, many of the qualities which cut across the Menomini sociocultural system were matched by appropriate qualities which cut across the modal personality patterns of Menomini people. We may then assume that, in substantial measure, the integration of the sociocultural system was facilitated by the personality structure of the society's members. It is of special interest to note, furthermore, that those Menomini who chose the path of acculturation were progressively less like the traditionalists and more like whites in personality, depending on the degree of acculturation. We may say, then, that the pattern of social change was also in significant degree influenced by modal personality patterns.

The Menomini are a small enough group, and the least acculturated are sufficiently homogeneous, to allow us some confidence in results coming from a sample of only 17. This is, unfortunately, no longer the case when we approach modern national states. It is an odd fact that there are relatively more complete modal personality studies for nonliterate peoples than there are for modern nations. Soviet Russia may serve to illustrate the problem of integrating social structure and personality modes in a modern society. Considering the extreme inaccessibility of Soviet citizens, this may seem a strange choice. The political interest in Soviet Russia has, however, stimulated studies which have not been undertaken for other populations. Unfortunately, only refugees from Soviet totalitarianism were available as subjects. But this group has been extensively studied by several independent researchers utilizing psychiatric clinical interviews, extensive psychological testing, and careful participant observation. In two studies, an explicit purpose was to derive modal personality patterns and to assess their relation to the individual's adjustment in the sociopolitical system. In these two studies, rather careful attention was also given to subgroup differences in personality modes. I shall base my argument mainly on the clinical testing program of the Harvard Project on the Soviet Social System as reported in Inkeles, Hanfmann, and Beier [33]. It should be noted, however, that the conclusions reached through this testing program accord well with those presented by Dicks [14] on the basis of clinical interviews and those of Pfister-Ammende [54], based on direct observation of the behavior of Soviet refugees living in Switzerland.

The Harvard clinical study included 51 subjects drawn from a larger sample of several hundred interviewees. Compared to the Soviet parent population, the clinical group was disproportionately male, young, educated, and well placed occupationally and politically. But it was internally well balanced, representing equally those over and under thirty-five, in manual versus white-collar jobs, living in urban or rural areas, and having education above or below the secondary level. The test battery included the Rorschach, TAT, a 60-item sentence-completion test, a set of "projective questions," and a specially developed "episodes" or problem-situations test. These tests were supplemented by interviews focused on childhood experience and adult adjustment. Each test was independently analyzed, but the conclusions for all tests were later combined to develop a profile of modal personality traits in the group as a whole. In developing this profile, the interpretation of the test results was strongly influenced by contrasts and similarities in parallel materials drawn from a matched sample of Americans.

The Harvard study gave special attention to the way in which the modal personality patterns which emerged were related to the adjustment of these subjects to the Soviet sociopolitical system. It is quite reasonable to doubt whether these refugees are at all representative of the parent population, although there are grounds for believing that in personality terms they are. The accuracy of this interpretation is not an important issue here. Rather, we should focus on the study reported below as merely illustrating an approach we may wish to see used with samples better drawn and more clearly representative of important parent populations.

The Soviet refugees manifested a very strong need for affiliation, which many distinctive features of the Soviet sociopolitical system seemed almost calculated to frustrate. The study notes, for example, that "the regime has placed great strains on friendship relations by its persistent programs of political surveillance, its encouragement and elaboration of the process of denunciation, and its assignment of mutual or 'collective' responsibility for the failings of particular individuals." The authors also comment that the breakup or official infiltration of many primary face-to-face groups, such as the village community, the traditional extended family group, the church, and the professional society all interfered with "the desire for involvement in the group, and the insistence on loyalty, sincerity, and general responsiveness from others" [33, p. 13].

Another of the most salient and distinctive characteristics of the Russian subjects was their emotional aliveness and expressiveness, their tendency to give way to impulse and freely to express criticism. This too was a source of difficulty in their adjustment to the Soviet sociopolitical system, since the regime emphasized and rewarded such qualities as control and formality and demanded discipline and orderliness. The study then concludes that the refugees' "expansiveness and tendency freely to express their feelings, including hostile feelings, exposed them to retaliation from the punitive police organs of the state. And in so far as they did exercise the necessary control and avoided open expression of hostile feelings, they experienced a sense of uneasiness and resentment because of this unwarranted imposition, which did much to color their attitude to the regime" [33, p. 15].

A third illustration is provided by the typical modes of conative functioning which characterized the Russian subjects. Compared to the American subjects, they showed much less vigorous striving and less concern for an instrumental-adaptive mastery of their environment. They were more passively accommodating and less persevering, although given to occasional great bursts of spontaneous energy. By contrast, the Soviet regime constantly demanded greater effort, long-range planning and deferred gratification, and an instrumental approach to problems. In the light of this contrast, it seems not surprising that "Soviet official sources have for many years constantly complained of the uneven pace at which work proceeds, with the usual slack pace making it necessary to have great, often frenzied, bursts of activity to complete some part of the Plan on schedule, followed again by a slack period" [33, p. 15].

These are but three of a considerable number of examples which permit testing the congruence between the personality modes and dispositions of at least one part of the Russian population and certain aspects of the sociopolitical system in which they lived. The authors conclude that the general pattern was one of noncongruence, which had

become an important factor in the refugees' maladjustment and subsequent defection from the system. They note:

Most of the popular grievances were clearly based on real deprivations
and frustrations, but the dissatisfactions appear to be even more intensified
and given a more emotional tone because they were based also on the poor
'fit' between the personality patterns of many Soviet citizens and the
'personality' of the leaders as it expressed itself in the institutions they
created, in their conduct of those institutions and the system at large, and
in the resultant social climate in the U.S.S.R. [33, p. 16].

Soviet leaders are not available for psychological testing. Nevertheless, the Harvard study developed some evidence indicating that in important respects the personality of Soviet leaders differs from the modal
personality type. The three defining characteristics of the modal pattern
were great strength of drive for social relatedness, marked emotional
aliveness, and general lack of well-developed, complex, and pervasive
defenses. Of 24 workers and peasants, 20 showed this pattern. By contrast, among the 13 holding professional and higher administrative positions only 1 showed this pattern.

Although we cannot be sure that the higher political elite in the
Soviet Union shares the personality characteristics of the better-educated
and occupationally more highly placed refugees, it seems not unreasonable to assume that the Soviet political elite is indeed even further along
the continuum from the point at which the rank-and-file workers and
peasants were found. As the report notes, "it seems plausible that persons in whom the affiliative need was particularly strong, expressiveness
marked and impulse control weak, and the defensive structures not well
developed or well organized would be handicapped in competition for
professional and administrative posts in any society; they certainly could
not be expected to strive for or to hold on to positions of responsibility
in the Soviet system" [33, p. 18].

In so far as the personality of the elite is in fact markedly different
from the patterns modal for the rank and file of Soviet industrial and
agricultural workers, this case provides another important illustration of
the earlier noted pattern of differential recruitment for occupations on
grounds of personality. It also provides an important illustration of the
relevance of personality for the integration of sets of specialized roles.
The presence of distinctive personality modes among the Soviet elite also
points up the system integration problem posed by the existence of distinct modal personality patterns in different segments of a national population. The qualities which facilitate a person's mobility or recruitment
to elite status and which enhance his effective performance at that level
may be the very traits most alien to the ordinary citizen. The same quali-

ties may lead the elite to establish institutional arrangements not congruent with the modal personality patterns of the rank and file. This is by no means the only or necessary relation between elite modes and those of the rank and file. On the contrary, the German experience under Hitler suggests that the relation of the personality patterns of the elite to those of the rank and file may be one of similarity or complementarity. In either case, however, profound implications for the system's functioning follow from the degree and kind of congruence between the pattern of behavior of the elite and the modal personality patterns of the majority of the population.

It is a moot question whether the definition of a social system should include not merely its basic institutions and roles, which provide the framework for individual action, but also its cultural values and the particular set of personalities within it at any given time. In our opinion it is desirable not to include the component personalities in the definition of the social system, but merely to specify the statuses and roles and their interrelations. To estimate the quality of role performances, however, and to understand their coherence in institutional systems, it is important— indeed, one might say essential—to know the personality of the status incumbents. Just as a general theory of personality may be used as an intervening variable in specifying the behavioral consequences of any aspect of social structure, so the personality of the role incumbents may be treated as an intervening variable in specifying the quality of role performance. The "same" formal social system will produce different behavioral consequences, depending on the personalities in it, and the "same" roles will be performed differently, depending on the personalities of the status incumbents. This indicates the second major point of articulation between sociological problems and psychological facts. The student of social structure must have some means for assessing the special qualities and needs of the personalities acting in the social system if he is to maximize his estimate of role performance and general system functioning. For that assessment, he must rely on the personality psychologist.

SPECIAL PSYCHOLOGICAL THEORIES

In contrast to the general theories of personality and to the approaches for assessing personality modes, the special theories and findings of psychology such as those dealing with learning, cognition, or perception cannot at this time be easily integrated with sociological theory and research. This is not surprising, since it was only in the period immediately after World War II that some of these special materials were even partially articulated with general personality theory itself. We hear, for example, of the "new look" in perception research [9], only to discover that it is the readiness to relate certain aspects of perception theory to such personality factors as "need." We are still far from having systematically related variations in perceptual and cognitive patterns to factors in the individual or group's sociocultural background. Further development which will permit these theories to contribute effectively to our understanding of the functioning of sociocultural systems lies some distance in the future. It may be instructive, however, to consider briefly a few pioneering efforts to study learning, cognition, and perception as they influence, and are influenced by, other aspects of personality and sociocultural forces.

Of the "special" branches of psychology, the theories of learning have perhaps the most direct relevance for the sociologist. Implicit in the idea that the members of a society share a system of action is the assumption that they have *learned* the appropriate responses to the cues given by others. The adults in a society are the end products of a long process of prior conditioning. They are thus equipped with a large repertory of standardized responses to meet the situations their sociocultural system will present. Societies experience a continuous turnover in personnel while maintaining relative stability in culture and social structure. The key to this continuity lies, in large measure, in the fact that successive generations learn their culture in all its complexity. They must also acquire a predisposition to accept, and an ability to act in accord with, the requirements of that part of the culture embedded in laws, art patterns, and a host of institutions. The key to this learning lies in the forms and content of childhood and later training. In other words, a necessary condition for sociocultural continuity is a system of socialization which ensures that each generation will learn the culture patterns sufficiently well to play all the appropriate social roles in much the same manner as did the preceding generation.

It is a moot point whether the study of this learning should be primarily the responsibility of the psychologist or is equally the province of the sociologist. In my opinion, the process is most appropriately studied by developmental and child psychologists, if they will accept the burden. Very few students of learning have shown much serious interest in this problem. Since the study of child training is one of the major points of articulation between psychology and sociocultural studies and is not amenable to a clear-cut allocation of responsibility to either, we should perhaps encourage a pattern of collaboration between the psychologist of learning and the sociologist or anthropologist.

A full discussion of the sociologist's perspective on the study of child training is beyond my mandate and the scope of this paper. It is not inappropriate to say, however, that contemporary learning theories seem inadequate to account for the process which transforms the infant into the fully socialized culture-bearing adult. Academic psychologists who study learning are mainly interested in the effects on learning of the time which elapses between stimulus and response, in the sequence of stimulus, conditioned and unconditioned response, in reinforcement and extinction, and in stimulus generalization. An understanding of these processes is essential to an understanding of human learning. But psychological students of learning have dealt with these problems at an extremely general level. They study learning as manifested in any species, rather than mainly in humans. Their desire to control what they regard as extraneous variables has led them to screen out elements of content and context which are not only most interesting and relevant for the sociologist, but which in his opinion are decisive for an understanding of the learning process, its success or failure, and its consequences. For these reasons the sociologist turns away from the student of learning and looks to the student of personality. Even in the case of the most intensive and explicit utilization of learning theories in the study of socialization by Whiting and Child [72], it is apparent that traditional learning theories contribute substantially less to the analysis than does Freudian theory. The blending of the two accomplished in that work may, however, provide a model for other efforts along the same line.

Learning theory may be very important in explaining how certain traits come to be prevalent in the adult members of a society. Once a given predisposition is established, however, the sociologist will be less concerned with its past development and more interested in understanding how the given trait affects the quality of role performance, or how certain role demands may affect the psychic adjustment of persons with the given trait. At the level at which most sociologists work, much that concerns contemporary students of learning seems to have little immediate relevance, even though its significance may be substantial in the study of behavior at more molecular levels.

To increase the relevance of learning theory and research for sociologists would require going far beyond what is traditionally defined as an appropriate concern of psychologists working in that realm. It does not seem likely, however, that the range of problems and the type of situation now covered in psychological research on learning can indefinitely remain so circumscribed. In time, psychologists who define themselves as specialists on learning must either broaden the area of their concern or allow others to share responsibility for, and legitimate entry into, the ranks of "students of learning." Foremost among these new entrants into the ranks will be those who study the early learning of the child in the socialization process. In addition, learning theory would be of great relevance for societal analysis if it would deal more

systematically with the principles which account for *adult* learning and
for the failure of individuals and cultures to learn new ways. However
much one might be led to think so by the concentration of studies on
early socialization, significant learning hardly ceases at the age of six.
Social learning, often meaning unlearning and relearning, goes on all
through life. Indeed, in modern large-scale societies, learning in early
and late adolescence is extremely important in laying the bases for later
social participation, and much of the process continues at the adult
level as in socialization to a professional role. About such learning, however, there is little or nothing that I can find in the chapters on learning
produced by most psychologists—indeed, there is not very much by students of personality.

At least one major exception can be cited in the work of Miller and
Dollard. In their book *Social Learning and Imitation* [51], they attempt
to show how an application of learning theories can augment our understanding of a number of social patterns, including crowd behavior and
culture borrowing. In describing crowd or mob behavior, Miller and
Dollard use the concept of "inter-stimulation," and describe a sequence
in which—

. . . the first individual notices the response of the second, and the stimuli
given off by this response operate to intensify his own response. The first
person is now responding more vigorously than he would to the drive
stimulus alone. The second person, in his turn, is stimulated by the intensified
response of the first, and increases the vigor of his own response.

[But why should A increase his response because B does? Apparently because
of generalization from prior experiences similar to the following paradigmatic
case]:

Children have learned that when others are running toward the same
goal, it is advisable to speed up, if the goal is to be reached. They are frequently rewarded, in such situations, for running faster when they see others
run. The response of running faster when others run is therefore fixed to
the stimulus of seeing the other person run [51, pp. 227–228].

This theory of crowd behavior seems inadequate on a number of
counts. In the socialization process, especially in the schools in Western
society, great pains are taken to teach children *not* to run just because
others are running. To explain crowd behavior, therefore, we must not
only deal with previous learning which reinforced the impulse to reach
a goal. We must explain how interstimulation overcomes the previous
learning which sought to extinguish the running response. Crowd behavior depends on conditions of anonymity and the reduction of social
control and it varies with the degree of hostility or aggressiveness which
characterizes the crowd members. Neither these nor a host of other

factors important in understanding crowd behavior can be dealt with adequately, if at all, by most extant learning theories. Of course, there is no reason to expect learning theory alone to explain so complex a phenomenon. This illustration does, however, highlight the need to attempt further integration of learning theories with theories of personality and social structure.

The application of learning theory to explain culture borrowing is less satisfying than its use to explain crowd behavior. Culture borrowing, we are told, depends upon a prior experience with such borrowing which was successful or rewarding. Thus the Chinese, although for centuries in contact with the Mongols, who used milk, did not adopt it because "the Chinese . . . never tried out the use of milk and hence could not be rewarded for adopting it" [51, p. 265]. The authors confidently apply the same theory to explain the fact that some societies seem in general disinclined toward borrowing, stating, "We have no doubt that the conservatism in question is a result of former experience with copying and indicates negative results in earlier copying" [51, pp. 265–266].

This confidence will hardly be shared by most students of culture borrowing. Indeed, Miller and Dollard themselves find it necessary to introduce factors such as the "prestige" of the society from which borrowing will be done relative to the prestige of the society which borrows, and the "social attitude toward copying." Neither of these ideas, nor many others they find it necessary to introduce, finds a place in most learning theory. The reason is, of course, fairly obvious. Animal experimentation, which is the basis for most learning theory, hardly creates a great need for such concepts. As soon as the learning theorist ventures beyond the rat maze, however, he finds that he must have such concepts. Perhaps the significance of *Social Learning and Imitation* lies as much in making this so very evident as it does in increasing our understanding of mob behavior and culture borrowing.

Turning to perception, we face a problem similar to that encountered in the study of learning—the subject either leads back into general personality theory or it seems to lack relevance for problems of sociological analysis. This is most evident in Else Frenkel-Brunswik's [19] "personality centered approach" to perception. She is mainly describing a quality of personality rather than a principle of perception when she shows that those inclined toward perceptual dichotomization, to which they stick rigidly and with intolerance of ambiguity, are also ethnically prejudiced. Much the same point may be made about the interesting work of Witkin and his associates [73]. They deal with perceptions of the spatial orientation of objects in relation to the upright dimension. The objects studied included, notably, the human body. In Witkin's apparatus, the subjects can be rotated and tilted with such precision that any subject will experience precisely the same objective situation or stimulus. Witkin's research leads to the conclusion that "under the same field conditions and with a force of the same magnitude and direction acting on their bodies, people differ markedly in their perception" [73, p. 156]. These differences, furthermore, "represent a pervasive and deep-seated characteristic of the individual" [73, p. 156]. In other words, the differences in perception are not explained by external conditions. They are an attribute of the person. In addition, there seem to be distinctive patterns which distinguish youth from adults, and men from women, which leads us back to social-group analysis.

It is immediately apparent how a sociologist can apply to his problems of research the findings presented by Else Frenkel-Brunswik. The application of studies such as Witkin's or the pioneering study of the effect of values on perception by Postman, Bruner, and McGinnies [55] is perhaps not so obvious, but the relevance seems clear. It is much more difficult to see such relevance in the principles of "pure" perception theory—such as those which deal with the relations of figure and ground, or with closure and continuity. This is not to exclude these principles from relevance in sociological analysis, but simply to suggest that their usefulness, except as expressed through personality, still awaits a convincing demonstration.

When we turn to the study of cognition, much the same kind of difficulty confronts us. The study of cognition has yielded fewer "laws" as rigorously formulated as those developed by students of learning and perception. Both concepts and research method are here less firmly set in a fixed mold. This fluidity holds more promise that studies of cognition can be developed in such a way as to make their findings relevant to the sociologist. The promise of such carry-over is also enhanced by the fact that work on cognition is generally done with men rather than animals. Nevertheless, the direct relevance of many studies of cognition to problems of sociological analysis is not immediately apparent.

For example, Bruner, Goodnow, and Austin [8] report in their study of concept attainment that there seem to be four main methods for validating categorizations: recourse to an ultimate criterion, tests by consistency, consensus, and affective congruence. They also call our attention to a phenomenon they label "persistence forecasting," by which they mean the tendency "to fall back on cues that in the past have seemed useful, whether these cues have been useful in an analogous situation or not" [8, p. 237]. Now it may be that individuals (or even societies) will vary in their propensity to utilize one or another method of validating categories, will be more or less prone to persistence forecasting, or will require more or less information before being willing to reach a decision. To the extent that this is true, however, these tendencies are merely variable properties of individual or modal personality and can be adequately handled as part of the general description of personality.

An interesting illustration may be found in Gordon Allport's [5] study of prejudice, which makes explicit use of perceptual-cognitive processes as they are revealed in the categorization of people. He describes how the processes of selection, accentuation, and interpretation of sensory data lead to either monopolistic or differentiated categories. The monopolistic category is one that is relatively undifferentiated, usually containing only two values, such as good and bad, which are applied mechanically and rigidly. These categories serve not as causal principles, but rather as descriptive terms about personal *styles* in cognition. Their significance becomes evident only when we see them in the context of personality. It is noteworthy that when Allport comes to "perhaps the most momentous discovery of psychological research in the field of prejudice," it turns out to be the discovery that "the cognitive processes of prejudiced people are *in general* different from the cognitive processes of tolerant people" [5, pp. 174–175].

Thus, the cognitive-patterning characteristic of a person may be an important influence on his selection of a status or on his performance of roles. The special branch of psychology concerned with cognition is then of relevance to sociological study, but only indirectly, through the avenue of personality and its influence. There is no *direct* translation of principles of cognition into a factor influencing or explaining some pattern or feature of social structure. This is not meant to deny the relevance for sociological analysis of a study of cognition. It is only to indicate that as yet we await a convincing demonstration of how, apart from its role as a dimension of personality, a knowledge of principles of cognition can increase our understanding of sociocultural processes.

SOME COMMENTS ON CONCEPTS AND METHODS

I have not specified in any detail what range of problems I consider sociological, perhaps thereby limiting the psychologist's opportunity to decide how his discipline might be related to sociology's needs or problems. This was not an oversight. As practiced, sociology is an extremely sprawling discipline which breaks down into a great welter of fairly discrete topics. Thus we have the sociology of the family, of industry, of the law, of religion, and of knowledge. Some study "sociological factors" in politics, others in economic behavior. Stratification and mobility, deviance and social control, invention, imitation, and change may be added to the list. To discuss each item of even this partial array is obviously far beyond what is possible here and would, in addition, be not only tedious, but disconcerting. The central theme which ties sociology together as an intellectual discipline, I have suggested, is its concern with the development, integrated functioning, and change of social systems. The social system may be large or small, and it may have a self-sufficient system of action or not, i.e., be a society or merely a subsystem or group in a society. The articulation of psychology and sociology comes largely through the study of personality, both the general theory of personality structure and functioning and the assessment or measurement of discrete personality traits and syndromes.

So long as the personal system and the social system are kept clearly in mind as the distinctive foci of psychological and sociological research, the two disciplines seem to "share" few concepts or methods other than those common to all analyses of systems. Exception must, however, be made with regard to at least four foci of interest which seem to involve considerable overlap or sharing of concepts and methods: small-group research, choice patterns (sociometrics), attitude and opinion study, and the study of values and ideologies. The latter is indeed also of central importance in anthropology, and would undoubtedly qualify as one of the major "bridging" concepts in the behavioral sciences. It is characteristic of work done on these topics that it is extremely difficult to say whether the work was done by someone who is by professional identification a sociologist or a psychologist, judging only by the research design, the method of analyzing the findings, and the concepts and the general language used. Some people are dismayed by this, feeling it threatens the purity and distinctiveness of their discipline. Others are greatly heartened by the same fact. They see in it evidence that ultimately psychology and sociology "are the same thing," and the promise of a unified science of man which is yet to come. Both judgments seem to be overreactive.

Most recent studies of small groups follow a common pattern. They seek to find the "effects" on group processes of varying some aspect of the organization, setting, or composition of the group. The effects studied might be measures of the efficiency of the group or more psychologically oriented measures, such as the members' satisfaction with their participation or their sense of solidarity. Such studies fall under the heading of "social system analysis," as that term has been used here. They are certainly not predominantly studies of personality and its adjustment. They deal with the elements of a system of action produced or shared by a group of people and trace adjustments of that system in response to internal or external stimuli. There is, of course, much small-group research which deals mainly with individual behavior and adjustment, although the setting for studying the individual is a small group. Such investigations are "personality studies" in the sense in which we have been using the term.

The professional identification of the reasearcher by no means permits accurate prediction as to which of these two types of study he may be doing. There is perhaps no reason why it should. What is regrettable is the assertion often made by one or another worker in the field that "only" psychological or "only" sociological factors are important in an understanding of group processes. This is all the more deplorable because often the disputants have only the most imprecise notion of what is a psychological as against a sociological factor, and they would not agree too well even if they could define these factors more precisely. The argument is perhaps futile. In any event, a decision as to whether or not a factor is psychological or sociological is much less important than the question as to whether or not it is systematically built into the research design.

Perhaps the best-known contemporary sociological student of small groups had until recently introduced absolutely no systematic controls in selecting the personalities of those who were joined together in his discussion groups. Consequently, Bales's [6, 28] results presumably can be generalized only to groups in which the same methods of recruiting discussants are applied to the same or a matched population of college students. By the same token, the work of a personality-centered psychologist such as Schutz [61], who systematically composes his group of individuals with certain personality traits, must be understood as applying only to groups working in sociocultural structure comparable to that in which he organized his groups. The results cannot be generalized to apply to groups having the same personality composition but different social structures—to groups in size other than four, to those with appointed or elected leaders, to those governed by formal rules of procedure, to groups having responsibilities to a larger structure of organization going beyond the immediate discussion group, and so on.

Greater understanding of group processes, including changes in formal structure, efficiency, emotional tone, and solidarity, depends upon fuller control of variations in both structure and personality composition. Our ability to generalize the findings of research is also greatly enhanced by simultaneous control of both sets of variables. It probably matters little what the discipline of the researcher is, so long as he has adequate awareness of both types of variable and seeks to bring both systematically under control. It is the *articulation* of the study of personality with that of social structure, not their integration or reduction, that is required.

Much the same challenge is posed by sociometry and by the study of opinions and values. A person's choice of those he would most like to work or live with, the opinions he holds on world government, his beliefs about the trustworthiness of his fellow men, or the nature of good and evil are not basically different from any other behavioral datum. Each choice, opinion, or value can be related either to the personality or to the group and the social system of which it is a representative expression. Failure to recognize these different referents as analytically and concretely distinct entities leads to substantial confusion, since both psychologists and sociologists are in this case studying the same items of behavior.

Closer examination of most work in these areas will, however, reveal that there is almost always a personality or a social system referent. In sociometrics, for example, when the focus is on the girl who regularly makes many choices and rejects no one or who rejects many and chooses many, we are clearly dealing with an attribute of the girl's personality. When we say of a set of such choice patterns that, compared to most groups of similar size, this one yields an unusually high number of reciprocated choices, we are dealing with an attribute of the group. A set of such attributes constitutes the social system in which the group participates or the culture which it manifests [35]. There is no need to confuse the pattern characteristic of any person with that characteristic for the group. Within broad limits, either can change fundamentally without any basic change in the other. By the definitions used in this article, the first is a personality, the second a sociocultural, focus of analysis. In this context, it should be particularly noted that although the same *type* of data is used for both the psychological and sociological analysis, it is not strictly the same *body* of data which is used by each.

Much the same argument can be made with regard to opinions and values. Both psychologists and sociologists are and must be concerned with them if they are to understand personality and social system, respectively. To relate the values of a man to his typical pattern of perception is not the same as to relate the values in a society to its system of stratification. In any event, it is hardly the type of data which defines the problem. This is often a source of confusion for psychologists who venture into the use of group data. They assume that if values are a property of personality and therefore a focus of psychological concern, then the structure of values in a society is also primarily, or even exclusively, a psychological problem. It is an easy step to conclude that psychologists therefore have special competence to deal with the problem and can automatically carry over principles which hold for the integration of a person's values into the study of the integration of a culture's values. There is, of course, no reason why a psychologist should not study the structure of values in a society. But the laws which govern the coherence of a culture's values are not necessarily the same as those which govern the coherence of personal values. Much confusion and frustration can be avoided by keeping the two analytical referents distinct, at least until it can be demonstrated that systems of values in fact do obey the same laws of coherence, whether in persons or in cultures.

To suggest the value of maintaining the distinction between personality and social system is not to assert that it is in fact possible at all points to do so with clarity or precision. If a man chooses mainly dependent or aggressive friends or workmates, we have no difficulty seeing this as definitely a manifestation of personality. If many other men manifest the same pattern, especially when the men also share a common social status, then this fact is an attribute of culture or social structure. It may be so without each individual manifestation of the "rate of choosing aggressive workmates" being any less an attribute of personality. In sociometric study, however, we must reckon not only with the choices made by a person, but also with those received. Are the choices received by a person an attribute of his personality or an attribute of the group which bestows the choices? There are many advantages in conceptualizing "choices received" as an attribute of the person, but there are also obvious difficulties in making something which in itself includes no act of or by the person a part of his personality. In this case, therefore, it would seem mainly a matter of taste or convenience whether one would treat the problem as psychological or sociological.

A similar problem arises in the analysis of opinions and values. To relate a man's opinions to his needs or his motives to his values is clearly a problem in psychology. The relationship falls entirely within the personal system. But when we seek to relate a man's values or opinions to his social-class position, is the problem less one of personality? Part of the difficulty arises from the assumption that social class is mainly an attribute of the person, a confusion to which sociologists have greatly contributed by publishing numerous studies purporting to weigh the influence of a man's values or education as against his "social class," as if this were always a discrete variable. How confusing it must be to discover that many other studies include education in their measures of social class. A man's social class can, of course, be a quality attributed to him and reacted to by others in the same way as they react to his color or his personality. The "social class" in most sociological studies, however, generally turns out, on closer examination, to be not an attribute of the person, but a set of objective situational factors within which the person must act or to which he reacts, for example, his occupational level or setting.

The *adjustment* of any person to his objective class situation is clearly a problem in psychology. If all or most of those who occupy a given class position adjust to their condition in a fairly standard way, however, the individual psychological fact becomes a social regularity. It seems none too obvious that the psychologist must bow out simply because the problem has assumed the proportions of a social regularity, since the regularity remains one of personal adjustment. It is only in so far as interest turns to the significance of this regularity for other aspects of the social system that the problem again becomes clearly sociological. But to assess the general pattern of personal adjustment to social-class situation, we must again have psychologically trained sociologists or sociologically trained psychologists or some working combination of representatives from both disciplines.

Articulating Sociology and Psychology

Difficulties between sociologists and psychologists involving overlap of interest, as in the study of sociometrics and in attitude and value research, represent only one type of tension between the disciplines. Perhaps equally important are those situations which arise from efforts to articulate the disciplines, even when the sphere of action appropriate to each is perfectly clear. Tensions often develop when one discipline makes demands on or expresses need for the work of the other. For example, sociologists would like to have a large number of personality studies based on well-designed samples of different strata of the population. The design and conduct of such tests is largely the province of the personality psychologist. But, until very recently, personality psychologists have concentrated mainly on studies of the individual, as in clinical testing in support of psychiatric diagnosis and counseling. The dimensions of personality important for an assessment of the individual's personal *adjustment* are often quite different from those significant for an assessment of performance in different social roles or occupational positions. In addition, the problems faced in scoring and interpreting tests performed for clinical study of the individual are quite different from those which arise when such tests are used with large samples. In the latter case, scoring must be valid and reliable and objective and routinized as well. The probability that a sociologist will systematically use personality variables in his research is obviously slight if he must put each subject through a long and expensive process of clinical assessment which can be performed only by a highly specialized clinician and which, in any event, yields only rather imprecise clinical impressions of the personality of his subjects.

Many sociologists feel that personality psychologists have not been very responsive to this need. For their part, many psychologists may well complain that, however much they may wish to accommodate the sociologist, it is extremely difficult to design new tests or to use existing tests to measure qualities, attributes, or traits which the "client" sociologist cannot precisely specify or define. For it is a distressing fact, which psychologists often discover when they try to relate personality to role requirements, that the sociologist has not developed an adequate set of standard categories or dimensions for the analysis of role requirements. Furthermore, the sociologist is often hard put to specify the requirements of any role in a way that has clear psychological relevance. Consequently, it often happens that the psychologist's analysis of the personality of a status type seems to the sociologist to be greatly lacking in relevance to the social aspects of the role. In turn, the sociologist's description of the role requirements placed on a status incumbent can only with great difficulty be translated into the psychological qualities that might be relevant to role performance.

The problem does, however, yield to systematic analysis. Indeed, it yields with what seem extraordinarily promising results whenever the study design from the start holds to the demand that both the role description and the psychological test be designed with consideration for the final step of relating the two. Roe's studies [58] of personality among scientists in different fields, although quite promising, suffered particularly from inadequate conceptualization of the role demands peculiar to the disciplines of biology, physics, anthropology, and psychology. By contrast, Swanson's study [69] of the differences in personality between editorial writers and the sports and business staff on a college newspaper is a model of precision in separately specifying role demands and appropriate personality dimensions. In his case, however, he was fortunate to have available an existing psychological test which measured precisely the variables of personality which his role analysis indicated to be relevant.

The extremely fine work by Stern, Stein, and Bloom [67] in the study of divinity students, young physicists, and students at a liberal progressive college is particularly instructive here. The analysis of role requirements was actually the first major step in their assessment program. Happily, their previous experience alerted them to the realization that a psychologist assessing the qualities required by a particular role often operates exclusively in terms of his own image of good and bad performance, without giving due consideration to "whether or not these determinants are free to operate in the actual job situation." They call this the "psychological fallacy in assessment research" [67, p. 33]. At the same time, they note, the sociological description of roles often seems to assume "a passive participant who becomes adapted" to any set of demands. Their own approach is based on the "psychologically functional analysis of the roles." By this, they mean "the translation of the varieties of press . . . into statements of role-fulfillment in terms of the needs or personality characteristics which are required for most effective functioning.

Thus, the same psychological terms are utilized to characterize the individual as well as the environment" [67, p. 55]. For example, a job might be described as requiring frequent friendly reciprocal reaction with others, obviously related to the strength of need affiliation. Another might put a premium on rough contact, even body contact, with materials or with other persons, which would make the strength of the personal tendency toward "harm avoidance" a critical dimension.

This method of "functional analysis of the role," especially when combined with testing procedures which are adapted to the requirements of large-scale testing, represents an important methodological advance. It should serve to bring personality study out of the limited confines of the clinic into broad usefulness in social science research. At the same time, it holds substantial promise of providing a set of general categories which may be used for the analysis of many different kinds of roles.

Even when role requirements are stated in terms of the personality qualities most adaptive for those in a given status, there is still the problem of assessing the presence or absence of the required traits in status incumbents, in candidates for the position, and in the population at large. For purposes of sociological analysis, it is virtually indispensable that there be tests which permit rating personality on a series of fairly discrete variables by methods which require little in the way of special testing environments or conditions. The idea that any trait can be meaningfully measured or understood in isolation from the simultaneous measurement of virtually all other qualities of the person meets strong resistance in some psychological quarters. The consequence has been that we have made very slow progress in devising personality tests which can be simply administered and easily scored. Only a few clinically validated personality traits of sociological relevance, such as authoritarianism [2] and stereopathy [67], can now be scored by simple paper-and-pencil tests. Methods of administration and scoring which are more complex, yet amenable to large-scale application, are available for need achievement, affiliation, and power [47]. But there is a long list of personality traits which, from a sociological viewpoint, it would be desirable to measure and which cannot now be treated in this way. More of this in our concluding remarks.

In debating with the clinical psychologist the sociologist hears his critic decry the separation of the part from the whole and use of the routine test score in place of rich living analysis. The roles are strangely reversed in the sociologist's methodological disagreement with the experimental psychologist. Many sociologists decry the possibility of our learning anything meaningful about individual or social behavior in the context of most controlled experiments. They assume and assert that the individual's behavior in such settings is unnatural or unreal. For his part, the psychologist will often charge that the sociologist can never *really* *know* anything because too many of the relevant variables remain uncontrolled in all his studies.

Often the emotional quality of these arguments stands in the way of any increase in insight or understanding. These questions, in good part, concern matters of fact and can be answered only by the same tests we apply to other facts. Is their participation in a laboratory discussion group dealing with fraternity membership as "real" to participants as a discussion of someone's suitability as a member of their own fraternity would be? Is the jury deciding a case it heard on tape as involved as it would be if the case were actually on trial? Is a boy's achievement motive aroused to the same degree by a laboratory-test instruction and competition for a crucial scholarship? None of these questions can be properly answered in absolute terms. Reality and involvement are variables which can be measured. Each laboratory setting and each experimenter differs in the capacity to affect these variables. Increased experience will undoubtedly make for greater skill in eliciting involvement similar to that manifested outside the laboratory.

Many sociologists are too quick to reject experimentally controlled studies before having closely examined the comparability of the experimental with the original setting. Even "unreal" settings may permit important inferences with regard to "real" situations. Competitive feelings, for example, can be induced in group experiments. They can be as real as competitive feelings experienced in the classroom and may permit inferences with regard to other situations. At the same time, it must be recognized that the necessarily transitory and limited relationships developed in the laboratory can seldom match the significance for the individual of the great majority of the important roles which he plays in the social system. To deal with these, it seems indispensable to deal with them in nature. Considerable control over the relevant variables, however, is possible with smaller samples through careful matching on crucial variables, as in the Gluecks' delinquency study, or through the method of controlled cross tabulation with larger samples in the manner of most opinion surveys.

In so far as the degree of personal involvement necessary for the problem and dimension under study can be developed in the laboratory, it is ridiculous for sociologists to do less than welcome this development for the greater control it affords. To the degree that matched samples permit control over the crucial variables, the psychologist should be equally impressed. It is foolish for either to make the deficiencies that he cannot help a matter of virtue—for the sociologist to claim precision for his findings when he cannot control the relevant variables, or for the psychologist to claim generality for his findings when he has been able to control only incidental variables at the price of wholly excluding from consideration the only factor which could give social meaning to his experiment.

FUTURE PROSPECTS

Rather than attempt to predict future developments, I will indicate some of the requirements which may be preconditions for further advance. These are stated mainly from the perspective of the sociologist and describe what he needs and wants from the psychologist. Psychologists probably have an equivalent set of needs for the satisfaction of which they are dependent on the sociologist. As a sociologist interested in bringing psychology to bear on problems of sociological analysis, I look for development along three main lines.

The General Theory of the Normal Personality

The fact that Freud made most of his discoveries about the dynamics of personality through the observation of psychiatric patients has not as yet been outlived by students of personality. There must be 20 books on the abnormal personality for every 1 which deals with the normal routine processes of personality functioning. Except in the study of social deviance, including suicide, homicide, and delinquency, the sociologist has only limited use for the theory of the abnormal personality. He is, however, greatly concerned with the propensities and capacities of the normal person to adjust and adapt to the strains implicit in social living and in the social consequences which flow from different adaptive modes. In particular, there seem to be some relatively neglected areas.

Development of personality under varying social conditions. Despite its tremendous contribution to our understanding of the growth of personality, Freud's work has also had an important inhibiting effect on efforts to study normal personality development as preparation for adult life. The importance attached to the physiological, or better, erogenous zones, the sharp delineation of stages of development organized around the zonal concept, and the concentration on the crises of personality development (e.g., the Oedipus complex) have all deflected attention from certain aspects of personality development which directly affect the individual's role performance and adjustment to society. An outstanding example of the difference at issue would be Freud's stress on the stages of libidinal development as contrasted with Erikson's [17] later attempt to specify parallel stages of ego development. The Freudian concentration on the primary disciplines for training the sex, the excretory, and the oral drives led to relative neglect of other needs, such as those for affection, relatedness, and self-respect, and of other values not directly bearing on libidinal drives. Less neglected, but still relatively so, were the patterns learned for handling aggression, fear, and anxiety.

In addition, Freud's assumption about the universality of the crises of human development encouraged many to overlook the range of pos-sible and actual patterns of child development and the difference in the personality consequences which follow. This range of variation in child rearing modes, and some of the differential consequences, are now being brought under systematic scrutiny in the work of Whiting and Child [72] and Miller and Swanson [49, 50]. Whiting and Child have so far dealt with only five "systems" of behavior: the ubiquitous oral, anal and sexual, plus dependence and aggression. An extension of this analysis to other systems is to be hoped for. Miller and Swanson deal in addition with such problems as modes of expressive behavior and moral needs, and they give particular attention to the defense mechanisms typically favored by those exposed to different methods of child rearing. Their work has particular advantage over that of Whiting and Child— they are able to study the consequences of different methods of child rearing directly in the personality of the child rather than observing them indirectly in the presence of such cultural elements as belief in ghosts. Carrying forward the pioneering work of Davis and Havighurst [12], Miller and Swanson deal systematically with the effect of social class and other aspects of the parent's life situation on the kind of child rearing disciplines he will adopt. From the sociologist's point of view, it is of great importance that such studies be extended to deal with a greater range of "behavior systems" and developmental problems among occu-pants of a wider variety of statuses, using larger and more systematically drawn samples.

Growth of the normal personality. The concentration on infancy and childhood encouraged by Freudian theory has recently been some-what balanced by fuller study of adolescence and a growing interest in the process of aging. Nevertheless, this intense emphasis on the early years has hardly been matched by comparably intensive study of early adult-hood and maturity. Yet from the sociologist's point of view, and under-standing of the dynamics of the adult personality is crucial. The function-ing of a social system, including the crucial task of training the next gen-eration, falls predominantly on the young adult. A fuller understanding of the adaptation of the individual to adult status and the progressive adjustments required through maturing into old age is badly needed, and it is to be hoped that we will have a full-scale development of the beginnings represented in White's *Lives in Progress* [71].

Nonpathological adjustment to conflict and strain. It seems almost in the nature of the case that the complex institutional structure of mod-ern societies will provide the individual with so diverse a set of role demands as to induce conflict and strain. The response is often personal disorganization, deviant social behavior, or extremist social movements. At the same time, many individuals show surprising flexibility and adaptability in adjusting to role conflict. We are greatly in need of knowledge as to both the qualities of personality which make for greater flexibility and the combinations of social demands which are least and most tolerable to the average person. In addition, we need fuller understanding of the responses which different types of personal strain are most likely to produce. The frustration-aggression hypothesis [Dollard, 15; Lindzey, 45] is one of the few instances we can site of a systematic effort to develop a theory accounting for the effects of a ubiquitous psychic deprivation. We also need to discover the most likely consequences of the deprivation of needs, such as needs for dependence, for affiliation, for self-respect and others to which social situations and systems may systematically deny adequate satisfaction.

Advances in Personality Assessment

I have suggested that, through knowledge of personality data, the sociologist can increase his understanding of the patterns of recruitment to different statuses, the quality of role performance, and the integration of diverse elements of the social system. To undertake such analysis, he must have descriptions of personality along dimensions which are of major relevance for sociological analysis. He must also have methods for acquiring such descriptions simply and inexpensively. The main dimensions of personality which further invite the development of assessment procedures are easy to specify. Yet the focus of attention in early efforts will most likely be on traits selected more in accordance with the needs of some particular research program than on the basis of any generally agreed-upon priority list. The following list is not meant to be exhaustive, rather it is intended to illustrate the kind of personality traits which seem to have obvious social implications. There is a high degree of congruence between this scheme and that presented in Stern, Stein, and Bloom [67], even though they were arrived at independently and at several points combine certain traits in quite different components of personality.

Relations to authority and others. The problem of individual and society can be conceived of in large part as one involving the problem of authority—the necessity for the individual to control and channel his needs to meet the restrictions placed on him by life in society. The great impact of the research on the authoritarian personality [2] attests to the immediate interest this dimension has for sociologists. However, further work is needed to bring under control other aspects of the individual's orientation to authority than are tapped in the study of the authoritarian personality. For example, Henry Murray, in his introduction to Stern

[67], has suggested that we study what he calls "subordinate capacity," that is, "the capacity to comply with the decisions and to execute the plans of a duly appointed leader without covert resistance or overt fuss and fury" [67, p. 15]. Riesman's other-directed, inner-directed, and autonomous syndromes [56], viewed as models of conformity [7], may also be cited as concepts on which further empirical work needs to be done.

Conceptions of self. Despite impassioned pleas by Allport [3] and others for further development of ego theory, much remains to be done in developing this topic of great sociological interest. One of the most important effects of social interaction lies in its impact on the individual's ability to maintain a stable self-concept. His self-conception is also one of the main factors shaping the individual's choice of roles and his performance of them. Although Sullivan [68] organized a large part of his psychiatric theory around this theme, little has yet been done to carry his work forward systematically.

Dominant needs or motives. Although all human beings manifest the same basic needs, some needs may achieve unusual strength or assume a more central or commanding role in the organization of the personality. In such cases, we may expect the need to exert substantial influence on the individual's orientation toward social situations. Furthermore, the members of important subgroups in a population may have in common the same distinctive need strengths. To supplement the existing measures for need achievement, we need fuller development of measures of need for affiliation and the need for power or dominance. In addition, the needs for aggression, for succorance and nurturance, for deference, abasement, and autonomy all have obvious sociological relevance and invite further study.

Typical polarities and primary dilemmas. Quite apart from the strength of any need or motive, the dimension along which it falls may itself become a focus of central importance in the personality in the sense that the person is preoccupied with the *issue,* that is, with the choice of alternatives posed by the fact that most dimensions can be polarized. These are the polarized issues which each person must resolve in the course of psychological maturation, as described by Erikson [17]. For example, it seems that the problem of autonomy-versus-belongingness is a primary dilemma in the personality organization of many Americans, whereas optimism-versus-pessimism and trust-versus-mistrust of others play a similar role for Russians [33]. Further understanding of such typical polarities or dilemmas would be of substantial sociological interest.

Modes of impulse control. Although we are only beginning to develop a fuller understanding of how these qualities influence social action, certain elements of personality which might be grouped under the heading of impulse control have clear relevance for many sociological problems. For example, the degree of superego integration or conflict has, as we have seen, substantial influence on the probability that a particular boy will engage in juvenile delinquency. We need valid and reliable measures of the defensive modes of structures which are intimately connected with impulse control. Propensities toward blame avoidance, denial, projection, and other modes of defense should be fully explored, and it is to be hoped that the work of Miller and Swanson [50] in developing measures in this realm represents the beginning of a trend.

Expressive modes.   Examples of the kind of variable which should be given fuller attention are tendencies toward physical acting out as against intellectualization or symbolic expression, freedom and spontaneity of expression as against restraint or constriction.

Modes of conative functioning.   Whatever the content of goals, the ways of striving for these goals may take on distinctive character. We must be better able to isolate patterns such as the passive-accommodative versus the assertive-striving pattern. Stern, Stein, and Bloom [67] include as guides several dimensions we might study under this heading, namely, the concern with order; the conjunctivity and disjunctivity dimension, which involves mainly coordination and integration of activity; and the quality of deliberation, including caution and hesitancy in behavior.

Modes of cognitive functioning.   We have already noted the close connection between such traits as rigidity of perception and intolerance of ambiguity in the racially and religiously prejudiced. Further study of patterns such as the balance of endo- and exocathection, of extra- and intraception, and of projectivity and objectivity would clearly be of value.

With each of these dimensions and qualities, our need is, of course, not only for further study and understanding, but also for tests. For purposes of sociological study in particular, we need tests which have been shown to be clinically valid and yet can be easily and simply administered. Preferably, they should be in something like questionnaire form, to be scored in a routine method by semiunskilled help, and they should yield ratings which can be expressed numerically. We need to find ways of getting at the same elements and reaching the same depths of personality that were made accessible by the TAT or even the Rorschach without necessarily using those instruments. This is undoubtedly a tall order, but recent developments indicate it is certainly not beyond our capacity. In any event, until such tests are available, we can expect only very limited application of psychological variables in sociological analysis.

Applications of the Special Psychologies

Our examination of the fields of learning, cognition, and perception did not yield many suggestions for direct application to sociology except through a link with personality. Nevertheless, it seems difficult to believe that the situation must remain thus. We are in need of further pioneering efforts, such as that by Miller and Dollard [51], seeking to apply the general principles developed in these fields to problems of social analysis. How successful such efforts can be will depend in part on the extent to which research in these special fields of psychology is designed from the beginning with some attention to the possible use of the findings in sociological analysis. This requires of sociologists that they restate their problems in terms amenable to treatment by those working on perception, cognition, and learning. Although past experience suggests we should not be too sanguine about bringing the psychology of learning, perception, and cognition to bear on sociology, we should certainly continue efforts in that direction.

We are on the verge of substantial progress in articulating sociology and personality psychology. We may anticipate, in the next two decades, the development of increased clinical understanding of many qualities of personality which are of maximum importance in the individual's social functioning. Increased knowledge of the child rearing patterns which produce given traits and of the social environments which seem to induce the use of different child rearing techniques may be expected. More character traits will become measurable through the development of simple, easily scored, yet valid and reliable psychological tests. As this goal is attained, the psychological "mapping" or "census" of major subgroups and total societal populations will become feasible and actual. When this is accomplished, the sociologist will be able—indeed, will be required—to build into his analyses not only such traditional sociological variables as the degree of social integration or cohesion, the freedom of communication, and the rigidity of stratification, but also a series of psychological variables. Along with the distribution of income or power, he will be able and required to consider the strength and distribution of needs for achievement, of tendencies toward projection, and of resentment of authority. Although this attainment will not mean the end of either sociology or psychology as separate disciplines, it will usher in an era of distinctively new approaches to and advances in the analysis of some of the traditionally most important and difficult problems of sociological research.

REFERENCES

1. Aberle, D. F., et al. The functional prerequisites of a society. *Ethics,* 1950, **60,** 100–111.
2. Adorno, T. W., Frenkel-Brunswik, Else, Levinson, D. J., & Sanford, R. N. *The authoritarian personality.* New York: Harper, 1950.
3. Allport, G. W. The ego in contemporary psychology. *Psychol. Rev.,* 1943, **50,** 451–478.

4. Allport, G. W. *The nature of personality: selected papers.* Reading, Mass.: Addison-Wesley, 1950.
5. Allport, G. W. *The nature of prejudice.* Reading, Mass.: Addison-Wesley, 1954.
6. Bales, R. F. *Interaction process analysis: a method for the study of small groups.* Reading, Mass.: Addison-Wesley, 1950.
7. Brodbeck, A., Nogee, P., & DiMascio, A. Two kinds of conformity: a study of the Riesman typology applied to standards of parental discipline. *J. Psychol.*, 1956, **41**, 23–45.
8. Bruner, J. S., Goodnow, J. J., & Austin, G. A. *A study of thinking.* New York: Wiley, 1956.
9. Bruner, J. S., & Krech, D. (Eds.) *Perception and personality.* Durham, N.C.: Duke Univer. Press, 1950.
10. Cantril, H. *The psychology of social movements.* New York: Wiley, 1941.
11. Cooley, C. H. *Human nature and the social order.* New York: Scribner, 1902.
12. Davis, W. A., & Havighurst, R. J. *Father of the man.* Boston: Houghton Mifflin, 1947.
13. Dicks, H. V. German personality traits and Nazi ideology. *Hum. Relat.*, 1950, **3**, 111–154.
14. Dicks, H. V. Observations on contemporary Russian behavior. *Hum. Relat.*, 1952, **5**, 111–175.
15. Dollard, J., et al. *Frustration and aggression.* New Haven, Conn.: Yale Univer. Press, 1939.
16. Durkheim, E. *Suicide.* J. Spaulding & G. Simpson (Trans.). Glencoe, Ill.: Free Press, 1951.
17. Erikson, E. *Childhood and society.* New York: Norton, 1950.
18. Festinger, L., Riecken, H. W., & Schachter, S. *When prophecy fails.* Minneapolis, Minn.: Univer. Minn. Press, 1956.
19. Frenkel-Brunswik, Else. Intolerance of ambiguity as an emotional and perceptual variable. In J. S. Bruner & D. Krech (Eds.), *Perception and personality.* Durham, N.C.: Duke Univer. Press, 1950.
20. Freud, S. *Civilization and its discontents.* Joan Rivière (Trans.). London: Hogarth, 1930.
21. Freud, S. Totem and taboo. (1912) In A. A. Brill (Trans. & Ed.), *Sigmund Freud: the basic writings.* New York: Modern Library, 1938.
22. Freud, S. *Moses and monotheism.* Katherine Jones (Trans.). New York: Knopf, 1939.
23. Fromm, E. *Escape from freedom.* New York: Holt, 1941.
24. Gilbert, Doris C., & Levinson, D. J. Role performance, ideology and personality in mental hospital aides. In M. Greenblatt, D. J. Levinson, & R. H. Williams (Eds.), *The patient and the mental hospital.* Glencoe, Ill.: Free Press, 1957.
25. Glueck, S., & Glueck, E. *Unravelling juvenile delinquency.* Cambridge, Mass.: Harvard Univer. Press, 1950.
26. Goode, W. J. Norm commitment and conformity to role-status obligations. *Amer. J. Sociol.* 1960, **66**, 247–258.

27. Gurin, G., Veroff, J., & Feld, S. *Americans view their mental health.* New York: Basic Books, 1960.

27a. Gurin, G., Veroff, J., Atkinson, J. W., & Feld, Sheila C. The use of thematic apperception to assess motivation in a nationwide interview study. *Psychological Monographs,* 74, No. 499, 1960.

28. Hare, P., Borgatta, E. F., & Bales, R. F. (Eds.) *Small groups: studies in social interaction.* New York: Knopf, 1955.

29. Haythorn, W., et al. The behavior of authoritarian and equalitarian personalities in groups. *Hum. Relat.,* 1956, 9, 57–74.

30. Healy, W., & Bronner, A. F. *New light on delinquency and its treatment.* New Haven, Conn.: Yale Univer. Press, 1936.

31. Henry, A. F., & Short, J. F. *Suicide and homicide.* Glencoe, Ill.: Free Press, 1954.

32. Horney, K. *The neurotic personality of our time.* New York: Norton, 1937.

33. Inkeles, A., Hanfmann, E., & Beier, H. Modal personality and adjustment to the Soviet socio-political system. *Hum. Relat.,* 1958, 11, 3–22.

34. Janowitz, M., & Marvick, D. Authoritarianism and political behavior. *Publ. Opin. Quart.,* 1953, 17, 185–201.

35. Jennings, Helen H. *Leadership and isolation.* (2nd ed.) New York: Longmans, 1950.

36. Kardiner, A. *The individual and his society.* New York: Columbia Univer. Press, 1939.

37. Kardiner, A. *The psychological frontiers of society.* New York: Columbia Univer. Press, 1945.

38. Kluckhohn, C. The influence of psychiatry on anthropology in America during the past one hundred years. In G. J. K. Hall, G. Zilboorg, & H. A. Bunker (Eds.), *One hundred years of American psychiatry.* New York: Columbia Univer. Press, 1944. Pp. 589–617.

39. Kroeber, A. L. History of anthropological thought. In W. L. Thomas, Jr. (Ed.), *Yearbook of anthrop.* New York: Wenner-Gren Foundation, 1955.

40. Levinson, D. J. Criminality from a sense of guilt: a case study on some research hypotheses. *J. Pers.,* 1952, 20, 402–429.

41. Levinson, D. J. The relevance of personality for political participation. *Publ. Opin. Quart.,* 1958, 22, 3–10.

42. Lewin, K. *A dynamic theory of personality.* New York: McGraw-Hill, 1935.

43. Lewin, K. *Resolving social conflicts: selected papers on group dynamics.* New York: Harper, 1948.

44. Lewin, K., Lippitt, R., & White, R. K. Patterns of aggressive behavior in experimentally created "social climates." *J. soc. Psychol.,* 1939, 10, 271–279.

45. Lindzey, G. An experimental examination of the scapegoat theory of prejudice. *J. abnorm. soc. Psychol.,* 1950, 45, 296–309.

46. Lippitt, R. An experimental study of authoritarian and democratic

atmospheres. Studies in topological and vector psychology, I. *Univer. Iowa Stud. Child Welf.*, 1940, **16** (3), 44–195.

47. McClelland, D. C., et al. *The achievement motive.* New York: Appleton-Century-Crofts, 1953.

48. Mead, G. H. *Mind, self, and society.* C. M. Morris (Ed.). Chicago: Univer. Chicago Press, 1934.

49. Miller, D., & Swanson, G. E. *The changing American parent.* New York: Wiley, 1958.

50. Miller, D., & Swanson, G. E. *Inner conflict and defense.* New York: Holt, 1960.

51. Miller, N. E., & Dollard, J. *Social learning and imitation.* New Haven, Conn.: Yale Univer. Press, 1941.

52. Murray, H. A. *Explorations in personality.* New York: Oxford, 1938.

53. Pear, T. H. (Ed.) *Psychological factors of peace and war.* New York: Philosophical Library, 1950.

54. Pfister-Ammende, Maria. Psychologische Erfahrungen mit sowjetrussichen Fluchtlingen in der Schweiz. In M. Pfister-Ammende (Ed.), *Die Psychohygiene: Grundlagen und Ziele.* Bern: Hans Huber, 1949.

55. Postman, L., Bruner, J. S., & McGinnies, E. Personal values as selective factors in perception. *J. abnorm. soc. Psychol.*, 1948, **43**, 142–154.

56. Riesman, D. *The lonely crowd.* New Haven, Conn.: Yale Univer. Press, 1950.

57. Roe, Anne. Personality and vocation, *Trans. N.Y. Acad. Sci.*, 1947, **9**, (Ser. II), 257–267.

58. Roe, Anne. *The psychology of occupations.* New York: Wiley, 1956.

59. Rosen, B. C. The achievement syndrome: a psychocultural dimension of social stratification. *Amer. sociol. Rev.*, 1956, **21**, 203–211.

60. Sarbin, T. R. Role theory. In G. Lindzey (Ed.), *Handbook of social psychology.* Reading, Mass.: Addison-Wesley, 1954.

61. Schutz, W. C. What makes groups productive. *Hum. Relat.*, 1955, **8**, No. 4. 429–465.

62. Sears, R. R., Maccoby, E. E., & Levin, H. *Patterns of child rearing.* Evanston, Ill.: Row, Peterson, 1957.

63. Shaw, C. R. *Delinquency areas.* Chicago: Univer. Chicago Press, 1929.

64. Shaw, C. R. *The natural history of a delinquent career.* Chicago: Univer. Chicago Press, 1931.

65. Sorokin, P. *Contemporary sociological theories.* New York: Harper, 1928.

66. Spindler, G. D. *Sociocultural and psychological processes in Menomini acculturation.* Berkeley, Calif.: Univer. Calif. Press, 1955.

67. Stern, G. G., Stein, M. I., & Bloom, B. S. *Methods in personality assessment: human behavior in complex social situations. Glencoe,* Ill.: Free Press, 1956.

68. Sullivan, H. S. *Conceptions of modern psychiatry.* Washington: William Alanson White Psychiatric Foundation, 1945.

69. Swanson, G. E. Agitation through the press: a study of the personalities of publicists. *Publ. Opin. Quart.*, 1956, **20**, 441–456.

70. Weber, M. *The Protestant ethic and the spirit of capitalism.* T. Parsons (Trans.). New York: Scribner, 1930.
71. White, R. W. *Lives in progress.* New York: Dryden, 1952.
72. Whiting, J. W., & Child, I. L. *Child training and personality: a cross-cultural study.* New Haven, Conn.: Yale Univer. Press, 1953.
73. Witkin, H. A. The nature and importance of individual differences in perception. In J. S. Bruner & D. Krech (Eds.), *Perception and personality.* Durham, N.C.: Duke Univer. Press, 1950.
74. Worsley, P. *The trumpet shall sound: a study of cargo cults in Melanesia.* London: MacGibbon & Kee, 1957.

THE RELATIONSHIP OF ANTHROPOLOGY TO STUDIES IN PERCEPTION AND COGNITION[1]

DAVID FRENCH
Department of Anthropology
Reed College

INTRODUCTION

Contacts between anthropology and psychology have sometimes occurred in areas peripheral to the major problems of the two disciplines. There have been recent convergences, however, in fields of growing importance to both; facets of the anthropological study of culture parallel certain studies of perception and/or cognition by psychologists. There is a shared concern with the ways in which human beings relate themselves to the world around them; this concern is manifested in separate attacks on similar problems. These convergences have been chosen as the focus of this discussion, and selected examples of recent writing in the

[1] The author would like to acknowledge the assistance of his students and colleagues at Reed College and the suggestions of Profs. Roger Brown, Jerome S. Bruner, Elizabeth Colson, Melville Jacobs, M. Brewster Smith, and E. Z. Vogt. Final revisions on the manuscript were undertaken while the author was Visiting Professor of Social Anthropology and a research fellow at the Center for Cognitive Studies at Harvard. Support from the Center and the Laboratory of Social Relations is gratefully acknowledged. Volney Stefflre (at Reed) and Ellen Childs (at Harvard) served as research assistants, and their valuable services are appreciated. While at Harvard, Mr. Stefflre was again helpful.

two disciplines are examined. The potential contribution of anthropology to research in perception and cognition is considered; methodological contributions from psychology are emphasized as an aid to various new types of anthropological research. Since there are major differences between the disciplines, it will be necessary to explore each and establish a basis for the examination of interrelationships.

FIELDS OF ANTHROPOLOGY

Anthropology is a federation of subdisciplines that have a common interest in the study of human beings. Like many other disciplines, anthropology is both a body of knowledge and an orientation and methodology directed toward the phenomena it studies. Shifts between these definitions of the discipline, which usually remain implicit, are a cause of confusion to anthropologists and others. A corollary is the frequent confusion between descriptive categories and explanatory categories.

The bodies of knowledge that comprise anthropology may appear rather diverse. Certainly these subdisciplines—archeology or prehistory, physical anthropology, linguistics, and cultural or social anthropology— are not of equal relevance to this paper. Although indirect connections can be made between psychology and archeology/prehistory, it is not practical to explore them here. Physical anthropology, being concerned with primate (including human) biology, has many areas of overlapping contact with psychology, particularly in the comparative and experimental fields (Hallowell's article in this volume is germane to certain of the preceding relationships; a paper by Geertz [48], is also relevant).

Linguistics—in contrast to the teaching of foreign languages and literatures—is, on the one hand, a subdiscipline of anthropology; on the other, it is a separate field with a unity of its own. Like prehistory, linguistics is one of the sociocultural fields of anthropology. Because of its growing importance to certain aspects of psychology, the methodology of linguistic research will be discussed in this paper. The area which is probably most familiar to psychologists is cultural anthropology. Many anthropologists with a strong interest in social structure speak of "social" rather than "cultural" anthropology. Social anthropologists are somewhat more likely to emphasize theoretical rather than descriptive aspects of the discipline.

For a number of institutional reasons, the subdisciplines of anthropology do not correspond to the fields of psychology. While there are convergences in interest, they occur in somewhat different contexts in psychology and in anthropology. The study of personality comes closest to being an exception since it has formed the principal area for investigation for certain representatives of both disciplines. In contrast, neither the study of perception nor of cognition has begun to approach the status of being a subdiscipline of anthropology, and there are no anthropologists whose exclusive interests during any extended period have been in these areas. Consequently, it is necessary to search among a variety of anthropological activities and to remove from context research findings and theoretical constructs which are relevant to perception or cognition.

Because of special training, certain men who were or later became anthropologists have conducted studies, especially on perception among non-European peoples, which more or less approximated psychological research. A classic example is the work on perception done as part of the Anthropological Expedition to Torres Straits (and New Guinea) just before the turn of the century. On the initiative of Haddon [56] and, under his direction, Rivers, Seligman, Myers, and McDougall studied vision, hearing, smell, taste, "cutaneous sensations," and "muscular sense," as well as various phenomena not related to sensation and perception. Of these men, the first three are now known as anthropologists and the last two as psychologists. Unfortunately, Bartlett [7], who later explored relationships between culture and memory and perception, has been little read by anthropologists [cf. Barnett, 6].

In Germany, even before Wundt, there was an interest in comparative (i.e., cross-cultural) human psychology; work in this area came to be known as "ethnopsychology," "folk psychology," or "race psychology" [129, pp. 6–9]. In addition to theoretical writings about "primitive mentality," the movement stimulated field research comparable to that done in Torres Straits by such men as Thurnwald [discussed in 60, pp. 182–183]. These German developments have never been well known to British and American anthropologists and have had only an indirect influence on them.

Most American anthropologists who have worked in the perception-cognition area have not taken the role of psychologist; most could not have done so because they lacked adequate training. Sometimes—as part of the total study of a people or within a more limited framework—they have undertaken studies worth mentioning at this point. Whether or not such studies are labeled as dealing with perception, they rarely focus on the details of perceptual activity; they concentrate instead on culture —that is, certain aspects relevant to perception. Often the relationship is closer with cognition than with perception. Since they are neither perception nor cognition studies as such, precise classification is unnecessary. Under any circumstance, both are being considered in a broad, rather than a restricted, sense.

The work of Hallowell deserves early mention. He, for one, has written from an extensive background in both psychology and anthropology.

In addition to a general paper, "Cultural Factors in the Structuralization of Perception" [59], he has published more specific papers on temporal orientation, spatial orientation, and psychological aspects of measurement. His papers on the self are among the selections which can be considered relevant to perception and/or cognition in his collected essays [61]. Hallowell's papers have rich illustrative material from the Salteaux and northern Ojibwa and often use our own culture as an outside point of reference for comparison. In contrast to many anthropologists who write on similar topics, Hallowell views his material as relating to the *psychology* of the people he is discussing.

While projective tests are customarily regarded as instruments for the study of personality, responses to them clearly involve perception. An illustrative problem is this: Do such instruments involve projections from an assumed culture-free base of drives and defense mechanisms, or do they reflect learned perceptual organization and hence cultural regularities? Dennis, a psychologist with cross-cultural interests, has argued that control over the perceptual aspects of the testing procedure is a necessary preliminary to the assessment of the tests [37, pp. 154–158]. His paper and one which discusses comparable issues by Hallowell [63], provide an introduction to problems raised in the comparative use of the Rorschach test, the projective technique most frequently employed with members of other societies.

Cultural differences in Rorschach responses and a host of anthropological research findings with implications for perception and cognition are discussed by Kluckhohn in the *Handbook of Social Psychology* [77, pp. 931–940]. His chapter can provide the reader with a guide to recent work on the way other peoples handle space, time, color, closure, and beauty; he includes "cultural factors" in remembering and forgetting. Since much of the research cited was undertaken as part of general studies of particular cultures, Kluckhohn's survey could have been lengthened, had he so desired, by increasing the number of ethnographic accounts examined. The uncovering of scattered papers on additional topics, for example, Zborowski's "Cultural Components in Responses to Pain" [137], would have served only to reinforce Kluckhohn's impressive picture of the liveliness and diversity of recent research.

Before leaving Kluckhohn's paper, it should be mentioned that the topics above were all classified as applicable to perception, while almost all of his discussion of cognition (as well as parts of that on perception) was devoted to the relationship between *language* and thought. Included is a consideration of the hypotheses often attributed to Whorf, which have been variously phrased as the influence on, or the determination of, thought by language [10]. The hypotheses have several names (e.g., Sapir-Whorf, Whorf-Lee) in recognition of the numerous people who have formulated or considered them. A reasonably full name would be the Humboldt-Boas-Cassirer-Sapir-Whorf-Lee hypotheses. The issues raised when one considers the relationship between language and the rest of behavior are complex, and there have been a number of general discussions of them [17, 40, 70, 71, 91, 105, 115]. Fortunately, teams of psychologists and anthropologists, such as Lenneberg, Brown, and Roberts, have devised methods for testing specific hypotheses in this area [20, 87, 88]. Similar work in the American Southwest under the directorship of Carroll has been yielding reports [30, 31, 83], as has research in the Netherlands [124, 125]. Language is sufficiently crucial to the issues being considered in this paper to be introduced more than once in the pages that follow.

We have not yet exhausted the rubrics under which anthropologists have considered relevant topics. A people's knowledge or beliefs about the structures and processes of the universe has been receiving increasingly systematic attention by such anthropologists as Conklin [33, 34], Frake [43], and French [46] under the name "ethnoscience." An effort is being made in such well-established research areas as ethnobotany and ethnozoology to discover implicit as well as explicit native categories. These categories have their implications for cognition and perception, as have some of those discovered in research under the rubrics of "cosmology," "world view," "ethos," and the like [e.g., Forde, 41, Redfield, 112, and Honigmann, 72]. The same holds true for research in the area of *values* [1], for example, the research undertaken with Harvard sponsorship by Vogt [126, 127] and others. Lee's writings [85] could be classed under more than one of the above headings.

In a consideration of cross-cultural study in these areas, reference should be made to similar research and writing which constitutes part of the field called the "sociology of knowledge." Durkheim and Weber have stimulated a steady trickle of books and papers that describe the ideas of various non-European peoples and, in addition, attempt to find determinants for those ideas in social structure and activity. Possibly Sorokin's discussion of time, space, and causality [120] will come to be judged more important than the longer works concerned with his general system. Eisenstadt should be mentioned as dealing provocatively with the perception of space and time [38]. It is sometimes difficult to decide whether sociology or anthropology is the "proper" home for these interests. Scattered through the writings of British social anthropologists and others who were influenced by Durkheim are papers which relate ideas to social structures and processes [e.g., 136].

During recent years, anthropologists have been using the term "perception" to label certain new and traditional research topics [e.g., 51]. This is even more true of "cognition" and "cognitive," which are increasingly being employed to designate anthropological interests relevant to this paper. For example, a symposium on cognitive structures was organized for the 1959 annual meeting of the American Anthropological Association. The diversity of topics was impressive. They included situational determinants in the use of kinship concepts, equivalence structures, cognitive processes in Micronesian navigation, and relationships between house structures, beliefs about children, and child rearing practices. In his discussion of the papers, Kluckhohn discussed cognition as the common theme and cited ethnoscience as an additional field of special relevance. The papers are being published separately [e.g., Fischer's on the social determinants of art styles, 39]. During 1960–1961, a series of papers on cognition were read before the Anthropological Society of Washington; the contributions by Frake [44] and others are scheduled for later publication. For the 1960 meeting of the American Association for the Advancement of Science, a joint anthropology-psychology symposium on language and cognition was arranged, with Lenneberg, Fishman, Vera John, and Dorothy Lee as participants. A final example is Hymes's use of the phrase "cognitive style" in describing various types of patterning in languages [73]. His discussion ranges through grammar and lexicon and makes diverse linguistic phenomena more accessible to study by psychologists.

Shifts in terminology may be of little importance in themselves, and not all studies labeled "cognitive" by anthropologists would be of interest to cognitive psychologists. Of greater consequence than terminology alone are the analytic (not experimental) techniques developed by such men as Conklin [35, 36], Frake [43, 44], Goodenough [54], Lounsbury [92], and Wallace and Atkins [128] for the precise delineation of the concepts shared by a people in particular modalities of behavior. A framework for certain types of cognitive studies is thus provided. Examples will be presented of work in such areas as color, disease, and kinship concepts.

This hasty survey is intended to suggest some anthropological activities of immediate or potential relevance to the study of perception and cognition. The lack of formal coherence is a reflection of the fact that anthropology as a discipline does not group these topics and methods under a single heading. When they are so grouped, a high degree of overlap among them becomes evident.

The nature of the *limits* to the anthropological activities, which are of potential relevance to perception/cognition, is difficult—if not now impossible—to determine. One could even argue that a people's perception of the articles they manufacture—studied by anthropologists under the heading "material culture"—is of importance in their perception of other objects, whether manufactured or not. For example, Hallowell recounts a story that illustrates how difficult it is for us to perceive certain northerly stars except as organized in a form that is dipper-shaped [59, pp. 171–172]. Regardless of the problem of setting limits, it is nevertheless possible to say that certain aspects of sociocultural activity studied by anthropologists are more likely than other aspects to be relevant to perception and cognition. The form the relevance takes is to be discussed in due course, but the nature of some of the concepts in anthropology and psychology must be discussed first.

CULTURE AND THE ANALYSIS OF BEHAVIORAL REGULARITY

Most anthropological studies are *idiographic*, i.e., descriptive or particularistic, rather than *nomothetic*, i.e., generalizing and intended to establish the relationship between independent and dependent variables [109; pp. 1–3; 119, pp. 45–47]. In the editorial discussion outline for the present study, a useful distinction has been made between (1) *systematic variables*, which are related to the construct language of a theoretical system, and (2) *empirical variables*, which are factors that vary or are varied in a specific research situation. Unfortunately, anthropologists rarely make such distinctions. Furthermore, since they seldom experiment, their variables, at least their empirical variables, cannot be specified in the same sense that they often can be within psychological research. Many of the methods of anthropologists—for example, intensive interviewing of informants—more closely resemble the methods of clinical than of experimental psychology.

Variables can be discussed on a more general level, however. A proposition that has been found useful again and again in a variety of ways is this: *Culture* is one of the major determinants of human behavior. Commonly, even biological "factors" in human behavior are culture-mediated [77, pp. 921–923]; for example, different peoples define illnesses and treatments differently [cf. 43]. It follows that as aspects of culture vary, there will be variation in behavior. Since the relationship between culture and concrete behavior is a complex one, and since the patterns that constitute culture are differentially available from situation to situation, a one-to-one correspondence between variation in the culture of a people and the behavior of all the persons constituting the group is too simple a formulation.

A minimal definition of culture related to that arrived at by Kroeber and Kluckhohn [82, p. 181] is this: Culture consists of learned patterns of and for behavior. Patterning indicates that *regularities* in human behavior are involved. If such an approach reflected common usage among anthropologists more closely, it would be convenient to think of culture in terms of the high probability of the reappearance in the same

person and in separate persons of certain learned behavioral characteristics. The focus of attention is upon the matrixes of interpersonal behavior. Much of culture consists of shared symbols (some writers assert
that all of it does); these are of significance in the learning of culture.
The term "symbol" connotes awareness, however, and we are unaware
of many of the cultural regularities we learn, share, and transmit.

It is important to note that there is great variation in the *scope* of the
systems which comprise any culture. For example, probably all cultures
have patterns of expectations as well as patterns of performance regarding the stages or course of life of a person; Shakespeare [118, pp. 260–
261] offers data on one such pattern. There can even be expectations as
to the "normal growth curve" for a dynasty or a civilization. At the other
extreme, there are systems or regularities of much less scope, though perhaps of great frequency, in a society; examples are conventions in punctuation, pointing with an index finger, and the American custom of
wrapping objects in paper, as opposed to the cloth that is used in certain
parts of the world.

Because of problems which will be explored later, attention should
be called to the fact that cultural regularities are constantly being combined with each other. When these combinations have marked saliency
and a high probability of being transmitted to others we call them *inventions,* but the term may equally well be applied to *all* of the numerous
instances of combination, not previously specified by the culture, which
occur in everyday life. When one wraps an unfamiliar object in paper
for the first time, this can be called an invention. Whether an invention
not yet shared with another person is part of culture or not is a problem
that need not be discussed here; at least culture is a constituent of the
invention process.

It may not always be clear why anthropologists bring up culture so
often. A psychologist, M. Brewster Smith, raises this question and suggests
an answer:

Is is important to note that culture is a concept, not a theory. The term
itself embodies no articulated propositions from which consequences can be
drawn and put to test. It asserts nothing about reality. The psychologist
who turns to anthropology after studying his lessons in the logic of science
may therefore show some surprise when he encounters statements about the
importance of the concept as an anthropological contribution.

It would be grossly unfair, of course, to view the concept of culture in
splendid isolation. If it contains no assertions, its definition nevertheless calls
attention to phenomena that had previously been neglected. With the *concept* of culture goes an *orientation*, if not a theory, that a very wide range of
human phenomena is cultural in nature. The importance of the concept
rests, then, on the host of assertions in which it occurs, to the effect that

phenomena x, y, z, etc. are cultural in origin, or are influenced in specific ways by culture. It is through facts of this latter order, together with the broader cultural orientation, that the concept of culture has been influential on psychology [119, pp. 40–41].

For Smith's "x, y, z," one might substitute speech, motivation, and food preferences as examples of behavior in which culture is important. In such areas of human activity, analysis can demonstrate the patterning or systematic quality specified in the definition of culture that was given. The extent to which any culture as a whole constitutes a system was argued even before Benedict published her *Patterns of Culture* [9]. Regardless of any decision on over-all integration, anthropologists are in general agreement about the systematic nature of parts of culture. The same agreement exists on the fact that the regularities exist prior to their being learned by persons who enter the society by birth or immigration.

A common approach in the study of phenomena that are systematic in nature is that of structure-function analyses. Such analyses are known by various names—they can be called simply "structural"—but in all cases attention is paid to the "contribution" that structural elements make to the greater structures or systems to which they belong; parts are understood as they relate to wholes. Such relationships are one meaning of the term "function"; there are alternative meanings, just as there are for the term "structure" [96]. Passing over the use of this method in such areas as biology and literary criticism, let us turn to the intensive use of it in modern linguistics. Not long ago, languages were studied historically and descriptively without particular regard to the fact that they could be viewed as constituting *systems*. Beginning in the last century there were extensive studies of the sounds used in languages, and a sub-discipline called *phonetics* was developed. Universal alphabets intended to classify the speech sounds found in all languages were devised. Such alphabets were believed to be "objective," but in fact they were culture-bound in that the reference points within them were drawn from European languages and the exotic languages most familiar to the linguists. The sounds of a particular language never corresponded exactly to acoustical and articulatory characteristics of the alphabet.

Building in large part on the work of Boas, the Americans Sapir and Bloomfield, as well as certain Europeans, developed a structural approach to speech sounds called *phonemics*. Sound units, called *phonemes,* were defined in terms of their relationship to other phonemes and to the phonological system as a whole. The study of phonetic features of speech remained as an initial phase, but much of the physical variation in speech sounds, which phoneticians had been recording so laboriously, proved not to be significant to the speakers of the language. For example, it is easy to demonstrate that there are many variations in the *t* sounds (phones) that are uttered in speaking English. It can also be demonstrated that this variation displays regularities (e.g., in amount of aspiration), depending on the sounds' relation to other sounds (e.g., whether they are in initial position, between vowels, or following *s*). When coupled with other criteria, the regularity in this variation helps the analyst to assign the various *t*'s to the same phoneme. (In another language, some variants might belong to different phonemes.) "Free variation" in sounds also occurs, but it can be isolated or identified only after the above "conditioned variation" is understood. In the meantime, the distinctiveness of the *t* phoneme from other phonemes—such as *d* —is established by other techniques, such as determining whether changes in meaning (differential meaning) accompany a substitution of one for the other. In summation, the range and boundaries of phonemes are determined by the study of the phonological features of a given language in relation to each other and not on the basis of an observer's assumedly "objective" universal phonetic alphabet. Phonemes are thus the *significant* "sounds" of a language.

There are differences, largely minor, in the methodologies and techniques of structural linguists in regard to phonemics. The same is true in the study of other aspects of language, these being handled by methods analogous to those in phonemics. *Morphemes* are units of form (e.g., suffixes like the English *-ing*), and they are studied in terms of the regularities, or systematic properties, in the forms of a given language. The general term for such study is *morphemics*. (Perhaps someone has coined the term "morphetics" for the nonstructural approaches to speech forms, such as in the normative grammar traditional in our language textbooks.) Linguistics has many more facets than can be mentioned here. Lounsbury discusses language in his contribution to this volume, and excellent introductions, available to psychologists, are provided by Brown [17] and Carroll [26]. There are numerous additional writings covering special problems in language and psychology [e.g., 27, 98, 115]. It should be noted that it is still the exception, and not the rule, for the variables in psycholinguistic research to be established by structural techniques.

Various linguists and anthropologists have become convinced that other aspects of culture can be analyzed and described by methods much like those of structural linguistics [cf. 77, p. 958]. A spectacular attempt to do so was made by Hall and Trager [58], but they unfortunately rooted it in arbitrary categories of biological activity rather than in the notion of the systematic nature of culture [cf. also 57]. Starting with Warm Springs Indian ceremonies as wholes, K. French was able to analyze them into segments which correspond to the segmentation of speech [47]. In the preface to a monograph on the social organization of Truk, W. Goodenough says:

The problem of rendering an ethnographic account that can be of practical use to administrators boils down, we feel, to trying to give the readers a basis for learning to operate in terms of the culture described in somewhat the same manner that a grammar would provide him with a basis for learning to speak a language. To seek to do this implies that a culture is as susceptible of rigorous analysis and description as is any language . . . . The writer feels that the recent advances in methodological and conceptual rigor in descriptive linguistics present a serious challenge to descriptive ethnography; for patterned verbal behaviors, the basic data of linguistics, are but one branch of patterned behaviors in general, which are the basic data of ethnographic analysis [53, p. 10].

Goodenough then proceeds in his preface to describe the type of structural analysis and formulation of definitions necessary to achieve his aims; he contrasts these aims with those of cross-cultural analysis [55].

A linguist, Kenneth L. Pike [107, pp. 8–28], has also been interested in the possibility of structural analyses of a variety of kinds of phenomena. He would call Goodenough's approach an "emic" one; he compares this with another fundamental type of approach which is labeled "etic." (He coined these terms by subtracting them from the words phonemic and phonetic, discussed above.) Pike identifies the emic approach as a structural one. The investigator assumes that human behavior is patterned, even though the members of the society being studied may not be aware of many of the units of the structuring. In Pike's view, the goal of the emic approach is to discover and describe the behavioral system in its own terms, identifying not only the structural units but also the structural classes to which they belong.

In contrast, an etic approach can be characterized as an external one. Items of behavior are examined not in the light of the systems in which they occur, but rather in that of criteria brought to bear on them by the observer. The observer classifies all comparable data into a system which he is creating, using criteria which were in existence before the classification began. Among the common types of etic studies are those in which the behavioral data are ordered in terms of physical criteria, for example, the use of degrees centigrade in studying the perception of heat.

Pike's emic-etic distinction does not imply a value judgment. Value judgments are pertinent, however, if an analysis of one kind is used when an analysis of the other kind is appropriate to the problems at hand. The initial approach to a new topic must be etic because one must move from familiar categories into the categories of the system to be studied. Cross-cultural studies must also be etic, since *all of culture* cannot now be handled as a system which can be studied emically.

To illustrate the two approaches: (1) A study of weaning in a given society in terms of the total pattern of mother-child relationships, food habits, and/or other relevant aspects of that particular culture would involve an emic approach; (2) a comparative survey of weaning practices which used universalistic principles of biological maturation would be etic.

Psychologists and anthropologists are among those who use both etic and emic approaches. Many of the emic approaches employed by psychologists involve part-whole relationships within biological rather than cultural systems. Neither psychologists nor anthropologists have been consistently aware of the distinction between these approaches nor sensitive to their disparate implications.

Anthropologists have written hundreds of monographs and papers approaching their subject matter emically but employing lax, as opposed to rigorous or strict, methods and techniques of analysis. Malinowski's Trobriand monographs [e.g., 95], excluding the generalizing sections, and Benedict's descriptive writings [e.g., 9, chaps. 4–6] are familiar examples. Among the more rigorous emic analyses are those by writers who had linguistic analysis in mind as a model.

Aspects of culture other than language and social organization are being subjected to rigorous emic analysis. While gesture is sometimes regarded as "natural" or "spontaneous" in human beings [132, p. 6], anthropologists, observant travelers, and many others have long known that gestural patterns are customary and vary from society to society [cf. 77, pp. 930–931, 940–941; 116]. Birdwhistell [13] has been working out techniques for the emic analysis of gestural systems. Etic analyses are also possible, of course [cf. 69]. Music can also be analyzed in terms of systems and part-whole relationships. Kolinski [79, 80] and other ethnomusicologists are in the process of evolving methods and specific techniques which will permit more adequate emic analyses of musical systems.

Folklore, in the sense of oral literature, is being subjected to emic analysis by such writers as Jacobs [74], who has not, however, employed structural linguistics as his model. The formal analyses of folk tales and myths by Propp [108] and Lévi-Strauss [90] are called "structural," but they are not emically so in that they do not limit themselves to the versions of a single group at a single time.

Emic analyses of kinship systems have long been undertaken, and these have been sufficiently useful and rigorous to constitute something of a "showpiece" in anthropology. Certain recent developments in kinship analysis deserve special attention because they not only exemplify emic analysis, but they have a potentially close relationship with studies of cognition. In 1956 Lounsbury [92] and Goodenough [54] published a pair of papers, differing in details of technique, employing types of componential analysis to determine the semantic distinctions made in kinship terminologies. Romney and Epling [114] and Frake [42] have similar intentions but do not use abbreviated notational systems to indicate conceptual dimensions and distinctions in the kinship systems they analyze. Wallace and Atkins have surveyed some of the published and unpublished papers in this area and have discussed the assumptions, procedures, difficulties, and utility of the approach. It is of interest that they assert [128, p. 79] that semantic analyses such as these are concerned primarily with "cognitive processes in culturally organized behavior," rather than with such familiar anthropological topics as linguistics, personality, or social structure or culture as such.

Among other recent semantic studies by anthropologists, linguists, and psychologists are papers on the structure of pronoun systems by Austerlitz [5] and McKaughan [94]. Brown and Gilman [19] study the semantic dimensions of second-person pronouns in European languages and relate their analyses to sociocultural characteristics of speakers. When Frake undertook the study of certain disease concepts of a Philippine people [43], one of the many problems he faced was determining the level of contrast on which a concept existed; his procedures are being adopted by others. Haugen has written an excellent paper [64] interpreting Icelandic directional concepts in terms of areas of settlement and modes of travel. Lounsbury [93, pp. 192–193] uses the term "structural semantics" for the types of studies discussed above, including those on kinship. Other useful papers on semantic analysis include those by Nida [103] and Öhman [104].

While these studies have been selected as being essentially emic, as previously defined, some of the papers in this area include purely formal analyses by the observer. Even the most conscientious attempts to analyze and portray significant semantic dimensions and categories emically yield results which have an ambiguous relationship to the behavior of the actors (or subjects, or informants). In other words, the results are best viewed as models and display the familiar strengths and weaknesses of models. Methodological problems of this general nature are included in the Wallace and Atkins paper [128].

Despite the importance of structural linguistics, it is not the only source for the methodology of emic studies. Biological taxonomics, formal logic, and various behavioral science fields have played a part [cf. 128, p. 60]. At the same time it should be clear that not all of the recent anthropological work on the topics discussed in this section are emic in approach. Some unpublished work in ethnoscience will illustrate another possibility. The author showed an identical series of familiar and unfamiliar plant specimens to Chinookan Indian, Sahaptin Indian, and Euro-American informants. The members of all the groups attempted to *identify* as many of the plants as possible. Most of the Chinookans said nothing at all about the plants they could not identify. The Sahaptins and the Euro-Americans *likened* the unknown plants to other plants, or to plant names, on the basis of similarities. Although the Euro-Americans had had no botanical training, they were the only group who attempted to any significant extent, to *classify* the plants by placing them in overt (mainly *ad hoc*) taxonomic categories. The author has been endeavoring to interpret these differences in ecological terms. Although he has also undertaken emic analyses of data from these Indians, this study is etic; it is comparative and does not attempt to delineate conceptual structure in the culture of a particular group.

Before turning to psychology, which has consistently stressed scientific objectives, it should be pointed out that an emphasis on emic analyses is consistent with the traditional anthropological interest in *describing* as much as possible of the way of life of each group of people studied. While anthropologists hope that some of their work is adequate in terms of any criteria for natural science, they are reluctant to bar from the field the well-established research in the *natural history* of man. This appreciation for extensive ethnographic accounts extends even to those British social anthropologists who are oriented toward nomothetic studies and whose own field research is limited to certain aspects of behavior. An increasing number of Americans now agree with Steward [122] and the social anthropologists that generalizing or nomothetic objectives should receive more emphasis. Many would also agree that the following sequence of stages represents an ideal for many kinds of problems not only in anthropology, but for certain problems in such disciplines as sociology and psychology: (1) an initial etic approach using established categories; (2) an emic organization of the data; and (3) a well-considered etic approach (employing a meta-language) which preserves the insights gained from the emic analysis.

PERCEPTION, COGNITION, AND SOME VARIABLES USED IN STUDYING THEM

It would not be appropriate here to summarize recent psychological literature on perception and cognition, or to attempt in a comprehensive way to outline the concepts, methods, techniques, problems, and subdivisions of the fields. Psychology is well supplied—far better than anthropology—with reference guides and summary articles. For example, two publications by Allport [2] and Scheerer [117] are recent enough and comprehensive enough so that there is little an anthropologist could add. Two other quite recent works by Boring [16] and Leeper [86] discuss the place of perception and cognition in experimental psychology, as do many of the essays in Study I and Study II of *Psychology: a Study of a Science.*

The present state of such disciplines as anthropology and psychology is sufficiently dynamic so that a majority of the technical terms do not have fixed, or generally accepted, definitions. Properly enough, terms are defined as they relate to the theoretical systems or to the logic of particular problems and writings at hand. It follows that neither "perception" nor "cognition" could be said to have a *meaning,* since they have multiple *meanings.* Yet it seems that psychologists of differing persuasions can discuss such topics as perception and cognition in ordinary conversation with only occasional resort to questions of definition. This suggests that such terms are meaningful after all, but that they refer, unless specifically defined, to disjunctive rather than conjunctive concepts [cf. Bruner et al., 25, pp. 41–45]. The various meanings of "perception," for example, lack a common denominator; each selects a pattern of meaning elements from a large array.

We have now made a beginning toward an ostensive definition of cognition and perception by implying that this paper is concerned with the range of phenomena that have been customarily discussed under these terms. Useful substantive definitions would then necessarily need to be broad ones, and, even so, they would not cover all the facets of current usage. With these cautions in mind, *perception* can be defined as the processes of immediate experience in organisms. This links perception with *sensation;* such primitive terms as "seeing," "tasting," and "feeling" are refinable into perceptual processes. As experience becomes less immediate, and the amount of *inference* by the organism increases, processes of *cognition* have become involved. Among the primitive terms here are "knowing" and "thinking." (More inferences by the observer, incidentally, are needed in studying cognition than perception.) A relationship between perception and cognition was suggested by the definitional approach that was taken. In the rest of the paper, however, it has been convenient to write about them as if they were distinct processes or groups of processes. An anthropologist lacks the experience to have an enlightened opinion on such vexing questions as the primacy or distinctness of such processes.

In isolating variables in the study of perception, psychologists were long divided between nativist and empiricist positions [2, pp. 86–89, 299–303]. After the defeat of the most naïve of the nativists, further attacks on American empiricism took the form of criticisms of the mechanistic and atomistic tendencies which accompanied it. Gestalt psychology and related approaches, which together have been labeled "organismic" or "organic" [3, pp. ix–x], came to represent the nativist position in the sense that they interpreted perceptual acts in the light of "central states." Gestaltists saw these states as reflections of the structure or organization of the brain [78, pp. 53–67]. Their emphasis on organization in general and on the importance of understanding parts in terms of wholes is also worth mentioning here because of certain parallels with anthropology.

In regard to nonorganismic approaches to perception, there is a point relevant to positions taken by anthropologists that should be made. In varying the stimulus conditions in experiments, it once was common for empirically oriented psychologists to make objective, physical, etic distinctions; for example, in the study of visual or auditory perception, the wavelength of light or sound was varied in a regular manner as if an experiment in physics were under way. Subsequently, the use of psychophysical units (rather than physical units), which are related to the organism as a system, was guided by thinking that could be classified as emic. Modern psychology uses similar emic approaches in countless ways, especially in such fields as experimental esthetics and the design of personality tests. Etic distinctions are still frequently made, legitimately or illegitimately, but their role in psychology has shifted.

The usefulness of the concept of cognition has been much more controversial than that of perception. With Tolman as a conspicuous exception, a great many American psychologists have not felt that they could reconcile the study of cognition with their definition of rigorous methodology. Those who *do* discuss cognition are not a homogeneous group; the term was once relatively common property in psychology and is subject to revival [86, p. 736] in disparate contexts. Many, but not all, of the cognitive theorists of greatest relevance to this paper have been rather strongly influenced by gestalt psychology. It should be mentioned that those who discuss cognition commonly extend the scope of cognitive processes to include various phenomena, such as aspects of perception or learning [86, p. 739], handled by other psychologists under other headings.

While experimental studies of cognitive processes are often classified into two types—those on *problem solving* and those on *concept formation* —it should be noted that the distinction is not always easy to maintain. Leeper [86, pp. 739–755] discusses three types of concept formation: inductive, deductive, and inventive. Inventive concept formation, which is discussed in other terms by Bartlett [8], is especially relevant to this paper and will be mentioned again.

The distinction between abstract and concrete thought has been of great importance in cognitive theory. This dimension, whether viewed as a continuum or a dichotomy, has served as a point of reference even for those who use somewhat different terminology [cf. 67, pp. 211–212]. Developmental or genetic psychologists associate concrete thought with "primitive" levels of development. "Primitive" and "advanced" are logical rather than chronological stages of development in the writings of

Werner, despite the fact that he uses the behavior of children as well as nonliterate peoples to exemplify primitive cognitive structures. Along with such men as Goldstein, Kasanin, and Arieti [4, pp. 26–27] he also classifies certain kinds of pathological thinking, especially among schizophrenics, as "primitive" [129, pp. 330–336]. Werner regards an increase in differentiation and hierarchic organization as the fundamental law of development. In his analysis of stages, he employs not only the concrete-abstract distinction, but also the following paired terms: (1) syncretic-discrete, (2) diffuse-articulated, (3) indefinite-definite, (4) rigid-flexible, (5) labile-stable. It is not necessary to define these terms except for several of them to be used later. *Syncretic* refers to a failure to separate phenomena which are normally distinct; *rigid behavior* does not vary when variability is appropriate; *labile behavior* is fluid, as exemplified in the distractability of children. Scheerer [117, pp. 132–137] provides a sympathetic summary of Werner's system and suggest parallels with that of Piaget.

Leaving developmental psychology, reference should be made to *codability*, a concept used sometimes as a systematic and sometimes as an empirical variable. It is a measure of the efficiency or ease with which a concept or a sensory experience may be transmitted in a given language code [cf. 88, p. 20]. Subsequently there will be discussion of the measurement of codability, and it will be related to *availability*, which refers to the ease with which subjects can employ a concept, e.g., in nonlinguistic judgments of equivalence and difference [cf. 20, pp. 454–456, 460].

PSYCHOLOGY-ANTHROPOLOGY INTERRELATIONSHIPS

Before discussing the specific interrelationships with which this paper is principally concerned, it seems worthwhile to touch upon some of the other connections between psychology and anthropology. Several excellent papers dealing with the general relationships between the disciplines have appeared in recent years [60, 77, 119]. Instead of a broad discussion, therefore, only a few selected points will be made here.

As was implied previously, certain anthropologists and personality psychologists have become familiar with each other's findings. In understanding this, it must be recognized that personality theory is one of the least systematic of the fields in either discipline. In fields in which there has been more satisfying substantive work, this convergence has not occurred. To illustrate, specialists in the classical fields of psychology (such as learning) have been less likely to feel that there is a necessity for them to explore thoroughly some aspects of another behavioral science discipline. Their explorations have been mainly in the biological and physical sciences.

Fewer anthropologists are using personality to "account for" certain of their data than during the decade 1940–1950. There were then overly optimistic hopes that neo-Freudian approaches would solve many problems. Perhaps there is now a growing realization that personality is after all a concept—a human artifact—rather than an objective entity that has existed throughout the history of man. As a concept it is indeed an entity, a cultural one, with a broad base in our everyday thinking about ourselves. This indicates nothing about the utility of personality formulations in behavioral science research, and anthropologists—like psychologists—are not in agreement regarding this utility. At the moment, a sizable group of anthropologists use personality formulations, others use alternative psychological and sociocultural approaches, and still others are concerned with problems in which these choices do not arise. The percentages will shift with the emergence of new problems and with developments in research and theory. The issues in this area are difficult and have been discussed many times—for example, by the writers cited above—and they will need to be discussed again in the future.

Clinical psychologists, psychiatrists, and psychoanalysts have sometimes paid attention to the writings of anthropologists, and an influence in the other direction has strongly affected certain anthropologists. To a certain extent this is due to a shared interest in human pathology; theoretical questions involving general culture-personality interrelationships, however, have been more significant common interests. It has also been suggested that the mutual attraction here is based in part on the similarity in methodology [cf. 77, p. 964], for example, case studies, the use of a temporal dimension, and a qualitative exploration of the characteristics of the material being studied.

Reference has already been made to interests common to comparative and physiological psychology and physical anthropology. Anthropologists are writing on the evolution of human behavior; any increased anthropological interest in physiology should lead to additional convergences.

Learning is a central concept in anthropology as well as in most American psychology. Implicit or explicit in all definitions of culture is the idea that learned and transmissible behavior is involved. It is obvious, however, that the emphasis is completely different in the two fields: anthropologists lack the training to study the *processes* and *mechanisms* of learning in an intensive way. Instead, they take them for granted or consciously leave them for psychologists to study. With rare exceptions [e.g., 133], the concern of anthropologists is with *what* is learned, not *how*.

The problem of avoiding subjectivity, which has so long concerned behaviorists is, strangely enough, not as acute in anthropology as might be supposed, considering some of the kinds of subject matter in which anthropologists are interested. While there are, indeed, unintended lapses into subjectivity, ethnographic writing has been so overwhelmingly concerned with what people *do*, and so little concerned with what they "really think" that the question of avoiding "mentalism" has not arisen as an important problem. Even ethnographic writings purporting to deal with the intellectual life of nonliterate peoples consist typically of records of verbal accounts by informants, with only an occasional passage suggesting that these accounts refer to processes and structures within the "minds" of the people being studied. This does not mean that the average cultural anthropologist can claim credit for avoiding mentalistic statements; the point is not that he remembers to avoid them, but rather that usually the subject matter and research aims make them unnecessary.

Certain anthropologists are explicitly behavioristic in their writings; one textbook is based essentially on this position [32]. The compatibility of behaviorism with cultural formulations is illustrated by the use of behavioristic strictures in the methodology of structural linguistics. Bloomfield [14, 15] and the linguists (in anthopology or not) who have followed him most closely have based their study of language on verbal *behavior*. They have studied the formal patterns or regularities in speech; questions of meaning have been handled gingerly, with some linguists attempting to exclude them entirely. Such a categorical exclusion, however, minimizes the opportunities to explore many of the kinds of questions which are relevant to this paper (e.g., cross-cultural differences in semantic structuring).

In general, anthropologists have no grounds for conflict with experimental psychologists, including those who use stimulus-response formulations. Fortunately or unfortunately, the problems in the two fields rarely overlap.

Many of the connections between anthropology and social psychology are too obvious to require discussion. However, recent work on "social perception" or "perception of persons" should be mentioned because of its potential importance to the two fields [24]. Its relevance to anthropology has been explored in at least one recent article [51].

CULTURE IN RELATION TO PERCEPTION AND COGNITION

Earlier in this paper, various modalities of anthropological research were discussed, and the assertion was made that they were relevant to the study of perception and cognition. The relationship between cultural categories and cognitive categorization is not difficult to demonstrate. The relationship between culture and perception is another matter; many traditional approaches in psychology and anthropology fail to establish a convincing connection between these realms. The crucial question is:

Do people with differing cultures actually perceive differently? Theoretical considerations and certain research results, even as early as the Torres Straits expedition [56], and especially Hallowell's work make one kind of case for real differences in perception. For example, one of Hallowell's informants perceived, i.e., heard, a cannibal giant under circumstances in which a Euro-American would have perceived something else [59, pp. 181–184].

During recent years, Bruner, Postman, and others have been publishing results of experiments which provide another kind of evidence for cultural influence on perception [see 2, pp. 304–406 for a discussion]. Their approach, which has been called "directive-state theory," employs variables such as value and personality—variables which coincide with those sometimes used by anthropologists in discussing aspects of culture. While there have been criticisms [21, pp. 138–140; 29, 76] (for example, of specific techniques), their general case for the "projective nature of perception" is an impressive one: Such variables as values, reward and punishment, "personality characteristics," and disturbing or threatening stimuli affect perception. (Note that these are not all cultural, at least in an obvious sense.) The effects include the speed of perception and the size of objects perceived. To be relevant to this discussion, a translation of the terminology for the independent variables is necessary. The directive-state research is often phrased in terms of "individual differences" in perception within our own society. The kinds of learned differences in values and other characteristics that are discussed, however, can also be viewed as *subcultural* differences. This means that they are cultural in nature and could as easily vary from society to society as they could vary between subsocieties or other groupings among the Euro-Americans used as subjects. It is an obvious suggestion that comparable research should be carried on cross-culturally.

Hallowell has discussed at length the ways in which the above developments in the study of perception can facilitate a closer *rapprochement* between anthropologists and psychologists. In this context he said:

> Thus the door has been thrown open to the investigation of a wide gamut of problems in the functional area which, on the one hand, include the question of the cultural constituents of perception and, on the other, idiosyncratic determinants rooted in the personality structure of the individual [59, pp. 165–166].

Since the time that Hallowell wrote, developments both in neurophysiology and in the psychology of perception and cognition have increased the probability that cultural approaches will prove fruitful. One can conclude from Bruner's discussions [22, 23] of those developments that the idea of "gating" or "filtering" processes during perception and the renewed emphasis on central functions increase the relevance of learning in perception. In the study of humans, almost any increase in the scope of learning in behavior means that new areas for the applicability of cultural approaches are opened.

This does not mean that the roles of learning and of culture are easily understood. For example, Navahos leave openings in simple designs so that circles and other figures are often not quite complete from a White point of view. There is evidence that Navahos "fail to achieve closure" in other aspects of their culture as well. Michael [97] found, however, that Navaho experience with "nonclosure" did not lead them to perceive complete and incomplete circles in a manner that differed significantly from Whites in the same area.

It was implied earlier that it is difficult to determine whether certain anthropological research relates more clearly to perception than to cognition. The question of the relationship between these processes is best handled by psychologists. Anthropologists can do fruitful work in the emic analysis of those aspects of culture concerned with man's structuring of the universe without deciding in precisely what field it will be most helpful to psychologists. One example is anthropological research on color categories.

The problem of the lack of correspondence between our own names and categories for colors and those of other people has long been recognized. Earlier interpretations tended to be *etic* and thoroughly culture-bound. Groups who did not differentiate between blue and green in their verbal and other behavior were victims of "blue-green confusion." This approach persists in a scattered way in contemporary writings; Werner [129, p. 284] cites blue-green confusion as an example of labile thinking among "primitives." While on the Torres Straits expedition, Rivers observed "confusion" between colors among the natives [113, pp. 58, 69, *et passim*]. His general attitude toward color names also deserves attention, however. He had an etic interest in what the natives "really" saw, and this was related to his program for studying differences in color blindness. Although he made a collection of color terminology, he made every effort to keep the natives from using their own classification in matching the dyed wools he was showing them.

After observing experiments by Jacobs for the study of color constructs in American Indian languages, Ray evolved methods which were technically superior to those of Rivers and other early workers. For example, not only were the colored papers which were shown to the Indian informants classified in terms of hue or wavelength, but they were shown under carefully controlled conditions [110]. Some of Ray's results were presented in a paper [111] in which he emphasized the people's own terminology and indicated the boundaries between the color categories by wavelength designations. His emic position caused him to deny the existence of blue-green confusion; he implied that we are equally guilty of *βa'lamι-tskι'lkwu* confusion in applying the single term "yellow" to a spectral range which the Santiam Kalapuya differentiate.

Conklin [35] exploited even more systematically the possibilities of an emic approach to a color system in his collecting of data from a Philippine group. The Hanunóo system could not be understood in terms of our notion of color taken alone. Other aspects of culture seem to intrude into the system. Conklin also discovered that he needed to study colors in contrastive situations; otherwise there could be overlap at the "boundaries" between categories. He found that two distinct levels of color terminology were necessary in his analysis—one general and one specific. It will be noted that in his conclusion he linked the Hanunóo system, or organization, with perception, in contrast to sensation:

> In short, we have seen that the apparent complexity of the Hanunóo color system can be reduced at the most generalized level to four basic terms which are associated with lightness, darkness, wetness, and dryness. This intracultural analysis demonstrates that what appears to be color "confusion" at first may result from an inadequate knowledge of the internal structure of a color system and from a failure to distinguish sharply between sensory reception on the one hand and perceptual categorization on the other [35, p. 343].

The work of Brown, Lenneberg, and Roberts [20, 88] involves not only the study of color, but also several other matters of mutual concern to psychologists and anthropologists. The methodology of the color work itself was carefully considered; this led to appreciably more elaborate operations than any of the previous cross-cultural research. The published results, however, do not exhaust the possibilities for the emic analysis of the Zuni Indian color *system*.

The concepts of codability and availability used by Brown, Lenneberg, and Roberts deserve comment from an anthropological point of view. Culture can be regarded as including systems of categories. The members of a given society are aware of certain of the categories of their culture, but not others. Judgments of equivalence and difference are made in terms of the categories: judgments of equivalence refer to the treating of discriminably different phenomena as if they were equivalent; judgments of difference refer to the limits of these categories and permit the exclusion of other phenomena which are discriminably different. Such judgments are made continually in everyday life, but they are also characteristic of the behavior of subjects of experiments and can be of significance in the results obtained.

Language is one system of cultural categorization, and it is the one most exploited in research. Especially in discussions of the hypotheses of

Whorf et al., the proposition is advanced that varying linguistic systems encode the phenomena to which they refer in varying manners. Similarities between this linguistic coding and nonlinguistic behavioral judgments of equivalence and difference have been the subject of debate; supporters of Whorf have asserted that language functions as a determinant. There has also been interest in what might be called the "general mode of perception of the universe" which is characteristic of the speakers of a given language. It has been suggested that those modalities of experience which are more readily *codable* in a language system are more readily *available* to those utilizing this coding system.

Psychologists concerned with linguistic codability have used the frequency of a word's appearance and measures based upon this frequency as an indication of the codability of stimuli which are instances of the concept the word symbolizes. Brown and Lenneberg used a formulation based upon Zipf's hypothesis that word length was inversely proportional to the frequency of appearance; they derived from this the proposition that length is inversely proportional to the saliency of a word and the concept for which it stands [20, pp. 458–460; cf. Heidbreder's use of the frequency of word appearance, 65, p. 194, as given in Thorndike's *Teacher's Word Book*, 123, in the measurement of familiarity]. Brown and Lenneberg's behavioral indexes of codability included also degree of agreement among the subjects, speed of reaction time, and degree to which subjects repeated themselves when naming the color at different times.

The methodology and techniques employed by Lenneberg and his colleagues proved to have many advantages over those of their predecessors in studying the relationship between linguistic and nonlinguistic behavior. For example, they were able to conclude, after experimental work suitable for replication, that there was a high correlation between ease in "recognition" of colors and their linguistic codability [20, pp. 460–462]. The codability-availability work has been further discussed by Brown [18, pp. 229–263]; new research is being undertaken by others [e.g., 124, 125].

Language, however, is only one part of culture, and the availability and codability of *cultural categories* may not always be reflected in it directly, for example, by short common words. It is customary in crosscultural research on color to devalue the *ad hoc* terms the subject invents to encode phenomena for which he lacks a ready name. To illustrate, the *ad hoc* phrase "Swiss-cheese colored" is both lengthy and uncommon, but it is likely to communicate certain color characteristics quite reliably to most Americans (more so than simply "cheese-colored"). The same point could be made in areas other than color. We lack a name for a category encompassing cups and tumblers. We are forced to *invent* a phrase such as "something to drink out of," or "something to drink from." In a somewhat different sense from that of Lenneberg et al., availability and codability would seem to be high in these cases, but to study them one would have to pay attention to aspects of cultural regularity beyond linguistic regularity. In addition to named categories, there are unnamed categories in culture which are readily available and easily used for judgments of equivalence and difference [46, p. 226]. It should be understood that this is not a criticism of the color-recognition experiments, but rather a suggestion that nonlinguistic cultural categorization be explored in future work on cognition.

In discussing the availability of categories, whether conventionalized in language or not, it is important to pay attention to differences between situations. Heidbreder [65, pp. 191–195] found in her early work on concept formation that number concepts were formed more slowly than those involving a greater degree of "thing-character." This was true despite the fact that numbers such as "two," "five," and "six" are frequent in English and rank higher on Thorndike's list than "building" or "circle," for example. By varying the experimental conditions (or *situation*), the speed with which number concepts were formed was increased [68, p. 21]. One point that can be made is that the frequency of occurrence of a word does not indicate the frequency of judgments of equivalence or of difference. In certain situations in everday life, we count; in others, we identify forms; in still others, we make various kinds of comparisons. All of these activities involve the existing regularities of culture or inventions based on these regularities.

The convergence between invention as defined and used here and Leeper's discussion of inventive concept formation should be mentioned in this context. He cites several instances in which it was fairly clear that the person had not previously learned a specific response and yet was able to produce it without hesitation—a small child spoke of a museum as a "dead zoo," another spoke of wood shavings as "carpenter peelings" [86, p. 750]. The relative rapidity of attainment of concepts of the unfamiliar spatial forms in Heidbreder's experiments [65, pp. 191–195] might be interpreted as having been facilitated by inventive concept formation [cf. 12]. While the specific forms were unfamiliar and were unnamed in English, subjects combined familiar cultural elements into new combinations of forms and names which served as devices for the categorization of the instances of the concepts. One subject, for example, described Heidbreder's unfamiliar form "stod" as being "like a thickly salted pretzel, broken at one end" [66, p. 112].

Linguists sometimes speak of "productivity" in language, and an examination of this term may throw further light on the invention processes we have been discussing. Suffixes such as English -*s* or -*ed* are said to be productive in that they can be added to new nouns and verbs to form plurals and tense forms that will be meaningful to a listener who has never heard these combinations before. If we borrow a Russian word for a type of space vehicle, we pluralize it with -s, rather than the nonproductive form -en, as in *oxen*. Research by Berko and Brown [10, 11, 12] on the acquisition of language by children involves the concept of productivity. Children learn the principles of plural formation and extend them to new words. They also learn to generate grammatical and meaningful utterences they have never heard before, and in this sense all of language is more or less productive [cf. 99, pp. 144–158]. Not all combinations occur, but any speaker is constantly "inventing" new combinations of elements in forming sentences. Similarly, the nonlinguistic aspects of culture can be seen as differentially productive; many kinds of new combinations can be easily formed.

A cultural approach to problems in cognition has terminological implications. Except possibly when both terms are used to indicate some contrast in cognitive processes [cf. Bruner et al., 25, pp. 21–22], *concept attainment* seems preferable to *concept formation,* which suggests an emphasis on individual experience and achievement. Carroll [28, pp. 195–196] advances cogent reasons for using *concept evocation* in many experimental contexts. To an anthropologist, *concept learning* seems to be an appropriate term for the situations in which the subject is, in effect, learning whatever regularities the psychologist has built into the stimuli. There is a parallel here with many other learning situations. For humans (and domesticated and laboratory animals), learning typically consists of the acquisition of regularities which other humans are already displaying in their behavior. For example, pets learn to eat food that humans define as appropriate for their species.

A cultural interpretation is also pertinent to the work on cognition by developmental or genetic psychologists. As a means of studying "primitive" forms of cognition, Werner and Kaplan [130, 132] employ a technique in which the subject is asked to express a simple statement by a line drawing. They reject a dichotomy between experience and mediation (e.g., systems of symbols), and they emphasize the separateness from other media and at the same time the "naturalness" of the line-drawing technique [132, pp. 4–6]. Their general reasoning is that their subjects are capable of expressing experience in an "advanced language," namely, English. The line drawings they make are a more primitive kind of expression; consequently, they are comparable to the forms of expression found in such languages as Navaho and "Western Africa Sudan" [132, p. 10]. The investigators present some of their findings and discuss the problems faced by the subjects, including those in which a "forced choice" is required.

It is puzzling that the authors do not really explore the role of an English-language background in determining the kinds of drawings that are produced. An anthropologist is inclined to see the problem facing the subject as a situation in which he is required to *invent,* within limits imposed from the outside, a method of expression. Inventions were defined as new combinations of existing cultural materials. From the diagrams and other results presented by Werner and Kaplan, it seems evident that English orthography as well as speech was important in producing many of the regularities in the results. The most obvious regularity is not mentioned by the authors—the drawings are to be interpreted from left to right [132, p. 6]. One could point out that the same is true of the sample drawings given by the investigators; the samples might have influenced the subjects. However, English (as opposed to Arabic) writing conventions provide the most satisfactory explanation for the consistency. The use of linguistic habits in the inventions seems clear in the form as well as in the direction of the lines. The sample line goes down; we speak of feeling "low," "down in the dumps," "depressed," and the like. The downward lines expressing yielding or defeat can be matched by such English expressions as "to go down to defeat." In discussing an aberrant result from one subject, the authors do mention that she was not a native speaker of English. They do not, however, attempt to understand the bulk of the results by taking into account the fact that the subjects were native speakers. (One presumes they were; this was not stated.) Since it seems relatively easy to interpret certain results of Werner and Kaplan by referring only to the explicit verbalized aspects of culture, one suspects that more subtle cultural regularities, rather than "primitive forms of expression," might be adduced to explain other results they obtained.

Anthropologists who stress organization and integration, as opposed to those who are more atomistic, are praised by Werner [129, pp. 9–13]. Nevertheless, he fails to apply the notion of organization in some of the areas in which it would be most helpful to him. Specifically, when evaluating cultural phenomena, he does not do so in terms of the organization of the systems in which they are embedded. An emic approach to questions of similarity and difference would hardly have led to the use he makes of his classificatory concepts, such as "lability" and "rigidity." One of his illustrations of lability is that the Kamayurá of Brazil call blue and green by the same name [129, p. 248]. The pitfalls in discussing equivalence or difference in colors without knowledge of the total color system have already been covered. Every color classification is equally arbitrary, and we Euro-Americans could be accused of conceptual lability by any Indian group that makes a color distinction that we do not. Werner cites as an illustration of rigidity the fact that the Tsimshian of British Columbia, being "members of an essentially concrete-ritualistic culture," refused to accept rowboats as substitutes for their indigenous canoes. While he realizes that this is a question of perceiving "changes that seem slight to the Western man," Werner imposes external judgments of rigid ritualism on the phenomena, rather than interpreting canoes as a crucial element within the total complex of a maritime way of life [129, p. 112]. Were it not for the implied value judgment on this way of life, the Tsimshian behavior would be classed as stable in Werner's system.

Werner and other psychologists with an organic or organismic orientation raise many questions of relevance to anthropologists. This is made explicit in an article by Werner and Kaplan [130] addressed to anthropologists and in G. Allport's foreword to Werner's book, *Comparative Psychology of Mental Development* [3, p. x]. Anthropologists, however, can easily misunderstand the approach, in addition to any legitimate objections which they might find to it. When Glenn [50] questioned certain aspects of the Werner and Kaplan article, the authors answered [131] that they had been misunderstood regarding the temporal and logical criteria for primitivity. They add that they do not believe that changes occur in any single direction and not in the direction of increasing progress. Their writings, however, resemble so closely those of nineteenth-century writers who did make these assumptions that it is easy to overlook or disregard their explicit disavowals.

The idea of general stages of development is fundamental to most of the writings of Werner, as well as Piaget and others. Stage theories of human development frequently take the form of psychological or maturational "recapitulation theories." One of the grosser forms of these theories, as propounded by Freud, Ferenczi, and others, is as follows: The individual human being reexperiences the events and stages of the human race. If one's analysis of an individual's memories is penetrating enough, memories of the experiences of our common ancestors will be discovered. This theory is based on two familiar ideas, now generally abandoned or much modified: (1) the inheritance of acquired characteristics; and (2) Haeckel's "biogenetic law," in the form "ontogeny recapitulates phylogeny." Kardiner [75, pp. 133–134, *et passim*] criticizes Freud for the misuse of the concept of inheritance; Hallowell [62] discusses at length such recapitulation theories and their implications.

Although Hallowell notes the close relationship historically and logically between the concept of stages and recapitulation theory, Werner claims that he based his system on the idea of "parallelism" rather than recapitulation [129, pp. 17–35]. In Werner's view, pathological thinking of adults and the thinking of children, contemporary nonliterates, and prehistoric men are all "primitive," but this similarity is based on their failure to maintain or achieve "advanced" forms of thinking rather than on any principle which unites them. The circularity in his reasoning is not eliminated by his assertion that the similarities are not identities and that those with "primitive" forms of thought are using them to adjust in their own way to their environment. To avoid the charge that the characterization of "advanced" thought is not simply culture bondage in scientific guise, developmental psychologists will need a better methodological base and better data. On both logical and empirical grounds, the coexistence (in effect) of ancestors and descendants in the form of prehistoric and present-day "primitives" was long ago shown to be untenable. Furthermore, anthropologists have demonstrated striking differences in the forms of thought among contemporary nonliterates. Dispassionate use of Werner's categories (e.g., rigidity-flexibility) would not permit nonliterates to be placed in a single group; the time when one could speak simply of "primitive thought" is gone. Children are universally influenced by the adults in their own society—in their forms of thinking and in other respects. They, too, are not a homogeneous group about which one can generalize easily. The thinking of psychotics is also related to the thinking of others in a given society. It should be noted that the reference here is to the *form* of thought, which is Werner's interest, not simply to the content.

Werner's use of anthropological sources to provide examples for his developmental system—rather than to explore differences among forms of thought—obscures valid problems. It is legitimate to ask the question: What are the differences in forms of thought among human beings? Werner's analytic categories (e.g., syncretic versus discrete), if carefully defined, might be of great value in the cross-cultural study of cognition. They must be used flexibly, however, with consideration of alternative hypotheses—to be tested empirically—as to which characteristics will appear in combination. An investigator, rather than assuming that each American Indian group will necessarily display both rigid and syncretic thinking, might use such categories as analytic tools in making comparisons between groups. For example, they might prove useful in testing aspects of the hypotheses of Whorf et al. regarding language and behavior.

Before we leave organic/organismic approaches to psychology, reference should be made to classical gestalt theory, from which various present-day psychologies have developed. Such theory has been examined by the anthropologist Barnett [6]. Furthermore, it seems noteworthy that two of the men who were mentioned in connection with linguistic and nonlinguistic cultural patterning, Whorf [135, pp. 160–172] and Pike [107, p. 56], both paid especial attention to gestalt writings. Perhaps other anthropologists with interests in psychology would be wise to add gestalt (and related) systems to the aspects of psychology with which they are familiar. A reexamination of the formulations stemming from gestalt in the light of the concept of culture might yield results of value both to anthropology and psychology.

On a more general level, psychology may prove to be helpful in eliminating a formulation that has outlived its usefulness in anthropology. This formulation takes a variety of forms, all of which have in common the use of "individual" or "idiosyncratic" in contexts suggesting that these terms explain some aspect of human behavior. Except in the special sense of historical "explanation," i.e., charting the succession of *events*, it is difficult to see how anything can be explained or understood by reference to unique, idiosyncratic characteristics. Rather, *regularities* of one sort or another are central to understanding. It is apparently difficult for anthropologists to accept the proposition that cultural systems, like scientific or logical systems, operate in terms of classes of objects each containing several members. Not only are null classes absent, but so are single-member classes.

Numerous examples could be cited of the use in anthropology of formulations which emphasize individual characteristics. Some of these are the result of careless phrasing; others are related to fundamental aspects of the writer's methodology. In a quotation on directive-state theory (cited previously), Hallowell contrasts "cultural constituents in perception" with "idiosyncratic determinants rooted in the personality structure of the individual" [59, pp. 165–166]. The second half of this dichotomy is ambiguous as stated; he may be contrasting personality with culture, or he may be contrasting the unique aspects of individuals with culture. Hallowell himself has been in the forefront in stressing the importance of culture in understanding personality. If the second interpretation is correct, the nature of the contrast remains puzzling; in adults the unique aspects of "individuals" are culturally mediated, e.g., cripples become beggars if that is the expectation or regularity in the society to which they belong. Indeed, Hallowell essentially agrees with this position and makes good use of it, since later in the same article, in his discussion of "idiosyncratic or personal determinants" of perception, he interprets the case of an Ojibwa man who experienced a cannibal giant by referring to the culturally mediated events which preceded the experience [59, pp. 185–186].

A way to dissolve Hallowell's apparent dichotomy, while still taking into account all the Ojibwa material he presents in his paper, can be suggested. It is feasible to say that in certain situations there is a high probability that all Ojibwa will share similar perceptual experiences (e.g., they will follow the cultural pattern and perceive any of various kinds of berries as "snake berries" and therefore inedible). In certain other situations, there is a high probability that less than all the Ojibwa—perhaps only one, in fact—will perceive a culturally defined entity (e.g., a cannibal giant). Then the phrase "idiosyncratic determinants rooted in the personality structure of the individual" would refer to a certain probability of appearance of particular kinds of cultural patterning. This does not imply that the low probability of an event signals its low saliency. Rather, this is a function of the role matrix in which the person operates.

Hallowell himself uses phrasing in terms of probability, but when he raises the question of *which* individuals will have particular experiences, he chooses to use personality—perhaps as an intervening variable between earlier cultural experiences and a particular situation to be explained. Many anthropologists do not use probability formulations at all and do not relate variability in culture to situations. They make even greater use than Hallowell does of the concept of personality in explanatory statements, or leave a residual category—"the individual"—often implying that no explanation is possible.

Anthropologists sometimes mistakenly assume that psychology is principally concerned with the scientific study of the individual or individuals. Since this is an error—if unique individuals are meant—any increase in familiarity with the methodology of psychology should assist anthropologists in overcoming confusion in this area. Psychologists can be of assistance to anthropologists in methodology, whether in disposing of residual categories or in a variety of other ways.

METHODOLOGICAL CONSIDERATIONS

Cultural anthropologists have spent little time, relatively speaking, defining their fields of research and analyzing and perfecting a methodology. This has been defended from time to time as permitting them to devote more of their efforts to important matters—field trips and the publication of data. The fact is, however, that anthropologists as a group do not know what they know; they do not know the questions for which they have the accumulated answers. Compared with other behavioral sciences, anthropology is the least sophisticated so far as methodology, research design, and problem formulation are concerned. Recently, there have been assessment volumes, such as *Anthropology Today* [81] and its successors, and there is a growing appreciation of such men as Nadel [101, 102], Leach [84], Lévi-Strauss [89], and Steward [122], who have raised methodological questions.

There is, of course, a methodology of sorts implied in the activities of even those anthropologists who are least aware of it. Certain criticisms of anthropology have been based on misunderstandings of its largely implicit methods or on a mechanical transfer of the problems of one discipline to another. For example, both sociologists and psychologists have criticized anthropologists because they so rarely use statistics. F. Goodenough and Anderson [52, p. 6], for example, have said that anthropologists "have shown little awareness of the problem of typicalness or representativeness and have frequently disregarded the size of sample necessary for confidence to be placed in the results." In the emic, structure-function analyses which are so common in anthropology, typicalness or representativeness are matters of little importance. It is commonplace to recognize that the distributive properties (in the sense of frequency) of an event are at a different level of analysis from the structural or organizational aspects of those same events. [Kluckhohn has discussed questions of quantification and statistics in anthropology, 77, pp. 958–960.]

To the extent that anthropologists become concerned with the etic analysis of variables (after making emic analyses of particular systems), to that extent they will need to concern themselves with the possibility that statistics can help clarify the relationship between the variables [cf. 100, 134]. Since there is also a growing interest in the analysis of *events*, or raw behavior, in contrast to cultural patterning, certain questions of quantification and statistics should be raised in appropriate situations. With the recent development of nonparametric statistics, the applicability of statistical analyses to certain anthropological data is much increased.

It is possible that other behavioral scientists do not always realize the variety of methods and techniques currently employed by anthropologists. For example, in the study of kinship they commonly—

1. Collect kinship terminology
2. Collect genealogies
3. Note the actual usage of kinship terms and other types of behavior between relatives
4. Ask informants how the various relatives ought to behave toward each other
5. Ask informants how relatives do behave toward each other
6. Reexamine their data so as to take into account the "biases" (e.g., roles) of informants
7. Undertake analyses of the data to discover regularities which may not be known to the informants
8. Relate the different kinds of data to each other
9. Consider the light that can be thrown on kinship behavior by activities in other institutional areas
10. Make comparisons with other cultures

This list, while not exhaustive, shows a lack of reliance on a single method or technique. Leeper [86, pp. 737, 739] demonstrates that there has been a variety of methods in the study of cognitive processes and makes the point that only through such a diversity of approaches can they be understood. He includes a plea for more "ecological" studies, i.e., field studies, like those of anthropologists and those of Piaget on children. The same suggestions could be made for the study of perception. In passing, it might be noted that few anthropologists are more than barely aware of the research and writings of Piaget [106]. There are indications, however, that some of those who have studied child development and personality with a neo-Freudian approach are becoming interested in Piaget as an alternative.

The general approaches of the several behavioral sciences are complementary rather than contradictory. Anthropologists believe that disciplines such as psychology and sociology would benefit by additional field research in our own society and others. This does not mean, however, that present activities need to be abandoned. Similarly, anthropologists may find themselves in the future engaged in intensive research on problems of relatively small scope; particular research problems may require the laboratory conditions so common in psychology. Nevertheless, this does not mean that anthropologists need abandon their field trips. Nor need they give up their interests in the "natural history" of man.

As matters now stand, however, such psychologists as Brown and Lenneberg have received training in methodology and research design applicable to cross-cultural problems which is far superior to that of most anthropologists. Despite the growing interest in nomothetic propositions, few anthropologists would now phrase their objectives as did J. J. Gibson in a preface:

> The principal subject of this book is the visual perception of space. The essential question to be asked is this: How do we see the world around us? The question is at once a theoretical one, a factual one, and a practical one . . . . The intention is to formulate a consistent approach to the problem—a way of getting new facts and making new applications. The construction of a theory is most useful when the theory is "vulnerable," that is to say, when future experiments can but do not disprove it. A strenuous effort has been made to keep the propositions of this book explicit enough to be potentially incorrect. Needless to say, the author hopes that they will comprehend the facts and will predict the results of future experiments [49, p. vii].

It seems probable that the most fruitful interdisciplinary relationships as far as anthropologists are concerned will be ones in which psychology *stimulates* anthropology to pay more attention to methodology. Specific techniques can be learned from another field if the formulation of problems requires them or if collaborative arrangements can be solicited.

CONCLUSIONS

More than a decade ago, Goodenough and Anderson [52, p. 8] suggested that the problem of the organization of perceptions was one of joint concern to psychologists and anthropologists. Cognition was added to perception in focusing this discussion of the interrelationships between anthropology and psychology because significant convergences of interests have been occurring in both these areas. While anthropologists rarely study perception and cognition as such, certain facets of the study of culture appear highly relevant to the psychological study of these processes. Emphasis in the paper was placed on the systematic regularities in culture and on the relationship between these regularities and behavioral regularities in the areas of perception and cognition. No attempt was made to discuss new anthropological formulations regarding the evolution of culture and of human psychological processes; these are covered by Hallowell in this volume.

Stimulated by successes in structural linguistics, the analysis of kinship systems, ethnoscience, and nonanthropological methodologies, anthropologists and linguists have made advances in the study of the semantic aspects of cultural systems. It is becoming possible to specify with some precision the structure of the concepts that are significant in particular aspects of a culture. These approaches have a potential relationship to cognitive studies, and anthropological awareness of this is beginning to appear.

The relevance of anthropological research to studies of perception has been more indirect and general. This may be due in part to the facts that studies oriented toward sensory experience are often difficult to do in the field and that institutional arrangements rarely facilitate laboratory experimentation of a cross-cultural nature. There are, nevertheless, numerous unexploited possibilities for interdisciplinary research.

American psychologists are well aware of the anthropological use of the concept of culture in the study of non-European peoples. In certain contexts, all behavioral scientists know that we too "have a culture." Far less frequently is this culture made part of explanations of our own behavior. It is a function of the culture bondage we all share [45] that we "forget" our own culture, even after having become intellectually convinced of its existence. It is one of the special functions of anthropology during the present period to provide intermittent reminders that cultural interpretations can be valuable and to suggest specific applications of them. Such psychologists as Brown and Lenneberg are already making such applications.

In this paper, particular emphasis was placed on the concept of invention as a way to relate cultural regularities to perceptual and cognitive events. Many such events can be understood as involving a new combination of existing cultural elements. An examination of some of the concepts in cognitive theory, such as developmental stages and generalized "primitive" people, led to suggestions for revisions in the approach and in the applications of terminology.

Curiously enough, many anthropologists may derive from the methodological advances of psychology an interest in making *relatively* less use of cultural formulations. Particularly in America, anthropologists have been content to *describe,* sometimes with great elegance, selected cultural systems. Increases in methodological sophistication may lead increasing numbers of them to go beyond descriptive studies and raise nomothetic questions regarding the reasons for the appearance and persistence of one cultural system rather than another. Cultural variables are of great value for certain problems; on other levels, variables must be sought not in learned patterns, but in unlearned or external phenomena, for example, recurrent social and ecological relationships.

Questions can be raised as to ways to effect closer coordination between the work of psychologists and anthropologists. Suggestions relevant to interdisciplinary cooperation were implicit in the text at various points. Since it seems probable that programmatic suggestions and other verbalizations much more often derive from institutional arrangements than the reverse, explicit recommendations will not be elaborated. There exist a number of mechanisms to effect closer relations between anthropology and psychology. Interdisciplinary departments and institutes such as those at Harvard and Michigan, fellowships for interdisciplinary training, and interdisciplinary research programs are some examples.

Whether in the study of perception and cognition or in other areas, an understanding of the cultural orientation of anthropologists is perhaps the greatest general benefit that psychologists could derive from interdisciplinary association. Conversely, anthropologists might gain, through stimulation from psychology, an increased awareness of the importance of methodology. They can also receive help in setting limits to the applicability of the concept of culture. In the more specific areas emphasized in this paper, a number of promising beginnings—and they are only beginnings—have been made toward convergent and cooperative attacks on problems in perception and cognition.

REFERENCES

1. Albert, Ethel M., & Kluckhohn, C. *A selected bibliography on values, ethics, and esthetics in the behavioral sciences and philosophy, 1935–1958.* Glencoe, Ill.: Free Press, 1960.

2. Allport, F. H. *Theories of perception and the concept of structure.* New York: Wiley, 1955.
3. Allport, G. W. Foreword. In H. Werner, *Comparative psychology of mental development.* (Rev. ed.) Chicago: Follett, 1948. Pp. ix–xii.
4. Arieti, S. Some basic problems common to anthropology and modern psychiatry. *Amer. Anthrop.,* 1956, **58,** 26–39.
5. Austerlitz, R. Semantic components of pronoun systems: Gilyak. *Word,* 1959, **15,** 102–109.
6. Barnett, H. G. *Innovation: the basis of cultural change.* New York: McGraw-Hill, 1953.
7. Bartlett, F. C. *Remembering: a study in experimental and social psychology.* New York: Cambridge, 1932.
8. Bartlett, F. C. *Thinking: an experimental and social study.* London: G. Allen, 1958.
9. Benedict, Ruth. *Patterns of culture.* Boston: Houghton Mifflin, 1934.
10. Berko, Jean. The child's learning of English morphology. *Word,* 1958, **14,** 150–177.
11. Berko, Jean, & Brown, R. Psycholinguistic research methods. In P. H. Mussen (Ed.), *Handbook of research methods in child development.* New York: Wiley, 1960.
12. Berko, Jean, & Brown, R. Word association and the acquisition of grammar. *Child Develpm.,* 1960, **31,** 1–14.
13. Birdwhistell, R. L. *Introduction to kinesics: an annotation system for analysis of body motion and gesture.* Washington: U.S. State Dept., Foreign Service Institute, 1952.
14. Bloomfield, L. *Language.* New York: Holt, 1933.
15. Bloomfield, L. Linguistic aspects of science. *Int. Encyc. unif. Sci.* Vol. 1, No. 4. Chicago: Univer. Chicago Press, 1939.
16. Boring, E. G. *Sensation and perception in the history of experimental psychology.* New York: Appleton-Century-Crofts, 1942.
17. Brown, R. W. Language and categories. In J. S. Bruner, et al., *A study of thinking.* New York: Wiley, 1956. Pp. 247–312.
18. Brown, R. W. *Words and things.* Glencoe, Ill.: Free Press, 1958.
19. Brown, R. W., & Gilman, A. The pronouns of power and solidarity. In T. Sebeok (Ed.), *Style in language.* Cambridge, Mass.: Technology Press. New York: Wiley, 1960. Pp. 253–276.
20. Brown, R. W., & Lenneberg, E. H. A study in language and cognition. *J. abnorm. soc. Psychol.,* 1954, **49,** 454–462.
21. Bruner, J. S. Personality dynamics and the process of perceiving. In R. R. Blake & G. V. Ramsey (Eds.), *Perception: an approach to personality.* New York: Ronald, 1951. Pp. 121–147.
22. Bruner, J. S. On perceptual readiness. *Psychol. Rev.,* 1957, **64,** 123–152.
23. Bruner, J. S. Neural mechanisms in perception. *Psychol. Rev.,* 1957, **64,** 340–358.
24. Bruner, J. S., & Tagiuri, R. The perception of people. In G. Lindzey (Ed.), *Handbook of social psychology.* Vol. 2. Reading, Mass.: Addison-Wesley, 1954. Pp. 634–654.

25. Bruner, J. S., et al. *A study of thinking.* New York: Wiley, 1956.
26. Carroll, J. B. *The study of language.* Cambridge, Mass.: Harvard Univer. Press, 1953.
27. Carroll, J. B. Communication theory, linguistics, and psycholinguistics. *Rev. educ. Res.,* 1958, **28**, 79–88.
28. Carroll, J. B. Process and content in psycholinguistics. In R. Glasser, et al., *Current trends in the description and analysis of behavior.* Pittsburgh, Pa.: Univer. Pittsburgh Press, 1958. Pp. 175–200.
29. Carter, L. F., & Schooler, K. Value, need, and other factors in perception. *Psychol. Rev.,* 1949, **56**, 200–207.
30. Casagrande, J. B. The southwest project in comparative psycholinguistics: a progress report. *Soc. Sci. Res. Coun. Items,* 1956, **10**, 41–45.
31. Casagrande, J. B. The southwest project in comparative psycholinguistics: a preliminary report. In A. F. Wallace (Ed.), *Men and cultures: selected papers of the Fifth International Congress of Anthropological and Ethnological Sciences, Philadelphia, 1956.* Pp. 777–782.
32. Chapple, E. D., & Coon, C. S. *Principles of anthropology.* New York: Holt, 1942.
33. Conklin, H. C. An ethnoecological approach to shifting agriculture. *Trans. N.Y. Acad. Sci.,* 1954, **17** (Ser. II), 133–142.
34. Conklin, H. C. The relation of Hanunóo culture to the plant world. Unpublished doctoral dissertation, Yale Univer., 1954.
35. Conklin, H. C. Hanunóo color categories. *S.W. J. Anthrop.,* 1955, **11**, 339–344.
36. Conklin, H. C. Lexicographical treatment of folk taxonomies. In F. W. Householder & S. Saporta (Eds.), Problems in lexicography. Ind. Univer. Res. Center Anthrop., Folklore, & Ling., Publ. 21, 1962. Pp. 119–141.
37. Dennis, W. Cultural and developmental factors in perception. In R. R. Blake & G. V. Ramsey (Eds.), *Perception: an approach to personality.* New York: Ronald, 1951. Pp. 148–169.
38. Eisenstadt, S. N. The perception of time and space in a situation of culture-contact. *J. Roy. Anthrop. Inst.,* 1949, **79**, 63–68.
39. Fischer, J. L. Art styles as cultural cognitive maps. *Amer. Anthrop.,* 1961, **63**, 79–93.
40. Fishman, J. A. A systematization of the Whorfian hypothesis. *Behav. Sci.,* 1960, **5**, 323–339.
41. Forde, D. (Ed.) *African worlds.* London, New York: Oxford for the International African Institute, 1954.
42. Frake, C. O. The Eastern Subanun of Mindanao. In G. P. Murdock (Ed.), Social structure in Southeast Asia. *Viking Fund Publ. Anthrop.,* 1960, No. 29, 51–64. Published by Wenner-Gren Foundation, New York.
43. Frake, C. O. The diagnosis of disease among the Subanun of Mindanao. *Amer. Anthrop.,* 1961, **63**, 113–132.
44. Frake, C. O. Ethnographic study of cognitive systems. In T. Gladwin

& W. C. Sturtevant (Eds.), *Anthropology and behavior.* Washington, D.C.: Anthropological Society of Washington, 1962.

45. French, D. The concept of culture-bondage. *Trans. N. Y. Acad. Sci.,* 1955, **17** (Ser. II), 339–345.

46. French, D. An exploration of Wasco ethnoscience. *Yearb. Amer. phil. Soc.,* 1956. Pp. 224–226.

47. French, Kathrine S. Culture segments and variation in contemporary social ceremonialism on the Warm Springs Reservation, Oregon. Unpublished doctoral dissertation, Columbia Univer. Ann Arbor, Mich.: Univer. Microfilms, 1955.

48. Geertz, C. The growth of culture and the evolution of mind. In J. Scher (Ed.), *Theories of the mind.* Glencoe, Ill.: Free Press, 1962.

49. Gibson, J. J. *The perception of the visual world.* Boston: Houghton Mifflin, 1950.

50. Glenn, E. S. On the developmental theory of languages. *Amer. Anthrop.,* 1957, **59,** 537–538.

51. Goldstein, M. J. Perception and acculturation. *Davidson J. Anthrop.,* 1956, **2,** 155–164.

52. Goodenough, Florence L., & Anderson, J. E. Psychology and anthropology: some problems of joint import for the two fields. *S.W. J. Anthrop.,* 1947, **3,** 5–14.

53. Goodenough, W. H. Property, kin, and community on Truk. *Yale Univ. Publ. Anthrop.,* 1951, No. 46.

54. Goodenough, W. H. Componential analysis and the study of meaning. *Language,* 1956, **32,** 195–216.

55. Goodenough, W. H. Cultural anthropology and linguistics. *Monograph Ser. lang. & ling.,* P. Garvin (Ed.), 1957, No. 9, 167–173. Published by Georgetown Univer. Press, Washington.

56. Haddon, A. C. (Ed.). *Reports of the Cambridge anthropological expedition to Torres Straits.* New York: Cambridge, 1901–1935. 6 vols.

57. Hall, E. T., Jr. *The silent language.* New York: Doubleday, 1959.

58. Hall, E. T., Jr., & Trager, G. L. *The analysis of culture.* Washington: Authors, 1953.

59. Hallowell, A. I. Cultural factors in the structuralization of perception. In J. H. Rohrer & M. Sherif (Eds.), *Social psychology at the crossroads.* New York: Harper, 1951.

60. Hallowell, A. I. Psychology and anthropology. In J. Gillin (Ed.), *For a science of social man.* New York: Macmillan, 1954. Pp. 160–226.

61. Hallowell, A. I. *Culture and experience.* Philadelphia: Univer. Pa. Press, 1955.

62. Hallowell, A. I. The recapitulation theory and culture. In *Culture and experience.* Philadelphia: Univer. Pa. Press, 1955. Pp. 14–31.

63. Hallowell, A. I. The Rorschach test in personality and culture studies. In *Culture and experience.* Philadelphia: Univer. Pa. Press, 1955. Pp. 32–74.

64. Haugen, E. The semantics of Icelandic orientation. *Word,* 1957, **13,** 447–459.
65. Heidbreder, Edna. The attainment of concepts. II. The problem. *J. gen. Psychol.,* 1946, **35,** 191–223.
66. Heidbreder, Edna. The attainment of concepts. III. The process. *J. Psychol.,* 1947, **24,** 93–138.
67. Heidbreder, Edna. The attainment of concepts. VI. Exploratory experiments on conceptualization at perceptual levels. *J. Psychol.,* 1948, **26,** 193–216.
68. Heidbreder, Edna. The attainment of concepts. VII. Conceptual achievements during card-sorting. *J. Psychol.,* 1949, **27,** 3–39.
69. Hewes, G. W. World distribution of certain postural habits. *Amer. Anthrop.,* 1955, **57,** 231–244.
70. Hoijer, H. The relation of language to culture. In A. L. Kroeber (Ed.), *Anthropology today.* Chicago: Univer. Chicago Press, 1953. Pp. 554–573.
71. Hoijer, H. (Ed.) Language in culture. *Amer. Anthrop. Ass. Mem.* 79, *Comp. Stud. Cultures & Civilizations,* 1954, No. 3.
72. Honigmann, J. J. Culture and ethos of Kaska society. *Yale Univer. Publ. in Anthrop.,* 1949, No. 40.
73. Hymes, D. H. On typology of cognitive styles in language (with examples from Chinookan). *Anthrop. Ling.,* 1961, **3,** 22–54.
74. Jacobs, M. The content and style of an oral literature. *Viking Fund Publ. in Anthrop.,* 1959, No. 26. Published by Wenner-Gren Foundation, New York.
75. Kardiner, A. *The individual and his society.* New York: Columbia Univer. Press, 1939.
76. Klein, G. S., et al. The effect of personal values on perception: an experimental critique. *Psychol. Rev.,* 1951, **58,** 96–112.
77. Kluckhohn, C. Culture and behavior. In G. Lindzey (Ed.), *Handbook of social psychology.* Vol. II. Reading, Mass.: Addison-Wesley, 1954. Pp. 921–976.
78. Koffka, K. *Principles of gestalt psychology.* New York: Harcourt, Brace, 1935.
79. Kolinski, M. The structure of melodic movement: a new method of analysis. In *Miscelánea de estudios dedicados al Dr. Fernando Ortiz por sus discípulos, colegas y amigos.* Havana: Privately published, 1956. Pp. 881–918.
80. Kolinski, M. The determinants of tonal construction in tribal music. *Musical Quart.,* 1957, **53,** 50–56.
81. Kroeber, A. L. (Ed.) *Anthropology today.* Chicago: Univer. Chicago Press, 1953.
82. Kroeber, A. L., & Kluckhohn, C. Culture: a critical review of concepts and definitions. *Papers Peabody Mus. Amer. Archaeol. & Ethnol., Harvard Univer.,* 1952, **47,** No. 1.
83. Landar, H., Ervin, Susan M., & Horowitz, A. E. Navaho color categories. *Language,* 1960, **36,** 368–382.

84. Leach, E. R. *Political systems of highland Burma: a study of Kachin social structure.* Cambridge, Mass.: Harvard Univ. Press, 1954.

85. Lee, Dorothy. *Freedom and culture.* Englewood Cliffs, N.J.: Prentice-Hall, 1959.

86. Leeper, R. Cognitive processes. In S. S. Stevens (Ed.), *Handbook of experimental psychology.* New York: Wiley, 1951. Pp. 730–757.

87. Lenneberg, E. H. Cognition in ethnolinguistics. *Language,* 1953, **29,** 463–471.

88. Lenneberg, E. H., & Roberts, J. M. The language of experience: a study in methodology. *Int. J. Amer. Ling.,* 1956, Mem. 13.

89. Lévi-Strauss, C. Social structure. In A. L. Kroeber (Ed.), *Anthropology today.* Chicago: Univer. Chicago Press, 1953. Pp. 524–553.

90. Lévi-Strauss, C. The structural study of myth. *J. Amer. Folklore,* 1955, **68,** 428–444.

91. Lévi-Strauss, C., et al. Results of the conference of anthropologists and linguists. *Int. J. Amer. Ling.,* 1953, Mem. 8.

92. Lounsbury, F. G. A semantic analysis of the Pawnee kinship usage. *Language,* 1956, **32,** 158–194.

93. Lounsbury, F. G. Language. In B. J. Siegel (Ed.), *Biennial review of anthropology 1959.* Stanford, Calif.: Stanford Univer. Press, 1959. Pp. 185–209.

94. McKaughan, H. Semantic components of pronoun systems: Maranao. *Word,* 1959, **15,** 101–102.

95. Malinowski, B. *The sexual life of savages in north-western Melanesia.* New York: Liveright, 1929. 2 vols.

96. Merton, R. K. Manifest and latent functions: Toward the codification of functional analysis in sociology. In *Social theory and social structure.* (Rev. enlarged ed.) Glencoe, Ill.: Free Press, 1957. Pp. 19–84.

97. Michael, D. N. A cross-cultural investigation of closure. *J. abnorm. soc. Psychol.,* 1953, **48,** 225–230.

98. Miller, G. A. *Language and communication.* New York: McGraw-Hill, 1951.

99. Miller, G. A., Galanter, E., & Pribram, K. H. *Plans and the structure of behavior.* New York: Holt, 1960.

100. Murdock, G. P. *Social structure.* New York: Macmillan, 1949.

101. Nadel, S. F. *The foundations of social anthropology.* Glencoe, Ill.: Free Press, 1953.

102. Nadel, S. F. *The theory of social structure.* Glencoe, Ill.: Free Press, 1957.

103. Nida, E. A. Analysis of meaning and dictionary making. *Int. J. Amer. Ling.,* 1958, **24,** 279–292.

104. Öhman, Suzanne. Theories of the "linguistic field." *Word,* 1953, **9,** 123–134.

105. Osgood, C. E., & Sebeok, T. (Eds.) Psycholinguistics: a survey of theory and research problems. Supplement to *J. abnorm. soc. Psychol.,* 1954, **49,** No. 4, Part 2. *Ind. Univer. Publ. Anthrop. & Ling.,* 1954, Mem. 10.

106. Piaget, J. *Play, dreams, and imitation in childhood.* New York: Norton, 1951.
107. Pike, K. L. *Language in relation to a unified theory of the structure of human behavior.* Part I. Glendale, Calif.: Summer Institute of Linguistics, 1954.
108. Propp, V. *Morphology of the folktale. Ind. Univer. Res. Center Anthrop., Folklore & Ling.,* Publ. 10, 1958.
109. Radcliffe-Brown, A. R. *Structure and function in primitive society.* Glencoe, Ill.: Free Press, 1952.
110. Ray, V. F. Techniques and problems in the study of human color perception. *S.W. J. Anthrop.,* 1952, 8, 251–259.
111. Ray, V. F. Human color perception and behavioral response. *Trans. N.Y. Acad. Sci.,* 1953, 16 (Ser. II), 98–104.
112. Redfield, R. *The primitive world and its transformations.* Ithaca, N.Y.: Cornell Univer. Press, 1953.
113. Rivers, W. H. R. Vision. In A. C. Haddon (Ed.), *Reports of the Cambridge anthropological expedition to Torres Straits.* Vol. II, Part 1. New York: Cambridge, 1901.
114. Romney, A. K., & Epling, P. J. A simplified model of Kariera kinship. *Amer. Anthrop.,* 1958, 60, 59–74.
115. Rubenstein, H., & Aborn, M. Psycholinguistics. In P. R. Farnsworth & Q. McNemur (Eds.), *Annual review of psychology.* Vol. 2. Palo Alto, Calif.: Annual Reviews, 1960. Pp. 291–322.
116. Ruesch, J., & Kees, W. *Nonverbal communication: notes on the visual perception of human relations.* Berkeley, Calif.: Univer. Calif. Press, 1956.
117. Scheerer, M. Cognitive theory. In G. Lindzey (Ed.), *Handbook of social psychology.* Vol. I. Reading, Mass.: Addison-Wesley, 1954. Pp. 91–142.
118. Shakespeare, W. As you like it. In *The complete works of. . . .* New York: Oxford, 1914. Act II, Sc. 7.
119. Smith, M. B. Anthropology and psychology. In J. Gillin (Ed.), *For a science of social man.* New York: Macmillan, 1954. Pp. 32–66. (Pp. 40–41 quoted by permission.)
120. Sorokin, P. *Sociocultural causality, space, time.* Durham, N.C.: Duke Univer. Press, 1943.
121. Stefflre, V. An investigation of the role of language in E. Heidbreder's experiments of concept formation. Uupublished bachelor's thesis, Reed College, 1958.
122. Steward, J. H. *Theory of culture change: the methodology of multilinear evolution.* Urbana, Ill.: Univer. Ill. Press, 1955.
123. Thorndike, E. L. *A teacher's word book . . . .* New York: Teachers Coll., Columbia Univer., Bureau of Publications, 1932.
124. Van de Geer, J. P. Studies in codability I: Identification and recognition of colors. *Psychologisch Instituut van de Rijksuniversiteit te Leiden,* Rapport No. E001-60, 1960.
125. Van de Geer, J. P., & Frijda, N. H. Studies in codability II: Identifica-

tion and recognition of facial expression. *Psychologisch Instituut van de Rijksuniversiteit te Leiden,* Rapport No. E002-60, 1960.

126. Vogt, E. Z. *Navaho veterans: a study of changing values. Papers Peabody Mus. Amer. Archaeol. & Ethnol., Harvard Univer.,* 1951, **41,** No. 1.

127. Vogt, E. Z. *Modern homesteaders: the life of a twentieth century frontier community.* Cambridge, Mass.: Harvard Univer., Belknap Press, 1955.

128. Wallace, A. F. C., & Atkins, J. The meaning of kinship terms. *Amer. Anthrop.,* 1960, **62,** 58–80.

129. Werner, H. *Comparative psychology of mental development.* (Rev. ed.) Chicago: Follett, 1948.

130. Werner, H., & Kaplan, B. The developmental approach to cognition: its relevance to the psychological interpretation of anthropological and ethnolinguistic data. *Amer. Anthrop.,* 1956, **58,** 866–880.

131. Werner, H., & Kaplan, B. Reply. *Amer. Anthrop.,* 1957, **59,** 538–539.

132. Werner, H., & Kaplan, B. Symbolic mediation and organization of thought: an experimental approach by means of the line schematization technique. *J. Psychol.,* 1957, **43,** 3–25.

133. Whiting, J. W. M. *Becoming a Kwoma: Teaching and learning in a New Guinea tribe.* New Haven, Conn.: Yale Univer. Press, 1941.

134. Whiting, J. W. M. The cross-cultural method. In G. Lindzey (Ed.), *Handbook of social psychology.* Vol. I. Reading, Mass.: Addison-Wesley, 1954. Pp. 523–531.

135. Whorf, B. L. In J. B. Carroll (Ed.), *Language, thought, and reality.* Cambridge, Mass.: Technology Press; New York: Wiley, 1956.

136. Wilson, Monica H. Witch beliefs and social structure. *Amer. J. Sociol.,* 1951, **56,** 307–313.

137. Zborowski, M. Cultural components in responses to pain. *J. soc. Issues,* 1952, **8,** 16–30.

PERSONALITY, CULTURE, AND SOCIETY IN BEHAVIORAL EVOLUTION*

A. IRVING HALLOWELL

Department of Anthropology
University of Pennsylvania

INTRODUCTION

One of the most significant contemporary areas of discussion concerning the study of man centers on his social nature, varying modes of cultural adaptations, and their psychological consequences. Although in certain respects this is an old problem, conceptualization and analysis have been rapidly reaching a new level of sophistication. Particularly noteworthy is the convergence of interest manifested by representatives of disciplines which, in the recent past, made their own abstractions, pursued their own special problems, and often ignored, or paid little attention to, relevant data and theories in other fields. In the historical perspective of a little over a century, it would appear that a cycle is being completed. In the nineteenth century, psychology and anthropology were in their early stages. Boundaries were less sharply drawn; ideas were advanced and problems stated that transcended the more specialized concerns that later characterized both of these disciplines. At that time J. F. Herbart (1776–1841) is said to have "represented a departure from the

* Originally prepared for this volume, sections of the manuscript were contributed to the Darwin centennial celebration (University of Chicago, November 24–28, 1959), and were published in *Evolution after Darwin* [224]. Since then, the manuscript has been revised and a new introduction and conclusion included.

dominant associationist school, inasmuch as he conceived of the mind throughout in terms of dynamic forces rather than of passive mechanisms" [63, p. 23][1] and he maintained that "psychology remains incomplete as long as it considers man only as an isolated individual." In fact, "he was convinced that society was a living and organic whole, ruled by psychological laws that are peculiar to it [189, p. 51].

Both Theodore Waitz (1821–1864) and Adolph Bastian (1826–1905), who are numbered among the pioneers of anthropology, were influenced by Herbart. Waitz had published books on psychology a decade before his *Anthropologie der Naturvölker* (1859) appeared. It was soon translated into English. In this book he was concerned with differences in human mentality and the question of national character. He did not believe that national differences could be explained on the basis of race because there are different nationalities within the same race. "It is therefore probable," he said, "that the mental peculiarities of peoples are generally more flexible and changeable than the physical characters of the race, and are transmitted with a less degree of constancy [235, p. 381].[2] Bastian, a tireless world traveler, a voluminous writer, and director of the Berlin Ethnological Museum, argued that a science of mental life must take cognizance of ethnographic data because "the individual's thinking is made possible only by his functioning in a social group [152, p. 36].[3] Lazarus and Steinthal, both Herbartians, were the first to promote *Völkerpsychologie* and it was they who founded the *Zeitschrift für Völkerpsychologie und Sprachwissenschaft.* [See 189, pp. 60 ff.; 123, pp. 42 ff.]

At a later period, Wundt (1832–1921), the founder of experimental psychology, rounded out his life's work with his massive 10-volume *Völkerpsychologie,* in which he attempted to link the study of the individual mind with such historical social products as language, custom, and myth in a comprehensive system, following his principle of "creative synthesis." Allport says:

The most significant thing about Wundt is his insistence that the study of all higher mental processes falls in the province of *Völkerpsychologie.* He did not believe that individual psychology, especially as pursued in the psychological laboratory, could account for men's thought. Thinking is heavily conditioned by language, by custom, and by myth, which to him were the three primary problem areas of *Völkerpsychologie.* Wundt would have felt at home in modern-day discussions of "social perception" [5, p. 36].

[1] Flugel finds in Herbart's psychological system faint resemblances to Freud. For further information on the relations of Freud and Herbart, see [119, vol. 1, pp. 371 ff.].

[2] For the influence of Herbart on Waitz and Bastian, see [103, p. 380].

[3] For a more extended discussion of Bastian's sociopsychological interests, see [161].

But by the time Wundt had begun to publish the first part of his *Völker-psychologie* (1900), both anthropology and psychology had developed specialized and highly characteristic areas of inquiry.

The new specialization is exemplified by the roles which William McDougall, C. S. Myers, and W. H. R. Rivers played on the Torres Straits expedition (1898), which had been organized by the Cambridge anthropologist A. C. Haddon, and which was characterized by Allport as "a landmark in the collaboration of social scientists" [5, p. 35]. Rivers, for example, had been lecturing on the physiology of the sense organs at Cambridge since 1893 and was responsible for planning the first systematic course in experimental psychology to be given in England. His work in psychophysiology in Torres Straits led him to the conclusion that pure sensory acuity is much the same in all races. Rivers likewise developed the genealogical method, which later became of classical importance in the investigation of the social structures of nonliterate peoples. Looking back, we note that at this period his psychological work and his pioneer work in social anthropology remained unintegrated. By 1916, however, Rivers was asking: "How can you explain the workings of the human mind without a knowledge of the social setting which must have played so great a part in determining the sentiments and opinions of mankind?" [190, p. 2]. But though Rivers touched upon many vital issues, he never initiated serious research along sociopsychological lines [75].

In the early part of this century, it would have been difficult for anyone to have predicted the later convergence of interest which focused upon the social, cultural, and psychological dimensions of man as a social being. Yet if we consider the interests of individuals rather than the manifest programs of disciplines, there are discernible beginnings.

American anthropologists, under the influence of Franz Boas, opposed early instinct doctrines in psychology, the racial interpretation of intelligence tests, and the generic concept of a primitive mind inferior to that of civilized man. Boas, nevertheless, recognized the relevance of psychology at a time when the major interests in physical anthropology, archeology, and cultural anthropology were chiefly descriptive and historical. He held Galton in high esteem and, in his seminars early in this century, discussed Wundt's *Völkerpsychologie*. According to Lowie [153, p. 1011], Wundt was also read "to some extent" by his students (Kroeber, Goldenweiser, Lowie, Haeberlin, Sapir, Reichard). Besides this, Boas delivered a lecture on "Psychological Problems in Anthropology" [18] at the celebration of the twentieth anniversary of Clark University (1909), the historic occasion when G. Stanley Hall invited Freud, Jung, Ferenczi, and Jones, to participate. Lowie says, moreover, that Boas "unremittingly preached the necessity of seeing the native from within" [153, p. 1009], and Benedict has remarked that to him one of the central questions of anthropology was "the relation between the objective world and man's subjective world as it had taken form in different cultures" [15, p. 27].

Perhaps it was no accident that the pioneers in the study of culture and personality—Sapir, Benedict, and Mead—were trained in anthropology by Boas and that early students like Goldenweiser, Haeberlin, Radin, and Lowie were psychologically knowledgeable.[4] At an early date too, Sapir, Goldenweiser, Radin, and Kroeber familiarized themselves with psychoanalytic theory.[5] Kroeber has reported that he practiced psychoanalysis in San Francisco from 1920 to 1923. He says, however, that this experience gave him no insights that helped him "to understand culture any better" [133, p. 300; see also p. 299] and it was the clarification of culture which Kroeber considered "the most significant accomplishment of anthropology in the first half of the twentieth century" [132, p. 87]. Indeed, he showed no enthusiam for the culture and personality studies that emerged later and wrote a negatively toned review (1920) of Freud's *Totem and Taboo* which reflected the general anthropological attitude of the time.[6] Eventually, however, it was an early phase of psychoanalytic theory that inspired culture and personality studies.

Perhaps I have said enough, however sketchily, to indicate that— although psychological problems lurked in the background of anthropological thinking, and some anthropologists reacted strongly to psychological theories—no positive focus emerged to link anthropological and psychological concepts and theories during the period when both disciplines were developing their characteristic abstractions, concepts, and specializations. Since the concept of culture has always implied inherent behavioral plasticity and emphasized socially acquired traits as

[4] Haeberlin published an article on Wundt in the *Psychological Review* (1916), and Goldenweiser, besides making frequent references to Wundt in his writings, published an obituary notice in *The Freeman* (1921). For more explicit details, see [75, pp. 184, 188–189]. For other references to articles written in the twenties by Goldenweiser and Lowie representing their interest in the relations of psychology to the social sciences, see [75, p. 161]. Writing in England, Haddon observes that "in the United States of America, thanks to the influence of Boas, psychology has been well recognized by students as an essential factor in ethnology" [71, p. 68].

[5] For references to Sapir's book reviews, see [75, p. 204], for Goldenweiser's articles [75, p. 161]. In 1929, Radin expressed the opinion that "it is the application of the psychoanalytic theories of Jung that is most likely to have the most profound influence upon ethnology" [see 75, p. 208]—a prediction that has not been fulfilled.

[6] Kroeber's original review of *Totem and Taboo*, which appeared in the *American Anthropologist*, was succeeded by a later one in the *American Journal of Sociology* (1939). Both are reprinted in his collected papers [133]. He closes the 1939 review by saying that if he may speak for ethnologists, the latter "though remaining unconverted, have met Freud, recognize the encounter as memorable, and herewith salute him."

opposed to innate characters, anthropologists were inclined to react negatively to psychological concepts or theories which stressed innate behavioral determinants. This has been true with respect to all varieties of instinct doctrines. It was also an immediate barrier to the acceptance of certain aspects of orthodox psychoanalytic theory in its early stages. The same attitude emerged in the critical appraisal of intelligence tests as direct indexes to innate factors, particularly when such tests were used to measure the capacities of people with a cultural background different from our own. For the same reason, most anthropologists have been skeptical of anything that savors of racial or constitutional psychology. As a matter of fact, there were anthropologists of an older generation who held the position explicitly stated by Lowie in 1917:

. . . [Since] culture is, indeed, the sole and exclusive subject matter of ethnology, as consciousness is the subject matter of psychology, the science of psychology, even in its most modern ramifications of abnormal psychology, and the study of individual variations, does not grapple with *acquired* traits nor with the influence of *society* on individual thought, feeling and inclination. It deals on principle exclusively with *innate* traits of the individual [149, pp. 5, 16].[7]

Brewster Smith has also observed, "what runs through an otherwise heterogeneous history [of psychology] is a pervading focus on the individual" [217, p. 33]. It can thus be appreciated why it was difficult to bridge the gap between anthropology and psychology in any very positive fashion until recently.

As a matter of historical fact, it was not until the emergence of social psychology in its contemporary form that there was a shift in emphasis within psychology itself. Asch says:

The idea of such a discipline [involved the] culmination of a series of great changes in thinking about nature and society [and] in part a reaction against the narrowness of a general psychology which found no place in its scheme for some of the most essential properties of men. The scientific psychology from which it sprang restricted its observations to the relations between an individual and an environment that strictly excluded other persons; it was not concerned with relations between persons or between persons and groups. The movement toward a social psychology represented an insistence

[7] Wissler [250], in his address as chairman of Section H, AAAS, in 1915 expressed a similar viewpoint. "Psychologists," he said, "give their attention to innate phenomena, especially man's psychophysical equipment. If we extend the meaning of the term behavior so as to include consciousness, we may say that psychologists are concerned with the behavior of man as an individual." Both Wissler and Lowie served as chairmen of the Division of Anthropology and Psychology of the National Research Council. Wissler pursued his graduate work at Columbia under J. McKeen Cattell and had a Ph.D. in psychology (1901). He took some courses with Boas during his last year of graduate studies.

that these major and neglected parts of human psychology be taken seriously. It stood for the belief that no psychology can be complete that fails to look directly at man as a social being [7, p. 364].

At the same time, twentieth-century anthropologists were preoccupied with their own abstractions and conceptualizations. As they became more and more immersed in the study of culture, its analysis, functioning, and variant forms, they receded farther and farther from any direct concern with the actual behavior of individuals.[8] In contrast with traditional academic psychologists, psychoanalysts, and psychiatrists (whose emphasis was on the concrete behavior of the ever-present individual in the laboratory or on the couch or in the clinic or hospital), the abstractions of anthropologists led them into the realm of the description and comparison of the different cultural attributes of human societies.

It was a departure from traditional anthropology when some anthropologists in the twenties and thirties began to devote attention to the relations between cultural differences and the life history and personality organization of individuals in nonliterate societies. In its early days, as Singer says, "the field of culture and personality theory and research was considered an American heresy in anthropology." He adds, "Today it is no longer a heresy, and in a few more years it will no longer be distinctively American" [216, p. 9]. This movement arose from an appreciation of psychoanalytic personality theory, with its emphasis upon the vital importance of childhood experiences on the life history of the individual. However, these experiences were viewed by anthropologists in the setting of the entire culture in which the child was raised rather than in the narrower one of the family circle.[9] Instead of highlighting the customs, values, and institutions of a society and subordinating the individuals as psychologically undifferentiated *bearers* of a culture, they considered human beings as differentiated personalities for whom the culture specified patterns and values of social behavior and whose personality structure it molded in a characteristic way. Academic psy-

---

[8] The logical extreme of this line of thinking is represented by Leslie White's "culturology." "Culture thus becomes a continuum of extrasomatic elements," he says. "It moves in accordance with its own principles, its own laws; it is a thing *sui generis*" [248, p. 374]. "Relative to the culture process the individual is neither creator nor determinant; he is merely a catalyst and a vehicle of expression" [249, p. 80]. At the other pole, Radin, who published "The Autobiography of an American Indian" in 1920 [181], was a pioneer in the personal-document approach in anthropology [75, p. 204].

[9] See Rapaport [183, p. 102] for a discussion of the "Psychosocial Point of View" in psychoanalytic theory. He points out that although "the social determination of behavior is not alien to classic psychoanalytic theory, [at first] these social conceptions were not generalized into an explicit psychoanalytic social psychology" [see also 138].

chology was also soon drawn upon by a number of investigators to supply the model for a learning theory useful in studying the acquisition of culture in the socialization process.[10]

We are only now beginning to see the wider implications of this new movement. It has, in fact, sharply refocused attention upon the old problem of the social nature of man.[11] Concrete studies of the social relations of individuals in particular societies have been the basis for new hypotheses. These have considered the relations of culture to the psychodynamics of the individual as an integral part of organized systems of social action, and they have added new dimensions to the study of the social nature of man as he was more abstractly conceived in the past. The psychological aspects of the problem are being more explicitly formulated than ever before; in addition, they have been reinforced by the revitalization of social psychology following World War II. Brewster Smith has observed that the culture and personality movement "was thus an attempt to join together what should never have been held asunder in the first place" [217, p. 56]. And, more recently, Bert Kaplan has expressed the opinion that this field "stands at the crossroads of many of the most important problems of both individual and societal functioning" [122, p. 1]. In his *Epilogue*, he goes so far as to say that "the one prediction I feel most secure in making is that the [culture and personality] field as a whole will gradually encompass more and more of the central issues of man's existence and his efforts at control and transformation and will become, finally, the vital center of a future science of man."

For anthropology there have also been latent and very complex psychological problems inherent in the concept of culture itself as it was defined by Tylor in his *Primitive Culture* (1871): "Culture, or civilization . . . is that complex whole which includes knowledge, belief, art, law, morals, custom, and any other capabilities and habits acquired by man as a member of society" [cf. 135]. This classic definition was focused on the products of behavioral interaction in society, not on behavior itself. From that time on, anthropologists took it for granted that cultures are transmitted from generation to generation—without examining the

[10] E.g., Mowrer and Kluckhohn [160]. They explicitly state at the beginning of their exposition of a "Dynamic Theory of Personality" that they have drawn upon "three relatively independent lines of scientific development: psychoanalysis, social anthropology, and the psychology of learning." The learning theory used is of the S-R type.

[11] Allport writes: "Our intellectual ancestors, for all their fumbling, were asking precisely the same question we are asking today. How does one generation, they wanted to know, impose its culture and its thought-forms upon the next? What happens to the mental life of the individual when he enters into association with others? And long before social psychology became a science political philosophers sought an answer to the question, *What is the social nature of man?*" [5, p. 3].

process. Similarly, the diffusion of culture and the impact of the culture of one people on another (acculturation) were studied without an analysis of the psychological processes involved [12]. Broadly stated, what culture and personality studies did was to focus attention on the integral aspects of the primary process in human social adaptation by connecting the established facts of cultural variability and patterning with the psychological processes necessary for the need satisfaction and socialization of the child, the personal adjustment of the adult, and the maintenance of a sociocultural system. The special problems implicit in this whole area of inquiry, the methods employed in the investigation of them, and the results so far reported call for no comment here, since they have been widely discussed elsewhere [216, 74, 75, 101, 122, 235a].

If culture and personality studies have had any wider significance than their value as case studies, it lies in the fact that by directing attention to the conditions under which primary processes in human adjustment occur, they raised further questions of general anthropological and psychological interest. Mainly, these investigations have been concerned with specific differences in personality structure and functioning which can be shown to be related to cultural differences. But implicit in these data are indications that universal dynamic processes are involved —processes which are related to the psychobiological nature of modern man as a species. There are implications of capacities which must be related to generic psychological attributes of Homo sapiens that have deep roots in the evolutionary process. All human individuals, through learning, become psychologically structured for participation in discrete sociocultural systems. On the other hand, the hominids, considered psychobiologically as an evolving group of primates, became the "creators" of culture in the generic sense.

In conventional terminology, the psychological dimension of evolution has long been phrased as the evolution of "mind." But this terminology reflects the mentalistic concepts of an older period of psychology in which "mind," "intelligence," and "reason" were key terms. The fact that the psychological organization of the human being is just as much a function of his membership in an organized social group as it is a function of his inherited organic equipment was overlooked. John Dewey [51] emphasized this point prior to the initiation of culture and personality studies and before social psychology had assumed its present form. He said in 1917, "What we call 'mind' means essentially the working of certain beliefs and desires, and these in the concrete—in the only sense in which mind may be said to *exist*—are functions of associated behavior varying with the structure and operation of social groups." Thus, instead of being viewed as "an antecedent and ready-made thing," mind "represents a reorganization of original activities through their operation in a given environment. It is a formation, not a datum, a product and a cause only after it has been produced."[12]

One of the seminal contributions of the psychoanalysts—daily faced with people needing help in readjusting to their life situations—was hypothesizing a model of personality organization which was conceptualized in "structural" terms. Whether we accept their particular model or not, it has proved useful in clinical practice. It has also been helpful in analyzing the dynamics of human behavior in sociocultural contexts of all sorts. In phylogenetic perspective, the psychoanalytic model of personality structure suggests that one of the things we must account for in human evolution is a generic type of personality organization which did not exist at the earliest hominid level, not simply a "human mind" in the abstract. In the psychoanalytic model, the "rationality" of the human mind is counterbalanced by an irrationality linked with biologically rooted forces which are intelligible in an evolutionary perspective. In adopting the genetic point of view, psychoanalysts have shown concern for the universal process in the ontogenetic experiences of mankind which, in Freud's thinking in particular, were closely related to phylogenetic developments. In consequence, evolution has always assumed a prominent position in the structure of psychoanalytic theory [183, pp. 60, 69].

In principle, of course, anthropologists, like academic psychologists and psychoanalysts, have always been oriented to man as a whole. Consequently, explicit or implicit assumptions have been made about the nature of man. For a long period, anthropologists have assumed a psychic unity in man (i.e., Homo sapiens), although this has remained a vague concept. It has been one of the assumptions underlying the idea that all cultural and linguistic data are inherently comparable; it underlies the notion that all races and peoples have the same capacity for cultural development and are equally capable of readjustment through culture change. Although Kroeber [131, p. 619] some years ago recorded his impression that "psychologists have become very unwilling to discuss the inherent psychic nature of man,"[13] Asch asserts that "it is the goal of psychology to furnish a comprehensive doctrine of man, one that will

[12] Allport observes: "What was formerly ascribed to the mind of the *Volk* [i.e., ethnic psychology] is now largely subsumed under the current concept of *culture*. 'Personality in culture' promises to be a far more productive concept than 'the mind of the group' has been" [5, p. 37].

[13] He thinks that while the psychic unity of man "cannot be considered to be either a proved fact or an axiomatic principle . . . it is so overwhelmingly borne out by the run of total experience that the anthropologist or the sociologist feels warranted in assuming the principle of essential psychic unity as at least a sufficient approximation to truth, and to employ it as a working hypothesis, or at any rate as a convenient symbol" [131, p. 573].

provide a tested foundation for the social sciences." At the basis of these disciplines, he says, "there must be a comprehensive conception of human nature" [6, p. 5].[14] Long before this, Radin had asked:

Can we ever arrive at any satisfactory knowledge of what constitutes human nature? To say with Boas and so many ethnologists and sociologists that the culture picture hides this knowledge from us forever is a counsel of despair. Some significant light can surely be obtained, even if today the technique for this type of investigation has not as yet been perfected. Here again, I feel that a psychoanalyst like Jung is on the correct trail [182, p. 267].

Anthropologists have by no means given up in despair. Spiro has discussed psychic unity and human nature in terms of the distinctive characteristics of a human personality structure generic to man.[15] However, discussion about human nature and the psychic unity of man has not confronted the problem in evolutionary terms, despite the fact that both anthropology and psychology assume that modern man is a product of biological evolution. The attributes of man's psychic unity, or his human nature, have remained ambiguous. This is largely because the question of whether such attributes are not themselves the end product of earlier stages of hominid evolution has not been satisfactorily answered. Furthermore, there are other vital questions which cannot be dissociated from the nature of human nature or the psychic unity of man when an evolutionary frame of reference is adopted. For instance, it was not so long ago that the late E. A. Hooton pointed out that considerable "difficulties have been encountered in formulating a scientific definition of man" [104, p. 1]. Does this term apply primarily to Homo sapiens as ordinarily used in the social and psychological sciences; if not, what other extinct genera or species of the hominids are to be included? Are our criteria morphological, or are they behavioral as well?

The recent discovery of new fossil material now requires us to make distinctions in our terminology which are in accord with the paleontological facts. Of the new material, the remains of the Australopithecines are of paramount importance. Their over-all dental morphology conforms to that found in more advanced hominids. And, although their cranial capacity is lower than that of the more advanced hominids, they had achieved bipedal locomotion. Consequently these primates, associated with Villafranchian fauna of Lower Pleistocene date, are now placed

[14] Discussing behaviorism, Asch finds Malinowski's conception of human nature inadequate [6, p. 14]. Malinowski had written: "By human nature we mean the biological determinism which imposes on every civilization and on all individuals in it the carrying out of such bodily functions as breathing, sleep, rest, nutrition, excretion, and reproduction" [155, p. 75].

[15] For a summary of changing opinions in anthropological thinking about human nature, see [216, pp. 16–22].

among the Hominidae. Structurally and behaviorally they represent an earlier level of hominid development than the Pithecanthropus group, once considered to represent the earliest-known hominid type [105, 144, 145, 147, 242]. We now know that the earliest hominids were small-brained and newly bipedal. Large brains did not announce the advent of hominid evolution, as Sir G. Elliot Smith argued in 1912 and as Sir Arthur Keith did later with reference to Piltdown. "Recent finds of fossil men and other primates," writes Straus, "indicate that it is the brain that was the evolutionary laggard in man's phylogeny; indeed, the studies of Tilly Edinger of the phylogeny of the horse brain suggest that this may well be a general rule in mammalian evolution" [222, p. 370]. Darwin himself remarked, "We must bear in mind the comparative insignificance for classification of the great development of the brain in man" [quoted by Le Gros Clark, 145, p. 192].

In the light of this new knowledge, it is now apparent that the familiar terms "man" and "human" are colloquial terms. They are *not* equivalent to the zoological term *Hominidae* or to the adjectival form *hominid*. The australopithecines were early hominids, but they were not "human" in the sense that we are human. We represent the terminal product of hominid development. It is difficult now to make use of the colloquial term "man" in discussing evolution [144, pp. 6–9]. Our temporal predecessors in the zoological family Hominidae were not all "men" in the usual lay meaning of the term. This indicates a broadening of our knowledge, as well as the reality of the evolutionary process itself. In current zoological classification, the subfamily *Homininae*—as distinguished from the subfamilies *Oreopithecinae* and *Australopithecinae* —serves to differentiate later from earlier groups of hominids. And the term *euhominid* is coming into use to designate "men"—both living and extinct—belonging to the most evolved group of the family Hominidae, the Homininae [see 108, pp. 137, 351, and Glossary; 91]. Most specialists in the taxonomy and phylogeny of the primates are convinced that the australopithecines stand much nearer to the contemporary ancestors of man than any other group of primates.

Contemporary attention has been directed toward a more integral approach to the investigation of personality, society, and culture as observed in Homo sapiens, without reference to the fact that these interdependent variables occur in a species with a complex evolutionary history. Thus the question arises: Can a thorough comprehension of the nature of Homo sapiens be achieved without the perspective which an evolutionary frame of reference provides? Phylogenetically, we have to consider the gross morphological features which led to the initial hominid radiation and subsequent changes, such as the expansion of the brain, which imply important behavioral and psychological consequences. Ontogenetically, we have to consider the question of neoteny and the social and psychological consequences of an extended period of dependency and the lengthening of the life span. Socioculturally, we have to consider the social structures observed in living nonhominid primates in relation to the evolution of social organization in the hominids which eventuated in the cultural mode of adaptation familiar to us in Homo sapiens. The properties of nonlinguistic systems of communication and their relations to the attribute of speech in Homo sapiens are also relevant. Viewed ecologically, hominid adaptation—as compared with that of most other primates—is terrestrial; this involves questions concerning a change in food habits, the development of technology, and the localization of social groups and their interrelations (territorialism).

Since culture, in the generic sense, has been said by anthropologists to be the crucial attribute that differentiates man from other primates, we must inquire whether all aspects of culture as observed in Homo sapiens came into being together at an early hominid stage. Did the australopithecines manufacture tools, speak, pray, exercise property rights, draw, paint, and recognize moral values? Is there any relation between the expansion of the brain and cultural adaptation? Are "half-brained" hominids as capable of cultural adaptation as those with an expanded cortex? Is speech a necessary condition for the earliest phases of cultural adaptation? And is there any relation between toolmaking, as contrasted with tool using, and speech? Do nonhominid primates show any traces of what has been called "culture" in Homo sapiens? And what of psychological structure? What kind of psychological capacities and mechanisms underlie a cultural mode of adjustment? And what is the relation between the development of systems of social action in the primates and the emergence of cultural systems characterized by a normative orientation?

In this paper I have attempted to give the broad outlines of a *conjunctive* approach to human evolution. The organic, psychological, social, and cultural dimensions of the evolutionary process are taken into account as they are related to underlying conditions that are necessary and sufficient for a human level of existence. I have also devoted some attention to earlier opinions to bring into sharper focus the problems that need reconsideration in the light of contemporary knowledge. "Behavioral evolution" is, perhaps, the term which best defines the framework of a conjunctive approach. "Evolution" implies connected and continuing processes of change and development in behavior as well as structure. Biologists too are taking an increasing interest in behavioral evolution [191]. Some years ago, Nissen remarked that "one of the weakest links in the sciences dealing with evolution, the one most needed to strengthen its facts and theoretical framework is that dealing with behavior" [169, p.

106]. It is in behavioral perspective that we can best conceptualize the major categories of variables to be examined to determine the evolutionary status of Homo sapiens. Whether we consider hominid evolution ecologically, socially, psychologically, or linguistically, behavior is the unifying center to which we must return at each adaptive level. As we proceed to higher levels, we must consider new integrations of determinants brought about by potentialities for behavioral adaptations that did not previously exist, for example, the consequences of bipedal locomotion, the adoption of new food habits, the use and manufacture of tools, the expansion of the brain, the effects of a new level of pyschological integration in the later hominids, and the role of speech in the symbolic mediation and social relations. In the evolutionary process, differential behavior patterns provide major clues to significant variables. Modern man represents a late stage in a complex chain of evolutionary events. His "human" nature and the varieties of psychological and cultural adjustments that we observe in culture and personality studies imply capacities that must be related to generic properties of Homo sapiens which have a long evolutionary history of their own.

Any attack on problems of behavioral evolution, of course, has inherent methodological difficulties. A direct observational approach at all stages is not possible. For the past, we can only make inferences and deductions from nonbehavioral data. But we can observe and compare the behavior of different species of living primates—with full appreciation of the fact that they represent their own specialized modes of adaptation. In the case of the hominids, archeological data provide us with both material products and the consequences of social interaction as it is expressed in traditional usage (where the manufacture of tools can be established). But the archeologist is not concerned with the problem of behavioral evolution. His attention is chiefly directed to the forms, distributions, and temporal relations of objects; from this, the early cultures of the euhominids can be inferred. Questions of behavioral evolution, on the other hand, force us to look behind the tool and ask questions which neither the archeologist nor the physical anthropologist can answer by a direct appeal to his data. Tools as products of behavior raise questions of another order. To account for a toolmaking tradition or the lack of one, we have to consider the psychobiological capacities which are a necessary condition of toolmaking; intervening variables have to be inferred. Such problems must be faced sooner or later; indeed, behavioral criteria frequently have been invoked in dealing with questions of human evolution, but there has not been sufficient discussion of the psychological implications. Inevitably there will be different interpretations of the facts of behavioral evolution, but the areas of dispute will be narrowed with the accumulation of new data.

THE PSYCHOCULTURAL DIMENSION OF EVOLUTION

Darwinism helped to define and shape the problems of modern psychology as it did those of anthropology. An evolution of "mind" within the natural world of living organisms was envisaged. Now a bridge could be built to span the deep and mysterious chasm that separated man from other animals which, according to Descartian tradition, must forever remain unbridged. Darwin himself explicitly set processes of reasoning, long considered an exclusively human possession, in an evolutionary perspective and advanced an evolutionary interpretation of the facial and postural changes of man when expressing emotion [46, 47].[16] He argued that mental differences in the animal series present gradations that are quantitative rather than qualitative in nature.

To A. R. Wallace, on the other hand, the evolution of the brain represented a sharp mutational development in man that permitted adaptive capacities far beyond those necessary for survival on a primitive level of human existence. He had had more intimate contacts with primitive peoples than Darwin, and was immensely impressed with their abilities. The position he took was a challenge to Darwin's theory of natural selection. "Natural Selection," Wallace wrote, "could only have endowed the savage with a brain a little superior to that of an ape, whereas he actually possesses one but very little inferior to that of the average members of our learned societies" [quoted in 56, p. 63]. Eiseley points out that, in 1864, Wallace "set forth the idea that with the rise of man, natural selection was ceasing to act upon the body and was coming to act almost solely upon the human intelligence. Man, he contended, was old and had attained the upright posture long before the final changes in the skull and brain which characterize our living species. Other animals had continued to change and modify under evolutionary pressure; in man, by contrast, all but mental evolution has largely ceased" [56; cf. 57, p. 306].

Although Darwin was later accused of gross anthropomorphism by some of his critics, he stimulated scholars to think and write about mental evolution. On the other hand, Wallace's views were discounted because, in the end, he fell back upon a theological explanation. Romanes, a disciple of Darwin, coined the term "comparative psychology,"[17] and it was not long before a phylogenetic dimension had been added to the program of scientific psychology.

---

[16] [Cf. 236.] Margaret Mead relates Darwin's work to the developing interest in "the non-verbal aspects of human communication—the new science of kinesics."

[17] His *Animal Intelligence* [193], published in 1883, "is the first comparative psychology that was ever written, and its author used this term believing that comparative psychology would come to rank alongside of comparative anatomy in importance" [20, p. 473].

In its early stages, comparative psychology had little interest for anthropologists. Psychologists, in reaction against anecdotalism, demanded more rigorously controlled observations; lower mammals, such as the rat, and insects, became preferred laboratory subjects. Observational results, even though highly reliable, did not throw much light on the phylogenetic roots of human psychology. It was only when laboratory studies of infrahuman primates, like the chimpanzee, initiated by Yerkes, Köhler, and Schultz, developed to a high point that they engaged anthropological interest [252, pp. 289–301]. Henry Nissen's [165] pioneer field observations of the chimpanzee were published in 1931; the studies of C. R. Carpenter [25, 26, 27, 28] on New and Old World monkeys and the gibbon followed shortly. A new body of information on nonhominid primates began to accumulate. We now have reliable data on a few samples of the ecology and organization of primate societies [for bibliography to 1957, see 31] supplementing behavioral observations made under laboratory conditions. At the present time, experimental research on nonhominid primates is also expanding [e.g., 82, p. 273]. While hitherto both kinds of studies were made by psychologists, a few anthropologists (e.g., Imanishi, Washburn, and De Vore) have now begun to study nonhominid primates in the field.

Also under the stimulus of Darwin's ideas as applied to man historians, economists, sociologists, linguists, cultural anthropologists, and others began to apply evolutionary ideas to human institutions on a wide scale. Language, religion, art, marriage and the family, law, and economic organization were studied comparatively to discover whether orderly development sequences could be established. These efforts, however, were chiefly confined to developments in a single species of the Hominidae—Homo sapiens. Fossil material and archeological remains were scanty at the time, and field studies of nonhominid primates living in their native state were nonexistent. Besides, the evolutionary hypothesis was closely linked with the older idea of progress as it was applied by social scientists and humanists. This reinforced the reconstruction of series of unilinear stages which more or less paralleled the concept of orthogenesis in biology. In this form, theories of social and cultural evolution persisted into the early years of this century.

Since it was assumed that processes of evolution were not confined to the organic sphere alone, a corollary psychological question arose in conjunction with the attempts to establish the stages of cultural evolution in man's long struggle from savagery to civilization. Could it not be shown that in the cultures of present-day nonliterate peoples there was mirrored a reflection of primitive mind? J. G. Frazer, who adhered to the recapitulation theory, was among those who explicitly linked this problem with the generic question of mental evolution. He thought that ethnographic data were relevant, as were studies of the ontogenetic development of the child and of patients in mental hospitals. He said that "this comparative study of the mind of man is thus analogous to the comparative study of his body which is undertaken by anatomy and physiology" [65, p. 586].[18] But when unilinear stages of cultural evolution were rejected by most twentieth-century anthropologists, the notion of "primitive mind" as applied to nonliterate peoples collapsed with them. The conclusion was drawn that culture change and development in Homo sapiens is not primarily linked with an evolution in mentality. Outside of anthropology, the more inclusive concept of genetically determined mental evolution—in so far as it was based on the theory of recapitulation in its original extreme form—became generally defunct with the rejection of this theory by biologists [48, chap. 1; 75, pp. 167–170; 76, chap. 2].

Wayne Dennis has written—

. . . it would not be inaccurate to say that developmental psychology began with a theory—the theory of recapitulation. Child psychology, the most productive segment of developmental psychology, began shortly after the promulgation of the theory of evolution when all scientific minds were inflamed by this great conceptual achievement [50, p. 2].

But after the movement had arrived at the "concise hypothesis" that "ontogeny recapitulates phylogeny," its decline was imminent. "The evolutionary viewpoint had seemed to open up wide unconquered vistas to child psychology. On closer approach, these beckoning plains proved to be inhabited only by insubstantial figures and retreating will-o'-the-wisps. There was not a testable hypothesis in the entire landscape." While some psychologists of an older generation—men like G. Stanley Hall and J. M. Baldwin—had adopted the theory of recapitulation and made it an integral part of their thinking, as did Frazer and Freud, this working hypothesis is not a necessary assumption of "developmental psychology." Heinz Werner [244, p. 3] points out that the concept—

. . . is perfectly clear if this term is understood to mean a science concerned with the development of mental life and determined by a specific method [i.e., the observation of psychologists, when they employ this term, refers only to ontogenesis] . . . . The mental development of the individual is, however, but one theme in genetic psychology. [Related to it] is the developmental study of larger social unities, a field of interest intimately linked with anthropology and best known by the name of *ethnopsychology*. The question of the development of the human mentality, if not arbitrarily limited, must lead further to an investigation of the relation of man to animal and, in consequence, to an *animal psychology* oriented according to developmental theory [244, p. 3].

[18] In this paper Frazer expresses a preference for "the more general name of mental anthropology," rather than "social anthropology" for the division of the subject in which he worked.

Thus the psychological dimension of evolution, which to Darwin was an integral part of the total evolutionary process and of vital significance for our comprehension of man's place in nature, fell into abeyance.

It is true that animal psychologists continued to investigate some problems comparatively; but special areas of investigation, such as learning behavior in rats, emerged into the foreground, while a primary focus on evolutionary questions as such receded. Schneirla, in a review of trends in comparative psychology, emphasizes the fact that "most American animal psychologists at present seem to be *really* non-evolutionary minded, in the sense that they show no special zeal to find how man differs mentally from lower animals and vice versa, but rather focus strenuously on general problems without much attention to phyletic lines" [204, p. 563].

In anthropology, the rejection of nineteenth-century unilinear theories of cultural evolution, along with the notion of a demonstable level of primitive mentality in Homo sapiens, meant that evolution, once so inclusively conceived, was effectively reduced to investigations in the area of physical anthropology. Physical anthropologists, moreover, concerned themselves chiefly with morphological problems, not behavior. Only recently has a shift in interest become apparent. J. S. Weiner, reader in physical anthropology at Oxford, in an appraisal of the field, writes:

> There is one large baffling topic on which our evolutionary insight still remains very meagre—the emergence of the peculiar attributes of human intelligence, temperament, and social organization. Wide as the morphological gap is between men and apes, we know there are distant ancestral links between them. How far is this apparent also in the working of the brain, and in behavior? . . . It remains an unfortunate fact that of all aspects of physical anthropology this one, which carries so much promise to the sociologist and social psychologist no less than to the human biologist, should at the present time be the most neglected of all fields of study [243, pp. 34–35].[19]

At the same time, the fact that so many twentieth-century anthropologists were preoccupied with culture led to a somewhat paradoxical situation. While continuing to give lip service to organic evolution, they held a crucial evolutionary issue in abeyance. Culture was taken for

[19] Cf. the investigations of ethologists, reviewed by Hinde [95]. Lashley in his introduction to the classical papers of the ethologists, *Instinctive Behavior* [200], notes on p. ix: "They have traced patterns of instinctive activity among related species and have shown that behavior may be as clear an index of phylogenetic relationship as are physical structures." In contrast with American psychologists, these zoologists have focused their attention upon instinctive rather than learned behavior, and their observations have been made in the field rather than the laboratory. The chief animal groups studied so far have been invertebrates and lower vertebrates [see also 228, 229].

446   A. IRVING HALLOWELL

granted and stressed as the unique possession of Homo sapiens and of earlier types of hominines, dating far back to the Pleistocene. The chief evidence was the association of tools with these early euhominids. In the 1920s, Kroeber's paper on "Sub-human Cultural Beginnings" [129] was practically unique. So far as Homo sapiens was concerned, it was assumed that all living races possessed equally the necessary psychological capacities for acquiring culture. Culture, as an attribute of all human societies, was abstracted and studied as such. Culture "traits," "complexes," and "patterns" became key terms. This preoccupation with culture led to a *re*-creation of the old gap between man and the other primates—the gap which, it had been thought, the adoption of an evolutionary frame of reference would bridge. The repeated emphasis given to speech and culture as *unique* characteristics of man sidestepped the essence of the evolutionary problem.[20] Distinctive characteristics of the most highly evolved primate were asserted without any reference to the prior capabilities, conditions, or events in the evolutionary process that made these distinctive characteristics possible. For unless culture and speech be conceived as sudden and radical emergents, they must be rooted in behavioral processes which cannot be considered apart from behavioral evolution any more than the distinctive structural characteristics of man can be considered apart from morphological evolution. Unless the nature of such linkages is established, one must ask how far the emphasis on distinctive attributes of man has advanced understanding of his evolutionary position in the animal series beyond the descriptive epithets of an earlier day. One thinks of such characterizations of man as the rational animal, the toolmaking animal, the cooking animal, the laughing animal, the animal who makes pictures, or *animal symbolicus*. All these characterizations stress man's differences from other living creatures. Like the criteria of culture and speech, they emphasize discontinuity rather than the continuity inherent in the evolutionary process.

A statement made by Carpenter a few years ago clearly articulates an opposition to any such sharp descriptive dichotomization between man and other primates. He said he found untenable a number of assumptions that seemed acceptable to many of his colleagues. One of these was that "the phenomena known as 'mind,' language, society, culture and 'values' exist exclusively on the level of human evolution" [30, p.

---

[20] The emphasis on uniqueness has an analogy in earlier discussions of man's biological status. "The opposition to Darwin's thesis of the evolutionary origin of man," Le Gros Clark points out, "naturally led his critics to search for anatomical characters in which the human body could be said to be 'unique,' thus providing arguments for removing man in any system of classification as far as possible from other mammals (especially the apes). In some cases, indeed, these arguments were pushed to an extreme of absurdity, which today we are apt to find rather astonishing" [145, p. 186]. Reference is made to the wrangle over "hippocampus minor."

93]. And Hebb and Thompson say that "exposure to a group of adult chimpanzees gives one the overwhelming conviction that one is dealing with an essentially human set of attitudes and motivations" [90, p. 543]. Thus, while cultural anthropologists have continued to render formal homage to the idea of evolution, its significance has not been actively pursued. The statements of Carpenter and Hebb and Thompson should remind us that there remain crucial evolutionary questions which transcend the old problem of unilinear stages of cultural development in Homo sapiens and the morphological problems dealt with by physical anthropologists.

Some years ago Le Gros Clark, referring to the question of the zoological classification of the australopithecines, said:

Taxonomic difficulties of this sort, of course, are bound to arise as discoveries are made of fossils of a seemingly transitional type, and with the increasing perfection of the fossil record, probably the differentiation of man from ape will ultimately have to rest on a functional rather than an anatomic basis, the criterion of humanity being the ability to speak and make tools [143, p. 73].

We must ask, then, what special capacities and conditions underlie the phenomena of speaking and toolmaking. Effective use of such criteria is hardly possible without considering what these capacities and conditions may be. For, as Nissen observes, "To say that man differs from the other primates in his capacity for tool-making and language is not very useful until we have identified the mechanisms and processes which produce these complex end results" [169, p. 102]. We cannot depend on the evidence from human paleontology and archeology alone. In so far as speech is concerned, it is now known that reliable inferences cannot be made from brain anatomy [188, p. 92]. Furthermore, it seems doubtful that speech as observed in Homo sapiens possesses properties as a system of communication which can be treated as a phenomenal unity in phylogenetic perspective. The question is: How far can speech actually be projected into the past? Do we not have to know more than we now know about the properties of nonlinguistic systems of communication at subhuman levels in order to understand the position of speech in behavioral evolution?

Critchley notes that Sir Arthur Keith "believed that the faculty of speech could be traced back as far as Neanderthal man, but no further," although his anatomical evidence was not very convincing [42, p. 304]. On the other hand, L. S. Palmer, "basing his opinion upon the anatomical characteristics of the mandible," argues that perhaps the australopithecines could speak. The kind of evidence advanced in both instances seems even more indirect than older inferences from the details of endocranial casts, regarding which F. Weidenreich once said that this sort of evidence is no more reliable than any other form of phrenology. However, it is of some interest to note that whereas in the past speech was often given great historical depth, in recent years it is being argued by some [e.g., J. B. S. Haldane, 72, and R. J. Pumphrey, 180] that it is a very, *very* recent development. What may prove to be a more positive approach to the anatomical basis of the evolution of speech has been followed by Du Bruhl [53], who has considered the anatomical changes in the oral anatomy brought about by erect posture. Reviewing this author's book, H. L. Shapiro says:

Standing erect, he shows, shortened the length of the oral cavity, increased its angulation with the neurocranium, moved forward the foramen magnum and along with it, the position of the throat. These adaptive modifications, resulting from postural changes, have limited the space between chin and throat and have led to a drastic alteration in the laryngo-velar relations. As an accidental by-product of these anatomical arrangements, expelled air has been given access to the oral cavity where the formation of distinctive and varied sounds becomes possible through tongue movements established in feeding habits. Invoking "opportunism" and the "selective premium" of established neural mechanisms put to the new use of speech, Du Bruhl offers a concept that envisages the possibility that speech could have evolved at a very early stage of hominid evolution [214].

In Schneirla's [204, p. 582] opinion, an adequate comparative study of group communicative behavior "is long overdue, particularly to clarify the relationships of concepts such as 'sign,' 'signal,' and 'symbol,' as well as the criteria of 'language,' all of which appear to suffer from a heavy load of speculation and a minimum of systematic research" [cf. 41; 24, p. 156 ff]. Perhaps expanding research in the area of "paralanguage" in man, as defined by Trager [231], may provide some new leads.

Hockett has recently pointed out that—

. . . part of the problem of differentiating Man from the other animals is the problem of describing how human language differs from any kind of communicative behavior carried on by non-human or pre-human species. Until we have done this, we cannot know how much it means to assert that only Man has the power of speech [97, p. 570].

He has approached the problem by identifying seven "key properties" of the speech of Homo sapiens and comparing them with the available data on nonhuman systems of communication. Hockett discovered that there was considerable overlapping in the properties selected, although they did "not recur, as a whole set, in any known non-human communicative system" [97, p. 574]. This suggests that the combination of properties that characterize speech, those "design-features" which "seem to be of crucial importance in making it possible for language to do what it does" [98, p. 32], did not arise full blown. It is argued that this assemblage of properties, as related to man's lineage, "could not have emerged in just any temporal sequence. Some of them either unquestionably or with high likelihood imply the prior existence of some of the others" [97, p. 581]. Consequently, Hockett is led to suggest a tentative evolutionary reconstruction.

In a later article (1960) which is illustrated by many clearly designed charts and tables, Hockett says:

Although the comparative method of linguistics, as has been shown, throws no light on the origin of language, the investigation may be furthered by a comparative method modeled on that of the zoologist. The frame of reference must be such that all languages look alike when viewed through it, but such that within it human language as a whole can be compared with the communicative systems of other animals, especially the other hominoids, man's closest living relatives, the gibbons and great apes. The useful items for this sort of comparison cannot be things such as the word for "sky"; languages have such words, but gibbon calls do not involve words at all. Nor can they be even the signal for "danger," which gibbons do have. Rather, they must be the basic features of design that can be present or absent in any communicative system, whether it be a communicative system of humans, of animals or of machines [99, p. 89].

In his earliest paper, the author identified seven design features. In this article he discusses thirteen.

It is probably safe to assume that nine of the thirteen features were already present in the vocal-auditory communication of the protohominids—just the nine that are securely attested for the gibbons and humans of today. That is, there were a dozen or so distinct calls, each the appropriate vocal response (or vocal part of the whole response) to a recurrent and biologically important type of situation: the discovery of food, the detection of a predator, sexual interest, need for maternal care, and so on. The problem of the origin of speech, then, is that of trying to determine how such a system could have developed the four additional properties of displacement, productivity and full-blown traditional transmission. Of course, the full story involves a great deal more than communicative behavior alone. The development must be visualized as occurring in the context of the evolution of the primate horde into the primitive society of food-gatherers and hunters, an integral part, but a part, of the total evolution of behavior [99, p. 92].

One of the key properties of a human system of communication is "cultural transmission,"[21] a property absent in the communication sys-

---

[21] Hockett [98, p. 36] says: "A behavior pattern is transmitted culturally if it is not only learned but taught, and if the teaching behavior, whatever it may be, is also learned rather than genetically transmitted" [97, pp. 579–580].

tems of primates and other animals. This factor becomes highly significant chronologically and, I think, has wider implications than those developed by Hockett. He suggests, in effect, that although learning and the social transmission of habits, or what he calls a "thin sort" of culture, may have existed at a very early stage in the development of the higher primates, the associated system of communication that prevailed may have operated without "cultural transmission" [97, p. 36]. In other words, what I prefer to call a "protocultural" stage may have been chronologically prior to speech but not, of course, to some other system of communication. The evolutionary significance of this chronology as adapted to communication lies in the fact that the conditions which permitted a protocultural stage to develop were, at the same time, among the necessary prerequisites of a communication system characterized by the total assemblage of properties considered by Hockett.

This kind of evolutionary inquiry is, of course, a far cry from earlier approaches, particularly those which began by concentrating on the problem of "primitive" languages spoken by Homo sapiens. These proved as fruitless as attempts to discover evidence of "primitive mind" in our species. These failures, however, may have helped to expose genuine evolutionary problems more clearly. Hockett's approach permits us to have a fresh look at speech in greater evolutionary depth. And by direct observation, we know that whereas some of the great apes have been able to acquire a "thin sort" of human culture when closely associated with members of our species, they do not have the capacity to acquire and use our distinctive form of linguistic communication, even when systematically motivated [e.g., 88, chap. 8]. There seems little reason to doubt that psychological capacities of crucial importance lay back of the ultimate emergence among the hominids of a characteristic system of communication. While this system shared some design features with that of nonhominid primates, capacities that transcended those of other primates permitted the development and integration of novel features. These, in turn, resulted in the functional potentialities of speech as we know it in Homo sapiens.

Man has long been defined as the "toolmaker." Yet if tools are taken as an index of a human status, considerable preliminary analysis is required to make this criterion useful. Oakley [170, 171, 172, 173] has been more precise than previous writers in his *Man, the Tool Maker* [170]. Nevertheless, an English biologist, Pumphrey, has remarked that " 'Subman, the Implement Maker' would have been a more accurate if less impressive title at least for the first half of his book." Pumphrey sees "no valid reason for assigning intellect to a maker of implements. . . . The web of a garden-spider and the nest of a chaffinch are highly fabricated implements," whereas genuine tools, which he thinks cannot be assigned to early members of the Hominidae, "were made in order to make something else with them" [180, pp. 27–28]. Even if we define the tool concept in terms of some very general adaptive function, without further analysis it is not very useful for making distinctions in an evolutionary frame of reference. Bartholomew and Birdsell say, "In contrast to all other mammals, the larger arboreal primates are, in a sense, tool-users in their locomotion [since,] as they move through the maze of the tree tops, their use of branches anticipates the use of tools in that they routinely employ levers and angular movements" [8, pp. 482–483], which is a very broad interpretation of tool using. These authors draw the conclusion, moreover, that "protohominids were dependent on the use of tools for survival."

There is ample evidence that both biologists and psychologists have had their own difficulties in dealing with the question: What constitutes tool-using? [e.g., 166; 227, pp. 109, 332]. And because the phenomenon of "tool using" is not confined to the primates alone, it is necessary to understand the varying factors that underlie what has been called "tool using" in other animals, to interpret properly the phenomenon of tool using in the behavioral evolution of the primates and the differential factors that made tool*making* possible as a unique development within the hominids.

In psychological experiments with infrahominid primates, "instrumentation," as it is usually called, includes piling boxes to secure food, the manipulation of sticks to achieve a similar goal, or pole vaulting. Interestingly, high proficiency in instrumentation under laboratory conditions appears to be a function of previous experience in related situations. Harlow, referring to Köhler's earlier construct of "insight learning," says, "Insightful behavior on instrumentation problems apparently occurs only in animals that have had previous opportunity for experience in related situations" [81, p. 217]. However, it is individual learning rather than social learning that is involved in "tool using" of this order. Sultan's success in "making" a tool was a unique individual achievement. Nissen says, "The nearest thing to the manufacture of tools in the ordinary sense seen in primates is the observation reported by Köhler of a chimpanzee fitting together two short sticks in order to make a long one. This observation has not been repeated" [166, p. 562].

While there would seem to be no question of the capacity of some primates to use tools as a means of achieving a desired goal when sufficiently motivated, this potentiality is only one of the prerequisites for a more highly developed stage of tool using. However, it seems quite likely that, under natural conditions, some rudimentary habits of tool using in the narrower rather than the broadest sense may have been individually learned and socially transmitted in nonhominid or early hominid groups. If so, this would exemplify what I have called a "proto-cultural" stage [77]. Nevertheless, the conditions operative at such a stage in primate groups are not in themselves sufficient to account for the still more advanced level of *toolmaking*. If the latter is invoked as a functional criterion for human status, we need to do more than differentiate between tool using and toolmaking. We must ask whether toolmaking presupposes a higher order of psychological structuralization and functioning than tool using; whether it implies a social system different from that of nonhominid primates, or a different system of communication.[22]

Toolmaking as observed in Homo sapiens is a skilled act—learned in a social context where speech exists and usually performed with reference to a purposeful use at some *future* time. Many years ago, Kroeber noted the chimpanzee's inability "outside of posed problems to manufacture tools or lay them aside for the future" [129, p. 336]. And Linton noted the anticipatory dimension of the human toolmaking situation. "This indicates," he said, "a distinct type of psychology, the realization of operation [sic] in the time stream, which no other animal shows. I think this is the point, actually, where the human mind emerges, even more than in the capacity for reorganization of experience we call 'thinking' " [225, p. 266]. Straus observes, "Man is peculiar in the extent to which he lives in the three dimensions of time. It is this peculiarity that gives use to his remarkable degree of foresight or anticipation which is perhaps best expressed in tool-making, to use this term in its broadest sense" [221, p. 133]. Therefore, when interpreting the archeological evidence, do we not have to make up our minds whether toolmaking necessitates a sense of self-orientation in time—and possibly institutionalized property rights which assure continued control over the tool?

When we have direct evidence of the persistence of characteristic techniques of manufacture and tool styles, as well as evidence of innovation or invention (i.e., a toolmaking tradition), we have indexes to a human level of cultural adaptation. But this involves far more than tool-

---

[22] [See 24.] In 1937, Grace A. de Laguna [49] argued that "it is scarcely credible, even aside from the more theoretical psychological considerations, that the art of chipping stone implements could have been developed by men who had not yet learned to speak." In a later unpublished manuscript, de Laguna has expressed her thought by saying: *"Homo faber is Homo cogitans."* Compare Révész [188, pp. 92–93], who equates *Homo faber* with *Homo loquens.* Compare Vallois, who points out that toolmaking, "un phénomène essentiel de l'hominisation culturelle," undoubtedly was preceded by an earlier stage of utilization . . . "qui n'impliquait encore qu'une hominisation à ses débuts. Les processus qui ont permis la fabrication doivent au contraire correspondre à une cérébralisation déjà avancée ainsi que, peut-être, à un certain usage de la parole. Une telle fabrication suppose en effet l'apparition de nouveaux centres corticaux et de nouvelles connexions sensitivo-motrices. Elle suppose l'idée d'une transmission des techniques d'un individu à un autre" [232, p. 211].

making per se or mere social transmission. Heinz Hartmann, in discussing the "reality principle" in human adaptation, points out that it—

. . . implies something essentially new, namely the familiar *function of anticipating* the future, orienting our actions according to it and correctly relating means and ends to each other. It is an ego function and, surely, an adaptation process of the highest significance. We may assume that ego development enters this process as an independent variable, though naturally the ego function involved may secondarily yield pleasure" [87, pp. 42–43].

If toolmaking is interpreted as an early indication of the reality principle, involving ego functions among other things, a psychological dimension could then be added to our conceptualization of the personality structure of early hominids which would be correlative with the point made by Linton [225, p. 266] and Straus [221, p. 133].

The more perplexing evolutionary problems arise in cases where the material evidence is ambiguous. The problem is particularly difficult where the early hominids responsible for the archeological remains had a smaller cranial capacity than later hominids of the Middle Pleistocene and after. At first, the general opinion prevailed that the bipedal australopithecines of Villafranchian age were not toolmakers, although Dart maintained that, in addition to their hominoid anatomical characters, "they were human in employing skeletal parts to subserve the function of implements in the business of obtaining and preparing . . . food, in getting and dividing it" [44, p. 335]. With the Leakeys' recent discovery of *Zinjanthropus boisei*, however, dated as upper Villafranchian and classified as a new genus of the Australopithecinae [141, 142; cf. 239], the fact of toolmaking in one genus of this group is now established. For, in this case, the discovery is unique in that the hominid remains were excavated from a living site, where they were associated with pebble tools of Oldowan type, along with the broken bones of small animals which had apparently been eaten. Consequently, as Howell says, "the new australopithecine from Olduvai Gorge represents the oldest fully authenticated toolmaker so far known" [106; see also 105].

These new empirical facts serve to sharpen an old question: What is the relation between brain size and the psychological capacities for cultural adaptation as we know it in Homo sapiens? Although no final answer can be given at present, Le Gros Clark, writing prior to the discovery referred to above, has reminded us that the range of variability in the cranial capacity of modern man is very wide (900 cc.–2,300 cc.) and that "while the cranial capacity of fossil hominids can give information on the brain volume, it provides no information on the complexity of organization of the nervous tissue of which it was composed" [147, p. 312; cf. 175]. Oakley raises the question, is it possible that

. . . systematic tool-making arose, not gradually as most nineteenth-century evolutionists led us to imagine, but suddenly and spread rapidly? . . . The earliest tools and weapons would have been improvisations with whatever lay ready to hand. Although the hominids must have begun as occasional tool-users, ultimately they were only able to survive in the face of rigorous natural selection by developing a system of communication among themselves which enabled cultural tradition to take the place of heredity. At this point systematic tool-making replaced casual tool-using, and it may be that this change-over took place in the australopithecine stage. It would not be surprising, in view of the close correlation between culture and cerebral development, if there had been at this stage intense selection in favour of larger brains, with the result that the transition from the small-brained Australopithecus to the larger-brained Pithecanthropus took place in a comparatively short space of time [174, p. 207].

Washburn has indicated that there may be chronological questions that will have to be considered, that is, the sequential development of tool using, toolmaking, speech, and a fully developed cultural mode of adaptation. It may be, he says, that—

tool use requires much less brain than does speech and might have started as soon as the hands were freed from locomotor functions. Oral traditions essential for complicated human society probably were not possible with less than 700 or 800 cc. of brain, and there is no likelihood that elaborate traditions of tool making are possible at lesser capacities, although simple pebble tools might well be [240, p. 432; p. 428, table].

This brief discussion of speech and tools as behavioral criteria of a human status has, I hope, indicated some of the preliminary problems met with in applying them. The evolutionary problem becomes even more complicated if, to begin with, we attempt to operate with the concept of culture as the criterion of a human status—that "complex whole" of Tylor's classic definition which, he said, is acquired by individuals as members of society. How can we apply such an abstract generic concept, derived from empirical observations of a very concrete nature, in any meaningful analysis of the developmental aspects of human evolution and adaptation?

Wissler tried to solve the problem by assuming the phenomenal unity of what he called a "universal pattern" of culture.[23] His solution was reductionistic. He projected this pattern—including speech—full-fledged from the properties he conceived the "germ plasm" to possess. "The pattern for culture is just as deeply buried in the germ plasm of man as the bee pattern in the bee," he said. "The human pattern . . . is a part, if not the whole, of man's inborn behavior. . . . Man builds cultures be-

[23] Referred to by Kroeber as "that seed lightly tossed out by Wissler that has never germinated" [134, p. 198].

cause he cannot help it, there is a *drive* in his protoplasm that carries him forward even against his will" [251, pp. 264–265]. Wissler, however, did not specify any particular genus or species of the Hominidae. He did not say whether the same universal pattern for culture was embedded alike in the genes of Pithecanthropus and Homo, and, at the time he wrote, the problem presented by the australopithecines had not yet arisen. While it is doubtful that any simple biologistic approach to the evolutionary roots of culture can be any more fruitful than preformationistic theories in biology, at the same time it must be recognized that Wissler was grappling with a genuine problem. It seemed clear to him that, despite the plasticity of the behavior of Homo sapiens and the varying traits, complexes, and patterns of different cultures, there were constant and recurrent categories of culture that transcended any particular mode of cultural adaptation.

Thirty years later Kluckhohn, discussing the question of universal categories of culture, pointed out that, although in the earlier history of anthropology there were those who recognized universal categories for a decade or more before Wissler and for an even longer period subsequently—

The attention of anthropologists throughout the world appears to have been directed overwhelmingly to the distinctiveness of each culture and to the differences in human custom as opposed to the similarities. The latter, where recognized, were explained historically rather than in terms of the common nature of man and certain invariant properties in the human situation [127, p. 511].

The point I wish to stress here is that there are inescapable psychological as well as evolutionary questions raised by "cultural universals," once such phenomena are in any way thought to be related to the nature of man and the human situation. Even if we do not accept Wissler's "universal pattern" concept as such or his reductive explanation, he was correct in viewing universals in phylogenetic perspective. Jung's theory of archetypes is focused upon the same problem of universals, couched in psychocultural terms. His remark that man is probably "born with a specifically human mode of (general) behavior and not with that of a hippopotamus or with none at all" [120, p. 436] sounds much like Wissler. Jung's aim in exploring what he has called the "collective" unconscious, as distinguished from the repressed unconscious of Freudian thinking, has been to develop a hypothesis to explain recurrent and presumably generic psychic phenomena which manifest themselves in art, myths, dreams, psychoses, and other ways. *Archetypes* are psychic propensities or dispositions which are part of a human psychobiological heritage seen both in a historical and phylogenetic perspective. How, when, where, and in what particular form archetypes are concretely manifested depends upon many variables [121, pp. 292–294; see also 117]. Jung's reference to Wundt's rejection of Bastian's *Elementarge-danken* as part of a common psychological heritage of man savors of the same attitude that we find expressed by anthropologists concerned more with cultural differences than cultural universals [120, p. 377].

Quite aside from the specific hypotheses of either Wissler or Jung, the fact remains that cultural universals do not find a ready explanation in cultural-historical terms. Furthermore, it seems probable that a closer examination would indicate that some of them, at least, point directly to the functioning of basic features of a human personality structure that would appear to be a necessary condition for the existence of many aspects of cultural adaptation. For instance, categories of Wissler's "universal pattern" were subsequently elaborated by Murdock, who itemized a long list of what he called "common denominators" of culture which occur "in every culture known to history or ethnography" [163, p. 124]. Among the many items he lists is "eschatology." It is a particularly interesting item when its underlying psychological implications are con- sidered. For concepts concerned with a future life, in order to become functionally significant, require a concept of self as being in some sense indestructible and persistent in future time. Consequently, a capacity for self-awareness and self-identification must be assumed as psychological universals. Furthermore, since this future existence of the self requires a locale, a level of personality organization is indicated which not only implies ego functioning but a capacity for symbolizing self in space, as well as in time [cf. 76, p. 100]. In phylogenetic terms, the evolutionary status of Homo sapiens implies common psychological potentialities. These would appear to be as necessary for the functioning of notions of eschatology as for the manufacture of tools and other forms of cultural adaptation.

In the light of our present anatomical and archeological evidence, we oversimplify the problem of human evolution if we do not press beyond such general categorical correspondences as *man-speech* and *tools-culture*. Without qualification and further analysis, we cannot associate every aspect of the kind of cultural adaptation we find in Homo sapiens with all members of the Hominidae any more than we can attribute to them a common "human nature." This latter concept always has proved difficult [see 17, 134]. Sometimes it has been given a purely biological content. Among anthropologists, it often has received a rela- tivistic connotation, despite lip service to the "psychic unity of mankind" [218, p. 21]. Spiro has given the concept a more precise meaning by asserting that "the structure and functioning of human personality constitutes man's universal human nature, psychologically viewed. Its universality is not only descriptively true; it is analytically true, as well.

In the absence of human personality there could be no human culture" [218, p. 29]. In phyletic perspective human nature is, then, the consequence of an evolutionary process. However conceptualized, it cannot be attributed to the earliest hominids in any meaningful sense. In a psychological frame of reference, a human personality structure did not arise as a sudden mutation in the evolution of the hominids any more than a saltatory constellation of anatomical traits suddenly gave rise to man.[24] Howells said a number of years ago:

Heretofore we have been given to talking about "the appearance of man"—the tyranny of terminology—as if he had suddenly been promoted from colonel to brigadier general, and had a date of rank. It is now evident that the first hominids were small-brained, newly bipedal, proto-Australopith hominoids, and that what we have always meant by "man" represents later forms of this group with secondary adaptations in the direction of large brains and modified skeletons of the same form [107].

Analogically, it is equally doubtful whether we should any longer talk in terms of the "appearance of culture," as if culture, along with "man," had suddenly leaped into existence. Moreover, if the ancestral hominids were at all like the australopithecines, it seems unlikely that they could have had a system of communication that was fully the equivalent of human speech.[25] There is no positive evidence, it might also be noted, that they had fire [176]. Further discoveries and analysis, no doubt, will illuminate the nature of their toolmaking, particularly with respect to the degree of tool differentiation and standardization of technique and form which prevailed. In the light of our present knowledge, we can attribute neither a fully developed cultural mode of adaptation nor a human personality structure to all the Hominidae.

Thus, instead of assuming that culture possessed a phenomenal unity from the start and trying to identify its existence in the past, it seems

[24] See Washburn's important paper [237], also Heberer's article [91]. Heberer writes: "Wir dürfen wohl sagen, dass, wie bereits Nehring (1895) vermutete und heute vielfältig werden kann . . . der Mensch 'zuerst mit den unteren Extremitäten Mensch geworden' ist. Die Erwerbung des Bipedalismus schuf die Vorbedingung für die definitive Hominisation durch Cerebralization. Ein pronogrades Wesen konnte keinen humanen Status erreichen, ebensowenig wie dies einem Brachiator möglich war" [91, p. 537]. And "Die Hominisation begann mit dem Eisetzen des evolutiven Trends, der zur Erwerbung des Bipedalism und zur Reduktion des Gebisses mit fortschreitendem Ersatz der Zähne durch die Hände (Instrumentalhilfen) führte. Mit diesen Erwerbungen wurde die kritische Phase erreicht, in der sich die Übergang vom subhumanen zur humanen Zustand volbezog" [cf. 145, p. 196].

[25] Oakley [172] does not think it necessary to assume that the earliest hominid tool users, or even toolmakers possessed speech. He likewise believes that a system of gestural communication preceded speech [171].

more fruitful to consider certain aspects of behavioral evolution that are noncultural in nature, but which are among the indispensable conditions that made cultural adaptation possible in the later phases of the evolution of the hominids. The most important of these conditions are sociopsychological in nature. Our empirical data are derived from observation on subhominid primates in their natural habitat or under laboratory conditions, for deductions from comparative behavior are as methodologically legitimate as those from comparative anatomy. Nissen points out:

It might well be that if we had a record of behavior as complete as the fossil record of structures, this would yield as convincing a body of evidence for evolution as does the latter. As a matter of fact, a study of the behaviors of living species alone—together with the paleontological evidence regarding the order in which these forms appeared—provides in itself a substantial basis for postulating a process of evolution [169, p. 99].

THE DIMENSION OF SOCIAL STRUCTURE

Social systems are not unique to Homo sapiens. And, even at this highly evolved level, social structure is now frequently differentiated analytically from culture or personality organization. Eggan, for example, has expressed the opinion that "the distinction between society and culture, far from complicating the procedures of analysis and comparison, has actually facilitated them." He goes on to say that "social structure and culture patterns may vary independently of one another, but both have their locus in the behavior of individuals in social groups" [55, p. 746].[26]

In approaching the sociopsychological dimension of primate evolution, a distinction of the same order is useful. Life in structured social groups is characteristic of primates and long antedated anything that can be called a "cultural mode of adaptation" among the more advanced hominids. Social structure can thus be treated as an independent variable. While at the highest level of primate behavioral evolution there are no organized societies without culture (or the reverse), at lower levels there were societies without culture. In phylogenetic perspective, a necessary locus and an indispensable condition for a cultural system is an organized system of social action. It likewise seems reasonable to assume that systems of social action at lower primate levels require some system of communication for their operation. To characterize such a system as

[26] [Cf. 74, p. 600]. Parsons [177] has added an organic reference point in this exposition of his general theory of action to the other categorical abstractions previously distinguished, i.e., personality or psychological system, social system, and cultural system.

"language" is ambiguous and even misleading without further analysis of the design features of the system. Then, too, consideration of the sensory mode of communication is required [72, 90, 204, p. 582; 213, chap. 9]. Among primates, both visual and acoustic modes appear to be extremely important. Schultz speaks of the intricate "silent vocabulary" of the non-hominid primate.

Crouching down, presenting buttocks, extending hands in pronation, exposing teeth partly or fully, raising eyebrows, protruding lips, shaking branches, pounding chest, dancing in one place, walking backwards, etc.— all are actions full of definite meaning. . . . The long lists of different postures, gestures and facial movements characteristic of monkeys and apes have not yet been compiled, but any careful observer realizes that they represent an intricate and voluminous "silent vocabulary" of great aid in social intercourse. In the perfectly adapted arboreal life of monkeys and apes the limited variety of sounds, together with the great variety of meaningful gestures and facial expressions, is fully adequate for all social life within such close contact as permits seeing and hearing these detailed means of communication [211].[27]

So far as the utterance of sounds is concerned, Schultz says they "are the essence of primate life . . . ; the simian primates are by far the noisiest of all mammals." In species that have been closely investigated, like the howling monkeys of Panama and the lar gibbon, differentiated vocalizations have been shown to have functional significance in the social coordination of the individuals belonging to a group [22, chap. 8; 29, p. 242]. According to Schultz:

The primatologist regards language not as something radically new and exclusively human, but rather as the result of a quantitative perfection of the highly specialized development of man's central nervous control of the anatomical speech apparatus in the larynx, tongue and lips, the latter being as good in an ape as in man. . . . As soon as the early hominids had ventured into open spaces, had begun to use and even make tools and had cooperated in hunting, the total variety of all means of expression needed additions which could come only from an increase in sounds, since the comparatively little changed anatomy had already been fully used for all possible gestures, etc. . . . Gestures have always persisted in human evolution, but they have become overshadowed by an infinitely greater variety of sounds in increasing numbers of combinations [211, p. 62].

Oakley and others have suggested that early hominids may have depended primarily on gestures, "mainly of mouth and hands, accompanied by cries and grunts to attract attention," and that speech may

[27] Carpenter [29, p. 242] says: "Each known genus of primate has a repertoire of gestures which are employed consistently and which stimulate consistent reactions." Examples are given.

have been a comparatively late development [171, p. 75]. If so, a mode of communication, infrahominid in origin, would have persisted into the protocultural phase of hominid evolution. Unfortunately, this interpretation must remain speculative. Yet it may be that, when the neurological basis of speech is clarified, we may be in a better position to make chronological deductions [53; 219, p. 8]. It is difficult to imagine, however, how a fully developed cultural mode of adaptation could operate without speech. If one of the necessary conditions for the functioning of a typically human system of communication is a speech community, an organized social system is as necessary for human language as it is for a cultural mode of adaptation. This condition was present even at the nonhominid level. So what we can discern in primate evolution is a behavioral plateau which provided the necessary context but, at first, not all the sufficient conditions for speech and culture.

It will be unnecessary here to consider the structure and functioning of infrahuman primate societies in detail. But a few general comments and interpretations may be ventured, despite the limitations of our present knowledge, for our samples of reliable observations on primate societies in their natural state are woefully small, particularly for prosimian groups.[28] Besides this, it is not yet possible to consider nonhominid primate societies systematically in the larger perspective of mammalian societies [22, p. 221]. There are terminological difficulties also. Descriptive terms like "family," "polygamy," "harem," "clan," and even "culture" and "acculturation"—familiar enough when employed with reference to Homo sapiens—sometimes have been applied to primates at the infrahominid level. Since no systematic terminology has been developed, these labels must be used with caution, especially when evolutionary questions are at issue.

Variations in type of mateship, of course, have suggested the closest human analogies. Since lar gibbons, for example, live in groups which consist of one male and one female and their young, we have a close analogy to the "nuclear family" in man [164], which likewise represents a monogamous type of mateship. Some biological writers have applied the term "family" exclusively to this kind of primate social unit, despite the fact that in anthropological writing the connotation of the term "family" is never limited to the nuclear family. The gibbon type of mateship, in which the sexual drive of the male is low, would seem to be a limiting case in the range of social units found among the more evolved primates, and without evolutionary implications. In Homo sapiens we

[28] [For bibliography to 1957, see 31.] Imanishi's 1960 paper [116] is the first full length review in English of the work that has been done on *Macaca fuscata* at the Japan Monkey Center, although a brief review was previously published by Frisch [68].

find two types of polygamous mateships, polygyny and polyandry, and social structures based on these are ordinarily called "families." Relatively rare in man in an institutionalized form, polyandrous mateships appear to be absent in infrahuman primates. On the other hand, polygynous mateships are common in both monkeys and apes. Among the chimpanzee and gorilla, this type of mateship seems to furnish the basis of independent social groups. Among some monkeys (for instance, the baboon), "harems" occur as subgroups within larger "troops" or "bands." Monogamous mateships, on the other hand, do not occur in groups of larger size because females in heat mate with more than one male. Past attempts to establish any regular evolutionary sequence of mateship within Homo sapiens have failed. So have attempts to link any *particular* type of mateship in the infrahuman primates with early man, as Westermarck tried to do in the belief that there was evidence to show that the gorilla was monogamous. He urged that this "fact" was of significance in the study of sexual relationships and marriage in man.

Westermarck, however, was on the right track and must be evaluated in historical perspective. Hart points out:

What had really happened to evolutionary theory between 1859 and 1891 was that, while Huxley had spent his life labouring on the genetic front to get his contemporaries to accept "the unitary view of organic nature" and to reject the old dualistic view which saw man on one level, the rest of the animal world on another with an impassable gap eternally fixed between, the pass had been betrayed by Spencer and his followers, who, by assuming that society was one thing and biology another, had merely substituted a new dualism for the older one, and had opened up as big a gap between man and the rest of nature as had been there in pre-Darwinian days. The extraordinary thing is not that this should have happened, but that nobody seems to have been aware of what was happening until Westermarck pointed it out [84, p. 108].

In his *History of Human Marriage,* Westermarck said:

If we want to find the origin of marriage, we have to strike into another path . . . which is open to him alone who regards organic nature as one continued chain, the last link of which is man. For we can no more stop within the limits of our own species, when trying to find the root of our physical and social life, than we can understand the condition of the human race without taking into consideration that of the lower animals" [245, p. 9].

Etkin [60] argues for a monogamous protohominid social structure but on quite different grounds than did Westermarck at the turn of the century.

Perhaps it might be better to recognize that, since there are only a limited number of possibilities in mateships, it is not surprising to find

them recurring at both the nonhominid and hominid levels of evolutionary development in the primates and in social units of varying size and
composition. Whatever form they take, all these mateships serve the same
reproductive ends. Their importance lies in this constancy in biological
function rather than in any direct relation that can be shown to the
evolution of group organization. They all lie close to biologically rooted
central tendencies and continuities in behavioral evolution which link
Homo sapiens to his precursors. What we find as the common social core
of all but the lowest primate groups, despite their variation, is the continuous association of adults of both sexes with their offspring during the
portion of the latter's life cycle that covers the period from birth to the
threshold of maturity. This core pattern of associated individuals, when
considered with reference to their interrelated roles, is linked with the fact
that basic functions are involved—the procreation, protection, and nurture of offspring—born singly, relatively helpless at birth, and dependent
for a considerable period thereafter. Variations in mateship or size of the
group may occur without affecting these functions. Besides this, the sex
needs of adults and the food needs of all members of the group can be
taken care of. The role of the female in relation to her young does not seem
to vary widely nor does the behavior of infants and juveniles. The protective role of the male in relation to infants and juveniles is similar in
gibbon and howler, even though the young of the group in the latter case
are not all his own offspring and the actual zoological relationship
between these two species is remote. Among monkeys and apes, the
adult males never provide food for juveniles or females. After weaning,
the juveniles always forage for themselves. Whether we call nonhominid
primate groups "families," "clans," "troops," or "bands," their basic
social composition can be expressed by the same general formula:[29]

$$x \text{ males} + x \text{ females} + x \text{ infants} + x \text{ juveniles}$$

Whatever the mating types or size of early hominid groups may have
been, their social composition must have conformed to this fundamental

[29] Imanishi [116, p. 397] has recommended *oikia* "as a technical term designating the minimum unit of social life found in any species of animal, regardless of
the composition of that unit." In nonhominid primates then, "the clan in howling
monkeys, the family in gibbons, the small nesting party or sleeping group in redtail
monkeys, and the harem in chacma baboons, would each be describable as an
oikia." Larger groups would be aggregates of *oikiae*. Washburn [238, p. 405], however, doubts the usefulness of this term. Imanishi also holds the opinion that "a
band in which promiscuity prevails cannot be called a 'family' even though the
two males in it [as in Nissen's reference to a chimpanzee group in 1931] are a
father and his mature son. In other words, we may legitimately consider it a family
only if we can establish the absence of incest between this mature son and his
mother."

pattern. This generic type of social structure, associated with territorialism, must have persisted throughout the extremely long period during which major morphological changes occurred in the species of the primate order, including those which ultimately differentiated the Hominidae from the Pongidae and later hominids from earlier ones. Underlying it physiologically was the type of ovarian cycle characteristic of practically all the primates. In contrast with some mammalian species in which females have only one oestrus period a year, primate females, along with those of a limited number of other mammalian species, are characterized by the recurrence of successive oestrus cycles in the course of a year. The primates belong to this group of permanent polyoestrus species [22, p. 147]. While breeding has been said to be continuous rather than seasonal in the primates, recent observations of the Japanese macaque have reopened this question. It is of great importance in establishing reliable facts about reproduction in nonhominid primate species, and because the answer to this question is relevant to the importance of the sexual bond as a primary factor in primate social organization [for further details see 116]. In the course of primate evolution, however, as Beach [9, 11, 64] has pointed out, some emancipation from strictly hormonal control of sexual behavior occurred, and this further distinguished the higher primates from other mammalian species. Cortical control came to play an increasing role in sexual behavior, and this tendency reached its culmination in hominid evolution with the remarkable expansion of the brain. Thus, the way lay open for the development in human societies of a normative orientation toward sexual behavior.

The evolutionary significance of the social organization of primate groups cannot be fully appreciated, however, without considering behavior patterns other than those directly connected with reproduction. The structuralization of these infrahuman societies is by no means a simple function of differential roles determined by sex and age. Of central importance is the structuralization of interindividual patterns of behavior by an order of social ranking in the group, a dominance gradient. Males are quite generally dominant over females, and the females associated with them may outrank other females. While it appears that in different species the "slope" of the dominance gradient varies considerably, some kind of rank order occurs. The importance of this in the operation of the social structure lies in the fact that it serves to reduce aggression between males, it determines priorities to mates and food, it influences the spatial disposition of individuals within the group, affects the socialization of group habits, and may determine the relations of groups adjacent to one another.

The ranking position of individuals, nevertheless, is not fully determined once and for all; an individual's role in the dominance hierarchy may change. Psychological factors such as individual experience in inter-individual relations and social learning become involved in its functioning and affect the motivation of behavior, as Carpenter [27, pp. 256–257] has indicated. Individuals become socially adjusted from birth through the mediation of learning processes. "Descriptions of mother-infant relations in monkeys and chimpanzee leave no doubt as to the importance of learning in the filial responses of immature primates. The infant learns to obey gestures and vocal communications given by the mother and derives considerable advantage from her tuition and guidance," Beach says [10, p. 426].[30] Indeed, modern research is showing that the primates are by no means unique among gregarious animals with respect to the importance of social learning and a dominance gradient. J. P. Scott asserts:

In animals which are capable of learning, social behavior becomes differentiated on the basis of mutual adaptation and habit formation as well as on the basis of biological differences. As shown by Ginsburg and Allee (1942) the formation of a dominance order is at least in part related to the psychological principles of learning. Once such a relationship is formed and firmly established by habit, it may be extremely difficult to upset it by altering biological factors, as shown by Beeman and Allee (1945). . . . Experiments which modify the social environment have tended to bring out the general principles of socialization. Any highly social animal that has been studied so far has behavioral mechanisms whereby, early in development, an individual forms positive social relationships with its own kind and usually with particular individuals of its kind [212, pp. 217, 218].

With respect to the socialization factor in behavioral evolution, Collias points out: "In both insect and vertebrate societies, maintenance of cooperative relations depends to a large extent on socialization of the young. Among vertebrates, this trend reaches its climax in the primates" [38, p. 1087]. It seems reasonable to assume, therefore, that the intimate relation between learning and social structure, so fundamental to the functioning and elaboration of cultural adaptation, was well established in the nonhominid primates prior to the anatomical changes that led to both erect posture and the expansion of the brain.

Furthermore, by direct observation of both monkeys and apes, we know that learned habits may be socially transmitted, even in the absence of speech. The most striking cases have been reported by observers who have been studying *Macaca fuscata* at the Japanese Monkey Center dur-

---

[30] See also [203, p. 104 ff.] in regard to ontogenetic factors influencing group organization. Cf. Schiller [201], who believed there is evidence that primates have distinctive *manipulative* patterns of activity available that are not derived from experience.

ing the past decade. These "Japanese apes" have been lured from their forest habitat into open feeding places, where, among other things, they have been offered new foods. Systematic observation has shown that newly acquired food habits, such as eating candies, became quite socialized. Imanishi points out, moreover, that young macaques acquire the candy-eating habit more quickly than adults and that some mothers learned to eat candies from their offspring, rather than the other way round [115, p. 51]. It has likewise been observed that the spread of a new food habit may be directly related to the dominance gradient which is a central feature of their social structure. Adult females of high rank were observed to imitate the wheat eating of a dominant male very quickly and the habit was passed on to their offspring. Females of lower rank, in a more peripheral position in the group, only later acquired the habit from their offspring, who, in turn, had picked it up through association with their playmates. The rate of transmission was extremely rapid in this case, the entire process occurring within two days [68, p. 589]. In another instance, a young female initiated the habit of washing sweet potatoes before eating them. This habit, having been transmitted to her playmates as well as to her mother, was slowly transmitted to a number of groups during the next three years. The same class of phenomenon in the anthropoid apes is illustrated by nest building among chimpanzees [169, p. 106] and the transmission of the technique of working the drinking fountain at Orange Park, which chimpanzees learned from each other [252, p. 52].

The social transmission of culture has sometimes been stressed as one of its chief earmarks. But to my mind, it is only one of the necessary conditions of cultural adaptation rather than a distinguishing characteristic. It only confounds the conceptualization and the investigation of hominid evolution if the term "culture" is applied without qualification to the phenomena of social transmission of simple habits in infrahuman species. J. P. Scott writes:

> The more the capacities for learning and for variable organization of behavior are present, the more it is possible for an animal to learn from its parents and pass the information along to the next generation. As we accumulate greater knowledge of natural animal behavior, we find more and more evidence that many animals possess the rudiments of this new ability, which we can call cultural inheritance. The migration trails of mountain sheep and the learned fears of wild birds are two of many examples . . . At the present time all our evidence indicates that cultural inheritance exists only in quite simple form in animals other than man, but future research may show that it is more common and complex than we now suspect [213, p. 237].

Social transmission is more usefully conceived as a prerequisite of culture and an earmark of a protocultural behavioral plateau. Concepts of culture that lay primary emphasis on shared and socially transmitted behavior without qualification do not enable us to make a necessary distinction of degree between different levels of behavioral evolution. Voegelin has made the acute observation that, while there is a general agreement that all culture involves learned behavior, "additional conditions are generally invoked before learned behavior is granted the status of culture," and that "if ever the converse statement were made (*that all learned behavior is culture*), it would necessarily imply that infrahuman animals have culture" [233, p. 370]. Harlow clearly discriminates between infrahominids and Homo sapiens when he says, "In a limited sense, however, any animal living in a group and capable of facile learning must develop a *semblance of a culture,* since it must have learned to be influenced in its behavior by the ways of its fellows." At the same time, he points out that "no animal other than man has a *true culture* in the sense of an organized body of knowledge passed down from generation to generation" [79, p. 127; italics mine]. The facts that some animals besides the primates may learn from each other, that in primate groups there seems to be good evidence that social learning and socially transmitted habits do occur, and that some chimpanzees in social interaction with members of our species have acquired "culture traits" do not indicate that a full-fledged level of cultural adaptation has been reached in these species.[31] Other capacities and conditions are required before this higher level can be realized. Indeed, neither learning nor the socialization and transmission of learned habits seems to have reached an optimum level of functioning in any nonhominid species. While it is true that a variety of gregarious animals possess the *rudiments* of an ability to be influenced by the behavior of other individuals of their species, the part which this ability plays in their total life history, their social relations, and their ecological adjustments needs more precise analysis. Phylogenetically, it is *only* in the primates that capacities and conditions arose which led to the transcendance of more than a protocultural stage.

---

[31] Yerkes thought the characterization of chimpanzee as "cultureless" to be "a seriously misleading statement, if not demonstrably false." He says that "the elements or makings of cultural exhibits are present" but that "they are relatively unimpressive because unstable, fragmentary, variable, and seldom integrated into functionally important wholes. Probably they should be described as intimations or primitive stages in patterns of behavior which have as yet acquired few functional relations" [252, p. 52]. Nissen [169, pp. 105–106], referring to nest building in chimpanzees, writes: "There is pretty good evidence . . . that this nest-building is not instinctive, as in birds, but is, rather, transmitted by imitation or tuition from one generation to the next; it is, therefore, one of the very few items of behavior seen in these animals which may be classified as cultural" [cf. 167, p. 426].

What appears to be of significance in the framework of behavioral evolution is that some primates are distinguished from other animals by a higher capacity for *observational* learning. Munn concludes that "it is only in monkeys and apes that anything clearly approximating such observational learning can be demonstrated and even at this level the problems solved by imitation are relatively simple" [162, pp. 129–130. Instances of spontaneous imitation on the part of Viki (the chimpanzee) were operating a spray gun, and prying off the lids of cans with a screw driver, 89].

If we use the term "culture" to refer to different levels of behavioral evolution, our vocabulary fails to discriminate the quantitative and qualitative differences between cultural adaptation in the hominines and the more rudimentary "cultural" manifestations found in infrahuman animals—to say nothing of possible differences between primates and nonprimates. Dobzhansky, in a brief discussion on the "Rudiments of Cultural Transmission among Animals," singles out one essential difference between what I have characterized as protocultural and cultural levels of adaptation, although he does not analyze specific cases in detail, and his chief citations refer to birds[32] rather than to primates.

In animals the individuals of one generation transmit to those of the next what they themselves learned from their parents—not more and not less. Every generation learns the same thing which its parents have learned. In only very few instances the evidence is conclusive that the learned behavior can be modified or added to and that the modifications and additions are transmitted to subsequent generations [52, pp. 340–341].

Simple conditioning and possibly observational learning account for these facts. The greater capacity for observational learning in primates also accounts for the socialization of nest-building habits among chimpanzees and the spread of the habit of washing sweet potatoes observed in the macaque group referred to. But so long as social transmission was dependent on capacities of this sort, the kind of acquired habits transmitted or any innovations which could become significant in the adaptation of the group were severely limited. Intervening factors, probably of a neurological order, were required before either the number or the kind of innovations possible at this level could be transcended and become effective through new mechanisms of socialization. As Bidney has said, "The identification of culture with the social heritage is, to my mind, not only a misnomer but also a serious error, since it implies that the essential feature of culture is the fact of communication and transmission,

[32] See Hochbaum [96] for a discussion of tradition in birds. The use of the term "tradition" by ornithologists clearly differentiates the existence of socially transmitted habits from the phenomenon of culture in human adaptation.

whereas I maintain that the essential feature is the combination of invention and acquisition through habituation and conditioning" [17, p. 27].[33]

Moreover, learning and the transmission of acquired behavior patterns could not acquire paramount importance until they could function in social structures of a higher order and wider geographical range than those represented among the infrahominid primates. At this level, social structures were highly provincial systems of social action because of their association with discrete territories. The phenomenon of territoriality, according to Carpenter, "reduces stress, conflict, pugnacity, and non-adaptive energy expenditure" [32, p. 245] in each group by isolating it from other groups; at the same time, it sets up a barrier to the integration of groups and the development of social structures of a wider range and more complex order [30, p. 98]. In the case of the Japanese macaques, for example, groups are almost totally isolated from each other in their natural state. It is said that "even where several groups live in contiguous territories, the inter-group relations are practically non-existent. Encounters between distinct groups are extremely rare, and even when they occur both groups keep at a safe distance from each other" [68, p. 591]. Offspring do not associate with parents after sexual maturity has been reached. They leave their primary group and form new groups. Individuals of two or more generations are not continuously associated in the same group during their lifetime. Consequently, continuity in learned habits is strictly limited. There is no way for experience to become cumulative, either spatially or temporally, beyond the narrowest range. Thus, in order for a cultural level of adaptation to be reached, structures of a wider range were required as a necessary social setting. This further step was contingent upon the development and functioning of psychological capacities that transcended those which had been sufficient for narrow-range social structures. In short, the social integration of larger groups, distributed more widely, and characterized by a greater diversity in role required a transformation in psychological structure.

We do not know what objective factors underlay the increase in the size and range of early hominid groups. Change to a carnivorous diet and hunting have been suggested. Washburn says:

Whether early man scavenged from the kills of the big carnivores, followed herds looking for a chance to kill, drove game, or followed a wounded

---

[33] Cf. the remarks of Kroeber [131, p. 253] on the use of the term "social heredity." Bidney distinguishes between "culture in general" and human or "anthropo-culture," which is peculiar to man. For him, "all animals which are capable of learning and teaching one another by precept or example are capable of acquiring culture." He maintains that "this implies an evolutionary approach to the concept of culture which recognizes degrees of culture from the sub-human to the human level" [17, pp. 125, 127].

animal, his range of operations must have been greatly increased over that of arboreal apes. The world view of the early human carnivore must have been very different from that of his vegetarian cousins. The interests of the latter could be satisfied in a small area, and the other animals were of little moment, except for the few which threatened attack. But the desire for meat leads animals to know a wider range and to learn the habits of many animals. Human territorial habits and psychology are fundamentally different from those of apes and monkeys [240, p. 434].

THE BIOLOGICAL DIMENSION: NEOTENY AND BRAIN ENLARGEMENT

A concomitant condition for the maximization of the sociopsychological importance of learning appears to have been the extension of the period during which the young become socialized. In the late nineteenth century, John Fiske, an ardent follower of Spencer and Darwin, linked such an extension of the learning period in man directly with evolution through what he called the "prolongation of infancy." In this fact alone, he thought he had discovered the essential key to man's distinction from other animals and the explanation of human psychological, familial, and cultural development. Fiske was impressed both with A. R. Wallace's account of the behavior of an infant orang raised by hand after its captured mother died[34] and by Wallace's suggestion that "natural selection, in working toward the genesis of man, began to follow a new path and make psychical changes instead of physical changes" [62, p. 28]. Fiske developed the thesis that the human being was born "in a very undeveloped condition, with the larger part of his faculties in potentiality rather than in actuality" [62, p. 9]. The period of helplessness is the period of "plasticity. . . . The creature's career is no longer exclusively determined by heredity . . . it becomes educable . . . it is no longer necessary for each generation to be exactly like that which has preceded" [62, p. 2]. Thus, "man's progressiveness and the length of his infancy are but two sides of the same fact"; "it is babyhood that has made man what he is." Infrahuman primates approached the point where "variation in intelligence" came to be "supremely important, so as to be seized by natural selection in preference to variations in physical constitution." But in a remote period, "our half-human forefathers reached and passed this critical point, and forthwith their varied struggles began age after age to result in the preservation of bigger and better

[34] Fiske [62, p. 26] says it occurred to him immediately that "if there is any one thing in which the human race is signally distinguished from other mammals, it is in the enormous duration of their infancy"; a point he did not recollect ever seeing any naturalist so much as allude to. But Fiske was not quite as original as he thought [e.g., 148].

brains, while the rest of their bodies changed but little. . . . Zoologically the distance is small between man and the chimpanzee; psychologically it has become so great as to be immeasurable" [62, p. 11].

We can see from these passages that Fiske anticipated a number of points frequently emphasized later in cultural anthropology and in evolutionary biology. But the theory he develops, while emphasizing the important role of learning in human experience and the potentialities of man for cultural development, does not account for the biological foundations of the extended period of dependency. He likewise makes "bigger and better brains" chronologically subsequent to the distinctive human condition that fired his imagination. Nor could he have anticipated the fact that later knowledge of the social organization of the nonhominid primates would fail to support his conviction that the prolongation of infancy "must have tended gradually to strengthen the relations of the children to the mother, and eventually to both parents, and thus give rise to the permanent organization of the family." For in Fiske's view, when this step was accomplished, "the Creation of Man had been achieved" [62, pp. 12–13].

While Fiske's theory, although once so widely known, is seldom referred to today, the fact should not be overlooked that the relations between the factors dealt with by him have not yet been satisfactorily resolved. Even now it is sometimes forgotten that an extended period of dependency and opportunities for social learning in man do not explain the genesis of cultural adaptation, even though these conditions may be of primary categorical importance in understanding the adjustment processes that relate an individual to his culture. While we now know more about the phylogenetic basis of what Fiske called the "prolongation of infancy," its precise psychological significance is a matter of dispute.

From comparative anatomy the fact seems well established that the larger apes, and particularly the gorilla, develop adult characteristics much earlier than does Homo sapiens. The latter has been called a "fetalized" animal by Bolk [19]; that is, certain features that are characteristic of the fetal stages of apes persist in human adults. It is an example of a well-known evolutionary process which, generically, is usually referred to as "neoteny": fetal and/or juvenile features of an ancestral form persisting in the adult stage of descendants [33, 34, 48]. In man, the rate of development of some characteristics has been retarded. On the other hand, De Beer says:

The reproductive glands have probably not varied their rate of development, for the human ovary reaches its full size at the age of about five, and this is about the time of sexual maturity of the apes and presumably of man's ancestors. The human body is, however, not ready for the reproductive glands to function until several years later. The retardation is due to the action of hormones which play an important part in regulating the speed of development. . . . At the same time, of course, in other directions, the evolution of man has involved progressive changes of vast importance, some of which, however, might not have been possible (e.g., the development of the brain), had it not been for certain features of neoteny (e.g., the delay in the closing of the sutures of the skull) [48, pp. 75–76].

It is the combination of various characters, considered with reference to their rate of ontogenetic development, that is peculiar to man.[35]

While such anatomical facts are well established, the psychological inferences drawn from them have varied in emphasis. Roheim maintains that the temporal disharmony between the development of what he calls the "Soma" and the "Germa" is the crucial point. Human sexuality becomes precocious because it develops at about the same rate as in other higher primates, but in our species full bodily growth is delayed. The consequence is that unconscious psychological mechanisms have come into play to repress, project, or transform sexual impulses before the individual is mature enough in other respects to engage in actual sexual activities. The Oedipus complex is universal not because it is derived from past events that have become inherited,[36] but because it "is a direct derivative of our partly premature, partly conservative (prolonged or retarded) rate of growing up" [192, p. 424].[37] "Our sexual ethics are based on juvenalization" [192, p. 413]. (Perhaps it should be added that in *both* man and the anthropoids sexual organs reach maturity earlier than full body growth, but in man the time difference is greater.) Montagu, on the other hand, sees in neoteny an evolutionary step whose major psychological significance is related to man's potentialities for learning. He says:

[35] Schultz [208, p. 53]. And see his 1956 publication for an authoritative comparative treatment of the details of growth and development in various primate species. Schultz concludes that it is erroneous to emphasize retardation exclusively in man's ontogenetic development, since "ontogenetic specializations can consist of accelerations as well as retardations in man as well as in all other primates" [209, p. 959].

[36] Roheim [192, p. 424] says, "This ultra-Lamarckian point of view is untenable," i.e., Freud's primal-horde theory.

[37] Roheim says: "It is a curious fact that while man's delayed infancy is universally admitted hardly anybody uses this fact in the sense that I do. The usual statement is that the delayed infancy makes it possible to condition human beings and that it is why psychology depends on conditioning, i.e., on culture. What culture depends on is then of course the kind of question no well behaved anthropologist should ask, because looking for origins is 'outmoded,' in fact it is nineteenth century, a truly terrible thing, a word loaded with the worst possible kind of *mana*. Quite apart, however, from this aspect of the question, how is it that nobody recognizes that in this one fact we have one of the most important keys to the understanding of human nature?" [192, p. 409]

The shift from the status of ape to the status of human being was the result of neotenous mutations which produced a retention of the growth trends of the juvenile brain and its potentialities for learning into the adolescent and adult phases of development. It is clear that the nature of these potentialities for learning must also have undergone intrinsic change, for no amount of extension of the chimpanzee's capacity for learning would yield a human mind [159, p. 90; cf. 158, p. 22].

Besides this, account must be taken of the biological fact that in primate evolution the life span of individuals was progressively lengthened while the onset of puberty and the beginning of fertility was more and more chronologically delayed. Culminating in man, the outcome was that the interval between generations became greater. This fact needs to be considered with reference to the association of individuals in larger social groups and in relation to the need for the development of the kind of psychological structure that would permit the coordination of the behavior of individuals of both sexes and widely differing ages over a longer time period, in order that interindividual relations in these more complex social systems might be successfully integrated.

While it is impossible to sustain the view that fetalization is completely responsible for all of modern man's distinctive psychocultural characteristics,[38] perhaps we may follow Sir Julian Huxley's view that while—

. . . it will not account for all the special characters we possess, notably the special enlargement of the association areas of our cortex, and the full adaptation of our feet and legs to bipedal terrestrial existence, it has certainly helped us to escape from anthropoid specialization. It is this possibility of escaping from the blind alleys of specialization into a new period of plasticity and adaptive radiation which makes the idea of paedomorphosis [fetalization, neoteny] so attractive in evolutionary theory. Both its possibilities and its limitations deserve the most careful exploration [111, p. 20].

If so, important steps in sociopsychological evolution beyond the nonhominid or early hominid level may have been contingent upon the situational effects produced by biological factors. These factors prolonged dependency of the young, delayed reproduction, and increased the life span in an already advanced hominid. At the same time, psychological functions were being greatly enhanced through the enlargement of certain areas of the brain.[39]

---

[38] The unkindest cut of all has come from Cuenot [43], who has said that man "can be considered a gorilla fetus whose development and growth have been greatly retarded."

[39] Bernhard Rensch, who has been investigating the effects of increased body size on the relative size of the brain and its parts, and on higher psychological

With respect to this particular development, there may well have been a critical transition period. However, an arbitrary Rubicon of 750 cc. [125][40] between the higher apes and the australopithecines on the one hand, and the early Homininae and recent man on the other, while perhaps of some crude taxonomic value, does not in itself permit significant behavioral inferences. "It is quality of brain rather than quantity, absolute or relative, that is all important," as Straus says [225].

Today we know considerably more than we did a generation ago about the functioning of various parts of the cortex as well as other parts of the brain. And new insights and hypotheses with evolutionary reference are coming to the fore. Washburn, referring to the diagram in Penfield and Rasmussen [178] showing the way the body is represented on the cortex, points out that there is unequal representation but that "the areas which are largest are the ones of greatest functional importance." Thus, "when the brain increased in size, the area for hand increased vastly more than that for foot," a fact which "supports the idea that the increase in the size of the brain occurred after the use of tools, and that selection for more skillful tool-using resulted in changes in the proportions of the hand and of the parts of the brain controlling the hand." The areas concerned with speech are also large and so are the frontal lobes which have been said to be connected, in part, with foresight and planning.

Our brains are not just enlarged, but the increase in size is directly related to tool use, speech, and to increased memory and planning. The general pattern of the human brain is very similar to that of ape or monkey. Its uniqueness lies in its larger size and in the particular areas which are enlarged. From the immediate point of view, this human brain makes culture possible. But from the long-term evolutionary point of view, it is culture which creates the human brain [238, pp. 27–29].

---

functions, has advanced the hypothesis [184, pp. 197–198]: "In man's line of descent we may at least consider the increase of the cortex, the relative increase of 'progressive,' i.e., more complicated, cortex-regions, the absolute increase of the number of neurons and of dendritic ramifications, as . . . selectively advantageous factors. Thus the trend towards the human level of brain organization may be regarded as inevitable. Another important factor here is the prolongation of the juvenile phase found in many large animals. This could only occur where multiple births, and therefore intrauterinal selection for rapidity of development, had been eliminated. But once this had taken place, the prolongation of the juvenile phase was favored by selection because thereby the period of learning, that is to say the period of gaining experience and of exploration by play, is also extended. Thus the evolution of man, too, was inevitable" [cf. 185, 186].

[40] See comments by Schultz [208, pp. 49–50]. The Hayeses, however, suggest "the possibility that most of the fourfold increase in cranial capacity from anthropoid to man took place after the appearance of culture and language, and therefore after primate behavior had become essentially human" [89, p. 116].

In recent years, too, as a consequence of rapid advances in neuro-anatomy and physiology, there has been a revival of interest in, and many discussions of, the brain mechanisms which underlie the phenomena of awareness, consciousness, attention, memory, and the functional integration of experience [e.g., 2, 136, 178, 179, 234].[41] So far as integrative functions are concerned, the present weight of evidence appears to focus upon the influence exercised by the masses of nerve cells in the upper part of the brain stem upon the more recently evolved cortical areas. An older notion that the cortex itself was of prime significance because it was somehow the "seat of consciousness" no longer seems to make complete neurological sense. Although no unanimity of opinion has been reached, hypotheses should emerge in time which will lead to further clarification of the relations between neurological evolution, psychological functioning, and cultural adaptation. Of central importance in this complex web of relationships is the distinctive psychological focus of consciousness in Homo sapiens—the capacity for self-objectification which is so intimately linked with the normative orientation of all human societies.

SOCIOPSYCHOLOGICAL EVOLUTION AND NORMATIVE ORIENTATION

Although we can never check developmental stages in the enlargement of the brain by direct observation of behavior, we do know what the behavioral outcome was in the most highly evolved hominid. Here, along with a greater diversification in the forms of social structure in Homo sapiens, we are confronted with a radical change in their underlying dynamics. At this more advanced stage, a normative orientation becomes

---

[41] Penfield and Rasmussen write: "It is apparent that there are important connections which conduct both ways between areas of cortex and specific nuclei of the diencephalon, and that in the process of encephalization a varying degree of autonomy has been handed over to the large cortical projections. It does not necessarily follow, however, that all function, either new or old, has been handed over in this way nor that correlation between the activities of the different cortical areas is necessarily carried out in the cortex rather than in the diencephalon. . . . Popular tradition, which seems to be largely shared by scientific men, has taken it for granted that the cortex is a sort of essential organ for the purposes of thinking and consciousness, and that final integration of neural mechanisms takes place in it. Perhaps this is only natural since there has been an extraordinary enlargement of the cortex in the human brain, and, at the same time, man seems to be endowed with intellectual functions of a new order." However, "the whole anterior frontal area, on one or both sides, may be removed without loss of consciousness. During the amputation the individual may continue to talk, unaware of the fact that he is being deprived of that area which most distinguishes his brain from that of the chimpanzee" [178, pp. 204, 205–206, 226].

an inherent aspect of the functioning of all sociocultural systems, since traditionally recognized standards and values are characteristic of them. Techniques are appraised as good or bad; so are the manufactured objects themselves. Property rights are regulated according to recognized standards. Knowledge and beliefs are judged true or false. Art forms and linguistic expression are brought within the sphere of normative orientation. Conduct is evaluated in relation to ethical values. All cultures are infused with appraisals that involve cognitive, appreciative, and moral values [230, pp. 344–346; 128, pp. 388–433].[42]

It has been said by a biologist that the foundation of any kind of social order is dependent upon role differentiation.[43] The general principle underlying social organization at any level is that role behavior on the part of individuals is, within limits, predictable in a wide variety of situations.[44] This is what makes it possible to establish empirically characteristic patterns of behavior interaction whether in invertebrates, vertebrates, or primates, despite the fact that the relative importance of innate versus learned determinants may vary widely at different levels. Normative orientation in man implements regularities in social systems at a more complex psychological level of development through role differentiation that is mediated by socialized values and goals. While some contemporary biologists, like Darwin a century ago in his *Descent of Man*, have given particular emphasis to the moral sense of man,[45] this aspect of social adjustment is but one facet of man's normative orientation. If all the ramifications of the normative orientation of human societies are taken into account, we have a major clue to the kind of psychological transformation that must have occurred in hominid evo-

[42] A value orientation, whether "held by individuals or in the abstract-typical form, by groups," and varying from explicit to implicit, is defined by Kluckhohn et al. as "a generalized and organized conception, influencing behavior, of nature, of man's place in it, of man's relation to man, and of the desirable and non-desirable as they may relate to man-environment and interhuman relations" [128, p. 411].

[43] Jennings, assuming a phylogenetic perspective and speaking of infrahuman animals, said: "Only if the individuals play different functional roles is there social organization" [118, p. 105].

[44] Cf. the discussion of "role expectations" in Sarbin [198, p. 226 ff.]. "Persons occupy positions or statuses in interactional situations. Psychologically considered, positions are cognitive systems of role expectations, products of learning. Role expectations are bidimensional; for every role expectation of other there is a reciprocal role expectation of self. The organized actions of the person, directed towards fulfilling these role expectations, comprise the role" [198, p. 225].

[45] Dobzhansky says, "It is man's moral sense which makes him truly human" [52, p. 376]; cf. 52a, pp. 340 *req*. And Simpson, asserting that "man is a moral animal," says: "It requires no demonstration that a demand for ethical standards is deeply ingrained in human psychology. Like so many human characteristics, indeed most of them, this trait is both innate and learned. Its basic mechanism is evidently part of our biological inheritance" [215, p. 294]. See also Waddington [234a].

lution to make this level of adaptation possible, and some measure of its depth and significance for an understanding of the dynamics of human systems of social action.

In their analysis of the functional prerequisites of a human society, Aberle and his associates [1] introduce the concept of an "actor," with cognitive, affective, and goal-directed orientation, but they do not discuss the psychological prerequisites of this actor. While this is irrelevant in their frame of reference, in phylogenetic perspective the capacities of the actor are crucial. For the functioning of a system of action as a normatively oriented social order requires a capacity for self-objectification, identification with one's own conduct over time, and appraisal of one's own conduct and that of others in a common framework of socially recognized and sanctioned standards of behavior.[46] Without a psychological level of organization that permits the exercise of these and other functions, moral responsibility for conduct could not exist, nor could any social structure function at the level of normative orientation. Learning remains important, of course, but it functions at a higher level of sociopsychological integration. The relations between needs, motivation, goals, and learning become more complex. The analysis of Aberle and his associates inevitably includes the "normative regulation of means," the "regulation of affective expression," and the "effective control of disruptive forms of behavior." Value systems have an ordering function in social interaction; they promote the broad behavioral expectancies which are of the essence of role differentiation in a *sociocultural* system.

Man, for example, has departed very radically from his primate forerunners in ecological development through the invention and use of technological devices of all kinds and in economic organization. A normative orientation in these spheres of activity is epitomized by the standards applied to the distribution of goods and services and to the ownership of property. One of the universal functions of all systems of property rights, which are among the common denominators of culture, is to orient individuals in human societies toward a complex set of basic values inherent in their day-to-day operation. This kind of value orientation is just as crucial in relation to the motivation and interpersonal relations of individuals as are the values associated with sexual behavior. Property rights are not only an integral part of the economic organization of any human system of social action; they likewise implement the functioning of the social order in relation to the resources of the physical environment through normative means. Discussion of "property" among

---

[46] Consequently, it is thoroughly intelligible why role theorists, more than any other group, as Sarbin points out, "have developed and used the conception of the self as an intervening variable" [198, p. 238].

infrahuman animals have centered around such phenomena as food sharing, the defense of the nest, prey, territorial domain, and so forth. The question is: In what sense are such phenomena comparable with the socially recognized and sanctioned rights in valuable objects that characterize property in human societies? In the latter the basis of ownership is the correlative obligations others have to allow me to exercise *my* property rights. A owns B against C, where C represents all other individuals. It is an oversimplification to omit C and simply say A owns B [see 76, chap. 12]. Among infrahuman animals, we meet with entirely different conditions. All we observe is the utilization, or possession (in the sense of physical custody or use), of certain objects which bear some relation to the biological needs of the organism or group of organisms. We cannot properly speak of rights, obligations, and privileges in societies where there is no normative orientation. We can only refer to such abstractions when a cultural system as well as a system of social action exists. "Use values" may exist at a protocultural stage in the primates, but they function in social systems with different properties.

Another example of normative orientation in human societies is the well-known phenomenon of incest avoidance. With its associated manifestations of shame, guilt, and anxiety, it long presented a puzzling sociopsychological problem because the underlying psychological structure was not thoroughly understood.[47] Such patterns of avoidance, with both constant and variable features, do not and could not operate at a nonhominid level where genealogical relations between individuals are not known, where socially sanctioned value systems are not present, and where the phenomena of self-identification and moral responsibility for conduct does not exist. Kroeber has pointed out that "the incest taboo is the complement of kin recognition." Abstraction, in turn, "involves ability to symbolize, in other words, speech" [130, p. 206]. Consequently, incest taboos could not arise among primates incapable of self-other orientation in a web of differentiated moral relationships. In social interaction, the individual could not be held responsible for differentiated responses to kin until the latter were explicitly classified through linguistic or other means. Although precisely the same genealogical relationships existed at a lower level of primate social organization, they could not be consciously identified and utilized as a basis of differential social interaction until the individual "actors" participating in the system developed a personality structure that permitted self-objectification and the use of symbolic means in playing sanctioned roles within a common framework of values.

Further ramifications of the basic significance of normative orienta-

[47] Lowie, e.g., in his *Primitive Society* [150], expressed the view that incest taboos have an instinctive basis. Later he changed his mind [151, p. 67].

tion and its psychological correlate of self-awareness in the evolution of a fully developed mode of cultural adaptation cannot be considered here. But the question can be raised as to whether the capacity for self-objectification was common to all the Hominidae from the beginning. Perhaps we might venture to say that, although some of the psychological *anlagen* were present at a protocultural stage, a capacity for self-objectification and role differentiation functioning in intimate relations with socially sanctioned value systems were sociopsychological developments that only became established in typical form long after the initial steps in hominid anatomical differentiation had taken place. One of the reasons for this, as we shall see, is that these developments were contingent upon a system of communication that was not only socially transmitted but, through symbolic mediation, gave unique and characteristic scope to the novel psychological capacities that had been developing through the expansion of the hominid brain.

EGO AND SELF-OBJECTIFICATION

While it has been widely recognized that self-awareness is a characteristic phenomenon in Homo sapiens,[48] the psychological structure that underlies it has been seriously studied only since the rise of a more general interest in personality structure, mainly under the impact of psychoanalytic theories. The evolutionary aspects of the problem have been scarcely touched.[49] Indeed, there have been "many psychologists

[48] For example, Bidney at the outset of his *Theoretical Anthropology* [17, p. 3] writes: "Man is a self-reflecting animal in that he alone has the ability to objectify himself, to stand apart from himself, as it were, and to consider the kind of being he is and what it is that he wants to do and to become. Other animals may be conscious of their affects and the objects they perceive; man alone is capable of reflection, of self-consciousness, of thinking of himself as an object." The psychologist David Katz, writing more than twenty years ago, likewise stressed what he called "objectivization" as a human differential [124, p. 253]. More recently, Rollo May has given particular emphasis to human self-awareness. "We can never see man whole," he says, "except as we see him, including ourselves, as the mammal who has a distinctive capacity for awareness of himself and his world. Herein lie the roots of man's capacity to reason and deal in symbols and abstract meaning. And herein lies also the basis for a sound view of human freedom" [157, p. 313; cf. 156, pp. 84–85]. Other comparable opinions could be cited, e.g., Dobzhansky [52a, pp. 337 ff.].

[49] Stanley Cobb, in discussing the papers contributed to the symposium *Brain Mechanisms and Consciousness* [2], says: "Although some of the authors seem to confuse the concepts of 'mind' and 'consciousness,' Fessard seems to agree with me that 'consciousness' is but one attribute of 'mind.' I would say [it is] *that part which has to do with awareness of self and of environment.* It varies in degree from moment to moment in man and from fish to man in phylogeny. It may be that invertebrates and even plants have rudimentary forms of awareness of self" [37, p. 202]. It is difficult, however, to follow Cobb through to this point! Sir Julian

of the modern period," as Asch says, "who have spoken of the individual organism as of a congeries of capacities and tendencies without a self-character" [6, p. 276]. It has been pointed out, moreover, that "between 1910 and 1940, most psychologists preferred not to mention 'ego' or 'self' in their writings" [199, chap. 20]. The publication of G. W. Allport's article in 1943 [4] initiated a renewed interest in ego and self on the part of social psychologists in particular. Nowadays, "ego" and "self" are familiar terms, although the connotation given them is not standardized. However, no one uses the ego concept in any substantive sense but rather as a psychological construct useful in conceptualizing a subsystem of the total personality, objectively approached, with reference to its development, structure, and functioning. If we wish to be rigorous, it is best to speak of a group of ego processes or functions, although this is sometimes awkward. Ego functions have a wide range; they are intimately connected with such cognitive processes as attention, perception, thinking, and judgment, because ego processes are involved in determining adjustments to the outer world in the interests of inner needs, particularly in a situation where choice or decision, and hence delay or postponement of action, is required [cf. 223, p. 4].[50]

On the other hand, the concept of self carries a reflexive connotation: "I" can think of "me." I can discriminate myself from other objects perceptually; I can conceive of myself as an object; I can develop attitudes toward myself. Thus the self is a phenomenal datum, whereas the ego is a construct. "The self can be observed and described; the ego is deduced and postulated. The ego may be conceived in quasi-physiological terms as a sub-system of the organism" [154, p. 234; cf. 6, chap. 10; 223]. Furthermore, the self does not mirror the ego—the subject's capacity for self-objectification does not imply his objective knowledge of the psychodynamics of his total personality.

Huxley has suggested that since "*mind* and *mental* have various undesirable connotations, it is best to drop them and to speak of awareness. Psychology in the customary sense can then be regarded as part of the general study of awareness and its evolution." This would include "the way in which new possibilities of awareness are in fact realized, and also of the limitations on their realization . . . . There are two evolutionary prerequisites for a high organization of awareness involving the incorporation of individual experience by learning: (1) a long youth period . . . ; (2) homothermy, permitting greater uniformity and continuity of awareness. Prerequisites for the further organization of the awareness-system, to enable it to incorporate experiences from other individuals and from past generations, are (1) social life, (2) the capacity to organize awareness in the form of concepts, (3) true speech. These have permitted the evolution of the unique type of awareness-system found in man" [113, pp. 558–559; cf. 110].

[50] Hartmann [86] distinguishes ego, a psychic subsystem of the total personality, with functions distinguishable from the id and superego, from self, one's own person.

Considered in evolutionary perspective, the ego may be said to be the major "psychological organ" that structurally differentiates the most highly evolved members of the Hominidae from subhominid primates and probably other hominids of lower evolutionary rank. It lies at the core of a human personality structure as we know it in Homo sapiens. Hall and Lindzey, for example, point out that "among the theorists who, in some way, make prominent use of the ego or self concept are Adler, Allport, Angyal, Cattell, Freud, Goldstein, Jung, Murphy, Murray, and Sullivan" [73, p. 545; cf. 218, pp. 27–28]. It permits adaptation at a new behavioral level. Since, in ontogenetic development, the beginnings of ego processes can be identified in the first half year of life well before the acquisition of speech, we can say that, while ego development occurs in a context of social interaction, in its initial stages it is not contingent upon the prior existence of either speech or culture. The underlying capacities for ego functioning must have deeper psychobiological roots.[51] This is the area in which the evolutionary problem lies. Rapaport, discussing the general, or psychological, theory of psychoanalysis with reference to the drive-object conception of reality, writes:

While the instincts of animals on lower evolutionary levels appear to be directly and more or less rigidly coordinated to specific external stimuli, the instincts of animals on higher evolutionary levels appear to be less rigidly coordinated to such specific stimuli. This difference may be characterized as a progressive internalization of the regulation of behavior [which is] considered coterminous with the establishment of the ego [183, p. 98].

Heinz Hartmann has been a pioneer in the development of psychoanalytic ego psychology. He says that we must not overlook important relations between animal instinct and human ego functions. His point is that "many functions, which are taken care of by instincts" in the lower animals "are in man functions of the ego." But, he says, we should not identify the nature and role of instincts in animals with "drives" in man. "The id, too, does not appear to be a simple extension of the instincts of lower animals. While the ego develops in the direction of an ever closer adjustment to reality, clinic experience shows the drives, the id-tendencies, to be far more estranged from reality than the so-called animal instincts generally are" [85, p. 379 ff.]. With reference to ontogenesis, Hartmann has been responsible for stressing an early "undifferentiated phase," in contrast with the notion that the id is chronologically older than the ego, and the concept of a "conflict-free ego sphere" [86]. In the early undifferentiated stage of ontogenetic development, there are no ego functions and no differentiation of self from the world outside. With respect

---

[51] While there is a considerable literature on the body-image phenomenon, the relations between body image, ego, and self-concepts are still under discussion [61].

to phylogenetic development, Hartmann says that while psychoanalysts do "attribute a sort of ego to animals" [87, p. 48; no species indicated]—

. . . we cannot speak, in regard to the animal, of that kind of separation into ego and id which exists in the human adult. The very fact that the concept of instincts as it pertains to the lower animals is much more comprehensive than the concept of instinctual drives as it pertains to man prevents such a separation. It is possible, and even probable, that it is just this sharper differentiation of the ego and the id—the more precise division of labor between them—in human adults which on the one hand makes for a superior, more flexible relation to the outside world and, on the other, increases the alienation of the id from reality [cf. 85].

Discussing Hartmann's conception of reality, Rapaport says:

In animals of lower evolutionary levels the instincts are the guarantees of reality adaptedness; man's drives have lost much of this role, and thus inborn adaptedness is with him more a potentiality than an actuality; processes of adaptation outweigh inborn adaptedness. This potentiality for internalized regulation of behavior actualizes in the course of the development of the ego, which thus becomes man's organ of adaptation . . . Hartmann goes even further and conceives of the reality to which man adapts as one created by him and his predecessors [183, p. 100].

Related to Hartmann's views are those of H. E. Erikson. "Man is potentially preadapted . . . to a whole evolving series of such environments [which] are not 'objective,' but rather social environments which meet his maturation and development half-way" [183, p. 100].

These views are of central importance in a conjunctive approach to human evolution. They reinforce other evidence which indicates that the general evolutionary trend is one in which the role of central cortical functions, acting as intervening variables, becomes increasingly important. Ego processes and functions in Homo sapiens would appear to represent the culmination of this trend in the primates, laying the foundation, among other things, for the more psychologically complex "inner world" of man. At the same time, the potentialities for relative autonomy from the external environment, in the purely "objective" sense, can be appreciated as an inherent part of later hominid evolution and the role which culturally constituted "behavioral" environments came to play in man's psychosocial adaptation.

Since, in contrast to the more peremptory determinants of behavior, ego processes refer to those aspects of behavior which are delayable, bring about delay, or are themselves products of delay [59, p. 5], evidence for the phylogenetic roots of the ego may be sought in the functional equivalents of ego processes and functions at lower primate levels.

Although Nissen does not make the inference himself, I think that the examples he gives in support of his assertion that the higher anthropoids are "guided by a delicately balanced system of values," may be taken as evidence of the functioning of rudimentary ego processes:

The larger and stronger male chimpanzee deferring to his female companion in the division of food, even after the female is pregnant and no longer suitable as a sex partner—the animal "punishing" the misbehavior of his cagemate and in position to inflict serious injury, but contenting himself with merely nipping him painfully—the chimpanzee refusing to expose himself to the frustration of occasional failure in a difficult problem, although he could get a desirable tidbit 50 per cent of the time by merely continuing to make a simple and easy response—these are but a few of many instances of a finely adjusted hierarchy of values. Like man, the chimpanzee has many values only indirectly related to primary needs, as for food, sex, and knowledge [169, p. 108].

It need not be inferred, I think, that the values referred to by Nissen were socially sanctioned, or that the chimpanzee is capable of consciously relating or appraising his own conduct with reference to socially acquired values. These values of the chimpanzee do not represent fully articulated values in the human sense. We are still at a protocultural level of sociopsychological functioning where no normative orientation exists.

However, the intervening variables that appear to be determinative in these situations exemplify the behavioral outcome of the shift from physiological to cortical controls which laid the foundation that enabled the Pongidae and, no doubt, their protohominind relatives, to develop a new level of psychobiological adaptation. I cannot escape the impression, either, that the behavior of the chimpanzees at Orange Park exemplifies the integration of attention, perceiving, thinking, purposiveness, and the postponement of action, in a rudimentary form, which are among the ego processes and functions attributed to Homo sapiens. Seeing visitors arriving, they ran quickly to the drinking fountain and, after filling their mouths with water, quietly waited for the closer approach of the visitors before discharging it at them. Hebb and Thompson, who report this observation [90, p. 539], do not refer to ego processes or function but use the episode to illustrate the chimpanzees' capacity for what is called "syntactic behavior," which they consider crucial in phylogenesis. In involves an "increasing independence of the conceptual activity from the present sensory environment, and an increasing capacity for entertaining diverse conceptual processes at the same time." Among other things it "eventually makes speech possible." "At the lowest level, it is the capacity for delayed response or a simple expectancy; at the highest level, for 'building' not only a series of words but also of sentences, whose meaning only becomes clear with later words or sentences." To my mind, Hebb's concept of syntactic behavior falls along the psychological dimension in phylogenesis where we must look for the rudimentary phases of ego processes and functions.[52] At the same time, I do not think that behavioral evidence such as that cited, which appears to indicate the functioning of rudimentary ego processes, allows us to make the further inference that this behavior involves self-objectification.

The capacity for self-objectification represents a level of psychological integration that requires the operation of additional factors. On the one hand, self-objectification is rooted in a prior development of rudimentary ego functions; on the other, the representation and articulation of a sense of self-awareness is contingent upon the capacity for the symbolic projection of experience in socially meaningful terms, i.e., in a mode that is intelligible interindividually. There must be a functional integration of intrinsic representative processes with some extrinsically expressible means of symbolization. An extrinsic mode is necessary in order to mediate socially transmitted and commonly shared meanings in a system of social action. There must become available to an individual some means whereby inwardly as well as outwardly directed reference to his own experience and that of others, and to objects and events in his world that are other than self, can find common ground. Outward behavior can be perceived and imitated through observational learning in nonhominid primates. Emotional experiences can become contagious. But what is privately sensed, imaged, conceptualized, or thought cannot be imitated or responded to without an overt sign extrinsic to the experience itself. Working the drinking fountain at Orange Park or nest building in the chimpanzee can be socialized without the mediation of any form of extrinsic representation. There is no evidence to suggest that either the chimpanzee or any other nonhominid has developed a traditional means whereby it is possible for an individual to represent himself and other objects and events to himself as well as to others. Consequently, even though capacities for ego-centered processes may exist, they can attain only a limited functional range.

In phylogenetic perspective there is evidence that intrinsic symbolic processes (i.e., central processes that function as substitutes for or representatives of sensory cues or events that are not present in the immediate perceptual field) occur not only in subhominid primates but in some lower species. But even in the higher apes the functioning of these representative processes appears to be limited, as is a capacity for ego processes. But it is difficult to know precisely what these limits are. Schneirla, making reference to Crawford's experiment [40] on the cooperative solving of problems by chimpanzees, says that these animals

---

[52] Hebb and Thompson make a most illuminating comment: "It is probably a common experience to all who have worked at the Yerkes Laboratories to feel that the bare bones of human personality, the raw essentials, are being laid open before his eyes. At the same time, it is hard to convey this to others, and to support it with behavioral evidence" [90, p. 544].

. . . were able to learn a gestural form of communication and use it symbolically. [They were enabled] to summon one another by means of self-initiated gestures such as gentle taps on the shoulder. These were truly symbolic, and not merely signals to action. The chimpanzee who tapped was presenting, in anticipation of its social effect, a special cue which had come to symbolize, i.e., to stand for meaningfully, the expected social result. The symbolic, anticipative, and directive nature of this gestural cue was indicated by the fact that, when shoulder taps were insufficient, or slow in producing co-operation, the active animal would turn to pulling alone, or might act forcibly and directly to get the second animal involved in pulling. Although it is not known how far and in what ways such gestural devices may be involved in chimpanzee group communication under natural conditions, their use is probably very limited [205, pp. 64–65].[53]

Interpreted in this way, the gestures referred to may be considered a rudimentary and highly limited mode of displacement or extrinsic symbolization. The function of these gestures was, of course, imposed by the nature and circumstances of the experiment. In this framework, conditions were not favorable for the perpetuation of these gestures through social learning and transmission in a wider group.

A unique observation illustrates the presence of intrinsic symbolic processes in chimpanzees, tantalizing because of their incommunicability. It is reported that Viki sometimes played with what appeared to be an imaginary pull-toy which she towed around on an imaginary string [88, chap. 11]. Viki, of course, could not deliberately communicate the content of her experience to ape or man, even if she had so desired. She could only act out her fantasy. Mrs. Hayes could only observe what she saw and guess what the probable image was that motivated Viki's behavior. Viki did not have the capacity to abstract, objectify, and transform the content of her intrinsic symbolic processes into a symbolic form extrinsic to the experience itself. For the same reason, we can be certain that she could not think about herself as an object playing with her pull-toy. Because there was no system of extrinsic symbolization available as a means of communication, the world that Viki and Mrs. Hayes could share was very limited psychologically. It may be that one of the major reasons chimpanzees cannot be taught to speak is that they are not capable of manipulating second-order abstractions of the type necessary for

[53] In a later publication, Schneirla notes that "a child's attainment of sentences marks a new advance from the stage of unitary verbal symbols, and contrasts sharply with a monkey's inability to master symbolic relationships beyond the simplest abstractions. In a far wider sense, man's capacity for repatterning verbal symbols serially, or for attaining such symbols at all, is qualitatively far above the functional order represented by the gestural symbolic processes to which the chimpanzee seems developmentally limited, although not altogether dissimilar in its ontogenetic basis" [207, p. 102]. I am not concerned here with the introduction of symbolic cues into laboratory investigations by the experimenter [80, p. 493 ff.].

extrinsic symbolization even though lower levels of abstraction are possible for them.

The earliest unequivocal proof of the capacity of Homo sapiens for extrinsic symbolization in a visual mode is found in the cave art of the Upper Paleolithic. Here we find the graphic representation of such animals as mammoth, rhinoceros, bison, wild horse, reindeer, etc., which could not have been present in the perceptual field of the artist when the drawings were made. The location of them in most of the caves excludes this possibility.[54] The number of human, or human-like figures, is small in proportion to the hundreds of animal drawings. So far as the figures of wild animals are concerned, we can only infer that the men of this period had highly accurate and vivid memory images of the contemporary fauna (intrinsic symbolization). At the same time, their capacity to abstract essential features of their images and represent them in a material medium is demonstrated. When the animals themselves were not present, the drawings of them in a naturalistic style could convey to other men what was "in" the artist's "mind." While the iconic type of symbolization employed required some abstraction, there is a relatively close correspondence in form between the object seen, the memory image, and the graphic symbolization.

But there also seems to be evidence in the cave art of a related human capacity, that is, the ability to project graphically synthetic images of fabulous creatures, animal-like or human-like, which were not objects of ordinary perceptual experience. These belong, rather, to the world of creative imagination. The beast with two horns at Lascaux is the prime example of the representation of a fantastic animal.[55] Many examples of ambiguous human figures—synthesizing both

[54] In one cave I visited I remember crawling along a low gallery on my knees, with candle in hand, for a considerable distance before reaching the end of it. Discouraged at not finding any drawings, I turned over on my back for a rest. There above me were several drawings of wild horses. And Laming says: "At Arcy-sur-Cure the engravings are discovered only after a painful crawl of about 80 yards over slippery clay and sharp-pointed calcite. Such remote recesses, difficult of access and laborious of approach, are almost as numerous as the painted and engraved caves themselves. The placing of all these figures in remote parts of dark caverns seems to bear witness to a pursuit of the arduous, the magical, and the sacred" [139, p. 158].

[55] Breuil writes: "By its massive body and thick legs, it resembles a bovine animal or a Rhinoceros; the very short tail is more indicative of the latter; the flanks are marked with a series of O-shaped oval splashes; the neck and ears are ridiculously small for the body; the head with a square muzzle, is like that of a Feline; two long stiff straight shafts, each ending in a tuft, are like no known animal horns, unless, as Miss Bate suggested, those of the Pantholops of Thibet . . . . This is not the only example of a composite unreal animal in Quaternary art, but it is the most spectacular" [23, p. 118 and Fig. 89]. The drawing measures about 5 ft. 6 in.

human and animal characteristics—are known. It is these figures which have proved the most difficult to interpret in the whole repertoire of cave art, since in style they do not fit the realistic tradition of the animal art.[56] The older view that these semihuman figures were the representation of actual human beings wearing masks or the skins of animals has been steadily losing ground. In the cave of Trois Frères, the figure originally called a "sorcerer" by Breuil and Bégouën is now thought by them to be the representation of the "Spirit controlling the multiplication of game and hunting expeditions" [23, pp. 176–177]; in other words, it is a god or a personage of an other-than-human class.[57] If the humanly ambiguous figures are thought of as belonging to such a class, I believe that it may be argued that we have evidence suggesting that a system of beliefs is reflected in the art. If such be the case, this category of figures is equivalent to the personages that appear in the myths of living primitive peoples. In this case, the cave art would offer evidence of a level of imaginative functioning and conceptual creativity that transcended a purely naturalistic reproduction of what was perceived. It could be interpreted as revealing capacities in early representatives of Homo sapiens that are psychologically equivalent to capacities of living peoples studied in their full cultural context, where the details of world view and religious beliefs have been recorded.[58]

The symbolism embodied in speech is in a different mode, since sound clusters are given a meaning-content that is unrelated to the form or qualities of the objects or events represented. Nevertheless, it seems to me that we must assume that the same basic capacities for extrinsic

[56] For illustrations of 250 examples of these figures and a systematic classification and analysis of them, see [195].

[57] Laming is of the opinion that "the imaginary animals and the semi-human figures are . . . incompatible with the theory of sympathetic magic" which has been applied to the animal art. Considered as a whole, she also finds untenable "the theory that they represent hunting masks or have some connection with ritual hunting dances." "Why should the sorcerers, who were probably the artists of the tribe, depict themselves on the walls of the sanctuary wearing their masks?" she asks. It seems more likely that these drawings "represent mythical beings who were perhaps connected in some way with the history of the ancestors of the group" [139, pp. 191–192].

[58] Cf. the discussion of "persons" of an other-than-human class among Ojibwa [78]. Persons of this category are reified beings in the behavioral world of the Ojibwa and are equivalent to characters in their myths. Among them these narratives are true stories. Since metamorphosis is possible, a hard and fast line cannot even be drawn between the outward appearance of *human* persons and animals. Persons of the other-than-human class in particular, appear in myths and dreams in animal form. If the Ojibwa had an art similar to that of the Upper Paleolithic peoples and we had no other evidence, it can be imagined how difficult it would be to interpret the graphic representations they had made of persons of an other-than-human class.

symbolization are involved. Art forms are as indicative of these capacities as are speech forms. Among other things, graphic art in all its manifestations requires abstraction, or it could not function as a means of representation. In any case, it is hard to believe that the people of the Upper Paleolithic did not possess a vocal system of representation (although we have no direct evidence of speech) as well as a fully developed mode of cultural adaptation equivalent to that of the nonliterate peoples of historic times. Viki and other chimpanzees, if considered as representative of an advanced level of infrahominid behavior, manifest as little capacity for graphic symbolization of an extrinsic type as for vocal symbolization [see the colored reproductions of Viki's paintings in *Life,* Dec. 3, 1951]. By the time we reach the Upper Paleolithic, the infrahominids have been left far behind on the ladder of behavioral evolution.

Systems of extrinsic symbolization necessitate the use of material media which can function as vehicles for the communication of meanings. Abstraction and conceptualization are required since objects or events are introduced into the perceptual field as *symbols*, not in their concrete reality. Thus systems of extrinsic symbolization involve the operation of the representative principle on a more complex level than do processes of intrinsic symbolization. In the case of Homo sapiens, extrinsic symbolic systems, functioning through vocal, graphic, plastic, gestural, or other media, make it possible for groups of human beings to share a common world of meanings and values. A cultural mode of adaptation is unthinkable without systems of extrinsic symbolization.

From a phylogenetic point of view, the capacity for individual and social adaptation through the *integral* functioning of intrinsic symbolic processes and extrinsic symbolic systems enabled an evolving hominid to enlarge and transform his world. The immediate, local, time-and-space-bound world of other primates, who lack the capacity for dealing effectively with objects and events outside the field of direct perception, could be transcended. Speech, through the use of personal pronouns, personal names, and kinship terms made it possible for an individual to symbolize, and thus objectify, himself in systems of social action. Self-related activities, both in the past and future, could be brought into the present and reflected upon.[59] What emerged was a personality structure in which ego processes and functions had become salient at a high level of integration—self-awareness. The inner world of private experience and the outer world of public experience became intricately

[59] Cf. Révész, who writes, "Without the verbal formulation of subjective experience and ethical standards, self-consciousness is incomplete and self-knowledge and self-control equally so. To be conscious of one's own self, to examine one's own endeavors, motives, resolves, and actions, necessarily presupposes language" [188, p. 104].

meshed through symbolic mediation. In the human societies, the self-image became, in part, a culturally constituted variable; self-orientation became integrated with other basic orientations toward the world that enabled the individual to think, feel, and act in a culturally constituted behavioral environment [76, chap. 4]. As a result of self-objectification, human societies could function through the commonly shared value orientations of self-conscious individuals, in contrast with the societies of nonhominid and probably early hominid primates, where ego-centered processes remained undeveloped or rudimentary. In fact, when viewed from the standpoint of this peculiarity of man, culture may be said to be an elaborated and socially transmitted system of meanings and values which, in an animal capable of self-awareness, implements a type of adaptation which makes the role of the human being intelligible to himself, both with reference to an articulated universe and to his fellow men.

The central importance of ego processes and self-awareness that we find distinctive in Homo sapiens can be viewed from another angle. Since self-objectification involves self-appraisal in relation to sanctioned moral conduct, we can see the social as well as the individual adaptive value of unconscious psychological processes such as repression, rationalization, and other defense mechanisms. Culturally constituted moral values impose a characteristic psychological burden, since it is not always easy, at the level of self-awareness, to reconcile idiosyncratic needs with the demands imposed by the normative orientation of the self. For animals without the capacity for self-objectification, no such situation can arise. Freedman and Roe write:

Only in man is there simultaneously such a rigidity of social channeling and such a degree of potential plasticity and flexibility for the individual. Incompatible aims and choices which are desirable but mutually exclusive are inevitable conditions of human development. This discrepancy between possibility and restriction, stimulation and interdiction, range and construction, underlies that quantitatively unique characteristic of the human being: conflict [66, p. 461].

In Homo sapiens, unconscious mechanisms may be viewed as an adaptive means that permits some measure of compromise between conflicting forces. They relieve the individual of part of the burden not only forced upon him by the requirements of a morally responsible existence but by the fact that the normative orientation of any human social order permeates all aspects of living. A human level of existence requires an evolutionary price; man as a species has survived, despite proneness to conflict, anxiety, and psychopathology [cf. 66, p. 422]. Freud's interpretation is to be found in his *Civilization and Its Discontents:* "The price of progress in civilization is paid for in forfeiting happiness through the heightening of the sense of guilt" [67, p. 123]. There seems to be little question that one of the crucial areas of individual adjustment turns upon the sensitivity of the self to feelings of anxiety and guilt.

Psychoanalysts, in particular, have come more and more to recognize that psychological maladjustment centers around the structural core of the human personality. David Beres, for example, writes: "There is then in man this unique structure, the ego, which in its full function allows for the expression of those qualities which distinguish the human from the animal and which, in their malfunction, give to his behavior and thought the characteristically human forms of mental illness" [16, pp. 170, 231].

Leopold Bellak has recently reviewed the shift in focus that has occurred in psychoanalytic thinking:

The novelty in psychoanalysis was originally its introduction of the unconscious in the sense of the unconsciousness of feelings, the unawareness of previously experienced events, the covert nature of motivations, and the hidden meaning of dreams and symptoms. Slowly attention focused on the forces responsible for this unconsciousness, notably repression [13, pp. 25–26].

A new era, however, "dedicated to the analysis not only of the unconscious but of the ego and its defences," was initiated with Anna Freud's book *The Ego and the Mechanisms of Defense* (1936). So that now "the pendulum has swung nearly full cycle, in that there is so much talk about ego psychology today that the forces of the unconscious are possibly already somewhat in disregard" [13, pp. 25–26; cf. 220, p. 146].

Franz Alexander, commenting on the same shift of interest, says,

Mental disease represents a failure of the ego to secure gratification for subjective needs in a harmonious and reality-adjusted manner and a breakdown of the defenses by which it tries to neutralize impulses which it cannot harmonize with its internal standards and external reality. . . . The highest form of integrative function requires conscious deliberation. Everything which is excluded from consciousness is beyond the reach of the ego's highest integrative functions. . . . Psychoanalytic therapy aims at the extension of the ego's integrative scope over repressed tendencies by making them conscious [3, p. 78 ff.].[60]

Thus, in the terminology I have been using here, psychological functioning at a level of self-awareness is as important for rational personal adjustment as it is for the functioning of sociocultural systems. Furthermore, as Schneirla points out, it is an error stemming from an

[60] Cf. Hartmann's remarks on the synthetic or organizing functions of the ego [85, pp. 383–384].

inadequate comprehension of the complex nature of a human level of existence to assume "that man's 'higher psychological processes' constitute a single agency or unity which is capable of being sloughed off" even under extreme provocation. On the contrary—

. . . socialized man even under stress of extreme organic need or persistent frustration does not regress to the "brute level." Rather, he shifts to some eccentric and distorted variation of his ordinary personality, which varies from his prevalent socialized make-up according to the degree of integrity and organization attained by that adjustment system [202, p. 273].

This is why we find variations in the symptomatology and incidence of mental disorders in man when we consider them in relation to differences in cultural modes of adaptation. These phenomena often have been given a purely relativistic emphasis. But increasing evidence suggests that they probably can be ordered to psychodynamic principles and etiological factors that operate universally [14, 226]. Direct comparison, moreover, between the psychopathology of the "civilized" individual mind and the "primitive" mind savors more than ever of a pseudoevolutionary problem.

CONCLUSIONS

What we observe in the behavior of Homo sapiens is the evolutionary culmination and unique integration of structures and functions which had developed over a span of millions of years in the long and complex history of the primates. The human nature of Homo sapiens cannot be fully grasped outside this framework. The cultural level of adaptation which has been said to be the characteristic feature of a human level of existence requires a developmental conceptualization which includes prerequisite conditions of a noncultural order and a discrimination of organic, social, and psychological variables operating in the past. I have used the construct "protoculture" as a means of identifying the necessary, but not sufficient, conditions which appear to be the evolutionary prerequisites of the fully developed phase of cultural adaptation as represented in Homo sapiens.

On the assumption that the hominid line of evolutionary radiation initially involved the genetic establishment of the structural changes which led to a bipedal upright posture and a terrestrial mode of adaptation, two stages of protocultural development which preceded cultural adaptation may be tentatively postulated. The first stage can be associated with the prehominids, and evidence for it is derived from observations on living groups of nonhominids. In the chronology of behavioral evolution, this protocultural stage may be conceived as having great temporal depth; at the same time, its most distinguishing features may be thought of as continuous with the earliest level of hominid morphological differentiation. In its sociological and psychological dimensions, it links the prehominids with the *early* hominids, and also provides some of the necessary conditions for *later* hominid cultural adaptation.

The second stage of protocultural development can be conceptually associated with the earliest hominids *prior* to the genetic establishment of an expanded cortex in the more evolved members of this group, the subfamily Homininae. This differentiation of two levels of protocultural development, based as it is on structural changes which have behavioral implications, is not intended to be precise. But it enables us to distinguish behavioral continuities and differences in relation to known structural changes and ecological relations and it provides us with a somewhat more differentiated chronological sequence than would a simple dichotomous distinction between infrahominid and hominid levels. The second protocultural stage, in short, is a construct which enables us to distinguish an intermediate phase of behavioral evolution. In this phase, certain features of an earlier protocultural stage persisted, but were modified by the structural changes which adapted the early hominids to a new ecological niche. In turn, this second protocultural stage was transformed; with the expansion of the brain, a new level of behavioral evolution, characterized by a fully developed mode of cultural adaptation, came into being.

The most important feature of the earliest protocultural stage (exemplified by nonhominid primates) was the existence of social structures or systems of social action. These structures were based on role differentiation, which partially depend upon the socialization of individuals mediated by observational learning, some tutelage perhaps, and unlearned systems of sign communication, both gestural and vocal. The latter embodied some design features which were later incorporated in the more elaborated system of linguistic communication that we find associated with the later level of cultural adaptation. There was social transmission of some group habits at the earlier level; perhaps there was occasional tool using of the simplest kind. In other words, it was a form of social organization which, in so far as it was a system of social action in which learning was related to social structure and to the transmission of social habits, exemplifies some of the basic conditions which are required for cultural adaptation. Particularly striking, in the light of present knowledge, is the lack of any evidence that there were any socially transmitted forms of communication in nonhominid societies, even though some of the design features of the languages characteristic of Homo sapiens were already present.[61]

[61] Carpenter says: "The limitations of capacities for communication, especially for symbol communication, seem to stop non-human primate social development at the level of limited contemporary social groupings, to preclude the development of tribal kinship and to make it impossible for them to have any except the *anlagen* of cultural traditions" [29, p. 242].

So far as learned behavior is concerned, its importance in relation to culture has been both exaggerated and oversimplified. As Nissen said, "Experience will not make a man out of a monkey" [169, p. 105]. Learning in the form of simple conditioning is found far down the animal scale.[62] Cultural adaptation cannot be equated with learned and socially transmitted behavior, although it is one of the necessary conditions underlying it. Equally important in behavioral evolution is how much is learned and what is learned, relative to the psychological capacities and total life adjustments of the animal.[63]

In anthropological writing prior to the culture and personality movement, the vital connection between learning, social organization, and culture remained vague; the gap had not been bridged between abstracted culture patterns and the behavior of specific individuals through such concepts as socialization or enculturation, personality structure, status, and role. The fact had been overlooked that a culture can be perpetuated only through the characteristic psychological structuralization of individuals in an organized system of social action. At a protocultural stage, what was learned differed both quantitatively and qualitatively from what was observed at a later stage in behavioral evolution. Particularly significant in primate evolution is the fact that learning became linked with social structure and the transmission of habits through a socialization process at the subhominid level. Here learning already played a part in the life history of the individual and the functioning of the social order that closely parallels at many points the part it continued to play in human socio*cultural* systems. Nor has there been sufficient

[62] Harlow argues that "there is no evidence that any sharp break ever appeared in the evolutionary development of the learning process" [83, p. 288]. At the same time, "it is quite clear that evolution has resulted in the development of animals of progressively greater potentialities for learning and for solving problems of increasing complexity" [83, p. 269].

[63] Hilgard is not content with the implicit, if not always explicit, generalization from comparative studies that "there are no differences, except quantitative ones, between the learning of lower mammals and man." At the human level, he says, "There have emerged capacities for retraining, reorganizing, and foreseeing experiences which are not approached by the lower animals, including the other primates. No one has seriously proposed that animals can develop a set of ideals that regulate conduct around long-range plans, or that they can invent a mathematics to help them keep track of their enterprises. . . . Language in man is perhaps the clearest of the emergents which carries with it a forward surge in what may be learned. It seems plausible enough that other advances in the ability to learn must have come about as the nervous system evolved through successive stages below man. . . . There are probably a number of different kinds of learning which have emerged at different evolutionary periods, with the more highly evolved organisms using several of them. It is quite probable that these different kinds of learning follow different laws, and it is foolhardy to allow our desire for parsimony to cause us to overlook persisting differences" [94, p. 461].

stress on the fact that at the earliest protocultural level, characterized ecologically by arboreal adaptation and territoriality, arboreal trails had to be learned [32, p. 241].

Considered in evolutionary perspective, a cultural mode of adaptation required an environmental setting in which ecological relations provided a foundation for later developments, in addition to sociopsychological prerequisites and the functioning of some system of communication. Consequently, a second protocultural stage which distinguished the hominid line of evolution from that of the pongids was initiated concomitantly with the structural changes. Arboreal adaptation may have played a part in the earlier evolution of the primates, and this may have included the development of distinctive psychological capacities and behavioral patterns. But it is difficult, if not impossible, to imagine an arboreal domain as the ecological matrix of cultural adaptation as observed in Homo sapiens. If we take a long-range view of ecological adaptation in the primates (excluding cases in which terrestrial adaptation has been achieved by such Old World monkeys as the baboons, who retained their pronograde mode of locomotion), we can reconstruct a successive series of arboreal adaptations. The series begins high in the tropical treetops where lower primate forms occupy a niche, leads downward to lower arboreal habitats, and ultimately arrives at a terrestrial niche occupied by the hominids. Le Gros Clark says:

> [In the primates] each successive grade has developed a new ecological domain, leaving behind representatives of antecedent grades (more or less modified for their local habitat of course) in occupation of the particular arboreal environment for which they had already become adapted. It may be said, indeed, that the trees of African and Asiatic forests still retain in rough outline a stratified population of Primates which represents the successive grades of the evolutionary tree of this order. [The] smallest and more primitive types (tree-shrews), by confining their activities mainly to the more attenuated branches of the treetops, lead a secluded life within the protection of foliage and have thus become effectively segregated from the larger types [146, pp. 320–321].

Le Gros Clark does not specifically make the point, but it seems to me that the hominids, in developing upright posture and orthograde locomotion, have taken an almost predictable step in the series of ecological readaptations which characterize primate evolution. The new ecological domain of the early hominids subsequently became the theater of the cultural adaptation of the more advanced hominids (Homininae).

Terrestrial living provided the ecological framework of these later developments. When the necessary psychological capacities, accumulated experience, and technological traditions had been developed, the hominids were able to accelerate the behavioral differences between themselves and other primates, achieving greater independence of their environment through increasing knowledge of its inanimate resources and its fauna and flora and through a succession of discoveries and inventions. Even if capacities for *tool using* were present in arboreal primates, how could the properties of stone have been discovered, exploited, and developed into the lithic industries of a *toolmaking* tradition by creatures who spent little or no time on the ground? How could the domestication of animals and the cultivation of plants come about? How could fire become of importance in the life of primates confined to an arboreal niche? Terrestrial living was one of the necessary prerequisites for cultural adaptation. It provided the opportunity for discovering new food resources. Ultimately it made possible the shift, through a possible scavenging stage, to hunting large mammals, cooking meat, and the omnivorous diet of the Homininae. Eiseley has pointed out that, so far as organic inheritance is conceived, the hominid gut is not that of a true meat eater. Nevertheless, euhominids did become carnivorous and thus underwent, according to Eiseley, "a transition in food habits which is unique on the planet" [56]. Details regarding this transition during the second protocultural phase may, in time, be filled in by evidence from archeological research. So far, there is no positive evidence that fire was used in the earliest stage of terrestrial adaptation.[64] Since fire could be brought completely under control only by fire-making implements, or tools, it may well be that they were only developed along with other tools employed in hunting and cutting meat. (I refer to the most rudimentary of tools. Even very simple cutting tools could have made it possible to supplement a vegetarian diet with the meat of small animals.)

It can be assumed, I think, that territoriality persisted into the second protocultural stage. A question arises as to whether there was any change in the size of organized social groups. Oakley's estimated size for the range of australopithecine groups is 10 to 200 individuals. Washburn and DeVore point out that "this corresponds almost exactly to the range in size observed in baboons. Since both are plains-living, primarily vegetarian forms," they say, "the comparison is of particular interest" [241]. Sahlins has estimated the size of human hunting groups to range between 20 and 50 [197]. Present data suggests that the size of localized groups may not have increased during the earliest phases of a cultural mode of adaptation. Their composition, however, undoubtedly did change to include individuals of several generations, as psychological restructuralization provided the foundation for modes of social control

---

[64] Oakley thinks: "It is probable that the earliest paleolithic fire-users were not *fire-makers,* but collected this precious commodity from natural conflagrations, and conserved it." There is evidence that fire was used earlier in Asia and Europe than Africa. "The oldest acceptable indications of the use of fire by man in Europe and Western Asia are associated with Acheulian hand-axe culture" [176].

that were based on superego functioning as well as external social sanctions.

We assume that hominid differentiation involved selection for immaturity, as indicated by the fact that maturation was slower, dependency of the young longer, and menarche later, so that longevity increased and the generation span became greater than at the subhominid level. If this is correct, there must have been a feedback into the system of social organization which affected the length of the period of socialization and the social transmission of new habits.

We can also assume that the new ecological domain to which the early hominids were becoming adapted provided increased opportunity to exercise behavioral potentialities already present. Motor functions like grasping hands were freed for new uses, and the discriminatory function of binocular stereoscopic vision facilitated new developments in tactile skills, manual dexterity, and probably visual imagery. It would appear that toolmaking arose in this period if the later australopithecines may be taken as representative; according to Washburn, this development may have had a feedback effect upon the expansion of the brain. Washburn and Avis have expressed the opinion that tool using may require "much less brain than does speech and might have started as soon as the hands were freed from locomotive functions" [240, p. 432]. Since the cortex had not yet undergone expansion, cranial capacity may have only ranged from 450 to 600 cc (australopithecines) and communication may well have remained at the nonhominid stage, thus maintaining another link with the earlier protocultural period.

In a new ecological setting, with greatly expanded possibilities for life adjustment provided by bipedal locomotion and some minor changes in social structure and food habits, the early hominids might have continued their existence at this level of adaptation indefinitely if another organic change had not occurred. This was the rapid expansion of the brain. Through the addition of neurons and their intricate systems of cerebral organization, the brain became the neurophysiological basis of the mode of behavioral adaptation that has been called "cultural" in Homo sapiens and antecedent types of Homininae. Psychological restructuralization occurred; it became manifest through the generic type of personality structure observable in Homo sapiens, it released novel potentialities whose feedback into the already existing systems of social action transformed them psychodynamically through the now possible normative orientation. For example, while parents and their offspring previously had been associated in systems of social action, the development of incest taboos radically affected their relations psychologically. It likewise affected the roles of other individuals brought within the categories of kinship. Mediated by the development of extrinsic forms of symbolization which appeared in speech and in the arts, cultural adaptation may be viewed as the culmination of social evolution in the primates to which new dimensions were added. This development could not have occurred, however, without the distinctive combination of prerequisite conditions already found in the protocultural phases of behavioral evolution.

There was a quantitative maximization of social learning, reinforced by teaching; this led to qualitatively distinctive consequences because of the role which learning came to play in the formation of a human personality structure and the functioning of the higher mental processes. Cognitive processes were raised to a new level of functioning by means of culturally constituted symbolic forms; these now could be manipulated creatively through reflective thought, imagination, and novel forms of expression. Cultural modes of adaptation—or certain aspects of them— could also be thought about, objectified, analyzed, judged, and even re- modeled to some degree by hominids who had achieved a capacity for self-awareness and had become objects to themselves in a world of other objects. In the behavioral evolution of the primates, the great novelty was not simply the development of a cultural mode of adaptation. It was the psychological restructuralization that made this new mode of exist- ence possible and also provided the potentialities for cultural *rea*djust- ment and change. The psychological basis of culture lies not only in a capacity for highly complex forms of learning, but in a capacity for transcending what is learned—a potentiality for innovation, creativity, reorganization, and change.[65]

In time, men even initiated systematic rational inquiries into the nature of the inanimate world, the world of living things, and man him- self—despite the fact that this knowledge conflicted at many points with the traditional world view of their culture. In modern times, scientific investigations have demonstrated this extraordinary capacity of our species to the highest degree. We now feel far removed from the infrahominid level of societal organization or the level of thought and action possible for the earliest hominids. Yet our mode of existence, elaborate as it may be, is linked with theirs in the same sense that all higher forms of organic life are linked with antecedent forms through the evolutionary process. In fact, most of the categories of variables which appear again and again in the studies of contemporary man can be projected into the far-distant past. For a comprehensive understanding of the evolutionary roots of human behavior, a conjunctive approach is just as relevant as it is for a study of contemporary man. Too radical ab-

---

[65] Cf. Henry, who points out that "because his mechanism for determining personal relations lacks specificity," man's unique evolutionary path is set for him "by his constant tendency to alter his modes of social adaptation. Put somewhat in value terms, man tries constantly to make a better society, i.e., one in which he can feel more comfortable. When he makes a 'mistake,' he tries to change. This is one way in which he evolves" [92, pp. 221–222].

stractions of the morphological, sociological, ecological, or psychological variables considered above leads to fragmentary knowledge in either case.

In either framework, too, man's social nature emerges as a paramount fact which cannot be ignored. The higher primates, like the later hominids, were gregarious animals. But this must not be taken as a banal descriptive fact. Their social existence took the form of discretely organized systems of social action, even though these were more restricted in numbers and differentiation of roles than ours. Behavioral evolution must be thought of as the concomitant evolution of continuously present and changing social relations, structured in systems of social action—not as the evolution of the behavioral attributes of isolated individuals. Consequently the genetic changes which took place in the primates, as in other animals, present problems in population genetics, the population units in this case being the social groups referred to. Thus, organic, ecological, social, and psychological variables all need to be considered in relation to each other at all levels of behavioral evolution.[66]

In Homo sapiens, personality, society, and culture have been conceptually differentiated for special types of analysis and investigation. At the same time, their interdependence is now well recognized. They cannot be postulated as independent variables either in the study of modern man or in human behavioral evolution. Considered phylogenetically, we gain some insight into the temporal depth of their intimate connections, as well as their relation to organic and ecological variables. Besides this, the significance of these integral connections is brought into focus both with respect to the sociopsychological nature of modern man as a product of evolution and the primary adaptive processes inherent in the achievement of the socio*cultural* systems which have become characteristic of his mode of life.

REFERENCES

1. Aberle, D. F., Cohen, A. K., Davis, A. K., Levy, M. J., Jr., & Sutton, F. X. The functional prerequisites of a society. *Ethics,* 1950, **60,** 100–111.
2. Adrian, E. D., Bremer, F., Delafresnaye, J. F., & Jasper, H. H. (Eds.) *Brain mechanisms and consciousness.* Springfield, Ill.: Charles C Thomas, 1954.
3. Alexander, F. The evolution and present trends of psychoanalysis.

[66]Cf. the thesis expounded by Dobzhansky that "man has both a nature and a 'history,' " and that "human evolution cannot be understood as a purely biological process, nor can it be adequately described as a history of culture. It is the interaction of biology and culture. There exists a feedback between biological and cultural processes" [52a, p. 18].

Acta Psychol., 1950, **7**, 126–133. Reprinted in H. Brand (Ed.), *The study of personality: a book of readings.* New York: Wiley, 1954.

4. Allport, G. W. The ego in contemporary psychology. *Psychol. Rev.*, 1943, **50**, 451–478.

5. Allport, G. W. The historical background of modern social psychology. In G. Lindzey (Ed.), *Handbook of social psychology.* Vol. 1. Reading, Mass.: Addison-Wesley, 1954.

6. Asch, S. E. *Social psychology.* Englewood Cliffs, N.J.: Prentice-Hall, 1952.

7. Asch, S. E. A perspective on social psychology. In S. Koch (Ed.), *Psychology: a study of a science.* Vol. 3. New York: McGraw-Hill, 1959. Pp. 363–383.

8. Bartholomew, G. A., Jr., & Birdsell, J. B. Ecology and the protohominids. *Amer. Anthrop.*, 1953, **55**, 481–498.

9. Beach, F. A. Evolutionary changes in the physiological control of mating behavior in mammals. *Psychol. Rev.*, 1947, **54**, 297–315.

10. Beach, F. A. Instinctive behavior: reproductive activities. In S. S. Stevens (Ed.), *Handbook of experimental psychology.* New York: Wiley, 1951.

11. Beach, F. A. Evolutionary aspects of psychoendocrinology. In Anne Roe & G. G. Simpson (Eds.), *Behavior and evolution.* New Haven, Conn.: Yale Univer. Press, 1958.

12. Beals, R. Acculturation. In A. L. Kroeber (Ed.), *Anthropology today: an encyclopedic inventory.* Chicago: Univer. Chicago Press, 1953.

13. Bellak, L. Psychoanalytic theory of personality. In J. L. McCary (Ed.), *Psychology of personality: six modern approaches.* New York: Logos Press, 1956.

14. Benedict, P. K., & Jacks, I. Mental illness in primitive societies. *Psychiatry*, 1954, **17**, 377–389.

15. Benedict, Ruth. Franz Boas as an ethnologist. In Franz Boas, 1858–1942. Mem. 61, *Amer. Anthrop. Ass.*, 1943, **45**, No. 3, Part 2.

16. Beres, D. Ego deviation and the concept of schizophrenia. In *The psychoanalytic study of the child.* Vol. 11. New York: International Universities Press, 1956. Pp. 164–235.

17. Bidney, D. *Theoretical anthropology.* New York: Columbia Univer. Press, 1953.

18. Boas, F. Psychological problems in anthropology. *Amer. J. Psychol.*, 1910, **21**, 371–384.

19. Bolk, L. *Das Problem der Menschwerdung.* Jena: Fischer, 1926.

20. Boring, E. G. *A history of experimental psychology.* New York: Appleton-Century-Crofts, 1950.

21. Bourlière, F. Classification et caractéristiques des principaux types de groupements sociaux chez les vertébrés sauvages. In P. Grassé (Ed.), *Structure et physiologie des sociétés animales.* Paris: Centre National de la Recherche Scientifique, 1952. Pp. 71–79.

22. Bourlière, F. *The natural history of mammals.* (2nd ed.) New York: Knopf, 1956.

23. Breuil, H. *Four hundred centuries of cave art.* Montignac, Dor-

dogne: Centre d'Études et de Documentation Prehistoriques, 1952.

24. Brown, R. W. *Words and things*. Glencoe, Ill.: Free Press, 1958.

25. Carpenter, C. R. A field study of the behavior and social relations of the howling monkeys. *Comp. Psychol. Monogr.*, 1934, **10**.

26. Carpenter, C. R. A field study in Siam of the behavior and social relations of the gibbon (Hylobates lar.). *Comp. Psychol. Monogr.*, 1940, **16**.

27. Carpenter, C. R. Characteristics of social behavior in non-human primates. *Trans. N.Y. Acad. Sci.*, 1942, 4, (Ser. II), 248–258.

28. Carpenter, C. R. Concepts and problems of primate sociometry. *Sociometry*, 1945, **8**, 55–61.

29. Carpenter, C. R. Social behavior of non-human primates. In P. Grassé (Ed.), *Structure et physiologie des sociétés animales*. Vol. 34. Paris: Centre National de la Recherche Scientifique, 1952. Pp. 227–245.

30. Carpenter, C. R. Tentative generalizations on grouping behavior of non-human primates. *Hum. Biol.*, 1954, **26**, 269–276. Reprinted in J. A. Gavan (Ed.), *The non-human primates and human evolution*. Detroit, Mich.: Wayne State Univer. Press, 1955.

31. Carpenter, C. R. Soziologie und Verhalten freilebender nichtmenschlicher Primaten. In *Handbuch der Zoologie*. Bd. 8, Lief. 18. Berlin: Walter de Gruyter, 1958. Pp. 1–32.

32. Carpenter, C. R. Territoriality: a review of concepts and problems. In Anne Roe & G. G. Simpson (Eds.), *Behavior and evolution*. New Haven, Conn.: Yale Univer. Press, 1958.

33. Carter, G. S. *Animal evolution*. London: Sidgwick & Jackson, 1951.

34. Carter, G. S. The theory of evolution and the evolution of man. In A. L. Kroeber (Ed.), *Anthropology today*. Chicago: Univer. Chicago Press, 1953.

35. Chance, M. R. A. What makes monkeys sociable. *The New Scientist*, March, 1959.

36. Chance, M. R. A., & Mead, A. D. Social behavior and primate evolution. *Sympos. Soc. exp. Biol.*, 1953, **7**, 395–439.

37. Cobb, S. Awareness, attention, and physiology of the brain stem. In P. H. Hoch & J. Zubin (Eds.), *Experiments in psychopathology*. New York: Grune & Stratton, 1957.

38. Collias, N. E. Social life and the individual among vertebrate animals. *Ann. N.Y. Acad. Sci.*, 1950, **50**, 1074–1092.

39. Count, E. W. The biological basis of human sociality. *Amer. Anthrop.*, 1958, **60**, 1049–1085.

40. Crawford, M. P. The cooperative solving of problems by young chimpanzees. *Comp. Psychol. Monogr.*, 1937, **14**, No. 2.

41. Critchley, M. Animal communication. *Trans. Hunterian Soc. London*, 1958, **16**, 90–111.

42. Critchley, M. The evolution of man's capacity for language. In S. Tax (Ed.), *The evolution of man*. Vol. 2. *Evolution after Darwin*. Chicago: Univer. Chicago Press, 1960.

43. Cuenot, L. L'homme ce Neotenique. *Bull. Acad. roy. Belgique* (Brussels), 1945, **31**.

44. Dart, R. A. Cultural status of the South African man-apes. *Annu. Rep., Smithsonian Instn.* (*1955*). Pp. 317–338.

45. Dart, R. A. *Adventures with the missing link.* New York: Harper, 1959.

46. Darwin, C. *The descent of man.* London: Murray, 1871.

47. Darwin, C. *The expression of the emotions in man and animals.* New York: Appleton-Century-Crofts, 1873. (A new edition with a preface by Margaret Mead was published by the Philosophical Library, New York, 1956.)

48. De Beer, G. R. *Embryos and ancestors.* New York: Oxford, 1951.

49. De Laguna, Grace A. *Speech: its function and development.* New Haven, Conn.: Yale Univer. Press, 1927.

50. Dennis, W. Developmental theories. In *Current trends in psychological theory.* Pittsburgh, Pa.: Univer. Pittsburgh Press, 1951.

51. Dewey, J. The need for a social psychology. *Psychol. Rev.,* 1917, **24,** 266–277.

52. Dobzhansky, Th. *Evolution, genetics, and man.* New York: Wiley, 1955.

52a.Dobzhansky, Th. *Mankind Evolving. The Evolution of the Human Species.* New Haven, Conn.: Yale Univer. Press, 1962.

53. Du Bruhl, E. L. *Evolution of the speech apparatus.* Springfield, Ill.: Charles C Thomas, 1958.

54. Edinger, Tilly. Objets et resultats de la paleoneurologie. *Ann. Paleontol.,* 1956, **42,** 97–116.

55. Eggan, F. Social anthropology and the method of controlled comparison. *Amer. Anthrop.,* 1954, **56,** 743–763.

56. Eiseley, Loren C. Fossil man and human evolution. In W. L. Thomas, Jr. (Ed.), *Yearbook of anthropology, 1955.* New York: Wenner-Gren Foundation for Anthropological Research, 1955.

57. Eiseley, Loren C. *Darwin's century: evolution and the men who discovered it.* New York: Doubleday, 1958.

58. Erikson, E. H. *Childhood and society.* New York: Norton, 1950.

59. Erikson, E. H. Identity and the life cycle. Selected papers. With a historical introduction by D. Rapaport. *Psychol. Issues Monogr.,* 1959, No. 1. Published by International Universities Press, New York.

60. Etkin, W. Social behavior and the evolution of man's mental faculties. *Amer. Naturalist,* 1954, **88,** 129–142.

61. Fisher, S., & Cleveland, S. E. *Body image and personality.* New York: Van Nostrand, 1958.

62. Fiske, J. *The meaning of infancy.* Boston: Houghton Mifflin, 1909. (Reprinting of "The meaning of infancy" from *Excursions of an evolutionist,* 1884, and "The part played by infancy in the evolution of man" from *A century of science, and other essays,* 1899.)

63. Flugel, J. C. *A hundred years of psychology, 1833–1933.* New York: Macmillan, 1933.

64. Ford, C. S., & Beach, F. A. *Patterns of sexual behavior.* New York: Harper, 1951.

65. Frazer, J. G. Scope and method of mental and anthropological science. *Sci. Progress,* 1922, **16,** 580–594.
66. Freedman, L. Z., & Roe, Anne. Evolution and human behavior. In Anne Roe & G. G. Simpson (Eds.), *Behavior and evolution.* New Haven, Conn.: Yale Univer. Press, 1958.
67. Freud, S. *Civilization and its discontents.* London: J. Cape, 1930.
68. Frisch, J. E. Research on primate behavior in Japan. *Amer. Anthrop.,* 1959, **61,** 584–596.
69. Fuller, J. L., & Scott, J. P. Heredity and learning ability in infrahuman animals. *Eugenics Quart.,* 1954, **1,** 28–43.
70. Greenberg, J. H. Language and evolutionary theory. In Essays in linguistics. *Viking Fund Publ. Anthrop.,* 1957, No. 24. (Published by Wenner-Gren Foundation for Anthropological Research, New York.)
71. Haddon, A. C. *History of anthropology.* (Rev. ed.) London: Watts, 1934.
72. Haldane, J. B. S. Animal communication and the origin of human language. *Sci. Progr.,* 1955, **40,** 385–401.
73. Hall, C. S., & Lindzey, G. *Theories of personality.* New York: Wiley, 1957.
74. Hallowell, A. I. Culture, personality, and society. In A. L. Kroeber (Ed.), *Anthropology today.* Chicago: Univer. Chicago Press, 1953.
75. Hallowell, A. I. Psychology and anthropology. In J. Gillin (Ed.), *For a science of social man.* New York: Macmillan, 1954.
76. Hallowell, A. I. *Culture and experience.* Philadelphia: Univer. Pa. Press, 1955.
77. Hallowell, A. I. The structural and functional dimensions of a human existence. *Quart. Rev. Biol.,* 1956, **31,** 88–101.
78. Hallowell, A. I. Ojibwa metaphysics of being and the perception of persons. In R. Tagiuri & L. Petrullo (Eds.), *Person perception and interpersonal behavior.* Stanford, Calif.: Stanford Univer. Press, 1958.
79. Harlow, H. F. Levels of integration along the phylogenetic scale: learning aspect. In J. H. Rohrer & M. Sherif (Eds.), *Social psychology at the crossroads.* New York: Harper, 1951.
80. Harlow, H. F. Thinking. In H. Helson (Ed.), *Theoretical foundations of psychology.* New York: Van Nostrand, 1951.
81. Harlow, H. F. Primate learning. In C. P. Stone (Ed.), *Comparative psychology.* (3rd ed.) Englewood Cliffs, N.J.: Prentice-Hall, 1952.
82. Harlow, H. F. Current and future advances in physiological and comparative psychology. *Amer. Psychologist,* 1956, **11,** 273–277.
83. Harlow, H. F. The evolution of learning. In Anne Roe & G. G. Simpson (Eds.), *Behavior and evolution.* New Haven, Conn.: Yale Univer. Press, 1958.
84. Hart, C. M. H. Social evolution and modern anthropology. In H. A. Innes (Ed.), *Essays in political economy in honour of E. J. Urwick.* Toronto: Univer. Toronto Press, 1938.
85. Hartmann, H. Psychoanalytic theory of instinctual drives. *Psychoanal. Quart.,* 1948, **17,** 368–388.

86. Hartmann, H. Comments on the psychoanalytic theory of the ego. In *The psychoanalytic study of the child.* Vol. 5. New York: International Universities Press, 1950.

87. Hartmann, H. Ego psychology and the problem of adaptation. D. Rapaport (Trans.). *J. Amer. Psychoanal. Ass. Monogr.,* 1958, No. 1. (Published by International Universities Press, New York.)

88. Hayes, Cathy. *The ape in our house.* New York: Harper, 1951.

89. Hayes, K. J., & Hayes, Catherine. The cultural capacity of chimpanzee. In J. A. Gavan (Ed.), *The non-human primates and human evolution.* Detroit, Mich.: Wayne State Univer. Press, 1955.

90. Hebb, D. O., & Thompson, W. N. The social significance of animal studies. In G. Lindzey (Ed.), *Handbook of social psychology.* Vol. 1. Reading, Mass.: Addison-Wesley, 1954.

91. Heberer, G. von. Die Fossilgeschichte der Hominoidea. In H. Hofer, A. H. Schultz, & D. Starck (Eds.), *Primatologia.* Vol. 1. New York: Karger, 1956. Pp. 379–560.

92. Henry, J. Culture, personality, and evolution. *Amer. Anthrop.,* 1959, **61,** 221–226.

93. Herrick, C. J. *The evolution of human nature.* Austin, Tex.: Univer. Tex. Press, 1956.

94. Hilgard, E. R. *Theories of learning.* (2nd ed.) New York: Appleton-Century-Crofts, 1956.

95. Hinde, R. A. Some recent trends in ethology. In S. Koch (Ed.), *Psychology: a study of a science.* Vol. 2. New York: McGraw-Hill, 1959.

96. Hochbaum, H. A. *Travels and traditions of waterfowl.* Minneapolis, Minn.: Univer. Minn. Press, 1955.

97. Hockett, C. F. *A course in modern linguistics.* New York: Macmillan, 1958.

98. Hockett, C. F. Animal "languages" and human language. In J. N. Spuhler (Ed.), *The evolution of man's capacity for culture.* Detroit, Mich.: Wayne State Univer. Press, 1959.

99. Hockett, C. F. The origin of speech. *Scient. Amer.,* 1960, **203,** 89–96.

100. Hofer, H., Schultz, A. H., & Starck, D. (Eds.) *Primatologia: Handbuch der Primatenkunde.* Vol. 1. New York: Karger, 1956.

101. Honigmann, J. J. *Culture and personality.* New York: Harper, 1954.

102. Honigmann, J. J. Psychocultural studies. In B. J. Siegel (Ed.), *Biennial review of anthropology—1959.* Stanford, Calif.: Stanford Univer. Press, 1959.

103. Honigsheim, P. The philosophical background of European anthropology. *Amer. Anthrop.,* 1942, **44,** 376–387.

104. Hooton, E. The importance of primate studies in anthropology. In J. A. Gavan (Ed.), *The non-human primates and human evolution.* Detroit, Mich.: Wayne State Univer. Press, 1955.

105. Howell, F. C. The Villafranchian and human origins. *Science,* 1959, **130,** 831–844.

106. Howell, F. C. Commentary on Leakey's "The newest link in human evolution." *Current Anthrop.,* 1960, **1,** 76–77.

107. Howells, W. W. Origin of the human stock: concluding remarks of the

Chairman. *Cold Spring Harbor Symp. quant. Biol.,* 1950, **15**, 79–86.

108. Howells, W. W. *Mankind in the making.* New York: Doubleday, 1959.

109. Huxley, J. *Man stands alone.* New York: Harper, 1941.

110. Huxley, J. *Evolution in action.* New York: Harper, 1953.

111. Huxley, J. The evolutionary process. In J. Huxley, A. C. Hardy, & E. B. Ford (Eds.), *Evolution as a process.* London: G. Allen, 1954.

112. Huxley, J. Evolution, cultural and biological. In W. L. Thomas, Jr. (Ed.), *Yearbook of anthropology—1955.* New York: Wenner-Gren Foundation for Anthropological Research, 1955.

113. Huxley, J. Psychology in evolutionary perspective. *Amer. Psychologist,* 1956, **11**, 558–559.

114. Imanishi, K. Social behavior in Japanese monkeys, *Macaca fuscata. Psychologia,* 1957, **1**, 47–54. (In English)

115. Imanishi, K. Identification: a process of enculturation in the sub-human society of *Macaca fuscata. Primates,* 1959, **1**, 1–29. (English summary)

116. Imanishi, K. Social organization of subhuman primates in their natural habitat. *Current Anthrop.,* 1960, **1**, 393–407. (Comments by Bourlière, Carpenter, Chance, Emlem, Schultz, Washburn, De Vore, Zuckerman.)

117. Jacobi, Jolande. *Complex archetype symbol in the psychology of C. G. Jung.* R. Manheim (Trans.). New York: Pantheon Books (Bollingen Ser. 57), 1959.

118. Jennings, H. S. The transition from the individual to the social level. In *Biological symposia,* Vol. 8. R. Redfield (Ed.), *Levels of integration in biological and social systems.* Lancaster, Pa.: Cattell Press, 1942.

119. Jones, E. *The life and work of Sigmund Freud.* New York: Basic Books, 1953–57. 3 vols.

120. Jung, C. G. The spirit of psychology. In J. Campbell & Olga Frock-Kapteyn (Eds.), *Spirit and nature* (papers from the Eranos yearbooks, Ser. 1). New York: Pantheon Books (Bollingen Ser. 30, 1), 1954.

121. Jung, C. G. Commentary on the Tibetan book of the dead. In Violet S. de Laszlo (Ed.), *Psyche and symbol: a selection of the writings of C. G. Jung.* New York: Doubleday (Anchor Books), 1958.

122. Kaplan, B. Introduction and Epilogue. In B. Kaplan (Ed.), *Studying personality cross-culturally.* Evanston, Ill.: Row, Peterson, 1961.

123. Karpf, Fay B. *American social psychology: its origins, development, and European background.* New York: McGraw-Hill, 1932.

124. Katz, D. *Animals and men: studies in comparative psychology.* New York: Longmans, 1937.

125. Keith, A. *A new theory of human evolution.* London: Watts, 1948.

126. Kluckhohn, C. The personal document in anthropological science. In The use of personal documents in history, anthropology, and sociology. *Soc. Sci. Res. Counc. Bull,* 1945, No. 53.

127. Kluckhohn, C. Universal categories of culture. In A. L. Kroeber (Ed.), *Anthropology today.* Chicago: Univer. Chicago Press, 1953.

128. Kluckhohn, C., et al. Values and value-orientations in the theory of action. In T. Parsons & E. A. Shils (Eds.), *Toward a general theory of action.* Cambridge, Mass.: Harvard Univer. Press, 1951. Pp. 388–433.

129. Kroeber, A. L. Sub-human cultural beginnings. *Quart. Rev. Biol.*, 1928, **3**, 325–342.

130. Kroeber, A. L. The societies of primitive man. In *Biological symposia,* Vol. 8. R. Redfield (Ed.), *Levels of integration in biological and social systems.* Lancaster, Pa.: Cattell Press, 1942.

131. Kroeber, A. L. *Anthropology.* New York: Harcourt, Brace, 1948.

132. Kroeber, A. L. Anthropology. *Scient. Amer.,* 1950, **183**, 87–94.

133. Kroeber, A. L. *The nature of culture.* Chicago: Univer. Chicago Press, 1952.

134. Kroeber, A. L. On human nature. *S.W. J. Anthrop.,* 1955, **11**, 195–204.

135. Kroeber, A. L., & Kluckhohn, C. Culture: a critical review of concepts and definitions. *Papers Peabody Mus. Amer. Archeol. & Ethnol.,* 1952, **47**, No. 1. (Published by Harvard University Press, Cambridge, Mass.)

136. Kubie, L. S. Some implications for psychoanalysis of modern concepts of the organization of the brain. *Psychoanal. Quart.,* 1953, **22**, 21–68.

137. La Barre, W. *The human animal.* Chicago: Univer. Chicago Press, 1954.

138. La Barre, W. Influence of Freud on anthropology. *Amer. Imago,* 1958, **15**, 275–328.

139. Laming, Annette. *Lascaux paintings and engravings.* Baltimore, Md.: Penguin, 1959.

140. Lashley, K. S. Persistent problems in the evolution of mind. *Quart. Rev. Biol.,* 1949, **24**, 28–42.

141. Leakey, L. S. B. A new fossil skull from Olduvai. *Nature,* 1959, **184**, 491–493.

142. Leakey, L. S. B. The newest link in human evolution: the discovery by L. S. B. Leakey of *Zinjanthropus boisei. Current Anthrop.,* 1960, **1**, 76.

143. Le Gros Clark, W. E. *History of the primates: an introduction to the study of fossil man.* London: British Museum, 1950.

144. Le Gros Clark, W. E. *The fossil evidence for human evolution: an introduction to the study of paleoanthropology.* Chicago: Univer. Chicago Press, 1955.

145. Le Gros Clark, W. E. The study of man's descent. In S. A. Barnett (Ed.), *A century of Darwin.* Cambridge, Mass.: Harvard Univer. Press, 1958.

146. Le Gros Clark, W. E. *The antecedents of man: an introduction to the evolution of the primates.* Chicago: Quadrangle Books, 1960.

147. Le Gros Clark, W. E. The crucial evidence for human evolution. *Amer. Scient.,* 1959, **49**, 229–313.

148. Lovejoy, A. O. The length of human infancy in eighteenth century thought. *J. Phil.,* 1922, **19**, 381–385.

149. Lowie, R. H. *Culture and ethnology.* New York: McMurtrie, 1917.

150. Lowie, R. H. *Primitive society.* New York: Liveright, 1920.

151. Lowie, R. H. *The family as a social unit* (Papers of the Michigan Academy of Science, Arts, and Letters). Ann Arbor, Mich.: Univer. Mich. Press, 1933.

152. Lowie, R. H. *The history of ethnological theory.* New York: Holt-Rinehart-Winston, 1937.

153. Lowie, R. H. Reminiscences of anthropological currents in America half a century ago. *Amer. Anthrop.*, 1956, **58**, 995–1016.
154. MacLeod, R. B. The place of phenomenological analysis in social psychological theory. In J. H. Rohrer & M. Sherif (Eds.), *Social psychology at the crossroads*. New York: Harper, 1951.
155. Malinowski, B. *A scientific theory of culture and other essays*. Chapel Hill, N.C.: Univer. N.C. Press, 1944.
156. May, R. *Man's search for himself*. New York: Norton, 1953.
157. May, R. The historical meaning of psychology as a science and profession. *Trans. N. Y. Acad. Sci.*, 1955, **17** (Ser. 2), 312–314.
158. Montagu, M. F. A. Time, morphology, and neoteny in the evolution of man. *Amer. Anthrop.*, 1955, **57**, 13–27. Reprinted in *Anthropology and human nature*. New York: Porter Sargent, 1957.
159. Montagu, M. F. A. Neoteny and the evolution of the human mind. *Explorations*, 1956, No. 6, 85–90. Reprinted in *Anthropology and human nature*. New York: Porter Sargent, 1957.
160. Mowrer, O. H., & Kluckhohn, C. Dynamic theory of personality. In J. McV. Hunt (Ed.), *Personality and the behavior disorders*. Vol. 1. New York: Ronald, 1941. Pp. 69–135.
161. Mühlmann, W. *Methodik der Völkerkunde*. Stuttgart: Enke, 1938.
162. Munn, N. L. *The evolution and growth of human behavior*. Boston: Houghton Mifflin, 1955.
163. Murdock, G. P. The common denominator of cultures. In R. Linton (Ed.), *The science of man in the world crisis*. New York: Columbia Univer. Press, 1945.
164. Murdock, G. P. *Social structure*. New York: Macmillan, 1949.
165. Nissen, H. W. A field study of the chimpanzee: observations of chimpanzee behavior and environment in Western French Guinea. *Comp. Psychol. Monogr.*, 1931, No. 1.
166. Nissen, H. W. Primate psychology. In P. L. Harriman (Ed.), *Encyclopedia of psychology*. New York: Citadel Press, 1946.
167. Nissen, H. W. Phylogenetic comparison. In S. S. Stevens (Ed.), *Handbook of experimental psychology*. New York: Wiley, 1951.
168. Nissen, H. W. Social behavior in primates. In C. P. Stone (Ed.), *Comparative psychology*. Englewood Cliffs, N.J.: Prentice-Hall, 1951.
169. Nissen, H. W. Problems of mental evolution in the primates. In J. A. Gavan (Ed.), *The non-human primates and human evolution*. Detroit, Mich.: Wayne State Univer. Press, 1955.
170. Oakley, K. P. *Man the tool-maker*. London: British Museum, 1950.
171. Oakley, K. P. A definition of man. *Sci. News*, 1951, No. 20, 69–81.
172. Oakley, K. P. Skill as a human possession. In C. J. Singer et al. (Eds.), *History of technology*. Vol. 1. New York: Oxford, 1954.
173. Oakley, K. P. The earliest tool-makers. *Antiquity*, 1956, **30**, 4–8.
174. Oakley, K. P. Tools makyth man. *Antiquity*, 1957, **31**, 199–209. Reprinted in *Annual Report, Smithsonian Institution* (1958). Pp. 431–445.

175. Oakley, K. P. Tools or brains. Which came first? *Archeol. Newsltr.* (London), 1958, **6**, 48.
176. Oakley, K. P. On man's use of fire, with comments on tool-making and hunting. In S. L. Washburn (Ed.), *Social life of early man.* Viking Fund Publications in Anthropology, No. 31. New York: Wenner-Gren Foundation for Anthropological Research, 1961.
177. Parsons, T. An approach to psychological theory in terms of the theory of action. In S. Koch (Ed.), *Psychology: a study of a science.* Vol. 3. New York: McGraw-Hill, 1959.
178. Penfield, W., & Rasmussen, T. *The cerebral cortex of man.* New York: Macmillan, 1950.
179. Penfield, W., & Roberts, L. *Speech and brain-mechanisms.* Princeton, N. J.: Princeton Univer. Press, 1959.
180. Pumphrey, R. J. *The origin of language.* Liverpool: Liverpool Univer. Press, 1951. Reprinted in *Acta Psychol.,* 1953, **9**, 219–239.
181. Radin, P. The autobiography of an American Indian. *Univer. Calif. Publ. Archeol. & Ethnol.,* 1920, **16**, 381–473. A somewhat revised edition appeared in 1926 as *Crashing thunder.*
182. Radin, P. *The method and theory of ethnology.* New York: McGraw-Hill, 1933.
183. Rapaport, D. The structure of psychoanalytic theory: a systematizing attempt. In S. Koch (Ed.), *Psychology: a study of a science.* Vol. 3. New York: McGraw-Hill, 1959. Pp. 55–183.
184. Rensch, B. The relation between the evolution of central nervous functions and the body size of animals. In J. Huxley, A. C. Hardy, & E. B. Ford (Eds.), *Evolution as a process.* London: G. Allen, 1954.
185. Rensch, B. Increase of learning capability with increase of brain size. *Amer. Naturalist,* 1956, **90**, 81–95.
186. Rensch, B. *Homo sapiens vom tier zum halbgott.* Göttingen: Vandenhoeck & Ruprecht, 1959.
187. Révész, G. Is there an animal language? *Hibbert J.,* 1953–54, **70**, 141–143.
188. Révész, G. *The origins and prehistory of language.* New York: Longmans, 1956.
189. Ribot, T. *German psychology today.* New York: Scribner, 1886.
190. Rivers, W. H. R. Sociology and psychology. *Sociol. Rev.,* 1916, **9**, 1–13.
191. Roe, Anne, & Simpson, G. G. (Eds.) *Behavior and evolution.* New Haven, Conn.: Yale Univer. Press, 1958.
192. Roheim, G. *Psychoanalysis and anthropology.* New York: International Universities Press, 1950.
193. Romanes, G. J. *Animal intelligence.* New York: Appleton-Century-Crofts, 1883.
194. Romanes, G. J. *Mental evolution in man.* New York: Appleton-Century-Crofts, 1888.
195. Saccasyn-Della Santa, E. *Les figures humaines du paléolithique supérieur Eurasiatique.* Antwerp: De Sekkel, 1947.
196. Sahlins, M. D. The social life of monkeys, apes, and primitive man. In

J. H. Spuhler (Ed.), *The evolution of man's capacity for culture.* Detroit, Mich.: Wayne State Univer. Press, 1959.

197. Sahlins, M. D. The origin of society. *Scient. Amer.*, 1960, **203**, 76–86.
198. Sarbin, T. R. Role theory. In G. Lindzey (Ed.), *Handbook of social psychology.* Vol. 1. Reading, Mass.: Addison-Wesley, 1954.
199. Sargent, S. S. *Social psychology.* New York: Ronald, 1950.
200. Schiller, Claire H. (Ed.) *Instinctive behavior.* New York: International Universities Press, 1957. (Introduction by K. S. Lashley.)
201. Schiller, P. H. Innate motor action as a basis of learning: manipulative patterns in the chimpanzee. In Claire H. Schiller (Ed.), *Instinctive behavior.* New York: International Universities Press, 1957.
202. Schneirla. T. C. Levels in the psychological capacity of animals. In R. W. Sellars, V. S. McGill, & M. Farber (Eds.), *Philosophy for the future.* New York: Macmillan, 1949.
203. Schneirla, T. C. The "levels" concept in the study of social organization of animals. In J. H. Rohrer & M. Sherif (Eds.), *Social psychology at the crossroads.* New York: Harper, 1951.
204. Schneirla, T. C. A consideration of some conceptual trends in comparative psychology. *Psychol. Bull.*, 1952, **49**, 559–597.
205. Schneirla, T. C. The concept of levels in the study of social phenomena. In M. Sherif & G. W. Sherif (Eds.), *Groups in harmony and tension.* New York: Harper, 1953.
206. Schneirla, T. C. Interrelationships of the "innate" and the "acquired" in instinctive behavior. In *L'instinct dans le comportement des animaux et de l'homme* (Foundation Singer-Polignac). Paris: Masson, 1956.
207. Schneirla, T. C. The concept of development in comparative psychology. In D. B. Harris (Ed.), *The concept of development.* Minneapolis, Minn.: Univer. Minn. Press, 1957.
208. Schultz, A. H. Primatology in its relation to anthropology. In W. L. Thomas, Jr. (Ed.), *Yearbook of anthropology, 1955,* New York: Wenner-Gren Foundation for Anthropological Research, 1955.
209. Schultz, A. H. Postembryonic age changes. In H. Hofer, A. H. Schultz, & D. Starck (Eds.), *Primatologia.* Vol. I. Basel: Karger, 1956. Pp. 887–964.
210. Schultz, A. H. Past and present views of man's specialization. *Irish J. med. Sci.*, 1957, 341–356.
211. Schultz, A. H. Some factors influencing the social life of primates in general and of early man in particular. In S. L. Washburn (Ed.), *Social life of early man,* Viking Fund Publications in Anthropology, No. 31. New York: Wenner-Gren Foundation for Anthropological Research, 1961.
212. Scott, J. P. The analysis of social organization in animals. *Ecology,* 1956, **37**, 213–221.
213. Scott, J. P. *Animal behavior.* Chicago: Univer. Chicago Press, 1958.
214. Shapiro, H. L. Review of Du Bruhl's "evolution of the speech apparatus." *Man,* 1960, No. 199.
215. Simpson, G. G. *The meaning of evolution.* New Haven, Conn.: Yale Univer. Press, 1950.

216. Singer, M. A survey of culture and personality theory and research. In B. Kaplan (Ed.), *Studying personality cross-culturally*. Evanston, Ill.: Row, Peterson, 1961.
217. Smith, M. B. Anthropology and psychology. In J. Gillin (Ed.), *For a science of social man*. New York: Macmillan, 1954.
218. Spiro, M. E. Human nature in its psychological dimensions. *Amer. Anthrop.*, 1954, **56**, 19–30.
219. Spuhler, J. N. Somatic paths to culture. In J. N. Spuhler (Ed.), *The evolution of man's capacity for culture*. Detroit, Mich.: Wayne State Univer. Press, 1959.
220. Stierlin, H. Contrasting attitudes toward the psychoses in Europe and in the United States. *Psychiatry*, 1958, **21**, 141–147.
221. Straus, W. L. Closing remarks. In J. A. Gavan (Ed.), *The non-human primates and human evolution*. Detroit, Mich.: Wayne State Univer. Press, 1955.
222. Straus, W. L. The Great Piltdown hoax. *Annu. Rep. Smithsonian Inst.*, 1954.
223. Symonds, P. M. *The ego and the self*. New York: Appleton-Century-Crofts, 1951.
224. Tax, S. (Ed.) *The evolution of man*. Vol. 2. *Evolution after Darwin*. Chicago: Univer. Chicago Press, 1960.
225. Tax, S., Eiseley, Loren C., Rouse, I., & Voegelin, C. F. (Eds.) *An appraisal of anthropology today*. Chicago: Univer. Chicago Press, 1953.
226. Teicher, M. I. Three cases of psychoses among the Eskimo. *J. ment. Sci.*, 1954, **100**, 527–535.
227. Thrope, W. H. *Learning and instinct in animals*. London: Methuen, 1956.
228. Tinbergen, N. *Social behavior in animals*. New York: Wiley, 1953.
229. Tinbergen, N. Behavior, systematics, and natural selection. In S. Tax (Ed.), *The evolution of life*. Vol. 1. *Evolution after Darwin*. Chicago: Univer. Chicago Press. 1960.
230. Tolman, E. C. A psychological model. In T. Parsons & E. A. Shils (Eds.), *Toward a general theory of action*. Cambridge, Mass.: Harvard Univer. Press, 1951, Pp. 279–361.
231. Trager, G. L. Para-language: a first approximation. *Stud. Linguistics*, 1958, **13**, 1–12.
232. Vallois, H. Le problème de l'hominisation. In *Les processus de l'hominisation*. Paris: Centre National de la Recherche Scientifique, 1958.
233. Voegelin, C. F. Culture, language, and the human organism. *S.W. J. Anthrop.*, 1951, **7**, 357–373.
234. Von Bonin, G. *Essay on the cerebral cortex*. Springfield, Ill.: Charles C Thomas, 1950.
234a. Waddington, C. H. *The Ethical Animal*. New York: Athenuem, 1961.
235. Waitz, T. *Introduction to anthropology*. London: Longman, Roberts & Green, 1863. Edited with numerous additions by the author from J. F. Collingwood, *Anthropologie der Naturvölker*. Vol 1.
235a. Wallace, A. F. C. *Culture and Personality*. New York: Random, 1961.

236. Walters, R. H. Historical background of comparative psychology. In C. P. Stone (Ed.), *Comparative psychology*. (3rd ed.) Englewood Cliffs, N.J.: Prentice-Hall, 1951. Pp. 9–29.

237. Washburn, S. L. The analysis of primate evolution with particular reference to the origin of man. *Cold Spring Harbor Symp. quant. Biol.*, 1950, **15**, 67–78.

238. Washburn, S. L. Speculations on the interrelations of the history of tools and biological evolution. In J. N. Spuhler (Ed.), *The evolution of man's capacity for culture*. Detroit, Mich.: Wayne State Univer. Press, 1959.

239. Washburn, S. L. Tools and human evolution. *Scient. Amer.*, 1960, **203**, 63–75.

240. Washburn, S. L., & Avis, Virginia. Evolution of human behavior. In Anne Roe & G. G. Simpson (Eds.), *Behavior and evolution*. New Haven, Conn.: Yale Univer. Press, 1958.

241. Washburn, S. L., & DeVore, I. Social behavior of baboons and early man. Viking Fund Publications in Anthropology, No. 31. New York: Wenner-Gren Foundation for Anthropological Research, 1961.

242. Washburn, S. L., & Howell, F. C. Human evolution and culture. In S. Tax (Ed.), *The evolution of man*. Vol. 2. *Evolution after Darwin*. Chicago: Univer. Chicago Press, 1960.

243. Weiner, J. S. Physical anthropology: an appraisal. *Amer. Scientist*, 1957, **45**, 79–87. Reprinted in *Evolution and anthropology: a centennial appraisal*. Washington.: Anthropological Society of Washington, 1959.

244. Werner, H. *Comparative psychology of mental development*. New York: Harper, 1940.

245. Westermarck, E. *History of human marriage*. New York: St. Martin's Press, Inc., 1903.

246. White, L. A. The origin and nature of speech. In W. S. Knickerbocker (Ed.), *Twentieth century English*. New York: Philosophical Library, 1940.

247. White, L. A. On the use of tools by primates. *J. comp. Psychol.*, 1942, **34**, 369–374.

248. White, L. A. Ethnological theory. In R. W. Sellars, V. J. McGill, & M. Farber (Eds.), *Philosophy for the future*. New York: Macmillan, 1949.

249. White, L. A. The individual and the culture process. *Centennial*. Washington: American Association for the Advancement of Science, 1950.

250. Wissler, C. Psychological and historical interpretations of culture. *Science*, 1916, **43**, 193–201.

251. Wissler, C. *Man and culture*. New York: Crowell, 1923.

252. Yerkes, R. M. *Chimpanzees: a laboratory colony*. New Haven, Conn.: Yale Univer. Press, 1943.

253. Zukerman, S. L'hominisation de la famille et des groupes sociaux. In *Les processus de l'hominisation*. Paris: Centre National de la Recherche Scientifique, 1958.

PSYCHOLOGY IN ANTHROPOLOGY: APPLICATIONS TO CULTURE CHANGE

GEORGE AND LOUISE SPINDLER[1]
Department of Anthropology
Stanford University

INTRODUCTION

The aim in this paper is to analyze the ways in which anthropologists writing about culture change have used psychological materials. The

[1] We wish to acknowledge gratefully our indebtedness to our colleagues at the Center for Advanced Study in the Behavioral Sciences at Stanford for much stimulation in seminar discussions related to the topic of this paper during 1957 and again in 1960.

initial meaning we ascribe to "culture change" is any modification in the way of life of a people, consequent either to internal stimuli (such as invention) or to contact between two peoples with unlike ways of life. In anthropological usage this latter process is termed "acculturation" and it will be our major focus. The meaning of these terms will expand as we proceed. By "psychological materials" we mean concepts, theories or postulates, methods, or data that have been developed primarily by professional psychologists, and in some instances by psychiatrists.

Other anthropologists have reviewed the much larger range of relations between anthropology and psychology [13, 16, 16a, 23], and the other articles by anthropologists in this volume select differently from the possibilities afforded by contact between the two fields. The rationale for the focus of this paper is that as anthropologists attempt to describe and analyze culture change as a *process*, they will be most likely to use whatever they have learned from psychology (and elsewhere) that they find useful. This is so, we believe, because culture change is a process involving all dimensions of adaptation—cultural, social, and psychological. Changes in the norms for behavior shared within a society occur as antecedents, consequences, and concomitants of psychological adaptations on the part of individuals interacting in social contexts.

Influence of the Culture and Personality Movement

Between the early thirties and late forties "culture and personality" emerged and grew as a field of interest in anthropology to such an extent that it assumed the proportion of a fad. In 1954, Clyde Kluckhohn, one of the major contributors to the culture and personality development, said: "Work in this field has suffered as a consequence of its being so fashionable for the last decade or two . . . many publications have been hasty, overly schematic, and indeed naïve." He further points out that history and biology have been neglected in culture and personality studies, that there have been many unwarranted assumptions of homogeneity in the populations studies, and that in some cases there has been a ludicrous overemphasis upon a few aspects, or even a single aspect, of child training [25]. Kluckhohn's estimate appears to be widely shared among anthropologists at present. And these attitudes play a role in the use of psychology by anthropologists now.

Anthropologists who have done research in culture and personality or have taught a course in this field have developed some fairly systematic notions about psychological processes. Such anthropologists have also been influenced by the mood of the day on the subject of culture and personality. When they describe and analyze culture change as a process, a way of life in motion, they have need of concepts and methods to help them answer perplexing questions that are not raised in more static situations. Presumably they will use whatever concepts and methods are known and available to them unless they have turned against them as a matter of principle. Do they turn to psychology? When they do, what do they select to use? How do they use it? Are psychological usages by anthropologists decreasing? These are the kinds of questions with which the substantive part of the paper will be concerned.

Procedure

The culture concept of the anthropologists and some of the problems inherent in its use in the study of culture change will be discussed briefly to provide relevant background for the analysis to follow. Two approaches to the study of acculturation will be presented and differences in the conceptualization of the psychological dimensions in culture change will be analyzed. The first statement was published in 1936 [39], the second in 1954 [41], and both can be considered representative. Contrasts between them are symptomatic of certain trends in the anthropological utilization of psychological materials. After this, a sample of 94 books and articles on acculturation, represented in a volume of critical abstracts covering the period from 1929 to 1952, will be analyzed. Bernard Siegel, the compiler of the volume, states that "an effort is made to abstract all the major empirical studies reported by anthropologists in the setting of North America which are of importance in analyzing the processes of sociocultural change under conditions of cultures in contact" [40, p. v]. Further details of procedure in the analysis of materials cited in this volume will be provided later. The final step will be to present a similar analysis of all articles on culture change published in the *American Anthropologist* from 1952 to April, 1962. The paper will be concluded with a discussion of some recent developments.

THE CULTURE CONCEPT

The touchstone of anthropological theory, particularly in North America, has been the culture concept. Many articles have been devoted to it, and Kroeber and Kluckhohn have compiled and analyzed more than one hundred definitions of it [30]. A brief discussion of certain issues relating to this concept will aid in understanding the motivations of anthropologists who turn to psychology for help in culture-change analyses, as well as those who ignore psychology or have purposely spurned its use.

There are some anthropologists who conceive of culture as displaying dynamics of its own—abstracted from its human bearers—and as providing a self-sufficient analytic framework. There are other anthropologists who regard culture as an overly abstracted and insufficient construct that must be expanded by other concepts in order to provide a useful theoretical model of working relationships. The extreme "culturological" position is represented by Leslie White when he says, in an attack on psychological explanations, "culture has, in a very real sense, an extrasomatic character. Although made possible only by organisms of human beings, once in existence and under way it has a life of its own . . . its own laws . . . explained in culturology." And again, "The most realistic and scientifically adequate interpretation of culture is one that proceeds as if human beings did not exist" [56, pp. 693–694].

Professor White has recently extended and defended this position [57]. The "fallacy of pseudorealism" is his term for the view that people and not cultures "do things," and he charges that some influential anthropologists have tended to give over to psychology that which can be directly observed in human behavior. He maintains that "a consideration of human organisms is irrelevant to the solution of certain problems of culture."

He goes on to differentiate the subject matters of psychology and anthropology, stating that "symboling" is characteristic only of humans. "Symbolates" (any characteristically human act, thought, or material product) considered in relationship to the human organism, or somatic context, is the subject matter of psychology. The same symbolates, considered in relationship to each other—in an "extrasomatic" context—are the subject matter of anthropology. This class of phenomena is brought into existence by exercise of the symbol faculty of the human species. The class includes language, beliefs, customs, tools, dwellings, works of art, etc., collectively called "culture." Once brought into existence, symbolates are suprabiological and are transmitted by the mechanisms of social heredity [57].

Few anthropologists would deny that many analytic problems in cultural process can be settled without reference to the needs, motivations, or perceptual structuring of human beings. Nor would White claim that the dynamics of culture change, as we expand their meaning, can all be explained culturologically. But he would say that those which cannot should be dealt with by somebody else, not by anthropologists. His views have been influential, partly because they appeal to many anthropologists who are disturbed by the sprawling, diversified character of the discipline and feel the need for enclosure. To us his view seems too constricted to permit the flexible, open-ended, problem-oriented approach that appears to be necessary if certain crucial aspects of culture change are to be analyzed.

The lack in White's position is recognition of the fact that changes occur simultaneously in all cases of so-called culture change. These changes are in the areas of social structure and interaction (changes in social roles and statuses, group size, territoriality, etc.), symbolates (culture patterns and traits, ranging all the way from knowledge to tools), and psychological adaptations (restructuring of motivations, affective controls, self-concept, and perceptual and cognitive systems). We want to be able to study White's symbolates in change situations in relation to each other and to the organism and simultaneously. Not all studies of culture change need to be complicated in this way, but some of them should be. It seems to us that this is the road, precipitous and rocky as it may be, to a unified theory of human behavior in adaptation to changing conditions of survival.

The late Alfred Kroeber, perhaps the most influential American anthropologist since Franz Boas, agrees with the "as-if" rule, proceeding, as a convenience, *as if* culture were an autonomous realm, even though he grants that its locus is in persons. With White, he feels that our knowledge of the psychology of persons has failed conspicuously to explain cultural forms. Specific cultural effects cannot be explained on the basis of specific "psychic" causes: psychology does not help us to understand why Comanche Indians cut off the noses of unfaithful wives or why Chukchee share their wives with visitors, or why milk products are abhorred by Chinese and considered staple foods by Europeans and Mongols. Explaining cultural forms by psychic causes is a form of reductionism that tends merely to confuse analyses and make unnecessary labor. He turns to cultural antecedents in time and space to make the relations of cultural forms intelligible. He does not think this will lead to "laws" of efficient causality, for *final causes will continue to reside in the psychic or psychosomatic*. He does not ask for laws, but for qualified generalizations about the relations of culture forms [27, 28, 29]. Kroeber's position can be termed "modified culturological."

The majority of anthropologists would probably find this position acceptable. If one accepts the purposes and rules of the game on Kroeber's terms, the internal logic of this stance cannot be gainsaid. There are serious difficulties consequent to this position, however. Once culture is abstracted from human psyches in this way, it is almost impossible to talk about many processes relevant to culture change without using reifying or anthropomorphizing terms. Kroeber himself, for example, uses terms like "cultural fatigue," "the death of cultures," "the personalities of cultures" [28, pp. 135, 161, 403]. In a review of Kroeber's *Configurations of Cultural Growth*, Clyde Kluckhohn has pointed out much the same thing [24]. He says that statements like the following make him feel "uncomfortable," even though in part his review is a defense of Kroeber's position. The passage he refers to is this: "It is entirely possible for a culture not to seize upon its finest pattern potentialities; to be lacking in ability to select or concentrate, and instead, to dissipate its energies in random or conflicting endeavors at expression" [26, p. 796]. Kroeber has recognized the ambiguity of this and similar phrasing, and calls for nonreifying language [29, p. 407].

When the culture concept is used as the exclusive frame of reference for analysis of culture change, it is subject to severe stress. The "as-if" rule provides a way of talking, but it does not provide a satisfying theoretical basis for dealing with process.

Our Position Stated

In fairness to the reader it seems desirable to state our position now. (Our concept of culture and the multidimensional process of culture change is implicit in criticisms already stated and will be a factor in the selection and analysis of data in the remainder of the paper.)

Culture may be defined in various ways, depending on the purpose of analysis and the problem. For us, the definition which follows is most useful in culture-change analyses. Culture consists of the patterns for behavior, both explicit (verbalized) and implicit (usually not verbalized but inferable from behavior) which are shared by a group of people and transmitted to new members. These patterns are antecedent to the existence of any new member of the group, but are continually in transformation or modification as people react to and mediate them. Our construct includes definitions of personality traits, possessions, symbols of status, and conditions of being which are considered desirable by the group; norms for behavior in all roles and statuses available to members of the group; and patterns for subsistence activity, child training, ceremonials, medical practice, etc.; and patterns of belief that justify the behaviors required in the various areas mentioned.

Culture is represented in, though never identical with, the cognitive maps, motivations, perceptual structuring, affective controls, and ego defenses of individuals. These constructs we regard as the consequences, in individuals, of the life experience within a culturally patterned environment, and together constitute the personality. Each individual's personality is different in some degree from that of any other person's depending on idiosyncratic life experience. Both the derivation of personality and the expression of it are, however, bounded by cultural norms. The personalities of individuals and the cultural patterns of the group are modified by new experience.

In acculturation situations, the established culture significantly affects the adaptations people make to changes in the conditions of life which are created by the impact of another culture and its bearers. As changes in the conditions of survival occur, established cultural patterns at least temporarily lose their meaning. Under conditions of rapid acculturation they may even become dysfunctional and therefore threatening to the individual who is trying to adapt to the new situation. The binding of cultural patterns upon the individual becomes loosened. Behaviors become comparatively, though never wholly, randomized. New alternatives are perceived and reacted to differently by different individuals, but within a spectrum limited in part by prior cultural patterns. When a successful (i.e., functional) adaptation is reached by a number of persons, new cultural patterns emerge and are consolidated in coherent form.

Most groups (societies, in the larger sense) in the world today, particularly primitive or nonliterate groups undergoing rapid and disjunctive change, have not reached the consolidative phase of adaptation. They are, rather, in the adaptive phase of pattern loosening and comparative randomization of behavior.

Precisely because this is so, we feel that psychological concepts, tools, and methods must be utilized if the strategy of so-called "culture change" studies is to be satisfying. Individuals are thrown upon their own resources of adaptation to a greater extent when previously tight cultural boundaries are weakened or destroyed. Their psychology must be understood, including the cognitive maps, etc., that reflect the imprint of their traditions, their reactive mediation of these patterns under stress conditions, and their perception of and groping toward new solutions.

This is not to say that all culture-change phenomena must be "reduced" to the level of individual psychology. Precisely because antecedent patterns of culture are shared, even though shared with idiosyncratic variation, regularities in psychological adaptation may be expected. The fact that all culture bearers in adaptation are human beings also suggests that regularities of psychological process must exist in disintegrating and reformulating situations. In fact, one of the significant potential contributions of the study of peoples adapting to the exigencies of rapid culture change should be a fuller understanding of panhuman regularities in psychological adaptation. There is no logical reason why a psychologically oriented study must be a study of individuals as such any more than a culturally oriented study must be a study of abstractions from behavior as such. Psychological process exhibits regularities and structure. "Personality," "cognitive system," "ego structure," etc., are abstractions from minutiae of observation just as culture patterns, traits, and complexes are.

The strategies of this complex study are only beginning to be worked out. Much fumbling must be expected. But worked out we feel they must be. In part, this paper details how anthropologists have dealt with the problems of this strategy, variously conceived; in part, it is a prediction of what will happen as future resolutions are effected. We will term this emergent strategy a *psychocultural approach*.

ANTHROPOLOGICAL FIRST STEPS TOWARD A PSYCHO-CULTURAL APPROACH (1936–1948)

With the background of the problem established, we turn to some first attempts by anthropologists to supplement the formalistic cultural approach. Constructs such as "themes," "covert culture," "values," and "basic attitudes" have been applied to analyses of culturally patterned behavior. In the applications of these constructs, authors refer explicitly to their analytic utility in culture-change situations. They all seem to be movements toward a psychological dimension without being radical departures from the cultural frame of reference.

Morris Opler defines themes as denoting "a postulate or position, declared or implied, and usually controlling behavior or stimulating activity. They are represented in many different aspects of culturally patterned behavior which is tacitly approved or openly promoted in a society" [37]. That men are physically, mentally, and morally superior to women is such a theme in Chiricahua Apache culture. It is represented in patterned behaviors with respect to sorcery, sex, childbirth, public roles, feasts, and sacred sanctuaries. Opler points out that themes such as these help to explain culture change, and especially acculturation. He illustrates this with examples that show how new cultural forms are perceived and integrated in relation to different themes into Chiricahua and Jicarilla Apache culture.

The concept of "covert" culture has also been used. Though it is like themes in its permeative and integrative character, covert culture is by definition hidden, rarely verbalized, implicit. Kluckhohn (among others) has made use of the concept. Among the Navaho, for example, the unstated premise that "sexual rights are property rights" relates otherwise incoherent behavioral facts in the treatment of illegitimate children, in the behavior at squaw dances, and in the complex of marriage. Kluckhohn points out the utility of this concept as an analytic tool. Adopting only limited overt aspects of a new culture results in disorganization, because the accompanying covert cultural configurations which act as limiting and integrating controls in the other setting are not also acquired [22].

H. Scudder Mekeel was one of the first anthropologists to use values as a conceptual tool in the analysis of culture change. In his treatment, values are desirable features of character embodied in the "ideal man." He illustrates how the Teton Dakota (Sioux) values—bravery, generosity, fortitude, and moral integrity—have been retained "behind the concrete patterns" of radically changed cultural forms and how they survive despite their dysfunctional role in the modern situation. In traditional Sioux culture, for example, very high value is placed upon generosity expressed in gift giving at most important social occasions and in hospitality extended to relatives and friends. This makes the accumulation of property—necessary to the goal of material success in American culture—very difficult for those Sioux who still maintain this pattern for behavior [35].

Highly generalized attitudes, such as the belief in immanent justice, considered indicative of "world view," are used as analytic categories by Laura Thompson in her analysis of culture change among the Zuni, Navaho, Papago, Dakota Sioux, and Ojibwa Indians. She analyzes reponses to the thematic apperception, moral ideology, and emotional response tests by Indian children six to eighteen years of age. She finds evidence that the world view in each tribe is congruent with the aboriginal mode of life and that these world views have apparently persisted despite great changes in the economy, social structure, and overt culture resulting from the changes in the conditions of life that are brought about by the impact of Euro-American culture [49].

These concepts have much in common. They interrelate seemingly disparate aspects of culturally patterned behavior. They call attention to premises for behavior that are, in varying degrees, implicit and not ordinarily verbalized by agents of the culture. They all move from the formal cultural level toward a level of culture in personality. They take into account the mediative, reactive aspect of human behavior, and are therefore not purely culturological. But they are still essentially cultural in their formulation and suggest that anthropologists in this period were not willing to move far from, much less discard, the culture concept.

During the latter phase (the mid-forties) of the period during which these constructs and their applications were emerging, the more broad personality and culture group was gaining strength. A veritable flood of publications appeared—analyses of the effect of child training on personality development and the relation of both to the culturally patterned environment, the study of basic personality, of national character and of various forms of abnormality in cultural context. Although the influence of behaviorism and, to some extent, gestalt psychology was represented in these writings, the influence of psychoanalysis and psychoanalytic psychiatry was decidedly dominant. Some anthropologists made explicit use of psychological concepts or methods in the analysis of culture change.

Two of the most definitive attempts to develop a framework for analysis of culture change using explicit psychological concepts employed learning theory. In 1942, John Gillin published an article titled "Acquired Drives in Culture Contact." He equates custom and habit, refers to the extinguishing of old customs (as habits) when their observance is punished, discusses acquiring new secondary drives, and cites Hull, Mowrer, Neal Miller, and Dollard [10]. He argues that changes in specific cultural *content* brought about by new "acquired" or "secondary" drives can be handled efficiently in the framework of learning theory. But he also argues that the relations of new patterns of "customary response" can "seemingly be explained only by principles formulated on the strictly cultural level" [10, p. 547]. He is willing to grant the efficacy of a psychological framework for the segmental, but not the integrative, aspects of culture change. He too seems reluctant to go far from the cultural frame of reference.

In 1945, A. Irving Hallowell published a paper titled "Sociopsychological Aspects of Acculturation" [11]. He argues against the concept of abstracted cultural traits diffused from one culture to another as the mechanism of cultural change in contact situations. He argues for attention to readjustments in individual behavior. He points out that humans are never passive culture bearers and that abstract cultures never meet; only humans meet. He makes a case for examining both the barriers and the incentives to learning in contact situations to gain insight into the dynamics of acculturation. He too uses the framework of learning theory, and cites Miller and Dollard [36]. He discusses cues, drives (or motivations), stimuli, and responses, anxiety reduction, reward and punishment, and gives specific examples from contact situations in which acculturation has occurred. He departs farther from the formalistic concept of culture than does Gillin and does not apparently feel the need to reembrace it.

It is clear that some anthropologists during this period moved toward "psychologizing" in analyses of culture change but nevertheless tended to stay within the cultural fold. This is explicit in the case of Opler, with his themes; it is somewhat less true of Kluckhohn and covert culture, and Mekeel and values; it is perhaps least true in the case of Thompson and basic attitudes constituting a world view. Gillin made a distinctive move toward explicit use of a psychological frame of reference, but returned to the culture concept in the end. Hallowell moved the farthest from an exclusively cultural formulation. Some anthropologists concerned with culture change apparently felt a need to include a psychological dimension of behavior in addition to the cultural. A fuller exposition and analysis of what they actually did in response to this need throughout the past two decades and up to the present will now be presented.

MEMOS FOR THE STUDY OF ACCULTURATION

Recognizing that acculturation was becoming a focus of much anthropological interest and activity, in 1935, the Social Science Research Council appointed Robert Redfield, Ralph Linton, and Melville J.

Herskovits as a committee to analyze acculturation studies, the implications of the concept, and to explore new leads for investigation. An outline called "Memorandum for the Study of Acculturation" was drawn up and published in 1936 in the *American Anthropologist* [39].

In the summer of 1953, the Social Science Research Council sponsored a seminar on acculturation. Homer G. Barnett, Leonard Broom, Bernard J. Siegel, Evon Z. Vogt, and James B. Watson were included. The group spent two months in study and discussion, and, in 1954, published a statement of what the authors conceived to be an "orderly approach to the study of cultural change as it is generated by culture contact" [41].

These two memoranda will provide useful data for an examination of changes in the formulation of the psychological dimensions that have taken place since the emergence of acculturation as a recognized field for anthropological inquiry. They are products of a group of workers, so they should represent more of anthropology than might be the case with pieces written by individuals. They have high-status sponsorship and were published in the organ of the American Anthropological Association. They are both attempts to do essentially the same thing.

1936 Memo

In the 1936 memo, acculturation is defined as "comprehending those phenomena which result when groups of individuals having different cultures come into continuous first-hand contact, with subsequent changes in the original cultural patterns of either or both groups" [39, p. 1]. The phrase "groups of individuals" is of particular significance, for this category subsumes most of what can be considered psychological in the formulation.

The memo as a whole outlines "types of contacts," "situations," "processes," and "psychological mechanisms of selection and integration of traits under acculturation." Clearly, in that part of the formulation (the major part) which is devoted exclusively to the cultural dimension, cultural *traits* are considered as the unit of analysis. Under "processes," subheadings include "selection" of traits (by the "receiving" group), "determination" of traits (economic, religious, etc., considerations), and "integration" of traits (into the pattern of the accepting culture). This was in keeping with the intellectual framework in anthropology of the time; relations between culturally differentiated groups were conceptualized in terms of *diffusion* of particles of culture, rather than adaptation by one or both groups to changes in life conditions brought about by the impact of one group on the other's environment. This conceptualization, in turn, has its antecedents in the history of anthropology and in the status of the world's cultures and their relationships during the first three decades of the twentieth century.

Under "psychological mechanisms," the *individual* is the unit of analysis. The personality of the first individual to accept foreign traits, the personality and social status of individuals in contact from both donor and accepting groups, the personalities of those members of the accepting group who accelerate or retard acceptance of new traits—these are the kinds of topics included. "Basic" or "modal" personality structure did not receive attention; individual personalities did. More generalizable psychological process is referred to only once, under the subheading "Results of Acculturation." Here "contra-acculturative" movements, more frequently called "nativistic" (a return to traditional culture in the form of cult movements and selective integration of special elements from the culture of impact), are included as a "reaction."

The focus on *traits* as the unit of cultural analysis, and the focus on *individuals* as the center of psychological analysis is consistent. Individuals from "donor" cultures present (in various forms, with various motives, and in various situations) a *smörgåsbord* of culture traits. Individuals from receiving cultures (with various motives, memberships, and influence) select from this *smörgåsbord*. Then the trait selected by an individual is integrated and reworked into the receiving culture. There is a movement toward psychology and behavior in situation, apparently in an attempt to treat with processes the more formalistic concept of culture does not comprehend effectively. But there is no real conception of psychological *systems*. Only abstract culture has system.

Equation of the individual with psychological process leaves the problem at an idiosyncratic, unpredictable, *unique* level. This equation is one possible reason for the rejection of psychologizing by some anthropologists; they see such a focus as a form of reductionism (from the cultural level) that is likely to lead nowhere. As a matter of fact, the approach has not been particularly successful. For instance, Ralph Linton edited a book called *Acculturation in Seven American Indian Tribes,* and presented his conceptualization of acculturation intended as a frame of reference for the separate analyses. His presentation included the psychological dimension as developed in the 1936 memo for the study of acculturation. None of the separate treatments applied it systematically [32], however. Homer Barnett's massive book *Innovation* pays heavy attention to individual psychology [1]. It is one of the most advanced conceptualizations of the innovating process in culture change and it eclectically uses learning theory, gestalt psychology, theories of perception and cognition, and neo-Freudian psychological concepts. This book may be considered intellectually successful, but it has not as yet had a marked effect on anthropological analyses of culture change in respect to a psychological frame of reference.

Despite criticisms, the 1936 memo includes a form of psychology as a major dimension, and it is internally consistent. It is representative of the thinking at that time, and it indicates that anthropologists interested in culture change felt the need to move toward a more adequate formulation of the psychological process. It will be interesting to see whether this formulation has survived the nearly two decades between the 1936 memo and the 1954 statement.

1954 Memo

This formulation of acculturation is complex and frankly exploratory. Only a few points of direct significance for the present analysis will be discussed. Acculturation is defined as "culture change initiated by the conjunction of two or more autonomous cultural systems." The units of analysis are not culture traits, but "any given culture as it is carried by its particular society." The dynamics of acculturation "can be seen as the selective adaptation of value systems, the processes of integration and differentiation, the generation of developmental sequences, and the operation of role determinants and personality factors." This statement is made:

"It is recognized that individuals are empirically the culture bearers and that they are the mediators of any cultural process. Students of culture are, however, concerned only with individuals as functioning members of a society and with the shared patterns of behavior constituting a body of customs. Consequently, while it is individuals who change their habits of doing and believing under the influence of alien forms, it is the body of custom of the society to which they belong that is said to be acculturated" [41; pp. 974–975].

While individuals, as such, are not included as units of analysis, "intercultural roles" are. The network of intercultural roles is seen as providing the channels through which "the content of one cultural system must be communicated and transmitted to the other." Role-playing in intercultural contacts is seen as mirroring "one group's image of itself, in relation to the other," but always selectively, since no one individual in any given role mirrors the whole culture. Existing "ideological and motivational sets" and the "perceptual organization of the receptor" are considered decisive factors, influencing the flow of communication through the network of intercultural roles [41; pp. 980–981].

The formulation comprehends four major aspects in the phenomenon of acculturation: (1) characterization of the properties of the autonomous cultural systems that come into contact; (2) the nature of the contact situation; (3) the conjunctive relations established between the cultural systems upon contact; and (4) the cultural processes which flow from the conjunction of the systems.

The position taken exhibits continuity with and differences from the 1936 formulation. Though traits are not the unit of analysis, as they were in the 1936 memo, culture is held as the more or less exclusive consequence of the adaptive processes in acculturation. There is less emphasis on the individual as a legitimate unit of analysis. Individuals do not become acculturated, but customs do. Actually this difference may be more apparent than real. In the 1936 memo, the personality of individuals in contact was conceived as a variable—but only as it affected what traits were selected for incorporation. And the position of the individual in his group, cited as another influencing factor in the 1936 memo, is broadly equivalent to the concept of role used in the 1954 formulation. The latter, however, includes ideological, motivational, and perceptual sets as factors in role-playing that are not included in the earlier statement. In this respect, the more recent formulation seems advanced in its use of psychological concepts. But this is the only place where such concepts are really an integral part of the formulation. There is a hint that other psychological processes are included as a significant dimension but, as will be demonstrated, they are not integrated into the formulation.

The problem of how to talk about culture as a system without reifying or anthropomorphizing seems to be very much present. An organismic analogy is invoked to make it possible to use the dynamic terms that seem so necessary when culture change is discussed. The internal structures of cultural systems are characterized as relatively "rigid" or "flexible." In discussing "boundary-maintaining" mechanisms, the authors said that "a system is likely to be rigid or self-consciously resistant to alteration on contact, since it is already organized defensively probably as a result of external or internal challenges in the past." "Self-correcting" mechanisms are described as "the ability of the cultural 'organism' [their quotes] to shift function and adapt internally, irrespective of its outer protective devices." Typological distinctions between cultural systems are made along the most frankly organismic lines. Terms like "hard-shelled, vertebrate" and "soft-shelled, invertebrate" are used to describe the propensities of cultural systems for adaptive change. It is stated that under conditions of extreme acculturative pressure, the former may "crack up completely," and that under other conditions the latter "ingest . . . great quantities of alien cultural material and still preserve their basic patterns and values" [41, pp. 977–978].

While there is possibly some value in such typological analogs, they do not take us very far into specific process and leave unformulated what seem to be most of the significant dimensions. The variables that should be used to test any hypotheses about process (and the authors state that these characterizations are potential starting points for hypotheses) are left at such a general level that it would be difficult to formulate them in a testable way.

The authors of this exploratory formulation cannot seek much help from psychological concepts because they define the psychological dimension so narrowly. In what seems to be almost an afterthought in the presentation, under the heading "Personality and Acculturation," they say:

As far as acculturation is concerned, the psychological problem is to determine the depth of commitment to certain shared patterns and values and consequently to assess the difficulties of accepting changes. For what is important in this connection is not the structure or the orientation of personality itself but the extent to which certain basic values are internalized or rejected and the extent to which they function as selective mechanisms in acculturation [41, p. 993].

It is apparent that this statement of 1954 does not move very far toward a psychocultural approach. The frame of reference remains culture. As the process of acculturation is conceived, a coherent, organized system (culture) responds through people to the impact of another system. So long as a cultural system does in fact exist—is shared by a community of people—this formulation is useful. When that system begins to disintegrate and individuation takes place, the formulation is no longer adequate. It cannot really even explain satisfactorily why or how the system begins to disintegrate unless neopsychological formulations, such as "perception of new alternatives," "anxiety about the efficacy of traditional solutions," or "striving for prestige in emergent status systems," are utilized.

Neither the 1936 or 1954 formulation of an approach to the study of culture change appears to have handled the psychological dimension with marked success. The former included a systematic focus on the psychology of the individual, but it did not comprehend categories for the analysis of psychological systems concomitant with cultural systems. The latter explicitly discarded the psychology of the individual as a legitimate unit of analysis, but it provided only a very narrow framework for consideration of other formulations of psychological process. Both explicitly acknowledge the existence of a psychological dimension. Both appear to place a great burden upon the culture concept.

A CASE ILLUSTRATION

At this point, discussion of some case studies of psychological process in culture change should clarify the issues. We hope that we will be pardoned if we emphasize our own research. The rapidly acculturating Menomini Indians of Wisconsin studied by the Spindlers intermittently between 1948 and 1955 provide one case [42, 43, 44, 45]. The culturally similar Ojibwa Indians of Ontario and Wisconsin studied by Hallowell and his co-workers provide the other [12, 14].

The Ojibwa study was carried out in three areas representing three different levels of acculturation. The least acculturated "inland" sample was taken from the Berens River group. These people were largely out of contact with white men and their civilization, spoke only Ojibwa, hunted and trapped for a living, and carried on the traditional religion. The intermediate group lived near Lake Winnepeg. Its members were more in contact with the white man and more dependent upon his material goods and economic techniques, spoke both Ojibwa and English, and were mostly Christianized. Hallowell's most acculturated group, living on a Wisconsin reservation, had lost nearly all of the traditional culture. Members of the group were mostly living as poor whites.

Rorschachs were collected from 217 subjects, 120 men and 97 women, aged sixteen to eighty years. The Thematic Apperception Test technique was also employed for part of this and a more extended sample, but these data are not directly relevant to the discussion. In order to establish a psychological as well as cultural baseline that would help substantiate the hypothesis that the inland Ojibwa represented a close approximation to an aboriginal level, Hallowell studied the accounts of fur traders, explorers, and Jesuit missionaries who had intimate contacts with the Indians of the eastern woodlands during the seventeenth and eighteenth centuries.

Hallowell's conclusions are dramatic and merit quoting:

> The most striking fact is the continuity of the same basic psychological pattern through these stages of acculturation. There is a persistent core of generic traits which can be identified as Ojibwa. Thus even the highly acculturated Indians at Flambeau are still Ojibwa in a psychological sense, whatever clothes they wear, whatever their occupation, whether they speak English or not and regardless of race mixture. While culturally speaking they appear like "whites" in many respects, there is no evidence at all of a fundamental psychological transformation [12, p. 38].

Hallowell goes on to point out that this does not mean an absence of changes as the analysis proceeds through progressively more acculturated levels. While the outlines of an aboriginal personality structure persist, this outline becomes corroded at the later stages of acculturation—specific Rorschach signs of deterioration appear in reality perception and emotional control. But no general psychological reformulation takes place.

Doubtless, there are many questions about methods, assumptions, and interpretative procedure. Some of them will be anticipated in the discussion of strategy to follow; for now, let us turn to the Menomini study.

The Menomini live as one tribe in a Wisconsin reservation community. The presence of a Menomini-run lumber industry on the reservation has helped produce a situation of economic self-sufficiency that is so advanced that the Federal government has recently withdrawn all support and control. And yet we were able to distinguish four levels of acculturation in its most manifest aspects within this reservation:

The *native-oriented* group lives mostly back in the forest in a loosely defined community called Zoar. Here the people carry on the "Medicine Lodge" and "Dream Dance" ceremonials, participate in "ghost feasts," naming ceremonies, and war dances—all generically and aboriginally Menomini or "Pan-Indian" conservative cultural patterns.

The *Peyote Cult* group consists of people who have become dissatisfied with traditional solutions to life's problems or have entered into culturally intermediate situations and have become disturbed by their experiences of culture conflict. The Peyotists live scattered in the area of Zoar and elsewhere on the reservation. Peyote Cult meetings are held frequently and are centered on taking peyote, a narcotic alkaloid in the form of cactus buds, to produce visions. The meetings are intensely religious. Members tell their troubles with open emotion. Cures of emotional and physical illnesses occur dramatically. Participants ruminate over their sins and hope for salvation through self-knowledge revealed and acquired in vision experiences and prayer. The religious paraphernalia, ritual, and ideology are a unique combination of native and Christian elements. The cult appears to be a special solution to the strains of culture conflict, interpreted by the individual as personal conflict. It is a socioculturally deviant and tight-knit group in the reservation community and is recognized as such both by members and nonmembers.

The *transitionals* all had early socialization experience in the native-oriented group, but they have moved toward Catholicism and the white man's culture. In our sample, they are most clearly in between the two cultures and are not wholeheartedly committed to either. They are also the most individuated and the most unpredictable in social, political, and economic behaviors. Some are apathetic and withdrawn. Others are aggressively disorganized. A few are consistently attempting to achieve a higher standard of living.

The *acculturated* live as white men and retain no manifest behavioral attachments to native-oriented ways. They are subdivided into two socioeconomic groups. The elite acculturated hold managerial or supervisory positions in the lumber industry or tribal government, live in houses like those of middle-class residents of nearby white communities, and are generally accepted as equals by many of the people who live in those communities. The lower-status acculturated are committed to regular work for wages but as semiskilled or unskilled laborers. They live more or less like whites at the same economic level.

A continuum of acculturation running from the native-oriented to the acculturated groups was validated through statistical tests (tetrachoric correlation and chi-square) of 23 sociocultural indexes, such as house type, occupation, use of medical facilities, and education.

The Rorschach technique was applied to 68 adult males and 61 adult females distributed throughout the various acculturative categories named above. These data for the two sexes were treated separately—a strategy we will discuss shortly. Our further discussion will be limited to the males, excepting where specifically indicated. Twenty-four autobiographies were collected from selected individuals representing all groups and both sexes. Thematic Apperception Tests were collected from some, and extensive verbatim records and extended observational data were gathered in all cases. We will confine our discussion here to the Rorschach data.

"Exact-probability" statistical tests of differentiation were applied to comparisons of Rorschach scores and ratios between each of the acculturative categories. The differences proved to be significant, numerous, and consistent. The native-oriented and elite acculturated samples, for example, are differentiated in nine Rorschach scores. The native-oriented and transitional samples are differentiated in five scores. This is precisely what we would expect if we hypothesize that the two ends of the acculturative continuum, most unlike in the sociocultural dimension, should be more unlike in the psychological dimension than are the transitional and native-oriented samples. Perhaps even more significant is the fact that the highly deviant Peyote group is differentiated more frequently in Rorschach scores from every other Menomini group than is any other acculturative group. Apparently this group is both socioculturally and psychologically deviant within the Menomini community.

Even without interpretation of the presumed psychological meaning of distributions of Rorschach scores, this pattern of deviation and differentiation tells us much about the covariance of psychological and sociocultural process in acculturation. We did not stop here, however. Fully cognizant of the questionable validity of many standard interpretive hypotheses applied to Rorschach scores, we stated them beforehand and applied them consistently to the demonstrated differences between acculturative groups and to modal Rorschach profiles.

Stated in qualitative psychological terms, the results may be summed up as follows (in each case we refer to modal characteristics that differentiated the acculturative group from others in the continuum) : At the native-oriented level, we found a modal personality type that is intellectually uncomplicated, limited but not constricted, sensitive to nuances of interpersonal relationships, and lacking in overt emotional responsiveness. Among the Peyotists, the modal type was characterized by involved self-projective fantasy, a marked loosening of emotional and reality control, complex introspective tendencies, and consistent indications of anxiety and tension. The transitionals presented some difficulties in the construction of a modal type. This is psychologically and socioculturally the most individuated group, and the most rapid adaptive changes are taking place in this group. Indications of a loosening of emotional and reality control, coupled with diffuse anxiety, characterize the group most frequently. The Rorschach profiles of scores, as well as the qualitative character of the responses, place the transitionals in a clearly intermediate position between the elite acculturated and the native-oriented. The outlines of a native perceptual structure are evident, but they appear to be undergoing disintegrative processes in a modal number of cases. The transitionals share certain features of these tendencies—in so far as they apply to loosening of emotional controls and reality perception—with the Peyotists, but they lack the marked introspective tendencies and self-projective fantasy of the cult group. The elite and lower-status acculturated exhibit many features in common, but a modal type that we can term "reformulated" is most fully developed among the former. This type is characterized by high intellectual productivity, a broad range of interests, a relatively high degree of self-projective fantasy that lacks the ruminative quality of the Peyotists, open but controlled emotional expressiveness, sharp reality control, and tension, but not diffuse anxiety.

The above characterizations apply to the male sample. In analysis of the female sample, we adopted a different strategy and discarded application of standard Rorschach hypotheses with respect to the meaning of scores. We developed separate modal typologies for males and females, using an adaptation of Wallace's method with the Tuscarora [51], and identified the cases contributing to the modal types in the various acculturative categories. This led us to a series of interpretive hypotheses concerning the respective social roles of men and women and the effect of acculturation upon them [44, 45, 46].

In brief, this analysis indicates that women are both socioculturally and psychologically more conservative than men, and are more homogeneous as a group. The modal psychological type for women is native-oriented, for men transitional and lower-status acculturated. The occupational and public roles of men call for more sharply focused adaptation to the impact of acculturation. Women are insulated in some degree from the impact of acculturation, in that there is continuity in the roles of wife, mother, and homemaker. We remark here that it would have been a serious error to mix indiscriminately the male and female data, as is frequently done. Men and women play different roles in all societies, and we believe they represent different universes of adaptation.

In comparison to Hallowell's results, it is clear that the Menomini sample is more highly differentiated with respect to Rorschach scores. This applies most particularly, however, to the Peyote Cult group and the elite acculturated, neither of which is represented in his sample of Ojibwa. Upon a close examination of the comparable data of all of the samples, it is evident that the same processes have occurred. The Menomini transitionals exhibit the same tendency to carry through a perceptual structure with native-oriented outlines, but with definite indications of stress. It is also interesting to us that the modal Rorschach profile of the native-oriented Menomini is very similar to that of the least acculturated Ojibwa, and that Menomini and Ojibwa cultures are likewise very similar. Apparently there is consistency in the covariance of psychological and sociocultural adaptation in at least these two cases.

Some Remarks on Strategy

Both Hallowell and the Spindlers committed two fallacies in their research—from the psychologist's point of view. One may be termed the "global" fallacy, the other the "jumping" fallacy. They are both typical anthropological fallacies in so far as studies of the psychology of acculturation are concerned and they merit some discussion.

The *global fallacy* we define as the attempt to deal with a complex holistic construct like "personality" or "perceptual structure" as a variable. This is apparent in nearly everything that has been said about the Menomini and Ojibwa. It is a logical, virtually inevitable, strategy in the light of the nature of anthropology as a discipline. We will discuss the antecedents of this strategy at the end of this paper. To us it is a profitable one because it raises rich, complex issues with respect to the covariance of psychological and sociocultural process. It also raises serious methodological problems that cannot be lightly dismissed. Any strategy involves a certain amount of "cost accounting."

The *jumping fallacy* we define, following Leonard Doob [6], as the application of unvalidated interpretive hypotheses concerning the meaning of Rorschach scores and profiles. The strategy is doubly complicated by the fact that we are doing cross-cultural research. We do not excuse ourselves on the basis of having to take what the psychologists give us in the way of tools and theories. If we know psychological theory and methodology, we can invent our own—at considerable cost of time and ingenuity. But to us the jumping strategy has value. We could ask, "What will happen if we set up the most parsimonious standard interpretations available in the literature on projective techniques and apply them to a sample of persons whose characteristic overt behaviors are intimately known to us?" The results seem to us to justify the decision. The interpretations based directly upon Rorschach scores seem too functionally congruent with our other observations to be discarded. For example, the Peyotists are the only Menomini group consistently producing *FK* (vista and perspective) responses to the ink blots (in 11 of 13 cases). The ideology of the cult, the ritual, the search for salvation, the rumination over sin and self are specifically introspective in orientation and sanction. *FK* is interpreted, using standard hypotheses, as indicating introspective tendencies. Another example—the native-oriented consistently fail to produce any responses using color (12 of 17 cases). The standard interpretation for this is low emotional responsiveness. It is not an exaggeration to say that the most persistent theme in the culture of the native-oriented group is stoic control of overt emotional responsiveness. This is clear in the ritual commandments of ceremonial organizations, in the conception of the ideal man, and in the stated conceptions of proper child training. Many other examples of this sort could be furnished. They are all congruent with the by now well-established conception of functional correspondence between personality and social structure [17, 19, 48].

It is apparent that a clinical, phenomenological, interpretive approach is being applied. We are aware of the dangers of *ad hoc* reasoning and the closure tendencies we all exhibit in the search for plausibility, but this strategy has respectable antecedents in an honorable branch of psychology as well as in anthropology.

The consistent implications of the functional relationships between Rorschach data and sociocultural observation lead us to the inference that the Rorschach is tapping significant psychological process in depth, and with sufficient reliability to allow us to use it as a complex index of psychological process. The ultimate ramifications of this process may be resolvable into cognitive, perceptual, or ego-defense dimensions. There are many ways in which Rorschach data may eventually be interpreted, but most of this work must be done by psychologists. To us it seems clear that Rorschach responses reflect the introjection of cultural patterns by individuals. In fact, it seems to us that the Rorschach may well be more useful as a psychocultural technique than as a personality technique. If we are interested in the relationship between psychological and overt aspects of culture change (such as occupation and house type), the Rorschach seems to be a useful tool. It is one of the very few that permits presentation of the same culturally unstructured stimuli to different groups.

But since we are acutely aware of the disrepute into which the

Rorschach has fallen among some of the most respectable psychologists, we have attempted another strategy [46]. We have discarded all conventional interpretations of the meaning of scores and have analyzed the covariance of psychological process with manifest sociocultural adaptation—as described previously. In this analysis, we have dealt exclusively with the concentration and dispersion of Rorschach scores in the various acculturative categories of our sample and in comparisons of males and females. This approach has yielded useful results. We are at least able to say at what point in the acculturative continuum significant changes in psychological structure occur, whether sociocultural deviation is accompanied by psychological deviation, and how relatively homogeneous a group is psychologically. But we admit that this strategy is somewhat alien to our anthropological value system. We much prefer the rich, dubious, qualitative complexity of the jumping fallacy—tempered by contextual empiricism.

This discussion may help the reader to better understand the problems of the psychologically oriented anthropologist. It should also make clear why we feel that the formulations of approaches to the study of acculturation discussed previously give too narrow a scope to the psychological dimension.

THE LITERATURE ON CULTURE CHANGE, 1929–1952

The next phase of analysis will detail more systematically the ways in which anthropologists studying culture change from 1929 to 1952 have used psychological materials. As stated in the section on procedure, all articles and books written by anthropologists on culture change in North America during the named period, abstracted in the Stanford volume *Acculturation: Critical Abstracts, North America* [40], will be used as a sample for analysis. The abstracts are quite detailed and complete, so that preliminary categories for further analysis could be developed from them. Publications were read in their original form before final judgments on categories were made, with one exception—the category including writings where problem formulation and interpretive procedure required no psychologizing and where this was evident from the abstract.

The procedure followed was first to record all instances in this sample where works written by psychologists were actually cited by title and author. The second step was to examine the sample for instances where identifiable psychological concepts were used, but where no citations of specific works by psychologists were given. The third step was to divide the remaining writings by anthropologists into two categories: (1) cases in which no psychological citations or concepts were used, but where there is evidence they were needed with respect to the problem formulation and procedure; and (2) cases where no psychological citations or concepts are used and there is no clear evidence that they were needed.

It is apparent that a subjective, interpretive element is absent only with respect to the category of specific citations. Judgments had to be made in respect to all other categories of analysis. The grounds for these judgments will be stated, but the results must be regarded as rough, in some cases quite problematic, and certainly influenced by our biases. Nevertheless, the over-all trends thus revealed are judged to have enough validity to be significant.

The outline following will provide data on the uses that anthropologists writing on culture change have made of writing by psychologists and psychological concepts and terminology. An outline form is used because it is impossible to communicate the necessary information in the highly schematic form of a table. The conceptual breakdown of psychology follows in a general way the one provided in the *Handbook of Social Psychology* [31, vol. 1]. In most cases, it was not difficult to assign a cited psychological piece or concept to a category. A few pieces, however, could have been assigned to more than one category. In these instances, an arbitrary judgment was made.

Outline by Category of Psychological Usages in Culture-Change Analyses, 1929–1952

1. Psychoanalytic
   a. Citation of specific works: by Freud, 1; Roheim, 2; other followers of Freud, 4 7
   b. Without citation of specific works: use of concepts traceable to Freud concerning influence of child training on personality formation, 6; use of psychoanalytic terminology to describe dynamics of personality, 10 16

   Total 23
2. Neopsychoanalytic
   a. Citation of specific works: by Kardiner (with Linton), 7; by Kardiner, 2; Fromm, 1; Erikson, 3 13
   b. Without citation of specific works: use of concepts originating in the Kardiner-Linton formulation, 3; use of concepts traceable to Jung, 1 4

   Total 17
3. Projective techniques
   a. Citation of specific works on the Rorschach: by Klopfer, 7; by Beck, 1; on other projective techniques, 7 15

   Total 15

4. Stimulus-response reinforcement theory
    a. Citation of specific works in general learning theory: by
        Hull, 1; Mowrer, 1 2
    b. Without citation of specific works: use of concepts like
        "reinforcing stimuli" "acquiring secondary drives,"
        11 . . . . 11 __
        Total 13

5. Frustration-aggression hypotheses
    a. Citation of specific works: by Miller and Dollard, 1 . . . 1
    b. Without citation of specific works: use of concept that
        frustration manifests itself in aggression, 9 . . . . 9 __
        Total 10

6. I.Q. Tests
    a. Citation of specific tests: Grace-Arthur Performance
        Scale, 2; Goodenough Draw-a-man, 2; Army Wech-
        sler scale, 1 . . . . 5 __
        Total 5

7. Cognitive theory
    a. Citation of specific works: by Angyal, 1; Goldstein, 1;
        Allport, 1; T. French, 1 4
    b. Without citation of specific works: use of concepts like
        "achievement motivation," 6 . . . . 6 __
        Total 10

8. Gestalt psychology
    a. Citation of specific works: by Ellis, 1 1
    b. Without citation of specific works: use of concepts
        like "configurations," "logicoesthetic integration,"
        "ethos," that are at least distantly related to gestalt
        theory, 7 . . . . 7 __
        Total 8

9. Self-other concept
    a. Citation of specific works: by Krech and Crutchfield, 1;
        by Charles Morris, a philosopher who uses the self
        concept, 1 2
    b. Without citation of specific works: use of concepts
        traceable mainly to the G. H. Mead formulation, 4 . . 4 __
        Total 6

10. Role Theory
    a. Citation of specific works on psychodrama: by Del
        Torto and Cornyetz, 1; Moreno, 1 . . . . 2 __
        Total 2

In the outline, the universe of possibilities is provided by all the writings by psychologists and all the concepts and terms traceable to psychology that anthropologists have been exposed to in one way or another and may use. This means that one anthropological author may use citations or concepts and terms falling under one, several, or all of the headings in the outline. Frequently the anthropologists in this sample have been very eclectic in their use of psychological citations, concepts, and terms, not confining themselves in any single article or book to the materials provided by any one kind of psychological theory. A citation of a specific psychological work or use of a particular psychological concept is counted only once for each anthropological author, irrespective of the number of times that he may use the same citation or concept in a given article or book. The number of citations, or usages without citation, are given in the outline.

The table below summarizes the information gained from analysis of the sample in a different way. Here the universe of treatment is the number of articles and books [94] listed in the volume, not the possible number of usages of psychological materials reported in the outline. To make this form of analysis possible, each piece of anthropological writing that cited specific psychological works was counted as doing so, even though in more than a few cases there was also use of psychological concepts and terms without citation in the same anthropological piece.

TABLE 1. USE OF PSYCHOLOGICAL MATERIALS IN ANTHROPOLOGICAL ANALYSES
OF CULTURE CHANGE IN NORTH AMERICA, 1929–1952

Usages	Number	Percentage
Concepts, with citation...............................	18	20
Concepts or terms, without citation....................	22	23
No concepts, terms, or citations used, but needed..........	29	30
No concepts, terms, or citations used, and none needed.....	25	27
Total..	94	100

Discussion. The outline and the table provide a rather clear picture of the usages of psychological material by anthropologists for the period 1929–1952, but some discussion will highlight certain features. Whenever a specific piece of writing by an anthropologist is mentioned, the complete reference may be found in the Stanford volume of abstracts [40]. Exhaustive citation seems irrelevant, in so far as materials from this volume are concerned, so no attempt is made to provide it.

It is clear from both the outline and table that many anthropologists have used psychological concepts and terms without citation of specific psychological works. Apparently such concepts and terms have become a part of the working vocabulary of these anthropologists. The spread of usages throughout a wide range of psychological categories also suggests a rather eclectic selection from psychology.

Of the various possibilities provided by psychology, the outline shows that the psychoanalytic and neopsychoanalytic categories dominate. This conclusion is strengthened if concepts used in interpreting the projective techniques and the rationale of their usage are seen as essentially neopsychoanalytic. The theoretical framework associated with application of these techniques is, however, rather eclectic, and cannot be comprehended under the neopsychoanalytic label without some qualifications.

In the utilization of psychoanalytic and neopsychoanalytic theory proper, there are few references to Freud or his identifiable followers. What has apparently happened is that a set of concepts that had their genesis in Freudian theory have interpenetrated the field of anthropology to such an extent that they have become implicit analytic assumptions. They are integrated into the works of many anthropological authors without explicit self-consciousness. Terms such as "displacement," "rationalization," "ambivalence," "identification," "sublimation," and "internalization" are used freely, and usually without citation of specific psychoanalytic works. In respect to neopsychoanalytic theory, the formulation advanced by Kardiner and Linton has been the most influential, and concepts like "basic institutions," "basic personality," and "integrative systems" are used both with and without specific citation.

If stimulus-response reinforcement theory, the frustration-aggression hypothesis, and aspects of cognitive theory can be lumped together as broadly representing what can be called "learning theory," this field of psychology runs a close second to the psychoanalytic and neopsychoanalytic category in extent of influence upon anthropology. Here too the ideas and terms comprehended in this field have become an integral part of the working vocabulary and conceptualizing of many anthropologists to such a degree that they are used freely without specific citations. Terms like "reinforcing stimuli" and "acquiring new habits," drawn from conventional stimulus-response reinforcement theory, are used without citation much more frequently than with it. The same applies to use of concepts from the frustration-aggression formulation. And the concept of achievement motivation is also incorporated in the works of some anthropologists, both with and without citation of specific works.

Other fields of psychology fade into comparative insignificance in respect to their influence upon the anthropology of this period. Gestalt theory is represented—at least indirectly—most frequently in the use of concepts like "configuration" and "ethos," but specific citations of gestalt theory are rare indeed. Use of self-other concepts, stemming mainly from George H. Mead, plays a minor role in anthropological usage.

Role theory proper is almost unrepresented. "Sociological" social psychology had apparently not infiltrated the ranks of anthropologists to any great extent up to 1952. Formal concepts of perception from psychology have not as yet made their appearance, but limited aspects of an emerging cognitive theory have.

The categories of table 1. Table 1 makes it clear that a bare majority (57 per cent) of anthropologists writing on culture change up to 1952 *did not* use any psychological constructs at all. This is important information, for one might conclude from the outline of usages that all anthropologists used psychology in culture-change analyses. The table also makes clear what is already known from the outline—that psychological terms and concepts were used more frequently without citation of specific works in psychology than with citation.

The categories of psychological usages in the table call for explanation and support. The category "No concepts, terms, or citation used, but needed," is the largest single bloc in the table and required making inferential judgments that might have been made differently by someone else. Anthropological writings were placed in this category when it seemed apparent that the clarity and precision of the research reported would have been definitely increased if the authors had dealt with psychological processes named or merely suggested in the report. Only studies in which the authors themselves give evidence of a need for a psychological explanation of a phenomenon are included. This need is exhibited in a variety of ways.

Reification or anthropomorphization. This occurs when the author finds it necessary to write as though personalities were reacting to change when his frame of reference disallows the use of psychology. This usually results in using constructs such as sociocultural systems or culture patterns as though they had an independent existence, volition, or ability to make a choice. In some cases, there is what appears to be a confusion of psychological and sociocultural systems—as though they could be used interchangeably. For instance, reference may be made to "adaptable," "flexible," and "rigid" societies, as though one were speaking of personalities, in a discussion in which only differences in sociocultural systems are analyzed and without independent psychological data. Or an author may anthropomorphize by reference to a "subliminal" culture pattern, without giving it a psychological context.

Substitution of values for motivation. This is quite common among anthropological writers who do not use psychological concepts. This seems to simplify the problem for them, and values become a motivational dimension of the culture as represented by individuals. "Personality patterns" may be described, without independent psychological data, as being made up of miscellaneous cultural items, such as the value placed upon generosity and the recognition of kinship obligations. We grant, however, that this may approach being considered a legitimate usage, since shared motivations may be viewed as the psychological counterpart of shared values. We have therefore included only instances where the usage appeared to go beyond the acceptable identity of values and motivations and a more full exposition of the motivational level would have proved useful for clarification and completeness of analysis.

Psychological process as a given. This occurs where a writer refers to a psychological process required by the problem as though it were a given assumption, with no definitions, explanations, elaborations, or empirical data to support the assumption. It is almost as though such writers felt at times that the expression of certain psychological concepts and terms had a magical effect—a power to communicate themselves. For instance, in discussing women's roles, writers refer to "striking personality differences" that are associated with social status, with no elaboration concerning these differences. Other authors make passing reference to psychological concepts such as "readjustment," "hostility," "psychological excitation," "satisfaction of desires," "motivation of individuals," "release of aggression," "maladjusted misfit," with no explicit psychological data and no operational definition of what the references mean in the context in which they are used.

Some anthropological writings were placed in the category "No concepts, terms, or citations used, and none needed." There are, of course, many significant anthropological problems where psychology is not relevant. It is not always possible or necessary to emphasize the concomitance of on-going adaptive processes. Ethnohistoric studies have a different aim. These are represented in the sample by Codere's reconstruction of Northwest Coast cultures, Albrecht's study of Indian-French relations at Natchez, Lewis's historical study of cultural changes among the Blackfoot Indians resulting from the fur trade, and Kineitz's study of the Delaware Big House ceremony. The study of the Menomini by Keesing is a good example. The author did, however, seem to feel the need for introducing concepts which would call for further elaboration in psychological terms. He concludes his discussion of tenacity of cultural pattern with the hypothesis that the aspects least affected, i.e., foods, religion, primary-group relationships, "appear closely connected either with the immediate environment or with deep-seated mental and emotional patterns." [21].

Also included in this category (where psychological usages are judged to be unnecessary) are some traditional distributional diffusion-type studies made with cultural traits, elements, or limited complexes as the units of analysis. These included Spier's Ghost Dance study and Opler's study of the diffusion of the Sun Dance, as well as others. Some authors, however, were forced to reify certain aspects of culture even with this kind of problem and method.

Other studies assigned to this category include descriptive analyses of change dealt with at the more or less "pure" social and organizational levels, where reification did not seem to be exhibited. These include Collins's study dealing with class distinctions among the Skagit Indians, and Aginsky's on change in family types among the Pomo and comparable studies.

Several studies of limited aspects of culture in change were judged to fall in this category. These include linguistic studies related to acculturation, such as those by Lee and Barker; studies of change and stability in musical forms, as represented by Slotkin's study of jazz and Herzog's study of the Ghost Dance songs; studies of culture change made on the basis of museum pieces (Quimbly, Spoehr); and studies in mythology as related to culture change, such as Barker's study on North American Indian mythology and its influence on messianic movements.

THE LITERATURE ON CULTURE CHANGE, 1952–1962

From January, 1952, to April, 1962, the *American Anthropologist* has published 58 articles on culture change. The number of articles on this subject has been increasing steadily during this time until the past two years, when it has declined.

Of these 58 articles, 13 (22 per cent) use explicit psychological concepts as a significant part of the framework of analysis, and 9 (15 per cent) cite specific psychological works. Two of these nine include references to materials on the self-concept and role-playing [2, 3]. One uses similar concepts in conjunction with projective techniques [45]. Another cites psychoanalytic, neopsychoanalytic, and psychiatric works and some in the social psychology of the self [53]. The next lists medical literature on stress and psychosomatic illness [15]. Another refers to works on tolerance of ambiguity and authoritarianism [33]. A general work on motivation and goal realization is cited in the next [4]. A social psychological analysis of Ojibwa acculturation uses concepts like self image, marginal personality, release of hostility, and cites extensively from relevant psychologically oriented works by anthropologists and social psychologists [18a]. The most recent article analyzes value attitudes about sex-linked role behavior [4a] in two Japanese villages and cities relevant literature in the use and interpretation of projective tests.

One of the four articles that use psychological concepts but do not cite specific psychological works makes very eclectic usage of the frustration-aggression hypothesis, the notion of the social self, and some general psychodynamic propositions, such as "compulsive hostility and anxiety," all of which are probably classifiable as neopsychoanalytic (50). Another uses concepts that are explicitly psychoanalytic, such as "oral zone," "primitive superego," "ego-identity" (47). The other two articles in this category include psychological terms but do not make the concepts they denote a particularly significant part of the analytic framework.

Psychological usages during the 1952–1962 period are summarized in Table 2 to facilitate comparison with Table 1 (1929–1952). The criteria for inclusion in the four categories of psychological usages are the same for both tables.

TABLE 2. USE OF PSYCHOLOGICAL MATERIALS IN ANTHROPOLOGICAL ANALYSES OF CULTURE CHANGE PUBLISHED IN THE AMERICAN ANTHROPOLOGIST FROM 1952–1962

Usages	Number	Percentage
Concepts with citation.	9	15
Concepts or terms without citation.	4	7
No concepts, terms, or citation used, but needed.	7	12
No concepts, terms, or citations used and none needed.	38	66
Total.	58	100

Comparison with 1929–1952 Period

Some differences in the use of psychological materials in culture-change analyses are indicated between the two periods summarized in Tables 1 and 2. There is a definite decline in the use of psychological concepts, whether with or without citation, with 43 per cent of the earlier sample using them, and only 22 per cent of the most recent sample doing so. This suggests that there has been a refocusing of interests among anthropologists studying culture change and a disenchantment with the personality and culture movement; it is probably a reaction against the overselling that is inherent in intellectual fads.

There is also a marked shift in the category "No concepts, terms, or citations used, but needed," with 30 per cent in the 1929–1952 sample, and only 12 per cent in the 1952 to 1962 sample. Problem formulations have grown more limited, more sharply focused—and on problems that do not require psychologizing. Analysis of changes in kinship systems, technology, religious ritual, ecological adaptations, social organization, and concerning highly specific culture traits and patterns exchanged between communities characterizes the major share of publications in the latter period represented in Table 2. Fewer authors now indulge in gratuitous reifying or anthropomorphizing—their problems do not require it.

A shift in the category "No concepts, terms, or citations used and none needed" supports the interpretation just given. This is the most marked shift in the comparison of the two periods, with 27 per cent in 1929 to 1952 and 66 per cent in 1952 to 1962. Again, problem formulation is more sharply focused, and limited to questions that do not involve psychological dimensions.

Taken as a whole, the differences between the earlier and more recent periods suggest a sharp trend away from the use of psychology—particularly away from the excesses of the personality and culture movement. This may be considered a retreat, in one sense. The scope of problem formulation is less broad, and many anthropologists have given up the attempt to incorporate the psychological level into a coherent theoretical structure. These developments appear to parallel those taking place in sociology and psychology following the partially abortive interdisciplinary period which culminated in the late 1940s. Retreats back to the "solid core" of each field seem to characterize the past decade.

Though the developments just discussed are in one sense a retreat, they have had a good result. Fifty-three per cent of the works in culture change written between 1929 and 1952 either should have used psychological materials called for by their problem formulations, and did not, or used psychological concepts and terms without documenting their origin, their place in established theory, or their application in any other research. Only 19 per cent of the works published during the past decade (1952–1962) can be characterized this way. There is clearly less tendency to formulate problems and use concepts loosely, in so far as use of psychological materials is concerned. Conversely, there has probably been a definite tightening in problem formulation, interpretation of research results, and by inference, in methodology as a whole.

The smallest change has been in the category "Concepts with citation," with 20 per cent in the earlier and 15 per cent in the later period. Apparently the proportion of anthropologists who are interested in frankly psychologically oriented analyses and who use specific psychological materials for specific purposes has remained about the same. Probably the most substantial joining of anthropology and psychology has not been much affected by the waxing and waning of interest. The progressive disengagement between anthropology and psychology noted earlier may have occurred where the joining between the two fields was already loose. Now that anthropological use of psychological materials is no longer a "movement," the most solidly creative work may be yet to come.

SUMMARY

No attempt will be made to integrate the arguments in the paper as a whole up to this point. Stated parsimoniously, the major conclusions issuing from the analysis of selected writings on culture change are as follows:

1. Some anthropologists have exhibited a need for concepts that will enable them to deal with the mediative and reactive aspects of behavior in culture-change situations.

2. In attempting to satisfy this need, few anthropologists are willing to move very far from the analytic framework supplied by the culture construct.

3. Explicit formulations by anthropologists of approaches to the study of culture change incorporate a psychological dimension but tend to give this dimension narrow scope.

4. Of those anthropologists who have used psychological materials, a majority have used them, until recently, without citation of specific psychological works. Many psychological concepts have become a part of the working vocabulary of anthropologists.

5. Psychoanalysis, learning theory, and the projective techniques comprise the fields of psychology most extensively diffused into anthropology.

6. The trend is for fewer anthropologists to formulate problems in culture change in such a way that psychological materials would be useful.

7. The proportion of culture-change studies formulated in such a way that psychological materials are not relevant and not used has more than doubled during the period covered.

8. A minority of anthropologists cite specific psychological materials in culture-change analyses, and the proportion of anthropologists making the most explicit and significant use of these materials has remained fairly constant.

9. There has been a marked disengagement between anthropology and psychology in so far as anthropological studies of culture change are concerned.

10. Because much of the disengagement may have occurred where the joining between anthropology and psychology was already tenuous, and because the proportion of studies using psychological materials in apparently more rigorous ways has remained relatively constant, there is reason for optimism about the future of this relationship.

PROBLEMS OF COMMUNICATION

Probably everyone who has written a critical review of what has been done in a developing field feels the need to discuss certain ideas and studies which do not conveniently fall within the stated framework of his paper. We find our need acute and ask the reader's indulgence while we seek gratification.

Our evidence clearly indicates that there has been a progressive disengagement from psychology on the part of anthropology during the past decade. While our analysis has been limited to works on culture change, we have encountered no evidence that would negate this generalization and much that supports it. It is, therefore, surprising to find that during the past five years psychologists have researched among Zulus, Turks, Arabs, Israelis, Norwegians, Germans, Mexicans, Englishmen, Algerians, Indians (from India), Ghanians, New Zealanders, Japanese, Greeks, and Navaho Indians. It is true that many of the subjects were displaced persons—students attending our universities—but, nevertheless, they represent different cultural backgrounds. Without doubt, there has been a rapid development of interest in cross-cultural research on the part of some psychologists.

These studies appear to fall under three major headings: (1) identifying and manipulating differential characteristics of culture that may have a relationship to attitude formation—e.g., differences in degree of authoritarianism in various communities related to differences in children's attitudes toward interpersonal relationships; (2) studying the impact of one culture upon another, e.g., stereotype persistence and change in personal encounters in alien cultural settings; (3) studies of cross-cultural variations in relationships between language, conceptual processes, behavior and attitudes, e.g., the relationship between linguistic categories for colors and perception of colors [18].

Leonard Doob [5, 6] has made a major contribution to the study of the psychology of acculturation. He samples and criticizes the anthropological literature on the subject. He concludes that anthropologists frequently try for too much in their attempts to analyze major "personality" changes and presents evidence relating to 27 hypotheses such as the following: "People changing centrally from old to new ways are likely to become more tolerant of delay in the attainment of goals," and "After people change centrally from old to new ways, they are likely to value in others and in themselves traits which indicate initiative, independence, and self-confidence" [6, pp. 324–325]. He uses interview and other data collected by himself on three African societies and one in Jamaica, supplemented and extended by data from a wide variety of other studies, mostly by anthropologists.

Our comments are not intended as a review of Doob's interesting work. We cite it as evidence of a promising concern on the part of psychologists about cross-cultural, and particularly acculturation, psychology that bodes well for a firmer and more rewarding joining of forces between psychology and anthropology—providing the critical and consistent differences in strategy and criteria of credibility between the two disciplines do not function as impermeable barriers to communication.

What do we mean by this last phrase? Anthropologists usually approach their study in the field with a complex, functionalistic, holistic, comparative, and empirically based model in mind. Cultural patterns are seen in functional relationship with each other. Together they are thought of as an instrumental adaptation to the problems of group maintenance in a geographic area influenced historically by other areas. Individual personal characteristics are seen in the light of those characteristics shared as an adaptation to culturally required behaviors. Any observed event or characteristic is seen in as total a context as possible and compared, explicitly or implicitly, to other known events in other contexts. Limited variable relationships may be researched; statistical tests of significance may be used; but events and variables will be contextualized in both time and space where possible. The approach is that of the natural historian—the trained bird watcher with a global outlook and intimate factual knowledge of many kinds of birds in many kinds of environments.

If these statements read like sheer nonsense to many trained psychologists, working on highly selective, minutely defined, sharply operationalized laboratory problems, the point we are making is only strengthened. Academically respectable psychologists seem to work on isolable and limited variables and their interrelationships. But for the anthropologist, variables make sense only when seen in their natural context.

Most readers will realize that we have overstated the case. There are anthropologists and psychologists of many persuasions. Not a few of our colleagues would reject our description of anthropology with some feeling. Nevertheless, there is enough that is valid here to make the point. If anthropologists and psychologists by and large start from opposite ends of a continuum of beliefs about worthwhile procedure, can they meet on some middle ground?

Ten years ago there was a considerable flow of ideas and applications—for the most part from psychology to anthropology. It is no accident that the kinds of psychology contributing most to anthropology and receiving the most from it were primarily psychoanalytically oriented Psychoanalytic models were most analagous to anthropological models. But somehow fatigue has set in. Anthropologists have wearied of complicating further their already complicated professional lives. Unless the complications produced new, significant, and relevant knowledge, there seemed to be little point to them. Some of what was learned was most rewarding and stimulated new conceptualizations about behavior that are now incorporated in a wide variety of anthropological models. But many anthropologists also learned disrespect for psychologizing, because they eventually recognized in extreme (and not merely orthodox) psychoanalytic and psychodynamic theory a speculativeness that went far beyond anything the anthropologist could tolerate in the light of his careful natural historian's comparative empiricism. We do not mean to suggest that psychoanalytically oriented psychologists are necessarily careless of fact or that they are poor clinical observers. Perhaps the trouble is that what seems to be a reasonable inference about unconscious dynamics in a single cultural context is outrageous when applied cross culturally. In any event, the meeting ground between psychology and anthropology that was apparently suitable a decade ago is no longer usable for many of our colleagues.

Are there other meeting grounds for anthropologists and psychologists? The cross-cultural studies, carried out mainly by social psychologists, are an encouraging indication. But most of them will be unsatisfying to anthropologists. Even the studies of the psychology of culture change do not in many—if not most—cases consider the context of the variables isolated so that the more complete meaning of relationships uncovered between defined variables can be detailed. Most cross-cultural studies by psychologists use cross-cultural variation simply as a fortuitous circumstance that makes it possible to define a limited antecedent or independent variable. This is good if the object is to see how A relates to B, but most anthropologists could not care less whether A relates to B— unless they can see the ramifications of this relationship in context. A real anthropologist, it may be said, never trusts a correlation or a statistically significant difference without intimate acquaintance with its ancestors, parents, marrying and nonmarrying cousins, and descendants, *in situ*.

PROMISING POTENTIAL

There are some hopeful signals flying just now, however, that suggest that the future will be brighter. Daniel Katz, in his foreword to the recent special issue of the *Public Opinion Quarterly* on attitude change [20] hoists one of these signals:

This issue reflects the heavy emphasis in present-day psychology upon the problems of cognitive organization and the attempts of people to achieve unity and consistency in their own mental worlds. The older, mechanistic, nonrational model of behavioristic psychology has been replaced by a Gestalt conception according to which man strives for a unified, meaningful structure of his perceptions, beliefs, and attitudes [20, p. i].

A few anthropologists have already made significant usage of modern cognitive theory in cultural analyses, but very few have applied it to culture-change situations. Wallace and Atkins [55] have discussed the application of componential analysis to kinship structures. They utilize the technique to explicate a cognitive construct—classification of kin in native terms, as perceived by those who use the kinship system, in their own semantic space. Fischer has attempted to describe art styles as cultural cognitive maps [7]. Art styles from nonliterate cultures are codified in dimensions of straight versus curved lines, symmetry, repetition, and open space in relation to various sociocultural dimensions, such as egalitarian versus hierarchical social systems and matrilocal versus patrilocal residence patterns. Frake has studied the diagnosis of disease among the Subanum of Mindanao. He regards diagnosis as a pivotal cognitive step in the selection of culturally appropriate responses to illness and demonstrates that study of diagnostic categories produces clues for discerning how a people construe their world of experience. He analyzes terminological systems in a way which reveals the conceptual categories that generate them as an important step toward mapping a cognitive system that is learned in a cultural environment and communicated by language [8, 9].

Wallace has provided one of the very few explicit adaptations of cognitive theory to analysis of culture-change process [52, 54]. The concept of cognitive structure that he uses is more broad than the one used in the other instances cited. He develops his concept of a "cognitive map," which consists of cognitive residues of perception—generalizations about ways in which sensory data distribute themselves. And these generalizations are interrelated in a complex but systematic way in the brain's organized and codified archives. During culture-change process, the mazeway becomes increasingly discrepant with reality as the individual perceives the results and conflicts of culture change. This continues until the stress reaches a critical point. In some cases (prophets, messianic leaders, etc.), collapse occurs, possibly as a result of physiochemical processes activated by prolonged stress. During the collapse— and usually in a trance-like state accompanied by hallucinations—resynthesis of the mazeway occurs. The individual recovers and becomes an active proselytizer for a sociocultural reality that will be congruent with his resynthesized cognitive map. Under certain conditions of readiness shared by other members of his group, a rapid and radical transformation of culture may take place.

The utility of the model provided by Wallace for culture-change analyses is explicit, though there may be serious difficulty in reducing the complex cognitive map construct to operational terms. The utility of the other models described above for this purpose is potential. They all constitute segmental, but probably manageable, approaches to "world view"—a concept that anthropologists have long struggled with but which they have found too amorphous to apply in fine-grained research formulations. It seems probable that systems of classification, as systems of conceptualization that are probably linked with language as a codification of reality, are among the last aspects of culture in people that adapt to the conditions of life created by culture change. If Rorschach responses may be regarded as a complex expression of perceptual and cognitive process, the studies by Hallowell, the Spindlers, and others on shifts and persistence in these responses related to acculturation would support this hypothesis. Cognitive systems can, in any case, be regarded as one of the important determinant influences in how adaptive change can take place and in how quickly it will occur.

Let us try to concretize further some of the potential meaning of this growing emphasis on cognitive theory for culture-change studies by discussing the relevance of three postulates advanced by Charles Osgood [38] concerning cognitive process and attitude change:

1. *Cognitive modification results from the psychological stress produced by cognitive inconsistencies.*

This postulate makes it explicit that the search for and maintenance of symmetry, or consonance, in cognitive elements can be included among the significant human drives, e.g., it is cognitively inconsistent to believe one way and behave another. Incongruity may be reduced by changing belief to the point where the psychological stress becomes tolerable.

It is clear that rapid and disjunctive culture-change situations provide a legion of cognitive discongruities. For instance, a tradition-oriented Sioux Indian who believes in generosity to relatives and friends who drop in to "free-load" and in giving away goods at public "give-away" ceremonies finds that this tradition-based belief is incompatible with the required behaviors in the existing framework of contemporary life—that he and others be economically self-sufficient. The questions become: How long can he tolerate the stress induced by this discongruity? Under what conditions does reduction of discongruity occur? How does it occur?

These questions give us a starting point for analysis. To provide good answers we would need to know the sources and functions of his belief in the traditional culture, the degree to which it is reinforced in the present setting by extrinsic rewards issuing from his group memberships, the incidence and character of situations where this discongruity becomes punitive, and the incidence and character of discongruity-reducing decisions. Analytic categories like these can generate hypotheses that can be tested cross-culturally, taking care to study each culture case in depth, so the cultural context of the processes isolated to test the hypotheses would be known. Semi-experimental research could be combined with contextual research to good advantage.

2. *If cognitive elements are to interact, they must be brought into some relation with one another.*

While Osgood's meaning here may be somewhat more precise than what we would need in culture-change analyses, the postulate seems fertile. Acculturation brings potentially inconsistent cognitive elements together in the framework of individual experience. But segmentalizing of belief and behavior in different roles and situations occurs frequently as an acculturative adaptation. Anthropologists have often observed that many Western culture patterns are acquired as "necessary accessories" to getting along with Euro-Americans in situations which they dominate, but these accessory techniques are simply dropped in primary-group relationships. This can be interpreted as one way of resolving cognitive discongruity—by compartmentalizing the cognitive elements so that they are not brought together in such a way as to induce severe stress. Study of the processes and consequences of cognitive compartmentalization requires methodologies that we have only begun to develop, but their application to the study of culture change may prove to be very rewarding.

3. *The magnitude of stress toward modification increases with the degree of cognitive inconsistency.*

In rapid and disjunctive culture-change situations, the degree of cognitive inconsistency may become so great that the stress induced cannot be coped with and the individual stops trying to reduce inconsistency. He withdraws and becomes almost totally passive, or he escapes to a regressive reaffirmation of nonfunctional traditional cognitive consistencies. It seems probable that native-oriented groups on American Indian reservations recruit new members largely through this process. On the other hand, a point can be reached rather quickly in culture-change situations where inconsistencies become radical and stress intense, and the traditional forms of belief and behavior (the cognitive congruities stabilized in the traditional culture) are discarded in a rapid reformulation of belief and behavior, resulting in a new stabilization of cognitive congruities. It is possible to interpret what happened in the case of the Manus studied by Mead [34] and the Seneca Iroquois studied by Wallace [52] in this way.

We are not making a case for the adoption of cognitive theory as an exclusive frame of reference in the design of psychocultural-change problems or their interpretation. In the light of these postulates this application seems plausible, but other theories may serve as well. For instance, modern ego psychology seems highly suggestive. Here the motivations issue from ego defenses, such as the defenses of identification, rejection, and denial. The situations created by rapid culture change are ego-threatening, and consequently anxiety-arousing—the efficacy of ego-maintaining mechanisms functional in the traditional cultural context is challenged. Consequently all or any of the ego defenses may be utilized by persons caught up in rapid culture change. For instance, the defense of identification may be utilized—members of groups suffering the impact of an alien culture may identify with the cultural "aggressors," the bearers of the alien threat. The Manus' situation—where the people literally copied salient aspects of the military subculture of the American troops that fought over and occupied their island home in their rapid postwar cultural transformation—could be interpreted this way. Or defenses of denial may predominate at certain stages of acculturation and culture change. The Plains Indians equipped themselves with bulletproof vests and with amulets that would make them invisible during the late resistance movements against whites—when all other resources had failed. This indeed had specific traditional cultural antecedents, but the pattern grew to dysfunctional proportions. The white man's guns were believed to be ineffective against these protective devices, despite the fact that many warriors died from bullet wounds. This is one species of ego defense by denial of the reality of threat.

At this point, it is not possible to say that one theory is "better" than another. Both are plausible in their applications. Any internally consistent theory that helps explain observed phenomena and generates researchable problems is useful. Because culture change—particularly acculturation—creates a complex conflict situation, a psychological theory applicable to culture-change situations must deal systematically, and with internal coherence, with conflict recognition and resolution. Any psychological theory that regards man as striving and adapting must deal with conflict, but doubtless some will do it more elegantly than others.

The new developments in cognitive and ego theory are encouraging for those of us who seek a new meeting ground for anthropologists and psychologists interested in the psychology of culture change. The mechanistic, nonrational model of behavioristic psychology was never satisfying to anthropologists. The analogical, dynamic Freudian model was and will continue to be of use, particularly as the initial excesses of speculative interpretation are further reduced and a tighter model of ego structure and function emerges. The cognitive model is one of high potential utility because of its gestalt, drive-oriented conception and the possibility it affords of doing research on comparatively limited sets of relationships between operationally definable variables. It will be acceptable to anthropologists who have traveled some distance from the position of extreme holistic functionalism and to psychologists who have departed from the position of extreme experimental particularism.

We predict that during the next decade, or even the next five years, psychology and anthropology will join at the conceptual level to produce consistent, penetrating, and even elegant research and theory concerning the processes of psychocultural adaptation. The confusion, uncertainty, and disengagement of the past decade may appear then as the Dark Ages just before the Enlightenment.

REFERENCES

1. Barnett, H. *Innovation*. New York: McGraw-Hill, 1953.
2. Boggs, S. Culture change and the personality of Ojibwa children. *Amer. Anthrop.*, 1958, **60** (1), 47–58.
3. Bruner, E. Primary group experience and the process of acculturation. *Amer. Anthrop.*, 1956, **58** (4), 605–623.
4. Chance, N. Culture change and integration: an Eskimo example. *Amer. Anthrop.*, 1960, **62** (6), 1028–1044.
4a. De Vos, G., & Wagatsuma, H. Value attitudes toward role behavior of women in two Japanese villages. *Amer. Anthrop.*, 1961, **63** (6), 1204–1230.
5. Doob, L. W. An introduction to the psychology of acculturation. Part 2. *J. soc. Psychol.*, 1957, **45**, 143–160.
6. Doob, L. W. *Becoming more civilized, a psychological exploration,* New Haven, Conn.: Yale Univer. Press, 1960.
7. Fischer, J. L. Art styles as cultural cognitive maps. *Amer. Anthrop.*, 1961, **63** (1), 79–93.
8. Frake, C. O. The diagnosis of disease among the Subanum of Mindanao. *Amer. Anthrop.*, 1961, **63** (1), 113–132.
9. Frake, C. O. The ethnographic study of cognitive systems. Paper read at Anthrop. Soc., Washington, D.C., January, 1961.
10. Gillin, J. Acquired drives in culture contact. *Amer. Anthrop.*, 1942, (4), 545–554.
11. Hallowell, A. I. Sociopsychological aspects of acculturation. In R. Linton (Ed.), *Science of man in the world crisis.* New York: Columbia Univer. Press, 1945. Pp. 171–200.
12. Hallowell, A. I. The use of projective techniques in the study of sociopsychological aspects of acculturation. *J. proj. Tech.*, 1951, **15** (1), 27–44.
13. Hallowell, A. I., Psychology and anthropology. In J. Gillin (Ed.), *For a science of social man.* New York: MacMillan, 1954. Pp. 160–226.
14. Hallowell, A. I., *Culture and experience.* Philadelphia: Univer. Pa. Press, 1955.
15. Henry, J. Culture, personality, and evolution. *Amer. Anthrop.*, 1959, **61** (2), 221–227.
16. Henry, J., & Spiro, M. E. Psychological techniques: projective tests in field work. In A. Kroeber (Ed.), *Anthropology today.* Chicago: Univer. Chicago Press, 1953.
16a. Hsu, F. L. K. (Ed.) *Psychological anthropology: approaches to culture and personality.* Homewood, Ill.: Dorsey Press, Inc., 1961.
17. Inkeles, A. Personality and social structure. In R. K. Merton, L. Broom,

& J. Cottrell (Eds.), *Sociology today, problems and prospects.* New York: Basic Books, 1958. Pp. 249–276.

18. Jacobson, E., Kumata, H., & Gullahorn, J. E. Cross-cultural contributions to attitude research. *Publ. Opin. Quart.,* 1960, **24** (2), 204–223.

18a. James, B. J. Social-psychological dimensions of Ojibwa acculturation. *Amer. Anthrop.,* 1961,**63**, (4), 721–746.

19. Kaplan, G. Personality and social structure. In J. B. Gittler (Ed.), *Review of sociology: analysis of a decade.* New York: Wiley, 1957. Pp. 87–126.

20. Katz, D. Editorial. *Publ. Opin. Quart.,* 1961, **24** (2), i–iii.

21. Keesing, F. M. *The Menomini Indians of Wisconsin.* Vol. 10. Philadelphia: American Philosophical Society, 1939.

22. Kluckhohn, C. Covert culture and administrative problems. *Amer. Anthrop.,* 1943, **45** (2), 213–227.

23. Kluckhohn, C. The influence of psychiatry on anthropology in America during the past one hundred years. In J. K. Hall (Ed), *One hundred years of American psychiatry.* New York: Columbia Univer. Press for the American Psychiatric Association, 1944.

24. Kluckhohn, C. Review of A. L. Kroeber's "Configurations of cultural growth." *Amer. Anthrop.,* 1946, **51** (4), 336–341.

25. Kluckhohn, C. Southwestern studies of culture and personality. *Amer. Anthrop.,* 1954, **56** (4), 685–697.

26. Kroeber, A. L. *Configurations of cultural growth.* Berkeley, Calif.: Univer. Calif. Press, 1944.

27. Kroeber, A. L. History and evolution. *S.W. J. Anthrop.,* 1946, **2** (1), 1–15.

28. Kroeber, A. L. *Anthropology.* (2nd ed.) New York: Harcourt, Brace, 1948. Chap. 15.

29. Kroeber, A. L. White's view of culture. *Amer. Anthrop.,* 1948, **50** (3), 405–415.

30. Kroeber, A. L., & Kluckhohn, C., Culture: a critical review of concepts and definitions. *Papers Peabody Mus. Amer. Archaeol. & Ethnol.,* 1952, **47**, No. (1).

31. Lindzey, G. (Ed.) *Handbook of social psychology.* Vol. I. Reading, Mass.: Addison-Wesley, 1956.

32. Linton, R. (Ed.) *Acculturation in seven American Indian tribes.* New York: Appleton-Century-Crofts, 1940.

33. Maher, R. F. Social structure and cultural change in Papua. *Amer. Anthrop.,* 1960, **62** (4), 593–602.

34. Mead, Margaret. *New lives for old.* New York: Morrow, 1956.

35. Mekeel, H. S. *The economy of a modern Teton Dakota community.* New Haven, Conn.: Yale Univer. Press, 1936.

36. Miller, N. E., & Dollard, J. *Social learning and imitation.* New Haven, Conn.: Yale Univer. Press, 1941.

37. Opler, M. E. Themes as dynamic forces in culture. *Amer. J. Sociol.,* 1945, **51** (3), 198–206.

38. Osgood, C. E. Cognitive dynamics in human affairs. *Publ. Opin. Quart.,* 1960, **24** (2), 341–365.
39. Redfield, R., et al. Memorandum for the study of acculturation. *Amer. Anthrop.,* 1936, **38** (1), 149–152.
40. Siegel, B. J. (Ed.) *Acculturation: critical abstracts, North America.* Stanford, Calif: Stanford Univer. Press, 1955.
41. Social Science Research Council (summer seminar on acculturation). Acculturation: an exploratory formulation. *Amer. Anthrop.,* 1954, **56** (6), 973–1002.
42. Spindler, G. D. *Sociocultural and psychological processes in Menomini acculturation.* Culture and society series, Vol. 5. Berkeley, Calif.: Univer. Calif. Press, 1955.
43. Spindler, G. D., & Spindler, Louise S. American Indian personality types and their sociocultural roots. *Ann. Amer. Acad. pol. Soc. Sci.,* 1957, **311**, 147–157.
44. Spindler, Louise S. Menomini women and culture change. Memoir 91, Amer. Anthrop. Assoc., February, 1962.
45. Spindler, Louise S., & Spindler, G. D. Male and female adaptations in culture change. *Amer. Anthrop.,* 1958, **60** (2), 217–233.
46. Spindler, Louise S., & Spindler, G. D. A modal personality technique in the study of Menomini acculturation. In B. Kaplan (Ed.), *Studying personality cross-culturally.* Evanston, Ill.: Row, Peterson, 1961. Pp. 479–492.
47. Spiro, M. E. The acculturation of American ethnic groups. *Amer. Anthrop.,* 1955, **57** (6), 1240–1252.
48. Spiro, M. E. Social systems, personality and functional analysis. In B. Kaplan (Ed.), *Studying personality cross-culturally.* Evanston, Ill.: Row, Peterson, 1961. Pp. 93–128.
49. Thompson, Laura. Attitudes and acculturation. *Amer. Anthrop.,* 1948, **50** (2), 200–215.
50. Voget, F. W. The American Indian in transition. *Amer. Anthrop.,* 1956, **58** (2), 249–263.
51. Wallace, A. F. C. *The modal personality structure of the Tuscarora Indians. Bur. Amer. Ethnol. Bull.,* 1952, No. 150.
52. Wallace, A. F. C. Mazeway resynthesis: a biocultural theory of religious inspiration. *Trans. N.Y. Acad. Sci.,* 1956, **18** (Ser. II), (7), 626–637.
53. Wallace, A. F. C. Revitalization movements. *Amer. Anthrop.,* 1956, **58** (2), 264–281.
54. Wallace, A. F. C., Stress and rapid personality changes. *Int. Rec. Med. gen. Pract. Clin.,* 1956, **169** (12), 761–774.
55. Wallace, A. F. C., & Atkins, J. The meaning of kinship terms. *Amer. Anthrop.,* 1960, **62** (1), 58–60.
56. White, L. A. Culturological vs. psychological interpretations of human behavior. *Amer. sociol. Rev.,* 1947, **12** (6) 686–698.
57. White, L. A., The concept of culture. *Amer. Anthrop.,* 1959, **61** (2), 227–252.

LINGUISTICS AND PSYCHOLOGY

F. G. LOUNSBURY
Department of Anthropology
Yale University

THE FIELD OF LINGUISTICS

The linguistics of today has developed in a rather remarkable isolation from the psychological disciplines. Influences from psychology have been indirect, coming through the general intellectual climate of the recent decades—to which behaviorist psychology has contributed its share—rather than by direct contact. It is not our task here to account for this, but rather to sketch some areas of central concern in linguistics which may be considered as potential areas for psychological exploration. First we should note some of the commonly accepted limitations on the scope of the discipline.

Linguistics is concerned with the structure of the verbal response. Only within relatively narrow limits is it concerned with the stimulus conditions under which a verbal response is produced or with the nature of the stimulus-response connection and its establishment in the individual. It is primarily descriptive and formulative, rather than interpretive. In this, it is akin to certain behaviorist schools of experimental psychology. In the former respect, however, its goals are rather different from those of psychology.

It is concerned with verbal responses only up to a certain level of complexity. Levels of complexity or structural integration in the verbal response are of at least two sorts: phonological and grammatical. The former include the distinctive phonetic feature, the phoneme, the syllable, one or more orders of stress groups, one or more kinds of pause groups, and several intonationally defined groups. The latter include the distinctive morphemic feature, the morpheme, and several intermediate levels of morphological and syntactic structures, on up to the sentence in its various types. Languages differ from one another considerably in the way in which units in one of the hierarchies tie in with units in the other hierarchy, but they agree at least to the extent of a fair correlation—not quite perfect— between certain maximum units of the one kind and certain maximum units of the other kind. These are the sentence types of a language. Linguistics deals with all of the levels of either type, up to and including the sentence. Except when a linguist ventures into logic, discourse analysis, content analysis, or literary criticism, his field of investigation does not extend to verbal responses of a larger magnitude or of a higher order of internal complexity than these.

The research problems which linguists undertake are generally not of the sort that psychologists undertake when they study verbal behavior. This is not to deny psychological relevance to the former or linguistic relevance to the latter, however. Many of the problems of linguistics do relate to questions that are properly a concern of psychology or of one or another of its subdisciplines. And psychological studies of verbal behavior throw light on particular points in linguistic theory.

The linguist's special concern is with the "structure" of language in its grammatical, phonological, and—somewhat less frequently— semantic aspects. Many of the problems of special concern to psychologists are of secondary concern to the linguist. Some of these are the acquisition of language, concept formation, the instrumental use of language, the study of individual differences in various specific verbal skills, the measurement of these, their relation to problem solving, second-language learning, etc., the relation of verbal patterns to various types of nonverbal behavior and to personality, the study of the statistical properties of language, or word associations, response latencies, symbolism, phenomena of interference, speech pathology, etc., and even perception. They are all relevant to linguistics ultimately, but are subordinated to the study of structure in language. The linguist wants to see them not as isolated items or as illustrations of psychological principles, but rather as they can be related to the total theory of language structure. We proceed to sketch a few of the aspects of this. The selection and presentation are from the standpoint of linguistics and the interests of its practitioners rather than from the point of view and the interests of psychologists. We do not attempt a review of the psychological literature on language. That is the function of another paper in this series [65]. Rather, we attempt a brief synoptic view of topics which are in the foreground in current literature on structural linguistics.

THE STRUCTURES OF AN UTTERANCE, OF A LANGUAGE, AND OF LANGUAGE

Utterances can be said to have "structures," languages to have "structural patterns," and language (in general) to have certain "structural characteristics" or "general properties." There are differences between these. For short, one often uses the term "structure" indiscriminately—not only of utterances, but also of a language, and of language. Its special sense in each of these contexts must be understood. The structure (i.e., structural pattern) of a language is a phenomenon of a different order of abstraction and of greater generality and comprehensiveness than the structure of an utterance. The structural characteristics or general properties of language are, in turn, of a still different order. In this case, one refers to the properties which are common to the structural patterns of all languages, that is, of language in general, or of the phenomenon of language.

For linguists the starting point in analysis is the utterance—or rather a corpus of these from a single speaker or several speakers from one speech community. From the study of these—and with continued recourse to native speakers so that the corpus can be amplified as becomes necessary—one arrives at a formulation of the structural pattern of the language. The study involves various kinds of data processing, analysis, abstracting, hypothesis formulation and testing, and carrying out experiments. The approach is both "clinical" and "experimental." It is directed toward the construction of a theory of the forms of the language in question, such as will account for the data at hand at any one time and will also have predictive power so as to stand the test of any further accumulation of data from the same language.

From the comparative and contrastive study of the structural patterns of many languages and, most importantly, from the progress which is made toward an analytic method of equal applicability to all languages, there are the beginnings of an understanding also of the "structure" of language, that is, a theory of the general nature of the organization of language behavior.

It is this third kind of structure—whatever can be said about the properties of languages in general—that would seem to be of the greatest relevance to psychology. Only this can be said to characterize the behavior of man as a species. Generalizations of a lower order, which are the principal product of linguistic researches, characterize the linguistic behavior of men in particular societies—Englishmen, Americans, Germans, Chinese, Iroquois, or some subgroup within these or other societies. These are of interest to linguists and to culture historians. They may, however, be of interest to psychologists also, in so far as one or another of the structural patterns of these particular languages can be shown to *exemplify* a structural characteristic of language in general. That is to say, they may be of some interest as illustrations of general principles.

Unfortunately for present purposes, the general science of language is still in its infancy. Despite notable successes in the construction of theories of particular languages, the general theory of language structure and of language universals is still in the stage of tentative formulation, and its relation (or reduction) to psychological laws is still largely speculative. A few of the more obvious general characteristics of language structure are sketched below, together with comment—where such is possible—on their psychological relevance. We beg indulgence for the excursion into grammar. If it does not seem to relate immediately to psychological problems, we should not on this account pass it by. At least it points up some aspects of the rather amazing complexity of the behavior that goes into the production of sentences. Surely this is in some sense a problem for psychology, especially as psychology may be concerned with the hierarchical organization of behavioral sequences. If at certain points we seem to be describing not so much the nature of language as what linguists do with it or to it, it should be confessed that this is true. We are concerned with the models that linguists construct in order to account, in as simple and comprehensive a manner as possible, for the regularities that they observe in specimens of linguistic behavior.

THE PROPOSITION

The propositional sentence is a universal in human language. This is not to say that all utterances are statements of propositions;

it does mean that there is no human society whose speech patterns do not permit of both *a primary reference* and *an ascription* (of something to it, or of it to something) within a single speech act.[1] This is a uniquely human attribute. The proposition is absent, to the best of our knowledge, from the possible communicative vocal acts of all other species. The specific form or set of alternative forms which the proposition assumes in different languages shows considerable variation. This variation, however, does not controvert the universality of the proposition itself.

Inherent in this statement of a simple and obvious fact are some rather large questions for comparative psychology and neurology. A young child's first statement of a proposition—his first subject-predicate equation or complete sentence, e.g., "Baby, crying!" (an actual case)—is preceded by the development of a very extensive naming vocabulary based on recognition of both static and dynamic qualities of things in his environment, with the vocabulary in part already morphologically differentiated. In turn, all of this rests upon the unfolding—prior to and concurrently with the growth in vocabulary—of a phonological system which is not yet that of adult speech, but which already has a fair degree of internal differentiation and a structure of its own. None of these—the phonological capacity, the naming capacity, or the constructional capacity—seems to have a true analog in the vocal behavior of other animal species. The quasi analogs which do exist appear to differ drastically both in degree and in quality.[2]

---

[1] Phrasing this in terms of a reference and an ascription is, of course, a semantic description. The correlated units of linguistic form can be given nonsemantic formal definitions for particular languages, but not for languages in general.

[2] On crucial differences between human and infrahuman communication see Hockett [28, pp. 569–586; 29] and White [78, 79]. On the notion of evolution in language see Greenberg [21]. It should be noted that neither linguistics nor cultural anthropology has much to offer that is relevant to the question of the origin of language [cf. Sturtevant, 73, pp. 40–50]. On the semiotic base present in gesture and its interpretation in animal behavior, see G. H. Mead [60]. For an insightful speculation concerning the nature of the transition from the prelinguistic species of Homo to Homo sapiens, see Krantz [36] on pithecanthropine brain size, the relation of its probable growth curve to the maturation cycle, and its linguistic and cultural consequences. It should be noted that no transitional stage in the origin and evolution of languages has survived for observation by modern man. Note also that, contrary to popular notions, as well as to earlier scholarly interpretations [45, 46, 72; contrast 35, 38], the languages of even the most primitive peoples cannot be characterized as "primitive" languages by any valid or consistently applied criterion. All languages—so far as their phonological base, their formal syntactic apparatus, their lexical derivational potential, and their adaptability to communicative needs are concerned—appear to be quite on a par with one another. This statement applies to their formal resources, not to their semantic content. Primitive levels of lexical development of particular semantic areas are well known.

BRANCHING AND LAYERING

In speaking of the structure of an utterance (proposition or otherwise), one understands that it is a unit of some sort which is made up of parts. There are fair reasons for assuming that if more than two parts are present in the make-up of a unit, more than one level must be involved in its construction.

Linguistic structures can be described as "branching" and as "layered." The import of these terms may perhaps best be seen by way of an example. Consider the latter portion of the first sentence of this section: *one understands that it is a unit of some sort which is made up of parts*. The first few layers of its structure divide (i.e., branch) as follows:

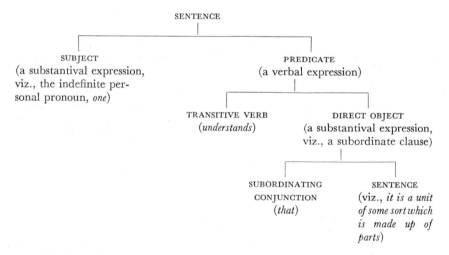

The reader may be disappointed to note that this is nothing more than the traditional parsing which he learned in grammar school. He might have expected something more novel and revealing from linguistics. There is, in fact, considerably more to it than meets the eye. A few of these matters are taken up briefly in following sections. It is, moreover, a representation of but one aspect of the structure of the sentence, other aspects of which would require different representations. The choice of an English example is undramatic because of our familiarity with this type of structure. A sentence from an exotic language could have been used to show structures of quite different sorts.

The remaining layers may be left for the reader to take apart. The first of these, the resolution of the inner sentence into a subject and a predicate, is the same as that for the outer sentence, of course. Beyond that, different structures appear.

RECURSION

In the above diagram of a branching and layering structure, we began with a sentence (*One understands that . . .*) and ended with a sentence (*It is a unit of some sort which . . .*). Though different in specific content and different in structure on the second and further lower layers, they are identical in structure on the first lower layer and are members of the same form class (tokens of the same type), viz., SENTENCE, i.e., the SUBJECT-PREDICATE construction of English.

This points up a characteristic and important feature of language structure in general, namely, its recursive potential. It is a special case—a peculiar and pervasive one—in the general derivational potential of a language. It is an aspect of the capacity for using constructions of a particular type as constituents in other constructions, which may be of a different type or (immediately or ultimately) of the same type as the original. This latter possibility—especially as it involves encapsulating sentences within sentences—makes for theoretically indefinite expandability, limited in practice only by certain external considerations of another order.[3] The mechanics of such encapsulation differs greatly from language to language—some exotic varieties of it strike us as quite bizarre—but the basic functions performed and the general consequences for the adaptability of the language tool are essentially the same.

The inner sentence can be subjected to its own analysis of branches and layers, as was the first, or outer, sentence.

ALTERNATIVES

At the third layer of the inner sentence, we find that the predicate does not resolve into TRANSITIVE VERB + DIRECT OBJECT as in the outer sentence, but into COPULA + PREDICATE NOUN. These are but two of the substitutable alternative types which may serve as predicates in English sentences. Other common ones are INTRANSITIVE VERB (a "nonwanting" verb, which is therefore potentially complete in itself as a predicate) and COPULA + PREDICATE ADJECTIVE.

"Alternatives" are different in their internal structure and identity, but are the same in their external structural relations. They are members of the same form class (tokens of the same type) at the next higher layer of structure.

Other examples of alternatives which concern the form class of substantival expressions are noted in the next section.

[3] On recursion in syntax and its import for an adequate model of language structure, see Chomsky [7, 9, 10].

IMMEDIATE CONSTITUENTS

As is apparent from the preceding sections, an utterance, a complex verbal response, cannot be regarded merely as a unidimensional concatenation of unit response-segments, in spite of its apparently linear array in time; it must be seen as a many-layered edifice, a construction of parts, each of which is in turn a construction of parts, and so on from the highest to the lowest in the order of layers.

Most constructions are seen as two-part constructions. Longer chains which may—in the context of certain problems—be viewed as many-part constructions are resolvable on further analysis into successive layers of two-part constructions.

The parts of a construction are its "constituents." Every linguistic unit except the highest and the lowest dealt with is seen simultaneously (1) as a construction made up of smaller constituents, (2) as a constituent in a particular larger construction, and (3) as a member of a form class defined by its "distribution," or range of possible constructional contexts. It must be characterized in each of these capacities and may be named accordingly. Thus, the expression *that it is a unit* . . . in our diagram sentence is a subordinate clause when described as a construction. When described as a constituent in the construction in which it finds itself in this sentence, it is a direct object of a transitive verb. When described as a member of a form class, it is a substantival expression (along with nouns, noun phrases, pronouns, etc.). All of these roles need to be specified in its grammatical characterization.

The members of a form class may represent several different kinds of constructions. Thus, as noted, there are many varieties of substantival expressions, as these are considered from the vantage point of the next lower layer. Also, any member of a form class may enter into a number of different kinds of constructions and accordingly be different kinds of constituents. Thus, a substantival expression may be the subject of a predicate, the direct object of a transitive verb, the object of a preposition, a predicate-noun expression, an appositional complement to a noun, etc. To be a member of the form class substantival expressions is, by definition (for English), to be capable of serving in any of these constituent roles; for a form class, as noted, is defined in terms of its distribution.

Linguistic analysis proceeds by the method of "immediate constituents," i.e., by division of a larger unit into two immediate constituents. The brief illustration given above of the branching and layering in structure proceeded in this fashion. The parsing above no doubt appeared simple. In fact, however, the determination of the hierarchy of immediate-constituent divisions in longer forms always presents serious problems. In the illustrative sentence which was used above, there are at least two other places that might seriously be considered as choices for the first immediate-constituent division. These would yield not a SUBJECT-PREDICATE construction at the top layer of analysis, but would give constructions of other sorts requiring different characterizations. In the end, a systematic pursuit of a different set of policies in immediate-constituent division would, in fact, produce a different grammar of the same language. Among the alternative procedures which may be considered, there is one which is based strongly on phonological considerations—especially those of juncture—as applied to the spoken forms of sentences in their textual environments.

In general, the guiding consideration in making such choices is one which involves (1) maximum substitutability of parts on both sides of the division, (2) maximum productivity of the end formulation, and (3) maximum simplicity in the statement of the total structural pattern. These are not independent criteria, but are related ultimately to the same thing.

In working toward a solution that satisfies these desiderata, there are some who are willing to believe that they are discovering the structural pattern which inheres in the language, while others consider that they are merely constructing a model of the simplest and most highly predictive form that can generate the forms of utterances in the given language. The latter view would seem to be the safer. It leaves open the question of *the* structure of the language, and it carries no suggestion or commitment as to the psychological validity of the formulation. It leaves the field open for alternative analyses and it can entertain, without prejudice to itself, the posing of psychological questions which may be asked in connection with language structure in its varied facets and alternative interpretations.

At the present time, a point of view which holds that linguistics offers not so much a discovery as an evaluative procedure is gaining ascendancy. It permits one to choose from among different grammars or models of a language that which is the "best" according to a stated set of criteria.

Languages differ greatly in their roster and hierarchy of specific constructional patterns. An illustration from another language, especially from a non-Indo-European language, might have shown some of the novelty that was lacking in the English example excerpted from this paper.[4]

---

[4] On immediate constituents see Wells [77], Gleason [15, chap. 10], Hockett [28, chap. 17].

HISTORY AND ACTUALITY

Of two constructions made according to the same pattern, one may be an *ad hoc* construction of the moment and the other may be a repetition or reuse of one coined long ago, often heard, and much employed as a whole unit, e.g., as an idiom, a cliché, or a high-frequency phrase of some sort. It is apparent that as behavioral events they are quite different and that in some sense their psychological statuses in the structure of the actual speaking behavior may be quite different. This may be reflected in a number of ways other than that of their grammatical structure, which is presumed constant. They may be characterized by different internal entropy profiles. They may have different text frequencies. They may have different latency patterns, these being reflected in observably different timing patterns and in differences in the introduction of hesitation pauses. Yet in terms of their grammatical structure, they may be the same.

The point to be made is that the structural pattern of a language —its grammar—serves as a guide for the manufacture of one's speaking stock in trade. Some of this is old, familiar, and quite automatic at any given time—some of it is new as of the moment and may even be hesitatingly put together. Old and new alike exhibit the same structural patterns (except for the relatively rare cases where there is a legacy of old forms which were coined in a no longer productive pattern). The old, in fact, furnish the models for generating the new. In a psychological account taking of linguistic behavior, more than the grammatical structure of utterances needs to be reckoned with. In particular, indexes of latency must be attended to. Usage as well as system requires study.[5]

TRANSFORMATIONS

We turn again to the excerpted sentence which was used for purposes of illustration. In *Branching and Layering*, its analysis was carried to the point of recursion to another sentence. In *Alternatives*, the next two layers in the structure of this inner sentence were indicated. A further step would lead to the next lower layer, which divides into a NOUN PHRASE (*a unit of some sort*) and an ADJECTIVAL EXPRESSION consisting of a relative clause (*which is made up of parts*). The next step leads to the analysis of the relative clause.

[5] On hesitation pauses and their relation to the transitional-probability structure of a language (as opposed to the grammatical structure), see Lounsbury [57], and Maclay and Osgood [59]. Also of interest in this connection are Goldman-Eisler [16, 17].

Here again, alternative analyses present themselves. All clauses, relative included, share the SUBJECT-PREDICATE construction. An immediate-constituent analysis of the relative clause might then follow this division, identifying the relative pronoun as the subject and the remainder as the predicate. In the evaluative procedure which must follow any decision and which weighs the merits of the decision (in terms of final simplicity and potential account-taking capacity) against other possible decisions, two weaknesses are inherent in taking the SUBJECT-PREDICATE division as the first in the analysis of the relative clause. One is that the relative pronoun is in certain respects fundamentally different from all other members of the class of substantival expressions which may serve as subjects or objects or predicate nouns. The other and more serious weakness is that this decision fails to identify or take account of an important and fundamental relationship between any relative clause and a corresponding independent clause of the sentence form—as, for example, the analysis of the subordinate clause above showed its relation to a corresponding independent sentence.

In such cases, one identifies the construction as a "transformation" of some other construction (i.e., of one of the so-called "kernel" constructions), states the relationship between the two, and then proceeds to analyze the constituency of the latter. In the present case, that of the relative clause in our illustration, this amounts to a different decision as to where to place the first immediate-constituent division. It involves the suppression of one of the canons of immediate-constituent analysis, viz., a rule not to divide within a word prior to dividing between words, the justification for which may perhaps be called into question. It is as though in the present case we were to regard the relative pronoun *which* as consisting of, or representing, a relative morpheme (*wh-*) and a pronominal morpheme (identifiable with the morpheme of *it*), and then make an immediate-constituent analysis of RELATIVE SUBORDINATOR (*wh-*) + SENTENCE (*it is made up of parts*) instead of an immediate SUBJECT + PREDICATE analysis.

The concept of transformation is needed to account for aspects of structure (of which the present example represents only one type among many) which would escape an accounting by immediate-constituent analysis of phrase and clause structure except by a *tour de force* such as indicated above. In particular, transformation analysis uncovers a great many *masked recursions* that would otherwise remain undetected. Since the degrees and manners of masking of recursive structures vary greatly from language to language, one result of transformational analysis, which undercuts this masking, is to lead linguistics a step closer to a general model for the syntax of language.

It also raises the question of the status of the word as a linguistic unit. Clearly, in the analysis of one aspect of language structure, the word can be violated. Yet it is surely a unit in another aspect of structure. We are dealing with linguistic units of some sort in each case.[6]

CONDITIONED VARIANTS

A frequent phenomenon in the structure of languages is that the context in which a unit appears imposes certain constraints upon the form which the unit may assume. A unit may thus appear differently in different contexts. This kind of contextual determination may be found at all levels:

1. In phonology, in the determination of allophones of phonemes (e.g., whether a *t* in English is an aspirated stop, an unaspirated stop, an unreleased stop with simultaneous glottal closure, a lightly articulated voiced or voiceless flap, a simple glottal stop, etc.);

2. In morphophonemics, in the determination of allomorphs of morphemes;

3. In syntax, in the determination of alternant forms (allotagmas) which particular constructions (tagmemes) must assume in particular larger constructional contexts;

4. In morphology, in the determination of the particular form of an inflectable word—the "allolog," we might say—which it must have in a particular syntactic context.

All of these result in a redundancy between a form and its context, each implying something of the other.

The last case just mentioned, which concerns inflected forms of words, is the weakest as an example of the phenomenon of contextual determination, but it is one of the most interesting. We return once more to our earlier sample sentence for illustrations. In the outer sentence, in the context of the subject *one*, the verb of the predicate must take the form *understands*, not *understand*. Similarly, in the inner sentence, in the context of the subject *it*, the copula of the predicate must be *is*, not *are*.

Inflection in some languages is carried into several dimensions of variation, resulting in multidimensional paradigms running into hundreds or even thousands of forms. Dimensions may be such famil-

[6] On transformations see Harris [24], Chomsky [9, 10], Lees [41, 42], Householder [33], and Gleason [15, chap. 13]. The notion of transformation is a recent innovation in structural linguistics, though unformalized analogs to it are old in traditional school grammars—such as, for example, the rules for "converting" an active sentence into a passive sentence, those for converting indicative into interrogative sentences, etc.

iar ones as those of person, number, mode, aspect, tense, voice, etc., or they may involve quite novel criteria (criteria of context, with or without definite correlates in reference). A single form from such a paradigm may be characterized in each of several dimensions.—For example, it may be second person, singular, preterite, subjunctive. The person and number specifications may be required by the particular subject with which the verbal predicate is in construction; the modal specification may be required by a part of the outer context in which this subject-predicate construction (as an inner sentence) finds itself; while the tense specification may perhaps be restricted by still another part of the context.

In the case just described, each of the inflectional features of the word is a *conditioned* feature of that word, and the resulting form of the word may be described as a *conditioned variant*, or allolog of the word. There is a resulting condition of redundancy; given the context of the word, the particular form of the word—with its special features —may be predicted. And conversely, the special features of the word are an index to the nature of its context, permitting prediction of the latter (within limits) or at least narrowing down its possibilities. Given this situation, the features by which inflected forms differ may be said to be "conditioned," "determined," or "nondistinctive" features.

This type of case, however, represents something of an ideal case. The sentences in which this state of affairs obtains may be termed "model sentences." Actual discourses, however, may occasionally or even frequently contain sentences which deviate from the model by the omission of parts of the model context which are fully predictable from the particular variant of the word. Thus, for example, in Portuguese one may sometimes hear simply *sei* in place of *eu sei* (*I know*), or *sabes* in place of *tu sabes* (*you know*). In such instances, where the presumed conditioning part of the model context is absent, the inflectional feature can no longer be described as contextually determined or as nondistinctive.

This is the state of affairs with much of the morphological inflection of words. In many sentences a particular inflected form can be regarded as a conditioned variant in the proper sense of the term. Yet in other sentences it may be the only source for a feature of the message. It may thus alternate between the status of a conditioned variant and the status of a syntactic construction internal to the word. Inflectional categories are only rarely devoid of referential (denotational) content. In optimum cases, they may be semantically defined —e.g., second person, plural. In some of the more frequent cases, however, the referential content is irregular, shifting from instance to instance, often null, and without common feature (cf. the gender distinctions in German, French, etc.). The semantic definitions, even where these are possible, give no clue to the linguistic status of the inflectional categories. Their linguistic definitions are contextual ones, in terms of their distributions or their "privileges of occurrence." (The latter is not quite the same as the former. A definition in terms of privileges of occurrence is essentially a definition in terms of a form's distribution in what were called "model sentences" above.)

It is rather surprising to see how different languages can be from one another in this particular respect. This kind of interconditioning between syntactic environments and inflectional morphology of words can be virtually nil in some languages (e.g., Chinese) but can be carried to staggering lengths in others. This can be disconcerting to the linguist or psychologist who inclines to a view of the basic sameness of all languages in their fundamental structural characteristics. What is true of the interconditioning between syntactic environments and the inflectional morphology of words is also true of the relations between environment and the forms of morphemes. Some languages have hardly any morphophonemic irregularities (e.g., the Cuzco dialect of Quechua), while others have incredible amounts of it (e.g., the Iroquoian languages). It does not seem that there is as much difference between languages in respect to the corresponding phenomenon on the phonemic level. All languages have a good deal of it. Some may seem to have more of it than others, but this is a function of our ethnocentricity. A case in point is described in the next section.

STIMULUS EQUIVALENCE

Linguistics has developed a considerable apparatus for handling problems of what might be regarded as stimulus equivalence in language structure. This phenomenon in language and the apparatus to deal with it in linguistics seem most often to have attracted the attention of psychologists. It relates (in a very general way) to the problems of constancy, conditioned similarity, and criterial attributes which have interested perception psychologists, learning theorists, and those who study concept formation.

Linguists themselves never cease to be amazed at the identifications and groupings into equivalence classes which they discover in the structures of the languages they work with. They find them in phonological equivalences, in grammatical equivalences, and in lexical equivalences. Many of them are indeed novel and unusual, given the conditioning of one's own different language background. It is on these that the so-called "Whorf hypothesis," or the "linguistic-relativity hypothesis," is based. We consider here an example from phonology. Examples from lexicon are found in the next section.

The writer has done intensive field work on a language—Cayuga, one of the languages of the Iroquoian family—which exhibits conditioned alternations and resulting stimulus equivalences of types such as those in the following pairs of disyllabic and monosyllabic sequences: *gahẽn* and *k'hãin*; *diho* and *t'hyo*; *gũha* and *k'hwa*; *driho* and *t'hryo* (or *čhryo*). The paired types are quite unlike in over-all acoustic properties, and they are perceived as very unlike by listeners (like ourselves) who have a different perceptual preconditioning to speech sounds from that which native speakers of this language have. When the differences between the alternants in these pairs were pointed out by the writer to his language informants, however, they declared that they never were aware that there was any difference between them.

Cayuga speech also has a liberal sprinkling of "whispered" syllables. (They are syllables—*ka*, *tro*, *nyũ*, *wi*, for example, which are pronounced entirely without voice. Phonetically this is not quite the same as whispering, for a whisper has another added articulatory feature.) These voiceless syllables alternate in a regular way with voiced syllables which are followed by *h*. Speakers who have been questioned about this and informed of the point at issue have replied that they had never noticed before that these syllables were whispered, or that there was any difference between them and the voiced types (followed by *h*) with which they alternate.

Besides these, Cayuga has many metathesized pairs in similar alternation, where the metatheses affect the relative order of vowels and the glottal stop (as it does with vowels and *h* in the first examples cited). These alternations too escape detection by the very ones who produce them.

The Cayuga words pronounced *onũhsagáhẽn* (*window*) and *deyonh^usák'hãin* (*two windows*) produce drastically different auditory impressions on a phonetician or on an English-speaking listener or on one who speaks almost anything but Cayuga. But to the Cayuga they sound the same, except that the second word begins with *de-* (a prefix associated here with reference to *two* things). So it is also with *g'oník'hwa'* (*her mind*) and *godi'nigũha'* (*their minds*). The second word has a syllable *-di-* which makes it a plural form. Here again the acoustic impression to the outsider is drastically different as between the two words, but not at all so to the native speaker, who notices only the presence or absence of the syllable *-di-*. Similarly in *ẽhat'hryó'daat* (*he will work*) and *ẽhẽnadrího'daat* (*they will work*), the difference in the pronominal prefixes *-ha-* (*he*) versus *-hẽna-* (*they*) is noticed, but the remaining differences are not.

The Cayuga listener is obviously not responding to the same features of the acoustic stimulus that an outsider would pick up. We would probably not be far wrong if we concluded that in the native speaker there is a learned *nonperception* (a conditioned indifference) to some of these features. If, instead of objectively reporting the total acoustic stimulus as we have done above in our phonetic transcriptions, we should obliterate the distinctions (1) between voiced and voiceless sounds both in consonants and in vowels; (2) between the two possible orders of a vowel and a laryngeal, e.g., between *aʔ* and *ʔa*, and between *ah* and *ha*, etc.; (3) between syllabic and nonsyllabic vocalic segments; (4) between stressed and unstressed vowels; and (5) if we drop the special mark of nasalization, the tilde, on the two nasalized vowels, we would probably come closer to representing what the native speaker hears. We should then write the above examples as *onuhsakahɛn* and *teyonuhsakahɛn* (instead of the phonetically more accurate *onũhsagáhẽn* and *deyonhᵘsákhʻãin*), *koʔnikuhaʔ* and *kotiʔnikuhaʔ* (instead of *gʔoník'hwaʔ* and *godiʔnigũhaʔ*), and *ɛhatrihoʔtaat* and *ɛhɛnatrihoʔtaat* (instead of *ɛhat'hryóʔdaat* and *ɛ̃hẽnadrího ʔdaat*). Now the paired members begin to look as much alike in transcription as they seem to sound alike to the Cayugas. What we have accomplished is to suppress from our transcriptions the representation of features of the acoustic stimulus (voicing, syllabicity, laryngeal order, and position of the accent) which do not serve as cues for differential responses on the part of native subjects and to retain a representation only of those features which do serve as cues—the distinctive features of this language.[7]

This process is called "phonemicizing" the transcription.[8] For an outsider, one must give rules for converting the phonemic representation back into phonetics. Otherwise it would be impossible for him to read the transcription to make it sound like the original

[7] The above is a slight oversimplification of the facts. Fuller details are presented in another paper [58]. It is possibly also an overinterpretation of the facts because it can be argued that perception is of a total whole, a gestalt, and that within this no feature can be said to be devoid of stimulus value, whatever its redundancy and predictability from context. It should be remarked in this connection that linguists generally make a point of avoiding psychological interpretations of the structural facts of a language—a rule of caution which the present writer has allowed himself to neglect for the moment.

[8] A transcription which suppresses all but the cue-bearing phonetic features (the *independent variables* of a phonological system) is known as a "phonemic" transcription. This contrasts with a "phonetic" transcription, which registers all features that a given phonetician is able to discriminate and report, without regard to their structural status or cue-bearing function in the particular language at hand.

language. For the native speaker, however, the rules are built into his habits already. The basis of the Cayuga rules—as the reader may already have observed from the examples—is syllable count, the distinction between even and odd-numbered syllables. The details of the rules are too complex to be given here. An almost identical system was found by Sapir in Southern Paiute. It is described in his monograph on that language [68] as well as in the famous paper "The Psychological Reality of Phonemes" [67]. The two cases are of independent historical development. Cayuga and Southern Paiute are neither phylogenetically related nor influenced by geographic proximity.[9]

The method of phonemics is not one of psychological experimentation; rather, it involves the search for circumstantial evidence as to the distinctiveness or nondistinctiveness of phonetic features in naturally occurring speech data. The only "psychological" test which the linguist performs is to ascertain whether two phonetically different forms are the same or different as linguistic stimuli to natives. The specific purpose of the same-or-different test is to determine whether a particular feature of phonetic difference is a result of *free variation* or of *contrast*. Beyond this, one studies the distributions of phonetic types (the inventory of phonetic environments in which they occur). In particular, one seeks to determine whether two phonetic types which are similar in some features but different in others are in *complementary distribution* or in *contrast*. If a rule can be formulated whereby the occurrence of one or another of two such phonetic types is shown always to be a function of the phonetic context, then they can be regarded as conditioned variants of one unit. The "phoneme" is generally regarded as a class of phone types which have a phonetic feature in common and whose differences are either in complementary distribution or in free variation in respect to their environments. Alternatively, it can be regarded as the phonetic feature (or bundle of features) shared by all the members of such a class, i.e., the defining features of the class, or necessary and sufficient conditions for membership in the class. Given the specification of a phoneme and of the environment in which it occurs in any instance, the selection of the allophone—i.e., the particular member of the class of conditioned variants—follows automatically.

[9] Sapir's paper [67] is one of the classic pioneer papers in the then (1933) new theory of phonemics. It contains interesting data on the interpretive responses of a native speaker to one of the phonological problems of Southern Paiute, and it gives a partial phonemicization of the phonetic data. Sapir's phonemicization—or "phonologic orthography" as he called it in this paper—does not go far enough, however. It misses the solution of both the geminate stops and the voiceless syllables. Lounsbury [58] suggests a reinterpretation based on the structural analogies with Cayuga.

It is generally assumed that the allophones of a phoneme are in some sense equivalent stimuli. They are defined so that they share the same distinctive features (features that function as cues for differential responses in the given language) and differ from one another only by nondistinctive features (those which do not function as cues). Granting the assumption, one may see in this phenomenon in phonology—as some psychologists have seen in it—an analog to the phenomenon of constancy, which has been studied by perception psychologists largely in connection with visual-concept formation. The notion may perhaps be extended also to analogs in lexicon, such as those described in the next section.

Examples just as pertinent as the Cayuga ones could be found in English. It is difficult to make the point with English examples, however, for the phonetic differences which would have to be described in distinguishing the allophones of English phonemes would seem like phonetic hair-splitting to an English-speaking reader. But one society's hair's breadth can be another's chasm. Every linguist has struggled in a strange language over distinctions so subtle (from his point of view) that he has wondered how the speakers of that language can ever pick up the cues. These same distinctions, however, seem gross and obvious to the native speakers. On the other hand, some differences that seem gross and obvious to us (such as those mentioned for Cayuga) may escape detection by others, including the very ones who produce them. There seems to be no absolute metric that can be applied to acoustic space when, in langauge behavior, it is subject to so much learned perceptual distortion.[10]

THE CLASSIFICATORY FUNCTION OF LINGUISTIC FORMS

Linguistic forms act as classifiers of their referents, for it is through the use of the forms that distinctions are drawn and ambiguities allowed in the construction of messages which report on (or otherwise relate to) things, situations, and events. We will use the term "first-line distinctions" to designate distinctions of reference which are made, in usage, by the naming vocabulary of a language; and the term "first-line ambiguities" to refer to the ambiguities of reference which are present in that same usage. Sharper distinctions

[10] In regard to the learned perceptual distortion of phonetic space, Liberman et al. [50] have designed experiments to test whether the observed sharper stimulus discriminations in the region of phoneme boundaries are an effect of learning, and, if so, whether this represents "acquired distinctiveness" near phoneme boundaries or "acquired similarity" within the ranges of variation of phonemes. The results support the assumption that the discrimination peak at phoneme boundaries is a result of learning, and they point in the direction of acquired distinctiveness.

than those given by the naming vocabulary can, of course, be drawn by the addition of modifying constructional devices, and some of the first-line ambiguities may be thereby eliminated. Every language has qualifying and limiting constructions by means of which reference may be sharpened, when necessary, beyond the degree provided by the conventional usage of its naming vocabulary.

The first-line distinctions and ambiguities are of considerable interest in their own right, however. These are the referential distinctions which are most economically made and the hardest to avoid (those most accessible and inevitable in the "code"), and the ambiguities in reference which are the likeliest to be present and the most cumbersome to remove. Anthropologists, linguists, and psychologists have entertained numerous interesting hypotheses concerning these. The referential classifications made through lexicon often vary strikingly from language to language and are seen to exhibit different classificatory principles in different languages. It is posited that the principles of referential classification embodied in lexical usage in a given speech community bear some relation to their relative utility in communication in that community and to the frequency with which the distinctions implied by them are of crucial significance. This, in turn, it is posited, may be a function of the ways in which a people's social interactions and their activities in relation to their natural and man-made environments are organized.

Some of the best cases in support of this hypothesis come from special vocabularies such as those of kinship systems, numeration, ethnobotanical, ethnozoological and ethnometeorological terminologies, etc. Other convincing examples can be found in the vocabularies and/or inflectional apparatus related to the forms of respect and familiarity, authority and deference, social distance and solidarity, etc. Some of those who have speculated on these matters see language as organizing a very large part of one's perceptual habits, and would see even the grammar of a language as related to an underlying "world view" or perceptual orientation which may characterize the culture of a particular speech community. Clearly this is a fertile field for hypothesis formulation.[11] As an example of the classificatory function in lexical usage, we shall cite a few instances from kinship terminologies.

Lexical units in kinship terminologies can differ, as between different societies, in two aspects of their meanings: the "personnel-designating" aspect and the "role-symbolizing" aspect.[12] Thus the

[11] In fact, it has been a favorite field for quite untrammeled speculations [cf. Whorf, 80, especially pp. 57, 134, 160, 207, 233; Lee, 39, 40; and Hoijer, 31].

[12] This distinction is drawn from Schneider and Roberts [71].

meanings of the "father" terms of various kinship systems may differ in regard to who may be named "father" (or the equivalent) and what it means to be a "father" in that society. In our society, as the term is applied to real relatives (i.e., excluding the metaphoric extensions to nonrelatives), the reference term is applied by an individual to but one person: the one whom we understand as one's father (though as a term of address it may be extended to a step-father and to a father-in-law as well). In a great many societies (those having what anthropologists call Iroquois-type kinship systems), the "father" term is applied not only to one's father, but to one's father's brothers and male cousins as well. In still other societies (those having Crow-type kinship systems), the "father" term applies to one's father, father's brothers, father's sister's sons, father's sister's daughter's sons, and sometimes to the father's mother's brothers as well. Aside from the question of who may be classed under the same kinship label as the father, there is also the question of what the label implies in the way of expected behavior. In one society, the relevant term may mean an authoritarian figure who is the head of the family; in another, the analogous term may mean something quite different.[13] The personnel-designating aspects of the meanings of kinship terms are analyzed by isolating the dimensions of referential features which are distinctive in the given system and by defining each labeled kin class in terms of the distinctive features of that class, i.e., in terms of those which state the necessary and sufficient conditions for membership. The role-symbolizing aspects may be analyzed from associated behavioral data in somewhat analogous ways.

The effects of different classificatory principles applied to the same set of elements can be seen in the following examples. Consider the following pairs of kin types:

1. Brother, sister
2. Father's brother's son, father's brother's daughter
3. Mother's sister's son, mother's sister's daughter
4. Father's sister's son, father's sister's daughter
5. Mother's brother's son, mother's brother's daughter.

In our kinship usage, the types of 1 are classed as brother and sister, while those of 2, 3, 4, and 5 are classed as cousins. In the Iroquois-type usages, the 1, 2, and 3 types are all brothers and sisters, while only those of 4 and 5 are cousins. In Crow-type usages the types of 1, 2, and 3 are again brothers and sisters, while those of 4 are classed as father and aunt, and those of 5 are son and daughter to a man, but nephew and niece to a woman. In Omaha-type usages, the types

[13] Cf. Schneider and Gough [70, especially Schneider, pp. 1–29; Fathauer, pp. 247–249; Basehart, p. 291; Gough, pp. 363–366].

of 1, 2, and 3 are brothers and sisters, while those of 4 are nephew and niece to a man, but son and daughter to a woman, and those of 5 are uncle and mother. (There are no cousin classes in Crow- or Omaha-type usages.)

These different classifications result from the recognition of different dimensions of distinctive features. In our system, the primary dimension is degree of collaterality, with generation as a secondary dimension of limited applicability. (Our cousin class, which consists of second and higher-degree collaterals, extends into ascending and descending generations.) In systems of the Iroquois type, the primary dimensions are those of generation and bifurcation (the distinction between "parallel" and "cross" kin types). In those of the Crow type, the primary dimensions are a skewed generation measure (in whose computation females rank a social generation higher than their male siblings in certain contexts) and bifurcation. In those of the Omaha type, they are a differently skewed generation measure (the mirror image of Crow generation, in whose computation the roles of the sexes are reversed) and bifurcation.[14] It should be noted that the particular generation measure, whether straight or skewed, must be applied first in the Iroquois, Crow, and Omaha systems, inasmuch as the reckoning of bifurcation (whether a kin type is to be regarded as parallel or as cross) is dependent on the prior specification of generation in all systems.

The different principles of classification are not arbitrary quirks of particular languages, but linguistic reflections of important legal and social realities in particular societies. The first-line distinctions drawn by a kinship lexicon are simply the most useful ones for the given society. The fact that certain types of systems recur independently among peoples in distant parts of the world reflects the phenomenon of convergence in basic aspects of social structure, i.e., of similar adaptive responses to similar conditioning factors.

THE RELATIONS OF A LINGUISTIC FORM

The primary relations of a linguistic form have been variously categorized. C. W. Morris's familiar partitioning of these [63, 64], which puts them as "pragmatic," "semantic," and "syntactic" at a first level of categorization, was intended to apply to the relations of

---

[14] The above is not a sufficient description of the modes of generation reckoning in these systems. Actually there are four different varieties of so-called "Crow-type" generation reckoning, and a mirror-image set of four varieties of "Omaha-type." The formal analysis of these systems, their typology, and hypotheses concerning their social determinants are presented in papers by the present writer [55, 56].

linguistic forms as well as to those of other and more general kinds of signs. We shall speak only of its application to linguistic forms, but we shall preserve Morris's terminology in referring to the latter as "signs."

1. Of the three varieties of relations, the "pragmatic" is the least well defined. It was meant to embrace the "expressive" aspects of the linguistic act, relating a linguistic sign to its users. "User" appears here to include both the producer for whom the linguistic sign is consciously or unconsciously an instrument, and whose disposition it expresses, and any additional audience upon whom the sign acts as a stimulus, and whose interpretant response it also expresses [63, p. 7]. Of the three relations specified by Morris, "pragmatics" is the one of most traditional interest to psychologists. The full gamut of psychological writings concerned with language, ranging from Freud to Skinner to Osgood, bears witness to this. It is, incidentally, the one of least traditional interest to linguists.

2. The "semantic" relation in this scheme of things is that between linguistic signs and "the objects to which [they] are applicable" [63, p. 6]. "Object" here is an overly concrete term for what is intended, viz., objects, qualities, conditions, etc., whether actually existent or only describable or imaginable. Semantics in the present scheme, then, has to do with "reference," in the widest sense of this term. It is not a traditional interest in either psychology or linguistics, though linguists have not avoided dealing with it in at least an offhand, practical sort of way, and anthropologically oriented linguists (or linguistically oriented anthropologists) have made it a subject of theoretical, as well as practical, concern. It has, of course, long been a subject of theoretical concern in philosophy. (In the anthropological approach to reference, since this is based on usage representing a society-wide pragmatism of sorts and reflecting a so-called "linguistic relativity," the line of division between pragmatics and semantics becomes somewhat blurred.)

Semantic analysis is facilitated by recognizing different *modes of reference* in the relationship between a linguistic sign and its object, viz., the relation between a sign and its *object as a thing*, and the relation between a sign and its *object as an exemplar of a kind or member of a class*. The former relation has been called "denotation" and the latter "designation" [63, p. 5].

Although some writers have used "kind of object" and "class of objects" as essentially equivalent terms [*ibid.*], it is important in descriptive semantics to make a further distinction between them. A semantic *class* may be defined merely by the sign which is its label, i.e., as the set of objects to which a given linguistic sign is applied. This tells us nothing about the *kind*, however; i.e., it does not tell us what distinctive qualities the members of the class have in common, other than their name. But any naturally formed class of things, arrived at pragmatically by stimulus generalization, is assumed to have some distinctive quality or combination of qualities in common, which furnished the basis for the generalization manifested in the common labeling response. A natural class of this type contrasts with unnatural classes, or pseudoclasses, which have no distinctive inherent qualities in common at all except their name (e.g., the class of girls named Mary as opposed to the class of those named Helen) or a feature of their name (e.g., the class of things named by masculine nouns in German as opposed to the class of things named by feminine nouns in German). Such classes are not based on stimulus generalization, but on random individual acts of name bestowal from out of a limited stock (as in the first example) or upon a traditional but arbitrary classification whose presumed former natural basis, if any, is a matter of prehistory (as in the latter example). It is the task of descriptive semantic analysis to isolate and abstract from the members of a label-defined class of objects what are their common distinctive inherent features that also make them a "kind," if indeed they are. We may restrict the use of the term "designation" to the relation of a sign to the class of its objects, and adduce a later term of Morris, "signification," for the relation of a sign to the distinctive features of the class of its objects, i.e., to the attributes which specify the kind of object to which it is applicable [64, pp. 17, 20, 354].

While theoretical semantics, as already noted, is one of the traditional interests of philosophy, its applied aspect—the descriptive or "structural" semantic analysis of the lexicons of natural languages—is at present a concern of linguistically oriented anthropologists and psychologists. Areas of lexicon investigated by them include such lexical sets or semantic "fields" as the vocabularies of spatial and temporal orientation [27], color terminologies [5, 11, 37, 43, 44], pronominal categories [4, 12, 74], native botanical ("ethnobotanical") taxonomies [12], primitive taxonomies of disease [14], and above all, systems of kinship terms [18, 20, 52, 55, 56, 75, 76]. The usual procedure in such undertakings is to move from (a) the compilation of raw lexicographic data on particular denotations, to (b) the assembling of the denotata of each single linguistic form as a semantic class of objects, or designatum, to (c) the discovery—when possible—of the classificatory dimensions imposed upon the field by native linguistic usage, and (d) the specification of the distinctive features defining each of the constituent semantic classes as a kind, to (e) an ordering of the semantic units of the various hierarchical levels within the total structure of the system.

Success in the third and fourth of these steps, viz., in the discovery of the significant variables of stimulus features and the specification of the defining features of each semantic class, is not always assured—especially when working with exotic systems such as anthropologists most often work with; for one can never know in advance what cues the people of a given society may be responding to in their linguistic classificatory behavior (cf. *The Classificatory Function of Linguistic Forms*). Analytic successes, however, as they accumulate in solving problems of this kind, may lead—and in some lexical domains have led—to a fairly comprehensive theory of the psychological and sociological possibilities for variation in linguistic classificatory behavior. As such a theory develops—as it has already in the field of kinship organization—it becomes increasingly easier to arrive at the solutions to newly discovered, or old but as yet unsolved, individual systems. Moreover, the determinants of the classificatory structures are often revealed, and this aspect of structure in language can be seen as related to other social and cultural phenomena.

3. The "syntactic" relation, the third of the varieties recognized in Morris's outline, is "the formal relation of *signs to one another* . . . in abstraction from the relations of signs to objects or to interpreters" [63, pp. 6, 13]. It is the aspect of language which is the principal concern of linguistics. It is the one of least traditional interest in psychology, although in recent times with the advent of information theory there has been an interest on the part of some psychologists in the probabilistic aspects of this relation [61, chap. 4; 62; 66; esp. §§2.3, 5.1-5]. Since then, however, it has been adequately demonstrated that no stochastic model can generate the syntactic structures of a language [7, 9, 10].

The "formal relations which signs have to one another" are generally viewed as belonging to two elementary varieties: (*a*) those of a constituent to its partner-constituent within a construction, and (*b*) those of a constituent to an alternative constituent which may take its place in a similar construction with the same partner. The types of relations in this basic dichotomy have been variously categorized as "syntagmatic" and "associative," "*in praesentia*" and "*in absentia*," "contiguity" and "similarity," "combination" and "selection," "distribution" and "commutation," etc. [34, part II; 69, part II, chap. 5; 54].

R. Jakobson has noted that aphasic disturbances may affect one or the other or both of these facets of linguistic structure. He has referred to the resulting disturbances as the "contiguity disorder" and the "similarity disorder," respectively [34, part II].

Responses to word-association tests show the same two associative relations between words: the sequential contiguity variety and the substitutional similarity variety. The familiar special cases of antonyms and synonyms as associative responses may be due to either contiguity, or similarity relations: contiguity, because both antonyms and synonyms are frequently linked in conventional phrases (*black and white, great and small, summer and winter*); and similarity, because of both syntactic and semantic similarity. (*Syntactic similarity:* membership in the same substitution class and substitutability in many of the same syntactic frames. *Semantic similarity:* sharing of all defining features but one—all but the last in the hierarchy of defining referential features in the case of antonyms, and all but one of context in the case of synonyms.) Selection of the antonym is a fairly frequent form of tongue slip with some persons.

The same relations are involved also in the well-known and long-classified figures of speech, metaphor and simile on the one hand, and metonymy and synecdoche on the other. The nineteenth-century American philosopher C. S. Peirce recognized them in a typology of signs, in the dichotomy of "icon" and "index, "the former owing its special character as a sign to the similarity principle, and the latter to the contiguity principle. Sir James G. Frazer recognized the same principles operating in a special form of sign behavior, primitive magic, and in his *Golden Bough* made these the criteria for defining the two main subdivisions of sympathetic magic: "homeopathic," based on the similarity principle, and "contagious," based on the contiguity principle. These same notions of similarity and contiguity relations were fundamental to nineteenth-century association psychology, and they survive into twentieth-century learning theory in a refined form as two of the basic variables in stimulus conditioning.[15]

These relations, manifest in the sequential arrangement of forms and in the replaceability of forms, are the fundamental syntactic relations within any layer of structure in language. Passing from layer to layer, there are the relations of constituent to construction, of form to transform, etc., which characterize the derivational structures of sentences and the derivational patterns of a language. Something of the nature of these relations was suggested in earlier sections. Their specification constitutes the major part of the descriptive syntax of a language.

Morris, in his sketch of the "syntactic" branch of the theory of signs, focused on the "logical syntax" of Carnap as an example of the kind of investigations that were to be included under the heading of "syntactics." He noted how this "deliberately neglects what has

[15] These two paragraphs are adapted from a previous publication of the writer [54].

here been called the semantical and the pragmatical dimensions of semiosis to concentrate upon the logico-grammatical structure of language, i.e., upon the syntactical dimension of semiosis" [63, p. 14]. The nature of the analysis envisioned for descriptive syntactics is indicated in his précis of logical syntax:

> In this type of consideration a "language" becomes any set of things related in accordance with two classes of rules: *formation rules*, which determine permissable independent combinations of members of the set (such combinations being called sentences), and *transformation rules*, which determine the sentences which can be obtained from other sentences. These may be brought together under the term "*syntactical rule*." Syntactics is, then, the consideration of signs and sign combinations in so far as they are subject to syntactical rules. It is not interested in the individual properties of the sign vehicles or in any of their relations except syntactical ones, i.e., relations determined by syntactical rules [63, p. 14].

"Logical syntax," however, is at best a very special case in the syntactics of languages, being "the pure syntactics of *the language of science*" [64, p. 279]. This last restriction imposes drastic limits on the kinds of sentences and the kinds of discourses to which it is applicable and even to the "language" to which it is applicable; since the language is not necessarily any one of those employed in scientific discourse (e.g., English, German, etc.), but a sort of international and artificial one consisting of a relatively small set of logical relations expressible (though in different ways) in all of these and abstracted from these; and whose selection from the total set of syntactic relations possible in a natural language introduces certain considerations of both a semantic and a pragmatic sort.

As for the syntactics of natural languages, Morris noted correctly that grammar, as usually developed in linguistics (which should be the syntactic description of natural languages) "is both semantical and syntactical in nature" [64, p. 280]. The inclusion of semantic specifications has become something of an issue. The post-Bloomfieldian dogma in American linguistics has long upheld the desideratum of exclusion of semantic considerations from linguistics. Though certain theorists have attempted to formulate the analysis of phonology in such a way that it might—in theory, though only clumsily in practice—be carried out without recourse to questions of meaning differentiation [1, 8, 9, 23, 26], it has generally been considered impossible, or at least unfeasible, to eliminate it from grammar. (We have included it above when constructions were identified not only by the form classes and the order of the constituents which comprise them, but also by the functions of the constituents in the given constructions.) Thus, grammar has remained functional, and the identification of grammatical constructions has included specification of the semantic relations between constituents. Recently, however, a new school of linguists in this country has undertaken a completely semantics-free theory of grammar, fulfilling Morris's prophecy for "syntactics" in its linguistic application, as well as the post-Bloomfieldian dream of getting rid of meaning altogether. (In another sense also this new linguistics would seem to be a fulfillment of Morris's forecast, for it is the first to incorporate an explicit theory of sentence transformations.)

There is, of course, no compelling reason why studies of language *must* be compartmentalized in precisely this way. As intimated earlier, we are reporting not so much on what language *is* (for it cannot be said with certainty that any one view of this is adequate) as on what linguists do to it. And this is what they are doing to it now.

LINGUISTICS AND THE PSYCHOLOGY OF LANGUAGE

It would perhaps be desirable to conclude this paper with some suggestions of a programmatic sort for the development of the psychology of language—suggestions which might represent the linguists' points of view toward this subject. Actually, few linguists have given much thought to the subject (at least not in print). And the writer hardly feels competent to formulate linguistic problems as psychological questions, in spite of the fact that he feels that many of the issues that divide linguists of different schools are at bottom questions for the psychology of language.[16] The best that he can do at present is to give a sketch—as has been done in the preceding sections of this paper—of the things that linguists see in language and let the psychologists themselves decide whether any of these look as though they might hold something worth exploring by their methods. The writer is of the opinion that all aspects of linguistic behavior—from the molecular components of articulation and perception to the highest levels of behavioral organization that are involved in speaking and in the comprehension of speech—are appropriate topics and provide important problems for psychological inquiry into language. The foregoing sketch is far from an adequate map of this territory. If, however, it should reveal a few features of the terrain that are not yet common knowledge among psychologists, it will have served its purpose.

[16] For a discussion of some of the basic issues upon which linguists disagree, and the psychological questions underlying these issues, see an account in the *Biennial Review of Anthropology* 1961 [53, pp. 279–299].

REFERENCES

1. Bloch, B. A set of postulates for phonemic analysis. *Language,* 1948, **24,** 3–46.
2. Bloomfield, L. *Language.* New York: Holt, 1933.
3. Brown, R. W. Language and categories. In J. S. Bruner et al., *A study of thinking.* New York: Wiley, 1956. Pp. 247–312.
4. Brown, R. W., & Gilman, A. The pronouns of power and solidarity. In T. A. Sebeok (Ed.), *Style in language.* New York: Wiley, 1960.
5. Brown, R. W., & Lenneberg, E. H. A study in language and cognition. *J. abnorm. Psychol.,* 1954, **49,** 454–462.
6. Chomsky, N. Review of B. F. Skinner, *Verbal behavior. Language,* 1959, **35,** 26–58.
7. Chomsky, N. Review of C. F. Hockett, *A manual of phonology. Int. J. Amer. Ling.,* 1957, **23,** 223–234.
8. Chomsky, N. Semantic considerations in grammar. *Inst. Lang. Ling. Monogr.,* 1955, No. 8, 141–150.
9. Chomsky, N. *Syntactic structures.* The Hague: Mouton & Co., 1957.
10. Chomsky, N. Three models for the description of language. *IRE Trans. Inf. Theor.,* 1956, **IT-2**(3), 113–124.
11. Conklin, H. C. Hanunoo color categories. *S.W. J. Anthrop.,* 1955, **11,** 339–344.
12. Conklin, H. C. Lexicographical treatment of folk taxonomies. *Int. J. Amer. Ling.,* 1962, **28,** 119–141.
13. Cooper, F. S., et al. Some input-output relations observed in experiments on the perception of speech. In *Second International Congress on Cybernetics.* Namur, Belgium: Association International de Cybernétique, 1958. Pp. 930–941.
14. Frake, C. O. The diagnosis of disease among the Subanun of Mindanao. *Amer. Anthrop.,* 1961, **63,** 113–132.
15. Gleason, H. A., Jr. *An introduction to descriptive linguistics.* (2nd ed., revised). New York: Holt, 1961.
16. Goldman-Eisler, F. A comparative study of two hesitation phenomena. *Lang. Speech,* 1961, **4,** 18–26.
17. Goldman-Eisler, F. The predictability of words in context and the length of pauses in speech. *Lang. Speech,* 1958, **1,** 226–232.
18. Goodenough, W. H. Componential analysis and the study of meaning. *Language,* 1956, **32,** 195–216.
19. Goodenough, W. H. Cultural anthropology and linguistics. *Inst. Lang. Ling. Monogr.,* 1957, No. 9, 167–173.
20. Goodenough, W. H. Property, kin, and community on Truk. Yale Univer. Publ. Anthrop., 1951, No. 46.
21. Greenberg, J. H. Language and evolution. In B. J. Meggers (Ed.), *Evolution and anthropology: a centennial appraisal.* Washington: Anthropological Society of Washington, 1959.
22. Greenberg, J. H. Order of affixing: a study in general linguistics. In

J. H. Greenberg, *Essays in linguistics* (Viking Fund Publ. in Anthrop., No. 24). New York: Wenner-Gren Foundation, 1957. Pp. 86–94.

23. Halle, M. The strategy of phonemics. *Word,* 1954, **10,** 197–209.
24. Harris, Z. S. Co-occurrence and transformation in linguistic structure. *Language,* 1957, **33,** 283–340.
25. Harris, Z. S. Distributional structure. *Word,* 1954, **10,** 146–162.
26. Harris, Z. S. *Methods in structural linguistics.* Chicago: Univer. Chicago Press, 1951.
27. Haugen, E. The semantics of Icelandic orientation. *Word,* 1957, **13,** 447–459.
28. Hockett, C. F. *A course in modern linguistics.* New York: Macmillan, 1958.
29. Hockett, C. F. Animal "languages" and human language. In J. N. Spuhler (Ed.), *The evolution of man's capacity for culture.* Detroit, Mich.: Wayne Univer. Press, 1959. Pp. 32–39.
30. Hockett, C. F. Biophysics, linguistics, and the unity of science. *Amer. Scientist,* 1948, **36,** 558–572.
31. Hoijer, H. Cultural implications of some Navaho linguistic categories. *Language,* 1951, **27,** 111–120.
32. Hoijer, H. (Ed.). *Language in culture.* (Amer. Anthrop. Assn. Memoir No. 79.) Chicago: Univer. Chicago Press, 1954.
33. Householder, F. W. On linguistic primes. *Word,* 1959, **15,** 231–239.
34. Jakobson, R., & Halle, M. *Fundamentals of language.* The Hague: Mouton & Co., 1956.
35. Koppers, W. Lévy-Bruhl und das Ende des "prälogischen Denkens" der Primitiven. *Sonderabdr. d. 18. int. Sozialkongresses.* Bd. IV. Rome, 1950.
36. Krantz, G. S. Pithecanthropine brain size and its cultural consequences. *Man,* 1961, **61,** 85–87.
37. Landar, H. J., Ervin, S. M., & Horowitz, A. E. Navaho color categories. *Language,* 1960, **36,** 368–382.
38. Laycock, D. C. Language and society: twenty years after. *Lingua,* 1960, **9,** 16–29.
39. Lee, D. D. Conceptual implications of an Indian language. *Phil. Sci.,* 1938, **5,** 89–102.
40. Lee, D. D. Linguistic reflection of Wintu thought. *Int. J. Amer. Ling.,* 1944, **10,** 181–187.
41. Lees, R. B. Review of N. Chomsky, *Syntactic structures. Language,* 1957, **33,** 375–408.
42. Lees, R. B. The grammar of English nominalizations. *Ind. Univer. Res. Cent. Anthrop., Folkl., Ling. Publ.,* 1960, No. 12.
43. Lenneberg, E. H. Color naming, color recognition, color discrimination: a reappraisal. *Percept. mot. Skills,* 1961, **12,** 375–382.
44. Lenneberg, E. H., & Roberts, J. M. The language of experience: a study in methodology. Ind. Univer. *Publ. Anthrop. Ling.,* 1956, Mem. 13.
45. Lévy-Bruhl, L. *La mentalité primitive.* Paris: 1922.
46. Lévy-Bruhl, L. *Les fonctions mentales dans les sociétés inférieures.* (3d ed.) Paris: 1918.

47. Liberman, A. M., et al. Minimal rules for synthesizing speech. *J. Acoust. Soc. Amer.*, 1959, **31**, 1490–1499.
48. Liberman, A. M., et al. Some results of research on speech perception. *J. Acoust. Soc. Amer.*, 1957, **29**, 117–123.
49. Liberman, A. M., et al. The discrimination of relative onset-time of components of certain speech and nonspeech patterns. *J. exp. Psychol.*, 1961, **61**, 379–388.
50. Liberman, A. M., et al. The discrimination of speech sounds within and across phoneme boundaries. *J. exp. Psychol.*, 1957, **54**, 358–368.
51. Liberman, A. M., Delattre, P. C., & Cooper, F. S. Some cues for the distinction between voiced and voiceless stops in initial position. *Lang. Speech*, 1958, **1**, 153–167.
52. Lounsbury, F. G. A semantic analysis of the Pawnee kinship usage. *Language*, 1956, **32**, 158–194.
53. Lounsbury, F. G. Language. In B. J. Siegel (Ed.), *Bien. Rev. Anthrop.*, 1961, 279–322.
54. Lounsbury, F. G. Similarity and contiguity relations in language and in culture. *Inst. Lang. Ling. Monogr.*, 1959, No. 12, 123–128.
55. Lounsbury, F. G. The formal analysis of Crow and Omaha-type kinship terminologies. In W. H. Goodenough (Ed.), *Explorations in cultural anthropology*, Univer. Pennsylvania Press, in press.
56. Lounsbury, F. G. The structural analysis of kinship semantics. *Proceedings Ninth International Congress Linguists*. Cambridge, Mass., in press.
57. Lounsbury, F. G. Transitional probability, linguistic structure, and systems of habit-family hierarchies. In C. E. Osgood and T. A. Sebeok (Eds.), *Psycholinguistics: a survey of theory and research problems, Ind. Univer. Publ. Anthrop. Ling.*, 1954, Mem. 10, 93–101.
58. Lounsbury, F. G. Voiceless vowels, their phonological status and conditioning factors in Cayuga, Comanche, and Southern Paiute. To appear in *Language*.
59. Maclay, H., and C. E. Osgood. Hesitation phenomena in spontaneous English speech. *Word*, 1959, **15**, 19–44.
60. Mead, G. H. (C. W. Morris, Ed.) *Mind, self and society*. Chicago: Univer. Chicago Press, 1934.
61. Miller, G. A. *Language and communication*. New York: McGraw-Hill, 1951.
62. Miller, G. A. Speech and language. In S. S. Stevens (Ed.), *Handbook of experimental psychology*. New York: Wiley, 1951. Pp. 789 810.
63. Morris, C. W. *Foundations of the theory of signs*. Int. encycl. of unified science. Vol. 1, No. 2, Chicago: Univer. Chicago Press, 1938.
64. Morris, C. W. *Signs, language and behavior*. Englewood Cliffs, N.J.: Prentice-Hall, 1946.
65. Osgood, C. E., see p. 244.
66. Osgood, C. E., & Sebeok, T. A. (Eds.) Psycholinguistics: a survey of theory and research problems. *Ind. Univer. Publ. Anthrop. Ling.*, 1954, Mem. 10.
67. Sapir, E. La réalité psychologique des phonèmes. *J. de Psychol. normale*

et pathologique, 1933, **30,** 247–265. Also in D. G. Mandelbaum (Ed.), *Selected writings of Edward Sapir.* Berkeley, Calif.: Univer. Calif. Press, 1949. Pp. 46–60.

68. Sapir, E. Southern Paiute, a Shoshonean language. *Proc. Amer. Acad. Arts Sci.,* 1930, **65,** No. 1.

69. Saussure, F. de (C. Bally and A. Sechehaye, Eds.). *Cours de linguistique générale.* Paris: Payot, 1916. Also W. Baskin (Trans.), *Course in general linguistics.* New York: Philosophical Library, 1959.

70. Schneider, D. M., & Gough, K. (Eds.) *Matrilineal kinship.* Berkeley, Calif: Univer. Calif. Press, 1961.

71. Schneider, D. M., & Roberts, J. M. Zuni kin terms. *Lab. Anthrop. Note Book,* 1956, No. 3, 1–23.

72. Sommerfelt, A. *La langue et la société: caractères sociaux d'une langue de type archaïque.* Oslo: H. Aschehoug & Co. (W. Nygaard), 1938.

73. Sturtevant, E. H. *An introduction to linguistic science.* New Haven, Conn.: Yale Univer. Press, 1947.

74. Thomas, D. Three analyses of the Ilocano pronoun system. *Word,* 1955, **11,** 204–208.

75. Wallace, A. F. C., & Atkins, J. The meaning of kinship terms. *Amer. Anthrop.,* 1960, **62,** 58–80.

76. Wallace, A. F. C. Culture and cognition. *Science,* 1962, **135,** 351–357.

77. Wells, R. S. Immediate constituents. *Language,* 1947, **23,** 81–117.

78. White, L. A. On the use of tools by primates. *J. Comp. Psychol.,* 1942, **34,** 369–374. Reprinted in L. A. White, *The science of culture.* New York: Farrar, Straus, 1949. Pp. 40–48.

79. White, L. A. The symbol: the origin and basis of human behavior. *Philos. Sci.,* 1940, **7,** 451–463. Reprinted in L. A. White, *The science of culture.* New York: Farrar, Straus, 1949. Pp. 22–39.

80. Whorf, B. L. (J. B. Carroll, Ed.). *Language, thought, and reality: selected writings of Benjamin Lee Whorf.* New York: Wiley, 1956.

POLITICAL SCIENCE AND PSYCHOLOGY

ROBERT E. LANE
Department of Political Science
Yale University

POLITICAL SCIENCE

One comes best to an understanding of the nature of political science as a discipline through a brief introduction to the larger questions members of the discipline seek to answer. In this area of macropolitics, such central questions would include: What is the nature of power? How is it distributed? In whose interest is it exercised? What is the nature of man in this context? Are all men capable of sharing in power, or is there a necessary division between an elite that must rule and others who must follow? How shall governmental power be organized so as to achieve a "just" distribution of benefits? How can government be made both efficient and responsible, and what are the relationships between these two goals? What is the relationship between majority rule and minority rights? How do nations relate to one another, in what terms, through what channels, with what results? What is the nature of law, and how does law develop, how is it interpreted? What are the ingredients, the premises, the merits of the great ideologies of the world: socialism, communism, democracy, and fascism? It is of such stuff that this most disparate of disciplines is formed.

In the pursuit of answers to these questions, some men have sought to discover the "essence" of the field, to reduce it to some particular line of inquiry which to them represented the core of the discipline. This would, of course, be most appropriate as applied to political theory. Thus Barker, upon the occasion of his accession to a chair of political science at Cambridge in 1928, considered that political theory, while based in history and law, was most properly an effort to "determine the end, or ultimate value, which governs and determines the life of political society [and] . . . to discover the appropriate and congruous means by which that end may be realized" [9, p. 42]. Its closest relative was moral philosophy. Harold Laski, a few years earlier, upon a similar occasion at the University of London, reported his views of the field whose principles he was about to teach. "A true politics," he said, "is above all a philosophy of history" [100, p. 10]. Here political theory is conceived both as an interpretation of past events and as the history of ideas in their appropriate context. Of course, these views are now thirty-five years old, but their relevance is not merely historical; even today these views of the office of theory in political science and of the discipline itself are everywhere significant, and in many places unchallenged.

Although in Britain philosophy and history seemed between them to smother their political science offspring, across the Atlantic a different approach to the discipline soon developed. In Chicago, Charles E. Merriam (after studying in Germany) picked up the theme of "power" as a central feature of political science, a theme also developed by George Catlin. Both reached back into traditional literature of Hobbes, Treitschke, Michels, and others for precedent [30, 129]. At the same time, the most significant voice in the field, Harold Lasswell, began a series of definitions of political science which have left a permanent imprint upon the thinking in this area. In 1934 he said, "Political analysis is the study of changes in the shape and composition of the value patterns of society" [104, p. 3]. Four years later Lasswell said, "The study of politics is the study of influence and the influential" [101, p. 3]. In 1950, Lasswell and Kaplan, after referring to political science as the "study of the shaping and sharing of power," gave a broader formulation, one more in keeping with the behavioral "operational" orientation: "The subject matter of political science is constituted by the conduct of *persons* with various *perspectives* of action, and organized into *groups* of varying complexity" [107, pp. xiv, 1]. Finally, most appropriately in this series, is David Easton's definition of politics, building on Lasswell's views: "Political life concerns all those varieties of activity that influence significantly the kind of authoritative policy adopted for a society and the way it is put into practice" [45, p. 128]. Here Easton deals with three concepts: "policy," which is roughly equivalent to the distribution of values suggested by Lasswell; "authoritative," which is the residuum of the idea of power, combined with the concept of legitimacy; and "society," which distinguishes what is political from what is private or religious or falls in some other category. This is where the situation rested in 1961. Although there are those who deprecate the effort to define a discipline and think of it as a latter-day search for essences [39], there can, in fact, be no doubt that a reformulation of the central questions of an area of study can, and does, have enormous consequences.

For our purposes, however, there is a superior approach to the definition of the field, an approach which depends upon a more conventional view of the way in which political problems are allocated among specialists in the area. History is divided according to area, time, and subject, and psychology may be considered to fall into several parts, experimental, social, personality, abnormal, clinical, etc. In the same way, political science has developed specialized areas of research with specialized training and specialized teachers in each area. A bulletin of the U.S. Department of Labor breaks the field down into the following fields of specialization [183, p. 12]:

American government and comparative government
International law and relations
Political parties and public opinion
Constitutional and administrative law
Political theory and philosophy
Legislature and legislation
Government and economic enterprise

The fields defined for specialized graduate work at Yale University, which is probably representative of most universities, are given in the Yale Graduate School Bulletin as follows:

Political theory
Political analysis and research methods

Comparative government
Public law
Politics and policy formation
Public administration
International politics and organization

Neither division reveals the specialized attention which is sometimes accorded to state and local government.

No one who has been associated with current thinking in the social sciences can contemplate this division with satisfaction; yet radical and abrupt revision runs the risk of establishing empty categories divorced from the literature, devoid of meaning to the practitioners in the field, and without the demonstrated capacity to facilitate research more fruitful than what has gone before. A cautious approach is indicated. One goal is postulated as "functional coherence," that is, an organization of a discipline such that similar processes are grouped for study together. This, of course, contributes to the cumulative growth of understanding of these processes and the maximization of generalizability. *If* the field of political science could be grouped so that all mass phenomena, all small-group phenomena, all intrapsychic phenomena, all problems of attitude formation, and so forth, could be treated separately, much would be gained. This would greatly facilitate the development of laws of politics, and the theory of political behavior would flourish in properly behavioral terms. What are the impediments to such a functionally coherent arrangement?

The first of the obstacles to the reorganization of the field in these terms lies in the fact that the phenomena to be studied have an *intrinsic* importance. It is important to know the precise distribution of electoral preferences as well as the laws of electoral behavior. It makes a difference who is elected, however this may have been achieved. The content of the President's messages are as important as the interactive processes which produced them. This means that the reporting of raw data as contrasted to relationships, incidence as contrasted to dynamics, has a justification in political science which cannot be ignored. This difficulty, moreover, is shared with economics and, to some extent, sociology but, with the possible exception of clinical psychology, it does not lie athwart the path of the student of psychology.

In the second place, the particular relation of political processes to historical antecedents offers obstacles to functional coherence. Thus at many stages of explanation, two types of data are relevant, one dealing with the operational forces at the moment, the other dealing with the genesis of these operational forces. We can partially "explain" a given foreign policy in terms of currently operational concepts of internationalism and isolation, developing hypotheses about their effect on decision makers at a given time. Or we can explain the same policy in terms of the history that has created these attitudes and values and has defined current views on what is in the national interest. A concentration upon the current relationships makes functional coherence easier than a genetic explanation of how we came to our present position. One is reminded in this connection of Seeley's rhyme:

> History without political science has no fruit
> Political science without history has no root.

Third, political science is saturated with the problem of the use and abuse of authority. Consequently, it deals with such concepts as "freedom," "rights," and "privileges," which are normative in their implications and in their historic modes of analyses. Other aspects of the problem of authority and of the problem of distribution of goods and services in society are included in the concept of "justice" or associated with views on "equality." Two questions emerge in this connection: Should the discussion of the "goals" of society, the normative aspects of political science, be included as part of the political science discipline? If so, how can they be integrated with nonnormative analytical modes of analysis?

With respect to the first of these, the analysis and clarification of goals, it should be said immediately that this is certainly a proper function for the political scientist. Here is a constant and urgent need to be met, and nothing is gained by turning the matter over to either the philosopher or the historian, who is even more remote from insight into social forces at work in a society. But there are three conditions to be met in this regard. First, goals and values must be explicit. Second, they must not enter the discussion of political processes in such a way as to alter the estimates of probable relationships (probable consequences of a given course of action). And third, the premises of the postulated values must be examined. Very often a so-called "goal" is adopted because it is believed to be associated with a certain state of affairs—a belief which may be factually wrong. Thus, a person may posit a goal to be "free enterprise" because he believes this to be necessary to freedom of speech. This theory about the relationship between a goal and some other factor must not be permitted to remain implicit and unexamined.

Can justice, equality, and freedom be treated as elements of a social process on a par with other less value-laden concepts? Of course. What is required is the specification of the goal in operational terms, that is, a specification of a procedure to indicate to what extent the goal has been achieved, a procedure which, if followed, will give two different observers the same information. Without further elaboration, we may say that the analysis of the normative aspects of political science can be put on a par with other aspects of the discipline and will allow the same degree of "functional coherence" as, but no more than, the rest of the discipline.

Fourth, partly because of its concern with the use and abuse of power, political science has focused very considerably upon questions of law, since law is the vehicle whereby power is formally granted and withheld in most Western societies. The interpretation of law, the legal process, embodies a number of techniques—the discovery of intent on the part of a legislature or a constituent assembly, the embodiment of cultural norms into legal form, the interpretation of what the public will and will not tolerate, and so forth. But among these processes is a kind of formal reasoning involved in searching precedent for the closest analogy to a given situation or the differentiation of the instant case from previous situations. This is a process of reasoning in which many nonrational elements play very significant roles. Because of the high logical content of this analogical reasoning, however, it does not fit easily into the types of behavioral analysis which have heretofore been employed—any more than the study of mathematics is advanced by a study of the psychological and sociological conditions of the mathematical decision makers. Although one may think of such logical processes as having functional coherence, this is a coherence which must be considered apart from other aspects of the political process.

Finally, even when the political scientist does focus upon process, it is not a functionally coherent process. He is interested in the representative process, the legislative process, the administrative process, and so forth. Could these be interpreted as functionally coherent? Only, I think, in a strained sense. While it is no doubt true that some rubric such as "action theory" or "decision-making process" might cover these diverse acts, the full utility of these rubrics has yet to be explored. Political science is, by the nature of its subject matter, interdisciplinary. If psychology and sociology each have difficulty achieving functional coherence, political science, which must also include elements of history, is certain to have even more trouble. For these and other reasons, political science is more likely to be organized along the lines of problems as they are presented by the society, rather than functions as they are organized by a discipline.

None of these considerations, of course, alters the attractiveness of the goal, the grouping of common processes according to a scheme facilitating the development of empirically verifiable laws in the general area of politics and government. We may, with a full knowledge of the difficulties involved, attempt to group the areas of inquiry into a division which does minimal damage to historical division of function and achieves maximum coherence in terms of the institutions and processes involved. Something like the following might be a solution:

1. Electoral and public opinion processes
2. Legislative (policy) processes (including certain functions of party, executive, and bureaucracy as well as legislature)
3. Administrative processes
4. Judicial and legal processes
5. International processes
6. Integrative processes analyzing the above in terms of their interrelationships and combined effects.

These processes may be studied in many different ways. They may be studied comparatively so that the special features of the process in one country are highlighted by contrast to similar processes in other countries. They may be studied at different levels of government (national, state, and local), and the interrelationships among these levels brought into focus. They may be studied in isolation from other institutions or as part of larger cultural complexes—as is the case with certain area studies. They may be studied historically, as has been true in American history courses for a long time. Concepts regarding the way in which they ought to function may be analyzed separately from the way they do function— a study method common to courses in political theory. We shall concentrate on the problems of a functional analysis of the way these six processes operate in their separate cultures of the modern period.

The advantage of functional coherence, as we have said, is in the facilitation of hypothesis and theory formation in operational and empirically testable forms. Such hypotheses are properly stated as relationships between two or more variables, one of which is usually taken to be independent and the other dependent. We have further specified criterion variables which indicate the attributes of the dependent variables we are interested in. If the six processes indicated above were to be analyzed in this fashion, what independent, dependent, and criterion variables might be selected as most relevant? In no other place has the question been put this way, hence the formulation must proceed in a highly tentative fashion. Perhaps something like the arrangement on pages 590–592 would be useful, or at least suggestive.[1]

A sweeping formulation of this nature should be interpreted with great care, and its utility should be carefully defined. In the first place, it is illustrative, not comprehensive. In addition, the independent variable at one level of study is inevitably the dependent variable at the next level —"lower down," so to speak—in an endless chain of association. With-

---

[1] The above formulation may be criticized on the grounds that the criterion variables imply a series of democratic values. This is true, and hence the scheme might not be so useful in the analysis of dictatorships and non-Western politics. An alternative and normatively more neutral scheme might employ some variants of the "power" or "influence" concept as the criterion variables.

Independent variables	*Dependent variables*	*Criterion variables*

1. Electoral and public opinion processes

Electoral laws and institutions	Acts and attitudes	Participation: opportuni-
Group memberships of the pub-	of members of	ties, rates, channels,
lic and their personal mean-	the electorate,	modes
ings	party leaders,	Orientation: attitudes on
Cultural, subcultural, and per-	and candidates,	parties, issues, candi-
sonal norms and values	chiefly votes and	dates, ideologies
Exposure to mass media and	opinions	Leadership: selection, ex-
other sources of information		pression, distribution
and indoctrination		
Attachment to symbols and		
ideas which have become ego-		
involved for some segment of		
the population		
Economic and other stakes in		
decisions of government as		
perceived by the public		
Historical events significantly		
related to the above		

2. Legislative (policy) processes

Representative institutions and	Laws, resolutions,	Patterns of value alloca-
legal structure	appropriations,	tion: economic reward,
Constituency, party, bureau-	executive policies	legal protection, etc.
cratic, and interest-group	with the force of	Responsibility measured
pressures	law and other	in terms of long-run
Reference-group identifications	governmental	congruence between
of legislators (party, class,	policy formula-	public demands and
ethnic)	tions	legislative action
Values, attitudes, and per-		Effectiveness in solving
sonalities of legislators		social problems includ-
Recruitment processes of		ing both speed and
legislators		adequacy of solution
Group dynamic processes in the		
legislature		
Place of legislature in institu-		
tional matrix (separation of		
powers, relation to bureauc-		
racy, etc.)		
Legal (and customary) boun-		
daries of authority		

3. Administrative processes

Administrative structure and	Orders, rules, and	Efficiency measured in
organization	other "products"	terms of input and
Intraorganizational flow of	of the adminis-	output
communications, formal, and	trative branch	Morale measured in
informal		terms of satisfaction of
Extraorganizational flow of		participants
communications to and from		Responsibility measured

Independent variables	*Dependent variables*	*Criterion variables*
the public, interest groups, legislature, the executive and his staff		in terms of long-run congruence between executive-legislative policy and administrative action
Legal and other authority patterns		
Personnel selection		
Resources available and terms of their receipt		

4. Judicial and legal processes

Structure and formal organization of the judiciary	Decisions and opinions of the court; decisions to prosecute by government attorneys	Substantive allocation of values among individuals and groups in the population
Legal authority and competence of the judiciary		Congruence of decisions with precedent and legislative intent
Recruitment of judicial personnel		Autonomy of judicial processes in relation to electoral and legislative processes
Relation of judiciary to the bar, legislature, executive; and public values, attitudes, skills, and personalities of members of the judiciary		

5. International processes

Comparative national size, population, productivity, military potential	Acts of diplomacy, including making treaties, alliances, and war; exchanges of information, demands, goods, promises, etc.	Tension between nations, including official and popular attitudes
Cultural themes in each nation of war and peace, imperialism, internationalism, etc.		Balance of power in terms of military potential and alliance systems
Historical events influencing current attitudes (encirclement, entangling alliances, etc.)		Cultural assimilation and diffusion arising from communication, trade, and exchange of persons
Internal political forces finding expression in foreign policies (ethnic minority pressure, diversionary tactics of insecure regime, etc.)		
International institutions, their nature, power, operation		
International communication		
Geographic and strategic factors affecting international processes		

6. Integrative processes

Relation of each of the five processes and the complex of processes to the culture, modal personality, the econ-	Pattern of and interrelationship among the five processes men-	Production of satisfactions in terms of facilitation of the economy, advancement of cul-

Independent variables	*Dependent variables*	*Criterion variables*
omy, other social institutions, historical events	tioned above	tural values, reduction of conflict and other social disutilities
		Distribution of values in the society as affected by governmental institutions and processes
		Efficiency of governmental operation in terms of coordination of purpose and action among the several branches of government
		Normative judgments on the above in terms of minority rights, freedom of choice, equality, self-expression, etc.

out operational indexes for the terms employed, only a loose manner of formulation is possible. And, finally, there has been less effort to achieve logical exactitude in this formulation because of the greater value assigned to a generalized statement of what political scientists are in fact interested in.

Grouped in this way, however, the field achieves some minimal coherence in three senses. There is a consolidation and focus upon relatively fewer dependent variables; the targets for research are made more explicit. Second, the institutions and processes of government are brought together in a manner which gives a clearer picture of their interrelationships. Third, and political science badly needs monitoring in this respect, analysis of structure is made to serve the needs of process analysis; the articulation of an organization, the legal bones of an institution, are significant only as they affect the results of organizational and institutional processes. But, of course, in spite of these advantages, the actual molecular interaction schemes in each of the process categories are extremely heterogeneous. We have come but a short way toward functional coherence but, for now, a greater step would involve a loss of view of the institutions and processes which the discipline has been called upon to explain.

PSYCHOLOGY FOR POLITICAL SCIENTISTS

Looking across the boundary into a cognate field, one's perspectives are inevitably warped and one's vision is myopic. The farther reaches of the field seem less promising; only the parts near at hand offer adequate "pasture," so to speak. So, as the political scientist examines the areas of psychology, his attention focuses inevitably on literature such as that dealing with leadership, public opinion, authoritarianism, and other topics which have the clearest substantive applicability to his own problems. Physiological psychology, sensory perception, psychology dealing with orders lower than humans on the phylogenetic scale, and child psychology seem somewhat less fruitful. The enormous literature of these fields seems harder to profit from, although future research may well discover considerable political relevance in these areas.

These remarks inevitably raise the question of the place of learning theory in the application of psychology to political science. Courses are given in "psychological laws and theory for social scientists," in which the "laws" are learning theory laws. This area of psychology claims a universality, precision, and deductive quality which should make it broadly useful to other disciplines. The kind of behavior which political science seeks to explain is learned behavior. But in spite of these factors, learning theory is not the favored medium for informing the political scientist of the reasons for his respondents' behavior. This may be partly because of the paucity of literature. Aside from works by Dollard, Miller, Skinner, Logan et al., Osgood, Kubie, and a few others [133, 44, 163, 120, 139, 140, 95], little applied literature is available. But allowing for this aspect of the problem, it has been the author's experience that the common, and perhaps too facile, criticisms of "rat psychology" have some merit:

1. The translation of a theory derived from experiments with non-verbal animals in satisfying largely physiological needs to verbal animals in their more complex (political) response patterns becomes too tenuous.

2. In the S-*O*-R paradigm, the desire for purity of inference has led to the stripping from the *O* of those subjective, intrapersonality, or postulated qualities which give social science its most fruitful (and often measurably verifiable) ideas.

3. It offers small utility in the first step of the research process—the isolation of the "best" variable.

What are the secondary drives, the operating incentives, the precise habits in a complex social situation? Learning theory does not help very much in answering such questions, and if it is applied without information from other areas of psychology, it will lead to positively wrong conclusions.

What, then, are the areas of psychology which offer the greatest contribution to the political scientist? Broadly speaking they are the two fields of social psychology and clinical psychology and, we might add, the interrelationships of the two. Each of these fields of psychology, of course, has its more or less standardized subdivisions, as a glance at any of the current texts will show. Rather than review these familiar categories, however, we shall attempt to outline the divisions of the field which appear to give the greatest commutability between psychology and political science. We are interested in social behavior and attitude formation as this is relevant to the six political processes outlined above. How, then, does psychology come to grips with these processes?

Social Interaction and Influence

Let us look at the problem first in terms of social interaction and influence. This occurs in many different *contexts*. It is modified by the *numbers of people involved*. The *vehicle of influence* is significant. The *degree or level of influence* and *role of influencer* are important and may be summarized as matters of leadership. The *content* of communication affects the nature of interactive responses and is a matter of importance in predicting their outcome. Psychology offers material and ideas of the greatest significance to political scientists in these several problem areas. One recent diagram of the interrelationship of these and other elements of interaction is presented by Janis, Hovland, et al. [79, p. 4].

Contexts. The political scientist is well aware that the context of a decision is a most relevant consideration in every political process; indeed, he may be more aware of the context than of the nature of the processes taking place therein. The division of psychology into the separate study of psychological processes in different situations facilitates the borrowing process and tends to minimize errors of application. Thus industrial psychology offers to the student of public administration a fund of information and theory of particular utility; he will be familiar with the Hawthorne studies [127, 146, 147], the work of William Foote Whyte [191], Guetzgow [64], Chapple [33], Bavelas [10, 12], and others working in this area in their several ways.

The community or neighborhood context is of prime significance in voting and public opinion studies. Whether the psychological principles and research come from an anthropologist, a sociologist, or a psychologist will be a matter of indifference to the political scientist (as indeed it seems to be for others in the social sciences). He will profit from the studies of Yankee City, Plainville, a southern town, Jonesville, Akron, Decatur, Middletown, Atlanta, New Haven [43, 44, 74, 82, 86, 121, 122, 186, 187, 189], and so forth, in searching for the dynamics of power or the pattern of influence. Such neighborhood studies as those dealing with Westgate and Regent Hill have also been fertile in their suggestiveness and direct application to political problems [52, 53].

The same is true of other contexts. Research on the social movement [25, 68, 99, 174], the radio audience [24, 109, 154], and the problem-solving group [66] is more transferable if the context of the interactive principles is similar in both the psychological study and the political problem to be investigated.

Numbers of people involved. Psychology has, fortunately, devoted attention to psychic phenomena of groups of all sizes. For the political scientist, the focus of attention is sometimes partially defined by the size of the group; he may become interested in small elite groups when he studies political parties and in mass phenomena when he examines the electorate. The organization of this latter area of mass phenomena by Roger Brown in the *Handbook of Social Psychology* may serve as an excellent starting point for the student of public order, revolutions and social movements, and even audience research [16, pp. 833–876]. Students can borrow freely from the principles elaborated in psychological studies of these phenomena. And the same is true of the study of small groups which has flourished in the postwar decades. As Katz and Lazarsfeld point out, the discovery of the small group by the Mayo, Dickson, and Roethlisberger studies in industrial research, by Lloyd Warner and associates in community studies, by Stouffer and associates in the Army studies, and by their own research in communications has highlighted the significance of the face-to-face personal community in different phases of social behavior [86, pp. 34–42]. The political scientist is not without awareness of the significance of such groups—as the studies of various "kitchen cabinets," revolutionary cabalas, and political caucuses will show—but he has no systematic theory. Thus the separate treatment of social interaction among groups of different sizes offers assistance to the political scientist in a more easily transferable form.

The vehicle of influence. To take two broad categories, the vehicles of influence may be divided into mass media and mass communication sources on the one hand and personal influences on the other. The literature on mass communication and propaganda is extensive and rich, as the bibliography *International Communication and Political Opinion* [164] by Bruce Smith and Chitra Smith shows. The recent work of Hovland, Lazarsfeld, and others further documents the fact. Within this category, of course, distinctions may be made regarding the various influences of radio, newspapers, magazines, libraries, and, after World War II, television. Studies on the relation between exposure to these sources and voting behavior by Lazarsfeld and associates, Berelson and associates, and Campbell and associates now form an integral part of the political science literature [13, 22, 111].

Personal influence, for the moment, will be taken to mean face-to-face influence of one person on another without benefit of intervening media. It has been studied in a number of situations—institutions [81, 136], housing projects [52, 53], factories [147], communities [74, 132], street corners [190], and in the voting studies mentioned previously. The study of personal influence merges, in one sense, into the small-group studies of the induction of opinion and the roles people take in problem-solving groups; in another sense, it merges into the study of leadership, of which personal influence is a part. The clear relevance of personal influence to the decisions not only of voters, but of candidates, legislators, executives, administrators, and judges has been insufficiently exploited, but some steps have been taken in this direction in the analysis of the administrative and the electoral processes.

Levels of influence (leadership). Dividing political phenomena in terms of the relationship between what might be called different "levels" of influence and not according to the nature of the source, we move into the sphere of leadership proper. Here those phenomena of personal influence mentioned above might be grouped with more distant leadership relations. Among others, two kinds of distinctions are made in political science in this regard: distinctions between elite and mass, and distinctions between formal and informal leadership. The former refers to differences in any society or community between those who have ascribed or achieved status of a given order and who have easy access to official or titular leaders and those who do not. In this area, there is little psychological literature of importance, although there could be. The distinction between formal and informal leadership refers to the contrast between those occupying offices (roles) which give their possessors formal authority and those who have no such offices. Here the psychological and sociological literature is rich and informative and, indeed, the distinction merges into a host of other fruitful distinctions of types of leadership [8, 48, 59, 62].

Although in general the study of leadership has turned away from trait analysis [58], etc., the qualities that are salient in a given situation are a significant area of inquiry. They may be significant because they refer to the needs which the leader fulfills by his acts, or they may be qualities which make his leadership effective. In this latter group, the interpersonal skills, the intellectual powers, and the task skills serve as foci of attention in some analyses [15]. In other studies, the situation is the major variable; in still others, it is the nature of the followers [151]. Whatever the focus, it is clear that the problem is significant for such relations as may exist between candidates and voters, political bosses and ward heelers, prime ministers and back benchers, bureau chiefs and their subordinates—in short, across a wide range of political phenomena.

Content of communication. As is well known, the content of discussion or the themes of communication affect responses in significant ways. One of the reasons why people are said to avoid politics and religion in discussion is the divisive influence of these themes, which is partly a function of the high affective content of such topics [150]. On the other hand, it is sometimes said that political knowledge serves as a social lubricant in discussion [149]. Obviously content and audience are inter-related in complicated patterns. Some of the psychological research on different content items of significance to political scientists are ethnic prejudices [3, 187], class identifications [32], support for the United Nations and internationalist sentiment generally [182], challenges to property arrangements [82], and others.

Some Significant Personal Variables

We have been examining some selected kinds of interactive situations, their participants, and their content. Psychology has much to say on these subjects which is of relevance to political science. But psychology has equally important material on the nature of the individuals participating in these processes. In some ways, of course, this is the reciprocal of the earlier material, but since we have by no means limited ourselves to logically exclusive categories (nor does the discipline so divide itself), we may examine these elements briefly to indicate their relevance. Among these relevant personal variables, *knowledge, attitudes and opinions, ideologies,* and the "deeper" *personality needs* of the individual are especially significant.

Knowledge. One general area of inquiry—suggested by such terms as "cognition," "information theory," and "theory (sociology?) of knowl-edge"—offers to the interdisciplinary specialist, if we may use this title, an open sesame to new understanding of political phenomena. Democratic theory assumes a given level of information among the electorate and, even more important, among the legislators, diplomats, and judges. Studies showing the way in which information is contaminated by prefer-ence and the uses to which data may be put in the service of a prejudice have shaken the foundations of this theory. Political science needs to know not only who knows what, but also why knowledge in selected elite and mass populations assumes its particular proportions and content at a given time. Belief systems serve social and psychic needs for the individual which are most easily analyzed in what may be called "psychosocial" terms [19, 94, 155].

Attitudes and opinions. It is probably true that attitude and opinion research represents the area of psychological science which first made contact with political science along a broad front. After all, opinions are the data of primary reference for the analysis of electoral and legislative processes, particularly when expressed in some such register as an election or a roll call. It is, moreover, no accident that a judicial decision is referred to as an "opinion." Furthermore, many of the earlier attitude studies dealt with attitudes having political content—liberalism and con-servatism [88, 123], attitudes toward fascism and communism [85], attitudes toward issues of the day [35, 67]. Thus theories of attitude formation such as the synthesis offered by Sherif and Cantril [158] and the theories of dogmatism and opinionation developed by Rokeach [148] have an obvious relevance and application—in this case, not merely by analogy or theoretically, but also in their specific content.

Ideologies. The analysis of combinations of attitudes, information, beliefs, and values into what is loosely called an "ideology" is still relatively unsophisticated in both disciplines—indeed, each asks wholly different questions in this area. The political scientist wants to know the merits of the arrangement of institutions proposed by each ideology. He argues the case for democracy, for socialism, for the welfare states, and, elsewhere, for communism or monarchy or fascism. He argues in familiar terms, employing logic, historical illustration, assumed facts about the nature of man, deductions from ethical premises, and so forth. The psychologist is interested in why the individual has adopted this particular ideology and penetrates the merits of the case only in so far as its postulates about the human mind requires correction. In asking what an ideology is, the political scientist wants to know what system of ideas logically coheres, given certain premises; the psychologist wants to know what items of belief are associated in what ways and for what reasons. Both political scientists and psychologists want to know who has accepted a particular ideology, but for different reasons. The political scientist usually is more interested in the results of a given pattern of acceptance, the psychologist in the light a given distribution can shed on the etiology of the belief. The differences in interest have produced differences in methods. The psychologist can describe the particular acceptance pattern of a belief system in a given population with some accuracy [21, 22, 173]. He can do this by survey methods, giving absolute and relative distributions; he can show the dimensions of acceptance and relative intensities; he may say something about which beliefs are "prior" to other beliefs; by use of such factorial schemes as those employed by Cattell [31], he can give a particular interpretation of ideological patterns with multiple dimensions [1, 5, 49, 167, 168, 169, 170, 171, 172].

As for the analysis of ideologies or other attitudes in an etiological fashion, each discipline has something to contribute. Political science may be able to say something about why certain groups of Southerners are ethnocentric conservatives or why the Germans did not happily adopt the democratic tenets of the Weimar Republic. But the psychologist can say something about why Mac, in Lindner's *Fifty-Minute Hour,* became a Communist walking the Baltimore streets [115], and why the Germans found a totalitarian regime so congenial [41, 55, 152]. Each has a claim to special skill in interpreting some facet of the origins of political belief and, as always, only the combination of these skills will produce that full and manifold interpretation which is scientifically most satisfactory.

Personality needs. We turn now to the general question of personality research and theory and its relation to political science. The theoretical relevance is obvious and has long been recognized without benefit of the data which psychology now makes available. But the specific interpretation of a given event is very difficult. Consider, for example, the problem of interpreting the outcome of the Yalta conference in terms which give appropriate scope to the personalities of the three great participants. Everyone will recognize that their feelings—hostility, dependency, cynicism, paranoic fear, intelligence, sense of reality, and even wit and humor—were relevant. But how to appraise their operation? Each of the principals was operating within a framework of certain national objectives; each had advisers whose influence was intermittent but often crucial; each said things for bargaining purposes which should be appraised as only partially representing a belief or attitude held at the time. And so forth. Under these circumstances, the correct procedure is not to abandon the field, but to study the congruence of the psychological factors present with the pattern of choices made in the context of the historical, institutional, and social forces active at the time, and to interpret the findings cautiously. Perhaps such speculation is uncongenial to the psychologist, just as it often is to the political scientist, although anyone who has read Freud's interpretation of Leonardo da Vinci and of Michaelangelo's *Moses* will understand how very absorbing such an exercise can be. But, of course, there are psychologists of many persuasions.

However difficult to appraise, the personality of the judge, the legislator, the executive, the voter, or the foreign minister is in almost every case an independent variable of significant proportions. What have the psychologists to offer along these lines? First, I think, is a point of view. This is best expressed by the opening sentence of the Smith, Bruner, and White study, *Opinions and Personality:* "Of what use to a man are his opinions?" [165, p. 1]. Once the question is put in this fashion, the individual's psychic needs served by his beliefs, attitudes, and decisions inevitably come into view—although by themselves they do not by any means provide a full answer to the question. How does the adoption of a fascist ideology by some Middle Western American help him to solve his intrapsychic problems? Legislators with similar constituencies, faced with the same evidence, decide differently. What needs are served by the conformist? By the rebel? These questions urgently need further research. Personality theory has paid too little attention to the way that a given role or institutional setting will evoke latent attributes and structure response patterns among persons of different personality qualities.

The second element of personality research which political science can find useful is the isolation of variables or personal qualities which are psychologically viable. The language of the political scientist is the language of the layman in this respect; he has tended to focus upon moralistic terms such as "integrity," "idealism," "strength of character," or terms thought to be qualities of leaders, such as "decisiveness," "courage," "independence." There has been a focus upon qualities which, in spite of the slightly bad repute of the term, one might call "traits." They have emerged from clinical experience (dependency, autism, split libido) and from projective and questionnaire techniques in testing situations (anti-intraception, which a clinician might call "resistance," instrumentalism, anomie) and they have given the political scientist interested in the qualities of his actors something to work with. In the development of concepts of authoritarianism in particular, the political scientist has found scope for new interpretation of old phenomena [36, pp. 123–196].

Along with borrowing views on what the salient features of personality are, political scientists have borrowed psychodynamic concepts which give a clue to the way the mind may deal with political or other material. One of the first—and still one of the best—formulations of political belief is expressed in Lasswell's formula $p\}d\}r = P$, stating that private motives displaced onto public objects and rationalized into some political belief system constitute "political man" [105, p. 75]. An understanding of the processes of repression, sublimation, reaction formation, identification, generalization, and so forth, is essential to a comprehension of the working out of this formula. The formula, however, is only a partial statement of the dynamics of political belief, and the more comprehensive scheme of Smith, Bruner, and White gives a closer approximation of reality. One of the most useful concepts involved in such analysis, incidentally, lies in conflict theory, where the "closeness of opposites" finds a legitimate rationale. For example, Fillmore Sanford has found that authoritarians tend either to reject or wholeheartedly to accept a domineering figure, while nonauthoritarians, free of authority tension, treat the problem of his domineering manner with calm detachment, thus showing how the theory of the closeness of opposites explains apparently irrational authoritarian behavior [151].

A working knowledge of adult psychic processes, traits, syndromes, and types might be adequate for most political analysis, but there are occasions when it is necessary to go further. In the discussion of ideology above, we noted that the psychologist and psychiatrist can help to explain why some single individual such as Lindner's Mac becomes a Communist or Adorno's Mack becomes an authoritarian. In order to do this, of course, more than an understanding of the mechanisms of the adult mind is necessary; it is also necessary to know such bodies of genetic theory as are included in Fenichel's *The Psychoanalytic Theory of Neuroses* [50].[2] In such an instance, the wide panoply of psychiatric theory is called upon, for the analyst of the origins of political belief is

[2] This work has a bibliography of 1,646 items.

required to know something about why childhood experiences create the qualities in people which later produce politically significant choices. In the case studies of Almond, Gilbert, Lasswell, Lindner [5, 60, 105, 115] and others, the genesis of the predispositions which were receptive to deviant beliefs can only be fully appreciated with a working knowledge of psychoanalytical theory. It is essential to be conversant with Oedipal theory, the theory of libidinal development, the roles of id, ego, and superego at various points in this development, for example, either in their pristine Freudian form, as modified by Fromm and Horney, or as interpreted through the anxiety theory of Sullivan as it departs from the basic Freudian doctrines [55, 56, 57, 70, 71, 176, 177].

In order to avoid misunderstanding, it is best to point to the limited applicability of this part of personality theory in understanding the decision-making process. To understand the judicial process, we do not need to know the resolution of the Oedipal situation by the judges. We need not interpret most voting decisions in terms of father cathexis [cf. 20, pp. 262–280, 399–436]. Only when we are dealing with central, salient, and "deep" features of a person's political orientation is it useful to enter these further reaches of personality theory and borrow from theoretical hypotheses which, it must be confessed, are still somewhat speculative.

We turn now from a focus on individual psychology, where problems imply questions about the personality of specific persons, to areas where questions relate to the psychic qualities of groups, subcultures (such as classes and ethnic groups), and entire populations. Here is a vast new area of special relevance to political science which has been somewhat unevenly explored. This is the area of national-character analysis. Handicapped by earlier unscientific formulations, a sequence of authors, including Wilhelm Reich (at least in his earlier work), Fromm, Dicks, Adorno and associates, and more particularly Kardiner and Inkeles and Levinson, has recently contributed a wealth of theories and data for the inquiring political scientists [1, 41, 42, 55, 76, pp. 977–1020; 83, 84, 143]. Indeed, seldom have psychological theories found their way into the body of political science as quickly as these national-character studies have done. Nor is the reason far to seek. The unit of analysis for much of political science is the nation as embodied in studies on the relation between nations, the governmental structure of the nation, the ideologies prevalent in the nation, national political responses to crisis situations, and others. In this sense it is a holistic science. Theories of national character fit easily into such a comprehensive analytical scheme and offer insights into events which previously were quite mysterious. (It is not suggested that all mysteries have now been resolved, by a very wide margin.)

The possibilities and the limitations of using national-character concepts as tools in explaining political phenomena may be illustrated by a glance at some of the work done on the rise of the Nazi regime in Germany. A political scientist can find excellent historical reasons for the rise of Nazism. Among them would be lack of experience with democratic processes, the unpopular sponsorship of the Weimar Constitution, the loophole afforded by Article 48 (providing for emergency powers) in that constitution, the challenge from the Left, the destruction of familiar and orderly status lines, the ideological heritage of imperialist thought and the glorification of the military, the late unification of Germany, the fright of propertied interests, the destruction of part of the middle class through inflation, the heritage of anti-Semitism, and so forth. But the persistence of these institutional arrangements and preferences and the ideological content of popular attitudes and belief patterns are not self-explanatory. In any event, why the growth and final selection of Nazism by such a substantial portion of the public, when other possibilities might have offered equal relief? Underlying institutions and beliefs and influencing the content of Nazism were personality factors which contribute to an explanation of this particular historical event. The concept of *Einklang* between ideology and personality, first brought out by Fromm and developed by Dicks, has great utility to the political scientists [41, 55]. And in studying the relationship between nations, and even warlike attributes of nations, the study of the modal distributions of personality may be important.

As in the study of individual ideological choices, some scholars have sought to go beyond the present configuration of character traits and assault the problem of the genesis of these traits. Here, of course, the work of Kardiner and his anthropological associates Linton, DuBois, and West, together with the fine summary by Child of recent studies on the socializing process are most significant [34, pp. 655–692; 83, 84]. Taking seriously the aphorism "The hand that rocks the cradle rules the world," such studies seek to link the culturally prevalent means of socializing the child with the modal personalities of adults in their respective cultures. These, in turn, become the bases of belief systems which support particular institutional arrangements.

Here again, a caveat is in order. Those who seek to make a direct link between a given basic personality type and given formal institutional arrangement transcend the implications of the theory and violate the data. It is certainly possible that nations whose citizens tend to rank high on the authoritarian personality scale may have democratic institutions, while those whose citizens tend to rank low may have hierarchical institutions with a minimum of shared power. There is some suggestion in comparative studies not yet made public that Belgians rank high in authoritarianism along with Germans, but Belgium has representative institutions which have endured for generations. It is at least possible that an even balance between conflicting ethnic groups within a country will make for a distribution of power which is best arranged to the satisfaction of the public by some parliamentary system where each group can veto the acts of the other. A dictatorship would not serve this need. Yet, with this caveat in mind, within the interstices of the formal arrangements, so to speak, one may still find the expression of modal personality characteristics; a dictatorship may operate in an equalitarian style, and representative government may behave in an authoritarian way. As with the study of personality itself, the clues for the operational principles of a governmental system may be subtle and hard to ferret out. Probably because of some doubts about the national-character hypotheses and a desire to get closer to the immediate causes of political behavior, research will now turn increasingly to belief systems, cultural values, and anthropological concepts.

In this brief overview, we have spoken of the areas of psychology which have marked or partially exploited relevance for the problems of political science. We have first noted that psychology offers specialized studies in different contexts, thus making their application to political problems more visible. We have noted the utility in dividing the interaction process according to the number of participants. Then, in examining the kinds of stimuli to which persons respond in political situations, we have referred to the applicability of research in mass communications and in more intimate personal influences. The area of leadership studies—small perhaps in social psychology, but significant for political science—is a central area for further investigation. The analysis of different themes and contents offers the political scientist data of immediate utility. The nature of knowledge, opinions, and ideologies—all subjects of psychological research—is relevant to many political problems. We have suggested that by looking at the areas of psychology which might be included under the heading "personality," political scientists have found informative material for their studies of the six political processes noted earlier. Finally, the implications of national-character research for larger-scale, macroscopic investigation have been indicated. Now we turn to the more difficult task of attempting some theoretical formulations which will serve to bring the substantive findings of these areas into focus on political science problems.

A FRAMEWORK FOR PSYCHOPOLITICAL STUDY

With some analysis of the relevant elements of the two fields behind us, we are in a position to consider the possibility of systematic laws and theories covering the area where the two fields converge. A thorough analysis of this area of convergence would require a thorough compilation of the relevant psychological hypotheses deriving from theory and experimental work. These hypotheses should be annotated to show the differences in measuring instruments and in terminology, synthesized into a smaller set of overarching laws, and put into the unique settings of the political decision maker. We will, perforce, be more modest and set forth a framework into which such a general theory might be placed, giving a few exemplary laws to illustrate our intention.

What kind of framework? One might employ a Freudian model; the emphasis would be placed upon the intrapsychic structure and tensions which produced certain response patterns. This is unsuitable, however, in a situation where the elements of the environment are often the most important features of the analysis. Simon offers a number of specific models referring, among other things, to group equilibrium and group survival, but they are too limited for the broad problem here at stake [160, 161]. Snyder and his associates suggest a fruitful model for decision theory; he emphasizes the nature of the decision and the process by which it is to be made, who is to make it in terms of the properties of the decision makers and their social roles, and where (at what level of society, in what context) the decision is to be made [166]. Tolman employs a model which is comprehensive and penetrating and which synthesizes in a coherent pattern elements of learning theory, Freudian psychology, and Lewinian psychology [180]. Either of the latter two might serve our purposes, but we prefer to simplify the model and to focus upon three elements: the decision, the decision makers, and the environment. In doing this we are erecting a simple S-O-R paradigm; the decision is the response (R), the decision makers are the organisms (O), and the environment is the stimulus (S).

Now let us clarify a few points with respect to this model. First, although "stimulus" language is notoriously ambiguous, we prefer the S to Lasswell's E (for environment) because it suggests a specification of the features of the environment which are operational or effective in any given instance. Second, we use it without implying that changes in response patterns are always the product of changes in the environmental stimuli. Of course, the personality has a dynamic of its own, attitudes and beliefs extinguish, the processes of "cognitive dissonance" may be at work—and all of this can produce response changes while the environment remains as constant as it ever can. In the third place, we specify two types of environmental stimuli, the general social environment S_{se} and the institutional environment S_{ie}. This is merely for convenience in analyzing political situations where, for the most part, the decision makers are located in institutional settings such as a legislature, a bureaucracy, or a court. This model, of course, is not a new one, even for social or political analysis. Roethlisberger uses it in his study of the behavior of factory workers [146, p. 21]; Leighton employs it in his analysis of *The Governing of Men* [112, p. 384]; and Berelson and associates find it useful in their study of voting behavior [13, p. 278].

One further question emerges: What is the relation of this S-*O*-R model to the stipulation of independent, dependent, and criterion variables in the six political processes discussed earlier? The relationship is a simple one. In the S-*O*-R model, we speak only of a chain of events with a specified outcome (R). In the earlier analysis, we combine S and *O* and refer to them as independent variables. Furthermore, we indicate the attributes or qualities of R in which we are especially interested and which will be used as criteria in appraising and analyzing R. Now let us turn, in order, to the analysis of the decision makers, the decisions, the institutional environment, and the social environment.

The Deciders

The *O*, which in the original paradigm stood for organism, is here to be represented by men in selected offices, but the office is not part of the organism. In focusing on the *O*, we are interested in the flesh and blood men, the occupants of the offices, not the rules and regulations, customs, and so forth, which bind them. These men might be designated as follows:

Process	*O = decision maker*
Electoral (in broad sense)	Electors and other participants
	Candidates
	Party officials
Legislative	Legislators
	Chief executives (President, governor, mayor)
Administrative	Administrators
	Chief executives
Judicial	Judges, jurymen, and prosecuting attorneys
International	Secretary of State and advisers, including National Security Council, etc.
	Diplomatic and military personnel
	Chief executive
Integrative	Combined interaction of these decision makers ($O_1, O_2, O_3, \ldots O_n$)

A political scientist glancing at this arrangement will be quick to point out that, in the legislative process, the decisions of the leaders of interest groups are important; in the administrative process, the decisions of the members of the legislative appropriations committee are crucial; and in the international process, the decisions of the electors are a most significant matter. Of course, this is true but, since all the world is interrelated, it is best to take it segmentally for analytical purposes. In doing so, we may treat one man's decision as another man's stimulus. That is the way we proceed in this case.

We are interested in the qualities of each such decision maker which will provide internal stimuli for action or which will screen the stimuli of the outside and institutional world in such a way as to affect the decision. We are, therefore, interested in their attitudes, information, values, skills, and personalities with particular reference to psychic needs. We are interested in the recruitment processes for these offices and the effects of these offices on the individual because of the possibilities of systematically skewed distributions of attitudes and skills. Thus the hypothesis that men seek office in public life because they are attracted to positions of power which serve to compensate them for their own low estimates of themselves is a crucial one [102, p. 39]. Another hypothesis dealing with the training and self-selection of administrators in such a way as systematically to incapacitate them for broad policy decisions is an equally important idea for investigation [130]. Lane finds that people who, in a specified sense, can be described as "strong," "happy," and "moral" are more likely than others to participate in political life [98, pp. 147–162].

This latter idea of Merton's suggests a particular facet of study, the analysis of the O as a dependent variable over time, with the influences of the office as the several independent variables. Certain hypotheses are currently "in the air," so to speak. It is thought that judges change their values in a conservative direction as a result of their tenure of office on the bench; it is believed that parochial politicians become more "statesmanlike" after several terms in Washington. But the dimensions, scope, and even direction of these attitude changes remain for investigation.

Perhaps the skills of the decision makers is one area which has been more readily appreciated by the public and political scientists than any other. The skills of the candidate for judicial position may be considered formally to be legal skills, and informally to be "political" or interpersonal skills bringing him to a position of high visibility and influence. The skills of the civil servant are likely to be examined in some detail at the threshold of his career through tests which have much in common with the testing done by psychologists in other areas. For the foreign service, certain language-aptitude tests have been employed as screening devices.

Qualities of personality which may be considered useful or requisite for different kinds of office have occasionally been examined and more frequently discussed. For elective office, the lore informs us of certain allegedly necessary qualities such as extraversion, energy, strong personality (suitable for father imagery), but little is actually known. Perhaps such findings as Fillmore Sanford's discovery that both equalitarians and authoritarians are more likely to select leaders for face-to-face relationships from persons who rated low on authoritarianism [151] will find a place in political history. The skills and personalities of those who become decision makers through elective office should be more nearly specified in further research along these lines. However that may be, the qualities of the O persons (decision makers), the selective processes which give bias to the distribution of these qualities, and the influence of their training and experience in office upon these qualities will serve as the substance of the hypotheses to be made in this area. Further research on the influence of location in the structure of a group (particularly location at communication centers) and upon leadership selection and certification (legitimation) will prove helpful in this area of study [86, pp. 100–115]. A start has been made in the elite studies of the Radir project at Stanford [113].

The Decisions

We have the decisions designated as the R in the paradigm. These decisions might be analyzed in a number of ways,[3] but we have limited ourselves here to two: a classification which remains close to the substantive or topical content of the decisions, and a classification which abstracts certain dimensions common to decisions on a wide variety of topics. With respect to each of these classes of decisions, the questions we ask are these: What psychological dimensions are most likely to affect decisions of this class? How do they affect them?

The following categories of decision contents, close to common modes of perception, may serve as a starting point:

Decisions affecting the security of the entire nation vis-à-vis other nations (expenditures for armaments, declaration of war)

Decisions allocating scarce resources to one group within the nation (public housing, tidal oil lands)

Decisions regulating the activities of some group within the nation (Sherman act, Taft-Hartley act)

Decisions on personnel selection with implied reference-group identifications: regional, ethnic, class, party (elections, appointment of Cabinet officer [46, 106, 166])

Decisions affecting culturally sanctioned traditional beliefs (use of the flag, "desegregation," national honor)

[3] There is a growing literature on decision making [46, 106, 166] which may soon occupy a place in the literature comparable to that of attitudes and opinions at the present time. For the most part, however, we shall refer to the more general theory of response.

Procedural decisions (administrative reorganization, speeding up the
judicial calendar)

The nature of the decision to be made is a significant datum for
the psychologist for several reasons. In the first place, certain kinds of
decisions seem to have a close relation to certain specific attitudinal complexes; they seem to call forth specific qualities of an affected person's
personality. Illustrative of this operation is the relationship between
World Politics and Personal Insecurity discussed by Lasswell [104]. Also,
as the California authoritarian-personality study makes clear, reference
to foreign affairs tends to evoke in-group out-group dichotomies among
people of an ethnocentric orientation. Following this latter theme, one
might suppose that a President or senator with ethnocentric sentiments
would hesitate to trust allies, seek to concentrate resources under the control
of his own nation, place the worst interpretation on the motives of foreign
diplomats, regard the acts of foreign nations in different perspectives according to whether or not the acts were performed by Western nations,
and in other ways reveal his ethnocentrism in an important degree. This
area of decision making, then, might tap qualities in a decision maker which
would be irrelevant in other areas. And the theory of ethnocentrism,
prejudice, and authoritarianism would help to explain decisions in this
area, regardless of whether the decision maker was a judge looking at the
constitutionality of marital law in Hawaii during the war, or an administrator making a report on aid to underdeveloped countries, or the Secretary of State negotiating a treaty.

Although the above classification, since it is so close to the descriptive
level, yields relatively little theory of a broad generalizability, nevertheless
one can find in the literature some suggested relationships between psychological variables and these classes of decisions. For example, on matters of foreign policy and personality, some illustrative hypotheses supported—though, of course, not validated—by research evidence may be
stated as follows:

The greater the degree of basic psychosexual conflict a person has, the
less will he generalize his everyday pattern of aggressive behavior to
foreign policy questions [35, p. 231].

The less a person is willing to examine his own motives and character
(anti-intraceptive,) the more likely he is to view the world as made
up of in-groups and out-groups [1].

The more personally insecure a person is, the more he is likely to use
foreign policy material in a projective and unrealistic manner [104].

Decisions allocating scarce resources have not been so clearly linked to
personality or attitudinal traits; the economic interests are more visible
in many of these decisions, and, as is often the case, they tend to smother

other attitudinal or motivational variables. Nevertheless it would be interesting if the fact that the anxious man is more future-oriented than others had a bearing on the conservation issue and on receptiveness to appeals for preserving resources for the future. Regulatory activities offer scope for punitiveness. Is it the case that men with similar economic situations respond to issues of regulation according to their extrapunitive, intrapunitive, or impunitive dispositions? Work along these lines has proved fruitful in examining the psychological foundations of foreign policy attitudes; it might also be helpful here [35].

Personnel decisions involve, among other things, the self-selection of the men themselves. A recent study in New Haven suggests that politicians who run for office are substantially different from those who are appointed to office: the electoral candidates have a uniform pattern of high need achievement, high need for power, and low need for affiliation. The appointed politicians (ward chairmen, city officers) did not follow this pattern [17]. But, here, of course, the main focus is upon the decisions of those doing the selecting.

Decisions on the selection of personnel are, to a very large extent, decisions with a reference-group basis. At the electoral level, party identification and ethnic identification play enormously significant parts in the decision-making process. At the level of presidential appointment, party preference is, of course, often a preliminary screening question—followed by considerations of regional representation, ethnicity, and other matters of public importance. Often equally important, though a matter of private consideration only, if possible, are more intimate associations such as "old-school-tie" connections (Sumner Welles and F.D.R.), Battery D (General Vaughn and Truman), or neighborhood friends (Morgenthau and F.D.R.). The study of the salient reference groups in a voting situation has taught us of the overwhelming importance of party identification, even where the party is a distinct minority [134, 2], and of intensity of ethnic group attachment in party preference [13, pp. 64–76]. The study of reference-group identifications among appointing officers of the government might contribute to a better understanding of the appointment process.

Decisions affecting cultural norms and culturally approved symbols elicit the above attitudes in varying degrees, but also seem to open up challenges to feelings about conventional behavior, tradition, and the usual order of things. Conventionalism is a feature of the authoritarian syndrome and, indeed, it has been shown that ethnocentrics become anxious when, in the process of attacking the minority out-group, traditional symbols are also attacked [14]. Such conventionalism is, of course, a kind of noneconomic conservatism and probably the best measure of noneconomic conservatism of this kind is McClosky's conservatism scale.

McClosky finds that, compared to others, "the extreme conservatives are easily the most hostile and suspicious, the most rigid and compulsive, the quickest to condemn others for their imperfections or weaknesses, the most intolerant, the most easily moved to scorn and disappointment in others, the most inflexible and unyielding in their perceptions and judgments" [123, p. 37]. In the same way procedural decisions open certain issues dealing with order, authority, and stability to which some are especially sensitive [160].

We have sought to show that certain types of decisions evoke attitudinal dimensions which are, so to speak, peculiarly their own: they have a psychological domain where they have a special home. The point is not that all attitudes are topic-bound, but rather that some issues come to people's attention in such a way as to evoke one underlying structure rather than another. Yet the classification used, close as it is to the way the political world structures our thinking, may not be the best one for this purpose. Consider five other possibilities:

1. One of the most usual situations in politics is characterized by the conflict between diffuse, distant, less visible, benefits to a large number of unorganized people, and a concentrated, immediate, highly visible, benefit to a smaller and well-organized group. We call this, rather loosely, a conflict between the public interest and a special interest. Although special interests clothe themselves with "public interest," and the merits of the case are often obscure, the decisions characterized by this situation (patients versus doctors, passengers versus railroads, future consumers versus lumber interests) are often easy to recognize.

2. Berelson and associates have drawn our attention to the distinction between issues which engage noneconomic values, such as ethnic loyalties, moral sentiments, personality appeals of candidates, or concepts of duty on the one hand, and the issues which enlist a person's economic interests on the other. The first, they call "style" issues, the second, they term "position" issues. Individual (idiosyncratic) motivational and attitudinal qualities are usually more influential in determining a person's views on style issues than they are on position issues [13, pp. 184–85].

3. Decisions on some issues are divisive; others reinforce the national consensus. Some decision makers stress the national unity, the high moral purpose of the nation, the approved norms of tolerance, honesty, individual effort; others tackle the allocation of income and power between labor and management, between retired and working groups, between farmers and urban consumers. Among the most divisive of issues is the "style" issue: desegregation. Is it the constituencies alone which frame a man's disposition on these matters, or do the personal attitudes toward conflict, "giving offense," and punishing enemies lead some to select divisive issues rather than consensual ones?

4. Most decisions favor one of several competing groups; most groups differ with respect to income, status, power. Thus, again and again a decision maker is tested on some aspect of equalitarian-inequalitarian attitudes. Authoritarianism is related to this dimension, but so are many other attitudes, needs, and motives.

5. Government is a policing operation. Decisions affecting the degree of discretion to be vested in individuals, as contrasted to the degree of control and limitation desirable for optimal behavior, are common, as in civil liberties and censorship matters, control of drugs and liquor, restriction on economic behavior, and so forth. Often these represent choices between market or private restrictions on the one hand, and authoritative governmental controls on the other. Whether or not there is a common theme or several differentiated themes in this tangle, many decisions pose some aspect of this question of freedom versus control.

Here, then, are five ways of classifying decisions irrespective of their political or topical import. In teasing from the topics these more abstract qualities, we have sought to prepare them for theoretical formulations of a more comprehensive nature. What we have lost in our power to answer certain questions of immediate political relevance, we have gained in our capacity to frame answers to questions dealing with the politics of other times and places. For the very reason that they are less topic-bound, they are more likely to show persistent relationships to the kinds of psychological variables which have been in the literature: extrapunitiveness, dogmatism, anti-intraceptiveness, and other aspects of the authoritarianism syndrome, the several need complexes outlined in McClelland's work, low self-esteem, and many others.

Moreover, they are more likely to reveal enduring relations to historical or environmental situations. For example, situations favoring the public interest as opposed to special interests might include places of expanding community income or a sense of solidarity engendered by outside threats. Situations favoring position issues, as contrasted to style issues, might include places where there was an educational system influenced by Lucy Sprague Mitchell's emphasis on "here and now," or the absence of a political tradition of *personalism*. An equalitarian-policy tendency might rest in part on the triumph of philosophies focused on *this* world or places where there was a widely held land tenure during the period of the great struggles for the extended franchise.

Institutional Environment (S_{ie})

It may be considered straining at the usages of ordinary English to refer to the laws and rules and customs of an institution or an office as stimuli. Are they not better grouped together under some such heading as "formal and informal regulations," "grants and limitations of power," "roles and conventions," and so forth? This is the case for a more refined analysis, but here we need some term to cover the external cues which prompt decisions of different kinds, and "stimuli" may appropriately serve this function. We focus first upon those cues connected with the offices of the decision makers.

It is here that the phenomena of law have their most obvious and immediate application. The law does three things. In the first place, it establishes the skeletal framework of the basic institutions—legislative, electoral, judicial, executive, administrative. The organic law defines the structure of government in terms of such principles as bicameralism, federalism, and separation of powers; statute law establishes the various administrative agencies to carry out the purposes of government. In the second place, the law grants powers to the various institutions and imposes limitations upon them. In the third place, the law orders procedures to be followed in decision making at the governmental level. At the electoral level, of course, the decision-making procedures are, for the voter, without much legal circumscription.

A decision made within this context of law is, one might say, part prescribed and part "free." Because political scientists have focused in the past upon that part which is prescribed, a wealth of excellent literature has developed on the powers of Congress, the powers of the executive, the required procedures of administrative agencies, the inevitableness, or at least the narrow range of choice, of a judicial opinion. Often, indeed, the limits on the possibility of choice are fully as important as the particular choice made within that range. But now attention is turning to the choice processes themselves, not to the limiting conditions of the choice. This took the form first of an examination of the "pressures" on congressmen, the executive, administrative agencies, and, to a lesser extent, upon the judiciary, but has recently broadened to include a variety of other factors. Therefore, in an examination of decision making within an institutional framework, the question now becomes: How does the law operate as a stimulus for a given kind of response?

The first point to note is the obvious one that it is not the law but the perception of the law which guides men's choices. Perception, as we know from the work of Sherif, Bruner, Asch, and others, is influenced by internalized values, conformity needs, considerations of status, wish-fulfillment mechanisms, and so forth [7, 18, 157]. Thus at the outset the problems of defining the "powers of Congress" or the attribution of concepts of "dual federalism" to the framers of the Constitution become freighted with psychological meaning. Perhaps it would be not too far off the mark to consider the reinterpretation of the intent of the framers of the Constitution in conformity with the needs and ideologies of each unfolding era as a kind of socialized projection.

In the second place, the uses and abuses of the law, however defined, are illustrative of a range of attitudes concerning its place within the manifold stimuli bearing upon an office. President Theodore Roosevelt is said to have made a distinction between his conception of the powers of the presidency and Buchanan's conception along the following lines. Whereas Buchanan sought to find reasons for inaction in the formal powers of his office, Roosevelt sought to find support for whatever, on other grounds, he wanted to do [141]. One man will, according to his temperament, seek to use the law as a vehicle for change, another will seek to employ it to prevent change. Neustadt has recently shown how attitudes toward the use of power affected the performance in office of three other Presidents: F. D. Roosevelt, Truman, and Eisenhower [137]. The range of attitudes and values, then, which are tapped by the legal stimuli are significant variables in every decision, as the biographies of great political leaders make only too clear.

The concept of "office" has meanings quite apart from, and fully as important as, the legal definition of official powers and limitations. Although the literature on the nature of an "office" is meager, by extension the idea may come under the concept of "role," on which there is considerable material [116, pp. 113–131; 117, pp. 77–82]. Of the several definitions of "role," we shall here employ the idea as a complex of expectations associated with a given position in a social structure [91, pp. 42–43]. These expectations may differ among relevant populations. For example, workers expect from their foremen behavior very different from the behavior expected by managers. Furthermore, these expectations may differ for the occupant of the role-office and the persons affected by it, in which case, of course, conflicts are certain to arise.

Among the classic choices of role interpretation, the choice required of the legislator is an important one. Henry Clay is able to say of his interpretation of the position [37, p. 135]:

I hold to the doctrine [of instruction] as it stood in 1789; that, in general, on questions of expediency, the representative should conform to his instructions, and so gratify the wishes, and obey the will, of his constituents, though on questions of constitutionality his course might be different.

On the other hand, Edmund Burke, in his speech to the electors of Bristol, explicitly denied such a view and claimed that his role was not to act as his constituents demanded from time to time but rather to employ his independent judgment on their behalf. Perhaps it is true, too, that electors themselves divide upon their concept of the role of their representatives and hence, as voters, have different interpretations of their own office. Although the concept of role has been carried further by sociologists and anthropologists than by psychologists, further treatment by psychologists would make their work of greater service to political science in this crucial regard. A relatively simple piece of research on state legislators' concepts of gubernatorial responsibility and expectations of probable action under specified conditions compared to governors' expectations and concepts under the same conditions would be a very significant piece of information on role interpretation in a significant area. Current studies of legislative-role interpretations contribute to this end [8, 48].

A third facet of the institutional stimuli bearing upon a decision maker, after the interpretations of law and the office role, would be the patterns of personal interaction within the organization. These are, of course, not defined by law, although it would be a mistake not to pay due regard to the influence of formal organization as established by law upon these more fluid intimate patterns. As the Sherifs have shown, the formal organization of teams so structures interaction that friendships are made and broken on the basis of formal organization [159, chaps. 9, 10]. Even more spatial arrangement, as the Festinger, Schacter, and Back housing development study reveals, can be determinative in this respect [53].

Among the relevant problems for investigation in this area of personal interaction and intrainstitutional pressures would be the following: What is the effect of being a member of a collegiate body upon (1) a legislator, (2) a judge, (3) a member of a cabinet—presidential or parliamentary, (4) a delegate to the United Nations? In theory, one would expect many of the principles of group dynamics to apply in this area. The salience of the organization for the individual, his other group memberships, his strategic position in the organization, the *esprit de corps* or morale of the organization, the nature and intensity of factionalism in the organization, his sociometric position in the organization, the degree to which he derives his authority from the organization contrasted to the degree to which he derives his authority from outside the organization (professional membership, constituent approval, intimacy in an authoritative elite group), and so forth, will all contribute to the influence of "collegiality" in decision-making processes [29, 66, 175].

Hierarchical relationships or gradations of formal authority and status, a fourth category of intrainstitutional stimuli, partake of the three kinds of problems discussed—legal powers and limits, office and role definitions, and informal interpersonal relationships—and are probably best understood in this context. These relationships imply formal and informal authority, the nature of the authority depending upon (1) the formal powers, (2) the attitudes, skills, and values of the officeholder with the power, (3) the attitudes of the subordinates, and (4) the situation at any given moment in time [162]. Speakers of the House of Representatives have varying degrees of influence over the House as these factors vary; the difference between the influence of the "boss" of one city and the "boss" of another is a measurement of the variance in these factors, and so forth. In this context, the analysis and theory of leadership is a most significant area of applied psychology. When, as Redl suggests, a leader emerges to reinforce men's id-related antisocial tendencies and becomes a "seducer," political decisions of one character emerge; when the leader, or central figure, occupies the position of patriarch, another quite different pattern will be followed [142]. Inaccessible as these factors may be for controlled and objective research, they must be considered and given weight in the analysis of decision making at every level.

Social Environment (S_{se})

Moving now to a wider circle of events and pressures, we turn to the world outside the institutional framework. In some ways the widest currently useful frameworks for studying the confluence of social and psychological forces upon political acts are those deriving from Marx and Weber. Thus Lipset studies the social requisites of a democratic system with the aid of United Nations data [118]; W. Kornhauser develops a theory of the relationship between "accessible" elites and "available" masses to explain the circumstances of a stable and democratic polity [93]. These empirical theories embrace variables of the largest order offering an interpretation of the *system* within which the processes about to be discussed take place. Perhaps, too, one should mention the system-wide circumstances conditioning the intellectual framework of the decision makers, circumstances studied in the sociology of knowledge [125]. Here, however, we limit ourselves to asking more limited questions: How do extrainstitutional stimuli impinge upon the decider to affect his responses? How may the stimuli best be grouped to order the events in a meaningful way? To such problems as these we may now address ourselves.

In a penetrating article on the foundations of organizational analysis, Selznick draws attention to the point that the organization does not envelop the whole person, but only that part of him which is occupied in fulfilling his organizational role [156]. Yet the person is nevertheless a whole person and the nonorganizational role aspects of his life will inevitably affect and modify his role behavior. Therefore the nonorganizational life of a decision maker is a relevant point of inquiry. Here we find the phenomena of cliques, friendship groups, kin and family groups, associational memberships, and categoric group memberships, in so far as they are salient and serve as reference groups. In two somewhat broader inquiries, Lane and Lipset et al. analyze how religious—of one sort or another—economic, communication, and political institutions affect popular decisions to participate in political life [98, 119].

Now psychology has much to say along these lines, as do sociology and political science, too. The influence of interaction patterns outside of any given institution may be studied as they affect workers' morale or administrative behavior or the political influence of a boys' club worker upon a member of the city council, or the power elite of a metropolitan community [74; 147; 178; 190, pp. 247–252]. A very considerable body of information shows the effect of homogeneity and heterogeneity of friendship groups upon the voter [13, 111], and presumably the influence of this factor upon the legislator, judge, and bureaucrat would not be insignificant. It is a common assumption, for example, that the diplomat to an Asian country who confines his circle of acquaintances to the foreign-colony country-club set will jeopardize not only his standing in the country but also the accuracy of his perspectives and the utility of his advice. The same thing might be said of the Secretary of Labor who restricted his associates to management circles. But, with the exception of the voter, these hypotheses about the intimate personal environment and reference groups of governmental decision makers remain at the level of the common-sense hunch, with little research to inform them.

In particular, the influence of membership in certain demographic groups deserves further investigation. The class membership of the legislators of a nation is at the focus of attention of the Marxian attack upon democratic institutions. There is indeed considerable evidence to show that the income, educational, and occupational level of congressmen is substantially above the average [126], but it is not at all clear that higher-class status is associated with greater conservatism. Indeed, the selective processes which operate to recruit candidates for the legislature in different class strata may invert for the legislature the relationships between income and welfare-state liberalism in the electorate at large. If this is true, psychological explanations of such selective recruitment more sophisticated than the usual *noblesse oblige* or guilt over wealth might be revealing. In the same way, ethnicity, regionalism, and rural-urban categoric group memberships are undoubtedly significant in the attitudes they create among decision makers in the six political processes.

Intermediate between "own-group" and "other-group" identifications lies the unique phenomena of constituency pressures. For those who seek to explain the behavior of legislators and elected executives in strictly group-dynamic terms, representation poses a challenge. Here is a stimulus complex, ambiguous and hard to define, which comes from outside the institution of the legislature or office of the executive, and toward which the elected person may feel ambivalence. He is dependent upon some part of his constituency for reelection and he is possibly grateful for past election; he feels, in some degree, a responsibility to serve them; he finds them, usually, divided in their sentiments so that he must offend some group whatever course of action he takes; the articulate members of the constituency may irritate and annoy him with their threats and demands; sometimes these importunities violate some values which are sanctioned by a strong superego formation.

We have spoken of the importunities and demands of certain elements of a constituency and this may be generalized to the larger problem of the relation of pressure groups to legislators, administrators, and executives. The political science literature is rich in descriptive material on the nature and procedures of pressure groups [69, 108, 138, 153, 181], but there is virtually no psychologically informed literature on the interaction process on how the pressured individual receives and reacts to the pressure. The possibilities of interpretation are varied. Does the decision maker need rationalizations couched in morally acceptable terms to permit him to do what is politically advantageous? Is he sensitized to the power dimension so that he searches for and clings to the group with the greatest political resources? Is he, like relatively few of Asch's subjects [7], able to maintain his own perspectives when the pressures cumulate in a direction he believes unsound? Can he do this alone? With a few associates? With a majority of his party? President John F. Kennedy has investigated the records of a few select legislators who withstood the pressures of their constituencies—some to their political detriment [87]. Such men, and their living counterparts, present a challenge for psychopolitical inquiry. Is there some such dimension as other-directedness versus inner-directedness in the attitudinal constitution of the legislators which makes some seek the counsel of important interests and colleagues before making up their minds, while others seek the solitude of their week-end retreats?

While personal influences and the absorption of standards from reference groups of every kind are probably the most important sources of attitudes relevant to decision making, the mass media are significant, too. Of course, the two are not wholly separable in that the effect of the media is often filtered through personal influence as Katz and Lazarsfeld have shown [86], but whether direct or indirect, the media provide stimuli of a very significant character. Analysis of these media is appropriately summarized in the phrase "who says what to whom through what channel with what effect," but the words in this caption need analysis for careful usage [103, pp. 37–51].

Who? Study of the source of media content can be analyzed in terms of who makes the news, who interprets the news in columns and over the air, whose views are incorporated in secondary reports, and so forth, and this has value, particularly as it may reveal some systematic distortion in the selection of the "who." *What?* Systematic or unsystematic content analysis reveals the nature of the "what," but much of the work applied to this area is more concerned with the validity of the content, whom it favors, what lines of policy are implied, what the premises or conclusions of the statement may be and any illogicality conceived to lie therein, and so forth. Audience research tells something about the "to whom" aspects of the media and the data on circulation of the press, number of viewers and listeners of television and radio, book-reading habits, the use of libraries, and the specialized circulation of trade and professional periodicals. It is of no small significance that the Patterson-McCormack *Times-Herald* was unable to continue publication in Washington; that in New Haven there is a captive audience for the single local television station owned by Italian-Republican entrepreneurs; that all of the important daily papers in Chicago are Republican.

But all of this is reportorial material and hardly comes to a significant conclusion without the final phrase—"with what effect?" The discovery of the "sleeper effect" and of delayed reactions to propaganda from a disreputable source [72, 73] puts new meaning into the political phenomena represented by a Senator McCarthy or a Huey Long. The differential impact of one-sided and two-sided presentations among populations with different initial attitudes and different educational backgrounds opens up new interpretations of the impact of political campaigns, or of the differential persuasiveness of various presentations in committee hearings [72, pp. 201–227]. Information on the effectiveness of prestige labeling in attitude information [6], of the effectiveness of new knowledge where attitudes are already firmly structured [114], of the probable reactions to fear-arousing content in a communication [78], of being forewarned [80], and so forth—all have immediate and practical application to the problems of political decision making. The relationship between low self-esteem and persuasibility has implications for the politics of underdeveloped areas [79].

The influences of personal contact and association and of the media and the written word occur within a milieu which gives direction and form to their messages. This milieu is the culture or the subculture of a given section of society. Now the analysis of culture is, if the division is still meaningful, the province of the anthropologist, but the psychologist has much to say of political relevance in this area as well. Consider first the distribution of attitudes within a society or sections thereof. Richard Centers can tell us much of *The Psychology of Social Classes* and in so doing he gives insight into the content and consequences of class consciousness in political attitudes [32]. Kornhauser, in a study of social attitudes at different class levels, shows that the sources of discontent are different; therefore the overt impetus toward "radical" political formulations is different for working-class and upper-class and lower-middle-class groups [92]. One source of the unradical orientation of the American working class is revealed in Lane's analysis, "The Fear of Equality" [97]. Cross-cultural attitudes toward authority, as developed in McGranahan's study of German and American youth, reveal the working out of father identifications in the politics of the two cultures [124]. In his analysis of the relationship of class consciousness to property attitudes, Jones reveals a tendency toward "centrality," that is, a preference for middle or compromise positions, as one of the defenses of the *status quo* [82].

But more recently the growing application of psychoanalytic theory to the socialization processes of entire populations has produced a kind of literature which fits the needs of the political scientist interested in the dynamics of political change. The relationships of the largest categories of political theory—democracy, dictatorship, monarchy, pluralism, equalitarianism—to the modal needs of an entire population are given form. Both a theoretical framework and some substantive data have evolved from studies in this area. Aspects of culture previously regarded as irrelevant have now become significant for politics—the training of the individual from birth to adulthood, the interrelationships within the family, the source and nature of nurture, and many more [63, 75].

Yet there remain a number of areas of cultural investigation not explored in psychodynamic terms and perhaps not fully accessible to this kind of explanation. Whether these are called "expressive styles of adjustment," or "paths of life," or "value preferences," the kinds of characteristic responses of a people which inevitably affect the decision makers in the six political processes deserve further study. Among these one finds for the American public the qualities of "other direction" or conformism noted by Mead and Riesman [128, 145], the instrumentalist approach which Inkeles and Hanfmann and Getzels have suggested [65], preferences for individual as contrasted to collective action marked by Almond and others [4], materialistic values which De Tocqueville considered important [179], pragmatic attitudes which the American contributions to philosophic literature suggest is congenial to the American mode of life [77], and many others. Here, then, lies an opportunity for political psychology and psychological political science, first in factoring out the salient features of American culture, and then, together with the historian, systematically offering a theory of their derivation.

Feedback, Reinforcement, and Responsibility

One cannot leave this brief statement of various psychopolitical S-*O*-R relationships without considering the influence of R, heretofore the dependent variable, upon S and O. This focus brings us into touch with three areas of thought symbolized, rather than described, by the terms "feedback," "reinforcement," and "responsibility." The first of these refers to the way in which a decision or a communication sets in motion a chain of circumstances which affect the decider or change the stimuli which affect him. A decision to vote Republican will very often have effects upon the selection of conversational partners during campaign time which will reinforce the original decision. The term "reinforcement" suggests that when an act is rewarded through some incremental status, affection, power, or other value, this will reinforce the tendency to act in this way again in the next situation seen as similar. Without such a reinforcement that particular manner of response may be extinguished. Thus the candidate, searching for a formula to win elections and finding that specious and generous promises attract votes, will be reinforced in his decision to use these promises in his campaigns. And the term "responsibility" raises, in political science language, the question of who controls the rewards and punishments following political decisions. Often the rewards and punishments are not subject to control by the electorate or even by elected officials because the decisions are made anonymously by an unrecorded legislative vote, by unknown persons elected in the obscurity of a long ballot, or by officials in the depths of an autonomous bureaucracy.

Whichever of these frames of reference is chosen, and possibly only all three do justice to the problem, it is apparent that the estimation of consequences to the decider, the reinforcement of his habits, and the effect on those to whom he is responsible will be relevant in a study of the psychology of political decision making. In this connection, whether the decision is a public or a private one is important; the secret ballot may be good, but diffused (and therefore secret), administrative responsibility may be bad. Over time and also in anticipation, the response of one situation becomes a conditioning factor of the next; hence criteria for judging the response must include future perspectives which embrace this reversed relationship of S and R for the decider.

In this section we have sought to outline relationships between political science and psychology, not in terms of a series of formally stated hypotheses but rather in terms of improving our theories of decision-making processes in government. Viewed from one perspective, it is as though the political scientist focused upon the macroprocesses of politics, and the psychologist provided research and theory relevant to the microprocesses. In presenting this view of psychopolitical investigation, we have used the S-O-R formula, and have viewed each of these three elements in turn. Examining the O, we have located the decision makers and suggested a few of the qualities which may be relevant to their roles as decision makers. The responses we have defined as decisions; we have categorized them and pointed to different attitudinal dimensions tapped by different kinds of decisions. The stimuli we have divided into two groups, those arising within the institutional environment (S_{ie}) and those arising from the larger social environment (S_{se}). Of the first, we said that concepts of law and role were significant along with patterns of interaction and authority. Of the second, we said that extrainstitutional group membership and reference-group identifications—together with the selective processes which recruited decision makers from these various groups—offered scope for psychopolitical investigation. The phenomena of constituency and pressure-group interpretation by decision makers was discussed along with the nature and influence of the media. Some observations on cultural and subcultural themes focused attention on these molar areas of study. Finally, we have taken the dependent variable R and considered it as a factor affecting future external stimuli and internal psychic dispositions of the decision maker.

METHODOLOGICAL INTERRELATIONSHIPS

Although in one sense it may be said that the methodological tradition of political science is a combination of the normative and the descriptive, due to its origins in philosophy and history, this is an inaccurate account. Throughout the great tradition of politics, there have been a variety of deductive relationships and some empirically observed invariances which were thought to establish political laws of one sort or another. Harrington, Madison, and Marx all deal with the supposed relationships of property ownership to political systems; Machiavelli, Pareto, and Michels have much to say about the relationship between elite behavior and tenure in office; Plato and De Tocqueville discuss national character and the concentration and dispersal of power. And in the works of these and many other authors, the laws of politics are developed on a grand scale with the same expectation of capacity to predict that today is sometimes taken as a measure of a correct theory.

What the scientifically minded political scientist complains about, in relation to the body of literature of his discipline, is not only the heavy normative and descriptive emphasis, but also the fact that the analytical theory is not operational. It is not testable and was never meant to be except by the peculiar standards of historical interpretation. And it is the rapid advance of the other behavioral sciences in the area of measurement, validation, and the precise formulation of concepts and hypotheses which these have brought about that are viewed by political scientists with such acquisitiveness. Yet the metamorphosis of political science into a behavioral science is not easy. Consider for a moment the nature of the questions mentioned at the beginning of this essay: What is the relationship between majority rule and minority rights? How can government be made responsible? How shall power be shared? After the normative elements of such questions have been extracted so that the problems become problems of isolation of relevant variables and the discovery of invariant relationships, the difficulty of making the theoretical propositions testable still remains.

There are several problems in this connection which may be exceptionally frequent—if not unique to political science—in the study of politics. These may be examined in the context of the six processes discussed above. The first deals with the number and complexity of the decisions to be made. In electoral decision making, the decision is usually fairly well structured for the electorate so that a single clear choice is made by a large number of people. Thus the dependent variable is easily specified and the number of "cases" is large enough to control for a variety of factors while a given independent variable is examined. With respect to legislative decisions, at the roll-call stage (but not in other respects) something of the same situation exists, although the decisions are more complex, the deciders are less accessible for interview, and the number of cases is smaller. With the judicial process, where decisions can be grouped into roughly homogeneous categories and where they are of a recurrent nature, some factorial, correlational, or other quantitative analysis is possible. The possibilities are limited, however, and the purpose of the law is not only to find analogies (common categories of a sort), but also to discover distinguishing features in a case, thus making each case idiosyncratic in some respect. Administrative and executive decisions and decisions dealing with international affairs are very often unique. For example, how would one control the multiple factors involved in the decision to relieve General MacArthur? Or how would one do this for the decision to attempt to prevent the steel industry from carrying through an untimely price rise, or for the decisions reached by Stalin, Churchill, and Roosevelt at Yalta? Quantitative methods and the sophisticated methodologies associated with them partially fail in such situations—although, of course, greater sophistication in qualitative analysis would be useful [28, 38].

The second problem has to do with the scale of the questions asked by much political science literature. We are often interested in total systems, or large segments thereof. We want to know how the legislative process works *in toto*, and particularly how it works in several different nations. This has the effect of reducing the number of cases to one per nation. Now there are about one hundred nations in the United Nations and several more outside; hence one might think that there are enough cases to form a working group, but the problem of isolating relationships under these circumstances is difficult to solve. If one is interested, say, in the way in which the executive (cabinet) operates in Britain, Sweden, Holland, Belgium, and France, a comparative description is easily possible, but the relationship between the formal organization of the cabinet or the powers and limits of the relevant officers and certain modes of operation is inevitably linked to the cultural milieu of these five national systems. One cannot hold constant one factor while varying others because everything varies at once—the length of office, the pattern of recruitment, the formal powers, plus the attitudes and dispositions of the people, the number of parties, the history of executive leadership, the sense of crisis in foreign affairs, and so forth. Important steps can be taken in this direction and improved methods of keeping certain factors constant can help in this regard, but the problem is formidable.[4]

A third problem has to do with the time dimension. It is not an accident that political science is so saturated with historical analysis and methods. We are dealing with events in a historical stream and a stream, as we are reminded by the old philosophical paradox, is never the same at two different moments in time. Thus when a given legislative decision on labor problems is effected, and the issue comes up again, the context is inevitably changed. In 1935, Congress passed the National Labor Relations Act regulating the activities of employers with respect to unions, but not regulating union activities in any important sense. In 1947, Congress again tackled the problem and passed the Taft-Hartley Act regulating unions and relieving employers of certain restrictions on their activities. The contexts in which these two decisions took place had changed in so many ways that the behavior of the legislators, even of the same party and from the same constituencies, was different in many cases. It is hard to give rigor to the explanations of these differences because of the totality of the changed contexts. Each of the six processes occurs in a different historical, social, and psychological context each time it is analyzed, and although some of these changes can be controlled, it is hard to control enough of them at once to nail down the effect of any one. At this point, historical methods are likely to take over.

We cite some of these methodological difficulties not to detract from the effort of political scientists to employ greater rigor in their methods, nor to imply that a ceiling has somehow been reached in this respect, but to show the obstacles in their path. With this in mind, then, we may turn to psychological research methodology to see wherein it offers bor-

---

[4] A program of research in comparative state politics sponsored by the Social Science Research Council offers a promising approach to the problem of holding some factors constant while allowing others to vary. Unlike most comparative government studies, this study holds culture constant (to a large extent) while examining institutions and men.

rowable elements for political science. First with respect to the nature of the variables used, we think it would be accurate to say that political science is now searching for the appropriate psychic qualities operative in political decision making and also significant in the analysis of total systems. The tendency is generally to accept those variables which psychology offers in an eclectic fashion, whether it is Harrison Gough's "dominance" dimension, Fromm's automaton mode of escape from freedom, Adorno's authoritarianism, or Eysenck's tough tender-mindedness [61; 55, pp. 185–206; 1; 49]. Unfortunately, in our search for variables we are sometimes confounded by the tendency among psychologists to put together a few questions and discover a new "factor" or "dimension," particularly if these items do not hang together according to some substructure analysis. If the political scientist is to borrow with confidence, he must have better evidence of the way the alleged dimension operates behaviorally; its validity must be checked with care, preferably in populations at different socioeconomic levels. And its nomenclature should be restrained. In so far as the value of replication is a question in psychology, it should be said by a member of a borrowing discipline that replicated findings are particularly welcome at this end of the transaction. Political scientists should be eternally grateful to Washburn, Kepler, and others for replication of Moore's findings regarding radical-conservative differences in skills and temperament [135, 188]. In the replicated tests there were no differences; the alley turned out to be blind.

It is, perhaps, a commonplace that psychology can be "reduced" to sociology, and sociology can be "reduced" to psychology—that is, attitudes, values, and motives have causes in the external world, and the external world is perceived and shaped by men with operative attitudes, values, and motives. This is, in a way, inherent in the S-O-R formula, since one man's O-R relationship is another man's S. The methodological problem for political scientists lies in the question of which level of variables to use. In explaining voting behavior, shall we use income, or shall we use the private meanings of income? Shall we use region, or the regionally differentiated attitudes? Often the sociological variable is as closely associated as the psychological variable with the dependent political variable—and, of course, the data are much easier to come by. Explanation in the sense of prediction and correlation is then as effectively achieved in sociological terms as in psychological terms. This is, moreover, a very practical question in voting research, because it represents the difference between use of aggregate voting statistics and the use of survey methods.

I think it is true to say that ever since Graham Wallas wrote *Human Nature in Politics* [185], there has been a growing feeling that psychological variables are nevertheless necessary for an adequate explanation of the various political processes. This is so for several reasons. The first is that use of correlational techniques with external variables is useful for prediction only if conditions remain the same; if there should be a change in the situation, there would be no basis, without some knowledge of the psychic processes involved, for predicting how such changes would alter the relevant behavior.

Second, latent in most sociological investigations are various implicit hypotheses about the psychological factors associated with the sociological variable. Thus the analysis of the relation of recency of immigration to electoral behavior may be suggested by and interpreted in the light of theories about "underdog" psychology, in-group–out-group sentiments, rejection of parental generation, and so forth. A well-conducted survey can go directly to the heart of these aspects of the problem. A third reason why there is a tendency to psychologize the selection of variables is because of their greater utility in analysis of deviant cases. The rich radical, the Southern Republican, the Communist party member in England and the United States are rarely "explainable" in sociological terms; the private and idiosyncratic meanings of their life experiences must be tapped for satisfactory explanatory information. And, finally, a fourth reason lies in the greater insight provided, regardless of the correlational factors and predictability. Men are motivated to act in a given way by a combination of environment and psyche; one should study both. No doubt, to the psychologist this "admonition" is redundant; the issue is a real one for the political scientist who must answer the statement: I don't care what goes on in men's minds, I just want to know how they behave.

We turn now to the questions related to the collection of data and principally to four techniques: the survey, the experiment, field observation, and depth interviewing. The survey, of course, has been widely used to collect data on the electoral processes and material on public opinion relevant to administrative decisions [184] and the analysis of foreign policy. It has also been related to executive decisions [23], and to legislative action [27]. It has not, to our knowledge, been used in studying the judicial process, although there would be much value in doing so. For example, the following questions might find answers resting on survey material: How closely and in what respects do judicial decisions follow elite or mass opinion? What is the relation between public opinion and decisions to prosecute? How do juries' opinions relate to community opinion—before the trial and after the trial? In the light of the wide adoption of survey methods, however, and the increasing sophistication of political scientists in this respect, little more need be said.

Laboratory experiments represent the exact reverse of this situation— political scientists have never, to our knowledge, attempted a controlled laboratory experiment to ascertain the relation between relevant variables.[5] This, in spite of the clear relevance and excellent results of the Festinger study (now fourteen years old) on ethnic identifications in a voting situation [51], and the excellent work on administrative decision making by Bavelas [11, pp. 193–202] and others! The mock trial, the mock assembly, the mock hearing have been employed as teaching devices, not as research devices. Here, then, lies a golden opportunity for a combined assault by group-dynamics specialists, communications specialists of the Hovland school, and political scientists.

Field observation is, one is tempted to say, all too familiar to the political scientist, as it is to the journalist who also employs this method. Two things in particular are missing in political science observational techniques, however: (1) the use of techniques to objectify the findings and to assure the elimination of subjectively colored perception and interpretation, and (2) the frame of mind which constantly asks, "What are the invariances in these situations? What are the laws which are here at work?" In the absence of such techniques and modes of inquiry, a rich literature on the various processes has emerged, but it is eclectic, subjective, and nonadditive.

With respect to depth interviewing, not necessarily of the duration or penetration of the clinical interview, pioneer work has, in fact, been done by a political scientist, Harold Lasswell, by his colleague, Gabriel Almond, Adorno and his associates, Linder, and Brewster Smith. Bruner and White have contributed to this literature, and some of the interviewing of Nazi leaders at Nuremburg, and of Russian exiles has broadened the cultural base of the data thus collected [1, 5, 42, 60, 105, 115, 165]. The circumstances where such depth interviewing offers its greatest promise, for political science at least, is where (1) the decisions, attitudes, or beliefs in question are least likely to be structured by social pressures, (2) where the behavior is deviant and hence it appears that some idiosyncratic experience or psychic state must be at work, and (3) where the decision is unique and therefore survey or other means of comparing similar decisions by several people is least possible. The use of "clinical methods" promises to give new dimensions to the study of political thought and to reconstruct thought patterns into psychologically coherent (as contrasted to logically coherent) systems.

Something should be said of the use of mathematical models in political science, but perhaps in this case both political science and psychology are now only at the threshold of their development [110, 161]. The Hullian system, of course, has provided the basis for deductive

[5] Some recent experiments at Rand involving role-taking exercises have illuminated the decision-making process, although so far no publications have emerged on this topic from this source.

analysis, and hence lends itself particularly well to mathematical elaboration. The political scientist is disadvantaged by the absence of such a well-formulated set of empirically grounded interlocking laws in his discipline, but since the economists have done very well without them, perhaps the political scientists can do as well. As this line of approach goes forward, fruition is encouraged by the interaction of persons with empirical knowledge (who know what they are talking about, so to speak) with the model builders who can systematize and generalize this knowledge.

THE CONTRIBUTIONS OF POLITICAL SCIENTISTS AND PSYCHOLOGISTS TO THE STUDY OF POLITICAL PROCESSES

One of the truisms current in the social sciences is that the best kind of interdisciplinary research takes place in a single skull. There can be no doubt that a person who has mastered the relevant aspects of two disciplines is in a better position to undertake an integrated piece of research than two persons attempting to bring their own specialties to bear upon a problem. Not that the latter process is useless; it is merely less likely to produce a genuine synthesis. Collateral to this view is the belief that disciplines are artifacts and their boundaries had best be ignored. There should be a focus only on problems and methods, with each specialist combining a unique complex of substantive knowledge, methodological tools, and areas of interest. But that phase of the present drift toward a general behavioral science has not yet arrived, and we must start from the present situation.

In terms of collaboration in the existing situation, let us suggest first what the political scientist may contribute to collaborative efforts. In the first place, he asks *important questions,* important for human destiny and for the solution of major social problems. He can focus the psychologist's attention upon issues which, in some cases, might represent a better investment of the psychologist's time than those he is presently examining. The questions with which this paper started would represent some of these considerations.

Second, the political scientist, because of his knowledge of *laws and institutions,* precedents and operating procedures, can prevent the psychologist working in this area from making serious mistakes. Thus Erickson interprets the apparent preference for minimal action in Congress as a reflection of American family life, where the resolution of differences is said to be the selection of the course least unacceptable to any one member [47]. A political scientist, even accepting this in some degree, would have given additional emphasis to the system of staggered elections, becameralism, separation of powers, and a Federal decentralized party system impeding positive legislative action. And Berelson and associates interpret the utility of parties solely in terms of their representative functions, omitting entirely their functions as organs of government [13].

Third, in any explanation of political decisions, the political scientist, because he is so close to *history*, is likely to search for historical causes while the modern behavioral scientist seeks for causes in the immediate social and psychological situation. Thus, in explaining voting patterns in the South, the currently operational force is the set of attitudes now present in the minds of Southerners, but behind that lies the historical relation of each area of the South to the forces set in motion at the time of the Civil War or earlier. The peculiar similarity of the pattern of counties voting Democratic in 1928 and Dixiecrat in 1948 is understandable in terms of both current attitudes and historical experiences. And both are important [90].

Fourth, although there are limits to the *rationality and logic* of decision-making processes, the judicial process has long been interpreted with some success in precisely these terms—supplemented by a knowledge of the social problems and forces of the times. Although Judge Frank has shown the influence of personality upon a judge's sentence in various kinds of petty offenses [54], and Kinsey has data on the relation of a judge's personal sex life to his decisions in cases of sex offenders, there are limits, too, to this type of analysis. The development of Anglo-Saxon law is a remarkable achievement which cannot be psychologized away. The study of the law and judicial processes requires the collaboration of those who appreciate the limits of both types of analysis.

Fifth, the *situation* of the decision makers is often the most salient etiological factor. For example, in the study of international processes the concept of national interest is, no doubt, more often a block than an aid to understanding, but certain phenomena nevertheless seem to come under this category. The persistent pursuit of identical objectives by a nation over the years and over the centuries suggests that the idiosyncratic psychic qualities of any particular set of statesmen or rulers must be minimal in these decisions. Russia's efforts to establish a window on the world by way of a Baltic seaport is a case in point. A knowledge of the content of foreign policy objectives in situational terms must be brought to the attention of anyone seeking to understand the variables in international processes; and a political scientist is in a position to offer this knowledge at the right moment.

A political scientist then brings to collaborative efforts those and other contributions to the study of political processes. What may be properly expected of the psychologist? In terms of the S-O-R formula, he will be familiar with the dimensions of the O that are relevant and with the "laws" of human behavior. First, then, his knowledge of personality, attitudes, motives, and so forth, will form a nucleus of information comparable to the political scientist's knowledge of institutions and laws.

Second, he will be familiar with the dynamics of behavior in the sense that his theory of motivation and perception will suggest the mechanisms at work in a decision-making situation. This will serve the important purpose of taking the discussion of the decision-making process out of the realm of the naïve dynamics built upon the economists' "economic man" or the lawyers' "rational man" or the Marxian class-bound version of mankind.

Third, he will be able to offer a range of techniques and methods not familiar to the political scientist and hence facilitate data collection and interpretation. The use of depth interviewing, projective techniques, laboratory methods, and testing procedures provides a valuable contribution to joint research.

Fourth, the psychologist will help in the process of psychologizing sociological variables, giving class status, marginal cultural membership, and small-group membership the meanings which contribute greatly to the significance of the kinds of data which come most easily to hand for the inquiring political scientist.

Fifth, because of his understanding of the two- or three-dimensional level of the psyche, with its conscious, preconscious, and unconscious aspects, he can contribute to the latent function analysis of political acts both in social (Merton's) terms and in personal terms [131, pp. 21–81].

Finally, when the political scientist deals in normative terms, which is quite often, there is inevitably some hidden theory implied regarding the way in which men achieve happiness, self-expression, or moral stature. These are, by and large, lay versions of psychology or psychiatry. Much of the large fund of misinformation in this area could be reduced by the application of psychologically informed opinion at this point in the analysis.

SUMMARY

We have sought to outline the field of political science in terms of five central processes and a sixth synthetic analysis which unites them into a single system. We have discussed the areas of psychology which seem to have the greatest relevance and translatability, among them, attitude studies, communications research, small-group research, and psychoanalytic theory and case material. The utility of these areas of psychology to political science questions can best be seen with respect to the S-*O*-R model, and in this context a number of illustrative applications of psychology to political science were suggested. The methods of psychological research which can be employed to greater advantage in political science were briefly analyzed. Finally, the resources of the political scientist and the psychologist in collaborative efforts were noted in the hope that more collaborative work will be forthcoming.

REFERENCES

1. Adorno, T. W., et al. *The authoritarian personality.* New York: Harper, 1950.
2. Agger, R. Independents and party identifiers: characteristics and behavior in 1952. In E. Burdick & A. J. Brodbeck, *American voting behavior.* Glencoe, Ill.: Free Press, 1960.
3. Allport, G. Prejudice: a problem in psychology and social causation. *J. soc. Issues, Suppl. Ser.,* 1950, No. 4.
4. Almond, G. *The American people and foreign policy.* New York: Harcourt, Brace, 1950.
5. Almond, G. *The appeals of communism.* Princeton, N.J.: Princeton Univer. Press, 1954.
6. Arnett, C. E., Davidson, H. H., & Lewis, H. N. Prestige as a factor in attitude change. *Sociol. & soc. Res.,* 1931, **16,** 49–55.
7. Asch, S. E. Effects of group pressure upon the modification and distortion of judgments. In H. Guetzgow (Ed.), *Groups, leadership, and men.* Pittsburgh, Pa.: Carnegie Press, 1951.
8. Barber, J. D. *The legislator's first session.* New Haven, Conn.: Yale Univer. Press, in press.
9. Barker, E. *The study of political science and its relation to cognate studies.* New York: Cambridge, 1928.
10. Bavelas, A. A mathematical model for group structures. *Appl. Anthrop.,* 1948, **7,** 16–30.
11. Bavelas, A. Communications and patterns in task oriented groups. In D. Lerner & H. D. Lasswell (Eds.), *The policy sciences.* Stanford, Calif.: Stanford Univer. Press, 1951.
12. Bavelas, A., & Barrett, D. An experimental approach to organizational communication. *Personnel,* 1951, **27,** 367–371.
13. Berelson, B., Lazarsfeld, P. F., & McPhee, W. *Voting.* Chicago: Univer. Chicago Press, 1954.
14. Bettelheim, B., & Janowitz, M. Reactions to Fascist propaganda: a pilot study. *Publ. Opin. Quart.,* 1950, **14,** 53–60.
15. Borgatta, E. F., Couch, A. S., & Bales, R. F. Some findings relevant to the great man theory of leadership. *Amer. sociol. Rev.,* 1954, **19,** 755–759.
16. Brown, R. W. Mass phenomena. In G. Lindzey (Ed.), *Handbook of social psychology.* Reading, Mass.: Addison-Wesley, 1954.
17. Browning, R. *Businessmen in politics: motivation and circumstance in the rise to power.* New Haven, Conn.: Yale Univer. Library, 1960.

18. Bruner, J. S., & Krech, D. (Eds.) *Perception and personality: a symposium.* Durham, N.C.: Duke Univer. Press, 1950.
19. Bruner, J. S., & Postman, L. J. Perception, cognition, and behavior. *J. Pers.,* 1949, **18,** 14–31.
20. Burdick, E., & Brodbeck, A. J. *American voting behavior.* Glencoe, Ill.: Free Press, 1959.
21. Campbell, A., Converse, P. E., Miller, W. E., & Stokes, D. E. *The American voter.* New York: Wiley, 1960.
22. Campbell, A., Gurin, G., & Miller, W. *The voter decides.* Evanston, Ill.: Row, Peterson, 1954.
23. Cantril, H. America faces the war: a study in public opinion. *Publ. Opin. Quart.,* 1940, **4,** 387–407.
24. Cantril, H. *The invasion from Mars.* Princeton, N.J.: Princeton Univer. Press, 1940.
25. Cantril, H. *The psychology of social movements.* New York: Wiley, 1941.
26. Cantril, H. *The politics of despair.* New York: Basic Books, 1958.
27. Cantwell, F. V. Public opinion and the legislative process. *Amer. polit. Sci. Rev.,* 1946, **50,** 924–935.
28. Cartwright, D. Analysis of qualitative material. In L. Festinger & D. Katz (Eds.), *Research methods in the behavioral sciences.* New York: Dryden, 1953.
29. Cartwright, D., & Zander, A. *Group dynamics, research and theory.* Evanston, Ill.: Row, Peterson, 1953.
30. Catlin, G. E. C. *The science and method of politics.* New York: Knopf, 1927.
31. Cattell, R. B. *Factor analysis.* New York: Harper, 1952.
32. Centers, R. *The psychology of social classes.* Princeton, N.J.: Princeton Univer. Press, 1949.
33. Chapple, E. D. Anthropological engineering: its use to administrators. *Appl. Anthrop.,* 1943, **2,** 23–32.
34. Child, I. L. Socialization. In G. Lindzey (Ed.), *Handbook of social psychology.* Reading, Mass.: Addison-Wesley, 1954.
35. Christiansen, B. *Attitudes towards foreign affairs as a function of personality.* Oslo: Oslo Univer. Press, 1959.
36. Christie, R. Authoritarianism re-examined. In R. Christie & M. Jahoda (Eds.), *Studies in the scope and method of "the authoritarian personality."* Glencoe, Ill.: Free Press, 1954.
37. Clay, H. *The works of Henry Clay.* New York: Putnam, 1904. (Federal edition, Vol. VIII.)
38. Columbia University, Bureau of Applied Social Research. *Training guide on the techniques of qualitative interviews.* New York: Columbia Univer., 1948. (Mimeographed)
39. Dahl, R. A. The science of politics: new and old. *World Politics,* 1955, **7,** 479–489.
40. Dahl, R. A. *Power and democracy.* New Haven, Conn.: Yale Univer. Press, 1961.

41. Dicks, H. V. Personality traits and National Socialist ideology. *Hum. Relat.*, 1950, **5**, 111–154.
42. Dicks, H. V. Observations on contemporary Russian behavior. *Hum. Relat.*, 1952, **5**, 111–175.
43. Dollard, J. *Caste and class in a southern town.* New Haven, Conn.: Yale Univer. Press, 1937.
44. Dollard, J., & Miller, N. E. *Personality and psychotherapy.* New York: McGraw-Hill, 1950.
45. Easton, D. *The political system.* New York: Knopf, 1953.
46. Edwards, W. The theory of decision making. *Psychol. Bull.*, 1954, **51**, 380–417.
47. Erikson, E. H. *Childhood and society.* New York: Norton, 1950.
48. Eulau, H., Wahlke, J. C., Buchanan, W., & Ferguson, L. C. The role of the representative: some empirical observations on the theory of Edmund Burke. *Amer. polit. Sci. Rev.* 1959, **53**, 742–756.
49. Eysenck, H. J. *The psychology of politics.* New York: Praeger, 1954.
50. Fenichel, O. *The psychoanalytic theory of neuroses.* New York: Norton, 1945.
51. Festinger, L. The role of group belongingness in a voting situation. *Hum. Relat.*, 1947, **1**, 154–180.
52. Festinger, L., & Kelley, H. H. *Changing attitudes through social contact.* Ann Arbor, Mich.: Univer. Mich., Research Center for Group Dynamics, 1951.
53. Festinger, L. Schacter, S., & Back, K. *Social pressures in informal groups.* New York: Harper, 1950.
54. Frank, J. *Law and the modern mind.* New York: Brentano's, 1930.
55. Fromm, E. *Escape from freedom.* New York: Holt-Rinehart-Winston, 1941.
56. Fromm, E. *Man for himself: an inquiry into the psychology of ethics.* New York: Holt-Rinehart-Winston, 1947.
57. Fromm, E. *The sane society.* New York: Holt-Rinehart-Winston, 1955.
58. Gibb, C. A. The principles and traits of leadership. *J. abnorm. soc. psychol.*, 1947, **42**, 267–284.
59. Gibb, C. A. Leadership. In G. Lindzey (Ed.), *Handbook of social psychology.* Reading, Mass.: Addison-Wesley, 1954.
60. Gilbert, G. M. *The psychology of dictatorship.* New York: Ronald, 1950.
61. Gough, H., McClosky, H., & Meehl, P. E. A personality scale for dominance. *J. abnorm. soc. Psychol.*, 1951, **46**, 360–366.
62. Gouldner, A. *Studies in leadership.* New York: Harper, 1950.
63. Greenstein, F. I., The benevolent leader: children's images of political authority. *Amer. pol. Sci. Rev.*, 1960, **54**, 934–943.
64. Guetzgow, H. (Ed) *Groups, leadership, and men: research in human relations.* Pittsburgh, Pa.: Carnegie Press, 1951.
65. Hanfmann, E., & Getzels, J. W. Interpersonal attitudes of former Soviet citizens as studied by semi-projective methods. *Psychol. Monogr.*, 1955, **69**, No. 4 (Whole No. 389).

66. Hare, P., Borgatta, E. F., & Bales, R. F. *Small groups: studies in social interaction.* New York: Knopf, 1955.
67. Hayes, S. P., Jr. Voters' attitudes toward men and issues. *J. soc. Psychol.*, 1936, **7**, 164–182.
68. Heberle, R. *Social movements: an introduction to political sociology.* New York: Appleton-Century-Crofts, 1951.
69. Herring, E. P. *Group representation before Congress.* Baltimore, Md.: Johns Hopkins Press, 1929.
70. Horney, Karen. *The neurotic personality of our time.* New York: Norton, 1937.
71. Horney, Karen. *New ways in psychoanalysis.* New York: Norton, 1939.
72. Hovland, C., et al. *Experiments on mass communications.* Princeton, N.J.: Princeton Univer. Press, 1952. (The American Soldier Series, Vol. III.)
73. Hovland, C., & Weiss, W. The influence of source credibility on communication effectiveness. *Publ. Opin. Quart.*, 1952, **15**, 635–650.
74. Hunter, F. *Community power structure.* Chapel Hill, N.C.: Univer. N.C. Press, 1953.
75. Hyman, H. *Political socialization.* Glencoe, Ill.: Free Press, 1959.
76. Inkeles, A., & Levinson, D. J. National character: the study of modal personality and sociocultural systems. In G. Lindzey (Ed.), *Handbook of social psychology.* Reading, Mass.: Addison-Wesley, 1954.
77. James, W. *Pragmatism: a new name for some old ways of thinking.* New York: Longmans, 1943.
78. Janis, I. L., & Feshbach, S. Effects of fear-arousing communications. *J. abnorm. soc. Psychol.*, 1953, **48**, 78–92.
79. Janis, I. L., Hovland, C. I., et al. *Personality and persuasibility.* New Haven, Conn.: Yale Univer. Press, 1959.
80. Janis, I. L., Lumsdaine, A. A., & Gladstone, A. I. Effects of preparatory communications on reactions to a subsequent event. *Publ. Opin. Quart.*, 1951, **15**, 488–518.
81. Jennings, Helen H. *Leadership and isolation.* (Rev. ed.) New York: Longmans, 1950.
82. Jones, A. W. *Life, liberty, and property.* Philadelphia: Lippincott, 1941.
83. Kardiner, A. *The individual and his society.* New York: Columbia Univer. Press, 1939.
84. Kardiner, A. *The psychological frontiers of society.* New York: Columbia Univer. Press, 1945.
85. Katz, D., & Cantril, H. An analysis of attitudes toward Fascism and Communism. *J. abnorm. soc. Psychol.*, 1940, **35**, 356–366.
86. Katz, E., & Lazarsfeld, P. F. *Personal influence.* Glencoe, Ill.: Free Press, 1955.
87. Kennedy, J. F. *Profiles in courage.* New York: Harper, 1956.
88. Kerr, W. A. Correlates of politico-economic Liberalism-Conservatism. *J. soc. Psychol.*, 1944, **20**, 61–77.

89. Kerr, W. A. Untangling the Liberalism-Conservatism continuum. *J. soc. Psychol.*, 1952, **35**, 111–125.
90. Key, V. O. *Southern politics.* New York: Knopf, 1949.
91. Kluckhohn, C., & Murray, H. A. (Eds.) *Personality in nature, society, and culture.* New York: Knopf, 1949.
92. Kornhauser, A. W. Attitudes of economic groups. *Publ. Opin. Quart.*, 1938, **2**, 260–268.
93. Kornhauser, W. *The politics of mass society.* Glencoe, Ill.: Free Press, 1959.
94. Krech, D., & Crutchfield, R. S. *Theory and problems of social psychology.* New York: McGraw-Hill, 1948.
95. Kubie, L. S. Problems and techniques of psychoanalytic validation and progress. In E. Pumpian-Mindlin (Ed.), *Psychoanalysis as science.* Stanford, Calif.: Stanford Univer. Press, 1952.
96. Lane, R. E. Fathers and sons: the foundations of political belief. *Amer. sociol. Rev.*, 1959, **24**, 502–511.
97. Lane, R. E. The fear of equality. *Amer. polit. Sci. Rev.*, 1959, **53**, 35–51.
98. Lane, R. E. *Political life: why people get involved in politics.* Glencoe, Ill.: Free Press, 1959.
99. LaPiere, R. T. *Collective behavior.* New York: McGraw-Hill, 1938.
100. Laski, H. J. *On the study of politics: an inaugural lecture.* London: Humphrey Milford; New York: Oxford, 1926. (Pamphlet)
101. Lasswell, H. D. *Politics: who gets what, when, how.* New York: McGraw-Hill, 1936.
102. Lasswell, H. D. *Power and personality.* New York: Norton, 1948.
103. Lasswell, H. D. The structure and function of communication in society. In L. Bryson (Ed.), *The communication of ideas.* New York: Harper, 1948.
104. Lasswell, H. D. World politics and personal insecurity. In H. D. Lasswell, C. E. Merriam, & T. V. Smith, *A study of power.* Glencoe, Ill.: Free Press, 1950.
105. Lasswell, H. D. Psychopathology and politics. In *The political writings of Harold Lasswell.* Glencoe, Ill.: Free Press, 1951.
106. Lasswell, H. D. Current studies of the decision process: automation versus creativity. *West. polit. Quart.*, 1955, **7**, 381–399.
107. Lasswell, H. D., & Kaplan, A. *Power and society: a framework for political inquiry.* New Haven, Conn.: Yale Univer. Press, 1950.
108. Latham, E. *The group basis of politics.* Ithaca, N.Y.: Cornell Univer. Press, 1952.
109. Lazarsfeld, P. F. *Radio and the printed page.* New York: Duell, Sloan & Pearce, 1940.
110. Lazarsfeld, P. F. (Ed.) *Mathematical thinking in the social sciences.* Glencoe, Ill.: Free Press, 1954.
111. Lazarsfeld, P. F., Berelson, B., & Gaudet, Hazel. *The people's choice.* (Rev. ed.) New York: Columbia Univer. Press, 1948.
112. Leighton, A. *The governing of men.* Princeton, N.J.: Princeton Univer. Press, 1945.

113. Lerner, D. *The Nazi elite.* Stanford, Calif.: Stanford Univer. Press, 1951.
114. Lewin, K., & Grabbe, P. Conduct, knowledge, and acceptance of new values. *J. soc. Issues,* 1945, **1,** 53–64.
115. Lindner, R. *The fifty-minute hour.* New York: Holt-Rinehart-Winston, 1955.
116. Linton, R. *The study of man.* New York: Appleton-Century-Crofts, 1936.
117. Linton, R. *The cultural background of personality.* New York: Appleton-Century-Crofts, 1945.
118. Lipset, S. M. *Political man: where, how, and why democracy works in the modern world.* New York: Doubleday, 1960.
119. Lipset, S. M., Lazarsfeld, P., Barton, A., & Linz, J. The psychology of voting: an analysis of political behavior. In G. Lindzey (Ed.), *Handbook of social psychology.* Reading, Mass.: Addison-Wesley, 1954.
120. Logan, F. A., et al. *Behavior theory and social science.* New Haven, Conn.: Yale Univer. Press, 1955.
121. Lynd, R. S., & Lynd, Helen M. *Middletown: a study of contemporary American culture.* New York: Harcourt, Brace, 1929.
122. Lynd, R. S., & Lynd, Helen M. *Middletown in transition: a study in culture conflicts.* New York: Harcourt, Brace, 1937.
123. McClosky, H. Conservatism and personality. *Amer. polit. Sci. Rev.,* 1958, **52,** 27–45.
124. McGranahan, D. V. A comparison of social attitudes among American and German youth. *J. abnorm. soc. Psychol.,* 1946, **41,** 245–257.
125. Mannheim, K. *Ideology and utopia.* London: Routledge, 1936.
126. Matthews, D. R. *The social background of political descision-makers.* New York: Doubleday, 1954.
127. Mayo, E. *The social problems of an industrial civilization.* Boston: Harvard Graduate School of Business Administration, 1945.
128. Mead, Margaret. *And keep your powder dry: an anthropologist looks at America.* New York: Morrow, 1942.
129. Merriam, C. E. *Political power: its composition and incidence.* New York: McGraw-Hill, Whittlesey House, 1934.
130. Merton, R. Bureaucratic structure and personality. *Soc. Forces,* 1940, **18,** 560–568.
131. Merton, R. Manifest and latent functions. In R. Merton, *Social theory and social structure.* Glencoe, Ill.: Free Press, 1949.
132. Merton, R. Patterns of influence: a study of interpersonal influence and communications behavior in a local community. In P. F. Lazarsfeld & F. N. Stanton (Eds.), *Communications research, 1948–49.* New York: Harper, 1949.
133. Miller, N. E., & Dollard, J. *Social learning and imitation.* New Haven, Conn.: Yale Univer. Press, 1941.
134. Miller, W. E. One-party politics and the voter. *Amer. polit. Sci. Rev.,* 1956, **50,** 707–725.
135. Moore, H. T. Innate factors in radicalism and conservatism. *J. abnorm. soc. Psychol.,* 1925, **20,** 234–244.

136. Moreno, J. L. *Who shall survive?* Washington: Nervous and Mental Disease Publishing Co., 1934.
137. Neustadt, R. E. *Presidential power: the politics of leadership.* New York: Wiley, 1960.
138. Odegard, P. *Pressure politics.* New York: Columbia Univer. Press, 1928.
139. Osgood, C. E. The nature and measurement of meaning. *Psychol. Bull.,* 1952, **49,** 197–237.
140. Osgood, C. E., & Tannenbaum, P. H. The principle of congruity in the prediction of attitude change. *Psychol. Rev.,* 1955, **62,** 42–55.
141. Pringle, H. F. *Theodore Roosevelt: a biography.* New York: Harcourt, Brace, 1931.
142. Redl, F. Group emotion and leadership. *Psychiatry,* 1942, **3,** 576–583.
143. Reich, W. *The mass psychology of fascism.* (3rd ed.) T. P. Wolfe (Trans.) New York: Orgone Institute Press, 1946.
144. Renneker, R. E. Some psychodynamic aspects of voting behavior. In E. Burdick & A. J. Brodbeck (Eds.), *American voting behavior.* Glencoe, Ill.: Free Press, 1959. Pp. 399–413.
145. Riesman, D. *The lonely crowd.* New Haven, Conn.: Yale Univer. Press, 1950.
146. Roethlisberger, F. J. *Management and morale.* Cambridge, Mass.: Harvard Univer. Press, 1941.
147. Roethlisberger, F. J., & Dickson, W. J. *Management and the worker.* Cambridge, Mass.: Harvard Univer. Press, 1939.
148. Rokeach, M. *The open and closed mind.* New York: Basic Books, 1960.
149. Rosenberg, M. The meaning of politics in mass society. *Publ. Opin. Quart.,* 1951, **15,** 5–15.
150. Rosenberg, M. Some determinants of political apathy. *Publ. Opin. Quart.,* 1954–55, **18,** 349–366.
151. Sanford, F. H. *Authoritarianism and leadership.* Philadelphia: Stephenson, 1950.
152. Schaffner, B. H. *Fatherland: a study of authoritarianism in the German family.* New York: Columbia Univer. Press, 1948.
153. Schattschneider, E. E. *Politics, pressures, and the tariff.* Englewood Cliffs, N.J.: Prentice-Hall, 1935.
154. Schramm, W. *Communications in modern society.* Urbana, Ill.: Univer. Ill. Press, 1948.
155. Schramm, W. Information theory and mass communication. *Jour. quart.,* 1955, **32,** 131–146.
156. Selznick, P. Foundations of a theory of organization. *Amer. sociol. Rev.,* 1948, **13,** 25–35.
157. Sherif, M. *The psychology of social norms.* New York: Harper, 1936.
158. Sherif, M., & Cantril, H. The psychology of "attitudes." Parts I and II. *Psychol. Rev.,* 1945, **52,** 295–319; 1946, **53,** 1–24.
159. Sherif, M., & Sherif, C. W. *Groups in harmony and tension.* New York: Harper, 1953.
160. Simon, H. A. Some strategic considerations in the construction of so-

cial science models. In P. F. Lazarsfeld (Ed.), *Mathematical thinking in the social sciences.* Glencoe, Ill.: Free Press, 1954.

161. Simon, H. A. *Models of man: social and rational.* New York, Wiley, 1957.
162. Simon, H. A., Smithburg, D. W., & Thompson, V. A. *Public administration.* New York: Knopf, 1950.
163. Skinner, B. F. *Science and human behavior.* New York: MacMillan, 1953.
164. Smith, B. L., & Smith, C. M. *International communication and political opinion.* Princeton, N.J.: Princeton Univer. Press, 1956.
165. Smith, M. B., Bruner, J. S., & White, R. *Opinions and personality.* New York: Wiley, 1956.
166. Snyder, R. C., Bruck, H. W., & Spain, B. *Decision-making as an approach to the study of international politics.* Princeton, N.J.: Princeton Univer., Foreign Policy Analysis Project, Organizational Behavior Section, 1954.
167. Stagner, R. Fascist attitudes: an exploratory study. *J. soc. Psychol.,* 1936, **7**, 309–319.
168. Stagner, R. Fascist attitudes: their determining conditions. *J. soc. Psychol.,* 1936, **7**, 438–454.
169. Stagner, R. Correlational analysis of nationalistic opinions. *J. soc. Psychol.* (SPSSI Bull.), 1940, **12**, 197–212.
170. Stagner, R. Studies of aggressive social attitudes: I. Measurement and interrelation of selected attitudes. *J. soc. Psychol.,* 1944, **20**, 109–120.
171. Stagner, R. Studies of aggressive social attitudes: II. Changes from peace to war. *J. soc. Psychol.,* 1944, **20**, 121–128.
172. Stagner, R. Studies of aggressive social attitudes: III. The role of personal and family scores. *J. soc. Psychol.,* 1944, **20**, 129–140.
173. Stouffer, A. S. *Communism, conformity, and civil liberties.* New York: Doubleday, 1955.
174. Strecker, E. A. *Beyond the clinical frontiers.* New York: Norton, 1940.
175. Strodbeck, F. L. Small group research. *Amer. sociol. Rev.* (Special issue) 1954, **19**, 651–819.
176. Sullivan, H. S. *Conceptions of modern psychiatry.* Washington: William Alanson White Foundation, 1947.
177. Sullivan, II. S. *The interpersonal theory of psychiatry.* New York: Norton, 1953.
178. Tead, O. *Human nature and management.* New York: McGraw-Hill, 1933.
179. de Tocqueville, A. *Democracy in America.* H. Reeve (Trans.), P. Bradley (Ed.). New York: Knopf, 1945.
180. Tolman, E. C. A psychological model. In T. Parsons & E. A. Shils (Eds.), *Toward a general theory of action.* Cambridge, Mass.: Harvard Univer. Press, 1952.
181. Truman, D. *The governmental process.* New York: Knopf, 1951.
182. University of Michigan, Survey Research Center. *America's role in world affairs.* Ann Arbor, Mich.: 1952. (Mimeographed)

183. U.S. Department of Labor, Bureau of Labor Statistics. *Employment outlook in the social sciences.* 1954.
184. Wallace, H. A., & McCamy, J. L. Straw polls and public administration. *Publ. Opin. Quart.,* 1940, **4,** 221–223.
185. Wallas, G. *Human nature in politics.* Boston: Houghton Mifflin, 1909.
186. Warner, W. L., et al. *Democracy in Jonesville.* New York: Harper, 1949.
187. Warner, W. L., & Lunt, P. S. *The social life of a modern community.* New Haven, Conn.: Yale Univer. Press, 1941.
188. Washburn, M. F., Kepler, H., McBroom, N., Pritchard, W., & Reimer, I. The Moore Tests of radical and conservative temperaments. *Amer. J. Psychol.,* 1927, **38,** 449–452.
189. West, J. *Plainville, U.S.A.* New York: Columbia Univer. Press, 1945.
190. Whyte, W. F. *Street corner society.* Chicago: Univer. Chicago Press, 1943.
191. Whyte, W. F. *Human relations in the restaurant industry.* New York: McGraw-Hill, 1948.
192. Williams, R. M., Jr. The reduction of intergroup tensions: a survey of research on problems of ethnic, racial, and religious group relations. *Soc. Sci. Res. Coun. Bull.,* 1947, 57.

THE RELATIONSHIP BETWEEN PSYCHOLOGY AND ECONOMICS

GEORGE KATONA
Survey Research Center
University of Michigan

THE NEED FOR ECONOMIC PSYCHOLOGY

Introduction

During the last twenty years there has been substantial progress in the development of economic psychology. By now, economists in academic institutions as well as in business and government have become accustomed to regard studies of psychological variables as contributions to the understanding of economic processes. Psychologists, however, seem to be less aware of research in economic psychology than economists, although such research may contribute substantially to psychological knowledge.

In the past, many writings in economic psychology have been addressed to economists and have appeared in economic publications because the need for such material has been more pronounced in economic than in psychological research. Moreover, to the practitioners of economic psychology, it appeared more straightforward to address themselves to such economic problems as reactions to income and price changes or factors determining the demand for homes and automobiles than to analyze motivation, habit formation, and group belonging in the area of spending and saving. In either case the central problems were the same, only the labeling differed.

The belief that economic psychology is applied psychology often makes for difficulties in understanding. It is sometimes thought that established theorems of psychology can clarify the problems inherent in, say, inflation or business cycles. If this were true, economic psychology might serve to enhance the collective ego of psychologists and raise the income of some psychologists who might be called in as consultants on economic problems, but it would hardly contribute to psychological theory. But economic psychology is not applied psychology. Even a related, somewhat broader view appears to be insufficient, namely, that economic behavior can serve as a testing ground for psychological generalizations and hypotheses originally developed about noneconomic behavior. We shall attempt to show that studies of spending, saving, investing, and the like can contribute to the development of knowledge of motives, habits, groups, and other areas of psychology. Furthermore, we shall attempt to show that some important psychological problems are more susceptible to study through analysis of economic behavior than through work in areas more traditional to psychology.

It is necessary to find out first what economic psychology is. This task is best accomplished by describing certain developments in economics as well as the economist's need for psychological concepts and analysis.

The Need for Psychology in Economics

In economic literature the term "economic behavior" has been used in several ways. Some theorists have used the expression to mean the behavior of the "economic man," that is, the behavior postulated in their theory of rationality. After setting forth a set of basic assumptions or axioms—maximization of utility by each individual, perfect competition, full knowledge of and control over all means of achieving the postulated ends, and so on—a deductive science was developed which sets forth the required forms of behavior and their aggregate implications. That people frequently, or even generally, do not behave according to the deduced principles was not viewed as a cause for concern, because the theory was aimed at establishing how rational businessmen and consumers ought to behave in order to achieve the postulated goals. It was further assumed that deviations would cancel out and therefore would not influence average or aggregate behavior.

Secondly, in the realm of positive or descriptive rather than normative economics, the term "economic behavior" has been used to mean the behavior of prices, incomes, or the economy of a nation. Economists in this realm have been concerned with the relationships that exist among changes in supply, prices, incomes, consumption, and investment. Statistical analyses of covariations or lagged relationships, regression equations showing functional dependence, and the like were thought to explain what happens in the economy, except for some random variations. As an example, we may mention a recent symposium on the "behavior of unemployment." The papers dealt with the relation between different rates of employment and production, profits, inventories, and similar items. The analysis was restricted to interrelationships among results of human behavior. Neither the behavior of producers, distributors, consumers, or government agencies which might cause unemployment, nor the behavior of the unemployed persons was studied.

The third sense in which the term "economic behavior" has been used is represented by studies of how businessmen and consumers behave, through an analysis of decision formation, its circumstances, and its antecedents. Why are such studies needed? Suppose we accept for a moment the following statement of an economic theorist, which was probably intended to justify the second point of view (quantitative economics) given earlier: "It is the behavior of commodities not the behavior of man which is the prime focus of interest in economic studies" [1, p. 82]. Economic psychology holds that in order to understand "the behavior of commodities"—that is, the interrelationships between prices, demand, supply, and so forth—it is necessary, but not enough, to analyze such results of human behavior. It is necessary also to study the decision makers because their motives, attitudes, and opinions influence their actions and thereby what happens in and to the economy. In pragmatic terms we must ask the question: If we make psychological studies, in addition to the more traditional economic-statistical studies, do we gain a better understanding of economic processes (the behavior of commodities) and are we able to predict economic processes with greater accuracy? Economic psychology started out by answering this question in the affirmative on a priori grounds; by now empirical evidence supports its contention.

The theoretical grounds for the need of psychology in economics may be presented in terms familiar to psychologists. If it were true that economic stimuli completely determined economic responses, that is, if a one-to-one relationship existed between stimuli and responses, psychological studies would be neither necessary nor useful.

One-to-one relationships between stimuli and responses have been implicitly assumed in many areas of economic research. Propositions such as "Consumer expenditures are a function of income," or "Business investment is a function of profits" imply such relationships. Frequently, of course, more complex formulas have been used. For instance, time lags have been introduced or a larger number of variables have been taken into account. In most cases, however, such variations have served merely to provide a better description of the stimuli without altering the underlying assumption.

Many fundamental propositions of classical economic theory follow the same principle. "The lower the price, the higher the demand." This basic notion, derived from the so-called "law of supply and demand," may be read to mean: "Certain changes in prices serve as stimuli which necessarily bring forth certain responses, namely, predictable changes in demand." The fact that the reactions of human beings to price reductions may depend on their past experiences, attitudes, and expectations is disregarded. Or whatever latitude human beings have is thought to fall under the ceteris paribus clause and is classified as an unimportant deviation from the rule.

Economic behavior can be viewed, however, in either of two ways: as dependent exclusively on situational factors, or as dependent on situational factors as perceived by the decision maker. The second view attaches great importance to changes in habits, motives, and attitudes. Both views are applicable to business as well as to consumer decisions. Economic theorists have sometimes attributed importance to business attitudes and expectations in influencing capital outlays and changes in inventories. Recently, however, the importance of psychological considerations has also been demonstrated in the area of consumer behavior [11, 16].

Not so long ago it was widely held that consumers played only a negligible role in generating economic fluctuations. Of the three sectors of the economy, only two, the business sector and the government sector, were believed to have autonomy. Consumer income was thought to be determined by what business and government did, and consumer expenditures were considered a function of consumer income. In brief, the consumption function—the relation of consumer spending to consumer income—was held to be stable, or dependent on level and change in income in a simple and predictable manner.

Without relating here the American business-cycle developments during the past fifteen years, it may suffice to say that several times during that period forecasts based on extrapolations of consumer expenditures proved to be misleading. The assumption that consumers would continue to behave in the same way as before (i.e., that the relation of consumer expenditures to income would remain unchanged) was widely blamed for the incorrectness of the prediction that widespread unemployment would occur shortly after the end of World War II. During the recession of 1948–1949, the Korean War of 1950–1951, the upswing of 1954–

1955, and finally, the recession of 1957–1958, consumers proved to be powerful forces generating changes in economic developments. Thus, it has been shown that the recovery in 1954 appeared earlier in purchases of consumer durable goods than in consumer incomes or business investments. Disappointment with traditional methods of analyzing consumer expenditures enhanced the receptivity of economists for psychological studies.

Some contributions of psychological economics toward the understanding of fluctuations in the consumption function during the postwar years will be mentioned later in this paper. At this point, however, we must discuss a second consideration which has added to the acceptance of psychological analysis in economics. Dissatisfaction has developed with the exclusive use of aggregative or macroeconomic studies. Most of the economic-statistical work during the past twenty-five years has consisted of assembling and analyzing data on annual or quarterly changes of gross national product, national income, total consumer expenditures, and similar magnitudes relating to the performance of the entire economy. While these studies are of the greatest importance, many investigators now agree that aggregate data need to be supplemented by microeconomic data. In addition to data on total income, we need to know the distribution of incomes and income changes by size; in addition to data on total savings or bank deposits, we need to have information on the distribution of these assets.

Research on such distributions became concerned with demographic and sociological variables. What kind of people have very large or very small incomes, bank deposits, and so on? The race and age of the people, the number of children in the family, and location in urban or rural settings became important variables in studying spending and saving. The principal method of obtaining information on these variables, the sample interview survey, at the same time provided a bridge between economic and psychological studies [3, 25].

An example may illustrate how the availability of a methodological tool has helped to broaden the research objectives. Purchasing war bonds became the most important form of saving during World War II. The U.S. Treasury, of course, kept and published records about the amounts of bonds bought, owned, and redeemed. These over-all data could be correlated, along the traditional lines of economic studies, with changes in national income, but not with the incomes of individual bond purchasers, owners, or redeemers. (Buyers of war bonds did not have to state their incomes!) Therefore, sample interview surveys were needed and have been conducted regularly since 1942 to collect information on such questions as the following: What proportion of the bonds is bought and held by people in different income groups? What proportion of their income do people put into bonds? Are bond holdings concentrated among high-income people, or are they distributed as widely as income is? In the same surveys, information was obtained about the relation of purchases and holdings to age, family size, occupation, education, and the like. At a very early date, requirements of sales promotion led to an inclusion of psychological variables, such as motives and attitudes, in the bond surveys.

Why did people buy war bonds? This question could be studied by determining the differences between the people who bought bonds and those who did not. But information on income, assets, age, etc., of buyers and nonbuyers of bonds did not suffice. The investigation of psychological factors was necessary to gain new insights on why people bought bonds. Two methods were available. One consisted of asking people about their motives and attitudes, the second of correlation analysis. Thus it was established that people who were aware of several reasons for purchasing bonds (patriotic reasons as well as saving for the sake of buying a house or business later, for example) bought more bonds than people who had one reason only. At the same time, opinions about the relative advantages and disadvantages of bonds and other forms of saving revealed attitudes that shed light on bond purchases. The second method made use of questions about variables which did not appear in answer to direct questions but which were suggested by hypotheses about saving behavior. In this way, an association was established between personal solicitation at the place of work and bond buying [6] and between certain income expectations and bond buying.

Similar studies have been conducted in a variety of areas of consumer choice. Purchases of houses, automobiles and other durable goods, life insurance and common stock may be mentioned as examples of areas in which survey data on people's attitudes and expectations have contributed to the understanding of their behavior. To be sure, statistical studies are still being made which relate demand exclusively to financial variables. But, to put the matter in oversimplified terms, economists have increasingly accepted the fact that effective demand is a function of both ability to buy and willingness to do so. And, furthermore, they have accepted the fact that willingness to buy is susceptible to measurement and analysis [16, 19, 26].

The Need for Studies of Economic Behavior in Psychology

It is easy to make a case for the need of studies of economic behavior. Economic activities take up a substantial part of people's everyday lives. The housewife spends much of her time in purchasing goods. People who are engaged in business are preoccupied with economic activities. Many people who are not in business occasionally make economic decisions such as buying a car, saving money rather than spending it, or changing the form in which savings and investments are kept.

The psychologists' need for studies of economic behavior is much greater than references to the frequency of economic activities would indicate. The study of economic behavior occupies a unique position among studies of complex forms of social behavior in that here action can be isolated and measured readily. The term "action" is used in contrast to "verbal behavior." In most other studies of social psychology we face one of these two situations: either our dependent variables are expressed opinions and attitudes, or we study artificially simple conditions.

To illustrate the first situation, we may refer to an important topic of social psychology, the analysis of race relations and prejudice. If we recall the very few investigations in which action was studied (for instance, in interracial housing developments), it becomes clear that most studies were concerned with the explanation of different opinions (for example, "I am willing to dine with Negroes," or "I am opposed to my sister marrying a Negro") and of changes in such opinions. While it is true that attitudes are predispositions to action, it is important to include both attitudes and actions, as well as the relation between the two, in our studies. We learn a great deal by determining how people talk about "communism, conformity, and civil liberties"; the careful survey directed by S. A. Stouffer and published in a book having that title [43] is a clear indication of the value of this kind of investigation. However, this kind of survey affords little opportunity to study the relation of people's attitudes and opinions to their action. Or, to mention one more example, studies of political behavior which analyze the differences between Republicans and Democrats can be readily subjected to attitudinal research, but the study of the relation of attitudes to action is usually restricted to voting in presidential elections once every four years.

In experimental psychology, of course, action responses are frequently studied; primarily, however, in simple situations. In experimental studies of complex social behavior, responses in the form of doing something, rather than expressing a judgment or opinion, do occur occasionally, but usually in carefully controlled and perhaps not entirely realistic situations.

In a far too simple schematic way, we may describe the antecedents to action as follows:

1	2	3	4
Change in environment	Personality determinants	Change in attitudes or opinions	Action
(Stimuli, Situational determinants)	(Habits, Attitudes, Expectations, Motives, etc.)		

This does not imply that every action necessarily has all three ante-cedents; some automatic responses and action under compulsion may be viewed as lacking 2 and 3, or item 3 may be missing even though both 1 and 2 play a role.

The point emphasized here is that economic behavior presents unique opportunities for studying the entire chain. When the action variable can be identified clearly, it is possible to study those circumstances in which the "environment" and those in which the "person" is most relevant. That behavior is a function of both the environment and the person has been expressed by the equation $B = f(E, P)$. We wish to go further; we wish to clarify the respective roles of the two kinds of factors under different circumstances. Motives, attitudes, or expectations are treated as intervening variables, that is, as factors modifying the impact of changes in the environment and thereby altering the response.

Several types of action that occur in the economic area have been mentioned already. Some of these, such as buying groceries or small items of clothing or spending on carfare or newspapers, are not usually salient to the decision maker and not easily susceptible to psychological studies. It is easier to analyze the motives and attitudes regarding relatively rare and subjectively important decisions such as buying an automobile or life insurance and the like. Similarly, in the business area many things happen which are difficult to study from a psychological point of view. (As an example, we may refer to what economists call "involuntary changes in inventories.") But making capital outlays, changing prices, and choosing the location for a new plant are examples of major forms of business action that are susceptible to psychological study.

Turning to the beginning of our action chain, studies of economic behavior may also contribute to the clarification of situational determi-nants. Economic stimuli often consist of *information*. New orders re-ceived, changes in sales or costs, news about actions of competitors or consumers, news about business-cycle trends—all this variety of stimuli, whether transmitted by organs of mass communication, by letters and memoranda, or by word of mouth, represents information. How is infor-mation assimilated by the recipient, and under what circumstances does it affect action? These are central problems of the interaction between the environment and the person. These problems can be studied effec-tively in the area of economic behavior and can be related to education, group belonging, and attitudes; they can also be related to consumer resources, such as income or assets, which represent enabling conditions for economic action.

Enough has been said to illustrate the author's belief that economic psychology opens up new vistas for psychology. We shall now turn to a discussion of specific problems. In some past publications these problems have been grouped in economic categories. For instance, business investment or consumer spending for durable goods has been studied and the contribution of psychological variables to explaining changes in these economic activities analyzed. For our purposes, we shall adopt the opposite procedure of citing psychological problems and presenting the possible contribution of an analysis of economic issues to these problems.

HABITS AND PROBLEM SOLVING

Habitual Behavior

According to classical economics, economic behavior is rational. Although this thesis requires substantial qualification, a strong case can be made for the unique opportunities economic behavior offers to the psychologist for studying deliberate and carefully considered decisions and actions. Before turning to such studies, it is necessary to point to less complex processes which are likewise important in economic behavior. The acquisition of behavior patterns through association and reinforcement—learning through repeated satisfactory past experiences—represents a most accessible area to the experimenter, of course. Studies of economic behavior also offer valuable possibilities for an analysis of habit formation. These studies may be extended to an analysis of the circumstances under which behavior remains habitual and those under which habits are broken.

There can be no doubt that habits are powerful among businessmen and consumers. Following established procedure or rule of thumb or acting in a routine way have often been described in studies of business behavior. If businessmen were to consider every item of information they receive—every piece of news, each letter or telephone call—as giving rise to a problem which needs to be studied and analyzed, they would have no time to conduct their business. In larger firms, delegation of authority is necessary; employees with lower status usually are given instructions and rules to follow rather than permission to make independent decisions. Many well-established business procedures find their origin in conventions that prevail in the entire trade or industry; others have been used for long periods in the firm; others develop over relatively short spans of time. Similarly, consumers often adopt ways of spending and saving that prevail in their country, their family, or social group, or ways acquired through their own experience.

We may enumerate some few forms of habitual business behavior which have been described recently. Price setting by manufacturers, wholesalers, and retailers appears to be frequently habitual [8, 11]. First, there are accounting conventions, such as division of costs into variable and fixed costs, each of which is defined in specific ways. Second, there are rules about the usual margin to be added to fixed costs in order to determine the price. What is true about markups often applies also to markdowns. Retailers have developed habits that determine the selection of goods offered in clearance sales, as well as the extent of the price reductions. Accounting principles exist also as to depreciation charges, and habits have been developed with regard to the relation of depreciation charges to replacement costs. Inventory control and decisions about changes in inventories represent a further area in which principles, rules, and habits govern the procedures used on a wide scale.

Not much is known about how these forms of habitual practice developed. It is conceivable that they all originated in calculation, careful analysis, and extensive deliberation. New ideas devised by one or another theoretician or practitioner may have been first tried out tentatively, then formalized in memoranda or books, and finally accepted as standard practice. The end result may be described from a psychological point of view as follows: To predict how a businessman (or firm) will act under given circumstances, it is best to find out how he has acted before under similar circumstances.

Is this principle generally valid? More important still, is it true that the more often a given practice has been successfully applied in the past, the more probable it is that it will be applied again? Or do different principles determine under what conditions a habit or an established practice will or will not be followed?

We turn to a study of manufacturers' decisions to embark on an expansion project involving expenditures for new plants and machinery [17]. Such projects were most frequent among organizations whose executives described the current situation and the prospects of the firm as favorable. It was found that a rising trend of sales often induced manufacturing firms to undertake expansion projects as a matter of course. But the correlation between the two variables—(1) satisfaction with recent past and optimism about expected sales trends and (2) frequency of expansion projects—was far from perfect. A great many firms did not expand in spite of an optimistic outlook, and many firms decided upon expansion projects in spite of what their executives called "an unsatisfactory situation and unfavorable prospects." These instances are of particular importance for economic research because they may bring forth, or may contribute to, a reversal of prevailing economic trends. Detailed interviews with executives revealed that expansion under unfavorable conditions resulted from what the psychologist calls "problem solving." Under the impact of strong motivational forces, careful deliberation and the weighing of alternative courses of action took place. The firms experiencing strong pressures (by competitors or by the threat of large losses) embarked on a search among different possible courses of action, such as taking up new products, changing the quality of products, or closing certain plants. If expansion was undertaken, it was a deliberate choice among several possibilities. In contrast, expansion undertaken under the impact of rising sales was described as "automatic," or as "something that is always done."

Traditional norms, long-established rules, and habit have been found to play a dominant role in determining the borrowing practices of business firms [13]. The policy of certain firms calls for all financing to be done from the firm's own funds; the policy of other firms is governed by the principle that short-term bank credit should be used exclusively for short-term purposes, such as providing working capital or seasonal credit; in still other firms, all funds mingle, and business is regarded as making use of other people's money. Following the established principle is automatic; deviating from it calls for high-level decisions which are carefully considered under the pressure of strong motivational forces. Reorganization of the field is a good description of what takes place. Important new events, such as outbreak of war, change in government policies, or change in the management of the firm, may serve as precipitating circumstances. Attitudes and expectations of the managers play no significant role when the investment or financing decisions are habitual; changes in their feelings of security or confidence and in their hopes and fears play a large role when genuinely new decisions are taken. When no precipitating circumstances exist, no problems are seen and problem solving does not take place.

Turning to consumer studies, we find the most common instances of habitual behavior in frequent small purchases, in buying the same products in the same store, in what has been called "brand loyalty," and also in budgeting practices. In contrast, the assumption is sometimes made that rare purchases which involve large amounts of money are made with circumspection and careful deliberation. In a study of purchases of television sets, refrigerators, washing machines, and kitchen ranges, this assumption was not confirmed [33]. In a substantial number of these purchases there was no discussion among family members, no long planning period, no consideration of alternatives, no information seeking, no shopping around in several stores, and no consideration of different brands. Why should this be? Are high-income people or people of certain personality types the ones who do not care and purchase their large household goods without deliberation? The study revealed that there were more important factors than income and personality which accounted for an absence of deliberation. Some of these were urgent need for an article, the notion that a unique opportunity to buy was available, and satisfaction with a similar article previously used. These were some of the major conditions under which problem-solving behavior was not resorted to. In the absence of these conditions, problem solving was sometimes fragmentary or superficial, but not entirely lacking.

Exploration of the possible role of habit in consumer behavior has contributed to the clarification of a central problem of postwar economic research. During World War II, a large proportion of the American people acquired liquid assets (bank deposits, war bonds, and the like). Would ownership of liquid money stimulate spending because money "burns holes in people's pockets," or because it reduces the incentives to save? More generally, is spending or saving a function of asset holdings, in addition to being a function of income? Most economists answered these questions in the affirmative on a priori grounds, and these answers had grave consequences for predicting postwar economic trends. One way of testing the hypothesis was by asking this question: How does saving (the proportion of income saved) differ among families who are similar in many respects (especially regarding their income), but who differ in the amounts of their liquid assets? The finding most relevant for our problem was this: Among families with "large" liquid-asset holdings, there were more large savers (those who saved 25 per cent or more of their income) as well as more dissavers (those who spent more than their income) than there were among families with "small" liquid-asset holdings; the latter predominantly saved a small proportion of their income. In other words, overspending is encouraged by large liquid-asset holdings among some, but by no means all, people. The finding that many holders of large liquid assets saved a substantial proportion of their income should not have come as a surprise. It should have been expected on the basis of psychological considerations. Large liquid-asset holdings are most commonly the result of enduring past saving efforts; in attempting to predict the future saving behavior of people who have been large savers in the recent past, should it not be assumed that some of these people will continue to behave as they did before? Whether or not past saving habits are continued seems to depend on the attitudes and the level of aspirations of the savers.[1]

Expectations and Their Influence

Expectations represent a factor of great influence on spending and saving behavior. The study of the origin and the effects of economic expectations is of interest to the economist as well as to the psychologist. We shall first turn to a discussion of *price expectations* and their influence on demand.

[1] Economic research in contrast to psychological research is not satisfied with the finding that two different tendencies prevail among holders of large liquid assets. Economists are interested in the relative size of the two tendencies, that is, in the effect of large liquid assets on aggregate or mean saving [11, 16, 23, 24].

"What has happened in the past, people expect to happen in the future." This thesis is well grounded in certain psychological theories and has been frequently accepted by economists. In terms of economic experience, if prices (all prices or the prices of specific goods) have gone up for quite a while, it is probable that most people will expect further price increases; if they have gone down, it is probable that most people will expect further price decreases. On the other hand, it is also possible to argue that people form expectations on the basis of careful consideration of past developments (in our case, of a consideration of the causes and effects of past price changes). Then sometime they may discover that the current situation differs from the previous one, so that a continuation of past trends is not to be expected or even that their reversal is to be expected.

Before discussing findings about the development of price expectations, we may formulate certain generalizations about the effects of past and expected price changes. It follows from the so-called "law of supply and demand" that, other things being constant, if prices go up, the quantity demanded will decline; if prices go down, the quantity demanded will increase. This can be demonstrated for the entire economy and the general price level as follows: If the money available to buyers does not change and has been fully spent in period 1, then in period 2, in which prices are higher than in period 1, buyers can only purchase a smaller quantity than they were able to do in period 1. For individual products, the problem is more complicated because of differences in the price elasticity of the products; nevertheless, the thesis is believed to be overwhelmingly correct and rational.

Regarding the effect of price expectations, it has often been postulated in the light of assumptions about the rational or economic man that if people expect prices to go up, the quantity demanded will increase. Obviously, it is prudent to buy before the price increase takes place, and some people will be in a position to do so. Contrariwise, if people expect prices to go down, the quantity demanded will decline. In this case, people will wait with some postponable purchases until the prices have declined. These principles are assumed to apply to particular products as well as to the general price level.

From a psychological point of view, it is not permissible to consider the two principles relating to past and future price movements as separate and independent. People's time perspective extends both backward and forward in a selective manner. This is implicit in our earlier argument that price expectations might derive from the perception of past price movements. If, however, we assume that people expect what has happened before to happen again, then the postulates of the economists would not yield any clear conclusions. A typical or frequent instance would then consist of past price increases and the expectation of further price increases. Yet past price increases have been postulated to cause a decline and expected price increases to cause an increase in the quantity demanded. The converse is the case for past price decreases, coupled with the expectation of further price decreases.

We shall turn now to an enumeration of some findings obtained in recent studies in which the author participated [16, 36]. Generalizations from empirical research are difficult because "other things" are rarely constant. Therefore, the following propositions about consumer behavior may not be generally valid, but restricted to the circumstances under which they were obtained.

1. Past as well as expected price movements influence consumer behavior only when they are substantial. Small experienced or expected price changes usually do not induce consumers either to step up or to reduce their spending. What is substantial and what is small—in other words, how large the threshold is—may vary according to the situation and to past experience with price changes.

2. Expectation of large price increases following actual price increases occurs under conditions of "inflationary fever" or "runaway inflation," when distrust in the money prevails and causes buying waves. This has happened frequently in foreign countries under conditions of war or its aftermath. But in America, too, there have been certain relatively short periods when the fulfillment of expected price increases reinforced expectations of further increases.

3. Sometimes past and expected price increases do not increase demand; rather, they elicit a feeling of being worse off and resentment against the price increases. If these feelings are coupled with the notion that the expected price increases will be small ("creeping inflation"), then demand may decline. This was the case in the United States in 1951 and in 1957 when consumer demand for durable goods declined.

4. Expectation of price increases can originate at a time when prices have been stable because of an understanding of impending developments. If the new developments represent a complete break with the past and if substantial price increases are expected, then buying in excess of one's needs and stocking up may result. This was the case in the summer of 1950, after the outbreak of war in Korea. On the other hand, expectation of small price increases is often viewed as an adverse factor; people may feel that because of the price increases it will become harder to make ends meet. In the last few years, the great majority of people who expected some price increases said that these increases would affect them and the economy adversely.

5. The effect of past price declines on demand depends on price expectations. If price reductions are viewed as the beginning of further price reductions, the quantity demanded declines. If the price reductions

are considered temporary, so that unique buying opportunities are perceived, the quantity demanded increases. This principle applies to specific goods, for instance, to "bargains" obtainable through clearance sales or discounts. The expectation of a decline in the general price level is usually viewed as a favorable factor, namely, as one which adds to the purchasing power of one's income.

6. Experience that prices have been stable, coupled with the expectation that they will remain stable, stimulates buying. People become accustomed to prices that have persisted for quite a while, learn to consider them "right," and gain confidence from the expectation of price stability. Anxiety about overpaying or about being able to purchase the same article cheaper at a later time is a deterrent to buying, and the absence of such anxiety is a stimulant. Habituation to prices appears to be a slow process. After the substantial price increases of 1950–1951, it was possible to observe over a period of eighteen months how the impression "Prices are too high" gradually declined in frequency and intensity and gave way to "Prices are stable."

Two rather general principles follow from our research on reactions to price movements. First, it appears that the meaning of price movements varies under different conditions and depends on the whole situation. In addition to the immediate stimuli, certain general affective or cognitive notions—that inflation is bad, for instance—are of importance. Second, it appears that expectations may result either from repeated past experiences or from an understanding of the circumstances which bring forth certain new developments. In addition, of course, the studies on reactions to price increases are of practical importance. Different measures are needed to fight runaway inflation and creeping inflation because consumer attitudes toward the two kinds of inflation differ greatly.

Differences in the form of expectations were relevant for the analysis of *income expectations* also. It became necessary to analyze separately temporary and permanent increases or decreases in income. An income change which the recipient viewed as permanent or a step toward further changes in the same direction had to be distinguished from one which he considered a temporary windfall or a temporary calamity. Both kinds of situation were found to occur frequently [10].

The study of the effects of income changes was stimulated by principles of consumer behavior first announced by J. M. Keynes [21]. Only one aspect of these studies will be reported here briefly. Keynes assumed that the habitual standard of life would persist for a while after both income increases and income decreases. On the other hand, psychological principles made it improbable that both favorable and unfavorable developments (rewards as well as punishments) would elicit persistence of spending habits. Empirical studies during the postwar years in America confirmed the assumption that expenditures would not be universally restricted under the impact of income decline. But spending habits were readily altered by many people under the impact of rising incomes. Rather than maintaining their habitual standard of life, many families were found to have gone into debt or to have liquidated previously accumulated savings in order to acquire some needed goods when their incomes rose and were expected to rise further.

These studies indicated that borrowing is not generally associated with poverty or distress [9]. On the contrary, buying durable goods on installment and buying houses with a large mortgage debt occurs frequently with improved conditions and optimistic expectations. Not uncommonly, debt is incurred when cash is available to purchase the desired goods. This apparently irrational behavior appears to be due partly to people's awareness of their own saving habits. Some people doubt that they would have the fortitude to replenish their depleted bank deposits, while buying on installment necessitates the repayment of the debt and leaves the bank deposits intact.

Since human beings are not calculating mechanisms, the concept of the rational man is of no use in economic psychology. On the other hand, the concept of rational behavior, representing one of several possible forms of behavior, is worth analysis, although such analysis has been greatly neglected in psychology [12]. Studies of business and consumer behavior make an operational definition of this concept possible. Careful deliberation, seeking of information, and consideration of alternative courses of action have been found to be characteristic features of rational behavior. Such behavior, then, resembles to some extent the behavior studied in problem-solving experiments. When psychologists experimented with problem solving, they usually started with giving a problem to the subjects, who were externally motivated to work on it. In contrast to such experiments, economic behavior offers opportunities to study the conditions under which problem solving occurs.

The major alternative to problem-solving behavior appears to be habitual behavior—doing what one has done before under similar circumstances—not impulsive or ununderstandable behavior. Businessmen and consumers abandon habitual behavior when they perceive themselves to be in a new situation, that is, when a reorganization of the psychological field is called for.

SOCIAL PSYCHOLOGY

Instability of Attitudes and Social Learning

When we referred to the influence of attitudes on business-cycle trends in the preceding sections, we implied that very many consumers may have changed their attitudes in the same direction at the same time. If economic attitudes and expectations were fairly stable, being dependent solely on personality factors, the optimism of some people and the pessimism of others might cancel out without affecting the economy as a whole. Economic attitudes are of importance only if this does not happen, as a rule. Studies carried out over the last ten years have brought ample confirmation that optimistic and pessimistic attitudes frequently do not cancel out. These studies support the following generalizations, which are in accordance with established principles of social psychology:

1. New information will be apprehended in similar ways by very many people and especially by people with similar interests or by members of the same group, such as all, or many, businessmen.

2. When information is apprehended in the same way by broad groups of people, similar attitudes will arise among many people and they will act in a similar manner.

3. Action by some members of a group (e.g., by some businessmen) will facilitate similar action by other members of the same group.

The spread of rumors has long been recognized as an important topic of social psychology. The same should be true of the spread of economic attitudes, such as price expectations, business outlook, feelings of confidence and security, or of distrust and insecurity. A major generalization which has emerged regarding the change and spread of such attitudes is this:

If successive measurements yield similar aggregate distributions in economic attitudes or expectations, then it is likely that many individuals have changed their attitudes in one direction and many others in the opposite direction. If, however, in the aggregate there was a radical and substantial change in attitudes and expectations, then the direction of the change tends to be the same among most people and tends to bring forth similar changes in behavior [14].

This generalization was derived first from an analysis of American business-cycle developments associated with the Korean War. The outbreak of this war had marked effects on the domestic economy [18]. The news of military reversals—in the summer of 1950, when the American troops were driven back to the southeastern corner of Korea, and in the winter of 1950, when American armies retreated several hundred miles from the Yalu River after the intervention of the Chinese—came as a shock to most people. Within a short time most businessmen and consumers reacted to the news by expecting a third world war, which, it was thought, would bring about shortages in civilian goods and rapid price increases. The behavior of very many people underwent a sudden change. Businessmen stocked up on raw materials at sharply rising prices, and consumers purchased houses, automobiles, and other durable goods at an unprecedented rate.

Early in 1951, consumer attitudes again changed radically. The situation at that time was described as "cold war." Cold war was understood to mean many years of tension and friction, a disagreeable state of the world in which taxes would be high because of large defense expenditures. However, in the absence of a shooting war there would not be shortages in civilian goods. The sharp price rise in 1950–1951 was resented. Although some further price increases were anticipated, consumers generally reduced their rate of spending.

The twelve months beginning with the summer of 1951 represented a period of gradual habituation to the cold war and the new price levels. There was no marked change in the attitudes of the American people as a whole, and increased optimism of some coincided with increased pessimism of others.

Uniform and substantial changes in mass attitudes were observed again in the summer and fall of 1954. Relief that the then widely advertised depression had remained small, satisfaction with the prevailing price stability, and confidence in continued improvements in standards of living were found among the reasons for this change in public attitudes, which was followed by a substantial increase in the purchases of consumer durable goods [19].

In 1955 and 1956, there were no substantial changes in the distribution of economic attitudes among American consumers. This plateau at a high level was, however, again characterized by frequent changes in the attitudes of individual people. Some people became more optimistic and others more pessimistic without significant changes in the aggregate.

In June, 1957, and more pronouncedly toward the end of that year, a marked decline in consumer optimism was observed [15]. The majority of consumers reported having heard of unfavorable news and expressed anxiety about forthcoming business trends. The sentiment of some other people remained unchanged, and there were scarcely any people whose opinions and attitudes showed an improvement.

The findings about the changes in the economic attitudes of the American people were derived from several surveys in which the same questions were asked from different representative cross sections of the population. By interrogating the same respondents in consecutive surveys, that is, through the panel method, further relevant information could be obtained [14].

We shall first illustrate the type of information that can be obtained through the two methods of inquiry. By making two successive measurements with different samples, data of the kind shown on the top part of Table 1 are collected. For instance, we may find that response A was given by 50 per cent of a sample the first time and by 55 per cent of a sample the second time. This would represent a small change in the aggregate distributions or in the "Marginals" (Case 1). Or regarding another question (or regarding the same question at another time), response A may be given by 50 per cent of a sample the first time and by 70 per cent the second time; this would represent a large change in the marginals (Case 2).

When we make two measurements with the same people, we also obtain information about how many individuals have changed their responses and in what way they changed them. Both small and large marginal changes may come about through either few or many individuals changing their responses. It is always possible to designate the "minimum turnover of individuals" which is required to bring forth a given marginal change, as well as the "maximum turnover of individuals" which is possible, given the marginal change. This is shown for simple distributions in Table 1, which also presents an intermediate degree of turnover.

In actual observations, neither the minimum nor the maximum rates of turnover will be found. But certain distributions recorded through the panel method may be close to the minimum rate, while others may be close to the maximum possible-turnover rate. In principle, after defining the terms "large" and "small," we may distinguish four situations:

Case 1*a*. Small marginal change and small turnover of individuals
Case 1*b*. Small marginal change and large turnover of individuals
Case 2*a*. Large marginal change and small turnover of individuals
Case 2*b*. Large marginal change and large turnover of individuals

Suppose we ask a sample of people about their ages on two successive occasions (say, six months apart). Then we obtain data corresponding to Case 1*a*. The two successive age distributions will be quite similar and, in spite of occasional errors and misclassifications, relatively few individuals will be found to have given different answers; thus, only a slight turnover of individuals will be apparent. Similar results were obtained regarding certain deep-seated and enduring attitudes. The question to be raised is: If we ask questions about people's financial notions and expectations, which sometimes yield small and sometimes substantial changes in marginal distributions, will we then obtain small or large turnover rates?

In studies carried out between 1954 and 1956, two consecutive answers were obtained to more than 30 questions about personal financial and general economic expectations from the same representative panel of urban people. Some of these attitudes showed small and others large marginal changes after intervals of six or twelve months. It was found that two similar aggregate distributions (small marginal changes) usually corresponded with a great many people changing their attitudes. Some people's becoming more optimistic and other people's becoming more pessimistic canceled out. Cross shifts were frequent, and the findings resembled what has been shown in Table 1 as "Intermediate turnover, Case 1." When, however, the two consecutive aggregate distributions differed greatly, then in most cases only relatively few people swam against the current, so that the findings were not very different from the "Minimum turnover, Case 2" in Table 1. When optimism increased greatly, for instance, practically the entire population fell in either of two cells, those who had unchanged expectations and those who had improved expectations about the business outlook.[2]

TABLE 1. MODELS OF MARGINAL CHANGE AND TURNOVER OF INDIVIDUALS

		Case 1			Case 2	
		I	II			I	II
Marginals	A	50	55	A	50	70
	B	50	45	B	50	30
		100%	100%		100%	100%
Minimum turnover	$50_{A,A}$	$5_{B,A}$	55_{IIA}	$50_{A,A}$	$20_{B,A}$	70_{IIA}
	$0*_{A,B}$	$45_{B,B}$	45_{IIB}	$0*_{A,B}$	$30_{B,B}$	30_{IIB}
	50_{IA}	50_{IB}	100%	50_{IA}	50_{IB}	100%
Intermediate turnover	35	20	55	35	35	70
	15*	30	45	15*	15	30
	50	50	100%	50	50	100%
Maximum turnover	5	50	55	20	50	70
	45*	0	45	30*	0	30
	50	50	100%	50	50	100%

I = first measurement; II = later measurement; A = frequency of response A; B = frequency of response B.

* This is the crucial cell indicating the frequency of changes contrary to the general trend.

These studies then yield confirmation of the principle stated before. Substantial changes in mass attitudes reflect usually fairly uniform changes among very many people. Absence of substantial changes in mass attitudes, on the other hand, does not justify the conclusion that the attitudes of most individuals remained unchanged.

In one instance, that of small marginal change, large turnover of individuals, Case 1b, we may speak of instability of attitudes. Studies of the origin of such instability revealed that both changes in the personal situation of the respondents and the crudeness of the measuring methods may have contributed to it. Changers and nonchangers were found to differ from each other in what happened to them between the first and

[2] Quantitative data and their statistical analysis are published in [14].

second measurement. The two groups also differed in many respects already at the time of the first measurement when some of their attitudes appeared to be the same.

In the other important and frequent instance—large marginal change, small turnover, Case 2*a*,—we may speak of "social learning." According to data obtained in the first survey, hardly any differences were found among those people who later changed and those who did not change their attitudes. Individual differences (e.g., income changes for some, but not for others) between the first and the second survey likewise did not provide an explanation of the findings. But one group was found to have learned something. It acquired information about the economy which corresponded to the change in expectations. The information was understood in a similar way by people belonging to the same group, and social facilitation reinforced the common attitudes. It appears that such learning represents a current against which it is rather difficult to swim. The current may counteract personal experiences of an opposite nature. A sharp increase in optimism about business trends, for instance, was found even among people with adverse personal experiences.[3]

We have limited knowledge about the circumstances in which a current of opinion will develop and bring forth substantial and uniform changes in expectations. A study of economic developments or a content analysis of economic news transmitted in the summer of 1954 or 1957, for instance, would not have sufficed to predict the impact of the news on consumers. After having determined the changes in people's attitudes, it was possible to relate the changes to certain information and thus to explain them. But it is not easy to determine in advance which news will become salient and influential. Therefore, measurement of attitudes and their changes remains indispensable. In 1951, in 1954, and again in 1957, it provided unexpected information on consumer sentiment and advance information on changes in the rate of consumer purchases of durable goods [16].

Explorations of Group Behavior

Acceptance of the thesis about the uniformity of substantial changes in the economic attitudes of masses of consumers leads to new problems. One basic problem is this: A hundred or even fifty years ago, when news spread slowly and most people were ignorant of happenings outside their limited personal spheres, it was more difficult for incipient recessions and inflations to spread and snowball than it is today. Now, with rapid mass

[3] Campbell and associates [4] make use of the author's study and, in analyzing voting behavior, distinguish between personal forces which move individuals selectively and social forces which move large sections of the population more or less simultaneously.

communication, every localized difficulty and small price increase becomes generally known and may give rise to mass hysteria. Therefore, too much information received by too many people may be thought to be detrimental to economic stability.

Do mass attitudes and expectations necessarily snowball and become cumulative and self-justifying? The fact that this may occur occasionally is well known. Some of us still remember the bank runs of the early thirties. Rumors led some people to withdraw their deposits from the banks, more and more people followed suit, and finally the expectation that a bank was not sound made itself correct; even strong banks could not withstand the runs. Similarly, we recall from the thirties the vicious circle in which a slight reduction in demand led to cutbacks in production, then to the expectation of lower incomes, to reduced incomes and curtailed demand, and so forth. Contrariwise, inflationary fever was experienced in Germany, France, China, and many other countries. People expected prices to go up, therefore spent their money rapidly, which made prices go up; then people expected prices to go up further, and so on. That such sequences can occur under certain circumstances is beyond doubt. The point to be made is that they need not happen. During the past ten years the typical reactions of the American people have been different. To characterize them briefly, reactions seemed to be based on the notion that what goes up must come down. We have repeatedly experienced small recessions and small inflationary movements which were soon arrested and did not develop into depressions or runaway inflations.

Determining the conditions under which the one or the other form of behavior is most likely is a crucial economic problem as well as a psychological one. Tentatively, the following hypothesis may be advanced: Mass behavior consisting of cumulative and self-justifying expectations may be viewed as a form of catastrophic behavior. The masses resist speculative fever or despondency unless their sanity is crushed by a series of repeated shocks. The basis of mass sanity may be found in the desire to understand the reasons for developments that take place. News and rumors which are not clearly understood may be accepted for a short while, but will not sustain action by very many people over long periods [16].

It hardly need be said that a variety of studies must be conducted under different conditions before these assumptions can be confirmed. Nevertheless, past experience permits us to draw a negative conclusion— the thesis that expectations are generally self-fulfilling cannot be accepted. For this thesis to be correct, most people would have to act according to their expectations, and expectations and corresponding action would have to be sustained over long periods. But, as shown before in analyzing their origin, expectations do not necessarily or generally follow past trends.

These considerations represent a beginning of an analysis of mass behavior. Probably there are always leaders whose attitudes and opinions change first and whose actions stimulate similar behavior by other people. The role of opinion leaders could have been mentioned in our earlier discussion of the developments in 1954; we could have reported that upper-income people became optimistic earlier than lower-income people. Are upper-income people necessarily opinion leaders in economic matters? In studying the change in attitudes during the downturn in 1957 and the upturn during 1958, no income differences were found. Information derived from sources other than surveys of consumer attitudes must therefore be consulted to answer the question.

Katz and Lazarsfeld [20] contrasted the popular notion that the process of influence is vertical with the idea that there is horizontal opinion leadership. In the latter case, influence does not move downward from high-status or high-prestige levels. Marketing leaders were found in almost equal numbers at high-, middle-, and low-status levels. The authors conclude that each status level has its own core of opinion leaders.

Yet some aspects of what may be called "American tradition," such as the importance attached to upward mobility, may seem to confirm the notion that the "rich" are the opinion leaders. We may put forth a more precise assumption as follows: The mode of living of the top income groups at a given time will be imitated by others; ten or twenty-five years later, similar modes of living will be found among broad population groups. Experience from the last few decades may serve to contradict the hypothesis. Fifty years ago "conspicuous consumption"—marked by large mansions with many servants, lavish parties, high expenditures on dress, jewelry, as well as on art objects—characterized the mode of living of the rich. There is, however, hardly any evidence that these expenditure patterns have been imitated by the broader upper-income groups—the size of which has been growing rapidly in the last twenty years—and possibly they have disappeared by now even among the very rich. Did this happen because today's rich are less wealthy, or because broad groups of upper-middle income people have become the opinion leaders? Without being able to answer this question, we may point to certain new and generally accepted forms of living which were not initiated by the highest income groups. The use of labor-saving household equipment, shopping in department stores and supermarkets (rather than in exclusive specialty stores), vacation trips by car with stops at motels (rather than trips to resort hotels) or fishing and camping trips—these are some examples of ways of life in which broad groups of the upper-middle class (say, in the $5,000 to $10,000 income brackets) appear to have been the leaders.

The last paragraph was intended to point to problems of social psychology about which we know far too little, but which may be studied in the area of economic behavior. The introduction and acceptance of new consumer goods represent specific problems of great social-psychological significance. Investigations by William H. Whyte, Jr., on new suburban developments—specifically on the spread of room air conditioners in certain neighborhoods—must be mentioned in this connection [46, 47]. David Riesman [39, 40] has provided us with valuable insights about the changes that have taken place in style of life as well as in the predominant character types. Changes in economic attitudes—for instance, in attitudes toward property and business—play a substantial role in Riesman's arguments, and one of his major points is that American society has become increasingly consumption-oriented. Regarding consumption patterns, Riesman notes a growing tendency toward uniformity and the acceptance of a "standard package." Of particular importance for social psychology are Riesman's observations on the influence of children on consumption patterns.

An analysis of the rate of acceptance of innovations must deal with psychological problems. Some technological innovations were quickly accepted by consumers and have become part of the American life within a short time. Television sets, automatic washing machines, and automatic gearshifts may serve as examples from the postwar period. Other innovations have been much less successful when measured by their rate of penetration. Neglecting any goods which may be classified as failures, dishwashers may be named as an example of slow penetration. Is the difference due to technological factors or to advertising and salesmanship? It is not possible as yet to give a definite answer to this question, but it appears that there have been other reasons too. Prior to the introduction of the innovations, people are not usually aware of needing them. Needs must be stimulated. It is probable that there are differences as to what kinds of needs can be successfully stimulated.

We may ask further about the kind of people who will accept new articles at an early stage. It appears that education as well as ownership of a large number of widely accepted articles are among the variables which differentiate between leaders and followers [34]. Is there, in addition, a separate factor of "innovation-mindedness"? Are people of certain personality types especially attracted by new or modern things? Here again, we cannot do more than point to an area worth studying.

We have made no reference yet to studies of face-to-face groups, which are among the most popular investigations of social psychology. The greatest contribution of economic psychology in this area is to be expected from business-enterprise research. The business firm, in addition to being a legal entity, is a group in the sociopsychological sense [2, 11]. Most commonly, executives of a firm and sometimes also lower-level employees identify themselves with the firm and strive for it, although they attribute to it an existence independent from their private lives. Naturally, there are exceptions, but nowadays in America executives whose sole aim is to profit from manipulating their firms (milking the enterprise) appear to be rare.

Personal relations play a substantial role in business life, both in an individual firm and among several firms. Studies of management and human relations have clarified relations in individual firms to some extent, although the relations between management and employees have been studied more thoroughly than the relations among executives. Only isolated observations of groups of several firms seem to be available. In interview surveys, business executives revealed, for instance, that the relations between their firm and their banks consisted to a large extent of personal relations between business executives and bankers. Tradition, habits, and personal friendship frequently determine not only to whom to turn for advice, but also from which bank to borrow money [13]. Acting in the same way as other business firms do—be it regarding plant expansion, introducing new products, or increasing or decreasing inventories—may be greatly facilitated by frequent personal contact between executives of all leading firms. Group membership may explain the observations that overexuberance or overcaution are manifested at the same time by very many businessmen. It is probable, then, that mutual reinforcement of attitudes is more common among business leaders than among the unorganized consumers [16, chap. 14].

MOTIVATION

Multiplicity of Motives

Whether all economic behavior is viewed as motivated behavior is a matter of definition. The broad definition is often derived from the notion that economic behavior is necessarily purposive and instrumental. Alternatively, however, one may choose a narrower definition of motivated behavior by excluding habitual or routine behavior, which hardly varies under the impact of different motives (or of different attitudes and expectations). This narrower view is in accord with the definition of a motive by McClelland and his colleagues as a "goal-oriented free choice with habit and situational factors controlled" [30, p. 38[4]]. Whether the broader or narrower definition of motivation is accepted, there can be no doubt that economic behavior offers vast opportunities for the study of motivation.

[4] See also p. 252, where motives are contrasted with habits and specific associations.

Two major considerations have governed the studies on motivation in which the author has participated. The first concerns the multiplicity of motives; the second deals with effects of the gratification of motives and the influence which the achievement of goals may have on levels of aspiration. Both principles reflect concern with changes in motives under changing circumstances.

Classical economic theory postulates a single, comprehensive motive —maximization of utilities or profits—and resembles in this formal sense a one-drive theory. In contrast, economic psychology starts with postulating multiplicity of motives. Motives of different people or the same person under different circumstances may differ; in addition, most units of behavior are multimotivated.[5] In field-theoretical terms, different forces play a role at the same time; some of them reinforce each other, while others conflict with each other. To be sure, it is possible to assume that ultimately all different forces reflect the operation of one single motive. By making this assumption, however, we lose information; the study of different effects of different motivational forces as well as the study of changes in motives is ruled out by such a comprehensive one-motive theory.

Some analysts of contemporary business life, dissatisfied with postulating only the profit maximization motive, have produced lengthy lists of other prevailing motives [among more recent American books, see 7 and 37]. Striving for power and for the approbation of others, as well as security motives, have been given great prominence. The mere listing of different motives is not of great usefulness, however. Progress will be achieved only if we can specify the circumstances in which certain motives (or, more correctly, certain configurations or patterns of motives) will be particularly prevalent and if we can also demonstrate different behavioral effects associated with different motives. Along these lines the author has advanced the hypothesis—evidence for which is still fragmentary—that striving for short-range pecuniary goals will be common under the impact of unfavorable developments, while under the impact of favorable developments, striving for long-range objectives and nonpecuniary goals will predominate [11, p. 206 ff.]. Differences in the prevailing time perspective of business executives have been observed and appear to be associated with different motives, as well as different forms of behavior.

Similarly, it will be important to specify the conditions—cultural, societal, and relating to the situation of the firm—under which (1) security motives prevail (to stay in business, to avoid losses, or maintaining one's share in the business), (2) slow and gradual growth is sought (to

[5] Cf. Maslow: "It is unusual, not usual, that an act or a conscious wish have but one motivation" [31, p. 28].

make "satisfactory" profits, to increase business volume without undue risks), or (3) speculative motives predominate (to get rich quick). Possibly the most fruitful research procedure will consist of a study of decision formation. In an analysis of decisions about plant expansion, for instance, it was possible to determine some of the forces which favored the decision to expand as well as some of those which worked in the opposite direction [17]. The same should be true of many other choices made by business executives about external financing, inventories, or production rates, for instance.

If business firms are "satisficing" rather than maximizing, as H. A. Simon [42] postulates,[6] an array of psychological problems arises. What profits will satisfy? Undoubtedly, what is regarded as satisfactory does not depend entirely on situational factors; therefore, the respective roles of personality, past experience, and aspirations need to be studied.

Diverse aspects of consumer motivation have already been mentioned in this paper. Reference may be made again to the finding that more United States savings bonds were bought when several motives pushed a person in this direction than when, apparently, a single motive prevailed. Similarly, life insurance holdings and purchases were found to be relatively large among people who, in addition to the common motive of protection against unexpected risks, thought of life insurance as a good way to save [32]. Furthermore, purchases of automobiles, television sets, and other large household items were found to occur more frequently among people who felt "better off" than before and who expected further progress in their financial situation. It may be assumed, therefore, that striving for advancement is a motivating factor which, in our present society, drives many people toward gratification of needs for durable goods rather than toward the accumulation of reserve funds. Motives of self-enhancement as well as such social motives as prestige and imitation also probably play a role in such purchases.

Recent studies of motives to purchase houses for owner occupancy indicated felt needs such as the desire for a larger house because of an increased number of children or the desire for modern conveniences; they also pointed up additional powerful motives such as the desire to live in a "nice" neighborhood (suburb) or the desire to be a home owner and thereby a "substantial citizen" rather than a renter. There are many instances in which dissatisfaction and discomfort appear to be the major driving forces, but in the recent years of increasing prosperity a growing proportion of purchases of houses and durable goods appears to fall into the category of "upgrading." Home ownership or location in a favorable

[6] The author also put forth the hypothesis that striving for satisfactory profits is a common feature of the currently prevailing motivational patterns in American business [11, p. 201 ff.].

neighborhood are viewed as positive values for which people strive. There is some indication that the rate of purchases increases when the purchases satisfy positive needs rather than when they derive from negative motives [16, 19].

Saturation

A discussion of the dynamics of gratification of needs may well begin with a description of an economic problem of great importance in recent studies of short-term business fluctuations. This is the problem of saturation with consumer goods. In speculating about the reasons for buying automobiles and other durable goods, one might start with the assumption that the needs of people who do not have these articles, or who have old articles which no longer function satisfactorily, are more pressing than the needs of those who possess technologically satisfactory goods. It might then be concluded that the major market for automobiles and electrical appliances would consist of people who did not have them or whose cars and appliances were old and worn out. It might further follow that periods of large purchases would inevitably lead to periods of slump; during the former periods many people would have satisfied their needs, and a downturn in the market would be inevitable until many articles had worn out or even ceased to function. Thus prosperity, consisting of large-scale buying, would be seen as its own gravedigger.

Similar mechanisms might be expected to operate regarding other economic satisfactions. Take, for instance, striving for higher income. Is this motivation stronger among people with low incomes than among people with high incomes? Does striving for advancement gradually weaken, the more one has achieved? A similar problem has already been mentioned regarding liquid assets. It follows from the assumptions just presented that people with substantial liquid assets would have less incentive to add to them than people with small assets. Yet we have referred to findings which appear to contradict the general validity of this assumption.

These problems concern basic issues of the theory of motivation. In the past, psychologists have frequently considered biological needs as the prototype of motivational processes and have regarded reduction of tension or of anxiety as the fundamental driving force. Do all motives derive from deprivation, discomfort, or the disturbance of the equilibrium? We know that gratification of needs may reduce motive strength. But is this generally true, or do different mechanisms operate in the case of social or economic motives?

Studies of economic behavior have provided evidence in support of the assumption that gratification of needs often arouses new desires.

Similarly, some findings about economic motivation seem to be in accord with the theory of levels of aspiration as developed by Lewin and his associates [e.g., 29]. It appears that contentment is not the typical response to achieving what one has been striving for. On the contrary, achievement commonly serves to raise one's sights and to induce striving for more. Failure and frustration, rather than accomplishment, serve to reduce motive strength.

Let us examine specific instances. A promotion or a raise in salary for which we strive may appear to us as something which, if obtained, will bring satisfaction and contentment. But after the better position or the higher income has been achieved, our outlook may change. The new position may then be seen as a step toward further advancement; gratification may create new ambitions. The level of aspiration may be raised with accomplishment.

Or we may consider the act of purchasing a greatly desired automobile. Before the purchase the car had priority in the buyer's and his family's thinking; before the car was bought, remodeling the kitchen or buying new furniture or a larger and newer television set appeared impossible and even unnecessary. After the car was bought, those needs may have assumed great importance. To quote Maslow, who postulated more broadly and with somewhat different notions in mind: "The most basic consequence of satiation of any need is that this need is submerged and a new and higher need emerges" [31, p. 108]. Is this the general rule, or can we specify the conditions under which this type of dynamic process is more or less likely to prevail? We turn to survey findings for a study of this problem.

It is well known that the ownership of homes and durable goods has increased greatly during the past ten years. At present, more than 60 per cent of urban families own their homes; cars, refrigerators, washing machines, kitchen ranges, and television sets are owned by 75 to 90 per cent of urban families. Furthermore, many of these goods are quite new and most of them are in what their owners call "good condition."

In recent sample interview surveys, it was found that the majority of American families had made some purchases of durable goods or spent money around the house during the preceding twelve months. Following the inquiry about past expenditures, respondents were asked the question: Regarding the future, are there any special expenditures you would really *like* to make this year or next year? In reply, most people mentioned certain expenditures which they would like to make and only 20 to 25 per cent said "No." Among the latter, some said that they could not afford to spend on anything. These people were in such strained circumstances that they did not even express wishes. Others said that they had no special desires or that they were quite well supplied. Those who made the latter response were predominantly older people rather than well-to-do people.

Some of the goods people wanted to buy were new goods not then owned by them. But regarding automobiles, washing machines, and refrigerators, for instance, only a small part of current demand stems from nonowners. Understandably, then, in our studies, most of those who spoke of needing a new car or a new household appliance thought of replacing an article already in their possession. A possible hypothesis to explain replacement demand is the one mentioned before: People who have articles which are no longer in good operating condition or are old are those who replace them. It was possible to contradict this hypothesis and to show that the majority of expressed replacement needs originated from people who said that their cars, refrigerators, television sets, etc., were in good condition and were relatively new [34].

Why should owners of durable goods which in their own opinion are in good condition wish to replace them? The most important reason revealed by our studies consists of new features or improvements in new models. Most of those who expressed replacement needs could be shown to be aware of and attracted by new features relating to appearance, performance, or comfort which the articles owned by them did not have. Upgrading, to use this marketing term again, represents a psychological process which consists of being attracted by certain articles and becoming dissatisfied with one's possessions.

It appears, then, that people who own durable goods in good condition are not necessarily satiated; moreover, saturation is not an inevitable consequence of large recent purchases. Yet these findings do not suffice. We know that durable-goods sales fluctuate greatly. We must therefore ask, "What can bring about absence of demand or even bring a feeling of saturation?" The best answer we can give to this question is "Adverse attitudes." Most American families have an abundance of unsatisfied needs. Under what conditions are needs most likely transformed into effective demand? When people feel optimistic, confident, and secure. On the other hand, they are saturated when they are pessimistic, insecure, and when their past endeavors have been unsuccessful.

In 1957 and in 1960 when, following a period of large consumer demand, there was a substantial decline in consumer purchases of durable goods, market analysts commonly attributed the decline to saturation. But surveys disclosed—even prior to the decline in demand—that consumers' attitudes and expectations toward their own as well as the country's economic situation had undergone a change. Saturation itself is an attitude. The feeling of being saturated and being contented is not a function of one's possessions or of one's recent purchases alone; it is influenced and may even be determined by intervening variables. In order to predict when feelings of saturation will arise, it is necessary to study changes in people's motives, attitudes, and expectations.

The large-scale demand for consumer durable goods which this country has experienced during the fifties can be understood only within a broad framework. Surveys have shown that during those years the American people on the whole have been satisfied. The great majority of urban families said, for instance, that they were satisfied with their occupational progress, that their current income was about what it should be, that they were satisfied with their standard of living, that they mostly had had good breaks in the past, and that they expected to have better positions and incomes a few years hence. The Depression of the thirties has been forgotten by most people and is viewed as something which cannot happen again. Improving a way of life by constantly acquiring new good things—this is considered something to which most people feel entitled [16, chap. 11].

It does not follow from these findings that good times are self-perpetuating. As said before, expectations do not always originate in past developments. Moreover, disappointments and frustrations occur even in good times, especially when levels of aspiration are set too high. The attitudes of the individuals and their social reinforcement, which—if our thesis is correct—have greatly contributed to the recent American prosperity, could undergo substantial changes in the future.

Toward the beginning of 1958, consumer demand for durable goods declined sharply, as did business investment, and unemployment rose greatly. Feelings of uneasiness, dissatisfaction with prevailing prices, and pessimistic attitudes toward financial prospects in the near future were found to spread among consumers as early as the summer of 1957; these feelings increased greatly toward the end of that year, when only unfavorable news was salient for most people. (There had been favorable business news in the fall of 1957, but most people were found to have paid no attention to it.) Yet the recession of 1958 did not last long. In addition to certain government measures and inventory policies of business firms, the behavior of consumers was responsible for the quick upturn in economic conditions. Only the immediate prospects appeared gloomy to the American people in 1958. Most consumers, even if hard hit, maintained the notion that the next several years would be years of favorable economic climate. Motivations to strive for improving one's standard of living were not abandoned. To be sure, the purchase of goods not immediately needed was postponed, but expenditures on nondurables and services remained high during the recession, and served as a stimulus to the economy. Possibly a recession—in contrast to a depression—is characterized by a deterioration of short-range expectations and a maintenance of optimistic long-range expectations [15, 16].

METHODS OF OUTLOOK

One important aspect of the relationship between psychological and economic studies has not yet been discussed in this paper. The major methodological tool of economic psychology is the sample interview survey. Sociologists, psychologists, and sampling statisticians have contributed to the development of survey methods. This is not the place to describe these methods [3, 5, 22],[7] which range from brief mailed checklists to detailed personal interviews that probe into elusive motivational forces. Obviously, studies of changes in motives, attitudes, and expectations require psychological techniques of interviewing and cannot be accomplished with census-type fact-gathering methods.

In whose attitudes are we interested when we make economic-psychological surveys? Even though the subjects of all behavioral research are individuals, some such research is oriented toward large groups or aggregates and some toward individual people. Economic research, market research, and research in economic psychology all seek to obtain data relating to aggregates. But in clinical psychology, for instance, research is often oriented toward uncovering the maladjustments of particular individuals. Similarly, selection of individuals for jobs or the improvement of working conditions and morale of particular individuals and groups are among the aims of industrial psychology. Market research, on the other hand, does not aim at pinpointing the individuals who will buy a given product, nor does economic psychology aim at pinpointing the individuals who will increase their rate of spending or saving.

Obviously, motives, attitudes, intentions, hopes, and fears exist only in individuals (although, of course, they may be group-determined or group-influenced). How can psychological studies about how individuals feel and think be relevant for the national demand for all goods or for particular products? The task consists in constructing a bridge between the study of individual motives and attitudes and the study of the markets or the economy.

The survey method, based on representative samples, constitutes such a bridge. It enables the investigator to find out which attitudes and motives are more or less frequent in the entire nation or among large

[7] Relevant also are the reports on the annual Surveys of Consumer Finances [43a, 43b, 44] and the evaluation of economic surveys by consulting committees established by the Federal Reserve Board [45].

subgroups of the population, such as the upper-income people or the inhabitants of large towns. Studies made with samples which are not known to be representative cannot give quantitative information on the frequency with which attitudes and opinions are held. Furthermore, such studies are not replicable and therefore do not yield measures about how attitudes have changed over time.

Deliberation and saturation, to mention just two of the concepts introduced and analyzed in this paper, occur in individual people. The studies of the conditions under which deliberation and saturation take place have been conducted with individuals. But these individuals were members of a sample which represented all consumers in the country. Therefore it was possible to arrive at generalizations regarding the effects, for instance, of saturation or its absence for the entire economy.

The two major functions of survey research are the establishment of time trends and the establishment of functional relations among variables. How current opinions or expectations differ from those held some time ago is not only of historical interest, but of the utmost significance for predicting what will happen. Determining which opinions and attitudes are correlated and what the relation is between psychological variables and action variables represent basic psychological research which is of great practical use at the same time.

The two research functions are often used jointly. Suppose we establish that the expectation of good times to come and confidence in the future are correlated with increased purchases of durable goods. Further, suppose that at a given time a representative sample of the American people expresses more optimistic expectations and greater confidence than it did six or twelve months earlier. Then we may conclude that an increase in spending on durable goods is likely [16]. These procedures were applied by the Survey Research Center in preparing and publishing an *Index of Consumer Attitudes and Inclinations to Buy* durable goods. The measurements required for computing the index have been made two, three, or four times a year since 1952 [16, 19, 35].

Individual motives are manifold and elusive. Even with the use of time-consuming clinical methods, the complete picture of underlying motivations of an individual can hardly ever be revealed. The survey method must remain on a rather superficial level. How deep is it necessary to dig? With what degree of superficiality and generality should we be satisfied?

In studying predispositions for a curtailment of total demand, that is, factors conducive to a depression, we may safely neglect such factors as the Oedipus complex or the influence of stern or permissive fathers. It is hardly possible to assume that the frequency of such influences was different in 1930 from what it was in 1928. Or if we analyze the current housing demand, we may restrict ourselves to studying such surface hopes and fears as desires for living in a "nice" neighborhood where children can be brought up without being in close contact with juvenile gangs; we need go no further in studying underlying psychological factors. Similarly, if we study the desire and demand for a second car, we may concentrate on such factors as the suburban wife's freely expressed dissatisfaction when her husband uses the family car to commute to work.[8]

The interviewing techniques used in economic psychology consist primarily of open questions or what has been called the "fixed-question–free-answer method" of interviewing. The questions are asked in a conversational atmosphere after rapport has been established between interviewer and respondent. Sometimes the open questions are made "projective" or are used in an impersonal way instead of referring to the respondent himself. Sometimes the question is put in the form of a story; for instance, the interviewer may tell about certain actions of a Mr. Smith and ask the respondent what he thinks of Mr. Smith. Presenting pictures and asking about them represents a similar technique. Whether a picture of a woman hesitating between a bank and a dress shop is used, a story told, or a set of open questions asked, the choice represents a difference in technique, not in fundamental research design. In any case, we need quantitative information about the frequency of the attitudes revealed and must, therefore, address the same set of questions to each member of a representative sample.

No mention has been made of experiments as yet. Although they probably can be used in economic psychology, up to now they have not contributed much to a better understanding of the economic behavior of businessmen and consumers. Experimental studies of the decision-making process have been intended primarily to investigate choice behavior under certain artificially restricted conditions (e.g., gambling situations in which complete or fairly complete information was given about chances and risks). It has not yet been shown that an experimental clarification of postulates of economic theory about rational behavior has direct relevance to the understanding of how businessmen and consumers actually behave.

Some progress has been made in this respect recently by Siegel and Fouraker [41] who, through ingenious experiments, have contributed to a description of the bargaining process. Yet, again, the bargainers

---

[8] On the other hand, in some phases of research on preferences for individual products it may be necessary to delve into deeper personality layers. Certain preferences and aversions for particular products may not be accounted for without such studies.

were given specific data on what profits they would make if they sold (or bought) different quantities of goods at different prices, and the study of interpersonal relations was excluded from the experiments. What needs to be introduced in experiments is uncertainty about future developments and acquisition of experience (learning) in the course of economic activity. In this respect, the ideas of H. A. Simon ("Economics and Psychology" in this volume) are challenging; simulation of behavior by computers represents a most interesting new methodological tool which may enhance our knowledge of economic behavior (see also 37*a*).

As described in this paper, economic-psychological studies carried out in the recent past contributed to a better understanding of economic behavior. We know more now than we did twenty years ago about the motives, attitudes, and expectations which characterize prosperous times and recessions, or inflationary and deflationary trends. Our knowledge is much less complete about the origin of changes in the motives and attitudes of masses of consumers and thousands of businessmen. Some of the challenging questions which need to be studied are these: How do feelings of insecurity, lack of confidence, fear of adverse trends, and the like come about in "good times"? How does confidence in improved business conditions arise in "bad times"? What kinds of actions, or what kinds of information, have the power of getting hold of the imagination of people?

The study of these and other related questions belongs in the domain of economic psychology. Progress in economic psychology will add to our understanding of basic features of social behavior.

This is true even though some aspects of economic psychology appear to deal with practical problems of the day. When, for instance, the Survey Research Center's Index of Consumer Attitudes points downward—as was the case in 1957 and in the spring of 1960—few of the readers of such newspaper reports realize the scope of the behavioral studies from which the findings are derived. Yet even short-term forecasting is closely linked with the analysis of such questions as the conditions under which expectations influence social action, the conditions under which new attitudes become accepted by many people (social learning), or the conditions under which gratification of needs stimulates the arousal of further wants—to mention some of the problems studied in this paper. Without basic research, any attempt to understand and to predict longer-range economic developments is bound to fail. The task undertaken in this paper was to demonstrate that such research directed toward an analysis of the role of habits and their abandonment, or the change in attitudes and motivational patterns among broad social groups, for instance, may yield psychological insights and contribute to psychological theory.

REFERENCES

1. Boulding, K. E. *The image.* Ann Arbor, Mich.: Univer. Mich. Press, 1956.
2. Bowen, H. R. *The business enterprise as a subject for research.* New York: Social Science Research Council, 1955.
3. Campbell, A., & Katona, G. The sample survey: a technique for social science research. In L. Festinger & D. Katz (Eds.), *Research methods in the behavioral sciences.* New York: Dryden, 1953. Pp. 15–55.
4. Campbell, A., et al. *The American voter.* New York: Wiley, 1960.
5. Cannell, C. F., & Kahn, R. L. The collection of data by interviewing. In L. Festinger & D. Katz (Eds.), *Research methods in the behavioral sciences.* New York: Dryden, 1953. Pp. 327–380.
6. Cartwright, D. Some principles of mass persuasion. *Hum. Relat.,* 1949, **2**, 253–267.
7. Griffin, C. E. *Enterprise in a free society.* Homewood, Ill.: Irwin, 1949.
8. Katona, G. Psychological analysis of business decisions and expectations. *Amer. Econ. Rev.,* 1946, **36**, 44–63.
9. Katona, G. Analysis of dissaving. *Amer. Econ. Rev.,* 1949, **39**, 673–688.
10. Katona, G. Effect of income changes on the rate of saving. *Rev. Econ. & Statist.,* 1949, **31**, 95–103.
11. Katona, G. *Psychological analysis of economic behavior.* New York: McGraw-Hill, 1951.
12. Katona, G. Rational behavior and economic behavior. *Psychol. Rev.,* 1953, **60**, 307–318.
13. Katona, G. (with A. Lauterbach & S. Steinkamp). *Business looks at banks: a study of business behavior.* Ann Arbor, Mich.: Univer. Mich. Press, 1957.
14. Katona, G. Attitude change: instability of response and acquisition of experience. *Psychol. Monogr.,* 1958, **72**, 1–38.
15. Katona, G. The psychology of the recession. *Amer. Psychologist,* 1959, **14**, 135–143.
16. Katona, G. *The powerful consumer.* New York: McGraw-Hill, 1960.
16a. Katona, G. Consumer investment and business investment. *Michigan Business Review,* 1961, **13**, 4, 17–22.
16b. Katona, G. Consumers—wasters or investors? *Challenge,* December, 1961, 14–16.
17. Katona, G., & Morgan, J. N. The quantitative study of factors determining business decisions. *Quart. J. Econ.,* 1952, **66**, 67–90.
18. Katona, G., & Mueller, Eva. Consumer attitudes and demand, *1950–1952.* Ann Arbor, Mich.: Survey Research Center, 1953.
19. Katona, G., & Mueller, Eva. Consumer expectations *1953–1956.* Ann Arbor, Mich.: Survey Research Center, 1956.
20. Katz, E., & Lazarsfeld, P. F. *Personal influence.* Glencoe, Ill.: Free Press, 1955.
21. Keynes, J. M. *The general theory of employment, interest, and money.* New York: Harcourt, Brace, 1936.

22. Kish, L. Selection of the sample. In L. Festinger & D. Katz (Eds.), *Research methods in the behavioral sciences.* New York: Dryden, 1953. Pp. 175–240.

23. Klein, L. R. Assets, debts and economic behavior. *Studies in income and wealth.* Vol. 14. New York: National Bureau of Economic Research, 1951.

24. Klein, L. R. Estimating patterns of savings behavior from sample survey data. *Econometrica,* 1951, **19,** 438–454.

25. Klein, L. R. (Ed.) *Contributions of survey methods to economics.* New York: Columbia Univer. Press, 1954.

26. Klein, L. R., & Lansing, J. B. Decisions to purchase consumer durable goods. *J. Marketing,* 1955, **20,** 109–132.

27. Lansing, J. B., & Morgan, J. N. Consumer finances over the life cycle. In L. Clark (Ed.), *Consumer behavior II.* New York: N.Y. Univer. Press, 1955. Pp. 36–51.

28. Lansing, J. B., & Withey, S. B. Consumer anticipations: their use in forecasting behavior. *Studies in income and wealth.* Vol. 17. New York: National Bureau of Economic Research, 1955. Pp. 381–453.

29. Lewin, K., Dambo, Tamara, Festinger, L., & Sears, P. S. Level of aspiration. In J. McV. Hunt (Ed.), *Personality and the behavior disorders.* New York: Ronald, 1944.

30. McClelland, D., et al. *The achievement motive.* New York: Appleton-Century-Crofts, 1953.

30a. McClelland, D. C. *The achieving society.* Princeton: D. Van Nostrand Co., 1961. (See review of this book by George Katona in *Amer. Econ. Rev.,* 1962.)

31. Maslow, A. H. *Motivation and personality.* New York: Harper, 1954.

32. Miner, J. L. *Life insurance ownership among American families.* Ann Arbor, Mich.: Survey Research Center, 1958.

33. Mueller, Eva. A study of purchase decisions. In L. Clark (Ed.), *Consumer behavior I.* New York: N.Y. Univer. Press, 1954. Pp. 30–87.

34. Mueller, Eva. The desire for innovations in household goods. In L. Clark (Ed.), *Consumer behavior III.* New York: N.Y. Univer. Press, 1956. Pp. 13–37.

35. Mueller, Eva. Effects of consumer attitudes on purchases. *Amer. Econ. Rev.,* 1957, **47,** 946–965.

36. Mueller, Eva. Consumer reactions to inflation. *Quart. J. Econ.,* 1959, **73,** 246–262.

36a. Mueller, Eva (with A. Wilken & M. Wood). *Location decisions and industrial mobility in Michigan.* Ann Arbor, Mich.: Survey Research Center, 1961.

37. Nourse, E. G. *Price making in a democracy.* Washington: Brookings Institution, 1949.

37a. Orcutt, G. (with M. Greenberger, J. Korbel & A. Rivlin). *Microanalysis of socioeconomic systems: a simulation study.* New York: Harper & Bros., 1960.

38. Paxton, E. T. *What people want when they buy a house.* Washington: U.S. Department of Commerce, 1955.

39. Riesman, D. *The lonely crowd.* New Haven, Conn.: Yale Univer. Press, 1950.

40. Riesman, D., & Roseborough, H. Careers and consumer behavior. In L. Clark (Ed.), *Consumer behavior II,* New York: N.Y. Univer. Press, 1955, Pp. 1–18.

41. Siegel, S., & Fouraker, L. E. *Bargaining and group decision making.* New York: McGraw-Hill, 1960.

42. Simon, H. A. *Models of man.* New York: Wiley, 1957.

43. Stouffer, S. A. *Communism, conformity and civil liberties.* New York: Doubleday, 1955.

43a. Survey Research Center. *1960 survey of consumer finances.* Ann Arbor, Mich.: Author, 1961.

43b. Survey Research Center. *1961 survey of consumer finances.* Ann Arbor, Mich.: Author, 1962.

44. Survey of Consumer Finances, reports in the *Federal Reserve Bulletin,* annually 1946 through 1959.

45. U.S. Board of Governors of the Federal Reserve System. Reports of consultant committees on consumer survey statistics, and on general business expectations. Washington: Author, 1955.

46. Whyte, W. H., Jr. The consumer in the new suburbia. In L. Clark (Ed.), *Consumer behavior I.* New York: N.Y. Univer. Press, 1954. Pp. 1–14.

47. Whyte, W. H., Jr. The web of word of mouth. In L. Clark (Ed.), *Consumer behavior II.* New York: N.Y. Univer. Press, 1955. Pp. 113-122.

COMMENTS ON THE RELEVANCE OF PSYCHOLOGY TO ECONOMIC THEORY AND RESEARCH[1]

JAMES TOBIN
*Cowles Foundation for
Research in Economics
Yale University*

F. TRENERY DOLBEAR, JR.
*Department of Economics
Yale University*

Recent developments in economic theory have emphasized the dependence of economics on assumptions regarding the motivations of economic behavior. Economists naturally turn to psychology in their quest for valid and fruitful assumptions, and they have learned with some disappointment that there are no ready-made answers. The motivations of economic behavior remain a challenge to both disciplines.[2]

Neoclassical economic theory was able to describe a determinate economic system and to infer many of its properties by making very simple assumptions about the behavior of the individual decision-making units of the system. The main assumption was *rationality*, in the sense that each individual chooses, among the range of alternative actions open to him, the one whose consequences he prefers to all the rest.[3] This requires that the individual have a consistent and transitive ordering of the objects of choice, in the following sense: If A and B are such objects, then either A is preferred to B, B to A, or there is indifference

---

[1] *Editor's note:* Dr. Tobin originally met our invitation with the counterproposal that he write a supplement to George Katona's paper, "The Relationship between Psychology and Economics." What resulted, however, was this compact but self-contained article on the relations of psychology to economics. The editor is happy to acknowledge the limitation upon his characteristic thesis that analytic *reach* is a condition to analytic bite, pointed up by this brief but highly illuminating paper.

[2] Herbert A. Simon [29] and S. P. Hayes [17] provide extended discussion of some of these problems. See also the articles of Katona and Simon in this volume.

[3] For a careful presentation of the economic theory of choice see [18, 26].

between A and B. Moreover, if A is preferred to B, and B is preferred (or indifferent) to C, then A is preferred to C.[4]

The assumption of rationality in this sense is of considerably greater generality than is conveyed by the caricatures of "economic man" that too often represent economic theory in the eyes of other social scientists and, indeed, of some economists themselves. No restriction is placed on the dimensions of objects of choice that are relevant to their ordering. Within the framework of the theory, workers may rank alternative job opportunities according to quite different criteria from wages alone. Businessmen may reckon profits as only one among a number of outcomes on which they decide among alternative courses of action. Rationality does imply that, other things being equal, a larger sum of money will be preferred to a smaller. But if other things are not equal, rationality means nothing more than subjective consistency in the ordering of alternatives. Thus it is a mistake to identify rationality with the motivation of materialistic self-interest.

One assumption that economists make about this preference field is often the basis for misunderstanding. This assumption concerns the phenomenon suggested by the phrase "diminishing marginal utility," although this phrase is an inaccurate description. "Diminishing marginal utility" suggests that the more an individual has of some object, the less his satisfaction will be increased by giving him an additional unit of the same thing. So stated, the proposition seems to contradict psychological findings concerning the relationship of aspiration to achievement. Basing his position on these findings, as well as on survey evidence regarding levels of aspiration for accumulation of durable goods and savings, Katona criticizes the "saturation" implications of economists' utility theory. Actually, however, the theory is noncommittal on the question whether marginal utility diminishes or increases as successive additions of the same goods are made. The theory does assume that it is generally possible to keep an individual at the same utility or satisfaction level when depriving him of a unit of commodity A provided he is compensated by adding an appropriate quantity of commodity B. The theory further assumes that the smaller the amount of A left to the individual—and correspondingly the larger the amount of B—the more compensation in the form of B will be required for loss of another unit of A. This can be interpreted to say that, whatever the absolute marginal utilities may be,

[4] Recently economists have recognized what psychologists have long maintained —individuals do not always make the same choice when faced with the same alternatives. To avoid the neoclassical conclusion that indifference must be assumed to explain inconsistencies, a theory of *probabilistic choice* has evolved. For a definition of rationality assuming probabilistic choice, e.g., if A is preferred to B, then the probability of choosing A rather than B is greater than one-half [see 5, 8, 10, 11, 21].

the marginal utility of B declines *relative to that of A* as the quantity of B increases relative to the quantity of A. Economists have always been impressed by the boundlessness of human wants and have denied the possibility of universal saturation.[5] They do assume, however, the need for maintaining some kind of balance between objectives. Individuals may aspire to even higher levels of consumption of all kinds, as well as to even higher levels of savings and leisure. Since means are limited, these goals conflict; one can be approached only at the expense of another. Although an individual cannot be absolutely saturated with any desirable object, he can become relatively saturated. If he is relatively saturated with liquid assets, for example, he would be glad to have more, but he would prefer to have more durable consumer's goods.

Economics has sought to be neutral with respect to the sources of preferences, but it has purchased this neutrality at the cost of substantive content. Results that are determinate when business decisions are assumed to depend only on maximizing profits, for example, become indeterminate in fact (though still determinate in principle) when less measurable objectives of business policy are admitted [25, 28a]. In the field of consumer behavior, the formation of preferences from experience, observation, and advertising is at least as important a phenomenon as purchasing based on given preferences.[6] But economics looks to psychology to explain the formation of preferences.

General as they are, the usual formulations of the preference fields of economic units have implicitly involved some questionable propositions. First, a consumer's rankings of alternative "market baskets" of goods and services have traditionally been taken to depend only on the amounts of various commodities *he* consumes, not on the amounts other consumers are simultaneously consuming. This disregard of social interdependence in consumption contradicts everyday observation as well as the presumptions of sociology and social psychology. In recent years, there have been a number of attempts to correct the traditional individualistic bias of economics [4, 12, 19, 20].

Second, as a legacy of Benthamite utilitarianism, economic theory has tended to formulate work as a source of disutility and thus to assume that it is preferred to leisure solely because of the income it brings. The discovery of "human relations" in industry, a subject on which there has been considerable convergence between psychology and labor economics, has taught economists that the satisfactions of life occur on the job as well as after hours.

[5] This is why economists, in general, have been less impressed than the general public with such books as John Kenneth Galbraith's *The Affluent Society* [15].

[6] A discussion of some factors which appear to influence consumer behavior may be found in [12, 23, 14a].

Third, the preference field of economic theory is an attribute of a single mind. Yet the basic economic decision-making units are really groups rather than individuals—households, corporations, governments, and trade unions.[7] So far, we lack any satisfactory theory of the manner in which the effective preference fields of groups are formed. Indeed, as a logical matter, it is not possible in general to derive an ordering of alternatives for the group from conflicting rankings by group members [3].

Rationality requires that the outcomes of alternative courses of action be known with certainty to the decision maker. Given such certainty, it is clearly irrational to choose any outcome other than the most preferred. But if outcomes are uncertain, there is no obvious definition of rational choice. A number of decision criteria for situations of uncertainty have been suggested [2, 22]. Among them is the "minimax" strategy: For every possible action, assume the worst outcome, then choose the action whose worst outcome is least bad. This was first suggested as the correct strategy in playing a zero-sum game where your strategy is known to your opponent, who is trying to do his best against you [31]. Even in a game situation, it is a highly conservative strategy, and the person who follows it may find himself sacrificing the chance of large gains merely in order to avoid the possibility of small losses [14]. In situations where the environment is neutral, it is even more clear that it is excessively conservative. Consequently, there is considerable doubt that the minimax criterion should be recommended to decision makers, and, of course, even greater doubt that it describes actual behavior.

An alternative decision criterion is maximization of expected (in the probability sense) utility. This requires that the decision maker rank not only outcomes but differences in utilities of outcomes. Not only can he say that he prefers A to B; he can say whether the degree of preference of A over B is greater or less than that of C over D. This implies that values (on a scale unique up to a linear transformation) can be attached to the outcomes themselves. The criterion also assumes that the decision maker attaches probabilities of occurrence to the various outcomes. Since economic decisions generally occur in nonrecurrent situations for which objective probabilities cannot be calculated, these probabilities must be subjective estimates.[8] This decision rule avoids the overconservative implications of the minimax strategy. But in the nature of the case, there can be no proof that it is more nearly optimal than other principles of decision. As to its descriptive realism, economics and psychology have

---

[7] A decision procedure for a firm with a team of decision makers who possess a single objective for the firm is described by Jacob Marschak [24].

[8] Methods for obtaining these subjective probabilities are described in Leonard J. Savage [27].

found another area of convergence in experimental measurement of utility and subjective probability. Experiments have been designed to test whether subjects' choices can be regarded as maximization of expected utility [9, 13, 13a]. These experiments involve procedures similar to the scaling of sensations and attitudes, which has a long tradition in psychology [7]. A major difference, however, is this: Since economists regard utility and subjective probability as personal to each subject, they cannot follow the psychologists' technique of treating the responses of different subjects as replications of observations from the same population of choices. This greatly complicates experimental testing of the expected utility hypothesis; at the moment, we have little idea of the size or characteristics of the population groups whose behavior can be represented as maximization of expected utility.

Even if these groups turn out to be significant in the economy, further questions remain: How are subjective estimates of utility and probability formulated? Is it useful to break the decision process into these components, or is it better looked upon as a unit? Lately economists have learned how difficult and costly it is to be rational—or, in the case of uncertainty, to apply any of the suggested criteria of "quasi rationality." Indeed the development of management science and operations research since World War II has opened a fertile field for economists, statisticians, and mathematicians, increasing the efficiency of business decisions [6]. If the economic model did not fit the world, one is tempted to wonder whether the world is being made over to fit the model. But in the last analysis, rationality cannot apply to situations of uncertainty. It may be that, instead of seeking a quasi rationality which can be applied to these situations, we should, as descriptive scientists rather than advisers, look more directly for the manners in which individuals and groups simplify and structure complicated situations in which they must make decisions whose outcomes they cannot control or predict.[9]

Psychologists and economists have barely begun to exploit the possibilities of fruitful collaboration in empirical research on economic behavior. The pioneering work at the Survey Research Center, led by George Katona, has shown that the social sciences have in the sample survey a powerful tool applicable to research on economic behavior as well as on public opinion. Considerable further development of the tool is necessary to utilize its full research potential. Two lines that such development might take may be mentioned.

1. Surveys of economic behavior can be designed specifically for research on the strategic relationships between variables, rather than for the primary purpose of making estimates of population frequencies and averages. Research-oriented surveys would place less emphasis on representative

[9] G. L. S. Shackle [28] attempts an approach of this kind [see also 1, 16].

sampling of the population, and more focus on observations strategic for measuring the relationships under study. Surveys would take on experimental design, in which some variables are deliberately held constant and others made to differ as much as possible. Successive reinterviews of identical respondents would be used to obtain information on reactions to change in circumstances over time.

2. Psychological characteristics of respondents can be measured in order to seek their relationship to economic behavior. Katona's work has concentrated on measuring a particular category of psychological variables, mainly respondents' optimism or pessimism about the economic future. These attitudes of optimism or pessimism are relevant to the short-term outlook for consumer spending. They cannot help very much in the making of longer-run economic predictions. For that task, it would be valuable to explore the relationship of economic behavior—e.g., spending and saving—to more fundamental and permanent dimensions of personality. Without measurement of such dimensions, there are some unresolvable ambiguities of interpretation of the results of economic surveys. For example, Katona cites findings that people with substantial liquid assets tend to add more, not less, to their total assets than people whose existing stocks are low. It is a matter of some economic importance whether this finding reflects (1) the fact that persons of a thrifty disposition have saved more in the past and continue to save more than persons of a different personality, or (2) a tendency for a given individual to save more in liquid form, the greater his initial holdings of liquid assets. If the finding reflects the former, then it still may be true that for persons of given personality, high liquidity promotes spending rather than saving [30]. But if, as Katona believes, it reflects the latter, then it would be foolish to worry about possible inflationary effects of high liquidity. Thus the relationship of economic behavior to personality attributes is not only a subject of interest in itself; it is also essential for correct interpretation of observed relations among economic magnitudes.

REFERENCES

1. Angell, J. W. Uncertainty, likelihoods, and investment decisions. *Quart. J. Econ.*, 1960, **74**, 1–28.
2. Arrow, K. J. Alternative approaches to the theory of choice in risk-taking situations. *Econometrica*, 1951, **19**, 404–437.
3. Arrow, K. J. *Social choice and individual values.* New York: Wiley, 1951.
4. Baumol, W. J. *Welfare economics and the theory of the state.* Cambridge, Mass.: Harvard Univer. Press, 1952.
5. Block, H. D., & Marschak, J. Random orderings and stochastic theories

of responses. In I. Olkin et al. (Eds.), *Contributions to probability and statistics*. Stanford, Calif.: Stanford Univer. Press, 1960.

6. Case Institute of Technology, Operations Research Group. *A comprehensive bibliography on operations research through 1956, with supplement for 1957*. New York: Wiley, 1958.

7. Clark, L. (Ed.) The choices consumers make: a panel on the technical problems of measuring preferences. In *Consumer behavior*. New York: N.Y. Univer. Press, 1954. Pp. 88–95.

8. Davidson, D., & Marschak, J. Experimental tests of a stochastic decision theory. In C. W. Churchman & P. Ratoosh (Eds.), *Measurement: definitions and theories*. New York: Wiley, 1959.

9. Davidson, D., & Suppes, P. (with S. Siegel). *Decision making: an experimental approach*. Stanford, Calif.: Stanford Univer. Press, 1957.

10. Debreu, G. Stochastic choice and cardinal utility. *Econometrica*, 1958, **26**, 440–444.

11. Debreu, G. Topological methods in cardinal utility theory. In K. J. Arrow et al. (Eds.), *Mathematical methods in the social sciences, 1959*. Stanford, Calif.: Stanford Univer. Press, 1960.

12. Duesenberry, J. S. *Income, saving, and the theory of consumer behavior*. Cambridge, Mass.: Harvard Univer. Press, 1949.

13. Edwards, W. The theory of decision making. *Psychol. Bull.*, 1954, **51**, 380–417.

13a. Edwards, W. Behavioral decision theory. *Annu. Rev. Psychol.*, 1961, **12**, 473–498.

14. Ellsberg, D. Theory of the reluctant duelist. *Amer. Econ. Rev.*, 1956, **46**, 909–923.

14a. Ferber, R. Research on household behavior. *Amer. Econ. Rev.*, 1962, **52**, 19–63.

15. Galbraith, J. K. *The affluent society*. Cambridge, Mass.: The Riverside Press, 1958.

16. Haring, J. E., & Smith, G. C. Utility theory, decision theory, and profit maximization. *Amer. Econ. Rev.*, 1959, **49**, 566–583.

17. Hayes, S. P. Some psychological problems of economics. *Psychol. Bull.*, 1950, **47**, 289–330.

18. Hicks, J. R. *A revision of demand theory*, New York: Oxford, 1956.

19. Johnson, H. G. The macro-economics of income redistribution. In A. T. Peacock (Ed.), *Income redistribution and social policy*. London: Cape, 1954.

20. Leibenstein, H. S. Bandwagon, snob, and Veblen effects in the theory of consumers' demand. *Quart. J. Econ.*, 1950, **64**, 183–207.

21. Luce, R. D. *Individual choice behavior*. New York: Wiley, 1959.

22. Luce, R. D., & Raiffa, H. *Games and decisions: introduction and critical survey*. New York: Wiley, 1957. Chap. 13.

23. Mack, Ruth P. Economics of consumption. In B. F. Haley (Ed.), *A survey of contemporary economics*. Vol. 2. Homewood, Ill.: Irwin, 1952.

24. Marschak, J. Theory of an efficient several-person firm. *Papers & Proc. Amer. Econ. Rev.*, 1960, **50**(2), 541–548.

25. Papandreou, A. G. Some basic problems in the theory of the firm. In B. F. Haley (Ed.), *A survey of contemporary economics*. Vol. 2. Homewood, Ill.: Irwin, 1952.

26. Samuelson, P. A. *Foundations of economic analysis*. Cambridge, Mass.: Harvard Univer. Press, 1947. Chaps. 5, 6, 7.

27. Savage, L. J. *The foundations of statistics*. New York: Wiley, 1954.

28. Shackle, G. L. S. *Expectations in economics*. New York: Cambridge, 1949.

28. Shackle, G. L. S. *Expectations in economics*. New York: Cambridge, *Quart. J. Econ.*, 1961, **75**, 345–375.

29. Simon, H. A. Theories of decision-making in economics and behavioral science. *Amer. Econ. Rev.*, 1959, **49**, 253–283.

30. Tobin, J. Consumer debt and spending: some evidence from analysis of a survey. In *Consumer installment credit*. Part II, Vol. 1, Board of Governors of the Federal Reserve System. Washington: U.S. Government Printing Office, 1957. Pp. 521–545.

31. von Neumann, J., & Morgenstern, O. *The theory of games and economic behavior*. (3rd ed.) Princeton, N.J.: Princeton Univer. Press, 1953.

ECONOMICS AND PSYCHOLOGY[1]

HERBERT A. SIMON
*Graduate School of In-
dustrial Administration
Carnegie Institute of
Technology*

[1] This paper has been prepared as part of the program of organizational studies supported in the Graduate School of Industrial Administration by research grants from the Ford Foundation. The author's burden of preparation has been very much lightened by the help he has received from his colleagues, and from six excellent previous reviews of parts of this field by Bowen [6], Edwards [22], Hayes [27], Katona [29], Papandreou [47], and Weisskopf [63]. Some of the topics considered here are discussed at greater length [37].

INTRODUCTION

In discussing the mutual relations of psychology and economics, I shall generally use psychological categories to divide the analysis. After considering the extent to which the two fields have areas of common interest, the next three sections are concerned with the motivation of the consumer, of the producer or entrepreneur, and of the employee, respectively. There follows a discussion of *oligopoly* (competition among the few) viewed as a conflict phenomenon. The sixth section reviews the cognitive aspects of economic behavior, including some important recently proposed modifications in the characterization of rational economic action.

The relations between psychology and economics run both ways. We are not concerned merely with possible applications of psychological methods *to* economics, but equally with the use of economic theory and data about economic behavior *in* psychology.

Economic behavior, family behavior, political behavior, and organizational behavior are all forms of human behavior. Each can be explained partly in relatively general terms that cut across these categories, and partly in terms that apply only to a particular area of behavior. The fruitfulness of the interaction between economics and other social sciences hinges on whether the same mechanisms operate in all these areas of behavior, and on how far human behavior in one area is relevant for testing theories in the others. The question is a pragmatic one that has to be asked and reasked as the sciences of man develop, and as our understanding of their interrelationship deepens.

The Subspecies of Economic Man

Psychology enters economics through the characteristics that are postulated for the several subspecies of economic man. These subspecies include (1) the buyer or seller of commodities in a market, (2) the entrepreneur or producer, (3) the consumer, and (4) the worker. In certain areas of economic theory the categories overlap, but they are convenient for classifying and examining economic man.

We must look first at the distinction between producer and consumer. When we understand this, we can study the motivations of each kind of economic man, and then the cognitive aspects of his behavior.

The separation of producer and consumer.   It is not strictly accurate to say that in economic theory there are producers and consumers. Each person is, of course, assumed to be both, but each role is kept rather distinct from the other. The line between them is defined by the clock: during the working day, economic man is a producer; during the remainder of the twenty-four hours, he is a consumer.

Interactions between producer and consumer.   In a strict version of the theory, there are only two possibilities of interaction between John Doe, producer, and John Doe, consumer. First, the length of the work day—and hence, the time boundary between his two roles—may depend on an economic decision that weighs the utility of the income obtainable by working longer against the disutility of substituting work for leisure. This decision is an essential part of any economic theory that seeks to explain the length of the work week.

Second, when he makes decisions as a consumer, John Doe's income is one determinant of his spending and saving behavior. Theories of consumer choice take income as a given, determined by the production segment of the economy.

The masters of classical economic theory were well aware that separating producer from consumer, and vice versa, oversimplified the facts of the real world—but still permitted a tolerable approximation to human behavior throughout most of the economic sphere. Alfred Marshall, for example, was careful to discuss the possible "psychic income" that the entrepreneur received from his activity, and was also quite aware that the daily work activity of the laborer might alter his tastes, and hence his utility function [39; 63, chap. 15]. Ricardo assumed that, in the long run, wages must sink to a subsistence level; hence, the wage rate might really be regarded as a "marginal cost of producing labor" [63, chap. 6]. In the Ricardian theory, the consumer was almost swallowed by the producer.

A few important economic theorists have rejected all or most of this classical analysis—Veblen and John R. Commons being prominent examples. The vast majority of contemporary economic theorists may be regarded, however, as disciples of the classical tradition; and, like most disciples, they sometimes ignore or underemphasize the qualifications that the masters were careful to acknowledge. In extreme cases, the result has been to change economics from an empirical science to a vast tautology in which entrepreneurs maximize profit by definition—for profit is defined as "that which entrepreneurs maximize"—and consumers maximize utility by definition—for the same reason.

The other subspecies.   I have mentioned four subspecies of economic man. One of these is the consumer, who tends not to be further differentiated in the theory. On the production side of the economy, however, the distinction between the entrepreneur and the worker is significant. About the buyer and seller, little needs to be said except that they observe the classical maxim "Buy cheap and sell dear." For the rest, they do not require separate discussion. I have omitted the investor as a separate sub-species. As a person who saves, his behavior is part of that of the consumer. As a person who lends to others, he is buyer and seller of the services of capital. As a person who holds the residual equity in a business in anticipation of profit, he is an entrepreneur.

What distinguishes the worker from the entrepreneur is that the former sells to the latter the right to apply his time and effort during working hours to the goals of the enterprise [55]. In agreeing to accept authority in the workplace, the laborer's productive services become "disembodied" from him, so to speak, and are turned over to the entrepreneur. In terms of this distinction, the hired executive, however exalted his position in the administrative hierarchy, is a worker and not an entrepreneur. We shall see that economists have become increasingly uneasy with this classification of roles—both with its factual accuracy and with its economic consequences, if accurate.

The Goals of Economic Science

Economics can be defined as the science that describes and predicts the behavior of the various kinds of economic man I have mentioned. This definition, while perhaps literally correct, conveys a false impression of the principal goals and focus in the literature of economics.

Work in economics may be classified as dealing with (1) the economy or industries as a whole (*macroeconomics*), or behavior of the individual economic man and individual firm (*microeconomics*); or (2) description of the economy and economic behavior within it, or norms either for purposes of public policy (*normative macroeconomics*) or advice to the consumer or businessman (*normative microeconomics*).

The dominant viewpoint in economics has been that of normative macroeconomics. Descriptive macroeconomics is, of course, the essential basis for policy prescription—but the specific research emphases have been determined in considerable part by relevance to policy (e.g., business-cycle theory). Normative microeconomics, while it has only been very recently cultivated on any extensive scale, is now a flourishing area of economic research having many contacts with statistical decision theory and other new areas, such as "management science," "logistics," and "operations research."

Economists have usually been interested in descriptive microeconomics—understanding the behavior of individual economic agents—only to the extent necessary to provide a foundation for macroeconomics. Hence, economic research at the microlevel has stemmed from a recognition that some aspect of the economy could be understood only by explaining a particular sector of individual behavior. We shall see this mechanism operating with particular clarity when we come to the topic of expectations.

Two economic principles operate to keep at a minimum the macroeconomist's concern with individual behavior [6, pp. 6–8]. The first is the assumption of objective rationality, which permits strong predictions to be made about human behavior without the painful necessity of observing people. The second is the assumption of competition, for where competition prevails, the individuals and firms that behave in conformity with the principle of rationality will survive at the expense of the others. Hence, the classical economic theory of markets with perfect competition and rational agents is deductive theory that requires almost no contact with empirical data—once the underlying assumptions are accepted or verified—to establish its propositions.

This preoccupation of economists with the economy as a whole (or with normative rules for individual agents), and the sealing off of macro- from microphenomena by the mechanisms of rationality and competition help to explain why there has been little interaction between economists and psychologists, and little dependence by either upon the literature of the other field. As we proceed, we shall consider how far this independence of economics from the behavioral sciences is justified by the present state of knowledge in these fields.

Our task, then, is to explore what has been a no man's land between economics and behavioral science—the area of descriptive microeconomics. Of course, we are not the first explorers and we shall be guided by what has already been learned of the territory—particularly by the economists who are usually called "institutionalists." The assumptions of economic theory that have been most challenged are its motivational assumptions—particularly the consistency of preferences of humans and their exclusive preoccupation with monetary rewards. In fact, there has been perhaps an excessive preoccupation with motivation and insufficient attention to the cognitive aspects of economic behavior. Hence, I shall pay particular attention to the psychological study of the limits of humans —regarded as learning and information-processing organisms—in their capacities for rational choice.

MOTIVATION: THE CONSUMER

I shall discuss separately the motivation of the consumer and the motivation of the producer, taking up the consumer first. A first section describes the apparatus—based on the concept of utility function—used by the economist to discuss consumer behavior. The second section explores psychology to determine what concepts in that field, if any, correspond to the economist's "utility." A third section considers the economist's interest in consumer behavior and the possible relevance of psychological research in answering his questions.

The Utility Function

The fundamental postulate in microeconomics about the consumer is that he possesses a *utility function*. This is roughly equivalent to saying that, for any pair of alternatives of action presented to him, he can tell which he prefers. In some variants of the theory, alternatives are assumed to be presented in the form of "bundles of commodities"; in others, as alternative courses of action with consequences attached.

For example, F. Modigliani and E. Brumberg [41] have developed a theory of consumption and saving that assumes that each consumer estimates the present value of his expected future stream of income; he then chooses among all possible time patterns of saving and spending consistently with his assumption. The consumer, in this theory, is assumed to be able to ascertain his preferences among these alternative streams of spending and saving.

Cardinal and ordinal utility.[2] There has been much discussion as to whether a *cardinal* utility function should be postulated, or only an *ordinal* function. Suppose that we assign the utility x_1 to one of the consumer's alternatives, and the utility x_2 to another where x_1 is greater than x_2 and the first alternative is the one he prefers. We say that the utility function is *ordinal* if the numbers x_1 and x_2 could equally well be replaced by any numbers y_1 and y_2, such that y_1 is greater than y_2. The set of functions y that have this property in relation to the function x are called the *monotonic increasing transformations* of x. By "equally well," we mean that the new function y leads to exactly the same predictions of the consumer's behavior as the function x.

Suppose, on the contrary, that only *linear transformations* of x preserve all the properties of the consumer's behavior

$$y_i = ax_i + b$$

where a is a positive constant and b is an arbitrary constant. In this case, the quantity of utility attached to alternatives is uniquely defined, except for the unit of measurement a and the zero point of the scale, fixed by b.

---

[2] A rather comprehensive discussion of the literature and issues on the topics considered in this and the following section will be found in Ward Edwards [22]. While I have departed from Professor Edwards's interpretations in a number of particulars, the analysis that follows owes a great deal to his review. See also Arrow's chapter in this volume and his review [2].

It is defined to just the same extent that temperature is defined by the Fahrenheit and centigrade scales. When utility is defined up to a linear transformation, we say that the utility function is *cardinal*.

Let us suppose that four alternatives are open to a consumer. If he has only an ordinal utility function, then a statement such as "The first alternative has greater utility than the third," is meaningful; but a statement such as "The advantage of the first alternative over the second is greater than the advantage of the third over the fourth," is not meaningful. For, by monotonic transformations of the utility scale, we can make the difference in utility between one pair of alternatives greater or less, as we please, than the difference between another pair of alternatives.

It follows that, if utility is ordinal, statements about increasing or decreasing marginal utility[3] are meaningless, i.e., we cannot say that a man gets more or less utility from his sixth dollar than from his one million and sixth. Conversely, it can be shown that if such statements are meaningful, then—implicitly or explicitly—a cardinal utility function has been defined.

Until about a decade ago, there was a tendency to prefer the ordinal function on grounds of parsimony and because Slutsky, Hicks, and other economists had demonstrated that no significant proposition in the accepted theory of consumer choice depended on the cardinal measurement of utility. This trend was reversed in 1944 with the publication by J. von Neumann and O. Morgenstern of *The Theory of Games and Economic Behavior* [62]. Up to that time, the theory of consumer choice had been concerned primarily with choice where no uncertainty about future events was involved. Von Neumann and Morgenstern treated the more general case where uncertainty was admitted. They showed that if a decision maker could make consistent choices among uncertain prospects (e.g., lottery tickets at various odds for various bundles of commodities), then cardinal utilities could be assigned to the commodity bundles after observing a sufficient variety of such choices [see also 34, 38, 48a].

The von Neumann-Morgenstern proposal provided cardinal utility with the same operational status that had previously been held by ordinal utility—utilities could be measured simply by observing acts of choice. Further study has shown that, where uncertain prospects are involved, there is an important interaction between subjective probabilities and cardinal utilities; to measure either one operationally calls for an experimental design that, in effect, permits the measurement of both. In the next paragraphs we shall consider this point more fully.

[3] The *marginal* utility of a commodity or money is the amount the utility will be increased by an increase of one unit in the amount of the commodity or money; that is, it is the first derivative of utility with respect to the other variable.

Utility and subjective probability. To understand the issues involved in utility measurement and their implications for psychology, let us consider them in a psychophysical framework. We confront a subject with a number of alternatives (e.g., we offer him any one of several phonograph records or, as suggested above, a choice among lottery tickets, each having different odds and different payoffs) and we observe the choices he makes. We wish to construct scales to measure the probabilities he has assigned to the occurrence of the various possible outcomes and the utilities he attaches to them.

Now if there were *objective* probabilities attached to each of the possible outcomes, and if the subject accepted these probabilities as the basis for his choices, then we would be faced with a straightforward task of constructing a utility scale. However, we must consider the possibility that there are no objective probabilities attached to events or that, if there are, they are not identical with the subjective probabilities that the subject himself attaches to the same events. A subject may prefer a particular risky alternative because one of the possible outcomes has a low subjective probability but a very high utility, or because this same outcome is judged to have a high probability of occurrence but only a moderately high utility.

It is not at all obvious that this interacting expectational-preference system can be analyzed into its components, but a rigorous formal examination of the question shows that in fact it can be. If we propose an appropriate set of alternatives to the subject, we can measure operationally both his probability estimates and his utility.[4]

There is one important "if" to be attached to this statement—an "if" involved in all psychophysical measurement. The scales can be measured operationally *provided that* the subject can make consistent choices. For example, no utility scale would be compatible with a preference for A over B, for B over C, and for C over A. By adopting a statistical viewpoint (i.e., percentage of trials in which A is preferred to B), we can weaken somewhat the requirements of consistency, but basically the possibility of constructing such a scale hinges on the consistency of the subject, and his consistency hinges on the transitivity and the stability of his choices [33, 35].

Thus the issue has been shifted. The question is no longer one of cardinal versus ordinal utility. If a utility scale can be defined, the additional assumption that it can be defined for choices among uncertain prospects guarantees its cardinality. The question now is whether a utility scale "exists" at all—is the behavior of consumers over the range of situa-

---

[4] This was first shown some decades ago by the English philosopher Frank Ramsey [48], but his proposal was not clearly understood and was largely neglected until the rediscovery of cardinal utility by von Neumann and Morgenstern.

tions relevant for economics sufficiently consistent and are consumer choices sufficiently transitive, to make the concept of utility empirically meaningful?

Joining the issue in these terms has given it interest for both economists and psychologists—and a number of philosophers and mathematical statisticians as well—with the result that several empirical investigations of these questions are going forward at the present time [an important study is 18; 38, including references]. The earliest investigation predates the present surge of interest; it was an attempt in 1931 by the psychologist L. L. Thurstone [61] to establish the ordinal utility function of a single subject.

The evidence available at the present moment is too scanty to permit very definite conclusions. The following observations are at least consistent with the experimental results:

1. Under a number of experimental conditions, significant differences can be observed between the probability estimates used by the subjects (subjective probabilities) and the objective probabilities known to the experimenter.

2. A fairly high degree of consistency is observed in choices when the payoff is in money; consistency is much lower with multidimensional payoffs (e.g., choice among phonograph records or among marriageable young ladies).

Psychological Analogs of Utility

The term "utility" has until recently had little currency in psychology —either because psychologists had not found a use for the concept, or because it was used, but under an alias. The truth lies somewhere between these extremes.

A construct like the utility function is needed to explain choice in the face of complex alternatives when the subject is trying to select the "best" alternative. If the alternatives can all be scaled along a single dimension (e.g., are all measured in money), or if the subject is merely looking for a "good" alternative, a theory of choice can be constructed that dispenses with a utility scale [57]. In *most* laboratory experiments where the subject is faced with a choice among alternatives, the situation is one of reward versus no reward, and even where alternative rewards are present, the consistency of the subject's preferences is not usually tested over a wide range of circumstances or a long stretch of time.

Contemporary work in the behavioral sciences aimed at defining and measuring "values" will undoubtedly raise questions of the relative strength of values as soon as attempts are made to predict behavior from a knowledge of a subject's value profile. Since little has yet been done empirically to make the jump from verbal attitudes about values to their behavioral consequences, this issue has not yet been faced. When the time arrives for dealing with it, social psychologists will find that the basic issues are precisely the ones that have arisen in the definition and measurement of utility.

Lewin, in his theory of "valences," treated choice with competing rewards and punishments as analogous to the situation in physics where a number of nonparallel forces converge on the same body. If the analogy were carried out strictly, the net valences of the Lewinian theory would have the formal properties of utilities. Lewin and those who have used his theoretical formulations as the basis for empirical work have not actually followed this path to its conclusion. If there are attached to a particular course of action *both* a large reward and a smaller punishment, for example, Lewinians and most other psychologists would predict that behavior will be different from what it would be if only a small reward—representing the difference between the original reward and the punishment—were attached to the action [31]. In contrast, utility theory would predict that, corresponding to any combination of punishments and rewards attached to an action, there would exist an exactly equivalent simple net punishment or reward.

We see, then, that although the Lewinian valence bears some resemblance to utility, the actual properties attributed to it on the basis of empirical study are quite different. The empirical facts—rather consistently observed with both human and animal subjects—are these: Choices bearing mixed consequences and choices where all alternatives have unpleasant consequences represent *conflict* situations for the subject, and behavior in a conflict situation is qualitatively different from behavior when conflict is absent [57]. For example, one kind of behavior has no place in classical utility theory, but it is frequently observed in conflict situations—this is the subject's refusal to accept the alternatives as given and his search for new alternatives [see 15 for an application of this notion in the theory of the firm]. Where the conflict is stronger, various kinds of neurotic behavior come into evidence—fixation, regression, aggression, withdrawal, and so on.

The empirical findings on choice in conflict situations challenge the validity of the utility function as a basis for conceptualizing decision-making behavior. Any microeconomic description of behavior that purports to fit empirical data will have to deal with this evidence. The study of choice under conflict may prove to be even more fruitful for reexamining the utility concept than the experiments on choice under uncertainty that were mentioned earlier.

The Economist's Interest in Utility

Returning now to macroeconomics, we may ask how much of the theory of utility and of consumer behavior is really needed to explain the operation of the economy. The answer is that the macroeconomist is ordinarily rather uninterested in detailed information about the shapes of consumers' utility functions—either the functions of individuals or aggregated functions. The broad aspects of consumer behavior with which he is actually concerned are discussed in the following paragraphs.

Consumer rationality. An important policy application of economic theory is to determine under what circumstances economic mechanisms lead to an efficient allocation of resources. This is the main topic of the branch of economic theory known as welfare economics. The important postulate about consumers required for welfare economics is rationality—that consumers maximize utility, that they attempt to allocate their income so as to purchase—from all possible baskets—the basket that will give them the greatest satisfaction. Hence the welfare economist has ordinarily no particular interest in the shape of the utility function, but a strong interest in its existence as the criterion of consumer choice.

Elasticity of demand. In economics, the consumer enters the market through his demand schedule—the schedule of quantities of a commodity he will buy at various prices. The summation of these quantities for all consumers gives the market-demand schedule. For many applications, it must be assumed that the market-demand schedule has a negative slope—that the quantity demanded decreases as price increases. For other purposes, it may be necessary to know the elasticity of demand—how sensitively the quantity demanded depends on price. The tendency even in these matters is to deal in generalities; only occasionally is the economist concerned with the numerical measurement of the elasticities of demand for specific commodities.

Many attempts have been made to derive certain characteristics of the demand schedule by deductive reasoning from the theory of consumer choice. However, where it is necessary to measure the elasticity of demand numerically, the usual procedure is to infer the elasticity from direct measurements of quantities purchased in the market at various prices. Hence the empirical study of demand has rested much more on the direct accumulation and analysis of data than on inferences from underlying psychological principles [50].

Saving and spending. In the modern post-Keynesian theory of the business cycle and national income, the consumer's decision as to what proportion of his income he will spend and what proportion he will save is of very great importance. The number of cents he will spend out of each additional dollar of income is the "marginal propensity to consume" of Keynes. In certain versions of Keynesian theory, one crucial assumption is that spending increases less than proportionately as income increases. Much effort has been devoted, over the last decade, to testing this assumption [29, chaps. 7, 8].

On the one hand, there have been attempts to measure spending and saving behavior by obtaining empirical data from consumers or analyzing secondary data from the economy. On the other hand, there have been attempts to deduce the spending and saving behavior of the consumer from the theory of rational consumer choice. The first course involves no particular framework of theory and, while it may yield data of interest to psychologists, it has borrowed little or nothing from psychology.

The second course, the deduction of the theory of saving from the theory of consumer choice, has also evolved almost independently of work in psychology. It illustrates the characteristic approach of the economist to individual behavior and the reason why he can formulate his assumptions with so little dependence on empirical observation (even though he may use aggregative data to test the consequences derived from his assumptions).

Modigliani and Brumberg [41] assume that the only motive for saving is retirement income and that the consumer adjusts his saving to give him a level annual expenditure over his lifetime. During periods of high income, he saves; during periods of low or no income, he dissaves. These are plausible assumptions—at least as approximations—and it is their introspective plausibility that the economist takes as his justification for adopting them. From these assumptions, together with assumptions as to how income expectations are formed and data on length of life and length of adult earning period, numerical estimates can be made of the fraction of total income that will be saved—that is to say, the saving-consumption function can be deduced from these assumptions. Up to the present time, the model has held up fairly well in explaining the actually observed data on consumer expenditures and savings.

Similar approaches have been used by economists to explain the fact —or supposed fact—that some individuals both gamble in lotteries and buy insurance [22, p. 393]. The explanation—like that outlined above— consists in showing that circumstances exist (i.e., can be postulated) under which the behavior in question *would be* rational behavior for a consumer bent on maximizing his utility. It is quite uncharacteristic of the economic theorist to test his explanation further by studying the consumer's attitudes or subjecting him to experimental situations. On the other hand, the psychological assumptions that underlie theories of this kind are not difficult to identify, and there are many possibilities here for direct testing by psychologists of the economic models.

Expectations.[5]   The third aspect of the consumer's behavior in which the macroeconomist has substantial interest is the formation of expectations. In a world of uncertainty, a theory cannot make a consumer's expenditure depend on future income, but only on *expectations* of future

---

[5] Expectations really belong to the cognitive rather than the motivational sphere, but it is convenient to discuss them here to round out our picture of contemporary research. For a panorama of recent approaches to the theory of expectations, see Bowman [7].

income. Hence the predictions of the theory will depend on assumptions about the formation of expectations.

Over the past decade, considerable data have been accumulated on consumers' plans and expectations from the Survey of Consumer Finances conducted for the Board of Governors of the Federal Reserve System by the Survey Research Center of the University of Michigan [7; 29, chap. 5]. These and similar data obtained by others begin to inform us to what extent consumers plan their expenditures in advance and for what kinds of purchases; what expectations they hold about their own income, and how well the expenditure plans predict actual behavior. It can hardly be said that these data have been linked with psychological generalizations from other areas of behavior; at present, they simply stand as brute facts.

Marketing.   Thus far we have left out of account the study of consumer behavior that has been carried out for its practical utility to the business firm—market research. The literature on selling and advertising has generally had a closer tie to psychology than has the economic literature on consumer demand. There have been attempts to apply principles of motivation and learning to the design of effective selling procedures.

The validity of general psychological principles applied to marketing behavior has had limited empirical test. There have been, for example, a number of controlled experiments comparing the relative effectiveness of different advertising copy or methods. An interesting development of the past few years has been the application of projective techniques to the study of consumer motivation. An early study of this sort, carried out by Mason Haire, showed that housewives had a quite different perception of an (otherwise unidentified) woman who bought instant coffee from a woman who bought ground coffee.

Much of the data of market research does not see the light of day, since it is gathered and analyzed for proprietary purposes. Hence, in spite of the great amount of discussion in the marketing field concerning "motivation research" and other applications of psychology to marketing, the number of good empirical studies in the literature is not large.

An important study, which may be a prototype of research to come on innovation and consumer adoption of new commodities, was carried out by the Bureau of Applied Social Research at Columbia University to determine the influence processes involved in the adoption of a new antibiotic by physicians [13]. While this study will hardly fit within the traditional static framework of utility theory, it points the way to possible approaches to the dynamics of consumer choice.

Summary: Consumer Motivation

Macroeconomics does not require for most purposes a detailed theory of consumer choice. The utility function has been the central theoretical construct here, but only a few qualitative features of the function are required for the theories derived from it. Moreover, much of the work on consumer demand—and particularly empirical work—is independent of the concept of utility.

The predisposition of economists to deduce behavior from assumptions of rationality and other "plausible" assumptions about behavior has limited the interaction of economics and psychology in the area of consumer behavior. The greatest potentialities for work of mutual value to the two disciplines lie at present in (1) testing the assumptions of utility theory and the existence of a cardinal utility function, (2) exploring the implications of behavior in conflict situations for economic theory, (3) extending the study of the spending-saving behavior of consumers and the formation of consumer expectations, and (4) extending the study of consumer market behavior in relation to individual products and specific marketing techniques.

MOTIVATION: THE ENTREPRENEUR

The entrepreneur is the man who holds the residual equity in the business firm. After all the other factors of production—including interest on invested capital—have been paid, his share is the remainder, be it large or small. Most important for the theory, he is the man who controls the decision variables of the basic productive unit, the firm.

Just as the central assumption about consumption is that the consumer strives to maximize his utility, so the central assumption about production is that the entrepreneur strives to maximize his residual share—his profit [47, pp. 205–210]. But the assumption of profit maximization is even more essential to the validity of classical economic theory than the assumption of utility maximization; hence the attack upon and the defense of classical theory has tended to focus upon the former postulate.

The hypothesis that the entrepreneur seeks to maximize his profit is a simple corollary to the general postulate of economic rationality. Attacks on the hypothesis have been frequent, and they range over many issues [29, chap. 9; 47]:

1. The theory leaves ambiguous whether short-run or long-run profit is to be maximized. If long-run profit is the criterion, then it is extremely difficult—because of the uncertainty in long-run consequences of action —to determine what course of action maximizes profit or to test whether a particular firm is in fact using the criterion. This is a serious difficulty for both descriptive and normative microeconomics.

2. The entrepreneur may obtain all kinds of "psychic income" from the firm, quite apart from monetary rewards. If he is to maximize his

utility, then he will sometimes balance a loss of profits against an increase in psychic income. For example, the high return from ownership of slum property is sometimes attributed to the negative psychic income attached to such ownership. But if we admit psychic income into the picture, the criterion of profit maximization loses all its definiteness and becomes identical with (and as ambiguous as) utility maximization.

3. The entrepreneur may not care to maximize, but may simply want to earn a return that he regards as "satisfactory." By sophistry and an adept use of the concept of psychic income, the notion of seeking a satisfactory return can be translated into utility maximization—but not in any operational way. As we shall see, the notion of seeking "satisfactory" levels of profits or sales is more meaningfully related to the psychological concept of aspiration levels than to any notion of maximization.

4. Under modern conditions, the equity owners and the active managers of an enterprise are usually separate and distinct groups of persons —the managers are really "labor" and not "entrepreneurs." Under these circumstances, there is no reason to postulate an identity of interests between entrepreneurs and managers or to assume that the latter are motivated to maximize profits.

All of these objections concern motivation; they assume, more or less, that the entrepreneur or the manager *could* aim at profit maximization if he wanted to. We shall see in the section on cognition that there are also serious cognitive questions as to the capacity of economic man to maximize profit, but I shall focus on questions of motivation for the moment.

Few data from psychology outside economics bear directly on the issues at hand. There have been some investigations, however, that are worth mentioning. These fall in two categories: attempts to determine the relative importance of economic and noneconomic motivation and studies of the dynamics of aspiration levels.

In addition to these psychological studies, there have been a number of inquiries directed specifically at these economic issues and carried out primarily by economists. Among these are studies of the formation of expectations by managers and business firms and studies of the making of particular classes of business decisions (pricing decisions, investment decisions, etc.). I shall consider each of these four classes of investigations, the two "psychological" and the two "economic," in turn. In a final part of this section, I shall discuss the identity and conflict of interest between owners and managers.

Economic and Noneconomic Motivation

The past twenty years has seen a strong reaffirmation of the importance of noneconomic as against economic motivation—for employees as well as for managers and entrepreneurs. This is one of the central points—and certainly one of the most widely quoted points—of Barnard's *The Functions of the Executive* [5]. It was earlier emphasized by Veblen and other institutionalists.

It is hard to determine the relative role of noneconomic and economic motivations because we do not have a metric for comparing them. We are really confronted again with the task of constructing a utility function in which monetary gain is one dimension in the commodity space, and status, prestige, power, and all the other things that men are supposed to work for are the other dimensions. Since no one has made the measurements needed to establish the shape of this function, the usual statements about the relative importance of the various motivations are nonoperational. They have about the same semantic status as the assertion "It is later than you think."

Really the situation is not so hopeless if we reject the economists' assumptions, which are implicit above, that there must be some marginal rate of substitution between profit and other goals and that "measuring the importance of the profit motive" is synonymous with measuring this marginal rate of substitution. From an institutionalist point of view, it would be equally satisfactory if we could simply describe the situations where profit would be sacrificed for other goals. Unfortunately, even this descriptive task has not been carried out in any comprehensive fashion. About the best we can say is that enough illustrations of response to other motivations have been collected to rule out the hypothesis that profit maximization (even long-run profit maximization) is an all-encompassing goal of business management. A measure of the "importance" of the deviations remains to be constructed.

Satisficing versus Maximizing

The notion of "satiation" plays no role in classical economic theory. However, in the treatment of motivation in psychology, this concept enters rather prominently. First, there is the widely accepted idea that motivation to act stems from *drives,* and that action terminates when the drive is satisfied. Second, there is the idea that the conditions for satisfaction of a drive are not necessarily fixed, but may be specified by an *aspiration level* that adjusts itself on the basis of experience [32, 52, 57, 60b].

The prevalent psychological treatments of motivation, then, hypothesize that drive satisfaction is an all-or-none phenomenon, but that the boundary between the satisfied and unsatisfied states (the level of aspiration) is variable. If we apply this point of view to the business firm, we would expect its goals to be stated not in terms of maximizing profit, but in terms of reaching a certain level or rate of profit, holding a certain share of the market, a certain level of sales, or the like [15a; 29, chap. 9]. There is considerable empirical evidence—most of it, unfortunately, of an anecdotal kind—that supports this interpretation of the goals of the business firm [21].

Here is one of the most interesting areas of relationship between economics and psychology. First, it does not seem unfeasible to test whether business behavior is governed by maximizing or by satisficing criteria. Second, the economic data required to choose between these hypotheses would extend previous theorizing about aspiration levels to a new area of human behavior.

It has sometimes been argued that the distinction between satisficing and maximizing behavior is not important for economic theory. In the first place, the psychological evidence shows that aspirations tend to adjust to the attainable. Hence, in the long run, the argument runs, the level of aspiration and the attainable maximum will be very close together.

A second argument is that even if some firms behaved in the manner of the aspiration-level hypothesis, they would gradually lose out to the maximizing firms, which would make larger profits and grow more rapidly than the others [1].

Both of these arguments assume that (1) firms know how to go about maximizing if they want to, and (2) the economic environment of firms changes slowly enough that the long-run position of equilibrium will be approached. Both hypotheses are dubious, but their discussion will have to be postponed to a later section where cognitive matters will be considered in detail. If we retain a reasonable skepticism—at least until the evidence is in—toward arguments that lean heavily on long-run equilibriums, then the test of the aspiration-level hypothesis is of substantial interest to economic theory as well as to psychology.

Business Expectations

Business expectations, like consumer expectations, are variables of crucial importance to macroeconomics and—unlike most other psychological concepts—cannot be exorcised from the economic model by assumptions of rationality. A considerable part of business-cycle theory hinges on postulates—most of them constructed in the comfort of armchairs—about the way in which business expectations are formed and how they change under changing environmental circumstances.[6]

Business expectations are currently a very active object of economic research, and several periodic surveys are now being conducted of busi-

---

[6] For an exploration of relations between business forecasting and partial reinforcement situations, see Feldman [23] and Cyert et al. [16].

ness forecasts of business conditions [29, chaps. 9–13]. The current empirical research is of two main kinds:

1. Surveys of businessmen's own forecasts of business conditions in the economy and in their own industries. These are obtained by straightforward questionnaire methods, which assume implicitly that businessmen can and do make such forecasts. In some uses to which the data are put, it is also assumed that these forecasts are used as one basis for businessmen's actions.

2. Studies of business decisions and the role of expectations in these decisions—particularly investment and pricing decisions. These will be the topic of the next paragraphs.

Studies of Business Decisions

I have commented earlier on the significance of Keynesian economics for the empirical study of consumer behavior. The controversy over the correctness of the Keynesian system had a similar impact on the study of business behavior. For one of the heretical doctrines of Keynes was that the amount of investment was very nearly independent of the rate of interest. The debate over this doctrine led to a number of empirical studies in the thirties by a group of Oxford economists who adopted the very direct procedure of asking businessmen whether the rate of interest was an important factor in their investment decisions; they concluded from the answers that it was not. This method of inquiry has been followed in virtually all the studies that have been published dealing with business decision making. A comprehensive list of such studies up to 1950 will be found in Hayes [27].

Stemming from a pioneer study by Hall and Hitch [26], there have also been a number of attempts to determine whether businessmen use marginalist principles in pricing their products,[7] as is predicted by classical theory. Different investigators have returned from their interviews with different conclusions. Hall and Hitch, for example, found average costs to be more significant in determining prices than marginal costs, while Early [21] has found an extensive use of marginalist procedures.

Conflict of Interest

We come finally to the actual or potential conflict of interest between owner and hired manager, a conflict that has been considered at length in the economics literature [47]. Two questions are involved:

1. Is the reward that the top management of modern industrial firms

---

[7] Under classical assumptions, profits will be maximized if the quantity produced is set so that the cost of producing one more unit would just equal the increase in revenue from selling the larger product.

actually receive closely related to the effect of their actions upon the firm's profits?

2. In so far as the correlation between management rewards and company profits is imperfect, what do members of top management in fact maximize?

Gordon [24] was able to show pretty conclusively that the correlation between management rewards and company profits is relatively low. On the second point, the evidence is less clear; it takes us back to some of our earlier questions about measuring the relative strengths of different motivations where there is conflict of interest. A formal comparison between the classical theory of the firm and organizational theories that come out of behavioral science, such as those of Barnard [5] and Simon [54], shows that they differ precisely at this point. Both the economic theories and the organizational theories of the firm assume that the firm will adopt a *viable* course of action, a course that will enable it to satisfy its various groups of participants (customers, investors, employees, suppliers) so that they will continue to participate. In general, any such course of action yields a *surplus*—i.e., income over and above that needed for distribution to the participants. The organizational theories leave indeterminate whether (1) the managers will try to maximize this surplus, or (2) all of it will be captured by the entrepreneur. The classical theory of the firm takes a definite stand on both points, asserting that the firm will be conducted in such a way as to maximize the surplus and that the surplus will go to the entrepreneur [56].

However inconclusive and anecdotal the evidence, most observers are persuaded that the organizational theory provides a more realistic picture of the behavior of large corporations than does the classical theory. The former is also consistent with a satisficing theory of the firm's decision making, while the latter is not.

Perhaps the most interesting psychological aspect of this topic is its connection with role theory. The conclusions of classical economics about the behavior of the firm can be valid in a world in which there is a considerable divorce of management from ownership only if the members of management are willing to play the *role* of profit-maximizing entrepreneurs, even though they do not receive the rewards of the entrepreneur. On the other hand, if the classical conclusions are wrong, then it becomes an empirical question to determine what premises the members of management do, in fact, employ in their decision making. Do they identify with the interests of some particular group of participants (e.g., investors), or do they perceive themselves as arbiters seeking to make a "fair" and acceptable division of the firm's surplus among its various participants? Again, the answers will have to come out of continuing empirical study of the firm's behavior.

Summary: Entrepreneurial Motivation

Over the past twenty years the motivational assertions embedded in the classical theory of the firm have been widely challenged. The challenge has stemmed partly from theory, and partly from a substantial body of data that is far from consistent with the classical theory. First, there has been emphasis on the noneconomic—as contrasted with the economic—motivations of the entrepreneur. Second, there has been argument that firms and individual persons do not maximize, but satisfice. Third, data on actual decision-making processes in firms has failed to confirm the universality or even the prevalence of marginalist principles of choice. Fourth, data on management and ownership has shown that, in large segments of modern business, those who hold active managerial control have no great personal economic inducement to maximize profits.

There has been some resistance among economists to accepting the cogency of the evidence for these assertions—even more resistance to admitting their relevance to normative macroeconomics if they are true. Edward S. Mason, for example, in commenting on Papandreou's essay, "Some Basic Problems in the Theory of the Firm" [47, pp. 221–222], states his defense as follows: "The writer of this critique must confess a lack of confidence in the marked superiority, *for purposes of economic analysis,* of this newer concept of the firm over the older conception of the entrepreneur." The italics are Professor Mason's, and the italicized phrase can be translated—I think without violence—as "for purposes of normative macroeconomics."

The matters discussed in these paragraphs are relevant for business-cycle theory largely for understanding how businessmen form their expectations and how these expectations affect their investment and pricing decisions. This is perhaps the weakest point in the empirical verification of business-cycle theories, and a point at which much on-going empirical work is directed.

The theory of the firm is relevant also for welfare economics—for determining under what circumstances the behavior of the firm will lead to efficient allocation of resources. The departure of the firm's behavior from the classical model vitiates all the conclusions about resource allocation that are derivable from that model when perfect competition is assumed. Hence the indifference of Professor Mason (and numerous other economists) is justified only if the firm's behavior turns out to be about the same in the newer theories as in the old ones. There is no reason so far for supposing that this will be so.

There are other questions of long-run economic policy which have been only slightly investigated in economics and for which an accurate understanding of motivation in the business firm may well have even more important implications than any mentioned thus far. The separation of ownership from control may well affect the risk-taking behavior of the firm. Most commentators on this point—solid evidence is almost completely lacking—assume that "business bureaucrats" will be more conservative in their attitudes toward risk and innovation than entrepreneur-owners. There is no very solid basis in psychological theory for making a definite prediction on this point, and the question can be answered only through empirical work.

MOTIVATION: LABOR

More can be said about the relations of economics and psychology in the area of labor relations than in the two areas previously discussed. By the same token, what has to be said is already well known to the specialists in labor relations, who have been less respectful of disciplinary boundaries than most of their colleagues in psychology and economics. I shall try here to steer a middle course. I shall not attempt a full exposition of the roles of economics, psychology, and sociology in labor economics and industrial relations, but point instead to a few key issues.

The motivation of the employee can be and has been approached from the classical standpoint as a pure question of "labor economics." At the other extreme, the same topic can be and has been approached as a pure question of the psychology of motivation. The field of labor economics and industrial relations is today an area of active communication—although not always complete agreement—for economists, psychologists, and sociologists [14].

The central issues are very similar to those considered in the two previous sections. We are interested in the job-taking and job-leaving behaviors of the employee, in his behavior while employed on the job, and in his activity in and through unions. Numerous predictions can be made about all these segments of behavior if we make the classical assumptions about economic rationality. The classical theory, for example, predicts movement from one job to another in terms of wage-rate differentials, and predicts the absence in equilibrium of differentials in wages for comparable jobs. The classical theory also permits predictions as to how employees will respond to wage incentive schemes—and most of the theorizing about piece rates in the early scientific management movement was thoroughly consistent with classical economic theory.

The empirical evidence, on the other hand, only partly supports these classical predictions. Geographical movements of the labor force, for example, are responsive to many forces other than wage differentials, although the influence of the latter, as one of several factors, is clearly demonstrable. In the matter of wage incentive schemes, employee responses have been shown to be far more complicated and dependent on far more complex relations than can be accounted for by a simple economic calculus. Unfortunately, we have as substitute for the classical model only a mass of empirical specifics that do not permit sharp predictions beyond the particular phenomena to which the data themselves relate. Thus, the situation is similar to that in the area of consumer motivation and entrepreneurial motivation [37].

The Authority Relation

One peculiar feature of the employment relation, which distinguishes it from most other economic arrangements and transactions, is this: The employee sells his "services" to the employer and then becomes a "factor of production" [55]. Here the classical assumption of the separation of production behavior from consumption behavior is clearly open to question.

The economic model of the employee—once the employment bargain has been struck—is that of a passive and neutral agent of production who will accept the authority of the employer. A considerable body of psychological evidence shows that the behavior of employees typically departs from this model of passivity and neutrality in a number of ways [28; 37, chaps. 3, 4]. Among the hypotheses that have been pretty well validated are these:

1. *The Hawthorne effect.* When special attention is given to a group of workers by management (say, by enlisting them in an experimental situation), production is likely to rise independently of changes in actual working conditions.

2. *The interaction hypothesis.* High morale and productivity in organizations are promoted if the employees have opportunities for interaction with each other. Conversely, when the work is organized in such a way as to discourage cooperation, teamwork, or social intercourse, low morale is likely to result.

3. *The participation hypothesis.* Significant changes in human behavior can be brought about rapidly only if the persons who are expected to change participate in deciding what the change shall be and how it shall be made.

4. *The cross-pressures hypothesis.* When the same individual has occasion for frequent and close contact with two or more groups that hold conflicting values and attitudes, he will find himself in internal personal conflict. The conflict is often evidenced by symptoms of frustration— withdrawal, aggressive behavior, and the like.

In view of the prominence of phenomena like these in research data, and in the everyday practice of management as well, there is less tendency to apply the economic calculus to supervisory problems than to most other areas of economic behavior. On the other hand, however significant these phenomena may be for the practice of management, they do not appear to have important implications for macroeconomics. Or to state the conclusion in a more precise way, if this revision of our picture of the employment relation has implications for public policy, these implications cannot be explored via the classical economic model for discussing welfare questions.

Labor Unions

In discussing the employment relation we must give great attention to labor unions. The effect of unions on the relation can be discussed more conveniently in the next section, where we consider the topic of competition among the few. Again, we shall see that the existence of unions provides new reasons for lowering the walls between economics and the other behavioral sciences and for bringing social and political considerations to bear upon an economic relationship.

CONFLICT OF INTEREST: OLIGOPOLY

Economic theory avoids any assumption of common goals and parallel interests among the participants in the economic system. Through the authority relation, employees can agree to accept the goals of their employers as guides to behavior; apart from this, each consumer is assumed to maximize his personal utility, each producer his profit.[8]

The conflict of interests creates no particular problems of theory so long as each participant in the system treats the other participants as parts of his given environment, and does not try to predict their behavior and anticipate it. But when this restriction is removed—when it is assumed that a seller takes into account the reactions of buyers to his actions or that each manufacturer predicts the behaviors of his competitors—the precision of prediction of the classical theory vanishes. The only case where the classical theory can then be applied with complete safety is to situations of perfect competition—where the number of competitors is so large that each competitor may safely assume that the market price is a given which is not affected by his own actions. Notice that we are not concerned here with the usual antimonopoly argument that competition is desirable from a welfare standpoint; what we are saying is that competition is an essential condition for unambiguous prediction of behavior from the classical assumptions of economic rationality.

[8] This does not rule out the possibility of nonselfish goals, for one person's pleasure may enter into another person's utility function; but since the utility functions are givens of economic analysis, their content is irrelevant to the theory.

The very assumptions of omniscient rationality that provide the basis for deductive prediction in economics when competition is present lead to ambiguity when they are applied to competition among the few. Awareness of this problem goes back a century to Augustin Cournot, but recognition of its fundamental character and sweeping consequences stems from von Neumann and Morgenstern's *The Theory of Games and Economic Behavior* [62], published in 1944. The central difficulty in competition among the few is familiar to every bridge or poker player: Rational play requires one to outguess one's opponents, but not to be outguessed by them—clearly not a consistent requirement, if it is applied to all the players.

Von Neumann and Morgenstern proposed a solution in the case of a game with two players and a zero-sum payoff—that is, a payoff in which one player would lose what the other won. In this case "omniscient" rationality generally calls for each player to randomize his play in a specified way in order to prevent the opponent from discovering his intentions. If the players accept this definition of rationality and behave this way, then their behavior is predictable at least in an average sense.

But when we attempt to extend the theory to situations that are not zero-sum or that involve more than two players, the ambiguities reappear in new forms (specifically in the form of bargaining among actual or potential coalitions of players), and the theory no longer makes specific predictions of behavior.

A further objection against the theory of games, at least as a descriptive theory, is that it requires of economic man even more fantastic reasoning powers than does classical economic theory. For the elimination of the ambiguities that "outguessing" introduces into prediction, we must seek more realistic assumptions that stem from limitations upon the human capacity for rational calculation [36, chap. 10; 57].

In general, analyses of economic behavior in situations of oligopoly draw at least as heavily upon theories of power and bargaining—initially developed to explain political phenomena—as upon economic theory. This is true of both competition among producers (e.g., the automobile, steel, or aluminum industries) and between unions and employers (particularly industry-wide collective bargaining). This framework does not lead to any more specific predictions of behavior than do other approaches to these phenomena. However, it introduces a greater emphasis upon description and actual observation and is modest in its attempts to derive predictions by deductive reasoning from a few "plausible" premises about human behavior [9, 49, 53].

Four important areas of social science and social policy—two in economics and two more closely related to political science—have as their central concern the phenomena of power and the processes of bargaining, the theory of political parties, labor-management relations, international politics, and oligopoly theory. Any progress in the basic theory applicable to one of these is certain to be almost equally important to the others.

COGNITION: THE CHALLENGE TO RATIONALITY

Up to this point I have emphasized primarily the relations between economics and motivational theory in psychology. It is true that cognitive considerations have not been absent—for example, the formation of expectations by the economic actor—but they have played a secondary role in the discussion. In the present section, cognitive matters will have the central place, while motivation and affect will be considered only as they interact with cognition. This shift in emphasis will allow us to view the relation of economics to psychology from a standpoint suggested by important recent trends in research on both sides of the interdisciplinary boundary.

Classical economics minimized its dependence upon motivational theory in psychology by taking utility maximization (for the consumer) and profit maximization (for the entrepreneur) as the sole motives of economic man. Similarly, economics got along almost without psychological hypotheses about economic man's intellective qualities by assuming him to be "objectively" rational—that is, rational in dealing with a given external environment as viewed by an omniscient being gifted with unlimited powers of computation [54, chap. 4]. Given these basic assumptions, motivational and cognitive, nothing more need be known about economic man to predict his behavior; it suffices to have information about his environment—e.g., the prices in the markets in which he trades, his production function, and so on.

Economists can claim—with considerable justification—that the classical model has had great predictive power in the areas of behavior with which they have been concerned. But economics has been moving steadily into newer areas where the power of the model has never been demonstrated and where its adequacy must be considered anew. Labor economics has been such an area, oligopoly or imperfect competition theory another, decision making under uncertainty a third, and the theory of economic development a fourth. I have already noted some difficulties the theory encountered in these new territories:

1. When the assumptions of perfect competition were removed, even the definition of rationality became ambiguous. New definitions had to be constructed (by no means as "obvious" intuitively as was simple maximization) to extend the theory of rational behavior to bargaining and outguessing situations. Moreover, these new game-theory formula-

tions do not give a univocal prediction of how a rational man would behave.

2. When the assumptions of perfect foresight were removed, the definition of rationality had to be extended in another direction to handle uncertainty about the environment. (There has been a strong tendency, under the influence of game theory, to wrap these two problems into one by treating "nature" as a malevolent opponent. While this solution appeals to some mathematicians and statisticians on aesthetic grounds, its logical or empirical basis is hard to find.)

But extending the classical theory to these new areas requires more than broadening the definition of rationality. In addition, it requires a distinction between the objective environment in which the economic actor "really" lives and the subjective environment that he perceives and to which he responds. When this distinction is made, we can no longer predict his behavior—even if he behaves rationally—from the characteristics of the objective environment; we also need to know something about his perceptual and cognitive processes [57, 58].

The classical model is a theory of a man choosing among fixed and known alternatives to each of which is attached known consequences. When perception and cognition intervene between the decision maker and his objective environment, this model is no longer adequate. Then we need a description of the choice process that recognizes that alternatives are not given but must be sought and a description that takes into account the arduous task of determining what consequences will follow on each of the alternatives [11].

The decision maker's information about his environment is much less than an approximation of the real environment. The term "approximation" implies that the subjective world of the decision maker resembles quite closely the external environment but lacks, perhaps, some fineness of detail. The psychological evidence contradicts this view—the perceived world is fantastically different from the "real" world. The differences involve both omissions and distortions and arise in both perception and inference.

Psychological research has paid most attention to the sins of commission—to the distortions of the external environment in perception and inference. In recent years, experimental work [e.g., Sherif, 51, Asch, 3] has emphasized affect as a cause of distortion. For our purposes, however —understanding the relations of psychology to economics—the sins of *omission* in perception are more important than the sins of *commission*. The decision maker's model of the world encompasses only a minute fraction of all the relevant characteristics of the real environment, and his inferences extract only a minute fraction of all the information that is present, even in his model. Under these circumstances, his choices cannot be predicted from a knowledge of the external environment without a knowledge also of the selective mechanisms that are part of his perceptual and problem-solving processes [37].

Perception is sometimes referred to as a "filter." This term is as misleading as "approximation," and for the same reason: It implies that what comes through into the central nervous system is really quite a bit like what is "out there." In fact, the filtering is not merely a passive selection of some part of a presented whole, but an active process involving attention to a very small part of the whole and exclusion, from the outset, of almost all that is not within the scope of attention. We need not argue the issue of "conscious" and "subconscious" perception; we need simply observe that every human organism lives in an environment that generates millions of bits of new information each second and that the bottleneck of the perceptual apparatus certainly does not admit more than 1,000 bits per second and probably much less.

Equally significant omissions characterize the processing that takes place when information reaches the brain. As every mathematician knows, it is one thing to have a set of differential equations and another to have their solutions. Yet the solutions are logically implied by the equations—they are "all there," if we only knew how to get at them! By the same token, hosts of inferences *might* be drawn from the information stored in the brain but they are not. The consequences implied by information in the memory become known only through active information processing, and hence through active selection of particular problem-solving paths from the myriad that might have been followed.

If we have a rat in a very small maze, with cheese at one branch point, and if we give the rat plenty of time to explore, we can predict where he will finally go without any very deep knowledge of rat psychology. We simply assume that he likes cheese (a given utility function) and that he chooses the path that leads to cheese (objective rationality). If we now transfer the rat to a maze having a number of pieces of cheese in it, but a maze that is several orders of magnitude larger than the largest maze he could possibly explore in a rat's lifetime, then prediction is more difficult. We must now know how a rat solves problems in order to determine where he will go. We must understand what determines the paths he will try and what clues will make him continue along a path or go back.

Classical economics was highly successful in handling small-maze problems without depending on psychology. Labor relations, imperfect competition, uncertainty, and long-run dynamics encase the decision maker in a much larger maze than those considered in classical short-run static theory. In these new areas the economist and the psychologist have numerous common interests in cognitive theory that they have not shared previously.

The Government of Attention: Roles

Short-run predictions of behavior, where there is a large discrepancy between subjective and objective rationality, require information both about the environment and about the frame of reference of the decision maker. In the longer run, the frame of reference may itself become the dependent variable for prediction, but a variable not easily eliminated from the analysis. For even if the environment is one of the long-run determinants of the frame of reference, there is no reason to suppose that there is any simple one-to-one relation between them. Although the individual and the social system to which he belongs must meet long-run tests of survival and efficiency, there are certainly multiple solutions to the survival problem (as evidenced, in another realm, by the large number of distinct biological species).

Although the distinction between the perceived environment and the objective environment is important in many parts of sociology, social psychology, and individual psychology, there has been little consensus as to what terms should be used to denote the perceived environments. Those in common use include "frame of reference," "set," "definition of the situation," and "role." None of these terms is exactly synonymous with the others—at least in the usage of a single writer—but all are used in a variety of meanings, and each has a large area of overlap with the others.

For the purposes of this essay, we need not solve this terminological problem—we can use the four terms above more or less interchangeably. But we must clarify the concepts to which the terms refer. Indeed, this clarification opens important possibilities for contributions of economics to psychology and vice versa.[9] In the following paragraphs I shall propose a revision in the concept of "role" or "frame of reference" that appears to me essential to the fruitful application of that concept.[10] In the next section, the redefined concept will be used to interpret some of the significant relevant current research.

A current definition of *role* [42, p. 278] that is representative of definitions in use in social psychology and sociology reads: "Each position carries with it definite prescriptions for behaving toward other persons in related positions. . . . Such ways of behaving toward others . . . are called *roles*." For brevity, we may say that roles are usually defined as *positionally prescribed sets of behaviors*.

There is, up to the present time, a great poverty of propositions about the characteristics of roles (as distinguished from propositions about how roles are acquired). This poverty can be traced in large part to the un-

---

[9] Bruner et al. provide a somewhat different example of important conceptual borrowing of psychology from economics and game theory [8].

[10] For a more detailed discussion of the proposal set forth here, see Simon [54].

satisfactory nature of the definition of role. The definition provides a name or label for a phenomenon but not a useful tool for its analysis. The difficulty resides in the term "behaviors," which designates the unit for the description of roles. A "behavior" or "action" is not a satisfactory unit for describing the cognitive orientations of persons to their environments.

The inadequacy of this basis for role description becomes apparent when we try to apply the role concept to rational and adaptive behavior. If roles were prescribed sets of behaviors, then there would be no place for rational calculation in role behavior. A person could decide whether he would conform to a role (and this is the topic most prominently discussed in the literature on roles), but having decided that he would conform, the role prescription would itself determine his behavior in that role.

A concept of role that does not admit processes of rational choice is obviously useless for describing the behavior of economic or administrative man. We need something like the role concept, for we need to distinguish between the objective and subjective environments of choice. At the same time, we must avoid substituting, in the theory, socially prescribed sets of behaviors for choice. We need a definition of role that accomplishes the former without implying the latter.

The difficulties with the role concept disappear if we introduce the *decision premise* as the unit of role description in place of the *behavior. A role—in terms of this definition—is a social prescription of some, but not all, of the premises that enter into an individual's choices of behaviors* [54, pp. 221–228; 19]. Any particular concrete behavior is the result of a large number of premises, only some of which are prescribed by the role. In addition to role premises, there are premises about the state of the environment based directly on perception, premises representing beliefs and knowledge, and idiosyncratic premises that characterize the personality.

A fanciful (but only slightly fanciful) example will help to make clear both the distinction between the new definition and the usual one— and the reason for making it. Suppose we were to construct a robot incorporating a modern digital computer and to program (i.e., instruct) the robot to take the role of a business executive in a specified company. What would the program look like? Since no one has yet done this [11, 17], we cannot say with certainty. However, several points are fairly clear. The program would *not* consist of a list of prescribed and proscribed behaviors, since what an executive does is highly contingent on information about a wide variety of circumstances. Instead, the program would consist of a large number of *criteria* to be applied to possible and proposed courses of action, of programs for *generating* possible courses of action, of computational procedures for *assessing* the state of the environment and its implications for action, and the like. Hence, the program—that is, the role prescription—would interact with information to produce concrete behavior adapted to the situation. The elements of such a program take the form of what we have called "decision premises," and what the computer specialist would call "instructions and data" [45].

Roles and the Process of Rational Decision

The definition of role in terms of decision premises is useful not only for clarifying concepts, but also for constructing actual detailed descriptions of concrete roles preparatory to analyzing the structure of these roles and their specific content. We can study the form of the role prescription and the cognitive and other central processes through which it is translated into action; at this point we can expect some genuine congruence to develop between the "economic" or "administrative" man and the "problem-solving" man who has been studied in psychology.

This is not a mere prospectus to be realized at some undefined future date. A substantial number of current research efforts in different fields are converging toward this point, as the following examples show:

Economics. Normative microeconomics seeks to advise the businessman in his decisions—whether to buy a piece of equipment, how much inventory to hold, what price to pay for a product, etc. Hence theories in this field take the form of decision-making procedures for handling particular problems. To mention just one example, linear programming theory has been used to construct a computational model for determining the most profitable blending policies in an oil refinery [10].

These decision models are not merely abstract "theories" of the firm, but actual decision-making devices. We can think of any such a device as a simulation of the corresponding human decision maker, in which the equations and other assumptions that enter into the formal decision-making procedure correspond to the decision premises, including the role prescription, of the decision maker [10a, 12].

In particular, the problems of subjective rationality must be faced in constructing normative decision models: (1) The latter can require for their application only data that are obtainable; (2) they can call only for practicable computations; (3) in so far as they utilize forecasts, they must specify a method of forecasting. These models, then, share many of the properties of less formal decision-making processes and provide us with concrete examples of decision-making roles described in terms of the premises used in deciding, the data, and the rules of computation.

Higher mental processes. Students of human problem solving have tried to describe in some detail the stages of the process and the steps taken by the problem solver. Although the studies that have been reported to date fall far short of complete descriptions of the process—in many respects less complete than the normative economic models mentioned above—they point clearly in the direction of describing the problem solver in terms of his "program," i.e., the premises that determine the course of the process [8, 20].

Electronic computers. Until very recently, the electronic digital computer was a device that, if instructed in painful detail by its operator, could be induced to perform rather complicated and tedious arithmetical operations. Recent research has enabled the computer to interpret and execute instructions given to it in languages that begin to have some of the power and flexibility of natural languages and to carry out tasks that, if performed by humans, we would certainly call "thinking" and "learning."

A few items will illustrate the stage that such research has reached. Several computers have been programmed to design industrial equipment (for example, small motors and transformers), and the persons who have devised these programs believe that their main processes simulate the decision procedures previously followed by the design engineers—hence describe the role of design engineer in these situations. Second, a computer program, the General Problem Solver [44, 46], is able to reason in rather general terms, solving problems of discovering proofs for mathematical theorems, proving trigonometric and algebraic identities, and a variety of other problems by applying means-end analysis. The program has been shown to simulate the main processes used by college students in solving some novel problems of moderate difficulty. Another computer program [10a, 11] simulates the decision processes used by a bank officer in investing the assets of a trust fund. A third [23] shows that the same basic cognitive processes can be used to explain on the one hand, certain economic predictions of businessmen and, on the other, the behavior of subjects in partial reinforcement experiments.

These computer programs contribute to economic theory by providing very concrete explanations of significant economic decision-making processes. At the same time, they are laying the foundations for an operational and rigorous information-processing theory of human thinking and problem solving. They bring promise of a far closer relation between economic and psychological theories of decision making than we have had in the past [60a]. So long as economics emphasized macroscopic events and ignored detailed process within the business firm and so long as psychology avoided the complexities of higher mental process in favor of rigorous experiments on simple learning and choice situations, the two fields had little common ground. With the appearance of computer programming as a tool powerful enough to allow the study of thinking and learning processes in situations as complex as those of everyday life, it will no longer be acceptable to explain the same phenomena with two different, and often contradictory, bodies of theory.

The Structure of Organizational and Economic Roles

We see that the *role* of a person who is behaving rationally or adaptively can be identified in large part with the decision premises he applies to the substance of his problem and the decision premises that govern his problem-solving processes. We see also that rapid progress is being made toward a more accurate and complete description of certain economic, executive, and technical roles (or parts of them). Apart from normative applications (e.g., substituting computers for humans in decision-making tasks), we are not primarily interested—as psychologists or economists— in the detailed description of the roles, but in broader questions—characterizing the structure of roles in general terms, understanding how roles come to be structured in the particular ways they do, and tracing out the implications for macroeconomics and other large-scale social phenomena of this version of role theory.

Characterizing role structure. Here we are concerned with generalizations about cognitive processes, particularly generalizations that are relatively independent of the substantive content of the role. A classical example is Dewey's description of stages in the problem-solving process and its use in Bales's categories for coding group discussions [4, 30]. Another example, of particular interest to economics, is the hypothesis that economic man is a *satisficing* animal whose problem solving is based on search activity to meet aspiration levels, rather than a *maximizing* animal whose problem solving involves finding the best alternatives in terms of specified criteria [57]. A third hypothesis is that *operative goals,* associated with observable criteria of success, and relatively definite means of attainment, play a much larger part in governing choice than *nonoperative goals,* lacking concrete measures of success or programs for attainment [37, chap. 6].

Understanding how roles emerge. Within almost any single business firm, certain characteristic roles will be represented—selling, production, accounting, and so on [16, 19]. Partly, this consistency may be explained in functional terms—a model that views the firm as producing a product, selling it, and accounting for its assets and liabilities simplifies the real world and provides the members of the organization with a workable frame of reference. Imitation within the culture provides an alternative explanation. It is exceedingly difficult to test hypotheses as to the origins and causal conditions for roles as universal in the society as these, but the underlying mechanisms could probably be explored effectively by studying less common roles—safety director, quality control inspector, or the like, that are found in some firms, but not in all.

With our present definition of "role," we can also speak meaningfully of the role of an entire business firm—of decision premises that underlie its basic policies [6, chap. 3; 17]. In a particular industry, we find that some firms specialize in adapting the product to individual customers' specifications; others specialize in product innovation. The common interest of economics and psychology includes not only the study of individual roles, but also the explanation of organizational roles of these sorts.

Tracing the implications for macroeconomics. If basic professional goals remain as they are, the interest of the psychologist and the economist in role theory will stem from somewhat different ultimate aims. The former will use various economic and organizational phenomena as data for studying the structure and determinants of roles; the latter will be primarily interested in the implications or role theory for the model of economic man and, indirectly, for macroeconomics.

Let us consider, by way of example, the economic theory of the size of firms. The classical theory is a static equilibrium theory: Firms of optimum size in terms of average cost per unit of output drive other firms to this size or out of business. Hence the "typical" size of firm in an industry will be that at which average cost per unit is a minimum. Attempts to determine empirically what this size is in specific cases have not been very successful; the theory is further embarrassed by the fact that in almost all industries there is an extremely wide dispersion of firms by size.

The empirical data are more easily reconciled with a model that assumes that the firm searches for growth opportunities than with one that assumes equilibrium at an optimum [6, pp. 72–73]. Thus research at the microlevel on the actual mechanisms of decision making and problem solving has important implications at the macrolevel for the size distributions of firms. The implications extend both to the explanation of the phenomena and the consequences for economic welfare of various kinds of governmental interventions to alter the size distributions of firms [60].

The topics of innovation and technological change provide somewhat more obvious links than the one just discussed between the firm and individual decision maker, on the one hand, and the economy and society, on the other. The factors determining the rate of a nation's economic and technological development are still very much matters of speculation. In particular, classical economics, built upon basically static models of the economy, does not readily handle the processes of invention, growth, and diffusion of knowledge as determinants of productivity or of the rate of capital investment. Some progress has been made in exploring the processes by which innovations are diffused through a culture [13, 25]. However, little or nothing is known of the determinants of the rate and direction of inventive activity or how technical know-how is "stored" and reproduced by a society. A better understanding of these processes would have obvious implications for the decisions that individual firms have to make in budgeting and directing research and development activities, for the decisions of governments relating to economic development, and for the encouragement of technological progress. Hence improved theories of human thinking and problem solving may have a major impact on economic and business policy.

Concluding Comments

This discussion of the mutual interests of economics and the behavioral sciences in cognitive processes—and particularly those of the rational decision maker—has necessarily been more speculative than earlier sections of this article. Here we are examining an area of investigation that is just emerging—just becoming an important element in the social scientist's model of the world. In describing this area, I have tried to point to a number of the diverse research activities that testify to its growing significance and its possible implications for the social sciences.

The relative lack of communication between economists and behavioral scientists on the topic of motivation can be attributed in considerable part to the economist's belief that his purposes are served by a very rudimentary theory of motivational processes, a theory he can construct without much outside help. Cognitive theory has been of great concern both to economics (rationality) and to behavioral scientists (learning, problem solving). What has limited communication here has been the great difference between the models of rational behavior that have prevailed in the several disciplines. There are strong indications today that a more realistic description of human rationality is emerging— one that may serve as common ground for a wide variety of social scientists [8, 20, 46].

METHODOLOGICAL BORROWINGS

A person who has occasion to wander into various territories in the social sciences is struck not only by the diversity of tribal customs relating to substantive matters—concepts and theories—but by the diversity of methodologies as well. If a social scientist is discovered computing a regression coefficient, he is almost certainly an economist; a factor analysis identifies him as a psychologist, probably working with test data, a t or chi-square test, or as a social or experimental psychologist, probably working with experimental data, etc. Mathematical statistics has provided a common meeting ground for the statistically sophisticated of all disciplines, but the statistical techniques they have brought back to their own tribes have tended to be somewhat specialized. Scaling techniques and latent structure analysis are hardly known outside social psychology, the country of origin; the work that has been done on the statistical identification problem is an even more closely held secret of the econometricians. The highly technical nature of some of these developments and the language in which they must be described have hindered their diffusion.

The same may be said about empirical methodology. For a traditional economic theorist, an empirical study means going to the reports of the U.S. Census or the Bureau of Foreign and Domestic Commerce. A social psychologist generates new data by experimenting with small groups of college sophomores in a laboratory. The anthropologist-sociologist buys a ticket to New Guinea or Newburyport. The ecologist-sociologist and the demographer-sociologist behave more like the economist, looking largely to official tabulations of aggregative data for their information. The public opinion specialist constructs a stratified random sample and asks questions of a number of respondents. These are some of the principal varieties of social scientists, viewed as data seekers.

Recent years have seen an increasing amount of borrowing of empirical methodologies among disciplines, although the average experience of social scientists trained in one discipline, but using the data-gathering techniques of the others, is very slight. A few economists are now using questionnaires and the interview as a means for learning about economic behavior. An even smaller group is exploring the possibilities of actually observing behavior within the business firm. A few studies, easily counted on the fingers, have attempted to elucidate economic phenomena by laboratory experimentation.

All of these activities seem to be growing—amidst a certain healthy skepticism of traditionally trained economists—and growing not merely in quantity but in their sophistication of technique. For example, the belief that the way to learn how a businessman makes decisions is to ask him (comparable to earlier beliefs in most public opinion polling studies) is gradually waning; one or two of the most carefully designed and controlled studies of utility functions show a high degree of sophistication with respect to introspective evidence.

The borrowing in the other direction—from economics to the behavioral sciences—lies more in the direction of statistics and mathematical formalization than empirical techniques. Mathematical theorizing is undoubtedly most highly developed in economics, where it has been intimately involved in the advance of theory over the last fifty years. Recently, the trend toward mathematical formalization of theories has spread to psychology and, to a lesser extent, sociology [30]. The number of social scientists capable of handling mathematics as consumers and as producers is increasing rapidly, and we may expect it to continue to do so under the impetus it has been given by the Social Science Research Council and the Ford Foundation.

As we survey the various aspects of methodology, then, we observe a slow but significant diffusion of empirical techniques from the behavioral sciences to economics and a return traffic in statistics and mathematics. These streams of diffusion of knowledge are bringing about important advances in the technical level of both empirical and theoretical work in the social sciences.

CONCLUSION

I shall not try to summarize further what is already a compressed survey of an alarmingly wide range of topics. The word "interdisciplinary" is in fashion again in the social sciences, but my review of the literature has not revealed any great excess of interdisciplinary fervor on the whole. On the contrary, the disciplinary boundaries remain rather effective barriers to the sharing of knowledge in areas that are certainly of common concern to economics and the behavioral sciences, and areas to which all these disciplines have much to contribute. It is doubtful whether the existing disciplines constitute a satisfactory frame of reference for the sciences of man. If the subjective rationality of the social scientist is to be adequate to the task of interpreting the objective facts of the real world of social phenomena, a more effective set of role definitions than those in current use needs to be found.

REFERENCES

1. Alchian, A. A. Uncertainty, evolution, and economic theory. *J. polit. Econ.*, 1950, **58**, 58–212.
2. Arrow, K. J. Utilities, attitudes, choices: a review note. *Econometrica*, 1958, **26**, 1–23.
3. Asch, S. E. *Social psychology.* Englewood Cliffs, N.J.: Prentice-Hall, 1952.
4. Bales, R. F. *Interaction process analysis.* Reading, Mass.: Addison-Wesley, 1950.
5. Barnard, C. I. *The functions of the executive.* Cambridge, Mass.: Harvard Univer. Press, 1938.
5a. Borko, H. (Ed.). *Computer applications in the behavioral sciences.* Englewood Cliffs, N.J.: Prentice-Hall, 1962.
6. Bowen, H. R. *The business enterprise as a subject for research.* New York: Social Science Research Council, 1955.
7. Bowman, M. J. *Expectations, uncertainty, and business behavior.* New York: Social Science Research Council, 1958.
8. Bruner, J. A., Goodnow, J. T., & Austin, G. A. *A study of thinking.* New York: Wiley, 1956.
9. Chamberlin, N. W. *A general theory of economic process.* New York: Harper, 1955.

10. Charnes, A., Cooper, W. W., & Mellon, B. Blending aviation gasolines. *Econometrica,* 1952, **20,** 135–159.

10a. Clarkson, G. P. E. *Portfolio selection: a simulation of trust investment.* Englewood Cliffs, N.J.: Prentice-Hall, 1962.

11. Clarkson, G. P. E., & Meltzer, A. H. Portfolio selection: a heuristic approach. *J. Finance,* 1960, **15,** 465–480.

12. Clarkson, G. P. E., & Simon, H. A. Simulation of individual and group behavior. *Amer. Econ. Rev.,* 1960, **50,** 920–932.

13. Coleman, J., Katz, E., & Menzel, H. The diffusion of an innovation among physicians. *Sociometry,* 1957, **20,** 253–270.

14. Coleman, J. R. The role of the local industrial union in contemporary collective bargaining. *Proc. eighth Annu. Mtg. industr. Relat. Res. Ass.,* 1955. Madison, Wis.: The Association, 1956. Pp. 274–286.

15. Cyert, R. M., & March, J. G. Organizational factors in the theory of oligopoly. *Quart. J. Econ.,* 1956, **70,** 44–64.

15a. Cyert, R. M. & March, J. G. *A behavioral theory of the firm.* Englewood Cliffs, N.J.: Prentice-Hall, forthcoming, 1962.

16. Cyert, R. M., March, J. G., & Starbuck, W. Two experiments on bias and conflict in organizational estimation. *Management Sci.,* 1961, **7,** 254–264.

17. Cyert, R. M., Simon, H. A., & Trow, D. B. Observation of a business decision. *J. Business,* 1956, **29,** 237–248.

18. Davidson, D., & Suppes, P. *Decision making: an experimental approach.* Stanford, Calif.: Stanford Univer. Press, 1955.

19. Dearborn, D. C., & Simon, H. A. Selective perception: a note on the departmental identifications of executives. *Sociometry,* 1958, **21,** 140–144.

20. de Groot, A. *Het Denken van den Schaker.* Amsterdam: Noord-Hollandsche Uitgevers Maatschapij, 1946.

21. Early, J. S. Marginal policies of "excellently managed" companies. *Amer. Econ. Rev.,* 1956, **46,** 44–70.

22. Edwards, W. The theory of decision making. *Psychol. Bull.,* 1954, **51,** 380–417.

23. Feldman, J. An analysis of predictive behavior in a two choice situation. Unpublished doctoral dissertation, Carnegie Inst. Technol., 1959.

24. Gordon, R. A. *Business leadership in the large corporation.* Washington: Brookings, 1945.

25. Griliches, Z. Hybrid corn: an exploration in the economics of technological change. *Econometrica,* 1957, **25,** 501–522.

26. Hall, R. L., & Hitch, C. J. Price theory and business behavior. *Oxford Econ. Papers,* 1939, No. 2, 12–45.

27. Hayes, S. P., Jr. Some psychological problems of economics. *Psychol. Bull.,* 1950, **47,** 289–330.

28. Homans, G. C. *The human group.* New York: Harper, 1950.

29. Katona, G. *Psychological analysis of economic behavior.* New York: McGraw-Hill, 1951.

30. Lazarsfeld, P. F. (Ed.) *Mathematical thinking in the social sciences.* Glencoe, Ill.: Free Press, 1954.
31. Lewin, K. *Principles of topological psychology.* New York: McGraw-Hill, 1936.
32. Lewin, K., et al. Level of aspiration. In J. McV. Hunt (Ed.), *Personality and the behavior disorders.* Vol. 1. New York: Ronald, 1944. Pp. 333–378.
33. Luce, R. D. A probabilistic theory of utility. *Econometrica,* 1958, 26, 193–224.
34. Luce, R. D. *Individual choice behavior.* New York: Wiley, 1959.
35. Luce, R. D., & Edwards, W. The derivation of subjective scales from just noticeable differences. *Psychol. Rev.,* 1958, 65, 222–237.
36. Luce, R. D., & Raiffa, H. *Games and decisions.* New York: Wiley, 1957.
37. March, J. C., & Simon, H. A. *Organizations.* New York: Wiley, 1958.
38. Marschak, J. Binary-choice constraints and random utility indicators. In K. J. Arrow, S. Karlin, & P. Suppes (Eds.), *Mathematical methods in the social sciences.* Stanford, Calif.: Stanford Univer. Press, 1959. Pp. 312–329.
39. Marshall, A. *Principles of economics.* (8th ed.) New York: St. Martin's Press, 1920.
40. Menzel, H., Coleman, J., & Katz, E. On the flow of scientific information in the medical profession. New York: Columbia Univer., Bur. Appl. Soc. Res., 1955. (Mimeographed report)
41. Modigliani, F., & Brumberg, E. Utility analysis and the consumption function. In K. K. Kurihara (Ed.), *Post-Keynesian economics.* New York: Knopf, 1954.
42. Newcomb, T. M. *Social psychology.* New York: Dryden, 1950.
43. Newell, A., Shaw, J. C., & Simon, H. A. Empirical explorations of the logic theory machine. *Proceedings Western Joint Computer Conference.* New York: Institute of Radio Engineers, 1957. Pp. 218–230.
44. Newell, A., Shaw, J. C., & Simon, H. A. Elements of a theory of human problem solving. *Psychol. Rev.,* 1958, 65, 151–166.
45. Newell, A., & Simon, H. A. The logic theory machine. *Trans. Inf. Theor., Inst. Radio Eng.,* September 1956, IT-2(3), 61–79.
46. Newell, A., & Simon, H. A. The simulation of human thought. In *Current trends in psychological theory.* Pittsburgh, Pa.: Univer. Pittsburgh Press, 1960.
47. Papandreou, A. G. Some basic problems in the theory of the firm. In B. F. Haley (Ed.), *A survey of contemporary economics.* Vol. 2. Homewood, Ill.: Irwin, 1952. Chap. 5.
48. Ramsey, F. P. *The foundations of mathematics and other logical essays.* New York: Harcourt, Brace, 1931.
48a. Restle, F. *Psychology of judgment and choice.* New York: Wiley, 1961.
49. Schelling, T. C. An essay on bargaining. *Amer. Econ. Rev.,* 1956, 46(3), 281–306.
50. Schultz, H. *The theory and measurement of demand.* Chicago: Univer. Chicago Press, 1938.

51. Sherif, M. *The psychology of social norms.* New York: Harper, 1936.
52. Siegel, S. Level of aspiration and decision making. *Psychol. Rev.*, 1957, **64**, 253–263.
53. Siegel, S., & Fouraker, L. *Bargaining and group decision-making.* New York: Macmillan, 1960.
54. Simon, H. A. *Administrative behavior.* New York: Macmillan, 1947.
55. Simon, H. A. A formal theory of the employment relation. *Econometrica*, 1951, **19**, 293–305. Reprinted in [59, chap. 11].
56. Simon, H. A. A comparison of organization theories. *Rev. Econ. Stud.*, 1952, **20**, 40–48. Reprinted in [59, chap. 10].
57. Simon, H. A. A behavioral model of rational choice. *Quart. J. Econ.*, 1955, **69**, 99–118. Reprinted in [59, chap. 14].
58. Simon, H. A. Rational choice and the structure of the environment. *Psychol. Rev.*, 1956, **63**, 129–138. Reprinted in [59, chap. 15].
59. Simon, H. A. *Models of man.* New York: Wiley, 1957.
60. Simon, H. A., & Bonini, C. P. The size distribution of business firms. *Amer. Econ. Rev.*, 1958, **48**, 607–617.
60a. Sprowls, R. C. Business simulation. In H. Borko (Ed.), *Computer applications in the behavioral sciences.* Englewood Cliffs, N.J.: Prentice-Hall, 1962. Chap. 23.
60b. Stedry, A. C. *Budget control and cost behavior.* Englewood Cliffs, N.J.: Prentice-Hall, 1960.
61. Thurstone, L. L. The indifference function. *J. soc. Psychol.*, 1931, **2**, 139–167.
62. Von Neumann, J., & Morgenstern, O. *The theory of games and economic behavior.* Princeton, N.J.: Princeton Univer. Press, 1944.
63. Weisskopf, W. A. *The psychology of economics.* Chicago: Univer. Chicago Press, 1955.

UTILITY AND EXPECTATION IN ECONOMIC BEHAVIOR

KENNETH J. ARROW
Department of Economics
Stanford University

UTILITY THEORY OF ECONOMIC BEHAVIOR

Choice Under Static Conditions

Theory. Broadly speaking, utility theory is concerned with the problem of choice by an individual from a set of alternative possibilities

724

available to him. The most usual economic context is that of choosing commodities. Suppose an individual has a given income. There are n commodities, each of which can be purchased in any quantity, but at a fixed price per unit. Then the individual is, in effect, permitted to choose only such amounts $x_1, \ldots, x_n$ of commodities $1, \ldots, n$, respectively, as do not exceed in cost the amount of income available to him. If $p_1, \ldots, p_n$ are the prices of commodities $1, \ldots, n$, respectively, then his total expenditures are $\sum_i^n p_i x_i$. If M is the individual's total income, then we are restricting the choice of commodities to those combinations which satisfy the condition $\sum_i^n p_i x_i \leq M$. If M or any of the prices p_i changes, then the chosen amount $x_1, \ldots, x_n$ will change. Thus for each i, x_i is a function of $p_1, \ldots, p_n$ and M. This relation is known as a *demand function*.

The prices and income together limit the range of alternative commodity bundles among which the consumer may choose. They thus define what Pareto has called "the obstacles." The utility theory of choice states that the choice in any given situation depends on an interaction of the externally given obstacles with the *tastes* of the individual and that the obstacles and tastes can be thought of as independent variables. The utility theory asserts, more precisely, that the tastes can be represented by an ordering according to preference of all conceivable alternatives. In the usual theory of consumption it is imagined that the individual could be asked in advance for his preference between any pair of given bundles.[1] It is assumed that these pairwise comparisons taken together have the property of *transitivity*—that is, if bundle A is preferred to bundle B in a choice between those two, and B to C in a similar pairwise choice, then A would be preferred to C if those were the two alternatives.

Preference among commodity bundles is thus assumed to constitute an ordinal scale. For any given set of obstacles—that is, any range of alternatives available to the chooser—there will be, under certain mathematical conditions that need not be elaborated here, one alternative which is preferred to all others. This alternative to be chosen can be predicted from a knowledge of the obstacles, which are presumably objectively given, and the tastes, which in principle are determinable from a series of experiments of a different type.

---

[1] From the point of view of proper experimentation, the above statement is much too simple. What is really desired is the actual choice an individual would make if confronted with a pair of commodity bundles, not his verbal responses to a question. The relation between verbally expressed and behavioral preferences is one of considerable methodological interest. If conditions could be found under which they could be expected to coincide, experimentation could be considerably simplified.

In economics, a convenient representation of this choice process has been given by means of a *utility function*. This is a function assigning to every alternative—that is, every commodity bundle—a number, in such a way that the utility of one bundle is greater than the utility of another if and only if the first bundle is preferred to the second. Notice that this is simply a convenient mathematical way of describing an ordinal scale and that it does not have any further significance at the present level of discussion. In particular, the utility function is unique only up to a monotone transformation. If we represent preference scales by utility functions, we can say the demand functions are defined by maximizing the utility function, subject to the constraints implied by the restriction that total expenditures not exceed total income.

This theory of the formation of demand is not a very strong theory, but it is not a tautology either. In many respects, it is very close to the hedonistic position in psychology which currently seems to be undergoing revival. However, psychological theory is usually much more explicit than pure economic theory[2] about the nature of pleasures and pains.

Time series verification.   Economists usually use two kinds of data to study consumption: budgets and time series of consumption of specific items. In the former, a sample of families at different income levels is taken and the consumption pattern of each family is found. Then, for any specific commodity—tea, for example—consumption can be related to income. Of course, other variables enter in. For the purpose of testing utility theory, this is not very satisfactory, since at any given moment in time, prices are the same for all families. Hence the only variation being studied is income.

The alternative is to take data on the total consumption of a commodity by years or by other time periods and relate it to prices of that and other commodities and to total national income. There is a somewhat illegitimate step here in that the theory relates to the consumption of the individual, while the data relates to the consumption of a national or other unit.

[2] I cannot help being struck by the parallelism between the economists' concepts of tastes and obstacles and Freud's pleasure principle and reality principle. The former, the phase of the "omnipotence of wishes," seems to correspond to a pure expression of tastes, while the reality principle corresponds to recognition that tastes can only be satisfied in so far as they are compatible with the obstacles presented by the external world, including other individuals.

Freud's use of the term "economic" in his discussions of metapsychology is remarkably precise. He is referring to the allocation of the scarce resources of the libido among competing uses, just as the individual allocates his scarce income among competing commodities. It might be interesting for the historian of thought to see what, if any, influence the thought of economists had in Freud's development. Vienna in the 1870s and 1880s was the center of a great school of economists who were very much interested in the utility theory—indeed, this group was one of its originators.

The utility theory implies that the demand function will satisfy certain conditions. One is that the demand function for any commodity is homogeneous of degree zero in prices and income—that is, if all prices and income were multiplied through by the same number, the demand would remain unchanged. (In effect, a change in all prices and in income is the same as a change in the name of the monetary unit and therefore should be of no consequence.) Virtually all time series analysis presupposes homogeneity and, since it is usual to get relations which fit very well, this may be taken as a confirmation of the homogeneity implication of the utility theory.

A more severe test is posed by the so-called "Slutzky relation." Let $f_i(p_1, \ldots, p_n, M)$ be the demand for commodity i as a function of prices and income; there is one such demand function for every commodity. Then the utility theory has the following implication:

$$\frac{\partial f_i}{\partial p_j} + f_j \frac{\partial f_i}{\partial M} = \frac{\partial f_j}{\partial p_i} + f_i \frac{\partial f_j}{\partial M}$$

There have been a few attempts made to verify this relationship. One is due to Wold and Juréen [63, pp. 300–302]. By regression analysis on data from 1921 to 1939 for Sweden, they estimated the demands for animal foods and vegetable foods as functions of the two prices and income. The estimated coefficients do not contradict the Slutzky relation, although they can hardly be said to support it very strongly. A similar conclusion is reached in a study of British data by Stone [56].

Experimental verification. Studies such as those by Wold and Juréen and Stone suffer, of course, from the uncontrolled nature of the underlying conditions. Many other properties of the economic system have changed during the period studied. It is not surprising that it is difficult to get any clear-cut results. It is this which has led some economists and psychologists to investigate the transitivity of preference and similar problems by experimental methods. Perhaps the earliest was the study of L. L. Thurstone [59]. He considered three commodities—hats, shoes, and overcoats—and assumed that the utility function had the form

$$\sum_{i=1}^{3} k_i \log x_i$$

Under these conditions, one may also consider the utility function for any two commodities, obtained simply by ignoring the third term. He first took a fixed bundle $x_1{}^0$, $x_2{}^0$ of the first two commodities; by repeated questions, he found which pairs x_1, x_2 were preferred to $x_1{}^0$, $x_2{}^0$ and which pairs found inferior. Verbal responses were used. By interpolation, an indifference curve could be found, which gave for each x_1 a value of

x_2, such that x_1, x_2 was indifferent to $x_1{}^0$, $x_2{}^0$. For the particular utility function assumed, this indifference curve should have the form

$$k_1 \log x_1 + k_2 \log x_2 = \text{constant}$$

The best fitting such curve was found (note that only the ratio k_2/k_1 is of consequence). This operation was repeated for alternative fixed bundles $x_1{}^0$, $x_2{}^0$. Since k_1 and k_2 are assumed to be independent of the fixed bundle, a pooled estimate of these parameters was obtained.

By a similar procedure, estimates of k_2 and k_3 were obtained. Since these estimates are defined only up to proportional changes in k_2 and k_3, they can be normalized, so that the two estimates of k_2 are the same. Under the assumptions made, the preference as between two bundles of commodities 1 and 3 is determined by the relative values of

$$k_1 \log x_1 + k_3 \log x_3$$

Actual preference statements as between pairs x_1, x_3 were tested against those predicted. From a graphical representation, it can be seen that the prediction is good, but not perfect. No tests of significance were used.

It should be made clear that in Thurstone's work, as in all subsequent work, the hypothesis of strict transitivity in a deterministic sense is not being seriously entertained; it is clearly rejected by the data. What is really tested is some concept of stochastic transitivity. In the studies reviewed in this section, the stochastic element is not analyzed in great detail but is added on to a deterministic hypothesis much in the way residual terms are added to a deterministic relation in the usual application of regression analysis to hypothesis testing. More recent attempts at a theory which encompass probabilistic choices in its structure are discussed below (see section on Probabilistic Choices).

Several rather ingenious studies have been made in recent years in testing the transitivity hypothesis. P. H. Benson [5] asked individuals to rank separately appetizers, entrées, and desserts from a specified list. Prices were given for the various items and the subjects were asked to choose a meal within a fixed budget constraint. He scaled the three separate rankings according to a modified form of the methods of paired comparisons and assumed that the utility of the meal was the sum of the utilities of the appetizer, entrée, and dessert, utility being assumed equal to scale found. It has been discovered that the choice of the meal could be very well explained by the assumption of utility maximization subject to the given prices and incomes. The assumption that the utilities are additive for the given scale is rather arbitrary. It is perhaps then even more surprising that agreement is so good.

More recently there have been two very carefully controlled experiments which tend to confirm the transitivity hypothesis. One was developed by Andreas G. Papandreou [47]. Individuals were asked to choose between pairs of combinations of tickets for different recreational events, e.g., to choose between two opera and two ballet tickets, and one opera and three ballet tickets. It was not assumed that the choice made between a given pair of alternatives would remain the same on repeated trials. Instead, it was hypothesized that the difference between the utilities of any two alternatives was a random variable, the alternative with the higher utility being chosen on any particular trial. This hypothesis was tested against the alternatives of any probabilities of choosing among alternatives. The evidence was overwhelming that the transitivity hypothesis was satisfied.

A similar result has been obtained more recently by Arnold M. Rose [50]. Rose asked opinions about the relative seriousness of different criminal offenses. The questionnaire consisted of pairwise comparisons and was repeated after two months. It was considered that observed circularities (intransitivities) could result from random choices between alternatives that are really very close, carelessness, or "true" intransitivity. No explicit model of the alternative hypothesis was formulated, but a number of observations which tended to minimize the possibility of true intransitivity were made. Three of the seventy-four subjects had no circularities on either test, and forty-seven did not repeat on the second test any circularity which occurred on the first. Less than 10 per cent of all circularities were repeated. It appears that most circularities could be attributed to carelessness. Of the repeated circularities, most were made on close alternatives (closeness being measured by the Thurstone scale based on paired comparisons for all subjects), and thus could be attributed to forcing a decision between alternatives that are virtually indifferent. It was concluded that "true" intransitivity was rare.

On the other hand, Kenneth O. May [37] found a considerable degree of intransitivity in choices by college students as to the qualities of three hypothetical marriage partners. Each potential wife was described in terms of intelligence, looks, and wealth, and the three possible partners were so chosen that if ranking was done by considering a majority of the three qualities, the result was circular. The subjects made pairwise choices among the three partners, who were given different designations but the same descriptions in the different choices. Seventeen out of sixty-two subjects had the circular preference pattern defined by a majority of the qualities; the remainder, close to three-fourths of the whole, had different transitive preference patterns.

The evidence seems mostly to be on the side of verifying the transitivity postulate, but obviously the data are far from conclusive. In particular, it would be useful to run experiments in which the individual could actually get some of the rewards so that the choice would be behavioristic rather than merely verbal.

Utilities and reference groups. Among other choices made by an individual with a given income, one is dividing it between consumption and savings. Although this division leads into dynamic problems to be discussed in the section on Choice in Dynamic Situations, it can be thought of first in the same way as a choice among commodities. In this context, there has been one line of thought which relates decisions about savings to the behavior of others in the community.

Dorothy Brady and Rose Friedman [7] studied budget data for different parts of the country. They found that the relation between savings and income was different by geographical areas. However, it could be shown that the ratio of savings to income could be explained in terms of the individual's *relative* position on the income scale of his particular geographical area. Thus an individual whose income was the median for the South would save the same proportion of his income as one who was at the median income position for the Northeast, even though those two median levels were very different.

This line of investigation was continued by James S. Duesenberry [13]. He argued that the utility derived by an individual for a given bundle, particularly a given level of consumption, was not absolute, but relative to the general consumption level of those whom he regarded as his peers. Thus there is a theory of changes in the individual's preference system. At any given moment—that is, at any given level of consumption by the community at large—the preference ranking of an individual for different amounts of consumption is well defined, but the ranking will change with changes in the community's consumption level.

This hypothesis has the advantage of explaining an apparent contradiction between time series and budget data. If one takes a given point in time and relates savings of families to incomes, the savings-income ratio tends to increase with income. On the other hand, time series data such as that of Simon Kuznets [29] show that the percentage saved by the community as a whole has been roughly constant since 1879. These two observations are apparently incompatible because, if the first relation held, a rise in income of the average member of the community would result in a higher savings-income ratio. Duesenberry's hypothesis would reconcile this paradox by arguing that individual preference rankings have shifted over time with the growth in real income and therefore consumption. He found further support for this view in such studies as those of Richard Centers and Hadley Cantril [9], which showed that the income to which an individual aspired tended to be related to differences between social status and economic status, in other words, peer-group influences.

A common general hypothesis in social psychology is that the desirability of alternatives is related to the standard set by the group of which the individual considers himself a member. An experiment which bears closely on the economic issues is that of Paul Hoffman, Leon Festinger, and Douglas Lawrence [23]. The subjects engage in a three-person game. The game is completely symmetric among all individuals and therefore the individual's only chance of winning is by forming a two-member coalition.

One of the hypotheses tested is that individuals are motivated by their scores relative to the scores of others whom they regard as comparable, not by their absolute scores. This hypothesis was tested by an ingenious experimental procedure. In each group of three, there was one instructed participant (unknown to the other two). It was arranged that he command an initial lead. The other two formed coalitions with each other to an extent significantly greater than chance, indicating a preference for reducing the instructed participant's lead rather than achieving a greater score.

On the other hand, a study of savings data from some highly selected groups by James Tobin [60] seems to show that savings depend on absolute income rather than relative income. However, this interpretation of the data has been challenged [18, pp. 169–182].

Choice in Dynamic Situations

Theory. Obviously, much choice behavior is forward-looking. Decisions made today have repercussions for the future and are themselves conditioned by what has happened in the past. In the field of consumption, the most obvious example is that of durable consumer's goods. The purchase of a refrigerator or automobile is made with a view toward the stream of benefits to be received over a future period. To put it another way, the decision to purchase durable consumers' goods will be influenced by the stock of such goods which have accumulated in the past.

A satisfactory theory which will logically account for consumption choices interrelated in time requires a modification—or more precisely, a reinterpretation—of the static model described earlier. Each individual is really choosing conceptually a set of commodities not only for the present, but also for each future instant of time. His choice is constrained then not merely by the current income that he receives and the prices that he pays, but also prices and incomes of all future times.

Let us formulate the theory of choice and dynamic conditions more precisely, following the exposition of John R. Hicks [22]. Let x_{it} be the amount of commodity i consumed in time period t, and let p_{it} be the price to be paid for a unit of commodity i in time period t. We will assume that the consumer plans for T periods ahead. Then his expenditures at time t will be

$$\sum_{i=1}^{n} p_{it} x_{it} \tag{1}$$

and his total expenditures for T periods are given by

$$\sum_{t=1}^{T} \sum_{i=1}^{n} p_{it} x_{it} \tag{2}$$

Let M_t be the income to be received at time period t.

We will now make an important assumption to simplify the exposition. It will be assumed at the present moment that the individual can borrow or lend money without interest, subject only to the condition that he have no indebtedness at the end of the period. This means that his expenditures and income do not have to balance in each time period separately, but only over the entire planning horizon of T periods.[3] This implies that, in making decisions in the initial period, the individual has available the total income which he has received during the entire period —that is

$$\sum_{t=1}^{T} M_t \tag{3}$$

which we will designate by M.

The choice between consumption and savings is now a part of the above analysis. In any particular time period, expenditures may fall short of income or may exceed them. If the individual is to go through a normal life cycle, we may expect him to save during the early and the middle years of his life and to dissave at the end. It is therefore implied that, in the year under consideration, the amounts consumed and the amounts saved are certain functions of the total or permanent income M, not of the income of a given year.

The situation is now formally analogous to the static case. The individual chooses now among commodity bundles which are enlarged to be extended in time. A single bundle is described by the coordinates x_{11}, . . . , x_{1T}, . . . , x_{n1}, . . . , x_{nT}. His preference ranking may then be described by a utility function $U(x_{11}, \ldots, x_{1T}, \ldots, x_{n1}, \ldots, x_{nT})$. He maximizes the utility function, subject to the restraint that the total

---

[3] The assumption that the lending and borrowing is without interest is not, of course, realistic; it is made here solely for simplification. In Hicks's presentation, interest is accounted for. The analysis above is not changed essentially, but the interpretation of future prices is somewhat different.

expenditure over the period does not exceed the total income—that is,

$$\sum_{t=1}^{T} \sum_{i=1}^{n} p_{it} x_{it} \leq M = \sum_{t=1}^{T} M_t \qquad (4)$$

In the problem as formulated, the obstacles now involve future prices and future income. This is not meaningful, of course, because the future is unknown. While the assumption of perfect foresight sometimes made by economists is not quite as absurd as it sounds for various reasons which we will not discuss here, there is no doubt that it gives an inadequate picture of reality. One approach is to assume that the individual forms expectations of future prices and incomes and acts as if he knew with certainty that his expectations were correct.[4] A more complicated assumption is that the individual is aware that he cannot know the future and anticipates it in the form of a range of possibilities, possibly a probability distribution.

The first form is, of course, more easily studied. In this form, the objection sometimes made to utility analysis—that it does not permit genuine decision making—is not valid. Decision making now comes in choosing the correct expectations. The utility theory does say that if expectations are the same in two situations, the choice of consumption and saving will be the same. Hence there is no contradiction between the hypothesis that choice is governed by utility maximization and the fact that an individual can change his mind in the light of new information. New information is incorporated in revised expectations of the future. However, it must be admitted that this formulation, while saving the utility theory, does so at the expense of putting most of its content into the expectations. Utility theory here serves mainly the method of suggesting which variables enter into the analysis and something about the way in which they affect current decisions.

Empirical evidence.   The main conclusion that we seem to have drawn from utility theory thus far is that consumption of commodities will be determined by the individual's permanent or lifetime income rather than by his current income. A number of writers have studied this question in different ways. George Katona [26, pp. 155–160], in an important pioneer study, showed that income increases resulted in a much greater increase in consumption when the individual expected the income change to be permanent rather than temporary. This study was based on questionnaire data. This result, of course, is compatible with the permanent-income hypothesis; an increase in income, accompanied by the expectation of its continuance, obviously results in the expectation of a much larger permanent income than does an income increase which

---

[4] For a very complete discussion of the incorporation of expectation into the theory of economic behavior, see Modigliani and Cohen [41].

is accompanied by the expectation that it will last for one period only. Similar results were found by Lawrence R. Klein [28, pp. 215–216].

The permanent-income hypothesis was stated explicitly and studied most extensively by Milton Friedman [18] and by Franco Modigliani and Richard Brumberg [40]. It is not possible to pursue the line of argument and the variety of empirical evidence here, but both conclude, mainly on the basis of studies of budget data, that the ratio of savings to permanent income tends to be quite constant.[5]

Until there is a more thorough understanding of the formation of expectations, the permanent-income hypothesis, when true, remains only a partial contribution to the understanding of consumption behavior.

Choice under Conditions of Uncertainty

Theory. Suppose an individual has to make a decision, the consequences of which he regards as uncertain. In a strict sense, of course, there is no decision which does not have this characteristic. For example, an individual who is contemplating the purchase of a house will be uncertain as to the future course of house prices. He might, for example, gain by postponing the purchase for awhile. He will also be uncertain about the future income he receives and about the length of time he will occupy the house. Each alternative is, of course, really a range of consequences. Which consequence will come true will depend on a whole series of other events which are sometimes termed "the state of the world."

A classic treatment of the subject in theory originates with Daniel Bernoulli [6]. Let there be m states of the world, and let their probabilities be $p_1, \ldots, p_m$, respectively. For any alternative x, let $U_i(x)$ be the utility of x if state i occurs. Then the utility to be attached to the alternative x, which is essentially a gamble or uncertainty, is the expected utility —that is,

$$\sum_{i=1}^{n} p_i U_i(x)$$

The alternatives are then ranked according to the expected utility associated with them and in any given situation that one of the available alternatives which maximizes the expected utility is chosen. The maximization-of-expected-utility hypothesis has the virtue of being capable of explaining certain real world phenomena. For example, insurance is typically actuarially unfair—that is, the expected money returned to the insured is negative. However, if we assume that the utility of different money outcomes is typically of a form showing decreasing increments to

---

[5] The definition of savings is somewhat different than the common-sense one because of the treatment of durable consumers' goods. The purchase of a durable consumers' good is considered to be an act of saving, not consumption, but the use of previously existing durable consumers' goods is added to consumption.

unit increases in money, the policy of taking out insurance may have a higher expected utility than the policy of not taking out insurance, even though the expected money income is lower for the first policy.

Although to this day there has been no serious rival to the Bernoulli hypothesis, it has been subject to much reinterpretation. A new line of development was initiated by Frank P. Ramsey, [49, chap. 7]. Instead of postulating that individuals maximize expected utility, a series of assumptions was made about behavior in the presence of uncertainty. These assumptions presumably defined how a "rational" man would behave.[6] While there are a number of assumptions involved, the basic one may be illustrated in the following special case. Let G_1, G_2, G_3, and G_4 be four possible options—that is, the choice of any one implies a probability distribution over the possible outcomes. Now let us consider two compound gambles or options: H_1, H_2. H_1 is a two-stage gamble in which first a choice is made between G_1 and G_2, G_1 being chosen with probability p, G_2 with probability $1 - p$. Similarly, let H_2 involve a preliminary stage where G_3 is chosen with probability p and G_4 with probability $1 - p$. After the initial random choice has been made, then the actual outcome is governed by the appropriate G_1, G_2, G_3, or G_4, as the case may be.

H_1 and H_2 have been defined as two-stage gambles, but they are clearly equivalent to a single-stage gamble which we can find by using the laws of compound probability. For example, if there is an outcome O which would be obtained under G_1 with probability r_1, and under G_2 with probability r_2, then under H_1, the probability of outcome O is $pr_1 + (1 - p)r_2$. The probability under H_1 for any possible outcome under either G_1 or G_2 can be found similarly.

With these preliminaries, we now state the basic assumption. Suppose that G_1 would be preferred by an individual to G_3, and that G_2 would be preferred to G_4. Then it is assumed that the compound gamble H_1 would be preferred to the compound gamble H_2. The intuitive appeal of this assumption is obvious, especially if we somehow think of rational decisions. It is surprisingly powerful in its implications; it implies that numerical values may be assigned to the different possible outcomes so that an individual's preference among options involving uncertainty can be described as the maximization of the expected numerical values. These numerical values may, in a natural way, be referred to as "utilities." Thus the Bernoulli expected-utility hypothesis can be derived from more primitive and intuitively plausible assumptions about the behavior of individuals in the face of uncertainty.[7]

---

[6] A similar point of view was developed later independently by John von Neumann and Oskar Morgenstern [61, Appendix].

[7] For an excellent exposition of the axiomatic approach to utility theory under uncertainty, see R. Duncan Luce and Howard Raiffa [32, pp. 19–34].

So far, the analysis has assumed that the different possible outcomes can be assigned probabilities. This may be satisfactory for the analysis of gambling or certain insurance situations in which the probabilities of events have been found by theory or empirical observations. However, an individual facing uncertainty—e.g., a consumer purchasing a second-hand car which may break down—frequently does not have available to him any set of objective probabilities. The question of rational behavior under these conditions was also studied by Ramsey and Bruno de Finetti [12]. A synthesis of these viewpoints has been made in a remarkable book by Leonard J. Savage [52]. This analysis brings us to the following conclusion: An individual acts as if he assigns probabilities to all possible events and utilities to all possible outcomes. Then he chooses among the available outcomes the one which maximizes his expected utility,[8] in very much the same way he would choose in a case where probabilities are known.

Other views of decision making under uncertainty have been developed, but usually with a reference to normative rather than descriptive application, particularly to serve as foundations for statistical method. One such theory, however, has been developed with reference to economic behavior by G. L. S. Shackle [53].[9]

Experimental verification. The expected-utility hypothesis in any of its forms gives rise to a utility function which is a ratio scale rather than an ordinal scale, as in the case of choice under conditions of certainty. The greater power of this theory has been a strong incentive to experimental work. The earliest such study was done by Frederick Mosteller and Philip Nogee [44]. The subjects were supplied with gambling situations in which the probabilities were known. By varying the rewards in money terms, it was possible to measure a utility curve for money—that is, a function of money such that the individual's choice of a bet is governed by utility-maximization hypothesis. If the individual is indifferent between taking and not taking a gamble with a stake of 5 cents and a probability p of winning an amount A, then

$$pU(A) + (1 - p)U(-5 \text{ cents}) = U(0)$$

If we let $U(-5 \text{ cents}) = -1$, $U(0) = 0$ (as we may, since origin and unit are arbitrary), we can solve for $U(A)$. This can be done for each A by varying p until the subject is indifferent between the two alternatives.

In one part of the experiment, utility curves were used to predict out-

---

[8] Excellent expositions of this and related theories are given in Luce and Raiffa [32, chap. 13], and by Jacob Marschak, in [30, chap. 4].

[9] For a general survey of theories of uncertainty and risk with special reference to economic applications, see [4].

comes in more complicated gambles than those from which the curve was derived. The measure of agreement was fair but not overwhelming.

The Mosteller-Nogee experiment had the difficulty—from the point of underlying theory—that it assumed individuals act subjectively in accordance with the objective probabilities. A much more careful series of experiments which seeks to control the subjective probabilities among other problems has been carried out by Donald Davidson, Patrick Suppes, and Sidney Siegel [11]. Their experimental procedure is first to isolate an event whose subjective probability is one-half. This can be determined, according to the theory, by finding an event E such that the individual is indifferent between the following two options: (1) receiving an amount of money a when E occurs and an amount b when E does not occur; and (2) receiving the amount b when E occurs and a when E does not occur. Here a and b are differing amounts of money—it being supposed, of course, that an individual always prefers a greater amount of money to a lesser. If an event E is such that options 1 and 2 are indifferent for some particular a and b, then, under the expected-utility hypothesis, the two options should be indifferent for all other values of a and b for which $a < b$. This implication was confirmed for all subjects.

Once E is determined, its subjective probability being one-half, the preferences between gambles on the occurrence of E can be established. For example, if one option is that an individual will receive x if E occurs, and y if E does not occur, and if a second option is that an individual will receive u if E occurs and v if it does not, then, according to the expected-utility hypothesis, a preference for the first option over the second is equivalent to the statement

$$\tfrac{1}{2}U(x) + \tfrac{1}{2}U(y) > \tfrac{1}{2}U(u) + \tfrac{1}{2}U(v)$$

The utility function for money can then be traced out with a limited number of observations and prediction to other choices can be made. For example, let a and b, $a < b$, be two fixed amounts of money. By varying c, we can find one value such that the option c if E occurs, b if E does not occur, is just indifferent to the certainty of a. Similarly, d is found such that the option d if E occurs, a if E does not occur, is indifferent to the certainty of b. Then the expected-utility hypothesis implies that the option d if E occurs, c if E does not, is indifferent to the option b if E occurs, a if E does not. The verification of the predictions is a verification of the expected-utility hypothesis. This was found to hold very well for 15 out of 19 subjects.

The question of the formation of subjective probabilities is not completely taken care of by this study, since only subjective probabilities of one-half entered. A second experiment tested some of the implications of the Ramsey theory for existence of subjective probabilities. For any event E and any amounts of money x, y, z, under Ramsey's theory, there should be a unique amount of money w, such that the options x if E, y if not E, and z if E, w if not E, are indifferent. Then the subjective probability of E would be

$$\frac{U(w) - U(y)}{U(x) - U(y) - U(z) + U(w)}$$

and, for given E, this magnitude should be independent of the amounts x, y, and z. Again there was confirmation, but one puzzling feature is that the subjective probability was lower than the objective probability. The situation was one of such complete symmetry that it is hard to believe there will not be inconsistencies with other experiments which involve more complicated gambles.

A subsequent study by Paul M. Hurst and Sidney Siegel [25] also confirmed the expected-utility hypothesis. The subjects were given a series of choices among pairs of options at even odds. Under the expected-utility hypothesis, the outcomes of any set of choices imposed constraints on the possible utility functions; in general, in fact, the results on a subset of the choices were sufficient to imply enough about the utility function to predict the remaining choices. The options concerned a numerical variable so that the expected value of each option was meaningful. It was found that the predictions made from the expected-utility hypothesis were significantly better than from the hypothesis that the individual always made a choice which maximized expected value. Additional results of the study relate to the experimental problem of determining indifference. As a rule, the experimental situation requires the individual to choose among alternatives, and if the individual is actually indifferent, there is clearly danger of introducing errors into the analysis. Hurst and Siegel found that the latency time for the cases where the expected-utility hypothesis failed was considerably greater than that where it succeeded. This suggests that the theory appears to fail only because of the difficulty of observing indifference.[10]

"Common-sense" empirical observations. The whole axiomatic approach can be thought of as crystallizing everyday or introspective observations. A very interesting use of casual empirical observation has been made in a paper by Milton Friedman and Leonard J. Savage [19]. They observed that some individuals gamble, others take out insurance, some do both, and finally that lottery owners find it profitable to offer several

---

[10] From the point of view of scaling theory, it is perhaps important to remark that while the expected-utility hypothesis theoretically gives rise to a ratio scale, it does so only when an infinite number of observations can be made. A finite number of observations give rise to something closer to an ordered metric scale; see Sidney Siegel [54].

prizes instead of one large one. It turns out that all of these phenomena can be explained on the expected-utility hypothesis provided the utility function of money is supposed to have first, a segment in which the derivative (in economic terms, the marginal utility) is decreasing, then a segment in which it increases, and finally a segment in which it decreases again. A modification of this theory designed to explain some further phenomena was introduced by Harry Markowitz [33]. The main innovation was that the utility should be thought of as a function of departures from the present situation rather than as a function of income. This hypothesis weakens very considerably the force of the original version and should be accepted, it appears to me, only with caution. It would be difficult to bring experimental evidence to bear on this question because it would be necessary to make a fairly large change in the individual's initial income to test the Markowitz hypothesis.

Mention should be made of a very severe criticism of the expected-utility theory due to Maurice Allais [1]. The argument in part consists of examples which are designed to show the counterintuitive character of some implications of the expected-utility hypothesis. Consider the following four gambles:

1. Certainty of receiving $1 million
2. $5 million with probability .1; $1 million with probability .89; 0 with probability .01
3. $1 million with probability .11; 0 with probability .89
4. $5 million with probability .1; 0 with probability .90

It can easily be seen that under the expected-utility hypothesis, an individual who prefers 1 to 2 must necessarily prefer 3 to 4. But, Allais argues, most people, especially if rather conservative in their attitude to uncertainty, would prefer 1 to 2 but 4 to 3. Similar arguments have been developed by Pierre Massé and Georges Morlat [36].

Probabilistic Choices

The theory of choice as formulated up to this point, whether for conditions of certainty or uncertainty, is stated in the form that for any two alternatives A and B, one of the two will be chosen and will be chosen every time the two alternatives are offered under the same conditions, except in the special case where the two are indifferent. This assumption implies a kind of perfect ability to discriminate which, of course, goes counter to the trend of virtually all psychological experiments. In fact, as we have seen above, all the experiments on transitivity described above have had to introduce *ad hoc* theories which permit the choice to be something less than perfectly invariable. A more general formulation is suggested: For any pair of alternatives A and B there is a certain probability, depending on the two alternatives, that A will be chosen over B. The classical theory then becomes a special case where this probability takes on only the values one, zero, and possibly one-half, the last to account for indifference. Some of the classical methods of psychophysics such as Thurstone's law of comparative judgment are special formulations of such a probabilistic theory of choice. Though a number of writers—R. Duncan Luce and Jacob Marschak, in particular—have raised the question in one form or another in connection with preference theory, no thoroughly satisfactory alternative has developed. They try to exhibit a utility function which has the property that the probability of preferring a to b depends monotonically on the distance between the two—i.e., on $U(a) - U(b)$. It seems quite difficult, however, to arrive at an appropriate set of assumptions which will not have very undesirable consequences;[11] in particular, difficulties arise when some, but not all, choices can be perfectly discriminated.

An attempt has been made by Richard E. Quandt to reformulate the theory of consumer behavior under certainty so as to admit a probabilistic element in choice [48]. He suggests two sources of random behavior. One is that the individual orders his preferences among commodity bundles in accordance with a set of basic characteristics of the commodities; however, in any given comparison he may consider only some of the relevant characteristics, the particular characteristics on which the choice is based being chosen according to some random process.[12] Secondly, the individual may be in error in regard to his *own* preference scale. This theory, however, has not been very much elaborated or subjected to any empirical tests.

Omar K. Moore [43] has suggested that the widespread use of divination methods can be regarded as a deliberate use of randomization in controlling behavior. Indeed, there seems to be evidence that most gambling originated as a form of divination. For example, Moore suggests as an interpretation that in hunting game, primitive tribes implicitly hit upon a method of deriving a mixed strategy in the sense of game theory.

Utility Theory and Motivation Theory

Economists' utility theory of behavior has many points of affinity with at least some studies of motivation and conflict in psychology. The pairwise comparisons of the utility theory are, in psychological terms, approach-approach conflicts. The consumer who has to choose among

---

[11] See, for example, Luce and Raiffa [32, Appendix 1], Luce [31], Jacob Marschak [34; 35]; Donald Davidson and Jacob Marschak [10].

[12] There is a similarity between this concept and the associationist theory of learning due to William K. Estes, described below.

all commodity bundles which he can afford is in a multiple-approach situation, with a continuum of alternatives. Mathilda Holzman [24] has shown that much of the apparent difference between economists' and psychologists' approaches to choice situations is due, not to any fundamental difference in assumptions about behavior, but to the different range of alternatives allowed. Choice tends to look much more like conflict when only two alternatives are permitted.

It should also be noted that there is no real distinction in economic terminology between approach-approach and avoidance-avoidance situations. Utility being an ordinal—or at most a ratio scale—there is no natural zero. This difference between economical and psychological theories is probably more semantic than anything else. In most psychological experiments, there is some available alternative of complete inaction, which can be ascribed a zero utility. Then positive utilities correspond to approach situations, negative utilities to avoidance situations.

To illustrate the relation between utility and motivation theories, we may look at the interesting papers of Neal Miller [38, 39].[13] Miller is concerned with an approach-avoidance situation. At the same spot, there is a pleasurable stimulus (e.g., food) and an unpleasant one (e.g., electric shock). A rat decides, in effect, how close he shall come to the spot in question. Miller's model may be formulated in economic terminology: Let x be the distance at which the rat stops; $U_f(x)$ the utility derived from proximity to the food, and $U_s(x)$ the (negative) utility derived from proximity to the shock situation. U_f is a decreasing function of x; that is, the larger x—therefore the more the distance from the stimulus—the less the satisfaction derived from the food. On the other hand, U_s is an increasing function of x. Miller's theory is that the rat chooses x so as to maximize $U_f(x) + U_s(x)$. The condition of maximization is that the first derivative of this utility function be zero and that the second derivative be negative. In symbols, $U_f' + U_s' = 0$, $U_f'' + U_s'' < 0$. In Miller's terminology, the first states that the avoidance and approach gradients are equal, the second that the avoidance gradient is steeper than the approach gradient.

The difference between the economic and the psychological formulations is not that they are contradictory in any way, but rather that they deal with different matters. The economist would usually be interested in saying simply that the rat has a utility function associated with distance, where the psychologist attempts to go into the structure of that utility function more carefully. The interesting implication of the deeper analysis is that the rewards and punishments which are strictly localized objectively nevertheless are generalized in space, which may be taken as a

[13] I am indebted to Daniel Berlyne for very helpful comments on Miller's work, though he may well not agree completely with the following interpretation.

paradigm for stimulus generalization along many dimensions of perception.

The role of stimulus generalization in economics is almost completely unexplored. The economic analog would be perhaps a case where new opportunities for consumption or for business arose. The economic agent would tend to respond by attributing to the new modes of behavior utilities related to their distance from the old and previously rewarded modes. Failures in economic development may be in some part related to this failure to evaluate new situations in terms different from the older ones.

DYNAMIC ASPECTS OF BEHAVIOR

Though, as we have already seen, utility theory of behavior by no means excludes dynamic aspects completely, there are many phenomena which are not encompassed by that theory, at least in its present form. We have seen in discussing choice in dynamic situations that expectations of the future are relevant. There have been a number of studies in recent years which cast some light on the role of expectations, both their impact on behavior and the process of their formation. The formation of expectations about the future is, of course, closely related to learning in a classical sense, and we will discuss below some of the relations between learning theory and economic theory.

The Influence of Expectations on Behavior

As far as consumers are concerned, the evidence of influence of expectations on behavior is at best fragmentary. The most complete study seems to be that of George Katona and Eva Mueller [27]. Interviews were used to get opinions as to the short-term and long-term business outlook, expectations of changes in individual income, subjective evaluation of changes in the financial situation, and expectations of price changes. These were related chiefly to opinions about the favorableness of buying conditions. The associations of the expectation variables to the intentions to purchase are in the expected direction. For example, expectation of better times was related to a more favorable opinion toward buying durable goods. However, the associations on the whole were quite weak. Also, of course, it would be more desirable to have a study on actual purchases rather than opinions of buying conditions.[14]

An elaborate study of expectations of business firms was made by

---

[14] There was a relation studied between evaluation of change in financial situation and purchases of durable goods during the preceding twelve months. Again this was in the expected direction but the association was by no means strong.

Franco Modigliani and Owen Sauerlender [42]. The data were derived from three sources: (1) forecasts of shipments made to railroads by shippers; (2) forecasts made for *Fortune* by a number of top executives, and (3) an interview survey of business expectations conducted by Dun and Bradstreet. By means of a rather elaborate statistical analysis, it was shown that the expectations are relevant to the firm's actual behavior— in the sense that, to some extent at least, changes in inventory and production policy can be predicted from changes in expectations.

From a practical point of view, the extent to which anticipations data can be used for short-term forecasting is very important, of course, but from the point of view of psychological theory it may be said that studies on the influence of expectations on behavior have at the moment methodological rather than substantive interest. In the case of any decision having consequences to be worked out in the future—for example, an investment by a firm in plant and equipment—we may reasonably postulate the existence of expectations or something equivalent as an intervening variable. Then the point of studies such as those of Katona and Mueller and of Modigliani and Sauerlender is rather to relate the expectation qua an intervening variable to verbally expressed expectations. If a relationship between the two can be established, then verbalized expectations may be used as an additional source of data in further research.

The Formation of Expectations

Evidence from time series. One theory which is frequently plausible is that the expectations about any variable are extrapolations of some type of the previous behavior of that variable. Though this general point of view has been usually accepted by economic theorists, very little has been done until recently to make it specific. An attractive hypothesis has recently been advanced by Phillip Cagan [8]. Suppose, for example, we are considering expectations by the individual of the price of a commodity. He suggests that there is a continuous adjustment in such a way that each expectation is compared with the reality when it is observed and the expectation for the following period is obtained by revising the previous expectation in the direction of the actual figure. Thus, let $\bar{p}_t$ represent the anticipation held at time $t-1$ of the price to prevail at time t, and let p_t be the actual price at time t. Then Cagan's hypothesis can be stated

$$\bar{p}_{t+1} - \bar{p}_t = a(p_t - \bar{p}_t)$$

where a is a number between zero and one. This theory may be termed that of *adaptive* expectations. It is analogous to the corrective mechanism used in firing a gun, where the accuracy is improved in successive rounds by adjusting toward the target and away from the previous aim. To give the theory another interpretation, it follows from the previous formula that

$$\bar{p}_t = a \sum_{u=1}^{\infty} (1 - a)^{u-1} p_{t-u}$$

that is, the expectation of current price is a weighted average of all previous prices, the weights decreasing as the price becomes more remote.

Cagan was particularly interested in studying the demand for holding cash balances under hyperinflationary conditions, such as those prevailing in Germany after World War I. The demand for cash balances ordinarily depends on a number of variables, but in hyperinflations it is reasonable to suppose that expected rate of change of prices is the dominant one. The particular formula suggested by Cagan as the explanatory variable for cash balances turned out to predict very well under a wide variety of hyperinflationary situations.

Another application of the same hypothesis has been made by Marc Nerlove [45; 46, chap. 2, sec. 1; chap. 8, secs. 1, 2]. A farmer, when deciding how much acreage to plant, cannot know the price at which the product will be sold, since this lies some months in the future. It is to be presumed that he acts in accordance with expectation of that price. The simple hypothesis that the price expected to prevail at the time of harvest is the same as the price at the time of planting has not been successful. Nerlove showed that the hypothesis of adaptive expectations yields an excellent explanation for the supply of corn and wheat in the United States.

The hypothesis has been used in a different form by Milton Friedman [18] in developing the theory of consumption as a function of permanent income described above. Since permanent income is really expected income, the hypothesis would imply that consumption in any year depends on an exponentially weighted average of past and present income. Friedman finds that this hypothesis applied to aggregate time series data yields a better explanation than rival ones.

Experimental evidence. Experimental evidence on the formation of expectations has been reported by Rotter [51, pp. 165–183]. The results are partially in accord with the theory of adaptive expectations but partially different. In repeated trials, the subjects were asked for their expectancy, measured either as an expected score or as an amount they were willing to bet on success in the next trial. Without going into details, the basic result seems to be that expectations are indeed revised regularly to bring them into line with observations, but in a repetition of similar situations the extent of revision tends to be inversely proportional to the number of trials already undertaken. This difference in results is presumably related to the degree to which the subject regards the situations as being really similar. In an economic context, an individual may feel that the world is steadily changing and therefore any new observation is not simply one more made under circumstances identical to those in the past.

Inferences from surveys of expectations. A new source of data which has become available in the postwar period is a survey of predictions by entrepreneurs conducted by the IFO—Institut für Wirtschaftsforschung in Munich. Each entrepreneur is asked about the direction of change of a large number of variables such as production, buying and selling prices, demand conditions, etc. The answers are qualitative—that is, the only three answers are "Increase," "Decrease," or "No change." These have been analyzed from a number of points of view. In the present context, the most relevant studies are two papers by Oskar Anderson, Jr., and collaborators at the IFO—Institut für Wirtschaftsforschung [2, 3, and a paper by Henri Theil and J. S. Cramer, 58; see also 57, chap. 6, sec. 3].

The studies by Anderson and his associates relate primarily to prediction of variables that are, in whole or in part, under the control of the firm, such as production and prices. These are really to be thought of as plans of the firm rather than expectations about events outside its control. Let x stand for the set of variables over which the firm has no control, and let y be its planned production, for example. Then if x were known, y would be a known function $f(x)$. At the time when the firm is asked for its expectations for the next month or two, it does not actually know the value of x and therefore uses an expectation $\hat{x}$. The expectation of the controlled variables, then, is $\hat{y} = f(\hat{x})$.[15] When the firm finds out the actual value of x, it would like to change y from $\hat{y}$ to $f(x)$. It may not succeed in carrying through the change completely since some commitments will have already been made, but the change will be in the direction suggested by the change from $\hat{x}$ to x. Thus if $f(x)$ is an increasing function of x, for example, production is an increasing function of price, the firm will have an actual production which is higher than its planned production if the actual price is higher than the planned price, and vice versa. These hypotheses are fully confirmed by the data.

They cast, of course, only an indirect light on the whole question of expectations. They do, however, suggest that the verbal expectations held by businessmen bear at least some relation to the hypothetical expectations which govern their behavior in economic planning. They also suggest that the expectations about the variables over which the firm has no control are of the adaptive type suggested in the last section. Similar re-

---

[15] Strictly speaking, $\hat{y}$ need not be the same function of $\hat{x}$ that y is of x if the firm recognizes that the expectation is, in fact, uncertain. However, there will be a general similarity in the two relations.

sults are obtained in the work of Irwin Friend and Jean Bronfenbrenner (Crockett) [20], based upon American postwar data of intentions to invest. Analysis of the departures between actual and planned investment showed that they could be partially explained by changes from expectations of the variables over which the firm had no control.

Theil and Cramer, in addition to other work, did a direct analysis of expectations of variables not under the control of the firm, buying prices in particular. They found that the expectation of a buying price was indeed related to its own past behavior. It was also related to the behavior of other prices that might be expected to influence it. Thus expectations about the price of leather correlated not only with the past prices of leather, but also with the past prices of hides. This suggests that the entrepreneur uses a multiplicity of cues in forming his expectations for the future, as indeed he should if he has any degree of rationality.

Statistical Learning Theory and Economics

The formation of expectations as a result of past experience is, of course, a learning process, and it might be instructive to consider some developments in statistical learning theory for their economic implications. As representative, we take the study of William Estes [15, 16]. Individuals are asked simply to predict occurrence or nonoccurrence of an event (rather than a continuous variable, as is more usual in economics). In fact, the event occurs randomly with a constant probability π, although this fact is not, of course, known to the subjects. Let p_n be the probability that the individual will predict that the event will occur at time $n + 1$. It is assumed that an observed success increases the probability of the individual's predicting the occurrence of the event and a failure decreases that probability and that these two effects are symmetrical. Then

$$p_{n+1} = p_n + \theta(1 - p_n)$$

if there was a success on the nth trial, and

$$p_{n+1} = p_n - \theta p_n$$

otherwise. These formulas bear a distinct similarity to the adaptive expectations discussed above. Under the experimental conditions assumed, it can be shown that the average of p_n over many individuals will approach π in a large number of trials. This theoretical implication has been confirmed experimentally.

If we assume that the aim of an individual is to maximize the expected number of successes—that is, that the expected-utility hypothesis holds with the number of successes as the utility function—then the individual's optimal behavior can easily be seen to predict success all the time if π is greater than one-half, and failure all the time if π is less than one-half. It is true that he will not adopt this behavior immediately if the value of π is unknown, but after a sufficient number of trials to "learn" the true value, he will—under the assumed conditions—behave as indicated. We have here a seeming contradiction between two theories of behavior.

There have been attempted reconciliations by Merrill M. Flood [17] and Siegel [55]. Flood has suggested two explanations. One is that the utility function is not simply the number of successes. There is disproportionately high utility to getting a perfect score, or—to put it another way—high utilities attached to guessing the less frequent event. The second is that the subject, not being aware that success and failure are generated by a random mechanism, may believe that there is a nonstationary process at work. His strategy, then, is in part a method of guarding against this possibility.

The first explanation in particular suggests that varying the reward attached to successes would alter the outcome. If the reward for a successful prediction and the penalty for an unsuccessful prediction were sufficiently high, one might expect a closer convergence to the economist's ideal. Experiments in which the reward was varied have been performed by Ward Edwards [14] and Siegel [55]. Both found that increased rewards increased the probability of choosing the more frequent response over the probability suggested by the probability-matching rule.

Siegel has advanced as explanations both an additional utility for predicting the less frequent event and a disutility for repeatedly making the same prediction. If the probability π is in fact known to the subject— as it presumably will be after repeated trials—and p is the proportion of times the more frequent event is predicted by the subject, then the utility of correct prediction is

$$ap\pi + b(1 - p)(1 - \pi)$$

where a and b are positive constants, and the utility of variability may be taken as

$$cp(1 - p)$$

this being a function with a maximum at $p = \frac{1}{2}$, the point of greatest variability in prediction. An experiment was performed in which the subject was given 5 cents for a successful prediction and penalized 5 cents for an unsuccessful one. It was assumed that under these conditions $a = b$, so that only the utility of variability remains as a factor. An individual who seeks to maximize his total utility would choose

$$p = (a/c)(\pi - \frac{1}{2}) + \frac{1}{2}$$

By running the experiment for a particular value of π and measuring p, an estimate of a/c was obtained. Since this ratio is, under the hypothesis, independent of π, the hypothesis can be tested by repeating the experiment with a different value of π and comparing the predicted value of p from the above formula with the actual. A very close confirmation was obtained. The general model, including both effects, has not been tested.

Hints of a Utility Theory of Learning

So far in this discussion, the theory of expectations has been treated as something to be added to a utility theory involving choice over time. However, some methods of forming expectations seem more rational than others and, at least formally, one can treat the learning process itself as a process of successive choices by the individual. His domain of choice now is a *strategy*—that is, in each stage he finds his next step as a function of all the information available to him up to the present time.

Some beginnings of a theory of this type have been made, though most often in a normative context. The most important development has been that of sequential analysis of statistical data by Abraham Wald [62]. Statistical observations are assumed to be collected one after another. After each observation one of two decisions must be made: to terminate the observations and draw whatever inference is called for, or to draw at least one more observation. The observations bear some kind of cost, but this incentive to stop must be weighed against the value of the additional information obtained. There is a close analogy to learning experiments which consist of a series of trials in which the subject's choices are sometimes rewarded and sometimes not. The individual, after making many choices, eventually begins to discriminate between the proper response and the improper one. At some point, presumably, he could terminate the experiment, at least in the sense of disregarding further observations and making the same choice each time.

Wald has developed the optimum rules for making sequential decisions, at least under simple conditions. Sequential analysis differs from standard learning experiments primarily in that there are no rewards for decisions made during the course of the observations; there is only a terminal decision. Attempts to incorporate the former have been made; they lead to great mathematical complexities, as shown in the important work of M. A. Girshick, Samuel Karlin, and Halsey L. Royden [21], for example.

Some modification must, of course, be made in the above theories in order to fit the experimental facts, such as those found by Estes and others. The chief trouble is that most optimal statistical procedures would eventually lead toward a convergence of choice on one or the other of two alternatives. Estes's hypothesis introduces the concept of a limited cognition of the stimulus elements at each stage in the learning process. This could be incorporated in a more complicated model of rational learning by introducing a cost to a complete scanning of the field of relevant information at each stage. Such developments, if at all appropriate, await future work.

REFERENCES

1. Allais, M. Fondements d'une théorie positive des choix comportant un risque et critique des postulats et axiomes de l'école Américaine. In *Économetrie,* XL, *Colloques Internationaux du Centre National de la Recherche Scientifique.* Paris: Centre National de la Recherche Scientifique, 1953. Pp. 257–332.
2. Anderson, O., Jr., Bauer, R. K., Führer, H., & Petersen, J. P. Short-term entrepreneurial reaction patterns. IFO—Institut für Wirtschaftsforschung, Munich, 1955. (Mimeographed)
3. Anderson, O., Jr., Furst, H., & Schulte, W. Zur Analyse der unternehmerischen Reaktionsweise. *IFO-Studien,* 1956, **2.**
4. Arrow, K. J. Alternative approaches to the theory of choice in risk-taking situations. *Econometrica,* 1951, **19,** 404–437.
5. Benson, P. H. A model for the analysis of consumer preference and an exploratory test. *J. appl. Psychol.,* 1955, **39,** 375–381.
6. Bernoulli, D. Specimen theoriae novae de mensura sortis. *Commentarii Academiae Scientiarum Imperialis Petropolitanae,* 1738, **5,** 175–192. Translated as Exposition of a new theory on the measurement of risk, *Econometrica,* 1954, **22,** 23–26.
7. Brady, Dorothy, & Friedman, Rose. Savings and the income distribution. In *Studies in income and wealth.* Vol. 10. New York: National Bureau of Economic Research, 1947. Pp. 250–266.
8. Cagan, P. The monetary dynamics of hyperinflation. In M. Friedman (Ed.), *Studies in the quantity theory of money.* Chicago: Univer. Chicago Press, 1956. Pp. 25–117.
9. Centers, R., & Cantril, H. Income satisfaction and income aspiration. *J. abnorm. soc. Psychol.,* 1946, **41,** 64–69.
10. Davidson, D., & Marschak, J. Experimental tests of stochastic decision theory. In C. W. Churchman & P. Ratoosh (Eds.), *Measurement: definitions and theories.* New York: Wiley, 1959. Pp. 233–269.
11. Davidson, D., Suppes, P., & Siegel, S. *Decision-making: an experimental approach.* Stanford, Calif.: Stanford Univer. Press, 1957.
12. de Finetti, B. La prévision: ses lois logiques, ses sources subjectives. *Ann. Inst. Henri Poincaré,* 1937, **7,** 1–68.
13. Duesenberry, J. S. *Income, saving, and the theory of consumer behavior.* Cambridge, Mass.: Harvard Univer. Press, 1949.
14. Edwards, W. Reward probability, amount, and information as determiners of sequential two-alternative decisions. *J. exp. Psychol.,* 1956, **52,** 177–188.

15. Estes, W. K. Individual behavior in uncertain situations: an interpretation in terms of statistical association theory. In R. M. Thrall, C. H. Coombs, & R. L. Davis (Eds.), *Decision processes*. New York: Wiley, 1954. Pp. 127–138.
16. Estes, W. K. The statistical approach to learning theory. In S. Koch (Ed.), *Psychology: a study of a science*. Vol. 2. New York: McGraw-Hill, 1959. Pp. 380–491.
17. Flood, M. M. Environmental non-stationarity in a sequential decision-making experiment. In R. M. Thrall, C. H. Coombs, & R. L. Davis (Eds.), *Decision processes*. New York: Wiley, 1954. Pp. 287–300.
18. Friedman, M. *A theory of the consumption function*. Princeton, N.J.: Princeton Univer. Press, 1957.
19. Friedman, M., & Savage, L. J. The utility analysis of choices involving risk. *J. polit. Econ.*, 1948, 56, 279–304.
20. Friend, I., & Bronfenbrenner (Crockett), J. Plant and equipment programs and their realization. In *Studies in income and wealth*. Vol. 17. *Short-term economic forecasting*. Princeton, N.J.: Princeton Univer. Press, 1955. Pp. 53–98.
21. Girshick, M. A., Karlin, S., & Royden, H. L. Multistage statistical decision procedures. *Ann. math. Stat.*, 1957, 28, 111–125.
22. Hicks, J. R. *Value and capital*. (2nd ed.) New York: Oxford, 1946.
23. Hoffman, P., Festinger, L., & Lawrence, D. Tendencies toward group comparability in competitive bargaining. In R. M. Thrall, C. H. Coombs, & R. L. Davis (Eds.), *Decision processes*. New York: Wiley, 1954. Pp. 231–254.
24. Holzman, Mathilda. Theories of choice and conflict in psychology and economics. *J. Conflict Resolution*, 1958, 2, 310–320.
25. Hurst, P. M., & Siegel, S. Prediction of decisions from a higher ordered metric scale of utilities. *J. exp. Psychol.*, 1956, 52, 138–144.
26. Katona, G. *Psychological analysis of economic behavior*. New York: McGraw-Hill, 1951.
27. Katona, G., & Mueller, E. *Consumer attitudes and demand, 1950–1952*. Ann Arbor, Mich.: Univer. Mich., 1953. Chap. 4.
28. Klein, L. R. Statistical estimation of economic relations from survey data. In L. R. Klein (Ed.), *Contributions of survey methods to economics*. New York: Columbia Univer. Press, 1954.
29. Kuznets, S. *Uses of national income in peace and war*. New York: National Bureau of Economic Research, 1942. (Occasional paper No. 6)
30. Lazarsfeld, P. F. (Ed.) *Mathematical thinking in the social sciences*. Glencoe, Ill.: Free Press, 1954.
31. Luce, R. D. *Individual choice behavior*. New York: Wiley, 1959.
32. Luce, R. D., & Raiffa, H. *Games and decisions*. New York: Wiley, 1957.
33. Markowitz, H. The utility of wealth. *J. polit. Econ.*, 1952, 60, 151–158.
34. Marschak, J. Norms and habits of decision-making under certainty. In *Mathematical models of human behavior*. Stamford, Conn.: Dunlap & Associates, 1955. Pp. 45–53.
35. Marschak, J. Binary-choice constraints and random utility indicators.

In K. J. Arrow, S. Karlin, & P. Suppes (Eds.), *Mathematical methods in the social sciences, 1959.* Stanford, Calif.: Stanford Univer. Press, 1960. Pp. 312–329.

36. Massé, P., & Morlat, G. Sur le classement économique des perspectives aléatoires. In *Économetrie, XL, Colloques Internationaux du Centre National de la Recherche Scientifique.* Paris: Centre National de la Recherche Scientifique, 1953. Pp. 165–193.

37. May, K. O. Transitivity, utility, and aggregation in preference patterns. *Econometrica,* 1954, **22,** 1–14.

38. Miller, N. E. Development and extension of conflict theory. In D. C. McClelland (Ed.), *Studies in motivation.* New York: Appleton-Century-Crofts, 1955. Pp. 507–516.

39. Miller, N. E. Liberalization of basic S-R concepts: extensions to conflict behavior, motivation, and social learning. In S. Koch (Ed.), *Psychology: a study of a science.* Vol. 2. New York: McGraw-Hill, 1959. Pp. 196–292.

40. Modigliani, F., & Brumberg, R. Utility analysis and the consumption function: an interpretation of cross-section data. In K. Kurihara (Ed.), *Post Keynesian economics.* New Brunswick, N.J.: Rutgers Univer. Press, 1954. Pp. 388–436.

41. Modigliani, F., & Cohen, K. J. *The role of anticipations and plans in economic behavior and their use in economic analysis and forecasting.* Urbana, Ill.: Univer. of Ill., Bur. Econ. Bus. Res., 1961.

42. Modigliani, F., & Sauerlender, O. Economic expectations and plans of firms in relation to short-term forecasting. In *Studies in income and wealth.* Vol. 17. *Short-term economic forecasting.* Princeton, N.J.: Princeton Univer. Press, 1955. Pp. 261–351.

43. Moore, O. K. Divination—a new perspective. *Amer. Anthrop.,* 1957, **59,** 69–74.

44. Mosteller, F., & Nogee, P. An experimental measurement of utility. *J. polit. Econ.,* 1951, **59,** 371–404.

45. Nerlove, M. Estimates of the elasticities of supply of selected agricultural commodities. *J. Farm Econ.,* 1956, **38,** 496–509.

46. Nerlove, M. *The dynamics of supply.* Baltimore, Md.: Johns Hopkins, 1958.

47. Papandreou, A. G. A test of a stochastic theory of choice. *Univer. Calif. Publ. Econ.,* 1957, **16,** 1–18.

48. Quandt, R. E. An probabilistic theory of consumer behavior. *Quart. J. Econ.,* 1956, **70,** 507–536.

49. Ramsey, F. P. *The foundations of mathematics and other logical essays.* London: Routledge, 1931.

50. Rose, A. M. A study of irrational judgments. *J. polit. Econ.,* 1957, **65,** 394–402.

51. Rotter, J. B. *Social learning and clinical psychology.* Englewood Cliffs, N.J.: Prentice-Hall, 1954.

52. Savage, L. J. *The foundations of statistics.* New York: Wiley, 1954.

53. Shackle, G. L. S. *Expectations in economics.* New York: Cambridge, 1949.
54. Siegel, S. A method for obtaining an ordered metric scale. *Psychometrika,* 1956, **21,** 207–216.
55. Siegel, S. Decision making and learning under varying conditions of reinforcement. *Ann. N.Y. Acad. Sci.,* 1961, **89,** 766–783.
56. Stone, R. The linear expenditure systems and demand analysis: an application to the pattern of British demand. *Economic J.,* 1954, **64,** 511–527.
57. Theil, H. *Economic forecasts and policy.* Amsterdam: North Holland, 1958.
58. Theil, H., & Cramer, J. S. *On the utilization of a new source of economic information.* The Netherlands, The Hague, Central Planning Office, 1954. (Mimeographed)
59. Thurstone, L. L. The indifference function. *J. soc. Psychol.,* 1931, **2,** 139–167.
60. Tobin, J. Relative income, absolute income, and saving. In *Money, trade and economic growth.* New York: Macmillan, 1951. Pp. 135–156.
61. von Neumann, J., & Morgenstern, O. *Theory of games and economic behavior.* (2nd ed.) Princeton, N.J.: Princeton Univer. Press, 1947.
62. Wald, A. *Sequential analysis.* New York: Wiley, 1947.
63. Wold, H., & L. Juréen. *Demand analysis.* New York: Wiley, 1953.

APPENDIX: THEMES OF ANALYSIS

EDITOR'S NOTE

The following is the main substance of a document that was sent to contributors when they were invited to participate in Study II. It attempts a detailed breakdown of types of analytic questions that might be entertained in considering field interrelations.

The role of the themes relative to other factors defining the "atmosphere" of Study II is characterized in the Introduction, pp. 16–18. There it will be seen that their primary purpose was to serve as a kind of check list of the many *particular* questions that can be considered relevant to issues of field structure and relationship, and thus to encourage concrete and differentiated analysis. Readers familiar with Study I will recall that a different set of analytic themes figured in defining the working atmosphere of that study. The respective themes of analysis, however, played quite different roles in the two studies. The objectives of Study I were such as to make it seem desirable to encourage adherence, at least in some degree. The aim of the present study was felt best served by encouraging the greatest possible play of individual predilection in the choice both of analytic questions and topics, and offering the themes essentially as *illustrative* of the range of questions falling within the scope of the study. This difference of intent may not be fully evident from the phrasing of the discussion outline per se, which—though affording many escape clauses—adopts the method of defining the requirements for an "ideal" analysis. But the letter of invitation to each contributor, a supporting memo, and most importantly, all the ensuing editorial contact, made amply clear to the contributor the illustrative intent of the themes.

The net effect of these circumstances (as already indicated in the Introduction, p. 18) is that the architecture of the present set of themes is reflected hardly at all the architecture of the essays. We think, however, that they did have the hoped-for effect of encouraging authors to raise more finely specified questions than have been usual in discussions of the present sort, and to approach their tasks with a set toward detailed and sustained analysis. Partly, then, for the historical record and partly for whatever intrinsic interest such a breakdown may contain, the Study II themes are presented forthwith. For brevity's sake, a "lead-in" to the original document, of little interest in the present connection, has been omitted.

753

RATIONAL FOR ARRANGEMENT OF ANALYTIC THEMES

Throughout the formulation of the discussion outline, the fields whose interrelations are under discussion by the given writer are referred to as *the field(s) of primary reference* and *the field(s) of secondary reference.*

A *field of primary reference* is the field (either subfield or total discipline, as the case may be) of which the contributor is a member, and whose relations to other areas he is subjecting to examination.

The *field (or fields) of secondary reference* is the area(s) whose relationship to his own field the contributor proposes to explore.

Thus, for a perception expert exploring the relations of his own field to psychology, perception is the field of primary reference and psychology (or various subareas thereof) is the fields(s) of secondary reference; for a sociologist analyzing the relations between sociology and psychology, sociology is the field of primary reference and psychology is the field of secondary reference.

In the sequence of discussion topics, item 1 (on the "mapping" of the fields of reference) and item 2 (on suggested revisions of "conventional" area breakdowns) are designed to lead to the "location" and definition of the fields of primary and secondary reference, together with some consideration of the internal structure of these fields. The purpose here is to lay the groundwork for treatment of cross-area interrelations. These cannot be meaningfully considered until the boundaries and inner structure of the fields of primary and secondary reference are assessed to whatever extent the limits of the present enterprise may permit. Item 3 (on "bridging laws" and formal relationships) raises the issues which are central to the present enterprise. Here the writer will be concerned with the assessment of those interrelations and interrelationship prospects which are in some sense implicit in, or suggested by, the extant bodies of lawful statements within the fields of primary and secondary reference.

Item 4 (on methodological interrelationships) seeks to supplement the picture of interrelations based on substantive research findings and systematic formulations thereof by inquiring into the interrelations of methods —both research and theoretical—which make such findings possible. Item 5 (on "overlap" of knowledge as between the fields of primary and secondary reference) seeks further supplementation of the picture by inquiring into that special class of cross-science or cross-area interrelations in which knowledge developed in a given area is incorporated without significant modification, or perhaps independently duplicated, in another. Finally, the issues introduced by item 6 are designed to lead the writer to derive from the preceding discussion any consequences which it may contain with respect to the optimal collaborative, administrative, and educational mechanisms for advancing *joint* interests of the fields of primary and secondary reference.

It would be meaningless to suggest any standard length for the manuscripts. Obviously, we should like to have a sufficiently sustained consideration of the discussion topics to ensure clarity for a heterogeneous audience and to derive maximum explicit benefit from the analyst's wisdom with respect to the problems at issue. On the other hand, we do not wish to burden the analyst with an overly laborious task. It should be emphasized that the task defined by the discussion outline is impossible, in any literal sense, and that the condition of psychological knowledge is such that only modest increments of insight into issues of the sort here envisaged are attainable. Nevertheless, even modest advance in the progressive definition of our emerging science, and its location in the matrix of general scientific activity, would seem an end worthy of substantial effort.

The Themes of Analysis

1. "Mapping" of Field(s) of Primary and Secondary Reference

For the field(s) of primary reference:

a. Identify, and, within the limits of feasibility, delimit the boundaries of the field(s) as conventionally conceived.

b. What are the chief independent and dependent variables, or classes of such, which seem to have emerged in a generally recognized way in the research of the last forty years or thereabouts?

c. Do these variables actually constitute a "functionally coherent" domain? That is, does one of these variables—or members of some given class of such variables having a specifiable common property (e.g., a criterion property of "drive" or of "performance change") —appear in all empirically determined functional relationships which are conventionally attributed to the name (e.g., motivation, learning) of the field(s) in question?

d. If the answer to c is negative, attempt a discrimination of the over-all field into functionally coherent domains of relationships.

e. For whatever "domains" emerge (one or many), estimate the chief subclasses of established functional relations; i.e., what are the chief research clusters discernible in each of the domains distinguished in c and d?

For the field(s) of secondary reference:

f. Attempt, if even in the most general way, an estimate of subject-matter boundaries and substructure on the basis of considerations in line with a through e above. (It is not necessary that the analysis here be as explicit or sustained as in the case of the field of primary reference.)

Explanation: The objective in item 1 is to identify and chart the geography of the fields of primary and secondary reference as a first step in preparation for all further considerations of interrelationship issues. Detailed and comprehensive treatment of these questions would be a monumental task of a sort entirely infeasible within the framework of the present study. What is called for here is a brief treatment guided by the various subspecifications of item 1.

For contributors dealing with the relations of the entire field of psychology to another discipline, or vice-versa, the task is even less manageable than for the subfield contributors. Nevertheless, it still may be possible to air relevant views with respect to those subareas of the sciences in question of most immediate concern to the individual writer.

In dealing with question *a*, the writer will no doubt wish to indicate which of the subparts (corresponding to his special interests) of the fields of primary and secondary reference he proposes to select for special attention. These specified subareas may then be highlighted in the ensuing treatment of questions *b* through *f* for more intensive consideration than is given other areas of the "assigned" fields of reference.

The force of all subquestions under item 1 must remain somewhat indeterminate, without some clarification of the terms *independent variable* and *dependent variable*. There has been a widespread failure to make a clear distinction, both in principle and in practice, between two senses of these expressions. An independent variable may be an expression in the *construct language* of a system, reducible to the chief classes of observable events which serve as operationally identifiable or measurable, and, wherever possible, manipulable antecedent conditions of the events that the theory is designed to predict. Or an independent variable may be an expression (strictly in the data language of the investigator) denoting any factor in an experimental or empirical research situation which is varied with the intent to observe and record a correlated change in another part of the system defined by the study. We may designate the first sense as the *systematic independent variable,* and the second as the *empirical independent variable.*

An obvious example of a *systematic* independent variable might be Hull's "conditions which produce drives" (C_D) or Tolman's analogous "states of drive arousal and/or drive satiation"; while characterizations of *each* of the many concrete operations or event-chains known to produce changes in drive states (including the alternate conditions resulting in changes of a given drive as well as those influencing quite varied drives) would be *empirical* independent variables. It should be evident that empirical independent variables may be (though not necessarily) specific "realizations" (operational or reductive "symptoms") of a systematic independent variable; they are not, however, to be identified with the systematic independent variables to which they are ordered. An analogous distinction can, of course, be made as between systematic and empirical *dependent* variables.

Empirical independent and dependent variables are, by definition, "theoretically neutral." Because the distinction between systematic and empirical variables is neither clearly made nor adhered to by most psychological investigators, there has been a marked tendency for intrusions of construct language *systematic variables* into contexts where *empirical variables* are more properly called for. Furthermore, even in areas where the degree of systematic development is not such as to warrant use of a term like "construct language," the desire of students to achieve reasonably general behavioral relationships has led to the grouping together, under a common designation, of empirical variables of widely disparate functional significance. These circumstances have tended in most areas to blur the contours of "theoretically neutral knowledge," and it is often an exceedingly difficult task to reconstruct the actual empirical variables corresponding to functional relationships reported in terms involving construct language intrusions, or other faulty "groupings" of empirical variables. It is not easy, for instance, to specify with accuracy all of the empirical variables to which expressions like goodness of perceptual form, stressfulness of a task, group cohesiveness, permissiveness of a therapist, similarity (as used in perception, learning, and performance studies), meaningfulness of material, amount of reinforcement, velocity of locomotion, amplitude, latency, and other characteristics of response, etc., are reducible. Yet these are the kinds of terms in which the so-called independent and dependent variables of specific empirical studies are reported and summarized in our literature.

From all of the above, it should be clear that the questions under item 1 (and, indeed, all further questions in which the terms "independent" and "dependent" variables appear) could be interpreted as having reference either to *systematic* variables, to *empirical* variables, or both. The objectives of the current study are such as to make it desirable for the analysis to be devoted mainly to the structure and interrelations of theoretically neutral knowledge. Nevertheless, it would be of extreme interest to explore the extent to which the writer's theoretical persuasion might lead to an altered discrimination of variables, and thus to a somewhat different geography of knowledge. It would therefore be ideally desirable to deal with mapping issues and certain of the subsequent more direct interrelationship issues (e.g., the isolation of "bridging laws," etc.; cf. item 3, Explanation) in two alternative forms. One of these would involve the discrimination of empirical (theoretically neutral) variables; the other would involve the identification of systematic variables in accordance with the author's theoretical viewpoint. It is hoped that writers will find this parallel mode of treatment feasible throughout the essay, but it is recognized that this may complicate an already laborious task. Should the writer decide that such an "alternative form" treatment is too demanding, it is at least desirable that the distinction between the two types of variables be held in mind so that the incidence of the writer's analysis can be clearly identified.

2. Suggestions for Revision of Conventional "Field" Breakdowns

a. If the analysis of item 1 above suggests that traditional lines of demarcation among subareas of the fields of primary and secondary reference (or of the fields of primary and secondary reference in their entirety) are in some sense "incorrect," or unfruitful, what new system of breakdowns, or what modifications of the conventional ones, would the writer suggest?

b. If the conventional lines of demarcation are found "defective," but the writer regards it as premature *currently* to suggest a more rational framework, what is the writer's estimate of the conditions or the steps necessary for the development of such a framework?

Explanation: Any study of the present sort must take its point of departure from the structure of current knowledge as currently conceived. This is why item 1—which calls for an exploration of the hypothesis that conventional area discriminations are functionally significant—is a necessary initial part of the undertaking. During the exploration, the analytic results may well disconfirm this latter hypothesis in certain respects. To the extent that this takes place, it would be interesting and useful for the writer to spell out the consequences of his analysis for the reassessment of conventional field breakdowns.

Should the author suggest some major realignment of conventional demarcations among subareas, he would then have the option of discussing further topics in terms of the revised breakdowns suggested at this place, in terms of the conventional breakdowns, or in terms of both.

3. **General Delineation of Interrelations between Field(s) of Primary Reference and Field(s) of Secondary Reference**

   a. Isolate the chief "bridging laws," or classes of such, which currently obtain between the field(s) of primary reference and the field(s) of secondary reference.

   b. Isolate the major variables, or groups of such, within the field(s) of primary reference and correlative variables within the field(s) of secondary reference which, in your estimation, have greatest promise for entering into bridging relationships in the (i) near future, (ii) long-range future.

   c. What formal or logical relationships (e.g., independence, deducibility, subsumability, equivalence or intertranslatability, conditional-causal, etc.) *currently* obtain between the field(s) (or any part thereof) of primary reference and the field(s) (or any part thereof) of secondary reference?

   d. On the basis of present indications, what will be the probable future formal relationship between (or among) the fields of primary and secondary reference?

   e. What is your personal evaluation as to the most desirable (fruitful, expeditious, etc.), formal relationship between (or among) the fields of primary and secondary reference?

   For contributors considering interrelations of subparts of psychological science ONLY

   f. To whatever extent feasible, consider the questions *a* through *e* above with respect to interrelations between the field(s) of primary reference and relevant scientific domains other than psychology.

Explanation: A *bridging law,* in the simplest case, would be a functional relationship between an independent and dependent variable such that one of the variables is a member of the class of variables regarded as characteristic of a given field, and the other variable is a member of the class of variables regarded as belonging to another field. In the case of a law (functional relationship) involving multiple independent variables, it is a sufficient criterion of a bridging law if there are at least two variables contained in the statement, each of which are members respectively of classes of variables regarded as characteristic of different fields. Both of these latter variables may appear in the multivariable bridging law as independent variables, or one may occur as an independent variable and the other as the dependent variable.

In all of the topics of item 3, as elsewhere, it is hoped that the writer will keep clearly distinguished *empirical* independent and dependent variables and *systematic* independent and dependent variables, as defined in item 1 above. As in the case of item 1, alternate treatments in terms of empirical *and* systematic variables would be desirable. This is particularly the case with respect to topics *a* and *b*.

Topics *c, d,* and *e,* usually in commingled form, have been at the heart of most discussions of interrelationship issues in recent decades, both at the level of interrelations between psychology and other presumably allied sciences, and in connection with the interrelations among the subparts of psychological science. The style of discussion prevalent in recent years with respect to such issues might be briefly sketched in terms of a few key contexts of inquiry.

To take one conspicuous example, discussion of the relations between psychology and physiology has been largely in the hands of philosophers of science. Proceeding from a context established by the traditional mind-body problem, they have shown the plausibility of translating most meaningful components of this problem into questions having to do with the relations between the "language systems" of psychology and physiology. But despite occasional half-hearted attempts to inquire into these relations over the past twenty-five years, they have come up with very little that an empirical scientist could consider useful. On the other hand, psychologists, even physiological psychologists, have proceeded within a framework of unanalyzed stereotypes (e.g., "all explanations must come from physiology"; "no explanations can come from physiology"; "psychological laws are derivable in principle from physiology, but psychology must first develop along 'purely behavioral' lines"). In general, there has been very little detailed analysis of: (1) alternate types of formal relationships which are logically possible as between any two sciences; (2) extant relations between psychology and physiology; (3) indicated trends with respect to the probable future relationship; and (4) evaluations as to the optimally desirable relationship. Moreover, when touched upon in past analyses, these classes of problems have often been hopelessly intermingled.

Again, attempts to explore the relations between psychology and sociology (or others of the social sciences) have adhered to a pattern similar to the above. Although such questions have been voluminously discussed by sociologists, social psychologists, and, to some extent, social philosophers, this area, too, is dominated by highly general prescriptions. For instance, assertions are often made to the effect that the two sciences deal with behavior at different levels of abstraction, independently of efforts to specify the formal or contentual characteristics of the abstractive levels in question. Assumptions may be made to the effect that it *is* or *is not* legitimate to transfer concepts from a psychological to a sociological context, or vice-versa, with little analysis of the grounds for the one belief or the other. It is sometimes expedient to assume that the sociologist provides the psychologist with descriptive information about the social aspects of the environment to which individual organisms must respond, but the detailed schema as to how this information may be integrated into the lawful statements of individual psychology has not been specified.

Though not generally discussed in as explicit a way as the above issues, questions having to do with the formal interrelations among the subparts of psychology are of equal importance. At the basis of the major theories of the recent past, there has uniformly been some prior judgment as to which empirical area(s) is *fundamental,* in the sense of providing empirical laws from which the empirical laws of other domains may in some sense be "deduced." It is only necessary to mention, in this connection, the presumption of classical Gestalt psychology that the laws of most psychological domains may be derived from a set of assumptions based on the facts of perception; the belief of reinforcement and conditioning theorists that principles based on simple CR situations suffice for generating all other psychological relationships, etc. Again, in recent times there has been much discussion in the literature as to whether laws of motivation are derivable from the laws of perception or vice-versa; whether perception is fundamental to learning or learning to perception; and so on.

The fact that authors will have already considered items 1 to 3 should impart a concreteness to the discussions of *c, d,* and *e* above which has not always been apparent in the treatment of formal interrelationship issues.

For contributors considering interrelations of subparts
of psychological science ONLY

Explanation of topic f: In clarifying the structure of psychological knowledge and its place within the sciences, it is as important to locate articulation points between given specialization areas and domains conventionally regarded as part of another science as it is to determine interrelations with other psychological areas. Though certain contributors will be specifically dealing with such cross-science interrelations, writers concerned mainly with cross-area relations internal to psychology may find the exploration of relations to other scientific domains helpful, or even indispensable, in getting their own field of primary reference into proper focus. For instance, a writer concerned with the place of sensory psychology in psychological science may not be able to do justice to this question without considering relations of the sensory area to certain sectors of physiological, biochemical, and even physical knowledge. Similarly a contributor concerned with the place of the personality area within psychological science may find it necessary, or at least helpful, to inquire into relations of knowledge in this field to relevant parts of genetics, endocrinology, or even embryology, on the one hand, and certain of the social sciences, on the other. Even in cases where such cross-science inquiries do not seem a *necessary* condition to clarification of the major interrelationship problem at issue, the over-all richness of the study would profit if the writer supplemented his discussion by consideration of articulation points with other sciences.

The present topic may, of course, be disregarded by those writers who have already considered similar issues as an organic part of their preceding discussions. It is appreciated that highly detailed treatment of this question could well multiply the writer's work by a large factor. Even a few hints concerning the writer's views, however, would be useful.

4. Methodological Interrelationships

    a. Estimate the extent to which experimental or empirical research methods developed within the area(s) of primary reference have been extended to, or incorporated within, the field(s) of secondary reference.

b. What is your estimate of the future prospects for the extensibility of research methods from the area(s) of primary reference to the field(s) of secondary reference?

c. Consider the two preceding questions with respect to extensions of research methods from the field(s) of secondary reference to the field(s) of primary reference.

d. Estimate the extent to which systematic devices, strategies, or techniques of systematization developed within the area(s) of primary reference have been extended to, or incorporated within, the field(s) of secondary reference.

e. What is your estimate of the future prospects for the extensibility of systematic devices, strategies, or techniques of systematization from the area(s) of primary reference to the field(s) of secondary reference?

f. Consider the two preceding questions with respect to extensions of systematic devices, strategies, or techniques of systematization from the field(s) of secondary reference to the field(s) of primary reference.

g. Estimate, in a general way, the kinds and priorities of refinements of research methodology, and refinements of techniques of systematization, in the field(s) of secondary reference which would be most fruitful for progress within the field(s) of primary reference.

For contributors considering interrelations of subparts of psychological science ONLY

h. If not already treated, consider at least briefly the line of questioning represented by *a* through *g* above with respect to interrelations between the field of primary reference and relevant scientific domains other than psychology.

Explanation: In this section the concern is with interrelations among the procedures employed for the discovery and systematization of knowledge in various areas, rather than the interrelations among the resulting bodies of knowledge. This dimension of analysis is perhaps more important—particularly in "young sciences"—than inquiries into the structure of formulated knowledge, and has been largely neglected in previous considerations of interrelationship issues.

By experimental or empirical *research methods*, we mean to encompass a broad class of procedures developed in the effort to discover functional relationships between (or among) empirical variables. These may include techniques for the variation of independent and recording of dependent variables, and techniques for direct control of, or compensation for, the effects of "irrelevant" variables. Such procedures have become institutionalized in various fields into characteristic types of "experimental designs," characteristic physically and psychologically defined research settings, types of apparatus, etc.

By *systematic devices* or *techniques of systematization* we have reference to identifiable components of the procedures developed in various areas in the attempt to formulate the results of empirical research with maximum generality, freedom from ambiguity, and predictive power, and generally, to establish orderly, logical relationships among the units of empirical knowledge. Because of the extreme variability in current modes of systematization, we hesitate to use the overstereotyped expression *theory* in this connection, though there would be marked overlap between what we designate *techniques of systematization* and what is generally called *techniques of theory construction*. From one point of view, past systematic effort in various areas of psychology can be regarded as involving a set of conceptual experiments in which attempts have been made to test the organizing and explanatory potentialities of alternate techniques for the identification and definition of variables, of alternate methods for the "measurement" or "scaling" of systematic variables, of alternate techniques for the construction of functional relationships between theoretical variables and for the precise description thereof, of alternate degrees of "axiomatization" or formal explicitness, and so on.

5. Overlap of Knowledge as between Fields of Primary and Secondary Reference

a. Estimate the extent to which substantive empirical findings developed within the area(s) of primary reference have been directly (or in slightly modified form) transposed to the field(s) of secondary reference, or independently duplicated within the secondary field.

b. Consider the same question with respect to transpositions (or other overlap) of findings from the field(s) of secondary reference to the field(s) of primary reference.

c. Estimate the extent to which systematic or theoretical concepts (and the laws into which they enter) developed within the area of primary reference have been transposed to, or independently duplicated within, the field(s) of secondary reference.

d. Consider the same question with respect to transpositions (or other overlap) of theoretical concepts and laws from the field(s) of secondary reference to the field(s) of primary reference.

For contributors considering interrelations of subparts of psychological science ONLY

e. If not treated above, consider, at least briefly, questions *a* through *d* with respect to interrelations between the field(s) of primary reference and relevant scientific domains other than psychology.

Explanation: One type of interrelationship, which may perhaps not come into prominence via the writer's treatment of preceding topics, is the limiting case of direct content overlap in the formulated knowledge characteristic of different subareas of a science, or of different sciences. Such overlap may be concealed by communication barriers associated with specialism, by purely terminological differences, and so on. Because the activities and results of activity of behaving scientists never fall into a rational, overall pattern, such interpenetrations of knowledge may be as much a part of the historically given picture at any time as is mutual supplementation and interdependence. In some instances, content overlap may result from actual "transposition" of materials developed in one area to another; in other cases, the overlap may result from independent duplication of the same materials within two or more areas.

Transposition of empirical findings, of concepts, and of theoretical laws from sociology and anthropology to psychology, and vice-versa, has been conspicuous in recent decades, as has, in certain instances, transposition from biological science to psychology. Occasionally, when such assimilation takes place without sufficient concern for the systematic significance of the assimilated materials within the new context (e.g., as in the direct transposition of psychoanalytic principles to social phenomena), important problems in the logic of science are raised.

Perhaps less generally noted than the phenomenon of cross-science transposition is the transposition of findings across specialty lines within psychology. Fields like *personality* and *social psychology* draw on research findings and theoretical formulations developed in virtually all other conventionally discriminated areas of the science, while the interpenetration of such classical fields as sensory psychology and perception is so great as to defy even a clear-cut setting of boundaries.

Though the fact of transposition or independent duplication of content may be easy to establish, extensive and concrete knowledge of the many contexts in which the resulting overlap exists is nowhere available. Some attempt on the part of the writer to chart such areas of overlap for his particular fields of reference would therefore be of considerable utility. If, as is entirely possible, such issues were already treated in the analysis of preceding items, the present item should, of course, be by-passed.

6. Collaborative, Administrative, and Educational Mechanisms

 a. What evaluation would the writer make, on the basis of the preceding analyses, of prevailing modes of research collaboration or interplay for advancing the *joint* interests of the fields of primary and secondary reference? What proposals with respect to the *most effective* modes of research collaboration or interplay for advancing such joint interests would tend to be suggested by the writer's discussion of preceding items?

 b. What evaluation would the writer make with respect to prevailing administrative, institutional, and organizational arrangements for advancing the joint interests of the fields of primary and secondary reference? What proposals with regard to *optimal* administrative, institutional, and organizational arrangements for advancing such joint interests would tend to flow from the writer's discussion of preceding items?

 c. What evaluations would the writer make of prevailing educational arrangements for the training of personnel equipped to advance the joint interests of the fields of primary and secondary reference? What proposals with respect to *optimal* arrangements for such training would tend to flow from the writer's discussion of preceding items?

NAME INDEX

Page numbers in **boldface** type indicate bibliography references; *n.* indicates footnote reference.

SUBJECT INDEX